Introducing Silverlight 4

Ashish Ghoda

Apress®

Introducing Silverlight 4

ISBN-13 (pbk): 978-1-4302-2991-9

ISBN-13 (electronic): 978-1-4302-2992-6

9 8 7 6 5 4 3 2 1

President and Publisher: Paul Manning
Lead Editor: Jonathan Hassell
Technical Reviewer: Damien Foggon
Editorial Board: Clay Andres, Steve Anglin, Mark Beckner, Ewan Buckingham, Gary Cornell, Jonathan Gennick, Jonathan Hassell, Michelle Lowman, Matthew Moodie, Duncan Parkes, Jeffrey Pepper, Frank Pohlmann, Douglas Pundick, Ben Renow-Clarke, Dominic Shakeshaft, Matt Wade, Tom Welsh
Coordinating Editor: Laurin Becker
Copy Editor: Mary Ann Fugate
Compositor: Bytheway Publishing Services
Indexer: BIM Indexing & Proofreading Services
Artist: April Milne
Cover Designer: Anna Ishchenko

Distributed to the book trade worldwide by Springer Science+Business Media, LLC., 233 Spring Street, 6th Floor, New York, NY 10013. Phone 1-800-SPRINGER, fax (201) 348-4505, e-mail orders-ny@springer-sbm.com, or visit www.springeronline.com.

For information on translations, please e-mail rights@apress.com, or visit www.apress.com.

Apress and friends of ED books may be purchased in bulk for academic, corporate, or promotional use. eBook versions and licenses are also available for most titles. For more information, reference our Special Bulk Sales–eBook Licensing web page at www.apress.com/info/bulksales.

The source code for this book is available to readers at www.apress.com. You will need to answer questions pertaining to this book in order to successfully download the code.

I dedicate this book to my grandparents (Nayansukhray and Kumud Ghoda, Mahavir and Sarla Majmudar), parents (Jitendra and Varsha Ghoda), sister (Kruti Vaishnav), and lovely family (Pratixa, Gyan, and Anand Ghoda) whose blessings, sacrifice, continuous support, and encouragement enabled me to achieve the dream.

—Ashish Ghoda

Contents

▓ **Contents**..**iv**

▓ **About the Author**..**xvii**

▓ **About the Technical Reviewer** ....**xviii**

▓ **Acknowledgments** ....**xix**

▓ **Introduction** ....**xx**

PART 1 ▓ ▓ ▓ **Introduction to Silverlight**...**1**

▓ **Chapter 1: Introducing Silverlight** **3**

Cross-Platform Frameworks...4

    Qt...4

    The Java Platform...4

    Adobe Flash/Flex/AIR..5

    Microsoft ASP.NET AJAX 5

    Microsoft Silverlight 5

The History of Silverlight 6

    Silverlight 1 6

    Silverlight 2 7

    Silverlight 3 9

    Silverlight 4 11

Design and Development Tools for Silverlight..14

    Visual Studio...14

    Expression Blend 15

    SketchFlow...15

Expression Encoder 16

Deep Zoom Composer 16

Eclipse Tools for Silverlight (eclipse4SL) 16

Creating a Silverlight 4–based Application 16

Working with Expression Blend 19

Demonstrating Local Image Files Integration Using Drag-and-Drop Functionality 21

Summary 26

▓ Chapter 2: Silverlight Concepts 27

Silverlight Architecture 27

Silverlight and XAML 29

Developing a Sample Application 29

Namespaces 33

Dependency Property System 34

Type Converters 39

Markup Extensions 40

Microsoft .NET for Silverlight 48

Core .NET Assemblies for Silverlight Applications 48

Managed Code-Behind .NET Integration 49

Summary 56

▓ Chapter 3: Silverlight User Interface Controls 57

Building Blocks 57

DependencyObject 58

Threading and the user interface 59

UIElement 59

FrameworkElement 63

The Control Class 66

Enhancements in Silverlight 4 68

Layout Management and Grouping Controls **69**

    Canvas 69

    StackPanel 70

    Grid 71

    DockPanel 74

    WrapPanel 77

    TabControl 78

    ViewBox 80

Forms Controls **81**

    The Button Controls 81

    TextBox 85

    PasswordBox 87

    RichTextBox 88

    AutoCompleteBox 91

Data Integration and Data Manipulation Controls **95**

    ItemsControl 96

    ListBox 96

    ComboBox 98

    TreeView 99

    HeaderedItemsControl 102

    ContentControl 103

    HeaderedContentControl 103

    DataGrid 104

    DataForm 104

    DataPager 105

    Label 105

    DescriptionViewer 105

    ValidationSummary 106

Functional Controls 106

Border 106

GridSplitter 107

TextBlock 109

Popup 111

ToolTipService 112

ScrollViewer 113

The RangeBase Class 115

Calendar and DatePicker 118

Image 121

MultiScaleImage 121

MediaElement 122

InkPresenter 122

Dialog Boxes 124

WebBrowser 133

Navigation 134

Summary 137

PART 2 ▓   ▓   ▓ Content Integration in Silverlight Applications 139

▓ Chapter 4: Media Integration 141

Media Integration Enhancements in Silverlight 4 141

Images 142

The Image Class 142

Bitmap APIs 147

Silverlight Hardware Acceleration 152

Multi-scale Images and the Deep Zoom Feature 155

Media (Video and Audio) 162

Supported Media Format 163

Unsupported Media Format 164

The MediaElement Class 164

Timeline Markers 172

Web Camera and Microphone Integration 174

Windows Azure Platform–based Hosting and Media Delivery Services for Silverlight
Applications 183

Subscribing to Windows Azure Platform Services 183

Publishing Silverlight Applications Video Content 183

Streaming Packaged Images and Media Files 184

Summary 184

■ **Chapter 5: Network Communication** 185

Networking Enhancements in Silverlight 4 185

Enabling Cross-Domain Communication 185

Cross-Domain Policy Files 186

Trusted Applications 189

Network-Aware Applications 191

Consuming Web Services with WCF 191

Creating a WCF Service Consumable by Silverlight 192

XAML to Consume Information 195

Invoking Services from Silverlight 196

Communicating Directly over HTTP 207

Communicating via Sockets 213

Controlling Client Access via a Socket Policy Server 213

The System.Net Namespace 214

Building a Socket-Based Sample Text Chat Application 217

UDP Multicast 232

The UdpAnySourceMulticastClient Class 232

The UdpSingleSourceMulticastClient Class 234

Considerations for Using Networking 236

Summary 236

▨ **Chapter 6: Working with Data**..**237**

Enhancements in Silverlight 4 237

Displaying Data..238

Data Binding 238

Type Converters... 262

StringFormat.. 263

BindingBase.FallbackValue and BindingBase.TargetNullValue Properties............................ 264

Binding to String Indexers 265

The DataGrid Control 266

The DataForm Control.. 279

The CollectionViewSource 284

WCF Data Services..284

Entity Data Model (EDM)... 285

Silverlight Client Library for WCF Data Services.. 286

Silverlight Application using WCF Data Service.. 289

Processing XML Data..299

Parsing XML... 300

Serializing XML... 301

Using LINQ 302

Saving State on the Client 303

Summary 309

PART 3 ▨   ▨   ▨ **Improving User Experience**...**311**

▨ **Chapter 7: Extending User Experience of LoB Applications**..............................**313**

Enhancements in Silverlight 4 313

Drag-and-Drop Functionality 314

Properties of UIElement to Enable Drag-and-Drop Functionality.. 314

Events of UIElement to Enable Drag-and-Drop Functionality 314

Processing Dropped File(s) 315

Developing an Example 315

Mouse-Wheel Support 324

Developing an Example 324

Limitations 326

Right-Click Context Menu Support 326

Printing Capabilities 329

PrintDocument Class 330

PrintPageEventArgs Class 330

Implementing the Printing Function 331

Clipboard Access 336

Globalization and Localization of Silverlight Applications 338

Globalization 338

Localization 342

Enhancements in XAML Features 352

Flexible Root XAML Namespace 352

XmlnsDefinitionAttribute 353

Direct Content 353

Whitespace Handling 353

Custom IDictionary Support 354

Summary 354

▓ Chapter 8: Styling and Templating 355

Enhancements in Silverlight 4 355

Using Styles 355

Style Inheritance/Style Cascading 360

Style Override/Style Resetting 361

Merged Resource Dictionaries 363

Implicit Styling 364

Style Setter 365

Using Control Templates 366

Creating a Control Template 366

Control Templates for Other Controls 376

Developing a Templated Control 378

Summary 380

▓ Chapter 9: Graphics 383

Enhancements in Silverlight 4 383

2D Graphics 383

Using Geometries 384

Using Shapes 391

Transforms 395

Translation 396

Rotation 396

Skewing 397

Scaling 398

Arbitrary Linear Transforms 399

Combining Multiple Transformations 401

Composite Transformation 401

3D Effects Using Perspective Transforms 403

Pixel Shaders 405

Brushes 407

The SolidColorBrush 408

The Tile Brushes 408

The Gradient Brushes 410

Transparency and Opacity Masks 412

Summary 414

▓ **Chapter 10: Animation** **415**

Introduction to Silverlight Animation 415

Timelines 416

AutoReverse 418

BeginTime 419

Duration 420

FillBehavior 421

RepeatBehavior 421

SpeedRatio 421

Storyboards and Animation 423

From/To/By Animations 423

Keyframe Animations 431

Animation Easing 437

Procedural Animation 441

Bubble User Control 441

DemoPage User Control 443

Animating with Expression Blend 447

3D Animation 451

Summary 452

PART 4 ▓   ▓   ▓ **Advanced Topics** **453**

▓ **Chapter 11: Advanced Silverlight Features** **455**

Silverlight Navigation Framework 455

Understanding the Navigation Framework 457

Implementing Custom Navigation 463

Deep Linking 471

Search Engine Optimization 471

Additional References 474

Out-of-Browser Functionality 474

Enabling the Out-of-Browser Functionality 475

Installing Out-of-Browser Applications 477

Uninstalling Out-of-Browser Applications 480

Trusted Out-of-Browser Applications 481

Customizing Out-of-Browser Applications 482

Working with the Networking and Offline APIs.. 484

Incorporating an Updated Version 488

Files Management 490

Notification API 494

COM Automation 497

Commanding Support 502

The Model Class 504

The ViewModel Class... 504

The View.xaml File.. 505

Cross-Silverlight Application Communication 506

Using the System.Windows.Messaging Namespace.. 507

Seeing an Example in Action 508

Summary 514

■ Chapter 12: Threading in Silverlight..515

Using Threading...515

The Thread Class 516

Creating and Managing Threads 519

The Dispatcher 521

The BackgroundWorker Class 522

Working with Shared Data... 526

Using Timers..529

Using the DispatcherTimer 530

Using the System.Threading Timer 531

Summary 532

▓ Chapter 13: WCF RIA Services and Silverlight for Mobile 533

WCF RIA Services for Silverlight 533

Setting Up a Development Environment 534

Introducing Silverlight Business Application Template 535

Additional References 545

Silverlight for Windows Mobile 546

Setting Up a Development Environment 546

Developing a Sample Twitter Application 546

Summary 553

▓ Chapter 14: Dynamic Languages and Dynamic .NET for Silverlight 555

Dynamic Languages 555

Dynamic Languages for Silverlight 556

IronRuby 556

IronPython 557

Dynamic Language Runtime (DLR) for Silverlight 557

DLR Scripting Assemblies 558

The Microsoft.Scripting.Silverlight.DynamicApplication Class 559

Setting Up the Development Environment 560

The Traditional Approach with the Chiron.exe File 560

The "Just-Text" Approach 561

Creating Silverlight Applications Using the "Just-Text" Approach 564

Hosting a HTML File 564

In-Line IronRuby/IronPython Code in Hosting HTML File 564

In-Line XAML Code in Hosting HTML File 565

Externalizing XAML and IronRuby/IronPython Code 565

Developing an Interactive Bing Maps Application with Silverlight and IronRuby 566

Installing Microsoft Bing Maps Silverlight Control SDK.. 566

Include Bing Maps Control to the Solution 566

Create a SilverlightMap.xaml File... 568

Creating a SilverlightMap.html File 568

Adding 3D Animation within the SilverlightMap.xaml File.. 569

Creating a SilverlightMap.rb IronRuby File and Adding Map Mode 570

Add Rotate Map Capabilities 571

Targeting Pre-defined Locations 575

Summary 577

▓ **Chapter 15: Security** **579**

NET Security in the CLR 579

Silverlight Security Model...580

Enhancements in Silverlight 4 582

Configuring Silverlight 4 Applications to Run with Elevated Trust 582

Digitally Signing Out-of-Browser Silverlight Applications 585

Elevated-Trusted Silverlight Applications vs. Partially Trusted Silverlight Applications 587

Application-Level Security...589

Securing Information in Transit.. 589

Securing Information with Cryptography... 589

Same-Domain and Cross-Domain Communication 607

Division of Responsibility.. 609

Summary 612

PART 5 ▓   ▓   ▓ **Testing and Deploying Silverlight RIAs**............................**613**

▓ **Chapter 16: Testing and Debugging**...**615**

Testing 615

Unit Testing 616

Automated User Interface Testing 627

Debugging 633

   The Debugging Process.. 633

   Conditional Compilation... 634

   Debugging Silverlight Applications with Visual Studio.. 635

   Handling Unhandled Exceptions.. 640

Summary 644

▓ **Chapter 17: Packaging and Deploying Silverlight Applications** **645**

Client Considerations.. 645

   Disabling Silverlight Plug-In Using Web Browser... 646

   Silverlight Configuration 647

Silverlight Deployment Package Definition... 650

   Core Runtime Library.. 651

   Silverlight Application Package (XAP File).. 651

   In-Package and On-Demand Files.. 656

Hosting Silverlight Applications 659

   Server-Side Silverlight RIA Deployment 661

   Custom Initialization Parameters.. 662

   Embedding Silverlight Plug-Ins to the Web Page 663

   Custom HTML Object Element Error Handling for Better User Experience 667

Silverlight and the Build Process.. 667

   Building a Silverlight Application Visual Studio Project (.csproj) with MSBuild................................. 668

   Building a Silverlight Application MsBuild Project (.proj) with MSBuild 670

Silent Installer for Silverlight Out-of-Browser Applications...................................... 673

Summary 674

▓ **Index** **675**

About the Author

■ Awarded with a British Computer Society (BCS) Fellowship, **Ashish Ghoda** is a customer-focused and business values–driven senior IT executive with over 13 years of IT leadership, enterprise architecture, application development, and technical and financial management experience.

He is founder and president of Technology Opinion LLC, a unique collaborative venture striving for strategic excellence by providing partnerships with different organizations and the IT community. He is also the associate director at a Big Four accounting firm.

Ashish actively contributes to the IT community. He provides strategic advice about achieving IT goals and defining the product and technology road maps of organizations, conducts training in and speaks on IT leadership areas and Microsoft technologies, and architects and develops customer-centric software services.

He is the author of *Accelerated Silverlight 3* (co-authored with Jeff Scanlon)and *Pro Silverlight for the Enterprise* from Apress, and several articles on Microsoft technologies and IT management areas for *MSDN Magazine*, TechnologyOpinion.com, and advice.cio.com. He is also the technical reviewer of *Silverlight Recipes Second Edition* and *Silverlight 3 Recipes*, also from Apress. Ashish reviews research papers submitted for the Innovative and Collaborative Business and E-Business tracks of the European Conference on Information Systems (ECIS) and World Multi-Conference on Systemics, Cybernetics, and Informatics (WMSCI).

He has a master's degree in information systems from New Jersey Institute of Technology (NJIT) and has earned Microsoft Certified Professional (MCP) and Microsoft Certified Application Developer (MCAD) certifications in .NET.

Visit his company site at www.technologyopinion.com, and blog site at www.silverlightstuff.net to get the latest information on the technology and different services.

About the Technical Reviewer

Damien Foggon is a developer, writer, and technical reviewer in cutting-edge technologies and has contributed to more than 50 books on .NET, C#, Visual Basic, and ASP.NET. He is the co-founder of the Newcastle-based user group NEBytes (online at www.nebytes.net), is a multiple MCPD in .NET 2.0 and .NET 3.5, and can be found online at http://blog.littlepond.co.uk.

Acknowledgments

I would like to thank Jonathan Hassell, my editor, for giving me another opportunity and remaining confident that I could finish one of the first few books on Silverlight 4 at a highly accelerated speed.

The schedule was really aggressive, and positive support from Laurin Becker (coordinating editor), Damien Foggon (technical reviewer), Mary Ann Fugate (copy editor), and other Apress team members enabled me to achieve this task successfully. They deserve special thanks for their thorough review and quick turnarounds, which helped me develop quality content in the given challenging timeline.

Jay Nanavaty, a senior consultant of Technology Opinion, has been working with me since my first book, *Pro Silverlight for the Enterprise,* published last year. He dedicated long hours helping me develop many examples for this book. Without his excellent work and through knowledge of Silverlight and .NET, it would have been very challenging for me to finish the book.

With blessings from God and encouragement from my grandparents, parents, and in-laws, I was able to accomplish this task successfully. My wife, Pratixa, and two little sons, Gyan (6 years old) and Anand (2 years old), have continued their positive support, which enabled me to finish my third consecutive book. I thank my family for their unbelievable cooperation and encouragement, and for keeping their faith in me during this ambitious endeavor.

Ashish Ghoda

Founder and President, Technology Opinion LLC

www.technologyopinion.com

Introduction

Microsoft Silverlight is a cross-browser, cross-platform, and cross-device plug-in for developing the next-generation, media-rich, interactive line-of-business (LoB) rich Internet applications (RIAs) in an agile and cost-effective way.

In only nine months, after releasing Silverlight 3 in July 2009, Microsoft released Silverlight 4 in April 2010. The Silverlight 3 version introduced out-of-browser capabilities to work in the disconnected mode and access to local file systems, and it helped professionals to develop data-driven applications easily. Silverlight 4 introduced support to Windows 7 Mobile phones and highlighted demanded features, such as printing, documents integration, reporting, rich offline capabilities, and local devices to develop line-of-business (LoB) data-driven RIAs. The following are some of them:

- Introduction of new and enhanced LoB RIA features, such as content printing capability, right-click context menus, drag-and-drop and copy-and-paste functionalities, notification windows, enhanced data controls and data binding features, full access to key boards, and integration with microphones and web cameras.

- Silverlight applications with elevated trust as out-of-browser applications enable access to "My*" Folders for Windows (and on Mac mapped to related places).

- Introduction of implicit theming and multicast UDP networking will help to improve the overall end-user experience.

- Visual Studio 2010 enables the user interface development for Silverlight 4 (and Silverlight 3) RIAs and introduces better data binding and WCF RIA services integration with other enhancements to improve the development experience.

- Silverlight 4 and Windows Phone development tools enable development of interactive Silverlight applications for Windows 7 Mobile Phone series.

This book covers all aspects of Silverlight 4 with numerous examples, providing you hands-on experience. Starting by covering Silverlight and its different versions, I will provide a detailed understanding of WPF, XAML, styling and templates, and Silverlight user controls (including new controls introduced in Silverlight 4) so you can build an effective presentation layer for your Silverlight applications. I will also cover the data integration capabilities and related user controls to show how to integrate with the different data sources using WCF services and LINQ. We will dive into details of seamless media integration and animations capabilities along with introducing Silverlight 4 key LoB features such as printing, right-click context menus, drag-and-drop functionalities, and notification windows. In addition, we will cover some advanced features such as the navigation framework, out-of-browser functionality, Windows mobile integration, and the networking and security capabilities of Silverlight 4. This book will also give you details on how to unit test Silverlight applications and the best way to build and deploy these applications.

Introducing Silverlight 4 aims to get you up to speed as quickly and efficiently as possible on Silverlight 4, and I hope you find what you're looking for within its pages.

PART 1

Introduction to Silverlight

CHAPTER 1

■ ■ ■

Introducing Silverlight

Silverlight is a Microsoft .NET Framework–based technology platform that enables IT professionals to develop next-generation, media-rich, interactive Line of Business Rich Internet Applications (RIAs) in an agile and cost-effective way. Cross-platform Silverlight-based line of business application can provide maximum customer satisfaction and help organizations to return maximum Return of Investment (ROI).

Silverlight provides a platform to develop cross-browser, cross-platform, and cross-device RIAs. All versions of Silverlight are a subset of Windows Presentation Foundation (WPF)—a strong and abstracted presentation framework—for defining interactive user interfaces that can be integrated seamlessly with media (audio, video, and images) and data. At the core of the Silverlight presentation framework is the XML-based declarative Extensible Application Markup Language (XAML, pronounced *zammel*). XAML enables designers and developers to define externalized and decoupled user interfaces and related style sheets. Thus, Silverlight is a natural extension to technologies that are already in existence, specifically .NET and WPF, enabling development and deployment of RIAs. In other words, if you strip out the parts of .NET that just aren't needed or that don't easily work across platforms, add in an implementation of XAML that is the core of WPF, and mix in a few new things such as browser interoperability and the ability to execute dynamic languages such as Python (IronPython, as the .NET implementation is called), you are in the world of Silverlight—a platform-agnostic, next-generation, web development platform.

Developing applications that work on multiple platforms is a difficult problem. What constitutes a platform is an important question, and for the purposes of this book, it is any unique host environment that provides an execution environment for code. If you give it some thought, it is easy to categorize operating systems such as Windows 7, Windows Vista, Windows XP, OS X, and Linux as platforms; but web browsers such as Firefox, Internet Explorer, Opera, and Chrome and devices such as regular computers and Windows 7 Series mobile phones also count as platforms. If you've done any web development targeting multiple browsers, you're familiar with the inherent headaches in getting a web site to render and operate in the same way on Internet Explorer as it does on Firefox and others. The goal of Silverlight is to create a consistent execution environment across different browsers, operating systems, and devices.

There is no magical reason why a cross-platform application is automatically "good." Any responsible software engineering starts with a careful examination of the business reasons for a project. If all users are on a single platform, such as Windows, there is no reason to spend extra development time ensuring that the software also works on other platforms. Also, a significant amount of software that enables business applications (data and business logic layers) has no need to work on multiple platforms (though it can potentially be *consumed* by different platforms), and in fact benefits from platform-specific optimizations.

However, cross-platform applications are definitely important and gaining more importance in today's Web 2.0 era—as is best evidenced by web sites that are usable, generally, on any browser. The ability to develop cross-platform applications is of the most importance when the potential users for an application are on multiple platforms. This is a rather obvious statement, but it is important to note that development of a cross-platform application offers no inherent benefits if all users are on a single platform; that is, unless the cross-platform aspect is free or nearly free (therefore helping to future-proof the application if the user base changes). This concept of "free or nearly free" is important—software engineering is already a challenging endeavor, and if making software cross-platform is difficult to implement, it requires either significantly more development time for a single code base, or a second code base for a different platform that replicates the functionality of the first (not to mention a third or fourth code base if other platforms must be supported). Without question, this means more time, more money, and more development resources are needed. Optimally, we want a relatively easy way to create cross-platform applications. Fortunately, a number of frameworks and platforms (including Microsoft Silverlight) have attempted to make the creation of cross-platform applications free or nearly free.

Cross-Platform Frameworks

Frameworks for developing cross-platform applications are not new. Even the C language is arguably cross-platform, since the source can be written once and compiled on each target platform, thus enabling portability of projects written in C. While arguments over what truly constitutes cross-platform can be interesting, they aren't of much practical use for us here, so let's take a brief look at the serious contenders for developing cross-platform applications.

Qt

Qt (pronounced *cute*) is a cross-platform application development toolkit mainly for C++; however, it has support for other languages, such as Java. The significant benefit of Qt is that programs execute natively after compilation (i.e., no new virtual machine is needed). The cross-platform nature of Qt is provided at the source level, as long as developers utilize Qt's platform-agnostic API. The major downsides to Qt are the learning curve for developers and the degree to which applications might become intertwined with Qt (though this might be acceptable to many organizations). Visit http://qt.nokia.com/products/ for more information.

The Java Platform

The Java platform (mainly Java Applet and JavaFX) is possibly the closest comparison to Silverlight on the market. Much like .NET Framework, the Java-based platform is a managed environment. Until Silverlight, though, .NET is mainly available on Windows. Both platforms provide the ability to compile a program and immediately execute it on multiple platforms. The Java platform and Silverlight approach this similarly: an execution environment (known as a virtual machine) is developed for each platform where programs might be run. Java source code is compiled to Java byte code, which is then executed by the Java virtual machine in a sandbox environment. The downsides to this approach are the plethora of virtual machines that can be created, each with potential quirks that sometimes affect existing applications, and the time cost of starting up a Java virtual machine on a web site (you've no doubt seen the gray rectangle and the loading symbol on web pages). Sun also has a more direct competitor of Silverlight called JavaFX, a framework that includes a scripting language to more easily create Java applications. This framework makes the most sense for institutions and developers who are already used to working in the Java environment or need to extend their existing Java applications. Visit http://java.sun.com/javafx/ if you are curious about learning more.

Adobe Flash/Flex/AIR

Adobe Flash is, by far, the most popular comparison to Silverlight. A browser plug-in that enables execution of rich content for the Web—doesn't that sound familiar? This comparison is made even more explicit with Adobe releasing Flex, an environment for executing rich applications in the browser and on the desktop. Adobe Flex provides a rich UI component library and uses MXML, a declarative XML-based language, to develop rich, interactive user interfaces. While there are some feature differences between Flex and Silverlight that can make one more appealing than the other, Flex is a viable alternative to Silverlight; however, it caters to a different set of developers than Silverlight does. Flex capitalizes on the languages people already know, including JavaScript, HTML, CSS, and ActionScript. Silverlight, however, provides a markup language, but is an incredibly natural platform to develop on if you're already a .NET developer. Visit www.adobe.com/products/flex/ if you want to learn more about Flex.

In addition to Adobe Flash and Adobe Flex, in February 2008, Adobe introduced Adobe AIR for developing desktop applications that you can extend as RIAs. Visit www.adobe.com/products/air/ to get more information about Adobe AIR.

Microsoft ASP.NET AJAX

Microsoft ASP.NET AJAX, a set of JavaScript libraries built into ASP.NET 3.5 and 4.0, is available as a separate download for ASP.NET 2.0. Being an integral part of ASP.NET 3.5 and 4.0 and the Ajax Library (comes with AJAX Controls Toolkit for ASP.NET 3.5), now ASP.NET AJAX client- and server-side libraries are more integrated with Visual Studio 2010 (and Visual Studio 2008). The client-side library allows you to implement client-level processing such as processing and validating information entered by the end user, refreshing a portion of the web page, and developing rich, interactive user interfaces. You can also efficiently integrate the client-side library components with the server-side ASP.NET controls library in asynchronous mode. The key technology driver of ASP.NET AJAX is scripting. In general, script-based web applications face several challenges due to different browser settings (e.g., JavaScript is not enabled by default) on PCs and mobile devices. As a result, scripting is often not always the best strategy for enterprises to use to develop secured and scalable RIAs. ASP.NET AJAX also supports limited features of RIAs and does not support effective multimedia integration, managed code-behind integration, or metadata and information management. Microsoft ASP.NET AJAX is a widely accepted model for building RIAs, but it is very likely that, having Silverlight as an option, .NET developers will migrate ASP.NET AJAX applications to Silverlight RIAs. Visit www.asp.net/ajax/ if you want to learn more about Microsoft ASP.NET AJAX.

Microsoft Silverlight

This section brings us to the subject of this book: Microsoft Silverlight. .NET Framework 3.0 included the first release of WPF, along with other key technologies. With WPF came XAML, essentially a way to create applications in markup (there is an almost one-to-one correspondence between XAML constructs and code). While XAML is not necessarily tied to presentation logic, the two most visible uses of it are in WPF and Silverlight. Microsoft Silverlight is a subset of WPF, which is part of .NET Framework 3.x and 4.0. Silverlight is integrated with the broad range of Microsoft tools and services like Microsoft Visual Studio 2010 and 2008, Microsoft Expression Blend, Microsoft Deep Zoom Composer, and Microsoft Silverlight Streaming by Windows Azure Platform for the easy development and deployment of Silverlight-based multimedia cross-browser, cross-platform, and cross-device RIAs. While Silverlight does contain a Common Language Runtime (CLR), it has absolutely no dependence on any of the .NET Framework versions. The free and small size (to be precise, the Silverlight 4 runtime is 5.96MB for Windows and 8.71MB for Mac) of the Silverlight runtime plug-in brings with it CLR and base-class library components all its own. If a user does not have the Silverlight runtime plug-in installed, (s)he will be automatically prompted to install it upon browsing the Silverlight application.

▓ **Note** Silverlight 4 runtime plug-in is backward compatible. It means, if an application is developed using Silverlight 3 (such as Netflix video player) and prior versions, it will continue working in your machine using Silverlight 4 runtime engine.

If you are already a .NET developer, you will be in familiar territory after learning XAML and its features. The correspondence of XAML to classes in .NET is a major strength, and tool support built around XAML for designers and developers is strong and continuously growing.

The History of Silverlight

Four versions of Microsoft Silverlight are available to date: Silverlight 1, Silverlight 2, Silverlight 3, and Silverlight 4.

Silverlight 1

Before the MIX07 conference in March 2007, Silverlight was known by the relatively boring but descriptive name WPF/E, which stands for Windows Presentation Foundation/Everywhere. While the details were sparse at the time, the rough goal of the technology was clear: a browser-hosted version of WPF. Silverlight 1 was unveiled at the conference and would no longer be known as WPF/E. This initial release of Silverlight 1 did not have CLR or anywhere close to the capabilities provided by Silverlight 2. What it did have, though, is support for a small subset of XAML and a variety of capabilities that foreshadowed the future of Silverlight. Possibly the most obvious aspect of Silverlight 1 is that applications are written either completely in XAML or in a mix of XAML and JavaScript with a Document Object Model (DOM) to manipulate the UI. Since there is no CLR, there is no compilation step, and the JavaScript is interpreted on the client. All Silverlight versions, including Silverlight 1, require a plug-in on the client side. The major features supported by Silverlight 1 follow:

Core architecture: This includes `DependencyObject` at the root and `UIElement` forming the base of the user interface classes (but no `FrameworkElement` class).

Basic layout: The Canvas is the only layout component, so user interface elements can only be placed using absolute positions.

Basic controls: The `TextBlock` and `Run` controls are provided to display text. In terms of handling user input, nothing specialized is provided. This limitation extended to Silverlight 1, and the full control architecture debuted when Silverlight 2 was first released in beta.

2D graphics: `Geometry`-based classes (which are flexible but can't be directly placed on a user interface) and `Shape`-based classes (which can be directly placed on a user interface) provide the ability to draw 2D shapes.

Media: Many early Silverlight applications showcased the image and video support provided by Silverlight. Also included is support for easily downloading media such as images, so that bandwidth can be utilized more effectively. The Silverlight Media Player controls support the WMA, WMV, and MP3 media file formats.

Animation: The Storyboard class from WPF became part of the XAML implementation in this first release of Silverlight, providing the ability to animate different user interface elements in a variety of ways.

Brushes and transforms: Brushes such as the image brush, video brush, and color brushes (solid colors and gradients) have been in Silverlight since this initial release.

Two of the most important parts of later versions of Silverlight not present in Silverlight 1 are a rich set of controls and performance and managed code-behind integration..

Silverlight 2

Soon after Silverlight 1 was released, the next version of Silverlight was released in preview form. This preview release was known as Silverlight 1.1, the most significant aspect of which is the cross-platform CLR. While Silverlight 1 could be used to develop some impressive and rich media-based applications, the possibilities greatly expanded with the ability to target the .NET platform and know that the application would run on multiple host platforms. The biggest missing feature from Silverlight 1.1 was a set of standard controls. This made developing useful user interfaces difficult. Handling input events was also difficult since events could only be captured on the root container. You then had to manually propagate the events to child objects. Input focus was also tricky.

After several months, as it got closer to the MIX08 conference in March 2008, Microsoft revealed that Silverlight 1.1 would actually be released as Silverlight 2 since the feature set grew so much. It was a big leap from the first basic version to version 2.

The following are key features of Silverlight 2:

- Provides a platform to develop cross-browser (Microsoft Internet Explorer, Mozilla Firefox, Apple Safari, and Google Chrome), cross-platform (Microsoft Windows, Apple Mac, Linux), and cross-device (desktop, laptop) RIAs.

- Silverlight 2 is based on Microsoft .NET Framework 3.5.

  - As a subset of WPF, the Silverlight user interface framework is based on .NET Framework 3.5, WPF, and XAML. Visual Studio and the Silverlight toolkit contain more than a hundred XAML-based user controls in the areas of layout management (e.g., Canvas, StackPanel, and Grid), form controls (e.g., TextBox, CheckBox), data manipulation (e.g., DataGrid, ListBox), functional controls (e.g., Calendar, DatePicker, ScrollViewer), and media controls (e.g., MediaElement) to develop rich, interactive applications.

  - Support for the CLR and the availability of .NET Base Class Libraries (BCL)— not the same BCL as the full desktop version—components enable the integration of Microsoft .NET managed code-behind using Microsoft .NET class libraries in Silverlight 2 projects.

  - Asynchronous loosely coupled data integration capabilities enable development of complex, media-rich, SOA-based enterprise RIAs.

  - Integration with WCF and Web Services via REST, WS*/SOAP, POX, RSS, and standard HTTP enables the application to perform various data transactions with external data sources (e.g., XML, relational databases) and feeds (e.g., RSS).

- ADO.NET data services, LINQ, LINQ to XML, and XLinq can be used for data transformation.

- Local data caching with isolated data storage capabilities support client-side data processing.

- Dynamic Language Runtime (DLR) supports dynamic compilation and execution of scripting languages like JavaScript and IronPython to develop Silverlight-based applications.

- Silverlight 2 provides effective media management, supporting secured multimedia streaming.

  - Adaptive media streaming helps to improve synchronization of media by automatically adjusting bit rates based on the network bandwidth.

  - Digital rights management (DRM) for media streaming enables protected distribution of digital media.

- Silverlight 2 supports rich graphics and animation.

  - 2D vector graphics are supported.

  - Deep Zoom provides an effective and easy-to-implement zoom-in and zoom-out feature.

  - With the use of the Deep Zoom Composer, professionals can smoothly enable navigation of large amounts of visual information, regardless of the size of the data, and optimize the bandwidth available to download it.

  - Object animation and embedded code-based animation provides high-performing graphics and animation support.

  - Seamless integration with Microsoft Expression Blend allows the development of compelling graphics with minimal effort.

- Silverlight 2 provides networking support.

  - Silverlight is capable of background threading and asynchronous communication.

  - JSON-based services integration is supported. LINQ to JSON support enables querying, filtering, and mapping JSON results to .NET objects within a Silverlight application.

  - Policy-based application development and deployment can occur with cross-domain networking using HTTP and sockets.

- Support for different deployment options (in-package and on-demand) and cross-domain deployment capabilities enable users to access Silverlight RIAs in a high-performing and secure environment.

- Silverlight 2 supports the open source and cross-platform Eclipse development platform by providing Eclipse Tools for Microsoft Silverlight (eclipse4SL, see www.eclipse.org/esl).

- The Silverlight XAML schema vocabulary specification (MS-SLXV) released under the Open Specification Promise (OSP) improves interoperability.

- End users need to have the Silverlight runtime installed to be able to create a sandbox environment to run Silverlight RIAs. No licensing is required for the Silverlight 2 runtime; it is free and a very small file for distribution and installation. The Silverlight 2 runtime is 4.68MB for Windows and 7.38MB for Mac. Silverlight 2 supports only Macs with Intel processors and does not support Mac PowerPC.

Silverlight 3

Microsoft kept the trend of releasing new versions of Silverlight at the MIX conference by releasing the Silverlight 3 Beta version during MIX09 in March 2009. Microsoft released Silverlight 3 along with Expression Blend 3 in a "Microsoft way"—in a virtual launch "See the Light" event (www.seethelight.com)—in July 2009. Silverlight 3 is an extension of Silverlight 2 and mainly provides improvements in graphics capabilities, media management, application development areas (additional controls, enhanced binding support, and out-of-browser functionality), and integration with the designers' Expression Blend 3 tool.

In addition to the features mentioned in the Silverlight 2 section, the following are the key enhanced features in Silverlight 3:

- Improved graphics capabilities to support a richer and more interactive user interface.

  - *Support for 3D graphics* enables designers to apply 2D content to a 3D plane with Perspective transforms. You can simulate live content rotation in the 3D space by applying the Perspective transform to the proper XAML elements. To achieve this functionality, developers do not need to write a single line of code. You can get this feature simply with the use of Expression Blend.

  - *Animation easing* allows users to generate impressive animation effects using the different animation easing functions available by default, such as BounceEase, ElasticEase, CircleEase, BackEase, ExponentialEase, and SineEase. You can also create your own custom, complicated, mathematical formula–based animation effects.

  - *Pixel Shaders* drive the visual behavior of the graphical content. By default, Silverlight 3 supports drop-down and blur effects. You can create custom effects using Microsoft's High-Level Shading Language (HLSL) and DirectX Software Development Kit (SDK).

  - *Theme application support* allows you to apply theme-based styles at runtime to Silverlight 3 RIAs. Developers can cascade styles by basing them on each other.

  - *Enhanced control-skinning* capabilities enable developers to define a common set of controls external to application, allowing the reuse of styles and control skins across applications. This enhancement helps organizations to apply, maintain, and control a consistent look and feel for applications.

- *Improved text rendering* enables efficient rendering and rapid animation of text. The use of *local fonts* improves overall application performance. *Bitmap caching* allows Vector graphics, text, and controls to be cached as bitmaps in the background, improving overall application-rendering performance.

- *Bitmap APIs* enable dynamic generation of bitmaps by reading and writing pixels in the bitmap. The capability to render visual elements to a bitmap makes it possible to edit images at runtime and develop different types of effects.

- Enhanced media management supporting high-quality and secured multimedia streaming.

  - *Support for new media formats*, such as H.264/Advanced Audio Coding (AAC)/MP4, and *the new RAW audio/video pipeline*, which supports third-party codecs, bring opportunities to develop a broad range of media formats that support RIAs and broaden the overall industry-wide acceptance of Silverlight as a main web-development technology platform.

  - *IIS Media Services* (an integrated HTTP media delivery platform) enable high-performing and smooth, live and on-demand, high-quality and high-definition (HD) (720p+) media streaming. Silverlight 3 also leverages Graphics Processor Unit (GPU) hardware acceleration to deliver a true HD media experience in both in-browser and full-screen modes.

  - *Silverlight DRM for media streaming* enables Advanced Encryption Standard (AES)–based encryption or Windows Media DRM of media files and allows protected distribution of digital media.

- Empowers developers to develop data-rich and media-rich interactive RIAs.

  - *New networking APIs* (to detect the connected, disconnected, and changed state) and the *new offline APIs Out-of-Browser functionality* allow Silverlight applications to run in disconnected mode as a rich client application in the sandbox environment. This feature lets organizations develop true RIAs that can support application functionalities in connected and disconnected mode.

  - *Silverlight 3 SDK* provides additional controls to develop rich and controlled applications in a rapid application development mode. The following bullet items outline some examples from Layout Management, Forms, and Data Manipulation.

  - *New Layout XAML Controls*, including `DockPanel`, `WrapPanel`, and `TabPanel`, help to control the application layout effectively.

  - *New Forms XAML Controls*, including `PasswordBox`, `AutoCompleteBox`, `SaveFileDialog`, and the Save-As File dialog box, make it easier to write operation implementations and additional `invalid` Visual State Manager (VSM) states to the `TextBox`, `CheckBox`, `RadioButton`, `ComboBox`, and `ListBox` controls.

- *New DataManipulation XAML Controls*, including a multi-select `ListBox` control; a `DataPager` control to display data in multiple pages; and a `DataForm` control to support dynamic fields generation, fields layout, validation, and data paging. An enhanced `DataGrid` control supports grouping and validation, and new data validation controls such as `DescriptionViewer`, `ErrorSummary`, and `FieldLabel` allow automatic validity checking of user input.

- *New Content XAML Controls*, such as `ChildWindow` and `ViewBox`, help to manage the content display more effectively in Silverlight applications.

- *Other user interface framework improvements*, including the *Element-to-Element Binding* feature that uses `ElementName` to bind two controls' properties to each other's value/state/position; `BasedOn` styling to enable changing the control's style at runtime dynamically; `CaretBrush` and access to `SystemColors`, which support high-contrast situations; and *DeepLinking*, which enables users to bookmark a page within an RIA.

- *Search Engine Optimization (SEO)* in Silverlight 3 resolves one of the key challenges of RIAs, the existence of the application in the search engine. With the use of business objects and ASP.NET controls and site maps on the server side, users can automatically mirror database-driven RIA content into HTML that can be easily indexed by the leading search engines.

Silverlight 4

Microsoft mainly focused on media-driven capabilities until the Silverlight 3 version. Silverlight 3 introduced key data integration capabilities to develop data-driven applications easily. However, if you want to develop Line of Business (LoB) data-driven RIAs with some core functionalities such as printing, documents integration, reporting, rich offline capabilities and local devices integration, Silverlight 4 is the version to start with.

Silverlight 4 Beta was quickly released at PDC 09 in November 2009, after the release of Silverlight 3 in July 2009. And Silverlight 4 is released on April 12, 2010 during the DevConnection conference.

In addition to the features mentioned in the Silverlight 3 section, the following are the key enhanced features of Silverlight 4:

- Introduction of new and enhanced LoB RIAs features, such as

    - *Content Printing capability* using new printing APIs enables developers to create default or custom visual print views that can be integrated with your local installed printers or can also be saved as files (XPS, PDF) based on the drivers installed on your machine.

    - *Right-click context menu* is now a default Silverlight capability, enabling a desktop application–like user experience for Silverlight RIA.

    - *Drag and Drop and Copy and Paste* features enable seamless integration of local files/data to Silverlight RIA.

    - *New controls*, such as the RichTextBox control, which allows developers to provide a rich text edit area, supporting text formatting, hyperlinks, and images within Silverlight applications. The new WebBrowser and

WebBrowserBrush controls enable integration of HTML content within the application while you are running the application in Out of Browser (OOB) mode.

- *Enhancements in existing controls* such as DataGrid with sorting/resizing and copy/paste rows capabilities, TextBlock with the new TextTrimming property and addition of the ViewBox control to manage the layout of the application.

- *Enhanced Data Binding* allows data binding to the properties of DependencyObject, string formatting within binding with the use of StringFormat, grouping collection of items using the GroupDescription property, and enhanced asynchronous validation and error management with IDataErrorInfo and INotifyDataErrorInfo interfaces.

- *Improved localization capabilities* add support for bi-directional text, right-to-left language support, and an additional 30 new languages. This is a significant achievement in terms of developing global Silverlight-based LoB RIAs.

- *Introduction of NotificationWindow* to provide a taskbar-based traditional notification ("toast") on the client machine (while Silverlight RIA is running in the OOB mode) will improve the end-user experience by providing a consistent approach, like many other traditional applications.

- *Support to keyboard access in full-screen mode* and *easy implementation of mouse wheel support* with the new APIs to handle MouseWheel events improve the usability significantly.

- *Integration capability with Webcam and Microphone* allows enterprises to implement interactive corporate and customer-facing applications to support voice interaction and video conferencing with regular data-driven and media-centric features, and to provide "One Box" solutions.

- Allowing Silverlight applications to be "trusted" as out-of-browser applications opens up a number of avenues, which you have implemented using traditional WPF-based LoB applications, by calling native code outside of the sandbox environment on the client machine. To make a Silverlight 4 application a trusted OOB application, you need to set the ElevatedPermissions property to Required in the OutOfBrowserSettings.xml file. The following are a few capabilities you can implement with the elevated trusted OOB RIAs.

  - *Support for Late Binding* allows late binding with the objects retrieved from HTML DOM (with IDynamicMetaObjectProvider interface) or from Automation APIs (with addition of the ComAutomationFactory class). This capability introduces features like integration with COM applications, such as Microsoft Office applications (e.g., Word, Excel, and Outlook) on the Windows client and other connected devices integration.

  - *Access to "My*" Folders from the application* allows access to all MyDocuments, MyVideos, MyPictures, and MyMusic folders for Windows (and on Mac mapped to related places) and to read and write files between these folders and the application running in the sandbox environment.

- Easy applications deployment and management by eliminating the need of cross-domain access policy files (`ClientAccess.xml` or `CrossDomainAcess.xml`) and the capability to create group policies to manage the trusted applications.

- Silverlight 4 does include a few key enhancements to protect, process, and deliver media-richer RIAs.

  - *Support for Offline Silverlight Digital Rights Management (DRM) powered by PlayReady* with the OOB applications will help to deliver the media in the offline mode in a more protected and managed environment.

  - As discussed earlier, integration capabilities with webcam and microphone and audio and video client-side recording capabilities provide numerous opportunities to develop audio/video interactive RIAs.

- The following core platform and components enhancements will help to improve the overall end-user experience and develop enterprise applications in the agile and rapid application development mode.

  - Official *support for the Google Chrome web browser* is probably a final step (for now—until a new widely-used browser pops up in the market) towards claiming Silverlight as a cross-browser platform and certainly will keep Google fans happy.

  - Introduction of *Implicit Theming/Styling* helps to develop a tighter control on the look and feel of specific types of controls based on the external definition.

  - Introduction of *Multicast UDP Networking* will help to improve the application performance and stability by utilizing networking resources more efficiently.

  - *WCF RIA Services* help the enterprise to develop n-tier applications, following the best practices in an agile and rapid application development mode.

  - Overall *performance optimization* improves the Silverlight 4 application start-up and execution performance compared to Silverlight 3 applications.

- Visual Studio 2010 enables the user interface development for Silverlight 4 (and Silverlight 3) RIAs and introduces better data binding and WCF RIA services integration with other enhancements to improve the development experience.

- Silverlight 4 and Windows Phone development tools enable development of interactive Silverlight applications for Windows 7 Mobile Phone series. You can develop high-quality media applications (including integration with video camera and microphone) to multi-touch and motion sensing gaming applications (using XNA framework) for Windows mobile phones. For further details visit - www.silverlight.net/getstarted/devices/windows-phone/.

▪ **Note** You can get detailed features matrix providing comparison between features capabilities in Silverlight 4 and prior versions (Silverlight 3, 2, and 1) by visiting `www.silverlight.net/getstarted/overview.aspx`

Design and Development Tools for Silverlight

It is no surprise that Microsoft has a set of design and development tools to develop Silverlight-based RIAs. One of the noticeable enhancements with Silverlight is that Microsoft created an opportunity for enterprises to bring the developers and artists/designers together to work on Silverlight RIAs independently, but without losing the development integrity. With the set of integrated designers' tools, such as Microsoft Expression Studio, and developers' tools, such as Microsoft Visual Studio, Microsoft development platform assists in a great way to develop interactive and rich Silverlight RIAs. The following is a quick summary of tools that can be used to develop Silverlight 4 and prior versions (mainly Silverlight 3) RIAs.

Visual Studio

Since Visual Studio 2010 supports .NET 4.0 and 3.x and Visual Studio 2008 SP1 supports .NET 3.x, WPF application support is already built in. However, Silverlight support is not provided out of the box.

Visual Studio 2010 supports development of .NET 4 and 3.5–based Silverlight 4 and Silverlight 3 RIAs. You can continue using Visual Studio 2008 SP1 for the development of Silverlight 3 applications. Note that for the development of Silverlight 4 applications, you must use Visual Studio 2010. With the appropriate version of Silverlight Tools for Visual Studio, Silverlight project type support is enabled. The Silverlight Tools for Visual Studio installs Silverlight Developers runtime, Silverlight SDK, and Silverlight Tools for Visual Studio.

Including the Silverlight 4 online and offline documentation, two more tools/services are available that can be integrated with Visual Studio for Silverlight development: Silverlight Toolkit and WCF RIA Services.

- The Silverlight 4 version of Silverlight Tool Kit provides additional Silverlight controls and related source code and themes supporting Visual Studio 2010 and .NET4.0. The Silverlight controls part of the tool kit uses open-source license. You can download them by visiting `http://silverlight.codeplex.com/`.

- If you are looking to implement mid-tier components to implement secured data access, the WCF RIA Services is an easy gateway to implement them easily, following the best practices. The WCF RIA Services provides a framework and integration capability with Visual Studio 2010 Silverlight projects to enable development of enterprise-level n-tier SOA RIAs using Silverlight and ASP .NET together. You can get more details on this topic by visiting `http://silverlight.net/getstarted/riaservices`. I will cover more on the WCF RIA Services in Chapter 13.

The key limitation introduced with Silverlight 3 and Visual Studio 2008 integration is the lack of designer support for Silverlight 3 projects. To define the user interface and preview interactively you have to use Expression Blend 3. However, Visual Studio and Expression Studio tools provide easy

Silverlight project integration between two development environments to switch back and forth between the presentation layer design and code-behind. This limitation is overcome in Visual Studio 2010. Visual Studio 2010 includes fully integrated Silverlight development support with interactive designer and debugging capabilities, which is applicable to Silverlight 4 and Silverlight 3 projects.

After you install the Silverlight 4 Tools for Visual Studio, Visual Studio 2010 gains support for building Silverlight 4 projects with Visual Basic and C# project templates. Default development features of Visual Studio such as design surface (including drag-and-drop Silverlight user controls on the design surface) and appropriate IntelliSense in the XAML editor are now available to Silverlight projects.

You can also use Visual Web Developer 2010 Express or Visual Web Developer 2008 Express SP1, instead of Visual Studio 2010 or 2008 for Silverlight 4 or 3 development.

Visit www.microsoft.com/visualstudio/ to get details on how to purchase Visual Studio 2010 or 2008 and get the free editions of Visual Web Developer 2010 or 2008 Express from www.microsoft.com/express/web/. You can visit www.silverlight.net/getstarted/ to download and install Microsoft Silverlight 4 Tools for Visual Studio 2010 and Silverlight 3 Tools for Visual Studio 2010 or 2008 SP1. Note that Silverlight 4 works only with Visual Studio 2010 and Visual Web Developer 2010 Express.

While Visual Studio is an established tool targeted to developers, tool support for WPF and Silverlight for both designers and developers is necessary. This need is satisfied by the Expression suite of products from Microsoft. Next we will discuss key products of Expression suite for Silverlight.

Expression Blend

Microsoft Expression Blend is part of the Microsoft Expression Studio and tightly integrated with Visual Studio, and it allows artists and designers to create rich XAML-based user interfaces for Silverlight applications.

Microsoft Expression Blend 3 introduced other key capabilities, such as integration with Adobe Photoshop and Illustrator to import files directly; sample data integration during the design and development phases, used to understand the visual and functional behavior of the data-driven RIAs without connecting to the live data in the development mode; and support for rich, graphics-based user interface development (e.g., 3D support, enhanced VSM).

With Silverlight 4 and Visual Studio 2010, a new version of Expression Blend—Expression Blend 4 RC for .NET 4.0—is available. Along with all capabilities of Expression Blend 3, the new version includes additional capabilities to integrate with Visual Studio 2010, .NET Framework 4.0, and Silverlight 4. You must use Expression Blend 4 RC for .NET 4.0 and 3.5 to develop Silverlight 4 and 3 projects and provide integration with Visual Studio 2010. Visit http://www.silverlight.net/getstarted/ to install Microsoft Expression Blend 4 RC for .NET 4.0 and visit www.microsoft.com/expression/products/Blend4RC_ReleaseNotes.aspx to get details on the Express Blend 4 RC.

SketchFlow

Rapid prototyping, or proof of concept, always helps to build the dynamic user interface, demonstrating the concept visually. To develop prototypes, Silverlight/WPF controls and components, imported images, and drawing tools can be used. The SketchFlow-based Silverlight and WPF prototypes can be extended as regular Silverlight/WPF projects within the Expression Blend and Visual Studio to transform a concept into reality without losing any major work done during the prototype phase. Visit www.microsoft.com/expression/ to install SketchFlow.

Expression Encoder

Microsoft Expression Encoder is part of the Microsoft Expression Studio and contains Silverlight Media Player templates used to author VC-1 or H.264 encoded media content, manage, and publish for Silverlight applications. Visit `www.microsoft.com/expression/` to install Microsoft Expression Encoder 3.

Deep Zoom Composer

The Deep Zoom feature allows Silverlight developers to implement zooming and panning capabilities to implement high-resolution imagery solutions. The Deep Zoom Composer allows professionals to create and prepare images to implement the Deep Zoom feature within Silverlight applications. If you have seen the Hard Rock Memorabilia (`http://memorabilia.hardrock.com/`) site, you have seen a product of the Deep Zoom Composer. This technology will be discussed when we take a closer look at media support in Silverlight in Chapter 4. Visit `www.microsoft.com/downloads/` and search for Deep Zoom Composer to download the tool.

Eclipse Tools for Silverlight (eclipse4SL)

Eclipse Tools for Microsoft Silverlight (eclipse4SL) enables development of Silverlight applications using the Eclipse open-source and cross-platform development platform. You can install this tool set by visiting `www.eclipse.org/esl/`.

Creating a Silverlight 4–based Application

Now let us get a quick hands-on experience with Visual Studio 2010, Expression Blend for .NET 4, and Silverlight by creating a simple but very powerful RIA. I will demonstrate the new capabilities of Silverlight 4, such as local file integration, with the new RichTextBox control, using the drag-and-drop functionality to insert JPG and PNG images within the RichTextBox control.

You can start creating a Silverlight 4 project using Visual Studio 2010 or Expression Blend 4 RC. Here we will start by loading Visual Studio 2010 and creating a new Silverlight Application project with the name FirstApplication under `C:\Users\<user name>\Documents\Books\Accelerated Silverlight 4\Source\Chapter 1\Project1\` (see Figure 1-1).

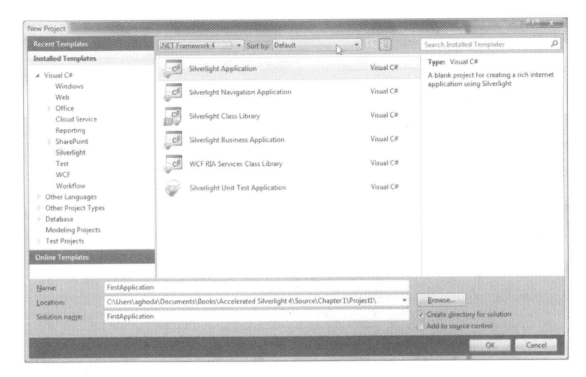

Figure 1-1. *The New Project dialog in Visual Studio 2010*

■ **Note** As you see in Figure 1-1, three new project templates are introduced in Silverlight 4 and Visual Studio 2010.

- *Silverlight Business Applications* creates a sample WCF RIA Services–based Lind of Business application. The sample project is created based on the Silverlight Navigation Application project template with WCF RIA services enabled and, by default, includes user authentication and registration services and Data Access helper classes.

- *WCF RIA Services Class Library* helps you to build reusable mid-tier and presentation-tier components and services to support multiple Silverlight-based RIAs. You can implement reusable user authentication, user registration, and data integration services using WCF RIA services class library. This template is available only if you have installed WCF RIA Services for Visual Studio 2010.

- *Silverlight Unit Test Application* helps to create a Silverlight unit test application to perform in-browser unit testing.

After you click OK, the next dialog allows you to create a new ASP.NET web site/web application project that hosts the Silverlight application (see Figure 1-2).

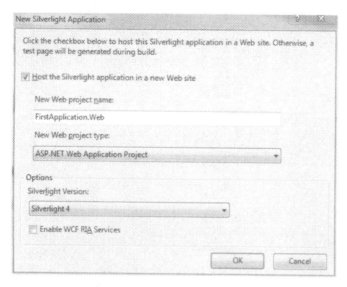

Figure 1-2. The New Silverlight Application dialog in Visual Studio 2010

For the purpose of the examples in this book, it does not matter if you use a web site or a web application project; however, web application projects are better for eventual deployment since they contain a project file suitable for MSBuild. Also, our project is going to be a simple demonstration project, so you do not need to select the "Enable WCF RIA Services" option.

Click OK, and the Solution Explorer will show two projects: the Silverlight application (FirstApplication) and the web site supporting it (FirstApplication.Web). If you now build the application, the Silverlight application is built to a XAP file (with the naming convention <SilverlightApplicationName>.xap) that is automatically copied to the ClientBin folder within the web site. This XAP file contains the Silverlight application with start-up assemblies and resources and will be downloaded by the client when he or she visits the web site.

If you now start the development server in Visual Studio (by pressing F5 or Ctrl+F5), you will see the Silverlight application start. If, however, you create a new web site in IIS, point the document root to FirstApplication.Web, and navigate to this site, you will get a 404 error when trying to load the Silverlight application in your browser. What's going on? IIS 6 must know about the new file extension .xap. You accomplish this by adding a new MIME type to either the root of IIS or to the specific web site you created. The file extension is .xap and the MIME type is application/x-silverlight-app.

■ **Note** If you are using IIS 7, the XAP Silverlight package file type is already related to the application/x-silverlight-app MIME type. No additional steps are required.

Working with Expression Blend

Now let's take a look at Expression Blend 4 RC, a tool used to lay out user interface controls and create animations in WPF and Silverlight. You can open the current Silverlight Project in Expression Blend directly from the Visual Studio. Right-click on any XAML file of the project and select the option "Open in Expression Blend..".

Alternatively, without closing Visual Studio, start Expression Blend, and from the Projects tab window, choose Open Project or go to File ➤ Open Project/Solution, and navigate to the solution file created in Visual Studio (in `C:\Users\<user name>\Documents\Books\Accelerated Silverlight 4\Source\Chapter 1\Project1\FirstApplication`, if you used the same directory structure).

The panes on the left in Expression Blend are devoted to managing project files (like the Solution Explorer in Visual Studio—see Figure 1-3), triggers and events, and the visual states of the UserControl or control template. The panes on the right in Expression Blend are devoted to properties for various user interface elements; resources, which include style templates; and the Data pane, which supports sample data integration to view the application with sample data (without connecting to the live data) while you are in development mode.

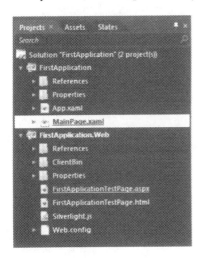

Figure 1-3. *The Projects tab in Expression Blend 4 RC*

▒ **Note** If you are familiar with Silverlight 2, you will notice that from Silverlight 3 and later version, the Page class Page.xaml file and the Page.xaml.cs code-behind file—representing the main application user interface (in Silverlight 2)—are renamed to MainPage.xaml and MainPage.xaml.cs (in Silverlight 3 and 4), respectively.

Along the left side of the Expression Blend screen is the toolbox. This provides access to both layout and input controls, and several tools used to modify the user interface, such as a paint bucket and a transform tool for brushes. Hold down the left mouse button when you select any icon with a white triangle in the lower-right corner, or right-click, and more tools will expand from it. Figure 1-4 shows an example of what clicking the Button icon (which looks like a mouse cursor hovering over a rounded rectangle) produces.

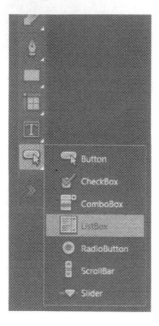

Figure 1-4. The control toolbox in Expression Blend

The Objects and Timeline area to the immediate right of the toolbox provides a place to create and manage animation storyboards, but more importantly for us right now, it shows the object hierarchy in XAML. After creating our application, we see [UserControl] and LayoutRoot. Click [UserControl] to highlight it and then click Properties in the top-right portion of the screen. The control with the gray highlight is the control that shows up in the Properties pane (see Figure 1-5).

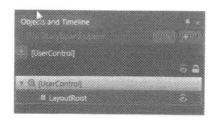

Figure 1-5. The Objects and Timeline pane in Expression Blend

Just for demonstration purposes, you can also set the Layout section of the Properties pane and set the Width and Height properties of the UserControl to 900 and 100, respectively, as shown in Figure 1-6.

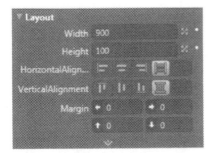

Figure 1-6. Defining Width and Height properties for a control in Expression Blend

You can also click XAML or Split along the right side of the design surface and view and edit the XAML directly. However, as interfaces get more complex, Expression Blend becomes an invaluable design tool for working with XAML indirectly. Hand-editing of XAML should generally be used for tweaking some XAML instead of creating full-blown user interfaces.

Demonstrating Local Image Files Integration Using Drag-and-Drop Functionality

One of the growing requests to develop a RIA is to ingrate with the local file system and have drag-and-drop functionality to insert/add/attach files to the application. Silverlight 3 introduces the Open File Dialog Box to insert files, and now Silverlight 4 introduces drag-and-drop capability to integrate with local files. Let's get started.

First, go back to the already-opened `FirstApplication` Visual Studio project so that I can also demonstrate some enhancements in Visual Studio 2010. Now if you double-click on the `MainPage.xaml` file to load the file, as shown in Figure 1-7, you will see the editable XAML design view to visually design the user interface, as well the XAML view to directly change the XAML code. The XAML code and the look and feel will be changed and reflected immediately in both views when a change is made in one of the views.

Figure 1-7. Design and XAML view in Visual Studio 2010

As you see in Figure 1-7, the main change in the definition of the UserControl is the inclusion of the DesignHeight and DesignWidth properties of the UserControl, which are set by default to 300 and 400. This helps you to design your user interface in a controlled and managed way at the design time, if you are not setting the UserControl's specific height and width. The design time height and width will not be reflected at runtime.

Now, in order to add a title and rich text area to insert images, add StackPanel control within the Grid control, as shown here.

```
<UserControl x:Class="FirstApplication.MainPage"
    xmlns="http://schemas.microsoft.com/winfx/2006/xaml/presentation"
    xmlns:x="http://schemas.microsoft.com/winfx/2006/xaml"
    xmlns:d="http://schemas.microsoft.com/expression/blend/2008"
    xmlns:mc="http://schemas.openxmlformats.org/markup-compatibility/2006"
    mc:Ignorable="d"
    d:DesignHeight="300" d:DesignWidth="400">
    <Grid x:Name="LayoutRoot" Background="White">
        <StackPanel>
        </StackPanel>
    </Grid>
</UserControl>
```

Next, from the ToolBox pane available on the left side, drag and drop a TextBlock control on the design surface to place it within the StackPanel. Then, through the property pane available on the right side, set the Text, FontSize, FontWeight, and Margin properties to make the title bigger and bold. This will be reflected in the related XAML code, as shown here.

```
<TextBlock
    Text="Drag and Drop Image File(s) from your Local Folder to the
          Following Rich Text Area"
    FontSize="15"
    FontWeight="Bold"
    Margin="25,0,0,0" />
```

Finally, after TextBlock control, add the RichTextBox control from the XAML view. At present the RichTextBox control is not available in the ToolBox within Visual Studio, so you need to add it using the XAML view. However, within Expression Blend you can drag and drop the RichTextBox control to the design surface. The RichTextBpx control allows the editing and display of rich text formatting (bold, italics, etc.), add hyper links and inline images.

To allow drag-and-drop you need to set up the AllowDrop dependency property of the UIElement to true allowing the element as a dropping target. Set the AllowDrop property of the added RichTextBox control to True, using the Properties pane. Set Name property to richTextBox. Next, set the key Drop event through the XAML to perform action when files are dropped on the RichTextBox control. Also change the TextWrapping property to Wrap, to allow text wrapping. Other modified self-explanatory properties are shown in the following code snippet.

```
<RichTextBox
    Name="richTextBox"
    AllowDrop="True"
    Drop="richTextBox_Drop"
    Background="#FFFCFCFC"
    Cursor="Stylus"
    FontFamily="Portable User Interface"
    TextWrapping="Wrap"
    VerticalScrollBarVisibility="Auto"
    HorizontalScrollBarVisibility="Auto"
    MinHeight="300" MaxHeight="600"
    MinWidth="300" MaxWidth="1200"/>
```

So far the XAML implementation is over. Note that we have added the Drop event in the XAML code and Visual Studio will add the related event handler automatically.

Go ahead and press F6 to build the application, and then Ctrl+F5 to start the application without debugging. You will see the application with the title and editable rich text area. You can enter only simple text to the rich text area because we have not coded to format the text. Now from the local file system, if you try to drag and drop file(s) on top of the rich text area, nothing will happen. To process dropped files, you need to implement the logic within the Drop event of the RichTextBox control, which we already defined through XAML. For this chapter, we would add logic to process each dropped file and insert JPG and PNG image files, one after another, to the rich text area. Each image will be added as a new paragraph. If you are dropping one or more files other than JPG or PNG files, for each invalid file type it will display a notification message window.

To start implementing the code-behind—MainPage.xaml.cs—first add reference to System.IO namespace to allow files processing (read and write files and obtain basic file profile information). Also add System.Windows.Media.Imaging namespace reference to process bitmap images, as shown here.

```
using System.IO;
using System.Windows.Media.Imaging;
```

Now implement the business logic of the richTextBox_Drop event, as shown here.

```
private void richTextBox_Drop(object sender, DragEventArgs e)
{
    if (e.Data == null)
        return;

    IDataObject dataObject = e.Data as IDataObject;
    FileInfo[] droppedfiles = dataObject.GetData
        (DataFormats.FileDrop) as FileInfo[];

    foreach (FileInfo droppedfile in droppedfiles)

        if (IsCorrectImageFileType
            (droppedfile.Extension.Trim().ToLower()))
        {

            using (var filestream = droppedfile.OpenRead())
            {
                var imgfile = new BitmapImage();
                imgfile.SetSource(filestream);
                var img = new Image();
                img.Source = imgfile;

                InlineUIContainer rtaImg = new
                    InlineUIContainer();
                rtaImg.Child = img;

                Paragraph inlineImg = new Paragraph();
                richTextBox.Blocks.Add(inlineImg);
                inlineImg.Inlines.Add(rtaImg);
            }
        }
        else
        {
            MessageBox.Show
                (droppedfile.Name + " is not valid file.");
        }
}
```

As shown in this Drop event, each dropped file is represented as a FileInfo object. The FileInfo object will allow opening and reading of the file and also provide a file profile. Before processing the JPG and PNG image files, you need to check whether each dropped file is a valid type of file. We used the Extension property of the FileInfo object to get the extension of the file. Next, validate the file extension by calling the IsCorrectImageFileType function. Each dropped JPG and PNG file is decoded, streamed, and loaded to the Image object. The InlineUIContainer allows UIElement-type (e.g., images) content to embed as inline content. The dropped valid image is added as inline content to the rich text area as a new paragraph.

If the file type is not valid then using the Name property of the FileInfo object notify user with the specific file is invalid. The following is a self-explanatory custom private method. IsCorrectImageFileType method returns true if the file is either a JPG or PNG; otherwise it returns false.

```
private bool IsCorrectImageFileType(string fileExtension)
{
    switch (fileExtension)
    {
        case ".jpg":
        case ".png":
            return true;
        default: break;
    }
    return false;
}
```

To build the application, press F6 and then Ctrl+F5 to start the application without debugging. As shown in Figure 1-8, I have dragged a JPG file from the Sample Pictures folder and dropped it on the rich text area, and the image is added as inline content.

Figure 1-8. Inserting image as inline image to the Silverlight 4 application by dragging and dropping a valid image file on the rich text area

Figure 1-9 demonstrates the received notification when you drop an invalid file to the application.

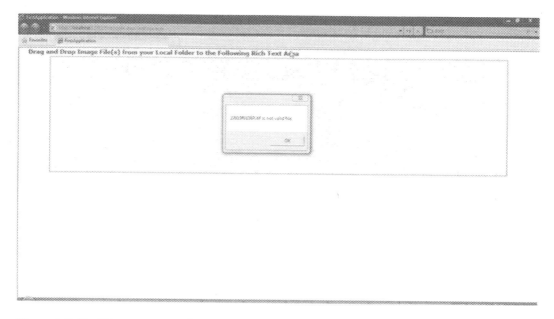

Figure 1-9. Notifying user upon dropping an invalid file type

Congratulations, you have now created your first Silverlight 4 application and learned the basics of developing Silverlight applications, using both Expression Blend and Visual Studio, as well as integrating code-behind managed code!

Summary

This chapter began with a discussion of Silverlight and its major competitors. We also learned the key differences between different versions of Silverlight. Next, we covered how to create a new Silverlight 4 application in Visual Studio 2010 with a supporting web site, how to modify the user interface, and, finally, how to build and execute an application in Visual Studio. While we built the application, I highlighted the key development aspect changes in Silverlight 4 compared to Silverlight 3. This should help if you are familiar with Silverlight 3 and would like to learn how to migrate Silverlight 3 applications to Silverlight 4. The migration of the existing Silverlight 3 applications may require some modifications based on the breaking changes between Silverlight 4 and 3. You can also visit - http://msdn.microsoft.com/en-us/library/cc645049(VS.95).aspx - to learn the key breaking changes between Silverlight 4 and 3. .

The next step on our journey through practical Silverlight development is to learn the basics of Silverlight and the role of XAML in Silverlight RIAs. Many of the core concepts needed to understand how Silverlight works are covered in the next chapter, including markup extensions, dependency properties, and previews of features such as data binding and styling applications.

CHAPTER 2

Silverlight Concepts

Now that you understand what Silverlight is and where it fits into the general technology landscape, and you have installed the tools necessary to develop in Silverlight and created your first Silverlight application, it is time to peel back the layers to understand the basic concepts of Silverlight. This chapter will start by detailing high-level Silverlight architecture and properly introducing Extensible Application Markup Language (XAML) (core platform of the presentation layer) and exploring its many features, such as property and event systems needed to support data binding, animation, and other key parts of Silverlight. The chapter will wrap up with more information on Silverlight applications, such as the project structure, key .NET assemblies for Silverlight applications, and connecting XAML to events in the code-behind.

▓ **Note** This chapter is intended to provide the basics of Silverlight technology platform, as well as XAML and its crucial role in developing the presentation layer of Silverlight applications. If you have already developed applications on earlier versions of Silverlight and worked on WPF-based applications, you can skip this chapter.

Silverlight Architecture

Silverlight provides platform-agnostic Rich Internet Applications (RIA) development and deployment platform by providing

- Lightweight runtime to run Silverlight applications within a sandbox on a client's cross-platform (different operating systems—Windows, Mac, Linux), cross-browser (different web browsers—Internet Explorer, Firefox, Safari, Chrome), and cross-device (regular computers and Windows Phone 7 mobile devices) environments.

- .NET Framework integration capabilities with the support of CLR (for Silverlight) to implement WPF-based user interface and managed code-behind .NET integration and support for WCF services, LINQ, and service-oriented features. In this chapter we will cover some of the areas of this topic.

- Support of dynamic languages via the Microsoft Dynamic Language Runtime (DLR) engine—a generic platform and hosting model for dynamic languages to run on top of the Microsoft .NET Framework Common Language Runtime (CLR). The dynamic languages for Silverlight are covered in Chapter 14.

- Extensible and flexible Silverlight applications package and deployment architectural options to balance start-up application performance, introduce reusability across Silverlight applications, and provide required security. We will cover this topic in Chapter 17.

Figure 2-1 shows the Silverlight architecture describing these key components and services. Visit http://msdn.microsoft.com/en-us/library/bb404713(VS.96).aspx to get more details on the Silverlight architecture.

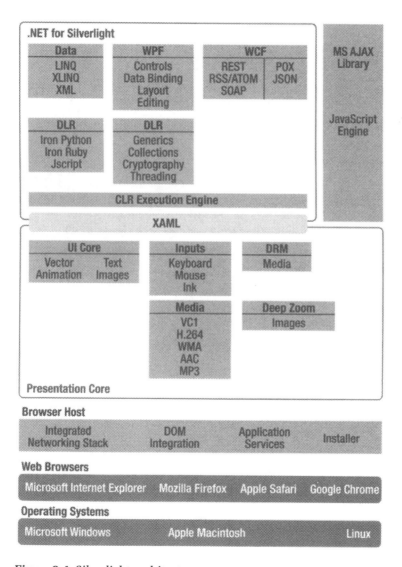

Figure 2-1. Silverlight architecture

Silverlight and XAML

All versions of Silverlight are a subset of Windows Presentation Foundation (WPF)—a strong and abstracted presentation framework—for defining interactive user interfaces that can be integrated seamlessly with media (audio, video, and images) and data. As a result, at the core of the Silverlight presentation framework is the XML-based declarative Extensible Application Markup Language (XAML, pronounced *zammel*). XAML enables designers and developers to define externalized and decoupled user interfaces and related style sheets. In this section I will provide you some basic information about XAML. If you are already familiar with XAML, you can skip this section to accelerate your learning of Silverlight 4.

▓ **Note:** The Silverlight XAML parser is different than the regular WPF XAML parser and has limited features. Silverlight 4 brings the Silverlight version of the XAML parser one step closer to the regular WPF parser. Originally, I would have covered this topic in this chapter, however, by the time XAML enhancements were introduced in Silverlight 4 RC, this chapter was already finalized. As a result, key XAML features enhancements introduced in Silverlight 4 are covered in Chapter 7.

Developing a Sample Application

Let's jump right in and look at a simple Silverlight application. For the sake of simplicity, this application will display only a basic login screen with a text entry area for username and password, and a button. There is no logic behind this screen—we will look only at the markup for now. Figure 2-2 shows a simple in-browser login screen developed in Silverlight using XAML controls.

Figure 2-2. A simple login screen developed using Silverlight

Silverlight being a cross-platform, cross-browser, and cross-device technology platform, unsurprisingly, if you try it on Windows or Mac machines, or Windows Mobile 7 phone, and use Internet Explorer, Safari, Chrome, or Mozilla FireFox web browser, the application looks the same on every platform. As long as this behavior holds true throughout Silverlight applications, it should reinforce the fact that Silverlight provides a viable cross-platform framework, delivering on its promise.

Defining User Interface Using XAML Code

Now let's look at the XAML that describes the login section of the application. If you create a new Silverlight application (XAMLTour in this book), you can copy and paste this code into MainPage.xaml (if your project name is different than XAMLTour, change the namespace in the x:Class attribute to match the project name). We'll discuss many aspects of this code in detail in later chapters, such as how the Grid and Canvas layout controls work.

```xaml
<UserControl x:Class="XAMLTour.MainPage"
    xmlns="http://schemas.microsoft.com/winfx/2006/xaml/presentation"
    xmlns:x="http://schemas.microsoft.com/winfx/2006/xaml"
    xmlns:d="http://schemas.microsoft.com/expression/blend/2008"
    xmlns:mc="http://schemas.openxmlformats.org/markup-compatibility/2006"
    mc:Ignorable="d"
    d:DesignHeight="300" d:DesignWidth="400">
    <Canvas Background="White">
        <Grid Height="140" Width="250" Canvas.Left="25" Canvas.Top="15">
            <Grid.RowDefinitions>
                <RowDefinition/>
                <RowDefinition/>
                <RowDefinition/>
                <RowDefinition/>
            </Grid.RowDefinitions>
            <Grid.ColumnDefinitions>
                <ColumnDefinition Width="Auto"/>
                <ColumnDefinition/>
            </Grid.ColumnDefinitions>
            <TextBlock HorizontalAlignment="Center"
                    Text="Please enter your information"
                    Grid.Column="0" Grid.Row="0" Grid.ColumnSpan="2"/>
            <TextBlock Text="Username:" VerticalAlignment="Top"
                    HorizontalAlignment="Right"
                    Grid.Column="0" Grid.Row="1"/>
            <TextBox VerticalAlignment="Top" Grid.Column="1" Grid.Row="1"/>
            <TextBlock HorizontalAlignment="Right" VerticalAlignment="Top"
                    Grid.Column="0" Grid.Row="2">
                Password:
            </TextBlock>
            <PasswordBox VerticalAlignment="Top" Grid.Column="1" Grid.Row="2"/>
            <Button Content="Login" Grid.Row="3" Width="100" Grid.Column="1"
                    HorizontalAlignment="Left"/>
        </Grid>
    </Canvas>
</UserControl>
```

Defining User Interface Using Code-Behind

XAML is a markup language that provides mechanisms for constructing and configuring object hierarchies that are traditionally done in code, such as C#. With the use of C#, you can generate similar XAML code instead of writing directly in XAML, as shown here:

```
Canvas canvas = new Canvas { Background = new
      SolidColorBrush(Color.FromArgb(255, 255, 255, 255))};
Grid grid = new Grid {
      Height=140,
      Width=250 };
grid.SetValue(Canvas.LeftProperty, 25d);
grid.SetValue(Canvas.TopProperty, 15d);

grid.RowDefinitions.Add(new RowDefinition());
grid.RowDefinitions.Add(new RowDefinition());
grid.RowDefinitions.Add(new RowDefinition());
grid.RowDefinitions.Add(new RowDefinition());
ColumnDefinition cd = new ColumnDefinition();
cd.Width = new GridLength(0, GridUnitType.Auto);
grid.ColumnDefinitions.Add(cd);
grid.ColumnDefinitions.Add(new ColumnDefinition());

TextBlock headerText = new TextBlock {
      HorizontalAlignment = HorizontalAlignment.Center,
      Text = "Please enter your information" };
headerText.SetValue(Grid.ColumnProperty, 0);
headerText.SetValue(Grid.ColumnSpanProperty, 2);
headerText.SetValue(Grid.RowProperty, 0);

TextBlock usernameText = new TextBlock {
      HorizontalAlignment = HorizontalAlignment.Right,
      Text = "Username:" };
usernameText.SetValue(Grid.ColumnProperty, 0);
usernameText.SetValue(Grid.RowProperty, 1);

TextBox usernameInput = new TextBox {
      VerticalAlignment = VerticalAlignment.Top };
usernameInput.SetValue(Grid.ColumnProperty, 1);
usernameInput.SetValue(Grid.RowProperty, 1);

TextBlock passwordText = new TextBlock {
      HorizontalAlignment = HorizontalAlignment.Right,
      Text = "Password:" };
passwordText.SetValue(Grid.ColumnProperty, 0);
passwordText.SetValue(Grid.RowProperty, 2);

PasswordBox passwordInput = new PasswordBox {
      VerticalAlignment = VerticalAlignment.Top };
passwordInput.SetValue(Grid.ColumnProperty, 1);
passwordInput.SetValue(Grid.RowProperty, 2);

Button loginButton = new Button {
      Content = "Login",
      HorizontalAlignment = HorizontalAlignment.Left,
      Width = 100 };
loginButton.SetValue(Grid.ColumnProperty, 1);
loginButton.SetValue(Grid.RowProperty, 3);
```

```
grid.Children.Add(headerText);
grid.Children.Add(usernameText);
grid.Children.Add(usernameInput);
grid.Children.Add(passwordText);
grid.Children.Add(passwordInput);
grid.Children.Add(loginButton);

this.Content = canvas;
canvas.Children.Add(grid);
```

The C# code is more verbose and thus more difficult to read and maintain than the XAML. Both the C# code and the XAML files require a compilation step: C# for obvious reasons and XAML files since they have the code-behind and must be packaged as part of a XAP file. C# also requires a software developer to create the user interface, either by hand or by using a designer, as with Windows Forms. XAML provides a way to create user interfaces such as the login screen in a straightforward and (relatively) easy-to-maintain fashion. Markup is easier to read (at least in small doses—complex user interfaces are a different story) and has far better tool support for creating and maintaining. XAML isn't just another markup language—its strength lies in its ability to model object hierarchies and easily configure object states via attributes or child elements. Each element name (e.g., UserControl, Canvas, etc.) directly corresponds to a Silverlight object of the same name.

The XAML Controls Structure

Let's look more closely at the XAML. The root element is UserControl, a container for other controls. A UserControl on its own has no visual representation—layout controls such as Canvas and Grid combined with standard controls such as text input boxes and buttons create the visual representation. User controls provide a way to compose controls into a reusable "master" control, not unlike user controls in ASP.NET. The next chapter will take a closer look at what goes into user controls in Silverlight.

Silverlight has rich support for composing what is ultimately viewed onscreen. Many controls can contain arbitrary content, such as a ListBox containing Buttons as items or even other ListBoxes! This makes composing a custom user interface possible using nothing other than markup. Since XAML is a dialect of XML, elements describing content are nested in a tree hierarchy. From the perspective of XAML, this tree is known as a *logical tree*.

■ **Caution** XAML is case sensitive. Since XAML is a dialect of XML, it possesses all of the characteristics of XML. Most importantly, all element names, property names, and so on, are case sensitive. Button is *not* the same as button. However, this does not necessarily apply to property values, which are handled by Silverlight's XAML parser.

By reading this XAML code closely, you can see that it describes a UserControl that contains a Canvas that contains a Grid that contains the various visual elements of the login screen. You can view the logical tree of these elements in Visual Studio by right-clicking the design surface and choosing Document Outline or, alternately, going to the View menu and choosing Other Windows ➤ Document Outline. This displays a window showing the logical tree of elements describing what's currently on the design surface. Figure 2-3 shows the document outline for the login screen. This view of the logical tree is slightly different from a similar logical tree in Windows Presentation Foundation (WPF), because the document outline focuses on what is explicitly found in the XAML. For example, if a ListBoxItem contains a Content attribute, the type-converted string is not shown. However, creating a Button as a child of a ListBoxItem will cause the Button to show up in the document outline.

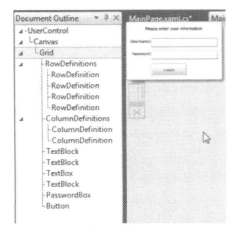

Figure 2-3. *The document outline describing the login screen*

▓ **Note** In Visual Studio 2010, if you mouse over one of the controls/elements within the document outline pane, you will see the corresponding user interface including all children controls. As an example, as shown in Figure 2-3, if you mouse over Grid, then you should see the login screen user interface displayed in the popup window.

Namespaces

We'll now elaborate on the XAML file structure. Two important namespaces, similar for regular WPF application XAML files, appear in the root element of each Silverlight application XAML files. (Expression Blend adds a couple of others, but we'll look at the two most important here.) The first is the default namespace, specified by xmlns="http://schemas.microsoft.com/winfx/2006/xaml/presentation". This namespace contains the various elements that correspond to objects in Silverlight, such as UserControl, Canvas, and Grid. If you remove this declaration from a XAML file in Visual Studio, blue squiggly lines will show just how much is defined in this namespace.

The other namespace declaration contains XAML XML namespace extensions. Elements in this namespace are assigned to the x scope. Table 2-1 describes the most important aspects of the XAML (x:) namespace.

Table 2-1. *Key Features of the XAML (x:) Namespace*

Feature	Description
x:Class	Joins different pieces of a partial class together. Valid syntax for this is x:Class="namespace.classname" and x:Class="namespace.classname;assembly=assemblyname". The XAML page generates code to a piece of the class that combines with the code-behind.
x:Key	Provides a unique identifier to resources defined in XAML, vital for referencing resources via a markup extension. Identifiers must begin with a letter or an underscore and can contain only letters, digits, and the underscore.
x:Name	Provides a way to give an identifier to an object element in XAML for accessing via the code-behind. This is not appropriate for use with resources (instead use x:Key). Many elements have a Name property, and while Name and x:Name can be used interchangeably, only one should be set. Identifiers must begin with a letter or an underscore and can contain only letters, digits, and the underscore.
x:Null	Corresponds to null in C# (or Nothing in VB .NET). Can be used via a markup extension ({x:Null}) or through a property element (<x:Null/>).

Dependency Property System

The dependency property system is a significant aspect of Silverlight. It provides a way for multiple discrete sources, such as animation and data binding, to gain access to object properties. You can see the top classes in this hierarchy in Figure 2-4. Notice that the top of the hierarchy is DependencyObject. This root object provides much of the infrastructure needed to support the dependency property system, though it has only a few public methods. Let's look more closely at what dependency properties are and then highlight a few aspects of DependencyObject that will make more sense in light of dependency properties.

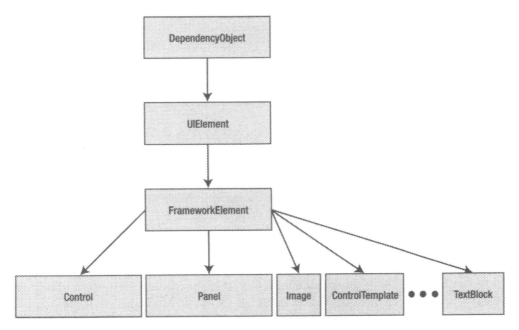

Figure 2-4. Top portion of object hierarchy relating to visual elements

Dependency Properties

A *dependency* property is a special type of property that backs a .NET property. The importance of dependency properties lies in the fact that the value depends on multiple sources (which is why it's called *dependency property*), and therefore, a standard .NET property is not enough. The value of a dependency property might come from data binding, animation, template resources specified in the XAML, styles, or local values. Figure 2-5 shows the precedence of these sources.

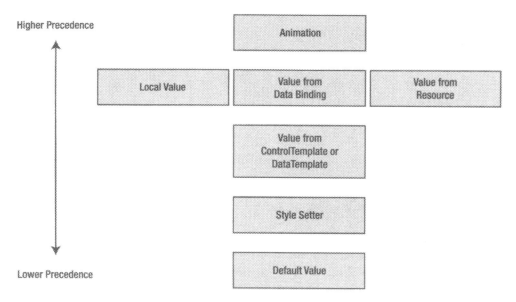

Figure 2-5. Precedence for sources of dependency property values

Animation has the highest precedence. Property values influenced by animation must be the values that take effect, or the user will never see the animation, since a different source will trump the animation values. Local values are those set via an attribute or property element. Local values can also be set via data binding or a static resource, so these are effectively local values—thus, at equal precedence (i.e., if you have set the local value using any approach, later, if you set the local value using another approach, it will replace the previous value entirely). Next lowest are values from a data template or a control template, which take effect if a local value does not override them. Styles defined in the page/application are next lowest, and if absolutely nothing is set, the dependency property takes on its default value.

▦ **Caution** The base value for a property is not the same as its default value. A property's base value is determined by applying the sources in the preceding precedence chart but stopping before getting to animation. A property's default value is its value when no other sources provide a value (e.g., a layout container's constructor may establish a default value for a size property, and if this is not modified anywhere else, its value remains untouched).

Let's examine an actual dependency property, one that you have already used. The Width property, defined in the FrameworkElement class, is first defined as a dependency property and then wrapped by a .NET property. This provides all the capability of a dependency property while providing a traditional approach to getting and setting its value. Let's examine how this particular dependency property is defined:

```
public static readonly DependencyProperty WidthProperty;
```

By convention, dependency properties end with the word `Property`, and this is adhered to throughout Silverlight. Notice that it is marked `public`—while this is also a convention, there is no compelling reason to not expose it publicly. The dependency property should be just as visible as the .NET property wrapper. The .NET property provides a shortcut, hiding the fact that there is an underlying dependency property, since it wraps the calls to `GetValue` and `SetValue`.

```
public double Width
{
   get {
      return (double) this.GetValue(WidthProperty);
   }
   set {
      base.SetValue(WidthProperty, value);
   }
}
```

Simply declaring the dependency property is not enough—it must be registered with the dependency property system using the `DependencyProperty.Register` static method. The `Register` method takes the following parameters:

```
public static DependencyProperty Register(
    string name,
    Type propertyType,
    Type ownerType,
    PropertyMetadata typeMetadata
```

Although you won't do much with it for now, let's create a new dependency property named `TextSize` in the `MainPage.xaml.cs` file. Add the following code to the class:

```
public static readonly DependencyProperty TextSizeProperty =
    DependencyProperty.Register("TextSize",
                                typeof(double),
                                typeof(MainPage),
                                new PropertyMetadata(new
                                    PropertyChangedCallback(onTextSizeChanged)));
   public double TextSize
   {
       get { return ((double)this.GetValue(TextSizeProperty)); }
       set { this.SetValue(TextSizeProperty, value); }
   }
```

The name of the dependency property (passed as the first parameter to `Register`) does not need to have `Property` appended to it—this convention holds only for the actual field name in the class. Now you have a new dependency property that can be used for data binding or any of the other various sources that can modify dependency property values.

There is one other useful aspect of dependency properties: property change notifications. This ability to capture property changes is vital for validating a property value at the last possible moment. This is useful for scenarios such as a progress bar, where there is a clear minimum and maximum value, and values greater than or less than these values should be constrained to their respective endpoints.

The final parameter to the Register method is where you specify a handler for the property change notification. Here's a handler for constraining TextSizeProperty to no larger than 36:

```
private static void onTextSizeChanged(DependencyObject source,
                                      DependencyPropertyChangedEventArgs e)
{
    if (((double)source.GetValue(e.Property)) > 36.0)
    {
        source.SetValue(e.Property, 36.0);
    }
}
```

■ **Note** A callback for property changes is the perfect place to validate and constrain dependency property values. It is also a great place to hold logic for modifying dependent properties, so when one changes, it affects other dependency property values of the DependencyObject that contains the properties.

The first parameter is the instance of DependencyObject—this is what you use to retrieve and set the value for the property. The Property member of the DependencyPropertyChangedEventArgs for this handler is then used as a parameter to GetValue and SetValue. If you try setting the value of the TextSize property to higher than 36 and then display its value, you will see it goes no higher than 36.

Attached Properties

An *attached* property is a special type of dependency property. Attached properties provide a way to assign values to properties on objects that do not actually have the property—the attached property values are generally used by parent objects in the element hierarchy. You have already seen several attached properties. Let's look again at the XAML code used to create header text for the login screen:

```
<TextBlock HorizontalAlignment="Center"
           Text="Please enter your information"
           Grid.Column="0" Grid.Row="0" Grid.ColumnSpan="2"/>
```

The Grid class defines several attached properties, including Column, Row, and ColumnSpan, which are used by the TextBlock object. If you look up the TextBlock object on MSDN, you won't find anything close to Grid.Row or Grid.Column properties. This is because Column, Row, and ColumnSpan are defined as attached properties on the Grid class. The Grid class defines a total of four attached properties: Column, Row, ColumnSpan, and RowSpan. The dotted syntax is used to specify the class that *does* provide these dependency properties. By using this syntax, it is possible to attach arbitrary properties to objects that do not have them. The attached properties for the Grid layout control provide a way for child elements to specify where they should be located in the grid. You can identify the attached properties by looking for an "Attached Properties" section in the MSDN documentation for a particular class. If you attempt to use a random dependency property as an attached property, the parser will throw an exception. Registering an attached property is accomplished in a similar fashion to normal dependency properties but uses RegisterAttached instead of Register.

The Root of Visual Elements: DependencyObject

Any class inheriting from DependencyObject, directly or indirectly, gains the ability to interact with dependency properties. You have already seen the GetValue and SetValue methods, probably the two most important methods of DependencyObject. This root object also provides the ability to obtain the value of the property (its base value) as if no animation occurred.

Dependency properties are important to many aspects of Silverlight and will be used often, generally transparently, throughout the rest of this book.

Type Converters

XAML introduces type converters in order to easily support setting of complicated property values. A *type converter* simply converts a string representation of an object to the actual object but allows for complex handling, such as wrapping a value in several objects. While not explicitly tied to Silverlight (or WPF or XAML), type converters are heavily used when parsing XAML. Let's take a look at the definition of the Canvas layout control in the login screen's XAML:

```
<Canvas Background="White">
```

The Background property is type-converted from a string to its actual type. If you were to create this Canvas in C#, the code would look like the following:

```
Canvas canvas = new Canvas { Background = new
        SolidColorBrush(Color.FromArgb(255, 255, 255, 255))};
```

If you had to guess, you might think that the Background property is backed by the Color type; however, it is actually backed by a Brush. Using a Brush for the background provides the ability to easily display solid colors, gradients, and other fancy backgrounds, thus providing much more flexibility for creating backgrounds. Brushes will be discussed in more detail in Chapter 9. Specifying the Canvas control's background as an attribute in XAML is the quickest way to provide a background and is known as *property attribute* syntax. XAML also supports *property element* syntax, which makes the fact that the Background is a Brush explicit.

```
<Canvas>
    <Canvas.Background>
        <SolidColorBrush Color="White"/>
    </Canvas.Background>
</Canvas>
```

When the property appears as an element, it must take the form of the object name, followed by a dot and then the property name, as in the case of Canvas.Background.

In many cases, content can also be provided via an attribute or inside an element's opening tag. Each approach is illustrated in the text labels for the title, username, and password entry boxes. The title and username label uses the content attribute Text:

```
<TextBlock HorizontalAlignment="Center"
    Text="Please enter your information"
    Grid.Column="0" Grid.Row="0" Grid.ColumnSpan="2" />
<TextBlock Text="Username:" VerticalAlignment="Top"
```

```
        HorizontalAlignment="Right"
        Grid.Column="0" Grid.Row="1"/>
```

The password label, however, is specified as a child of the TextBlock element:

```
<TextBlock HorizontalAlignment="Right" VerticalAlignment="Top"
                    Grid.Column="0" Grid.Row="2">
        Password:
</TextBlock>
```

The content attribute syntax, much like the property attribute syntax, is a useful shorthand, both in markup and when working with the code-behind. The content element syntax, however, is required when specifying more complex content than what can be captured by a simple attribute. Also note that content might be restricted based on which control you use—for example, a TextBox cannot contain a Button as content.

Markup Extensions

A *markup extension* is a special syntax used to specify property values that require interpretation. This interpretation is based on which markup extension is used. A markup extension takes the format of { (opening curly brace), followed by the markup extension name, optionally followed by parameters to the markup extension, and ending with } (closing curly brace). These are required to support some of the key features of Silverlight, including resources, data binding, and template binding. We'll briefly discuss each of these features here to highlight the syntax and usage of markup extensions.

▪ **Note** What's with the funny syntax? Markup extensions may seem strange at first and might leave you wondering why context can't dictate how a property value is interpreted (e.g., by utilizing a type converter). Markup extensions provide a mechanism to specify more than a simple value—they stand in for more complicated processing, such as completely changing the appearance of a user interface element via a style. If you want to explicitly show something in curly braces, such as a label, you must escape it by placing an empty set of curly braces in front—for example, {}{text here}.

Resource Dictionaries, Referencing Static Resources, and Implicit Styling

Applications must maintain consistency throughout in order to give users a predictable experience, including using the same colors, fonts and font sizes, styles, and templates (used to control how items in controls are rendered or to change the appearance of the default controls). The customization used to create this application consistency needs to reside in a place where multiple controls, and even multiple XAML pages, will have easy access (similar to the CSS approach for regular web applications). That way, when you need to change any details, such as colors, you need to go to only a single place.

The place where you can store these customizations is called a *resource dictionary*. Resource dictionaries associate a value with a key, much like you'd do in a Dictionary<string,object> instance. In XAML, the key is set via the x:Key property. Any object that contains a Resources member can contain resources. This includes the layout containers (such as Grid, StackPanel, etc. that you will encounter in the next chapter), and the App.xaml provides resources for the entire application.

Static Resource Dictionary

Let's revise the earlier developed login screen to use a static resource dictionary to specify font style information. This screen will look slightly different from the earlier example since the fonts are configured with different values. You can see the result in Figure 2-6. The use of a resource dictionary will make it easy to change the appearance of the header and labels.

Figure 2-6. *The login screen with font properties specified by a style resource*

The revised XAML code for the login screen is shown here, with the new additions in bold:

```
<Canvas Width="300" Height="Auto" x:Name="canvasTag">
        <Canvas.Resources>
            <Style x:Key="LoginHeaderFontStyle" TargetType="TextBlock">
                <Setter Property="FontFamily" Value="Times New Roman"/>
                <Setter Property="FontSize" Value="20"/>
            </Style>
            <Style x:Key="LoginLabelFontStyle" TargetType="TextBlock">
                <Setter Property="FontFamily" Value="Arial"/>
                <Setter Property="FontSize" Value="14"/>
            </Style>
        </Canvas.Resources>

        <Grid Height="140" Width="250" Canvas.Left="25" Canvas.Top="15">
            <Grid.RowDefinitions>
                <RowDefinition/>
                <RowDefinition/>
                <RowDefinition/>
                <RowDefinition/>
            </Grid.RowDefinitions>
            <Grid.ColumnDefinitions>
                <ColumnDefinition Width="Auto"/>
```

```xml
            <ColumnDefinition/>
        </Grid.ColumnDefinitions>
        <TextBlock HorizontalAlignment="Center"
        Text="Please enter your information"
        Grid.Column="0" Grid.Row="0" Grid.ColumnSpan="2"
            Style="{StaticResource LoginHeaderFontStyle}" />
        <TextBlock Text="Username:" VerticalAlignment="Top"
        HorizontalAlignment="Right"
        Grid.Column="0" Grid.Row="1"
            Style="{StaticResource LoginLabelFontStyle}"/>
        <TextBox VerticalAlignment="Top" Grid.Column="1" Grid.Row="1"/>
        <TextBlock HorizontalAlignment="Right" VerticalAlignment="Top"
        Grid.Column="0" Grid.Row="2"
            Style="{StaticResource LoginLabelFontStyle}">
            Password:
        </TextBlock>
        <PasswordBox VerticalAlignment="Top" Grid.Column="1" Grid.Row="2"/>
        <Button Content="Login" Grid.Row="3"
            Width="100" Grid.Column="1" HorizontalAlignment="Left"/>
    </Grid>
</Canvas>
```

To reference static resources, you need a way to tell the XAML parser that you want to use a resource and which resource to use. The markup extension name for referencing a static resource is simply StaticResource, and it appears after the open curly brace. The StaticResource markup extension takes a single parameter: the name of the resource to reference, which is defined as x:Key property of Style.

The x:Key property is used to give each style a name for referencing in the markup extension. While we will discuss styles in detail in Chapter 8, what's going on here isn't a big mystery. The TargetType property of the Style element is used to specify the object type the style is meant for, and the Setter elements are used to specify values for properties on this target type. In this case, we are defining two styles: one for the header text (the "Please enter your information" text) and the other for the labels next to the text input boxes. By changing the LoginLabelFontStyle, you affect both the username and the password labels at the same time. This is good—it makes styling applications significantly easier both because the style information is stored in a central place (such as defining an app.xaml file) and because the specific styles need only a single definition to affect potentially many elements of a user interface.

■ **Note** Although you can use {StaticResource} from a resource dictionary to reference other resources within the dictionary, you can reference only those resources that appear before the reference.

Merged Resource Dictionary

As you probably know, Silverlight 3 introduced further capability to the resource dictionaries via merged resource dictionaries. This makes it so you can reference resource dictionaries stored in content files within the XAP file, possibly even within another assembly within the XAP. The external resource dictionaries are referenced via the Source property of the ResourceDictionary class. The previous example used two styles, one for the header and one for the labels. Let's put each of these styles in a

separate, external XAML file. The style for the header goes into a resource dictionary defined in
ExternalResources1.xaml.

```
<ResourceDictionary
    xmlns="http://schemas.microsoft.com/winfx/2006/xaml/presentation"
    xmlns:x="http://schemas.microsoft.com/winfx/2006/xaml" >
    <Style x:Key="LoginHeaderStyle_External" TargetType="TextBlock">
        <Setter Property="FontFamily" Value="Times New Roman"/>
        <Setter Property="FontSize" Value="20"/>
    </Style>
</ResourceDictionary>
```

The style for the labels goes into a similar type of XAML file named ExternalResources2.xaml.

The key for these two styles was changed in order to distinguish the code from the previous
example. These files are added to the Visual Studio project as regular XML files (but with the extension
XAML), changing their build action from Page to Resource. This ensures these files are simply placed in
the XAP file as flat files. The Canvas no longer contains these styles—instead, it uses the
MergedDictionaries property to specify which external resource dictionaries to import and merge
together.

```
<Canvas.Resources>
    <ResourceDictionary>
        <ResourceDictionary.MergedDictionaries>
            <ResourceDictionary Source="ExternalResources1.xaml"/>
            <ResourceDictionary Source="ExternalResources2.xaml"/>
        </ResourceDictionary.MergedDictionaries>
    </ResourceDictionary>
</Canvas.Resources>
```

The Source property is a URI specifying in which file the external resource dictionary is located.
Resource dictionaries imported using the Source property cannot then create additional resources
directly within the file.

Implicit Styling

With Silverlight 4, you can define styles as a resource and target them to specific types of UIElement
implicitly. This would allow you to categorize the theme based on the control type to provide a
consistent look and feel of specific types of controls across the application.

We applied the static resource style to TextBlock controls of the login screen. Now we will use
implicit styling for the Button control. For that you need to add styling at the UserControl Resources
level (without x:Key attribute) targeting to the Button control by setting TargetType to Button, as shown
here.

```
<UserControl.Resources>
    <Style TargetType="Button">
        <Setter Property="Foreground" Value="Green"/>
        <Setter Property="FontWeight" Value="Bold"/>
    </Style>
</UserControl.Resources>
```

If you run the project you will see that Button control Font changes to Green and Bold automatically. If you add any other button, they will set to the same style automatically.

▓ **Note** If you set the Button control with {StaticResource} or with a specific style, the defined implicit styling will be overridden by them.

We will revisit the Merged Resource Dictionary and Implicit Styling features in Chapter 8 in the context of styles.

Data Binding

Data binding is a way to connect data between the user interface and a data source. It is possible to transfer data from a data source to the user interface once or each time the data changes, as well as to constantly keep the data source synchronized with the user interface. The markup extension controlling data binding is named Binding and has four possible syntaxes. Let's imagine the login screen authorizes access to an online bank. After customers log in, they're able to select one of their accounts to manage (and also instantly see their balance for each account), as shown in Figure 2-7.

Figure 2-7. Results of data binding Account objects to a ListBox

First, add a new class, Account.cs, to the XAMLTour Project. The following is what a simplistic business object for account information looks like:

```
public class Account
{
    public string AccountName { get; set; }
    public double AccountBalance { get; set; }
    public Account(string n, double b)
    {
        this.AccountName = n;
        this.AccountBalance = b;
    }
}
```

Next, create a new User Control within the XAMLTour project in Visual Studio and call it ChooseAccount. You can do this by right-clicking the project in the top right and clicking Add ➤ New Item ➤ Silverlight User Control. Give it the name ChooseAccount.xaml and click OK. Edit the

ChooseAccount.xaml.cs file, create a generic List containing the account type, and add a couple of accounts. This will serve as a data source for the data binding.

```
private List<Account> accountList;
public ChooseAccount()
{
    // Required to initialize variables
    InitializeComponent();
    //Create a generic account type list
    accountList = new List<Account>();
    accountList.Add(new Account("Checking", 500.00));
    accountList.Add(new Account("Savings", 23100.19));
    accountListBox.DataContext = accountList;
}
```

Notice the final line in the constructor—this is where the data source (accountList) is connected to the ListBox. The ListBox, named accountListBox, is our display control that we add to the XAML shown here. The markup extensions for data binding are in bold. (Here you will also notice that the Grid layout control is replaced by the StackPanel layout control.)

```
<UserControl x:Class="XAMLTour.ChooseAccount"
    xmlns="http://schemas.microsoft.com/winfx/2006/xaml/presentation"
    xmlns:x="http://schemas.microsoft.com/winfx/2006/xaml"
    xmlns:d="http://schemas.microsoft.com/expression/blend/2008"
    xmlns:mc="http://schemas.openxmlformats.org/markup-compatibility/2006"
    mc:Ignorable="d"
    d:DesignHeight="300" d:DesignWidth="400">
    <StackPanel Orientation="Horizontal" Margin="30 30 0 0">
        <TextBlock Text="Choose account to manage: "></TextBlock>
        <ListBox x:Name="accountListBox" Height="100" Width="300"
                    VerticalAlignment="Top" ItemsSource="{Binding Mode=OneWay}">
            <ListBox.ItemTemplate>
                <DataTemplate>
                    <StackPanel Orientation="Horizontal">
                        <TextBlock Text="{Binding AccountName}" />
                        <TextBlock Text=" ($" />
                        <TextBlock Text="{Binding AccountBalance}" />
                        <TextBlock Text=")" />
                    </StackPanel>
                </DataTemplate>
            </ListBox.ItemTemplate>
        </ListBox>
    </StackPanel>
</UserControl>
```

The Binding markup extension used in the ItemsSource property specifies that the items in the ListBox are data bound, and here you can specify how the data binding works (in this case, OneWay, which causes data to flow only from the data source to the user interface). A DataTemplate is used to format the data coming from the data source, in this case by using the Binding markup extension to access properties on the data source (accountList). The Binding markup extensions used to bind to

AccountName and AccountBalance treat the parent object (Account) implicitly. This is described in Table 2-2.

Table 2-2. Data Binding Markup Extensions

Syntax	Description
{Binding}	This signals data binding, configured with default properties (such as OneWay for Mode). See Chapter 6 for specific property values.
{Binding path}	This is used to specify object properties to pull data from. A dotted syntax is valid here, allowing you to drill down inside the objects from the data source.
{Binding properties}	This is used to set properties affecting data binding, following a name=value syntax. Specific properties affecting data binding will be discussed later.
{Binding path, properties}	The properties affect the data specified by the path. For example, a converter might be used to format data. The path must come first.

Until Silverlight 4, the data binding was possible only to the DependencyProperty of the FrameworkElement. Silverlight 4 extends the data binding capability to properties on DependencyObject also. That opens opportunities to develop the data-bound applications more effectively by extending the data binding to DependencyObjects such as Transformation. Visit Chapter 6 to get more details on this subject.

RelativeSource Markup Extension

The RelativeSource property of the Binding markup extension specifies that the binding source is relative to the location of the binding target. The RelativeSource markup extension is used to specify the value of the RelativeSource property of the Binding markup extension. It comes in the following two forms:

{RelativeSource TemplatedParent}: The source for the data binding is the control that has a ControlTemplate defined.

{RelativeSource Self}: The source for the data binding is the control in which this appears. This is useful for binding to another property on the control itself that is data bound.

The TemplatedParent is useful for properties in control templates that want to bind to properties of controls that are using the control template. For example, the TemplateBinding can be altered to retrieve the label from the Tag property of the Button.

```
<Style x:Key="ButtonStyle" TargetType="Button">
    <Setter Property="Template">
        <Setter.Value>
            <ControlTemplate TargetType="Button">
                <StackPanel Orientation="Horizontal"
                            Background="Gainsboro">
                    <TextBlock
```

```
                        Text="{Binding Tag, RelativeSource=
                                {RelativeSource TemplatedParent}}"
                        FontSize="16"/>
                    <ContentPresenter Content="{TemplateBinding Content}"/>
                </StackPanel>
            </ControlTemplate>
        </Setter.Value>
    </Setter>
</Style>
```

The text entered into the Tag property of a Button that uses this control template appears in the TextBlock via the TemplatedParent relative binding. The Self is even easier, because it simply provides a way to bind to a property within the control itself. The following TextBlock will show Tahoma since that is the value of the FontFamily property:

```
<TextBlock FontFamily="Tahoma" FontSize="24"
        Text="{Binding FontFamily, RelativeSource={RelativeSource Self}}"/>
```

We will delve deeper into data templates and data binding in Chapter 6.

Template Binding

Using something called a *control template* along with styles provides a mechanism to completely redefine how a control appears. This is one scenario where designers and developers can work independently—the designer fleshes out how the user interface looks, while the developer focuses on handling events and other logic related to the control. The TemplateBinding markup extension is used to connect the template to properties of the control that uses the template. Let's look at a brief example by creating a new UserControl named TemplateBindingExample, within the XAMLTour project that utilizes control templates, to enforce a consistent label on all buttons that use this template. Here's what the XAML looks like:

```
<UserControl x:Class="XAMLTour.TemplateBindingExample"
    xmlns="http://schemas.microsoft.com/winfx/2006/xaml/presentation"
    xmlns:x="http://schemas.microsoft.com/winfx/2006/xaml"
    xmlns:d="http://schemas.microsoft.com/expression/blend/2008"
    xmlns:mc="http://schemas.openxmlformats.org/markup-compatibility/2006"
    mc:Ignorable="d"
    d:DesignHeight="300" d:DesignWidth="400">
    <Canvas Background="White">
        <Canvas.Resources>
            <Style x:Key="ButtonStyle" TargetType="Button">
                <Setter Property="Template">
                    <Setter.Value>
                        <ControlTemplate TargetType="Button">
                            <StackPanel Orientation="Horizontal"
                                            Background="Gainsboro">
                                <TextBlock Text="Label from Template: "
                                            FontSize="16"/>
                                <ContentPresenter
                                        Content="{TemplateBinding Content}"/>
```

```
            </StackPanel>
          </ControlTemplate>
        </Setter.Value>
      </Setter>
    </Style>
  </Canvas.Resources>
  <Button Style="{StaticResource ButtonStyle}" Content="I'm a Button"/>
  </Canvas>
</UserControl>
```

The template is created as a style that the button references using the StaticResource markup extension. The first TextBlock contains the label that never changes, and the ContentPresenter is used to display any content the button specifies. In this case, the content is a simple string. The TemplateBinding is used to connect a property of a control in the template to a property on the control utilizing the template. Figure 2-8 shows the resulting user interface for this XAML.

Label from Template: I'm a Button

Figure 2-8. *What a Button looks like when using the ControlTemplate*

The bad news about this approach is also the good news: the Button's visual implementation is completely overridden, so if you try to click it, nothing will happen visually. Using a control template, though, provides a way to create any visual representation you want for when the mouse hovers over the button and when the mouse clicks the button. The button is still a button—it can just look drastically different from the default Silverlight button through the control template mechanism, which will be covered in Chapter 8.

Microsoft .NET for Silverlight

Now that you should be comfortable with many of the new concepts Silverlight introduces, let's take a closer look at the Silverlight application that gets created.

Core .NET Assemblies for Silverlight Applications

If you reveal the default referenced assemblies in the Solution Explorer of Visual Studio for any Silverlight application project, you will see seven assemblies listed. These assemblies provide the majority of what you need when writing applications supporting data integration, extensible Windows controls, networking, base class libraries, garbage collection, and the common language runtime (CLR) for Silverlight. Briefly, here are the important namespaces/classes in each assembly:

mscorlib: This is the CLR for Silverlight and thus provides the core functionality you always need, including collections, input/output, reflection, security, host interoperability, and threading. The important root namespace here is System, which includes System.Collections, System.Security, System.IO, and so on.

system: This supplements classes provided by mscorlib, such as by providing Queue and Stack classes in the System.Collections. Generic namespace.

`System.Core`: This contains LINQ support (in the `System.Linq` namespace) and cryptography support (`System.Security.Cryptography`).

`System.Net`: This provides a simple programming interface for many of the network protocols such as `HttpWebRequest`, `HttpWebResponse`, and `WebClient`. The `WebClient` class provides common methods for sending data to and receiving data from a resource identified by a URI.

`System.Windows`: This provides the bulk of what Silverlight uses, such as input-related classes in `System.Windows.Input` (mouse/keyboard event classes and stylus-related classes), image/video/animation-related classes in `System.Windows.Media`, the XAML parser in `System.Windows.Markup`, control classes in `System.Windows.Controls`, and many others. Chances are high that if you're looking for something, it's in this assembly.

`System.Windows.Browser`: This provides support classes for obtaining information about and communicating with the browser (via classes in the `System.Windows.Browser` namespace) and the managed host environment (via classes in `System.Windows.Hosting`).

`System.Xml`: This provides all XML-related classes (e.g., for an XML reader/writer/parser).

Managed Code-Behind .NET Integration

Support for the.NET Framework 4 and 3.5 with the Common Language Runtime (CLR) for Silverlight, and thus support for .NET managed code-behind code using the default .NET class libraries, is a key capability of Silverlight. The CLR basically provides memory management, garbage collection, type-safety checking, and exception handling. Additionally, the Base Class Library (BCL) contains a set of components that provide basic programming capabilities like string handling, regular expressions, input and output, reflection, collections, globalization, integration to WCF services, and networking capabilities.

So far, you have seen several user interfaces created in XAML. Each XAML file has a corresponding code-behind file; however, there is a third file that we have not yet discussed explicitly. If you open the XAMLTour project in Visual Studio, open the `MainPage.xaml.cs` file, right-click the `InitializeComponent` method call, and choose Go to Definition, you will be taken to the `MainPage.g.i.cs` file. This is a generated file based on the XAML. Any objects in the XAML that have an `x:Name` will cause a class member to get placed in this generated file. Partial classes in C# make this assemblage of different pieces easy, as illustrated in Figure 2-9.

▓ **Note** The x:Name property on objects can be set only in XAML. This is most likely because the object is either created in XAML (in which case it needs a corresponding member on the class for manipulation in the code-behind) or created in code (in which case you have a reference to it that you can name and store however you like).

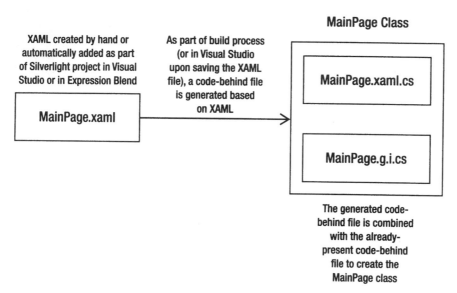

Figure 2-9. How the full class implementation for XAML comes together

Application and MainPage Classes

When you create a new Silverlight application in Visual Studio or Expression Blend, you might notice an App.xaml file along with an App.xaml.cs file. The application is based on the System.Windows.Application class—it supports centralization of resources for the application, it supports several important events, and it provides a direct connection to the browser/host environment.

The code placed in the initial project includes App.xaml and App.xaml.cs files. The App.xaml file doesn't have much in it, but there is one important feature to observe:

```
<Application xmlns="http://schemas.microsoft.com/winfx/2006/xaml/presentation"
             xmlns:x="http://schemas.microsoft.com/winfx/2006/xaml"
             x:Class="XAMLTour.App">
   <Application.Resources>
   </Application.Resources>
</Application>
```

The Application class contains a Resources element. Any resources specified in the Application class can be referenced throughout a Silverlight application. This is the perfect place to put style and template resources that are available to the entire application. The UserControl is actually turned into the main user interface for the application in the code-behind file, App.xaml.cs, as follows:

```
using System;
using System.Collections.Generic;
using System.Linq;
using System.Net;
using System.Windows;
using System.Windows.Controls;
using System.Windows.Documents;
```

```csharp
using System.Windows.Input;
using System.Windows.Media;
using System.Windows.Media.Animation;
using System.Windows.Shapes;

namespace XAMLTour
{
    public partial class App : Application
    {
        public partial class App : Application
        {
            public App()
            {
                this.Startup += this.Application_Startup;
                this.Exit += this.Application_Exit;
                this.UnhandledException += this.Application_UnhandledException;

                InitializeComponent();
            }

            private void Application_Startup(object sender, StartupEventArgs e)
            {
                this.RootVisual = new MainPage();
            }

            private void Application_Exit(object sender, EventArgs e)
            {
            }

            private void Application_UnhandledException(object sender,
                            ApplicationUnhandledExceptionEventArgs e)
            {
                // If the app is running outside of the debugger then report the exception
using
                // the browser's exception mechanism. On IE this will display it a yellow
alert
                // icon in the status bar and Firefox will display a script error.
                if (!System.Diagnostics.Debugger.IsAttached)
                {

                // NOTE: This will allow the application to continue running
                // after an exception has been thrown
                // but not handled.
                // For production applications this error handling should be replaced with
something that will
                // report the error to the website and stop the application.
                    e.Handled = true;
                    Deployment.Current.Dispatcher.BeginInvoke(delegate
                            { ReportErrorToDOM(e); });
                }
            }
```

```
    private void ReportErrorToDOM(ApplicationUnhandledExceptionEventArgs e)
    {
        try
        {
            string errorMsg = e.ExceptionObject.Message +
                    e.ExceptionObject.StackTrace;
            errorMsg = errorMsg.Replace('"', '\'').Replace("\r\n", @"\n");

            System.Windows.Browser.HtmlPage.Window.Eval
                    ("throw new Error(\"Unhandled Error in Silverlight 2↵
Application " +
                        errorMsg + "\");");
        }
        catch (Exception)
        {
        }
    }
}
}
}
```

The RootVisual property on the Application class specifies what will be shown when the application starts. The generated App.xaml.cs file also registers itself for all application-level events. The Startup method comes registered with a method that establishes where the main user interface comes from (RootVisual). This Startup event handler is where the connection to the MainPage class was established in the project code for this chapter. The Exit event comes registered with the empty handler method. The UnhandledException event comes registered with the method reporting exception using the browser's exception mechanism. The ReportErrorToDOM event comes registered with the method handling JavaScript exceptions. If you would like to have a XAML class other than MainPage class as a start-up page, then you need to update the application startup event appropriately.

These application events are the first events you've seen in this chapter. Many of the objects in Silverlight support events that can be hooked up either in the code-behind, as in the App.xaml.cs code, or through XAML.

The MainPage class represents the main user interface of the application by default. It contains the XAML markup—MainPage.xaml—derived from the UserControl and code-behind file—MainPage.xaml.cs—to perform application-level functionalities by integrating with the XAML user interface through events.

The MainPage.xaml defines the start-up main user interface of the Silverlight application. The default user interface is mainly derived from the UserControl and the Grid control as the root layout control, as shown here.

```
<UserControl x:Class="SilverlightApplication1.MainPage"
    xmlns="http://schemas.microsoft.com/winfx/2006/xaml/presentation"
    xmlns:x="http://schemas.microsoft.com/winfx/2006/xaml"
    xmlns:d="http://schemas.microsoft.com/expression/blend/2008"
    xmlns:mc="http://schemas.openxmlformats.org/markup-compatibility/2006"
    mc:Ignorable="d"
    d:DesignHeight="300" d:DesignWidth="400">

    <Grid x:Name="LayoutRoot" Background="White">
```

```
    </Grid>
</UserControl>
```

The code-behind MainPage.xaml.cs loads the main page XAML file and further defines the logic to the elements defined in XAML. The following is the default code calling InitializeComponent in the MainPage constructor.

```
using System;
using System.Collections.Generic;
using System.Linq;
using System.Net;
using System.Windows;
using System.Windows.Controls;
using System.Windows.Documents;
using System.Windows.Input;
using System.Windows.Media;
using System.Windows.Media.Animation;
using System.Windows.Shapes;

namespace SilverlightApplication1
{
    public partial class MainPage : UserControl
    {
        public MainPage()
        {
            InitializeComponent();
        }
    }
}
```

Events in Silverlight

When a user clicks a button, chooses an item in a list box, or uses the cursor keys, the application must be able to respond to these events. These events are *input events* and are actually forwarded to Silverlight by the browser hosting the Silverlight plug-in. Other events, such as the application events just shown, are defined within Silverlight itself.

Keyboard and mouse events are *routed events*. These events bubble up the tree of objects (until it is handled) starting at the first control to receive the input event. Let's create a simple example by adding a new UserControl named RoutedEventExample to the existing XAMLTour project and hook up MouseLeftButton down events.

■ **Note** If you have any experience with WPF, you should be aware that there is a vital difference between WPF routed events and Silverlight routed events. Silverlight routed events *only* bubble; they do not "tunnel" as they can in WPF. This means that events are only passed up the tree (bubbling); they cannot be passed down the tree (tunneling).

```xml
<UserControl x:Class="XAMLTour.RoutedEventExample"
    xmlns="http://schemas.microsoft.com/winfx/2006/xaml/presentation"
    xmlns:x="http://schemas.microsoft.com/winfx/2006/xaml"
    xmlns:d="http://schemas.microsoft.com/expression/blend/2008"
    xmlns:mc="http://schemas.openxmlformats.org/markup-compatibility/2006"
    mc:Ignorable="d"
    d:DesignHeight="300" d:DesignWidth="400">
    <Grid Background="Gray" MouseLeftButtonDown="Grid_MouseLeftButtonDown"
            Width="350" Height="250" >
        <Canvas Height="200" Width="300" MouseLeftButtonDown=
            "Canvas_MouseLeftButtonDown" Background="Black"  Margin="25">
            <StackPanel Height="150" Width="250" MouseLeftButtonDown=
                "StackPanel_MouseLeftButtonDown" Background="Yellow"
                Canvas.Top="25" Canvas.Left="25">
                <TextBlock Text= "'MouseLeftButtonDown' bubble up order" />
                <TextBlock x:Name="eventOrder" />
            </StackPanel>
        </Canvas>
    </Grid>
</UserControl>
```

In the previous code snippet, we placed a Canvas control inside the main container Grid. Inside the Canvas control we placed a StackPanel control. To differentiate them, we have set their Background property to Gray, Black, and Yellow, respectively. For these three controls, we also defined the MouseLeftButtonDown event handler in the code-behind. When the mouse button is pressed, the click event starts at the lowest control that is aware of the event. For example, when the StackPanel is clicked, the event starts there. Look at Figure 2-10 to visualize the mouse down event bubbling up the nested controls.

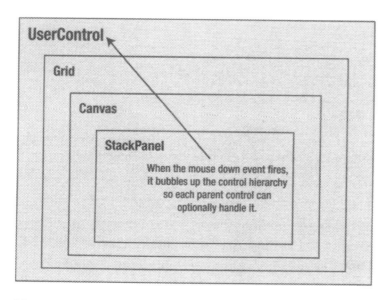

Figure 2-10. An input event bubbling up nested controls

The events are wired up to display which controls have received the mouse down event (which occurs when a StackPanel is clicked). The following is the code-behind showing the events handlers:

```
private void StackPanel_MouseLeftButtonDown(object sender, MouseButtonEventArgs e)
        {
            eventOrder.Text += " StackPanel";
        }

private void Grid_MouseLeftButtonDown(object sender, MouseButtonEventArgs e)
        {
            eventOrder.Text += " Grid";
        }

private void Canvas_MouseLeftButtonDown
          (object sender, MouseButtonEventArgs e)
        {
            eventOrder.Text += " Canvas";
        }
```

If you click StackPanel, the event originates at the StackPanel, gets sent up the tree to the enclosing Canvas control, and then gets sent up again to the enclosing Grid control. You can see the results of this in Figure 2-11. The controls receiving the event are shown in order in TextBlock eventOrder just beneath the message "MouseLeftButtonDown' bubble up order".

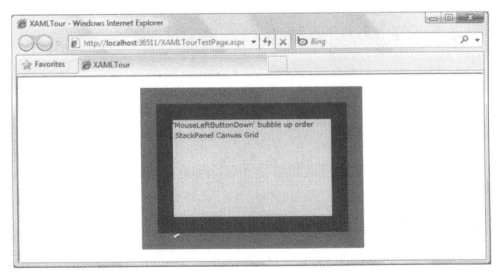

Figure 2-11. Clicking the StackPanel causes the event to bubble up to the control's parents.

▧ **Note** You can prevent events from bubbling up to the control's parents by adding e.Handled = true; to the event handler. For instance, in the previous example, you can add e.Handled = true; to Canvas and thus prevent the event from bubbling up to Canvas's parent control, which is Grid in our case.

Summary

This chapter covered the foundations of Silverlight. Before we can explore in detail more advanced topics such as theming, animation, handling media, and data binding, it is important to understand how these core features support the rest of Silverlight. Any exploration of Silverlight starts with understanding XAML and its many features, such as dependency properties, markup extensions, and resources. This chapter also showed how a Silverlight application is structured and how routed events work in Silverlight. You are now prepared to learn more about Silverlight. The next chapter explores creating user interfaces by using the layout controls and other standard controls, some of which you have already briefly seen.

■■■

CHAPTER 3

Silverlight User Interface Controls

Now that you've seen the Silverlight architecture, Silverlight concepts, and what XAML is all about, let's look at the basic user interface controls that Silverlight provides. Silverlight supplies *forms controls*, such as text boxes for display and for user input, list boxes, check boxes, radio buttons, and others; *data manipulation controls*, such as data grid, data form, and others; and *functional controls*, such as date picker, image, media element, and others. While a standard set of controls is important for building user interfaces, even more important is how these controls are placed on a user interface. This is handled by Silverlight's *layout controls*: one that enables absolute positioning and others that allow more intelligent layouts of controls. This chapter starts with exploring the building blocks of user controls to enable a detailed understanding of the base functionality of all controls. Later we will dive into the details of key layout, forms, data manipulation, and functional user controls. We will also cover new controls and enhanced existing controls introduced in the Silverlight 4 release.

■ **Note** This chapter is intended to provide a basic overview of key user controls of Silverlight. If you are already familiar with these controls, you can skip this chapter or just focus on the new controls introduced in Silverlight 4.

Building Blocks

Silverlight provides many useful controls for displaying information and handling data input. Before we get to the specifics of each control, it's important to understand the base functionality of all controls available for Silverlight. Figure 3-1 shows an abbreviated class diagram with a subset of Silverlight 4's controls and panels (used for positioning objects). While there is a Control class, not all elements of a user interface are controls, as you can see in Figure 3-1. In this chapter we will cover some of the key user interface controls and classes. The highlighted controls are introduced in Silverlight 4.

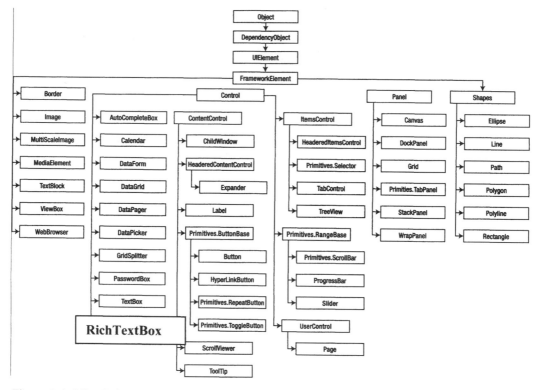

Figure 3-1. Silverlight 4 user interface class hierarchy

We had a high-level overview of DependencyObject in Chapter 2. The DependencyObject class provides the functionality for interacting with the dependency property system. The next class, UIElement, is the sign that a class has a visual appearance. The FrameworkElement class provides some interesting behavior such as data binding, but the only requirement for a visual appearance is that a class must inherit (directly or indirectly) from UIElement. Chapter 9 will detail some classes that inherit directly from DependencyObject, not from UIElement or FrameworkElement. Let's start at the top of this class hierarchy so you can see just what functionality is provided by each class before getting to panels and controls.

DependencyObject

The DependencyObject class is arguably the most important class in Silverlight. This object enables the dependency property system. In the previous chapter, you saw what dependency properties are and how to create them. The piece left out, however, is what enables the setting and reading of these properties. Any class that inherits directly or indirectly from DependencyObject can participate in Silverlight's dependency property system. Its most important features are the methods it provides, shown in Table 3-1.

Table 3-1. Methods of the System.Windows.DependencyObject Class

Method	Description
CheckAccess	Returns true if the calling thread has access to this object.
ClearValue	Removes the local value of the specified dependency property. The property might take on its default value or a value from another source. Visit Chapter 2 to understand different sources and precedence of dependency properties values.
GetAnimationBaseValue	Gets the value of the specified dependency property as if no animation were applied.
GetValue	Returns the current effective value of the specified dependency property. The effective value is the result of the property system having evaluated all the possible inputs (such as property-changed callbacks, data binding, styles and templates, and animation) that participate in the property system value precedence.
ReadLocalValue	Returns the local value of the specified dependency property or UnsetValue if the property does not have a local value. The UnsetValue specifies the static value indicating that the dependency property exists but its value is not set by the property system. This is used instead of the null reference, since the null reference can be a potential value of the property.
SetValue	Sets the local value of the specified dependency property.

Threading and the user interface

Silverlight is a multi-threaded environment. You can't modify elements of a user interface from a nonuser interface thread since it can lead to a number of problems. The proper way to modify a user interface from a different thread is by using a dispatcher. The DependencyObject class provides a single property, Dispatcher, which holds a reference to the associated dispatcher. If you want to set the value of a text block from a different thread, you must use Dispatcher.BeginInvoke to queue the modification on the main thread's work items queue like this:

```
Dispatcher.BeginInvoke(delegate() { textBlock.Text = "changed"; });
```

You'll get a closer look at threading in Silverlight in Chapter 12.

UIElement

The UIElement class is the next class you encounter as you walk down the inheritance hierarchy. This class forms the base for all classes that have the ability to draw themselves on a user interface, including keyboard, mouse and stylus input handling, focus support, and basic layout support. Table 3-2 lists methods of this class.

Table 3-2. Methods of the System.Windows.UIElement Class

Method	Description
AddHandler	Adds a routed event handler for a specified routed event by adding the handler to the handler collection on the current element.
Arrange	Positions objects contained by this visual element and determines size for the UIElement. Invoked by the layout system.
CaptureMouse	Sends mouse input to the object even when the mouse pointer is not within its bounding box. Useful for drag-and-drop scenarios. Only one UIElement can have the mouse captured at a time.
InvalidateArrange	Causes UIElement to update its layout.
InvalidateMeasurement	Invalidates the measurementstate for a UIElement.
Measure	Sets the DesiredSize property for layout purposes. Invoked by the layout system.
OnCreateAutomationPeer	Implemented by inheritors that participate in the automation system. Returns an AutomationPeer object.
ReleaseMouseCapture	Removes the mouse capture obtained via CaptureMouse.
RemoveHandler	Removes the specified routed event handler from the UIElement.
TransformToVisual	Returns a GeneralTransform that is used to transform coordinates from this UIElement to the object passed in.
UpdateLayout	Ensures all child objects are updated for layout. Invoked by the layout system.

Table 3-3 lists properties of UIElement.

Table 3-3. Properties of the System.Windows.UIElement Class

Property	Type	Description
AllowDrop	bool	Specifies that the specific UIElement is an allowed drop target to implement the drag-and-drop feature. New property in Silverlight 4.
CacheMode	CacheMode	Indicates that the render content should be cached when possible.
Clip	Geometry	Defines a clipping region for the UIElement.
DesiredSize	Size	Indicates the size of the UIElement as determined by the measure pass, which is important for layout. RenderSize provides the actual size of the UIElement.
Effect	Effect	Defines the pixel shader effect to use for rendering the UIElement.
IsHitTestVisible	bool	Gets or sets whether UIElement can participate in hit testing.
Opacity	double	Specifies the opacity/transparency of the UIElement. The default value is 1.0, corresponding to full opacity. Setting this to 0.0 causes the UIElement to disappear visually, but it can still respond to hit testing.
OpacityMask	Brush	Uses a brush to apply opacity to the UIElement. This uses only the alpha component of a brush. Do not use a video brush for this property because of the lack of an alpha component.
Projection	Projection	Defines the perspective projection (3D effect) to apply when rendering the UIElement.
RenderSize	Size	Indicates the actual size of the UIElement after it has passed through the layout system.
RenderTransform	Transform	Applies a transform to the rendering position of this UIElement. The default rendering offset is (0,0)—the top left of the UIElement.
RenderTransformOrigin	Point	Gets or sets the render transform origin. Defaults to (0,0) if not specified. This can be used to translate the UIElement.
UseLayoutRounding	Boolean	Determines whether rendering for the object and its subtree should use rounding behavior that aligns rendering to whole pixels.
Visibility	Visibility	Gets or sets the visibility state of the UIElement. Set this to Visibility.Collapsed to hide the UIElement (it does not participate in layout, is removed from the tab order, and is not hit testable). Set this to Visibility.Visible to restore the UIElement's position in its container.

UIElement also defines several important events, shown in Table 3-4.

Table 3-4. Events of the System.Windows.UIElement Class

Event	Description
DragEnter	Fires when the input system reports an underlying drag event with the specific event as the target. The event occurs only if the AllowDrop property of that element is set to true. Event args class: DragEventHandler. New event in Silverlight 4.
DragLeave	Fires when the input system reports an underlying drag event with the specific event as the origin. The event occurs only if the AllowDrop property of that element is set to true. Event args class: DragEventHandler. New event in Silverlight 4.
DragOver	Fires when the input system reports an underlying drag event with the specific event as the potential drop target. The event occurs only if the AllowDrop property of that element is set to true. Event args class: DragEventHandler. New event in Silverlight 4.
Drop	Fires when the input system reports an underlying drag event with the specific event as the drop target. The event occurs only if the AllowDrop property of that element is set to true. The Drop event is a bubbling event allowing multiple Drop events received by each object in parent-child relationship in the object tree. Event args class: DragEventHandler. New event in Silverlight 4.
GotFocus	Fires when the UIElement gains focus, if it doesn't already have it. Event args class: RoutedEventHandler.
KeyDown	Fires when a key is pressed. This event will bubble up to the root container. Event args class: KeyEventHandler.
KeyUp	Fires when a key is released. This event also bubbles up to the root container. Event args class: KeyEventHandler.
LostFocus	Fires when the UIElement loses focus. This event bubbles. Event args class: RoutedEventHandler.
LostMouseCapture	Fires when the object loses mouse (or stylus) capture.
MouseEnter	Fires if the mouse pointer is in motion and enters the UIElement's bounding box. A parent UIElement, if it also handles this event, will receive the event before any children. Event args class: MouseEventHandler.
MouseLeave	Fires when the mouse pointer leaves the UIElement's bounding box. Event args class: MouseEventHandler; however, the information provided in the event args is without meaning since the mouse has left the UIElement's bounds.

MouseLeftButtonDown	Fires when the mouse's left button is pressed down while the mouse pointer is within the bounds of the UIElement. Event args class: MouseButtonEventHandler.
MouseLeftButtonUp	Fires when the mouse's left button is released while the mouse pointer is within the bounds of the UIElement. Event args class: MouseButtonEventHandler.
MouseMove	Fires each time the mouse pointer moves within the bounds of the UIElement. This event bubbles. Event args class: MouseEventHandler.
MouseRightButtonDown	Fires when the mouse's right button is pressed down while the mouse pointer is within the bounds of the UIElement. Event args class: MouseButtonEventHandler. This is a new event in Silverlight 4 and supports the new right-click feature in Silverlight 4.
MouseRightButtonUp	Fires when the mouse's right button is released while the mouse pointer is within the bounds of the UIElement. This event will be fired only when the MouseRightButtonDown event is handled for that specific element. Event args class: MouseButtonEventHandler. This is a new event in Silverlight 4 and supports the new right-click feature in Silverlight 4.
MouseWheel	Fires when the mouse wheel is rotated while the mouse pointer is within the bounds of the UIElement or the UIElement has the focus. Event args class: MouseWheelEventHandler.
TextInput	Fires asynchronously when a UI element gets text in a device-independent manner. This event will be fired only when the KeyUp or KeyDown events are handled for that specific element. This event supports input from keyboard and other Input Method Editors (IMEs). Event args class: TextCompositionEventHandler. New event in Silverlight 4.
TextInputStart	Fires when a UI element starts getting text from the input devices. This event supports input from keyboard and other Input Method Editors (IMEs). Event args class: TextCompositionEventHandler. This event is a bubbling event allowing multiple TextInputStart events received by each object in parent-child relationship in the object tree. New event in Silverlight 4.
TextInputUpdate	Fires when text continues to be composed via IME. This event supports input from keyboard and other Input Method Editors (IMEs). Event args class: TextCompositionEventHandler. This event is a bubbling event allowing multiple TextInputUpdate events received by each object in parent-child relationship in the object tree. New event in Silverlight 4.

FrameworkElement

The next class, FrameworkElement, adds to the support introduced by UIElement. This class extends the layout support, introduces object lifetime events (such as when a FrameworkElement is loaded), and provides data binding support. The FrameworkElement class forms the direct base of Panel Control and

Shape, which are the base classes for object positioning support and most controls, such as Border, ContentPresenter, Image, MultiscaleImage, MediaElement, Primitives.Popup, and shape elements. Table 3-5 lists key methods of this class.

Table 3-5. Key Methods of the System.Windows.FrameworkElement Class

Method	Description
FindName	Searches the object tree, both up and down relative to the current FrameworkElement, for the object with the specified name (x:Name in XAML). Returns null if the object is not found.
GetBindingExpression	Retrieves the BindingExpression for a dependency property where a binding is established.
OnApplyTemplate	When overridden in a derived class, it is invoked whenever application code or internal processes (such as a rebuilding layout pass) call the ApplyTemplate method.
SetBinding	Binds a specified dependency property to a System.Windows.Data. Binding instance.

Table 3-6 shows the properties of FrameworkElement's properties.

Table 3-6. Properties of the System.Windows.FrameworkElement Class

Property	Type	Description
ActualHeight	double	Indicates the height of the FrameworkElement after rendering.
ActualWidth	double	Indicates the width of the FrameworkElement after rendering.
Cursor	System.Windows .Input.Cursor	Gets/sets the cursor that is shown when the mouse hovers over this element. Possible values (from the Cursors type): Arrow, Eraser, Hand, IBeam, None (invisible cursor), SizeNS, SizeWE, Stylus, Wait. Set to null to revert to default behavior.
DataContext	Object	Defines context (source of data) used in data binding.
FlowDirection	FlowDirection	Defines the direction (as enum) that text and other user interface elements flow within any parent element that controls their layout. The FlowDirection enumeration contains LeftToRight (default value) and RightToLeft members. New property in Silverlight 4 to support Right-to-Left languages such as Hebrew and Arabic languages.

Height	double	Indicates the asked-for height of the FrameworkElement.
HorizontalAlignment	HorizontalAlignment	Gets/sets the horizontal alignment. Behavior of this property is deferred to the layout control hosting this FrameworkElement. Possible values: Left, Center, Right, Stretch (default: fills the entire layout slot).
Language	System.Windows.Markup.XmlLanguage	Specifies localization/globalization language used by this FrameworkElement. Consult the XmlLanguage class documentation and RFC 3066 for details.
Margin	Thickness	Gets/sets the outer margin of the FrameworkElement.
MaxHeight	double	Defines maximum height constraint of the FrameworkElement.
MaxWidth	double	Defines maximum width constraint of the FrameworkElement.
MinHeight	double	Defines minimum height constraint of the FrameworkElement.
MinWidth	double	Defines minimum width constraint of the FrameworkElement.
Name	String	Gets the name of the FrameworkElement. When set in XAML, corresponds to the name of the variable automatically generated.
Parent	DependencyObject	Provides the parent object of the specific FrameworkElement in the object tree. It is a read-only property.
Resources	ResourceDictionary	Returns the resource dictionary defined on this FrameworkElement.
Style	Style	Gets/sets the style applied during rendering of this FrameworkElement.
Tag	Object	Places arbitrary information on a FrameworkElement. Restricted to the string type, although defined as an object.
Triggers	TriggerCollection	Provides the collection of triggers for animations that are defined for a FrameworkElement. It is a read-only property.

VerticalAlignment	VerticalAlignment	Gets/sets the vertical alignment. Behavior is subject to the container that has this control. Possible values: Top, Center, Bottom, Stretch (default: fills the entire layout slot).
Width	double	Indicates the asked-for width of the FrameworkElement.

Table 3-7 shows the events of FrameworkElement.

Table 3-7. Events of the System.Windows.FrameworkElement Class

Event	Description
BindingValidationError	Fires when a data validation error occurs as part of data binding. Event args class: ValidationErrorEventArgs.
LayoutUpdated	Fires when the layout of the FrameworkElement is updated. Event args type: EventArgs (this is a CLR event).
Loaded	Fires when the layout is complete and element is ready for interaction. Event args type: RoutedEventHandler.
SizeChanged	Fires when the ActualWidth or ActualHeight properties are updated by the layout system. Event args type: SizeChangedEventHandler.

The Control Class

The System.Windows.Controls.Control class forms the base of many controls in the complete Silverlight control set and uses ControlTemplate to define the appearance of the control. This class provides properties for setting the background and foreground of a control, configuring the appearance of text within the control, and enabling control templating (something we will look at in Chapter 8). Table 3-8 describes the properties the Control class introduces.

Table 3-8. Properties of the System.Windows.Controls.Control Class

Property	Type	Description
Background	Brush	Gets/sets the current brush used to paint the background of the control.
BorderBrush	Brush	Gets/sets the brush used to draw the border of the control.
BorderThickness	Thickness	Gets/sets the thickness of the control's border.

DefaultStyleKey	Object	Defines the key referencing to the default style for the control.
FontFamily	FontFamily	Indicates the font used for the text shown in the control.
FontSize	double	Gets/sets font size of the text shown in control. Defaults to 11 pt.
FontStretch	FontStretch	Gets/sets font compression/expansion for fonts that support it.
FontStyle	FontStyle	Gets/sets the font style. Possible values: Normal (default) and Italic.
FontWeight	FontWeight	Gets/sets thickness of font. Possible values range from Thin (100) to ExtraBlack (950). The default is Normal (400).
Foreground	Brush	Gets/sets the brush used to draw the foreground of the control.
HorizontalContent Alignment	HorizontalAlignment	Gets/sets the horizontal alignment of the control content (Left, Right, Stretch, and Center (Default value)).
IsEnabled	bool	Defines whether the user can interact with the control.
IsTabStop	bool	Gets/sets whether control participates in tab order.
Padding	Thickness	Gets/sets the space between the content of the control and its border or margin (if no border).
TabIndex	Int32	Gets/sets the position of the control in the tab order. Lower numbers are encountered first in the tab order.
TabNavigation	KeyboardNavigationMode	Controls how tabbing with this control works. Possible values: Local (default), None, Cycle.
Template	Template	Defines the control template used for the visual appearance of this control.
VerticalContent Alignment	VerticalAlignment	Gets/sets the horizontal alignment of the control content (Top, Bottom, Stretch, and Center (default value)).

The Control class contains two key methods: ApplyTemplate and Focus methods and 21 protected methods.

- The ApplyTemplate method loads the relevant control template so that its parts can be referenced. It returns true if the visual tree was rebuilt by calling this method, else it will return false, indicating that the previous visual tree was retained.

- The Focus method makes an attempt to set the focus on the control. It returns the Boolean value. It returns true if the focus is set to the control or control is already in focus. It returns false if the control is not focusable.

- OnDragEnter, OnDragLeave, OnDragOver, OnDrop, OnGotFocus, OnKeyDown, OnKeyUp, OnLostFocus, OnLostMouseCapture, OnMouseEnter, OnMouseLeave, OnMouseLeftButtonDown, OnMouseLeftButtonUp, OnMouseMove, OnMouseRightButtonDown, OnMouseRightButtonUp, OnMouseWheel, OnTextInput, OnTextInputStart, OnTextInputUpdate protected methods are called before any event handler for the respective event is called. The GetTemplateChild protected method retrieves the named element from the control template.

The Control class contains one event, IsEnabledChanged, which occurs when the IsEnabled property changes.

Enhancements in Silverlight 4

Before we dive into the details, the following points summarize the key enhancements of the Silverlight 4 version, supporting rich user interface controls and features to develop a line of business applications:

- Enhancements in the UIElement class to support drag-and-drop functionality

- Enhancements in the FrameworkElement class to support the bi-directional (left to right and right to left) languages support

- The ViewBox control matured enough and is migrated to the standard controls from the Silverlight Toolkit. It is a container control that allows precise positioning and flexible resizing of the child element filling the available space.

- The addition of Command and CommandParameter properties to the ButtonBase class will support implementation of MVVM (Model View ViewModel) pattern in your Silverlight application.

- New RichTextBox control is designed to facilitate rich text, which includes capabilities to format text (such as bold, italics, underline, font size, foreground color), insert in-line images, create hyperlinks and support left-to-right and right-to-left languages.

- New WebBrowser control to host HTML content within the Silverlight application when it runs in the Out of Browser (OOB) application mode.

Layout Management and Grouping Controls

Having a variety of controls and other visual objects gives us the raw material for user interfaces, but in order to form a full user interface, these objects must be positioned onscreen. This is accomplished via the Panel class—the base class of layout containers.

A layout container is used to contain controls and to oversee positioning of these controls on a user interface. In ASP.NET, layout of controls on a web page results from the application of styles to HTML tags that contain ASP.NET controls. In Windows Forms, layout is accomplished via absolute positioning, and there is no layout control; instead, controls specify their position and size. Silverlight (and WPF) strikes a balance between these two approaches, providing layout controls that work in conjunction with properties of its children controls (such as size properties). Silverlight provides many layout controls: Canvas, Grid, StackPanel, and, introduced with Silverlight 3 and Silverlight Controls Toolkit, DockPanel, WrapPanel, and Primitives (as a base class of many complex controls). The Canvas control provides the ability to absolutely position child elements, much like in Windows Forms. The Grid control provides support for laying out controls in a tabular configuration with rows and columns. The StackPanel control displays its child controls one next to the other, either in a horizontal orientation or in a vertical orientation. The DockPanel control is useful for easily placing controls at the edges of a container, similar to the behavior of the Dock property in WinForms controls. The WrapPanel control is similar to the StackPanel, but when the edge of the container is reached, new content is placed in the next row or column. The Primitives contains many complex controls–related classes and controls. Some examples of Primitives classes are RangeBase, TabPanel, and ScrollBar. Layout controls can be nested, so by combining multiple controls you can assemble some sophisticated user interfaces.

To create examples of key Silverlight user controls, first create a Silverlight 4 application project with the name chapter3. Now for each example we will add an associated user control to the project.

Canvas

The Canvas provides the ability to absolutely position elements. Controls that are added directly to a Canvas can use the Canvas.Left and Canvas.Top attached properties to specify where they should appear on the canvas. Figure 3-2 depicts several controls placed on a canvas, including a nested canvas.

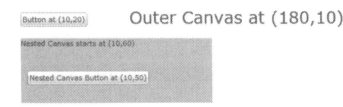

Figure 3-2. The Canvas panel example

The XAML for this screen looks like this:

```
<UserControl x:Class="chapter3.CanvasDemo"
    xmlns="http://schemas.microsoft.com/winfx/2006/xaml/presentation"
    xmlns:x="http://schemas.microsoft.com/winfx/2006/xaml"
    xmlns:d="http://schemas.microsoft.com/expression/blend/2008"
    xmlns:mc="http://schemas.openxmlformats.org/markup-
```

```
        compatibility/2006"
    mc:Ignorable="d"
    d:DesignHeight="300" d:DesignWidth="400">

    <Canvas x:Name="LayoutRoot">
        <Button Canvas.Left="10" Canvas.Top="20"
            Content="Button at (10,20)"/>
        <TextBlock Text="Outer Canvas at (180,10)"
            Canvas.Left="180" Canvas.Top="10" FontSize="26"/>

        <Canvas Canvas.Top="60" Canvas.Left="10"
            Background="LightSkyBlue" Width="300" Height="100">
            <TextBlock Text="Nested Canvas starts at (10,60)"
                Canvas.Left="0" Canvas.Top="0"/>
            <Button Canvas.Left="10" Canvas.Top="50"
                Content="Nested Canvas Button at (10,50)"/>
        </Canvas>
    </Canvas>
</UserControl>
```

StackPanel

A StackPanel stacks visual objects next to each other, either horizontally or vertically. The Orientation property of the StackPanel can be set to Vertical (the default) or Horizontal. Figure 3-3 shows stacking a label next to a text entry box in a horizontal orientation and are nested within vertically-oriented StackPanel with the title.

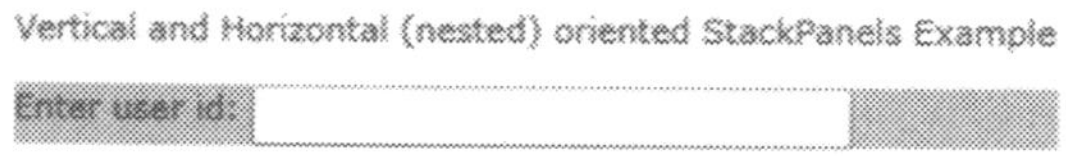

Figure 3-3. The StackPanel example

Here's the XAML for this control:

```
<UserControl x:Class="chapter3.StackPanelDemo"
    xmlns="http://schemas.microsoft.com/winfx/2006/xaml/presentation"
    xmlns:x="http://schemas.microsoft.com/winfx/2006/xaml"
    xmlns:d="http://schemas.microsoft.com/expression/blend/2008"
    xmlns:mc="http://schemas.openxmlformats.org/markup-
        compatibility/2006"
    mc:Ignorable="d"
    d:DesignHeight="300" d:DesignWidth="400">

    <StackPanel x:Name="LayoutRoot" Background="White"
        Orientation="Vertical">
        <TextBlock Margin="0,10" Text="Vertical and Horizontal
            (nested) oriented StackPanels Example"/>
        <StackPanel Background="LightSkyBlue"
```

```
                Orientation="Horizontal">
                <TextBlock Text="Enter user id: "/>
                <TextBox Width="200" Height="20" VerticalAlignment="Top"/>
            </StackPanel>
        </StackPanel>
</UserControl>
```

Grid

The Grid is the most complicated (relatively) and most capable layout container. It consists of one or more rows and one or more columns. Let's look at the XAML for a simple grid consisting of two rows and two columns:

```
<UserControl x:Class="chapter3.GridDemo"
    xmlns="http://schemas.microsoft.com/winfx/2006/xaml/presentation"
    xmlns:x="http://schemas.microsoft.com/winfx/2006/xaml"
    xmlns:d="http://schemas.microsoft.com/expression/blend/2008"
    xmlns:mc="http://schemas.openxmlformats.org/markup-compatibility/2006"
    mc:Ignorable="d"
    d:DesignHeight="300" d:DesignWidth="400" Height="300" Width="400">
<Grid x:Name="LayoutRoot" Background="White">
    <Grid.ColumnDefinitions>
        <ColumnDefinition/>
        <ColumnDefinition/>
    </Grid.ColumnDefinitions>
    <Grid.RowDefinitions>
        <RowDefinition/>
        <RowDefinition/>
    </Grid.RowDefinitions>
</Grid>
```

Four attached properties control where in the grid content is placed. Table 3-9 explains these attached properties.

Table 3-9. *Attached Properties of the System.Windows.ControlsGrid Class*

Property	Type	Description
Grid.Row	Int32	The row of the grid where content is placed. The first row is index 0. The default value is 0.
Grid.Column	Int32	The column of the grid where content is placed. The first column is 0. The default value is 0.
Grid.RowSpan	Int32	The number of rows the content will occupy. The default value is 1.
Grid.ColumnSpan	Int32	The number of columns the content will occupy. The default value is 1.

Placing content within a grid is a simple matter of creating content and then setting values for the various attached properties. Figure 3-4 shows the result of placing content in each column of the first row and then using ColumnSpan to cause the content to fill the second row.

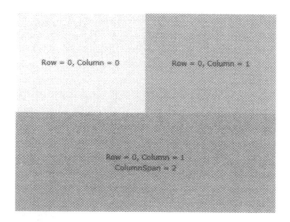

Figure 3-4. The Grid panel example

▓ **Note** There is an attribute called ShowGridLines that you can set to true on the Grid element to visibly see where the columns and rows are. This is incredibly useful when designing the Grid; however, the grid lines aren't especially pretty. If you want grid lines, look to the Border control later in this chapter.

Here's what the XAML looks like to create what's shown in Figure 3-4.

```
<UserControl x:Class="chapter3.GridDemo"
    xmlns="http://schemas.microsoft.com/winfx/2006/xaml/presentation"
    xmlns:x="http://schemas.microsoft.com/winfx/2006/xaml"
    xmlns:d="http://schemas.microsoft.com/expression/blend/2008"
    xmlns:mc="http://schemas.openxmlformats.org/markup-
        compatibility/2006"
    mc:Ignorable="d"
    d:DesignHeight="300" d:DesignWidth="400" Height="300" Width="400">

    <Grid x:Name="LayoutRoot" Background="White">
        <Grid.ColumnDefinitions>
            <ColumnDefinition/>
            <ColumnDefinition/>
        </Grid.ColumnDefinitions>
        <Grid.RowDefinitions>
            <RowDefinition/>
            <RowDefinition/>
        </Grid.RowDefinitions>
```

```
        <Border Grid.Row="0" Grid.Column="0" Background="Beige">
            <TextBlock HorizontalAlignment="Center"
                VerticalAlignment="Center" Text="Row = 0, Column = 0"/>
        </Border>
        <Border Grid.Row="0" Grid.Column="1" Background="BurlyWood">
            <TextBlock HorizontalAlignment="Center"
                VerticalAlignment="Center" Text="Row = 0, Column = 1"/>
        </Border>
        <Border Grid.Row="1" Grid.Column="0" Grid.ColumnSpan="2"
            Background="DarkKhaki">
            <StackPanel HorizontalAlignment="Center"
                VerticalAlignment="Center" >
                <TextBlock Text="Row = 0, Column = 1"/>
                <TextBlock HorizontalAlignment="Center"
                    Text="ColumnSpan = 2"/>
            </StackPanel>
        </Border>
    </Grid>
</UserControl>
```

The ColumnDefinition class has a property named Width that allows you to set the width of the column. Likewise, the RowDefinition class has a property named Height. These properties are of type GridLength, a special class that provides capabilities beyond a simple double value representing size. In XAML, the Width and Height properties can be set to the special value Auto, which is the default value. The Auto value causes the row/column to size automatically to the largest piece of content. More sophisticated control over space is provided by something known as *star sizing*.

The Width and Height properties can be set to the special value *, or a "star," with a number in front, such as 2* or 3*. This syntax gives a proportional amount of the available space to a row or a column. Figure 3-5 shows a grid with a single row and two columns given the star sizes * and 2*.

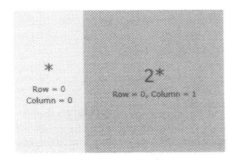

Figure 3-5. Using star sizing with a Grid

The XAML to create this grid looks like this:

```
<UserControl x:Class="chapter3.StarSizingDemo"
    xmlns="http://schemas.microsoft.com/winfx/2006/xaml/presentation"
    xmlns:x="http://schemas.microsoft.com/winfx/2006/xaml"
    xmlns:d="http://schemas.microsoft.com/expression/blend/2008"
```

```
    xmlns:mc="http://schemas.openxmlformats.org/markup-
        compatibility/2006"
    mc:Ignorable="d"
    d:DesignHeight="300" d:DesignWidth="400"
            Width="300" Height="200">

    <Grid x:Name="LayoutRoot" Background="White"
        Width="300" Height="200">
        <Grid.ColumnDefinitions>
            <ColumnDefinition Width="*"/>
            <ColumnDefinition Width="2*"/>
        </Grid.ColumnDefinitions>
        <Grid.RowDefinitions>
            <RowDefinition/>
        </Grid.RowDefinitions>
        <Border Grid.Row="0" Grid.Column="0" Background="Beige">
            <StackPanel HorizontalAlignment="Center"
                VerticalAlignment="Center">
                <TextBlock HorizontalAlignment="Center"
                    FontSize="16" FontWeight="Bold" Text="*"/>
                <TextBlock HorizontalAlignment="Center"
                    Text="Row = 0"/>
                <TextBlock HorizontalAlignment="Center"
                    Text="Column = 0"/>
            </StackPanel>
        </Border>
        <Border Grid.Row="0" Grid.Column="1" Background="BurlyWood">
            <StackPanel HorizontalAlignment="Center"
                VerticalAlignment="Center">
                <TextBlock HorizontalAlignment="Center"
                    FontSize="16" FontWeight="Bold" Text="2*"/>
                <TextBlock HorizontalAlignment="Center"
                    Text="Row = 0, Column = 1"/>
            </StackPanel>
        </Border>
    </Grid>
</UserControl>
```

The total width of the grid is 300. The second column is twice as big as the first, specified by the 2* property value for the width. If no number is specified before the star, it is treated the same as if the value were 1*. In this case, the first column is 100 since the second column is twice as big, and 200 added to 100 gives the total width of the grid, 300. If you combine the other sizing methods with star sizing, the value of 1* will equal whatever space is available.

DockPanel

The DockPanel is one of the new layout containers introduced as part of the Silverlight Toolkit. You need to add a reference of Systems.Windows.Controls.Toolkit.dll, delivered as part of the Silverlight toolkit under the Microsoft SDKs/Silverlight folder, to the project. Then add the reference of this namespace to the UserControl within the XAML file, as shown here (in highlighted fonts):

```
<UserControl x:Class="chapter3.DockPanelDemo"
    xmlns="http://schemas.microsoft.com/winfx/2006/xaml/presentation"
    xmlns:x="http://schemas.microsoft.com/winfx/2006/xaml"
    xmlns:d="http://schemas.microsoft.com/expression/blend/2008"
    xmlns:mc="http://schemas.openxmlformats.org/markup-
        compatibility/2006"
    xmlns:c="clr-namespace:System.Windows.Controls;assembly=
        System.Windows.Controls.Toolkit"
    mc:Ignorable="d"
    d:DesignHeight="600" d:DesignWidth="500">
```

The DockPanel is designed to place content around the edge of the panel. The Dock dependency property (which can be set to Left, Right, Top, or Bottom) defines the location of the child element. As its name suggests, the LastChildFill property of the DockPanel, if set to true (which is the default value), will allow the last added child element to cover the remaining size of the panel only if the added child element is allowed to resize. Otherwise, the element will appear in the originally-defined size and will not resize.

Figure 3-6 shows two example configurations of the DockPanel, along with the order that content was added to the DockPanel. The LastChildFill property is set to its default value of true, meaning the last child added to the DockPanel control will completely fill the remaining space.

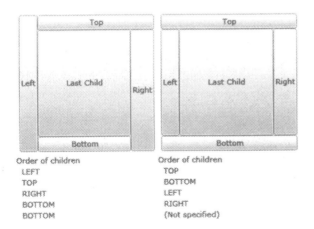

Figure 3-6. The DockPanel example with LastChildFill set to true (default value)

The XAML for the first configuration in Figure 3-6 sets the Dock property on all the child content, as shown here:

```
<c:DockPanel Height="200" Width="200" Grid.Column="0" Grid.Row="1">
    <Button c:DockPanel.Dock="Left" Content="Left"/>
    <Button c:DockPanel.Dock="Top" Content="Top"/>
    <Button c:DockPanel.Dock="Right" Content="Right"/>
    <Button c:DockPanel.Dock="Bottom" Content="Bottom"/>
    <Button c:DockPanel.Dock="Bottom" Content="Last Child"/>
</c:DockPanel>
```

The XAML for the second configuration in Figure 3-6 fills the remaining space with the last child button without specifying the Dock property, since its LastChildFill property is set to True by default (no need to specify explicitly),,as shown here:

```
<c:DockPanel Height="200" Width="200" Grid.Column="1" Grid.Row="1">
    <Button c:DockPanel.Dock="Top" Content="Top"/>
    <Button c:DockPanel.Dock="Bottom" Content="Bottom"/>
    <Button c:DockPanel.Dock="Left" Content="Left"/>
    <Button c:DockPanel.Dock="Right" Content="Right"/>
    <Button Content="Last Child"/>
</c:DockPanel>
```

The order in which child content is added is important. Content added to the left and right sides will completely fill the vertical space available to them. Content added to the top and bottom will completely fill the horizontal space available to them. You can observe this in Figure 3-6, since the left content was added first to the first configuration and the top content was added first to the second configuration. When LastChildFill is true, the Dock property of the last child doesn't matter, as you can see in the second configuration where the Dock property had no value. The picture changes, however, when the LastChildFill property is set to false, as shown here:

```
<c:DockPanel Height="200" Width="200"
             Grid.Column="2" Grid.Row="1"
             LastChildFill="False">
    <Button c:DockPanel.Dock="Top" Content="Top"/>
    <Button c:DockPanel.Dock="Bottom" Content="Bottom"/>
    <Button c:DockPanel.Dock="Left" Content="Left"/>
    <Button c:DockPanel.Dock="Right" Content="Right"/>
    <Button c:DockPanel.Dock="Top" Content="Inner Top"/>
    <Button c:DockPanel.Dock="Bottom" Content="Inner Bottom"/>
</c:DockPanel>
```

Figure 3-7 shows what the inner nesting of controls looks like.

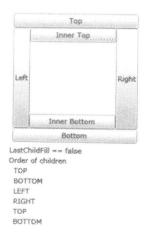

Figure 3-7. The DockPanel with inner nesting of controls with LastChildFill set to false

By preventing the last child from filling the space, it's possible to place more content around the edges of the container. The unfortunate consequence of this is that now the leftover space won't automatically be used by the last child added. One way to fill up the remaining space is by setting the width/height on the last child so that it fills up the space. Another technique is to nest a DockPanel within a DockPanel, giving you the ability to create the same interface as shown in Figure 3-7 without losing the fill behavior of the last child.

WrapPanel

The WrapPanel is the other layout container available as part of the Silverlight Toolkit. As you did in the DockPanel section, add a reference of Systems.Windows.Controls.Toolkit.dll, delivered as part of the Silverlight toolkit, to the project and add a reference of this namespace to the UserControl within the XAML file. Its behavior is similar to the StackPanel in that you can automatically place content adjacent to each other (left to right or top to bottom), but it adds the behavior of wrapping content to the next row or column of an invisible grid when the content reaches the end of its available space. Added images under the scope of the WrapPanel shown in Figure 3-8 and Figure 3-9 represent the behavior of the WrapPanel with the horizontal and vertical orientation.

Figure 3-8. Horizontal behavior of the WrapPanel

Figure 3-9. Vertical behavior of the WrapPanel

To develop the example shown in Figure 3-8, create a res folder under the project and then add the sample images, available in your machine, to the newly created res folder of the project and rename them 1.jpg to 5.jpg. Add the following code snippet to the user control to show the added images within the scope of the horizontally-oriented WrapPanel control, as shown here.

```
<StackPanel>
    <TextBlock Text="Horizontally Oriented WrapPanel Example"
        Margin="5" FontWeight="Bold"/>
    <c:WrapPanel Width="500" Height="250" Orientation="Horizontal">
        <Image Width="150" Height="100" Margin="2" Source="res/1.jpg"/>
        <Image Width="150" Height="100" Margin="2" Source="res/2.jpg"/>
        <Image Width="150" Height="100" Margin="2" Source="res/3.jpg"/>
        <Image Width="150" Height="100" Margin="2" Source="res/4.jpg"/>
        <Image Width="150" Height="100" Margin="2" Source="res/5.jpg"/>
    </c:WrapPanel>
</StackPanel>
```

Note that we have added the WrapPanel control within the StackPanel to display the title of the sample application.

The WrapPanel exposes three new properties, as shown in Table 3-9, all of which are also dependency properties. The Orientation property controls whether child content is stacked horizontally (wrapping to the next row) or vertically (wrapping to the next column). In the preceding code snippet, if you change the Orientation property of the WrapPanel to Vertical, increase the value of the Height property, and change the TextBlock's Text properly, you will get an outcome similar to Figure 3.9.

Table 3-10. Key Properties of the System.Windows.Controls.WrapPanel Class

Property	Type	Description
ItemHeight	Double	Specifies the height of each item. Can be set to Auto or a qualified value using the suffix px for device independent pixels, in for inches, cm for centimeters, or pt for points. The default is pixels.
ItemWidth	Double	Specifies the width of each item. Can be set to Auto (default value) or a qualified value using a suffix.
Orientation	Orientation	Specifies whether child content is stacked horizontally (wrapping to the next row) or vertically (wrapping to the next column). Can be set to Horizontal (default value) or Vertical.

TabControl

The TabControl is used to host multiple items sharing the same space on the screen, with each page accessible via a tab. Table 3-11 describes its key properties.

Table 3-11. Key Properties of the System.Windows.Controls.TabControl Class

Property	Type	Description
SelectedContent	Object	Specifies the content of the currently active TabItem.
SelectedIndex	Int32	Gets/sets the index of the currently active TabItem, or -1 if no TabItem is active.
SelectedItem	Object	Specifies the currently active TabItem, or null if no TabItem is active.
TabStripPlacement	Dock	Gets/sets how TabItem headers align relative to the TabItem content and thus defines the place where Tabs are displayed within the TabControl. The Dock enumeration has four possible values specifying the behavior of the TabControl. They are Left, Top (default), Right, and Bottom.

The TabControl provides one event, SelectionChanged (event args class: SelectionChangedEventArgs). The TabControl consists of TabItems, each with a Header property that is used to set the tab label and a Content property used to set the contents of the specific tab page. Figure 3-10 shows a TabControl with three tabs.

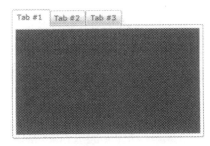

Figure 3-10. The TabControl example

Here's the XAML for this control. Notice that you need to add a reference of the System.Windows.Controls namespace to the UserControl:

```
<UserControl x:Class="chapter3.TabControlDemo"
    xmlns="http://schemas.microsoft.com/winfx/2006/xaml/presentation"
    xmlns:x="http://schemas.microsoft.com/winfx/2006/xaml"
    xmlns:d="http://schemas.microsoft.com/expression/blend/2008"
    xmlns:mc="http://schemas.openxmlformats.org/markup-
        compatibility/2006"
    xmlns:c="clr-namespace:System.Windows.Controls;
        assembly=System.Windows.Controls"
    mc:Ignorable="d"
    d:DesignHeight="300" d:DesignWidth="400">
<Canvas x:Name="LayoutRoot" Background="White">
```

```
    <c:TabControl Canvas.Left="20" Canvas.Top="40"
                  Width="300" Height="200">
        <c:TabItem Header="Tab #1">
            <Canvas Background="Red"></Canvas>
        </c:TabItem>
        <c:TabItem Header="Tab #2">
            <Canvas Background="Green"></Canvas>
        </c:TabItem>
        <c:TabItem Header="Tab #3">
            <Canvas Background="Blue"></Canvas>
        </c:TabItem>
    </c:TabControl>
</Canvas>
</UserControl>
```

ViewBox

Inherited from `System.Windows.FrameworkElement`, the `ViewBox` is included as part of the Silverlight 4 default standard controls, moved from the Silverlight tool kit. It is a container control that allows precise positioning and flexible resizing of the child element filling the available space. You can have only one child element per `ViewBox` control. To add multiple child elements within the ViewBox, you can use the panel control (such as `StackPanel`, `Grid`, and `Canvas`) and add multiple elements within the panel and then add the panel to the `ViewBox` control. Table 3-12 details the key properties of this control. The most common use of the `ViewBox` control is for 2D image source.

Table 3-12. *Key Properties of the System.Windows.Controls.ViewBox Class*

Property	Type	Description
Child	UIElement	Defines the child element of the ViewBox control.
Stretch	Stretch	Defines how content fills the available space by setting the Stretch mode. The Stretch is an enum and contains four possible modes: None, Fill, Uniform (default value), and UniformToFill.
StretchDirection	StretchDirection	Defines how scaling is applicable to the content. It prevents contents of the Viewbox from being scaled to a smaller or larger dimension than the original. The StretchDirection is an enum and contains three possible modes: UpOnly, DownOnly, and Both (default value).

The next example shows two `Viewbox` controls. The first 150x200 pixels `Viewbox` with default settings of `Stretch` set to `UniformToFill` and `StretchDirection` set to `Both` shows the 1024x768 pixels image is stretched uniformly to fill the entire smaller `Viewbox`. The second 150x200 pixels `Viewbox` with `StretchDirection` set to `UpOnly` shows only the small upper portion of the same image. This is because the image will only stretch up in size as specified by stretch direction, and since the container `Viewbox` is smaller than the image, the image will not stretch and only the upper portion is shown.

```
<StackPanel x:Name="LayoutRoot" Background="White">
    <TextBlock Text="ViewBox with Stretch=UniformToFill and
        StretchDirection=Both" Margin="5" FontWeight="Bold"
        HorizontalAlignment="Center"/>
    <Viewbox Height="150" Width="200" Stretch="UniformToFill"
        StretchDirection="Both">
        <Image Margin="2" Source="res/1.jpg"/>
    </Viewbox>
    <TextBlock Text="ViewBox with StretchDirection=UpOnly"
        Margin="2" FontWeight="Bold" HorizontalAlignment="Center"/>
    <Viewbox Height="150" Width="200" StretchDirection="UpOnly">
        <Image Margin="2" Source="res/1.jpg"/>
    </Viewbox>
</StackPanel>
```

ViewBox with Stretch=UniformToFill and StretchDirection=Both

ViewBox with StretchDirection=UpOnly

Figure 3-11. The ViewBox *example*

Forms Controls

User input is a vital part of virtually every web application. The Microsoft Silverlight platform is continuously enhanced to provide a fairly robust set of controls that enable you to quickly add rich UI elements and process user input effectively. Silverlight 4 made some vital improvements to existing Forms controls as well as a new addition of RichTextBox control that we are going to discuss in this section.

The Button Controls

Many specialized versions of buttons exist, all inheriting directly or indirectly from the ButtonBase class (in the System.Windows.Controls.Primitives namespace) inherited from the ContentControl. The ButtonBase class provides the basic pressing behavior that is common to all buttons. Table 3-13 describes its properties.

Table 3-13. Properties of the System.Windows.Controls.Primitives.ButtonBase Class

Property	Type	Description
ClickMode	ClickMode	Controls how the mouse triggers the Click event. Possible values: Hover (when the mouse moves over the button); Press (the left mouse button is pressed down); Release (the left mouse button is released while over the button). Defaults to Release.
Command	ICommand	Defines the command to be invoked when a button is pressed. The default value is a null reference. New property in Silverlight 4.
CommandParameter	Object	Defines parameter to pass to the Command property. The default value is a null reference. New property in Silverlight 4.
IsFocused	bool	true if this button has focus, false otherwise.
IsMouseOver	bool	true if the mouse pointer is hovering over this button, false otherwise.
IsPressed	bool	true if the button is in a pressed state, false otherwise.

The Command and CommandParameter are core properties for implementing MVVM (Model View ViewModel) pattern in your Silverlight application. We will discuss them further in Chapter 11.

The ButtonBase class provides a single event, Click (event args class: RoutedEventHandler). Figure 3-12 shows what the various buttons—Button, HyperlinkButton, RepeatButton and ToggleButton—look like by default.

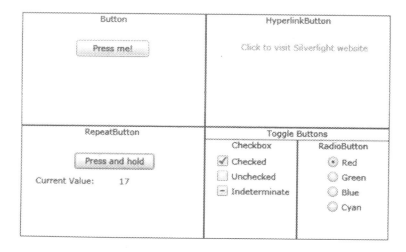

Figure 3-12. Collection of different button controls

Button

The Button control provides basic button functionality. Its implementation is supplied by its base class, ButtonBase. Here's a basic button in XAML where the content is set to text:

```
<Button Canvas.Left="74" Canvas.Top="20" Width="100"
        Content="Press me!" x:Name="button"
        Click="Button_Click" />
```

In the previous code snippet, the Click event of the Button control calls the code-behind Button_Click, as shown here:

```
private void Button_Click(object sender, RoutedEventArgs e)
{
    //Put your custom code here
}
```

HyperlinkButton

The HyperlinkButton control introduces the capability to cause the browser to navigate to a specific web site when it is clicked. Table 3-14 describes the key properties provided by the HyperlinkButton class.

Table 3-14. Key Properties of the System.Windows.Controls.HyperlinkButton Class

Property	Type	Description
NavigateUri	Uri	Gets/sets the URI to navigate to when the HyperlinkButton is clicked.
TargetName	String	Gets/sets the name of target window/frame where navigation happens

Here's the XAML for the hyperlink button shown in Figure 3-12:

```
<HyperlinkButton x:Name="hyperlinkButton"
        Canvas.Left="45" Canvas.Top="20" Width="200"
        Content="Click to visit Silverlight website"
        NavigateUri="http://www.silverlight.net"
        TargetName="_blank"/>
```

RepeatButton

The functionality introduced by a RepeatButton is the repeated firing of the Click event for as long as the button is clicked. You can set several properties to control how the Click event fires; Table 3-15 lists them.

Table 3-15. Properties of the System.Windows.Controls.Primitives.RepeatButton *Class*

Property	Type	Description
Delay	Int32	Number of milliseconds before the click action repeats, after the button is initially pressed. The default is 250.
Interval	Int32	Number of milliseconds between repeated Click events, after repeating starts. The default is 250.

Here's the XAML for the repeat button shown in Figure 3-12:

```
<RepeatButton Canvas.Left="73" Canvas.Top="20" Width="110"
    Content="Press and hold" Click="RepeatButton_Click"/>
```

An event handler shows the current value increment as the button is held down:

```
private int currentValue = 0;
private void RepeatButton_Click(object sender, RoutedEventArgs e)
{
    currentValue++;
    repeatButtonValue.Text = currentValue.ToString();
}
```

Toggle Buttons: CheckBox and RadioButton

The ToggleButton provides the base functionality for both radio buttons and check boxes, which are controls that can switch states. Table 3-16 shows its key properties.

Table 3-16. Key Properties of the System.Windows.Controls.Primitives.ToggleButton *Class*

Property	Type	Description
IsChecked	Nullable<bool>	Indicates true if checked, false if not, and null if in an indeterminate state. If IsThreeState is set to true, the user can cause this property's value to cycle between true/false/null.
IsThreeState	bool	Gets/sets whether the control supports three states. If false, the button supports only two states.

The ToggleButton class introduces three new events: Checked, Unchecked, and Indeterminate. These events use RoutedEventArgs as the event argument type and capture the various states a ToggleButton can switch into. The two classes that inherit from ToggleButton are CheckBox and RadioButton. The main distinguishing factor between check boxes and radio buttons is that radio buttons can be grouped, so only one specific radio button within a group can be selected at any given moment. Table 3-17 describes the key properties of RadioButton. If no group is specified, all ungrouped radio buttons within a single parent control become part of the same group.

Table 3-17. Key Properties of the `System.Windows.Controls.RadioButton` *Class*

Property	Type	Description
GroupName	string	Gets/sets the name of the group to which this radio button belongs.

To create the example shown in Figure 3-12, first we need to add check boxes and then radio buttons. Here's the XAML for the check boxes shown in Figure 3-12:

```
<CheckBox x:Name="checkBox1" Canvas.Left="25" Canvas.Top="20"
                IsChecked="True" Content="Checked"/>
<CheckBox x:Name="checkBox2" Canvas.Left="25" Canvas.Top="40"
                IsChecked="False"  Content="Unchecked"/>
<CheckBox x:Name="checkBox3" Canvas.Left="25" Canvas.Top="60"
                IsChecked="" IsThreeState="True" Content="Indeterminate"/>
```

The radio buttons are given unique names, but they share the group name to ensure the mutual exclusion functionality.

```
<RadioButton x:Name="radioButton1" GroupName="group1"
                  Canvas.Left="40" Canvas.Top="20" Content="Red"/>
<RadioButton x:Name="radioButton2" GroupName="group1"
                  Canvas.Left="40" Canvas.Top="40" Content="Green"/>
<RadioButton x:Name="radioButton3" GroupName="group1"
                  Canvas.Left="40" Canvas.Top="60" Content="Blue"/>
<RadioButton x:Name="radioButton4" GroupName="group1"
                  Canvas.Left="40" Canvas.Top="80" Content="Cyan"/>
```

TextBox

The TextBox control is used to get free-form text-based information from a user. It provides single-line and multi-line input and the ability to let the user select text. Table 3-18 describes its key properties.

Table 3-18. Key Properties of the `System.Windows.Controls.TextBox` *Class*

Property	Type	Description
AcceptsReturn	bool	Indicates true if the text box accepts/interprets newline characters enabling multi-line. The false is the default value.
BaselineOffset	double	Value by which each line of text is offset from the baseline, in device-independent pixels. The default value is NaN. New property in Silverlight 4.
FontSource	FontSource	Defines the font used for text within the text box.

HorizontalScrollBar Visibility	ScrollBarVisibility	Controls how/when the horizontal scrollbar is displayed. Possible values: Disabled (scrollbar never appears); Auto (scrollbar appears when content cannot fully be displayed within the bounds); Hidden (like Disabled, but the dimension of the content is not set to the viewport's size); and Visible (scrollbar is always visible).
IsReadOnly	bool	Indicates no edits from the user are allowed if true. Defaults to false.
MaxLength	Int32	Defines the maximum number of characters that can be entered into a text box. The default is 0 (no restriction).
SelectedText	string	Gets the currently highlighted text. If set, the highlighted text is replaced with the new string. Any change (including programmatic) causes the SelectionChanged event to fire.
SelectionBackground	Brush	Specifies the brush used to paint the background of selected text.
SelectionForeground	Brush	Specifies the brush used to paint the text within the selection.
SelectionLength	Int32	Defines the number of characters currently selected, or zero if there is no selection.
SelectionStart	Int32	Specifies the index where the selected text begins within the text of the text box.
Text	string	Defines the text currently stored in the text box.
TextAlignment	TextAlignment	Gets/sets alignment of text within a text box. Possible values: Left, Center, Right.
TextWrapping	TextWrapping	Controls whether text wraps when it reaches the edge of the text box. Possible values: Wrap, NoWrap.
VerticalScrollBar Visibility	ScrollBarVisibility	Controls how/when a vertical scrollbar is displayed. See HorizontalScrollBarVisibility for possible values.

Figure 3-13 shows a single-line TextBox control and a multiline TextBox control with scrollbars. Note that for scrollbars to appear on a TextBox, the AcceptsReturn property must be set to true.

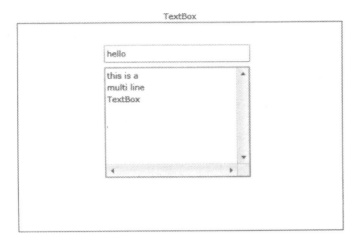

Figure 3-13. *The TextBox control*

Here's the corresponding XAML:

```
<TextBox Canvas.Top="30" Canvas.Left="120" Width="200"/>
<TextBox Canvas.Top="60" Canvas.Left="120" Height="150" Width="200"
        AcceptsReturn="True" HorizontalScrollBarVisibility="Visible"
        VerticalScrollBarVisibility="Visible"/>
```

PasswordBox

The PasswordBox control is designed to facilitate password entry. It provides the ability to enter a single line of non-wrapping content for a user to enter their password. Each entered character is displayed as a defined password character based on the defined PasswordChar property value. Table 3-19 describes PasswordBox's key properties.

Table 3-19. *Key Properties of the System.Windows.Controls.PasswordBox Class*

Property	Type	Description
PasswordChar	Char	Defines the password-masking character.
Password	String	Gets or sets the password held by the PasswordBox control.
MaxLength	Integer	Defines maximum length (characters) that can be entered in the PasswordBox control.

Figure 3-14 shows the use of the PasswordBox (with the masking character set to *) and the use of the PasswordChanged event to display the text entered in the PasswordBox control in a TextBox control. This event is raised every time there is a change in the Password property value.

Note that this is only for demonstration purposes; in practice you will probably not be using this feature due to security concerns.

Figure 3-14. *The PasswordBox control*

Here's the corresponding XAML:

```
<StackPanel x:Name="LayoutRoot" Background="White">
<TextBlock Margin="30,10,0,0" Text="Enter Password"
    FontWeight="bold"/>
<PasswordBox x:Name="EnterPassword" Margin="30,10,0,0"
    PasswordChanged="EnterPassword_PasswordChanged" MaxLength="11"
    Height="25" Width="150" HorizontalAlignment="Left" />
<TextBlock Text="Display Entered Password" Margin="30,10,0,0"
    FontWeight="bold"/>
<TextBox x:Name="DisplayPassword" Margin="30,10,0,0"
    HorizontalAlignment="Left" IsReadOnly="True" Height="25"
    Width="150" />
</StackPanel>
```

And here's the code-behind for the `PasswordChanged` event:

```
private void EnterPassword_PasswordChanged(object sender,
    RoutedEventArgs e)
{
    DisplayPassword.Text = EnterPassword.Password;
}
```

RichTextBox

We already took a quick look at the newly-introduced RichTextBox control in Chapter 1's sample application. Silverlight 4 drives for Line-of-Business (LoB) RIAs and rich text is one of the core requirements for most LoB applications. The RichTextBox control is designed to facilitate rich text, which includes capabilities to format text (such as bold, italics, underline, font size, foreground color), insert in-line images, create hyperlinks and support for left-to-right and right-to-left languages. This control supports paragraph blocks with different formatting of blocks of text. Table 3-20 describes RichTextBox's key properties.

Table 3-20. Key Properties of the System.Windows.Controls.RichTextBox Class

Property	Type	Description
Blocks	BlockCollection	Gets the content of the RichTextBox. The BlockCollection includes collection of the entered Paragraph elements.
HorizontalScrollBar Visibility	ScrollBarVisibility	Controls how/when the horizontal scrollbar is displayed. Possible values: Disabled (scrollbar never appears); Auto (scrollbar appears when content cannot be fully displayed within the bounds); Hidden (like Disabled, but the dimension of the content is not set to the viewport's size); and Visible (scrollbar is always visible).
IsReadOnly	bool	Defines if the rich text area is read-only or the user can change the content. The default value is false. The programmatic changes are allowed in the read-only mode. Inserted UIElements (XAML) and hyperlinks are active only in the read-only mode. The user can still perform selection of the text and get the cursor in the read-only mode. Also KeyUp and KeyDown events are marked as handled by default.
Selection	TextSelection	Gets the selected text within the RichTextBox.
TextWrapping	TextWrapping	Controls whether text wraps when it reaches the edge of the text box. Possible values: Wrap, NoWrap.
VerticalScrollBar Visibility	ScrollBarVisibility	Controls how/when a vertical scrollbar is displayed. See HorizontalScrollBarVisibility for possible values.

The Paragraph class (of the System.Windows.Documents namespace) is usually used to group different types of content and present them as a block. The Paragraph element can host simple text and Inline elements such as InlineUIContainer (for XAML UI element and images), Run (string of formatted or unformatted text), Span (to group other Inline content elements), Bold (format text as bold font weight), Hyperlink (to host hyperlinks), Italic (format text as italic font style), and Underline (decorate text as underlined text).

Figure 3-15 shows a very basic example of the use of the RichTextBox control containing simple text, formatted text, an inline image, and a Grid panel. Here we have used Paragraph elements to group the block of content and a LineBreak element to create a new line.

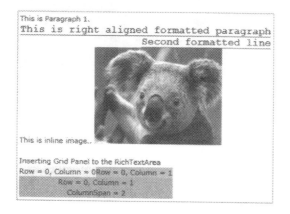

Figure 3-15. *The RichTextBox control example*

Here's the corresponding XAML:

```
<RichTextBox TextWrapping="Wrap" IsReadOnly="False">
    <Paragraph>
        This is Paragraph 1.
    </Paragraph>
    <Paragraph
        FontSize="16"
        TextAlignment="Right"
        FontFamily="Courier New">
            <Underline>
                This is right aligned formatted paragraph
                <LineBreak/>
                Second formatted line
            </Underline>
    </Paragraph>
    <Paragraph>
        This is inline image..
        <InlineUIContainer>
            <Image Source="res/5.jpg" Height="150" Width="200"
                Stretch="UniformToFill"/>
        </InlineUIContainer>
    </Paragraph>
    <Paragraph>
        <LineBreak/>
            Inserting Grid Panel to the RichTextBox
        <LineBreak/>
        <InlineUIContainer>
            <Grid>
                <Grid.ColumnDefinitions>
                    <ColumnDefinition/>
                    <ColumnDefinition/>
                </Grid.ColumnDefinitions>
```

```
                <Grid.RowDefinitions>
                    <RowDefinition/>
                    <RowDefinition/>
                </Grid.RowDefinitions>
                <Border Grid.Row="0" Grid.Column="0"
                    Background="Beige">
                    <TextBlock HorizontalAlignment="Center"
                        VerticalAlignment="Center"
                        Text="Row = 0, Column = 0"/>
                </Border>
                <Border Grid.Row="0" Grid.Column="1"
                    Background="BurlyWood">
                    <TextBlock HorizontalAlignment="Center"
                        VerticalAlignment="Center"
                        Text="Row = 0, Column = 1"/>
                </Border>
                <Border Grid.Row="1" Grid.Column="0"
                    Grid.ColumnSpan="2" Background="DarkKhaki">
                    <StackPanel HorizontalAlignment="Center"
                        VerticalAlignment="Center" >
                        <TextBlock Text="Row = 0, Column = 1"/>
                        <TextBlock HorizontalAlignment="Center"
                            Text="ColumnSpan = 2"/>
                    </StackPanel>
                </Border>
            </Grid>
        </InlineUIContainer>
    </Paragraph>
</RichTextBox>
```

AutoCompleteBox

The AutoCompleteBox control provides the ability to automatically show a drop-down list of items that match the partial input into a text box by a user. For example, if the AutoCompleteBox contains the items Blue, Red, Green, and Black and the user types **B**, a drop-down box will appear displaying Blue and Black. It is also possible to perform custom filtering on the AutoCompleteBox, making this control quite flexible. Although this control contains items (the data for the autocompletion), it is technically not an ItemsControl. Creating a simple AutoCompleteBox in your user interface is a matter of placing the control in the XAML and specifying the data source used for the autocompletion possibilities, like so:

```
<UserControl x:Class="chapter3.AutoCompleteBoxDemo"
    xmlns="http://schemas.microsoft.com/winfx/2006/xaml/presentation"
    xmlns:x="http://schemas.microsoft.com/winfx/2006/xaml"
    xmlns:d="http://schemas.microsoft.com/expression/blend/2008"
    xmlns:mc="http://schemas.openxmlformats.org/markup-
        compatibility/2006"
    mc:Ignorable="d"
    xmlns:input="clr-namespace:System.Windows.Controls;
        assembly=System.Windows.Controls.Input"
    d:DesignHeight="300" d:DesignWidth="400">
```

```
    <StackPanel x:Name="LayoutRoot" Background="White">
        <TextBlock Text="Choose a state"/>
        <input:AutoCompleteBox x:Name="stateSelection" Width="175"
            HorizontalAlignment="Left"/>
    </StackPanel>
</UserControl>
```

Notice that this control is in a different assembly than the other controls in this chapter:
System.Windows.Controls.Input, which is referenced at the UserControl level. You also need to add a
reference to the project. The constructor for this page creates a List<string> that is used to supply a list
of states in the United States to the autocompletion box:

```
List<string> stateList = new List<string>();
stateList.Add("Alabama");
stateList.Add("Alaska");
// ...
stateList.Add("Wisconsin");
stateList.Add("Wyoming");

stateSelection.ItemsSource = stateList;
```

Figure 3-16 shows this control in action after the user types **A**.

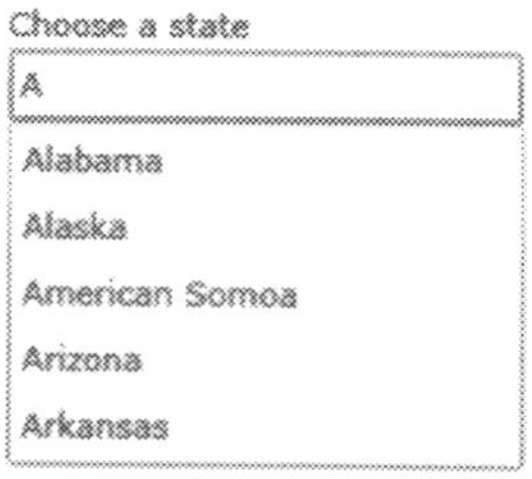

Figure 3-16. *The AutoCompleteBox control example*

Table 3-21 shows the key properties of the AutoCompleteBox control, and Table 3-22 describes its
key events.

Table 3-21. *Key Properties of the System.Windows.Controls.AutoCompleteBox Class*

Property	Type	Description
FilterMode	AutoCompleteFilterMode	Defines how text in the text box is used to filter items specified by the ItemSource property to display in the drop-down box. See Table 3-23 for the possible values. The default value is StartsWith.
IsDropDownOpen	bool	Returns true if the drop-down box is open, false otherwise. Setting this to true will open the drop-down box.

IsTextCompletion Enabled	bool	When set to true, the first match found during the filtering process will appear in the text box. Defaults to false.
ItemContainerStyle	style	Defines the style of the selection adapter contained in the drop-down box of the control. Default is a null reference.
ItemFilter	AutoCompleteSearch Predicate<Object>	Specifies the custom method to use for item filtering. When set, the SearchMode property is automatically set to Custom.
ItemsSource	IEnumerable	Specifies an IEnumerable data source used to populate the drop-down list.
ItemTemplate	DateTemplate	Specifies how items are displayed in the drop-down box.
MinimumPopulate Delay	Int32	Specifies the time, in milliseconds, before the drop-down box starts populating after a user starts to type in the text box. The default value is 0. Note that if the population of the drop-down box is a lengthy operation, the drop-down box won't appear immediately after the time specified in this property.
MinimumPrefix Length	Int32	Specifies the minimum number of characters the user has to type into the text box before the drop-down box will appear. The default value is 1.
SearchText	String	Specifies the text entered into the text box by the user and used for searching the list of items. This property is set after the TextChanged event and before the Populating event, so although it usually coincides with the Text property, it may not always.
SelectedItem	Object	Defines the selected item in the drop-down box.
SelectedAdapter	ISelectionAdapter	Defines the selection adapter used to populate the drop-down box with a list of selected items.
Text	String	Specifies the text entered in the text box of this control.
TextBoxStyle	Style	Specifies the style to apply to the text box of this control.
TextFilter	AutoCompleteSearch Predicate<String>	Specifies the custom method to use for filtering items based on the text in the text box. When set, SearchMode is automatically set to Custom.

ValueMemberBinding	Binding	Converts objects to strings so items shown in the drop-down box can be custom-converted to a form suitable for the text box.
ValueMemberPath	string	Defines value for the user-entered text and to filter items for display in the drop-down box.

Table 3-22. Key Events of the System.Windows.Controls.AutoCompleteBox Class

Event	Description
DropDownClosed	Occurs when IsDropDownOpen property is set to true and changes to false and the drop-down is changing from an open to closed state.
DropDownClosing	Occurs when IsDropDownOpen property is set to true and changes to false.
DropDownOpened	Occurs when IsDropDownOpen property is set to false, and changes to true and the drop-down box is changing from a closed to open state.
DropDownOpening	Occurs when IsDropDownOpen property is set to false and changes to true.
Populated	Occurs after the drop-down box is finishing populating.
Populating	Occurs right before the drop-down box starts populating.
SelectionChanged	Occurs when the selection in the drop-down box changes.
TextChanged	Occurs when the text in the text box portion of the control changes.

Table 3-23 defines the possible values of the SearchMode.

Table 3-23. Possible Values of FilterMode (from AutoCompleteFilterMode Enumeration)

SearchMode	Description
None	No filter; all items are returned.
StartsWith	Filters items that start with the text entered. Culture sensitive. Case insensitive.
StartsWithCaseSensitive	Filters items that start with the text entered. Culture sensitive. Case sensitive.

StartsWithOrdinal	Ordinal (comparison is based on the Unicode values of each character), case-insensitive filter based on items that start with the text entered.
StartsWithOrdinalCaseSensitive	Ordinal, case-sensitive filter based on items that start with the text entered.
Contains	Filters items that contain the text entered. Culture sensitive, case insensitive.
ContainsCaseSensitive	Filters items that contain the text entered. Culture sensitive, case sensitive.
ContainsOrdinal	Ordinal, case-insensitive filter based on items that contain the text entered.
ContainsOrdinalCaseSensitive	Ordinal, case-sensitive filter based on items that contain the text entered.
Equals	Filters items that equal the text entered. Culture sensitive, case insensitive.
EqualsCaseSensitive	Filters items that equal the text entered. Culture sensitive, case sensitive.
EqualsOrdinal	Filters items that equal the text entered. Ordinal, case insensitive.
EqualsOrdinalCaseSensitive	Filters items that equal the text entered. Ordinal, case sensitive.
Custom	Indicates a custom filtering is used, as specified by TextFilter or ItemFilter.

Data Integration and Data Manipulation Controls

Most of the Line-of-Business applications are data-driven applications and there is a need to integrate, process, and represent data in different ways. Although WPF from its first version provided rich data integration, the earlier versions of Silverlight were lacking in this department. The Silverlight platform initially focused on rich media integration. Starting with Silverlight 2, data controls were introduced as part of either default standard user controls or the Silverlight Toolkit. With the continuously improved data integration capabilities in Silverlight 3 and 4, using Silverlight 4 now you can truly develop data-driven and high performing LoB RIAs. In this section we will cover data integration and data manipulation controls at a high level, which will be covered more in detail in Chapter 6.

ItemsControl

Certain controls provide the ability to present a set of content as individual items. These controls are Primitives.Selector.ListBox, Primitives.Selector.ComboBox, TabControl, TreeView, and HeaderedItemsControl. The base class that provides the item handling behavior is ItemsControl. Table 3-24 describes its key properties.

Table 3-24. Key Properties of the System.Windows.Controls.ItemsControl Class

Property	Type	Description
DisplayMemberPath	string	Gets/sets the path to the property on the source object to display.
Items	ItemCollection	Defines a collection of items to display. If no items, it is null. The default value is empty collection.
ItemsPanel	ItemsPanelTemplate	Specifies the panel to use for displaying items. Defaults to an ItemsPanelTemplate that uses a StackPanel.
ItemsSource	IEnumerable	Similar to Items, provides the set of items to display, but provides more flexibility since any IEnumerable can be used.
ItemTemplate	DataTemplate	Specifies the data template used to display items. Used with data binding.

ListBox

The ListBox control is derived from the Systems.Windows.Controls.Primitives.Selector class and allows users to select one or more items from a collection of items. The ListBox provides a way to display one or more items and allows the user to select among them. Table 3-25 describes its properties.

Table 3-25. Properties of the System.Windows.Controls.ListBox Class

Property	Type	Description
ItemContainerStyle	Style	Gets/sets the style applied to the container for the list box's items.
SelectedIndex	Int32	Indicates the index of the first selected item, or -1 if no items are selected (inherited from the Selector class).
SelectedItem	Object	Indicates the first selected item, or null if no items are selected (inherited from the Selector class).
SelectedItems	IList	Defines the list of selected items for the ListBox controls.

SelectedValue	Object	Defines value of selected item (SelectedItem), received using the SelectedValuePath property (inherited from the Selector class). The default value is a null reference. New property in Silverlight 4.
SelectedValuePath	string	Defines the property path for the SelectedValue property of the SelectedItem (inherited from the Selector class). The default value is Empty. New property in Silverlight 4.
SelectionMode	SelectionMode	Defines the way the user selects items in the ListBox control. If set to Single, then the user can select only one item at a time. If set to Multiple, then the user can select multiple items with a mouse. If set to Extended, then the user can select multiple items by pressing a modifier key, such as Ctrl or Shift.

Inherited from the Selector class, the SelectionChanged (event args: SelectionChangedEventArgs) event occurs when the current selected item is changed.

Figure 3-17 shows a ListBox containing several simple items (text blocks).

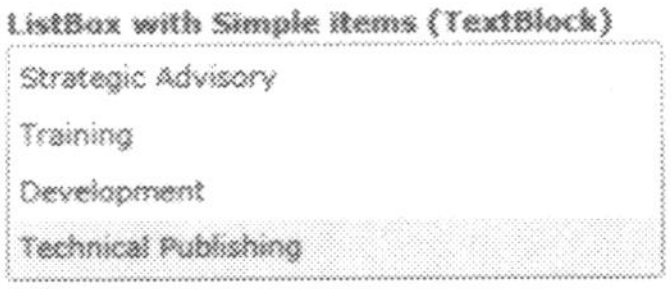

Figure 3-17. The ListBox control example

The corresponding XAML looks like this:

```
<TextBlock FontWeight="Bold">
    ListBox with Simple items (TextBlock)
</TextBlock>
<ListBox Canvas.Top="50" Canvas.Left="40" Width="200">
    <ListBox.Items>
        <ListBoxItem>
            <TextBlock Text="Strategic Advisory"/>
        </ListBoxItem>
        <ListBoxItem>
            <TextBlock Text="Training"/>
        </ListBoxItem>
        <ListBoxItem>
            <TextBlock Text="Development"/>
        </ListBoxItem>
        <ListBoxItem>
            <TextBlock Text="Technical Publishing"/>
        </ListBoxItem>
    </ListBox.Items>
</ListBox>
```

The ListBoxItem Class

The ListBoxItem class represents a ListBox's individual item. This class inherits from ContentControl and so can contain a wide variety of content. It exposes a single property of type bool, IsSelected, that is true when the item is selected. The appearance of the list box items can be controlled by setting the ItemTemplate property of the ListBox control. As implied by the properties shown in Table 3-25, the ListBox control supports single or multiple items selection. You can include a check box in the content for each item or create a custom list control (which can inherit from ListBox, or you can combine a ScrollViewer with a StackPanel). We'll take a look at displaying more complex items in a ListBox by using data templates in Chapter 6.

ComboBox

The ComboBox control is derived from the Systems.Windows.Controls.Primitives.Selector class and allows users to select an item from a collection of items. The ComboBox provides a way to display one or more items in a drop-down list (containing a list box) and allows the user to select one item among them (as a non-editable text box). The text box either displays the current selection, or looks empty if there is no selected item. Table 3-26 describes its properties, which are very similar to the ListBox.

Table 3-26. Properties of the System.Windows.Controls.ComboBox Class

Property	Type	Description
IsEditable	bool	Defines a value indicating if the user can edit text in the text box portion of the combo box. For Silverlight this property always returns a false value, since Silverlight does not support an editable combo box (which is not the case in WPF).
ItemContainerStyle	Style	Gets/sets the style applied to the container for the list box's items.
SelectedIndex	Int32	Indicates the index of first selected item, or -1 if no items are selected (inherited from the Selector class).
SelectedItem	Object	Indicates the first selected item, or null if no items are selected (inherited from the Selector class). You cannot select multiple items in combo box.
SelectedValue	Object	Defines value of selected item (SelectedItem), received using the SelectedValuePath property (inherited from the Selector class). The default value is null reference. New property in Silverlight 4.
SelectedValuePath	string	Defines property path for the SelectedValue property of the SelectedItem (inherited from the Selector class). The default value is Empty. New property in Silverlight 4.

It exposes one event—SelectionChanged (event args: SelectionChangedEventArgs), which is inherited from the Selector class.

Figure 3-18 shows a ComboBox containing several items.

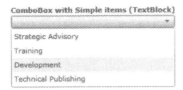

Figure 3-18. *The ComboBox control example*

The corresponding XAML looks like this:

```
<TextBlock FontWeight="Bold">
    ComboBox with Simple items (TextBlock)
</TextBlock>
<ComboBox>
    <ComboBox.Items>
        <ComboBoxItem>
            <TextBlock Text="Strategic Advisory"/>
        </ComboBoxItem>
        <ComboBoxItem>
            <TextBlock Text="Training"/>
        </ComboBoxItem>
        <ComboBoxItem>
            <TextBlock Text="Development"/>
        </ComboBoxItem>
        <ComboBoxItem>
            <TextBlock Text="Technical Publishing"/>
        </ComboBoxItem>
    </ComboBox.Items>
</ComboBox>
```

The ComboBoxItem Class

The ComboBoxItem class represents a ComboBox's individual item. This class inherits from ListBoxItem and thus ContentControl and so can contain a wide variety of content. Based on ListBoxItem, it exposes a single property of type bool, IsSelected, that is true when the item is selected. The appearance of the combo box items can be controlled by setting the ItemTemplate property of the Selector control.

TreeView

The TreeView control implements a tree display where items can be nested within each other, such as you'd see in Windows Explorer with its directory tree. Since this control inherits from ItemsControl, its behavior is much like you'd expect, only the organization of items is different. Figure 3-19 shows what the TreeView looks like with a few of the chapter examples listed from the following XAML. Notice that you need to add a reference of the System.Windows.Controls namespace to the UserControl:

```
<UserControl x:Class="chapter3.TreeViewDemo"
    xmlns="http://schemas.microsoft.com/winfx/2006/xaml/presentation"
    xmlns:x="http://schemas.microsoft.com/winfx/2006/xaml"
```

```
xmlns:d="http://schemas.microsoft.com/expression/blend/2008"
xmlns:mc="http://schemas.openxmlformats.org/markup-compatibility/2006"
mc:Ignorable="d"
xmlns:c="clr-namespace:System.Windows.Controls;assembly=
    System.Windows.Controls"
d:DesignHeight="300" d:DesignWidth="400">

<StackPanel x:Name="LayoutRoot" Background="White">
    <c:TreeView>
        <c:TreeView.Items>
            <c:TreeViewItem IsExpanded="True"
                Header="Layout Management and Grouping Controls">
                <c:TreeViewItem Header="Canvas" IsSelected="True"/>
                <c:TreeViewItem Header="StackPanel"/>
                <c:TreeViewItem Header="Grid"/>
                <c:TreeViewItem IsExpanded="True"
                    Header="Silverlight Toolkit Panel Controls">
                    <c:TreeViewItem Header="DockPanel"/>
                    <c:TreeViewItem Header="WrapPanel"/>
                </c:TreeViewItem>
                <c:TreeViewItem Header="TabControl"/>
                <c:TreeViewItem Header="ViewBox"/>
            </c:TreeViewItem>
        </c:TreeView.Items>
    </c:TreeView>
</StackPanel>
</UserControl>
```

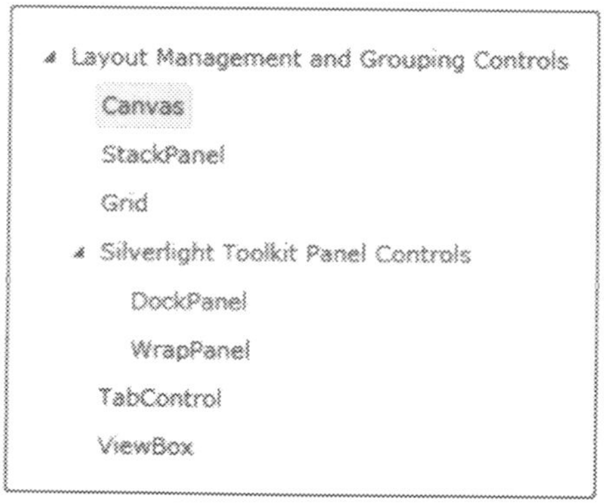

Figure 3-19. The TreeView control example

Table 3-27 defines the key properties of the TreeView control. Only one event is new to the TreeView class, the SelectedItemChanged event.

Table 3-27. Properties of the System.Windows.Controls.TreeView Class

Property	Type	Description
ItemContainerStyle	Style	Specifies the container around each item. See Chapter 8 for details about styles.
SelectedItem	Object	Specifies the currently selected item or null if no item is selected. This cannot be set because of a private setter.
SelectedValue	Object	Specifies the value of the SelectedItem property, or null if no item is selected. The SelectedValuePath specifies which property of SelectedItem to return.
SelectedValuePath	String	Specifies the property path used for the SelectedValue property.

The TreeViewItem Class

The most interesting functionality for the TreeView is provided by the TreeViewItem class. This class inherits from the HeaderedItemsControl (which is detailed in the next section), so it has the ability to store a header and content separately. Table 3-28 describes its properties, and Table 3-29 describes its events.

Table 3-28. Properties of the System.Windows.Controls.TreeViewItem Class

Property	Type	Description
HasItems	bool	Returns true if this TreeViewItem has items and false otherwise.
IsExpanded	bool	Returns true if this TreeViewItem is expanded and false otherwise.
IsSelected	bool	Returns true if this TreeViewItem is selected and false otherwise.
IsSelectionActive	bool	Returns true if this TreeViewItem has focus and false otherwise.

Table 3-29. Events of the System.Windows.Controls.TreeViewItem Class

Event	Description
Collapsed	Occurs when the value of IsExpanded is changed from true to false.
Expanded	Occurs when the value of IsExpanded is changed from false to true.
Selected	Occurs when the value of IsSelected is changed from false to true.
Unselected	Occurs when the value of IsSelected is changed from true to false.

HeaderedItemsControl

The HeaderedItemsControl provides a straightforward way to display a list of items with a header area. Figure 3-20 shows what this control looks like when displaying a few color names from a string array (via data binding, which we'll look at in Chapter 6). No selection is supported with this control (combine a ListBox with a HeaderedContentControl to accomplish selection).

Colors

Red
Green
Blue
Cyan

Figure 3-20. The HeaderedItemsControl example

Table 3-30 defines the key properties of the `HeaderedItemsControl` class.

Table 3-30. Key Properties of the System.Windows.Controls.HeaderedItemsControl Class

Property	Type	Description
Header	object	Specifies what is used as content for the header.
HeaderTemplate	DataTemplate	Specifies the date template used to dynamically supply data for the header. See Chapter 6 for details.
ItemContainerStyle	Style	Specifies the style of the container around each item. See Chapter 8 for details about styles.

The XAML used to render the HeaderedItemsControl in Figure 3-18 provides a static header, and the items are supplied in the code-behind:

```
<UserControl x:Class="chapter3. HeaderedItemsControlDemo"
    xmlns="http://schemas.microsoft.com/winfx/2006/xaml/presentation"
    xmlns:x="http://schemas.microsoft.com/winfx/2006/xaml"
    xmlns:d="http://schemas.microsoft.com/expression/blend/2008"
    xmlns:mc="http://schemas.openxmlformats.org/markup-compatibility/2006"
    mc:Ignorable="d"
    xmlns:c="clr-namespace:System.Windows.Controls;assembly=
        System.Windows.Controls"
    d:DesignHeight="300" d:DesignWidth="400">
    <Grid x:Name="LayoutRoot" Background="White">
        <c:HeaderedItemsControl x:Name="headeredItems">
            <c:HeaderedItemsControl.Header>
                <TextBlock FontSize="22" Text="Colors"
                    TextDecorations="Underline"/>
            </c:HeaderedItemsControl.Header>
```

```
        <c:HeaderedItemsControl.ItemTemplate>
            <DataTemplate>
                <TextBlock Text="{Binding}"/>
            </DataTemplate>
        </c:HeaderedItemsControl.ItemTemplate>
    </c:HeaderedItemsControl>
  </Grid>
</UserControl>
```

The data binding simply points the ItemsSource property in the direction of a string array:

```
string[] colors = { "Red", "Green", "Blue", "Cyan" };
headeredItems.ItemsSource = colors;
```

ContentControl

Many controls can define their content by using other controls. This provides an amazing degree of flexibility over how you construct user interfaces. One place where this is useful is in the ListBox control, where the items of the list box can be anything you can construct in XAML using controls. The controls that support this capability inherit from System.Windows.Controls.ContentControl. You can tell immediately that a specific control inherits from the ContentControl class by noticing it has a Content property in the IntelliSense window. Table 3-31 describes the properties of ContentControl.

Table 3-31. Properties of the System.Windows.Controls.ContentControl Class

Property	Type	Description
Content	Object	Defines the value of the ContentControl dependency property.
ContentTemplate	DataTemplate	Gets/sets the data template for this content control, used for data binding.

The controls that inherit from ContentControl are ChildWindow, Frame, Label, ListBoxItem, Primitives.ButtonBase, ScrollViewer, DataGridCell, Primitives.DataGridColumnHeader, Primitives.DataGridRowHeader, TabItem, and ToolTip.

HeaderedContentControl

Derived from the ContentControl and part of the Silverlight Toolkit, the HeaderedContentControl provides an easy way to display a header above arbitrary content. The following XAML creates the same list of colors as the HeaderedItemsControl example, using a StackPanel to display the colors vertically:

```
<UserControl x:Class="chapter3.HeaderedContentControlDemo"
    xmlns="http://schemas.microsoft.com/winfx/2006/xaml/presentation"
    xmlns:x="http://schemas.microsoft.com/winfx/2006/xaml"
    xmlns:d="http://schemas.microsoft.com/expression/blend/2008"
    xmlns:mc="http://schemas.openxmlformats.org/markup-
        compatibility/2006"
```

```
  xmlns:c="clr-namespace:System.Windows.Controls;assembly=
      System.Windows.Controls.Toolkit"
  mc:Ignorable="d"
  d:DesignHeight="600" d:DesignWidth="500">
  <Grid x:Name="LayoutRoot" Background="White">
      <c:HeaderedContentControl>
          <c:HeaderedContentControl.Header>
              <TextBlock FontSize="22" Text="Colors"
                         TextDecorations="Underline"/>
          </c:HeaderedContentControl.Header>

          <c:HeaderedContentControl.Content>
              <StackPanel Orientation="Vertical">
                  <TextBlock Text="Red"/>
                  <TextBlock Text="Green"/>
                  <TextBlock Text="Blue"/>
                  <TextBlock Text="Cyan"/>
              </StackPanel>
          </c:HeaderedContentControl.Content>
      </c:HeaderedContentControl>
  </Grid>
</UserControl>
```

Table 3-32 defines the properties of the HeaderedContentControl class:

Table 3-32. Properties of the System.Windows.Controls.HeaderedContentControl Class

Property	Type	Description
Header	object	Specifies what is used as content for the header.
HeaderTemplate	DataTemplate	Defines the template used to display the content of the control's header. See Chapter 6 for details.

DataGrid

One of the widely used controls for data integration and manipulation is the DataGrid control. The DataGrid control is useful for displaying data in the tabular format with rows and columns. It isn't part of the core Silverlight installation, so you must download the Silverlight SDK and distribute the System.Windows.Controls.Data assembly with your application by referencing it to your project. In order to use DataGrid in XAML, you must reference the System.Windows.Controls.Data namespace. The ItemSource property is a key property allowing the data grid to be mapped with the datasource and populate content in the control. Visit Chapter 6 to get more details on the DataGrid control.

DataForm

Forms are one of the key elements of data-driven applications. You can use the DataForm Silverlight control to achieve this functionality. While the DataGrid control is used to manipulate a list of items, the

DataForm control focuses on the item itself. Like DataGrid, DataForm is also not part of the core Silverlight installation, so you must download the Silverlight toolkit and distribute the System.Windows.Controls.Data.DataForm.Toolkit assembly with your application by adding it as a reference to the project. In order to use DataForm in XAML, you must reference the System.Windows.Controls.Data.DataForm.Toolkit namespace. We will discuss this control in more detail in Chapter 6.

DataPager

The DataPager control is a quick, configurable, and efficient mechanism for paging data that provides next/previous, numeric paging and data records management capabilities for data sets (with multiple records). The DataPager is also not part of the core Silverlight installation, so you must download the Silverlight SDK and distribute the System.Windows.Controls.Data assembly with your application. In order to use DataPager in XAML, you must reference the System.Windows.Controls.Data namespace. To accomplish the pagination you need to implement the IPagedViewCollection interface as the data source and use the IPagedCollectionView for the paging functionality. When DataPager is combined with WCF RIA Services, the WCF RIA Services ObjectDataSource automatically implements this interface. Visit Chapter 6 to get more details on the DataPager control.

Label

A Label control is used to display a caption, required field indicator, and validation error indicator to the user. When you need to indicate any data input control with required field and validation error indications along with the caption, you should use a Label control rather than TextBlock. To associate the Label control with other input UIElement controls, use the Target property of the Label control. You can use either the Content property of Label or DisplayAttribute property of the associated control to display the caption. Similarly, use either the Label's IsRequired property or the RequiredAttribute property of the associated control to display as a required field.

The Label control is available as part of the libraries in the Silverlight Software Development Kit (SDK). Download the SDK and add the System.Windows.Controls.Data.Input assembly as a reference to the project. In order to use Label in XAML, you must reference the System.Windows.Controls.Data.Input namespace and distribute the System.Windows.Controls.Data.Input assembly with your application. We will further cover this control in Chapter 6.

DescriptionViewer

Introduced in Silverlight 3, the DescriptionViewer control is used to display an information symbol (glyph) and when the mouse hovers on the symbol, a tooltip is displayed as a text description. This control can track error states for an associated control by implementing custom error. This can be useful for fields for which the label or content text alone is not sufficient and you want to provide some description for it.

The DescriptionViewer control is available as part of the libraries in the Silverlight Software Development Kit (SDK). In order to use DescriptionViewer in XAML, you must reference the System.Windows.Controls.Data.Input namespace, add as a reference to the project and distribute the System.Windows.Controls.Data.Input assembly with your application. The control has two key properties—the Target property to associate UI element control and the Description property to display the tooltip text. We will further cover this control in Chapter 6.

ValidationSummary

The easiest and most common way to display any (validation) error notification is to display it next to the UIElement control, such as with the use of the DescriptionViewer control. However, there are cases where you would like to display errors as a summary at the end of the form to improve the usability and user experience. The traditional way is to use the ListBox control at the end of the form and implement custom code to display these errors within the ListBox. However, Silverlight provides a ValidationSummary control as part of the Silverlight SDK. In order to use ValidationSummary in XAML, you must reference the System.Windows.Controls.Data.Input namespace, add as a reference to the project and distribute the System.Windows.Controls.Data.Input assembly with your application.

   This control provides a list of current validation errors for the container. For this you do not need to write a single line of code. For example, if we have a layout container such as Grid or StackPanel with input controls in it along with the ValidationSummary control, a list of current validation errors of the parent container will be displayed automatically. You can also point the ValidationSummary to that different layout container using the Target property. It will then detect and display validation errors that occur in any of the contained input controls of the targeted container. We will further cover this control in Chapter 6.

Functional Controls

Functional Silverlight controls help present information in a richer and more usable manner, in order to facilitate different actions such as date selection and to control or monitor application behavior using a slide bar or progress bar. We will explore key functional Silverlight controls in this section.

Border

The Border control is used to surround content with a border. It also provides the ability to easily add a background to a smaller part of a user interface. Table 3-33 describes its properties.

Table 3-33. Properties of the System.Windows.Controls.Border Class

Property	Type	Description
Background	Brush	Gets/sets the brush used to paint the background.
BorderBrush	Brush	Gets/sets the brush used to paint the border.
BorderThickness	Thickness	Gets/sets the thickness of the border.
Child	UIElement	Indicates the single child that the border is drawn around.
CornerRadius	CornerRadius	Gets/sets the degree of rounding used for each corner. Can be set to a single value to apply a uniform rounding for all corners.
Padding	Thickness	Defines the space between the child content and the border.

Figure 3-21 shows the Border control used in various ways.

Figure 3-21. The Border control example

The fanciest border uses a gradient brush. Figure 3.21 shows a button with a rounded border with the gradient brush. We'll take a closer look at brushes in Chapter 9. Here's what the XAML looks like:

```
<Border BorderThickness="10" Width="100" Height="100" CornerRadius="10">
    <Border.BorderBrush>
        <LinearGradientBrush StartPoint="0,1" EndPoint="1,0">
            <GradientStop Color="#FF000000" Offset="0"/>
            <GradientStop Color="#FFFF0000" Offset="1"/>
        </LinearGradientBrush>
    </Border.BorderBrush>
    <Button Content="BUTTON"/>
</Border>
```

Border can contain only one child object. So if you want to place a common border across a group of UIElements, you put all of them under layout container controls such as StackPanel and Canvas.

GridSplitter

The GridSplitter control, which is inherited from the Control class, is used to provide the user with the capability of changing sizes of rows and columns in a grid. It exposes three key properties, as described in Table 3-34.

Table 3-34. Key Properties of the System.Windows.Controls.GridSplitter Class

Property	Type	Description
PreviewStyle	Style	Gets/sets the style used for previewing changes.
ShowsPreview	bool	Gets/sets whether the preview is shown before changes from the grid splitter are applied.

Figure 3-22 shows a checkerboard pattern with a grid splitter between the first and second column, spanning all three rows.

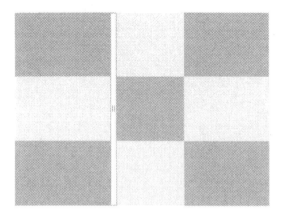

Figure 3-22. The GridSplitter control example

GridSplitter isn't part of the core Silverlight installation, so you must download the Silverlight SDK and in XAML, you must reference the System.Windows.Controls namespace. The XAML for this GridSplitter looks like this:

```
<UserControl x:Class="chapter3.GridSplitterDemo"
    xmlns="http://schemas.microsoft.com/winfx/2006/xaml/presentation"
    xmlns:x="http://schemas.microsoft.com/winfx/2006/xaml"
    xmlns:d="http://schemas.microsoft.com/expression/blend/2008"
    xmlns:mc="http://schemas.openxmlformats.org/markup-compatibility/2006"
    mc:Ignorable="d"
    xmlns:c="clr-namespace:System.Windows.Controls;assembly=
        System.Windows.Controls"
    d:DesignHeight="300" d:DesignWidth="400" Height="300" Width="400">
    <Grid x:Name="LayoutRoot" Background="White">
        <!-- 3 rows, 3 columns -->
        ......
        <!-- Border controls to draw a different
            background in each cell -->
        ......
        <c:GridSplitter Grid.Row="0" Grid.Column="1"
                Width="10" Grid.RowSpan="3"
                HorizontalAlignment="Left"
                VerticalAlignment="Stretch"/>
    </Grid>
</UserControl>
```

Note that we set the VerticalAlignment property to Stretch and the HorizontalAlignment property to Left allowing column resizing. Based on the values set for the HorizontalAlignment and VerticalAlignment attached properties, you can determine whether the added GridSplitter control to the Grid will allow column or row resizing.

Table 3-35. Defining Grid Row/Column Resizing using GridSplitter

HorizontalAlignment	VerticalAlignment	Row/Column Resizing
Stretch	Other	Row resizing
Other	Stretch	Column resizing
Stretch	Stretch	Column resizing if ActualHeight is greater than or equal to ActualWidth; otherwise row resizing

TextBlock

One of the most commonly used user control, the TextBlock control is used to display text on a user interface. This directly compares to the label controls in both Windows Forms and ASP.NET. Table 3-36 describes its key properties.

Table 3-36. Key properties of the System.Windows.Controls.TextBlock Class

Property	Type	Description
FontFamily	FontFamily	Gets/sets the set of font families. Each specified after the first is a fallback font in case a previous font is not available. Defaults to Portable User Interface, which encompasses several fonts in order to render the range of international language possibilities.
FontSize	double	Gets/sets the desired font size in pixels. Defaults to 14.666 (11 pt).
FontSource	FontSource	Gets/sets the font used to render text. The default value is null reference.
FontStretch	FontStretch	Gets/sets the degree to which a font is stretched. Possible values are UltraCondensed, ExtraCondensed, Condensed, SemiCondensed, Normal, SemiExpanded, Expanded, ExtraExpanded, and UltraExpanded, which are based on the usWidthClass definition in the OpenType specification. The default value is Normal.
FontStyle	FontStyle	Gets/sets the font style used for rendering text. Possible values: Normal (default) and Italic.

FontWeight	FontWeight	Gets/sets the desired font weight. Possible values are from the usWeightClass definition in the OpenType specification.
Foreground	Brush	Gets/sets the brush to apply to the text.
Inlines	InlineCollection	Gets/sets the collection of inline elements, such as Run and LineBreak, to render.
LineHeight	double	Specifies the height of a line of text in pixels. This property is used only when the LineStackingStrategy is set to BlockLineHeight.
LineStackingStrategy	LineStackingStrategy	Specifies how each line of text is stacked. Possible values: MaxHeight (maximum height of an element within the line dictates height of line) and BlockLineHeight (maximum height controlled by the LineHeight property).
Padding	Thickness	Gets/sets the amount of space between the border of the content area and the text.
Text	string	Gets/sets the text to display.
TextAlignment	TextAlignment	Gets/sets horizontal alignment of text. Possible values: Left, Center, Right.
TextDecorations	TextDecorationCollection	Gets/sets the set of decorations to apply to the text. Currently the only decoration available is Underline.
TextWrapping	TextWrapping	Controls how text wraps when it reaches the edge of its content area. Possible values: Wrap and NoWrap.

Similar to the newly introduced RichTextBox control, the TextBlock control can contain inline elements, providing an alternative way to piece text together. This approach is most useful when you want to apply specific font styles, such as different colors or sizes, to elements of a larger set of text. However, here you are limited to define rich text formatting and line breaks and cannot insert the XAML UI Element and in-line images. Figure 3-23 shows several uses of the TextBlock control.

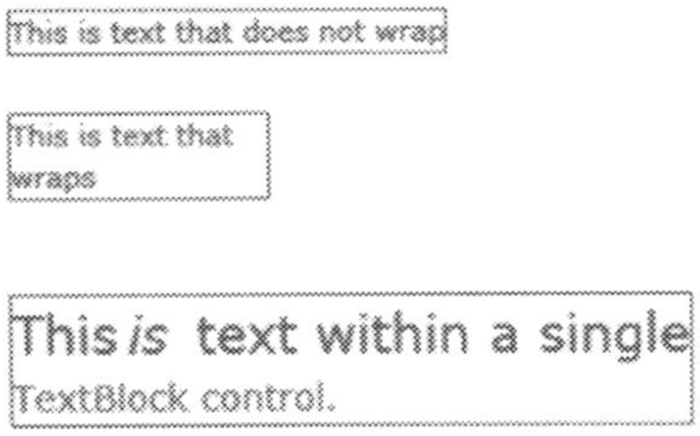

Figure 3-23. The TextBlock control example

Here's the XAML used for each of the TextBlock controls shown in Figure 3-23, including one where the TextBlock contains multiple inline elements:

```
<Border BorderBrush="Black" BorderThickness="1" Canvas.Left="20" Canvas.Top="20">
    <TextBlock Text="This is text that does not wrap"/>
</Border>
<Border BorderBrush="Black" BorderThickness="1" Canvas.Left="20" Canvas.Top="60">
    <TextBlock Text="This is text that wraps" TextWrapping="Wrap" Width="100"/>
</Border>
<Border BorderBrush="Black" BorderThickness="1" Canvas.Left="20" Canvas.Top="130">
    <TextBlock>
        <Run FontSize="20" Text="This"/>
        <Run FontSize="20" FontStyle="Italic" Text="is "/>
        <Run FontSize="20" Text="text within a single"/>
        <LineBreak/>
        <Run Foreground="Red" FontSize="14" Text="TextBlock control."/>
    </TextBlock>
</Border>
```

Popup

The Popup control is used to display content over the existing user interface, for example, showing a temporary message or providing mouse-over help to the end users. Table 3-37 describes its properties.

Table 3-37. Properties of the System.Windows.Controls.Primitives.Popup Class

Property	Type	Description
Child	UIElement	Gets/sets the content to display. It can be any UIElement control.
HorizontalOffset	double	Defines the horizontal offset used in displaying the pop-up. Defaults to 0 (left side).
IsOpen	bool	Gets/sets whether the pop-up is open.
VerticalOffset	double	Vertical offset used in displaying the pop-up. Defaults to 0 (top).

The Popup class provides two events: Opened and Closed. These events fire when the pop-up is opened or closed via setting of the IsOpen property. Figure 3-24 shows a button and the pop-up that opens when the button is clicked.

Figure 3-24. *The Popup control*

The XAML for the pop-up looks like this:

```
<Popup x:Name="xamlPopup" VerticalOffset="40"
            HorizontalOffset="270" IsOpen="False">
    <Border BorderBrush="Black" BorderThickness="5" CornerRadius="3">
        <Button Content="Click to close" Click="button_Click"/>
    </Border>
</Popup>
```

The showing and hiding of the pop-up is done programmatically by simply setting the IsOpen property of the Popup control to the correct value to show or hide the pop-up.

```
void button_Click(object sender, RoutedEventArgs e)
{
    xamlPopup.IsOpen = false;
}
private void showPopup_Click(object sender, RoutedEventArgs e)
{
    xamlPopup.IsOpen = true;
}
```

ToolTipService

The ToolTipService class is used to programmatically associate a UIElement describing content of the tool tip with the control. It provides an attached property (ToolTip) that is used in the XAML to create a tool tip without having to go to the code-behind. Figure 3-25 shows two buttons, the first with a tool tip already attached (displayed in the figure), and the second that gets a tool tip after the first button is clicked.

Figure 3-25. *The ToolTipService class example*

The XAML for the first button looks like this:

```
<Button Canvas.Left="20" Canvas.Top="40"
        ToolTipService.ToolTip="Click button to add a tooltip to the other button"
        Content="I have a tooltip!" Click="Button_Click"/>
```

The click handler programmatically adds the second button's tool tip via the SetTooltip method.

```
private void Button_Click(object sender, RoutedEventArgs e)
{
    Border b = new Border();
    b.BorderBrush = new SolidColorBrush(Color.FromArgb(255, 128, 128, 128));
    b.BorderThickness = new Thickness(5);
    TextBlock t = new TextBlock();
    t.Margin = new Thickness(5);
    t.Text = "I am another tool tip";
    b.Child = t;
    ToolTipService.SetToolTip(secondButton, b);
}
```

To set the tooltip using the code-behind, the ToolTipService class provides several key static methods (Table 3.38) to set the tooltip for the UIElement and define the placement.

Table 3-38. Key Static Methods of the System.Windows.Controls.ToolTipService Class

Static Method	Description
GetPlacement	Returns relative position of the specified tooltip.
GetPlacementTarget	Returns the UIElement for which the tooltip is set.
GetToolTip	Returns the value of the tooltip.
SetPlacement	Sets position of the tooltip relative to the target UIElement using the specified placement mode. The position is based on the value of the PlacementMode. The possible values are Bottom (bottom of the target element), Right (right of the target element), Mouse (current mouse pointer location), Left (Left of the target element), and Top (top of the target element).
SetPlacementTarget	Sets the position of the specified tooltip relative to the specified value element.
SetTooltip	Sets the tooltip for the target UIElement.

ScrollViewer

The ScrollViewer control is used to display content that is possibly larger than the allotted space, so scrollbars are used to let the user scroll to different sections of the content. It exposes a large set of properties that control the presentation of content, shown in Table 3-39.

Table 3-39. Key Properties of the System.Windows.Controls.ScrollViewer Class

Property	Type	Description
ComputedHorizontalScroll BarVisibility	Visibility	Gets/sets whether the horizontal scrollbar is currently visible.
ComputedVerticalScroll BarVisibility	Visibility	Gets/sets whether the vertical scrollbar is currently visible.
HorizontalOffset	double	Gets/sets the current horizontal offset of the content.
HorizontalScroll BarVisibility	Visibility	Gets/sets whether the horizontal scrollbar should be displayed.
ScrollableHeight	double	Defines the total vertical size of the content.
ScrollableWidth	double	Defines the total horizontal size of the content.
VerticalOffset	double	Gets/sets the current vertical offset of the content.
VerticalScroll BarVisibility	Visibility	Gets/sets whether the vertical scrollbar should be displayed.
ViewportHeight	double	Gets/sets the height of the viewport (the window into the content that is onscreen).
ViewportWidth	double	Gets/sets the width of the viewport.

Figure 3-26 shows a grid with a checkerboard pattern contained in a ScrollView control. The content is too large to display completely, so the vertical scrollbar is added automatically (the horizontal scrollbar is added automatically but must be set to Auto first).

Figure 3-26. The ScrollViewer control example

Here's the XAML to create the grid inside the scroll viewer:

```
<Canvas x:Name="LayoutRoot" Background="White">
    <ScrollViewer Canvas.Left="60" Canvas.Top="70" Width="250"
                  Height="200" HorizontalScrollBarVisibility="Auto">
        <Grid Background="White" Height="300" Width="400">
            <!-- 3 rows, 3 columns -->
            ...
            <!-- Border controls to draw a different background in each cell -->
            ...
        </Grid>
    </ScrollViewer>
</Canvas>
```

The RangeBase Class

The RangeBase class provides behavior to handle a range of values and a selected value within this range. It is the base class of the ScrollBar, Slider, and ProgressBar controls. The RangeBase class uses value coercion in order to ensure the current value is within the range (i.e., the value remains between or equal to the minimum and maximum defined values). An ArgumentException will be raised if any of the properties defining the end points of the range are set to a value that does not make sense, such as setting Minimum to NaN or SmallChange to a value less than zero. Table 3-40 shows the properties of RangeBase.

Table 3-40. Properties of the System.Windows.Controls.Primitives.RangeBase Class

Property	Type	Description
LargeChange	double	Specifies the value to add/subtract from the current value. Defaults to 1. Exact behavior is specified by the inheritor.
Maximum	double	Defines the highest value possible for this range. Defaults to 1.
Minimum	double	Defines the lowest value possible for this range. Defaults to 0.
SmallChange	double	Specifies the value to add/subtract from the current value. Defaults to 0.1. Exact behavior is specified by the inheritor.
Value	double	Gets/sets the current value. This property is subjected to value coercion to ensure it stays within range.

The RangeBase provides one event: ValueChanged event with event args class RoutedPropertyChangedEventHandler, which raises when the range value changes.

ScrollBar

The ScrollBar class is visually represented by two RepeatButton controls and a Thumb control that corresponds to the currently selected value within the range. You can see what horizontal and vertical scrollbars look like in Figure 3-27.

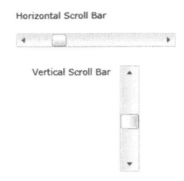

Figure 3-27. *ScrollBar controls*

Table 3-41 describes ScrollBar's properties.

Table 3-41. *Key Properties of the System.Windows.Controls.Primitives.ScrollBar Class*

Property	Type	Description
Orientation	Orientation	Gets/sets the orientation of the scrollbar. Possible values: Horizontal, Vertical. Default value is Horizontal.
ViewportSize	double	Specifies the amount of content that is currently visible according to the position of the thumb within the scrollbar. Defaults to 0.

The ScrollBar class provides one event: Scroll (event args class: ScrollEventArgs). This event fires only when the user changes the position of the thumb, not when the Value property is changed in the code-behind.

The XAML for the scrollbars shown in Figure 3-27 looks like this:

```
<Canvas x:Name="LayoutRoot" Background="White">
    <TextBlock Text="Horizontal Scroll Bar" Canvas.Left="20" Canvas.Top="40"/>
    <ScrollBar Orientation="Horizontal" Canvas.Left="20" Canvas.Top="70" Width="200"
                    Minimum="0" Maximum="100"
                    SmallChange="1" LargeChange="10" Value="50"/>
    <TextBlock Text="Vertical Scroll Bar" Canvas.Left="20" Canvas.Top="100"/>
    <ScrollBar Orientation="Vertical" Canvas.Left="150" Canvas.Top="100"
        Width="25"/>
</Canvas>
```

Slider

The Slider control is essentially a scrollbar, but it provides the capability to select a value from within a range. It inherits from RangeBase. Table 3-42 shows its properties.

Table 3-42. Properties of the System.Windows.Controls.Slider Class

Property	Type	Description
IsDirectionReversed	bool	Determines the direction of increasing value of a Slider. The default is a false value, which means increasing values when up for vertical sliders and right for horizontal sliders. Reverses the direction of increasing values if true: down for vertical sliders and left for horizontal sliders.
IsFocused	bool	Returns true if the slider currently has input focus.
Orientation	Orientation	Gets/sets the orientation of slider. Possible values: Vertical, Horizontal.

Figure 3-28 shows what a horizontal and vertical slider look like.

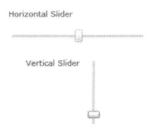

Figure 3-28. Slider control example

Here's the XAML used to create those sliders:

```
<Canvas x:Name="LayoutRoot" Background="White">
    <TextBlock Text="Horizontal Slider" Canvas.Left="20" Canvas.Top="40"/>
    <Slider Orientation="Horizontal" Canvas.Left="20" Canvas.Top="70" Width="200"
            Minimum="0" Maximum="100" SmallChange="1" LargeChange="10"
                Value="50"/>
    <TextBlock Text="Vertical Slider" Canvas.Left="20" Canvas.Top="100"/>
    <Slider Orientation="Vertical" Canvas.Left="130" Canvas.Top="100"
            Width="25" Height="100"/>
</Canvas>
```

ProgressBar

The ProgressBar control represents the progress of the defined operation. It also inherits from RangeBase. You can define the following two visual styles for the ProgressBar control using the IsIndeterminate property.

- Progress bar with a repeating pattern. You need to set the IsIndeterminate property to true.

- Progress bar that gets filled based on the value. You need to set the IsIndeterminate property to false and define the range by setting Minimum and Maximum properties and set the value using the Value property.

Table 3-43 shows its key properties.

Table 3-43. Key Properties of the System.Windows.Controls.ProgressBar Class

Property	Type	Description
IsIndeterminate	bool	Defines the progress bar's visual style as repeating pattern or filling bar based on the value.

Figure 3-29 shows the progress bar in repeating pattern and filled style.

Figure 3-29. ProgressBar control in two different styles

Here's the XAML used to create the different style progress bar:

```
<Canvas x:Name="LayoutRoot" Background="White">
    <TextBlock Text="Repeating Pattern Progress Bar"
        Canvas.Left="20" Canvas.Top="40"/>
    <ProgressBar Height="20" Width="200" IsIndeterminate="True"
        Canvas.Left="20" Canvas.Top="70"/>
    <TextBlock Text="Filling Progress Bar"
        Canvas.Left="20" Canvas.Top="100"/>
    <ProgressBar Height="20" Width="200" IsIndeterminate="False"
        Minimum="0" Maximum="100" Value="30"
        Canvas.Left="20" Canvas.Top="130"/>
```

Calendar and DatePicker

As part of the Silverlight SDK, the Calendar control provides a full calendar onscreen that the user can use to navigate to a month and select a date. It supports forbidding certain dates from being selected and constraining itself to a given date range. Table 3-44 shows the properties for the Calendar control.

Table 3-44. Properties of the System.Windows.Controls.Calendar Class

Property	Type	Description
BlackoutDates	CalendarDateRange Collection	Contains a set of dates that are blacked out and thus cannot be selected by a user.
CalendarButtonStyle	Style	Defines Style related to the control's internal CalendarButton object.
CalendarItemStyle	Style	Defines Style related to the control's internal CalendarItem object.
DisplayDate	DateTime	Specifies the date to display in the calendar.
DisplayDateEnd	Nullable<DateTime>	Specifies the last date to display.
DisplayDateStart	Nullable<DateTime>	Specifies the first date to display.
DisplayMode	CalendarMode	Controls how the calendar presents itself. Possible values: Month (displays a full month at a time), Year (displays a full year at a time), and Decade (displays a decade at a time).
FirstDayOfWeek	DayOfWeek	Specifies the day that marks the beginning of the week. Defaults to DayOfWeek.Sunday.
IsTodayHighlighted	bool	Returns true if today's date is selected in the calendar.
SelectedDate	Nullable<DateTime>	Used when SelectionMode is set to SingleDate. Indicates null if no date is selected, otherwise the selected date. If more than one date is selected, it will select the first date.
SelectedDates	SelectedDates Collection	Contains one or more selected dates, unless selection mode is None.
SelectionMode	CalendarSelection Mode	Gets/sets how the selection works in the calendar. The CalendarSelectionMode enum members are None (no selections are allowed), SingleDate (only one date can be selected), SingleRange (only one consecutive range of dates can be selected), MultipleRange (different, disconnected ranges of dates can be selected).

The Calendar control provides three events: DisplayDateChanged, DisplayModeChanged, and SelectedDatesChanged. These events occur when there is change in related DisplayDate, DisplayMode, and SelectedDates properties values.

Silverlight SDK provides another control, the DatePicker, which allows selecting a date. It consists of a TextBox, a Button, and a Calendar control. The user can enter a date in the TextBox control or click the

Button and select a date. The Calendar control appears only when the button is clicked. The DatePicker control carries many Calendar control properties. If the user types a date in the TextBox, the date can be retrieved using the Text property. If the entered value is not a valid date, then a DateValidationError event will be raised, unless the ThrowException property is set to false.

Figure 3-30 shows what the Calendar and DatePicker controls look like.

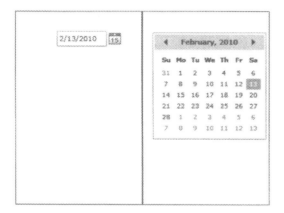

Figure 3-30. *The Calendar and DatePicker controls example*

The XAML for these controls looks like this:

```xml
<UserControl x:Class="chapter3.CalendarDatePickerDemo"
    xmlns="http://schemas.microsoft.com/winfx/2006/xaml/presentation"
    xmlns:x="http://schemas.microsoft.com/winfx/2006/xaml"
    xmlns:d="http://schemas.microsoft.com/expression/blend/2008"
    xmlns:mc="http://schemas.openxmlformats.org/markup-compatibility/2006"
    mc:Ignorable="d"
    xmlns:swcx="clr-namespace:System.Windows.Controls;assembly=
        System.Windows.Controls"
    d:DesignHeight="300" d:DesignWidth="400" Height="300" Width="400">

    <Grid x:Name="LayoutRoot" Background="White">
        <Grid.ColumnDefinitions>
            <ColumnDefinition></ColumnDefinition>
            <ColumnDefinition></ColumnDefinition>
        </Grid.ColumnDefinitions>
        <Border Grid.Column="0" Grid.Row="0" Grid.RowSpan="2"
            BorderBrush="Black" BorderThickness="1">
            <Canvas>
                <swcx:DatePicker x:Name="datePicker"
                    Canvas.Top="30" Canvas.Left="65"/>
            </Canvas>
        </Border>
        <Border Grid.Column="1" Grid.Row="0" Grid.RowSpan="2"
            BorderBrush="Black" BorderThickness="1">
            <Canvas>
```

```
            <swcx:Calendar x:Name="calendar" Canvas.Top="30"
                Canvas.Left="15" SelectionMode="SingleRange"/>
        </Canvas>
      </Border>
  </Grid>
</UserControl>
```

Image

The Image control inherits from `FrameworkElement`, so it inherits the bits from `FrameworkElement` and `UIElement`. Silverlight currently supports only PNG and JPEG formats. As mentioned earlier in Chapter 1, Silverlight 4 removed all restrictions on the PNG format support. Now all PNG image formats are supported with proper transparency. The simplest way to place an image on a user interface is by using the Image control and setting its `Source` property within the XAML code. You will see the image as shown in Figure 3-31:

```
<Image Source="res/Buddy.png" Width="300" Height="300"/>
```

Figure 3-31. The Image control example

In the next chapter, we will look at the `Image` class in detail.

MultiScaleImage

The MultiScaleImage control, inherited from the FrameworkElement, is used to render multi-resolution images, which can be zoomed in on and panned across. The `MultiScaleImage` class is one of the key objects of Silverlight's Deep Zoom technology and allows users to open a single multi-resolution image. By default, a user cannot zoom into or pan across the image loaded by `MultiScaleImage`. But `MultiScaleImage` provides methods to zoom and pan, which can be utilized to achieve zooming and panning of the loaded image. The MultiScaleImage control exposes some useful properties, methods, and events which are more appropriate for the next chapter.

MediaElement

The `System.Windows.Controls.MediaElement` is a central media control providing media integration capability in Silverlight. It represents an object that contains and plays audio, video, or both. By default, the media that is defined by the Source property plays immediately after the MediaElement object has loaded. To suppress this behavior, you can set the AutoPlay property to false. We will cover this control in detail in the next chapter.

InkPresenter

In the digital age the natural interaction through the touch screen or by stylus is gaining importance to provide real world user experience. With `System.Windows.Controls.InkPresenter`, Silverlight provides support to the ink feature. It represents a drawing surface supporting ink features input with a stylus, a mouse, or by touch.

As part of core Silverlight, InkPresenter derives from Canvas and can display one or more UIElement objects. The key property—Strokes—represents a collection of ink Stroke objects displayed on the surface as StrokeCollection. Here, Ink refers to handwriting or drawing content input through a stylus, a mouse, or by touch. Each stroke (Stroke object) contains a DrawingAttributes property representing Color, Height, Width, and OutlineColor, and a StylusPoints property with location coordinates (X and Y coordinates). You can capture theses ink strokes by wiring MouseLeftButtonDown, MouseMove, and LostMouseCapture events of the InkPresenter control.

Strokes and StylePoints

The `System.Windows.Ink` namespace provides three classes: DrawingAttributes (specifies drawing attributes that are used to draw a Stroke), Stroke (a collection of points that correspond to stylus down, move, and up movements) and StrokeCollection (a collection of Stroke objects). A Stroke represents the position/geometry through the StylusPoints property and appearance through the DrawingAttributes property. The StylusPoints property is a collection of StylePoint objects.

The `System.Windows.Input` namespace supports the Silverlight client input system including ink strokes. The StylusPoint structure represents a single point on an ink stroke by providing X and Y coordinates and pressure.

To see InkPresenter in action, let us create a basic InkPad application, as shown in Figure 3-32, to capture handwriting.

Figure 3-32. The InkPresenter control example

To create an InkPad application, here I have added a rectangle with the same size as the InkPresenter control to display the border of the InkPresenter. The InkPresenter control defines the `MouseLeftButtonDown`, `MouseMove`, and `LostMouseCapture` events and sets the `BackGround` property to Transparent. The `BackGround` property is crucial to display the ink strokes on the surface. Either you set up the solid color brush with `Alpha` set to 0, or through XAML set it as `Transparent`. The following is the related XAML code:

```
<UserControl x:Class="chapter3.InkPresenterDemo"
    xmlns="http://schemas.microsoft.com/winfx/2006/xaml/presentation"
    xmlns:x="http://schemas.microsoft.com/winfx/2006/xaml"
    xmlns:d="http://schemas.microsoft.com/expression/blend/2008"
    xmlns:mc="http://schemas.openxmlformats.org/markup-compatibility/2006"
    mc:Ignorable="d"
    d:DesignHeight="300" d:DesignWidth="400"
    Height="400" Width="500">

    <Grid x:Name="LayoutRoot" Background="White">
        <TextBlock Text="Ink Pad" Margin="10"
            FontWeight="bold" FontSize="12"/>
        <Rectangle Margin="10"  Height="330" x:Name="inkBorder"
            Stroke="#FF000000"/>
        <InkPresenter Margin="10"  Height="330" x:Name="inkPad"
            MouseLeftButtonDown="inkPad_MouseLeftButtonDown"
            LostMouseCapture="inkPad_LostMouseCapture"
            MouseMove="inkPad_MouseMove"
            Background="Transparent" Opacity="1"/>
    </Grid>
</UserControl>
```

The code-behind basically implements the MouseLeftButtonDown, MouseMove, and LostMouseCapture events to track and capture ink strokes. The code snippet is shown here:

```
public partial class InkPresenterDemo : UserControl
{
    Stroke newStroke;

    public InkPresenterDemo()
    {
        InitializeComponent();
    }

    void inkPad_MouseLeftButtonDown(object sender, MouseEventArgs e)
    {
        inkPad.CaptureMouse();
        newStroke = new System.Windows.Ink.Stroke();
        newStroke.StylusPoints.Add
            (e.StylusDevice.GetStylusPoints(inkPad));
        inkPad.Strokes.Add(newStroke);
    }

    void inkPad_MouseMove(object sender, MouseEventArgs e)
    {
        if (newStroke != null)
        {
            newStroke.StylusPoints.Add
                (e.StylusDevice.GetStylusPoints(inkPad));
        }
    }

    void inkPad_LostMouseCapture(object sender, MouseEventArgs e)
    {
        newStroke = null;
        inkPad.ReleaseMouseCapture();
    }
}
```

Here the MouseLeftButtonDown event creates a new stroke and adds to the stroke collection of the InkPresenter control. Every mouse move event adds the stylus point to the stroke and upon the last mouse capture, the stroke is completed.

Dialog Boxes

The default dialog boxes, such as open file dialog box, save file dialog box, and custom dialog box, are critical for any line-of-business application. Silverlight features the OpenFileDialog class and the SaveFileDialog class to access or store files to local file systems. Similarly it provides the ChildWindow template to create a custom modal dialog box.

OpenFileDialog

The OpenFileDialog enables users to select and open file(s) from Silverlight applications. The user can browse the local file system (or networked computer), filter file types, and select one or more files. The selected file(s) can be read and processed by the Silverlight application locally, without uploading to the server.

The OpenFileDialog class is contained in the System.Windows.Controls namespace. Table 3-45 shows the key properties of the OpenFileDialog class.

Table 3-45. Key Properties of the System.Windows.Controls.OpenFileDialog Class

Property	Type	Description
File	FileInfo	Gets a FileInfo object for the selected file. If multiple files are selected, returns the first selected file.
Files	IEnumerable	Gets a collection of FileInfo objects for the selected files.
Filter	string	Defines filter string that specifies the file types and descriptions to display in the OpenFileDialog. The default is Empty, which displays all files. Filter consists of a description of the filter followed by a vertical bar (|) and the filter pattern. You can specify one or more file types. You can use a semicolon (;) to define more than one file type for the same description (pattern). If you want to specify all files with the same extension you use start and full point (*.) followed by the file extension (e.g., *.png). If you want to select all files you use (*.*). You should not put any space before or after the vertical bars (|) in the filter string to avoid unexpected behavior. The filter description Image Files (*.JPG and *.PNG)|*.jpg;*.png will show Image Files (*.JPG and *.PNG) in the filter drop-down list and shows only *.jpg and *.png files when it is selected.
FilterIndex	Int32	Defines the index of the selected item in the OpenFileDialog filter drop-down list.
Multiselect	bool	Defines whether the OpenFileDialog allows users to select multiple files or not. Default is false (i.e., single file selection).

The OpenFileDialog exposes one method, ShowDialog, which displays an OpenFileDialog that is modal to the Web browser window. It returns true if the user clicks Open and false if the user clicks Cancel or closes the dialog box. It returns null reference if the dialog box is still open. It is not possible to specify the initial folder for the OpenFileDialog. For the first time the initial folder will be displayed based on the user's machine setting. The second time and onwards, the initial folder will be the folder last time the file was selected by the user.

The sample application as shown in Figure 3-33 allows opening the Open File Dialog box to select the text file type. The selected text file will be read and processed locally and will display the content within the application, as shown in Figure 3-34.

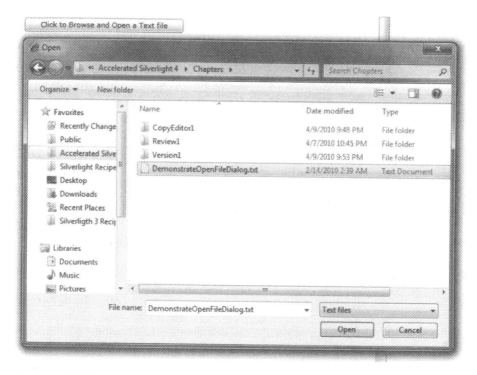

Figure 3-33. The OpenFileDialog example

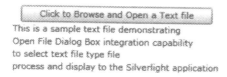

Figure 3-34. Displaying the selected file content within the application

The XAML code is very straightforward, containing a Button with the click event to open the open file dialog box and a TextBlock to display the selected text file text:

```
<StackPanel x:Name="LayoutRoot" Background="White">
    <Button Content="Click to Browse and Open a Text file"
        Width="250" Click="Button_Click"></Button>
    <TextBlock x:Name="txtContents" TextWrapping="Wrap"/>
</StackPanel>
```

As shown here, in the Button control's Click event, opens the open file dialog box by calling OpenFileDialog's ShowDialog method. In our example, we have set the Filter property to the text file

(.txt) type. The selected file is opened locally and the content is read as a StreamReader object. The read content is set to the Text property of TextBlock to display it:

```
private void Button_Click(object sender, RoutedEventArgs e)
{
    OpenFileDialog opendlg = new OpenFileDialog();
    opendlg.Filter = "Text files|*.txt";

    opendlg.Multiselect = false;

    if ((bool)opendlg.ShowDialog())
    {
        using (StreamReader reader = new StreamReader(dlg.File.OpenRead()))
        {
            txtContents.Text = reader.ReadToEnd();
            reader.Close();
        }
    }
}
```

Note that you need to add the reference to the System.IO namespace in order to create an instance of the StreamReader object.

SaveFileDialog

The SaveFileDialog enables users to save data as a file from a Silverlight application. The user can browse the local file system (or networked computer), filter file types, select the file type, define the file name, and save it. As OpenFileDialog, the SaveFileDialog class is also contained in the System.Windows.Controls namespace.

Table 3-46 and 3-47 show the key methods and properties of the SaveFileDialog class.

Table 3-46. Key Methods of the System.Windows.Controls.SaveFileDialog Class

Method	Description
OpenFile	This method opens the file, for writing, specified by the SaveFileName property. The SaveFileName property gets the file name (with no path information) for the selected file from using the SaveFileDialog box.
ShowDialog	This method shows the modal SaveFileDialog on the screen. It returns true if the user clicks Save and false if the user clicks Cancel or closes the dialog box. It returns null reference if the dialog box is still open. You can use the return value of the ShowDialog method to determine whether the user has selected a file.

Table 3-47. *Key Properties of the SaveFileDialog Class*

Property	Type	Description
DefaultExt	string	Defines the default file name extension applied to files saved with the dialog box.
Filter	string	Defines the filter string that specifies which file types and descriptions to show in the *Save as Type* drop-down list of the dialog box. The default is Empty. You can set up the Filter string similarly to how you set it up for the OpenFileDialog class. Visit the Table 3-45 to get more details.
FilterIndex	int	Provides the index of the selected file type from the *Save as Type* drop-down list of the dialog box.
SafeFileName	string	Provides the file name (with no path information) of the selected file associated with the dialog box. The default value is Empty.

The sample application as shown in Figure 3-35 allows text to be entered in the TextBox and opens the Save File Dialog box to save the entered text as text file to the selected location.

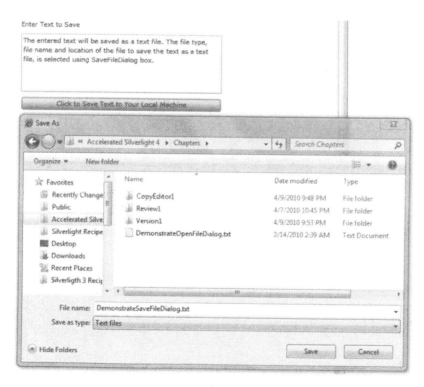

Figure 3-35. *The SaveFileDialog example*

The following is self-explanatory XAML code:

```
<StackPanel x:Name="LayoutRoot" Background="White">
    <TextBlock Text="Enter Text to Save" Margin="4"/>
    <TextBox x:Name="SaveText" Height="100" Width="350" Margin="4"
        TextWrapping="Wrap"/>
    <Button Content="Click to Save Text to Your Local Machine"
        Click="SaveFileButton_Click" Margin="5"/>
</StackPanel>
```

Now, in the Button control's Click event, with the use of SaveFileDialog's Show method, the user can define the file name and location to save the file. In the following example, we have set the Filter property to the Text File type to save the entered text as a file:

```
private void SaveFileButton_Click(object sender, RoutedEventArgs e)
{
    SaveFileDialog filesavedialog = new SaveFileDialog();

    //Set Save File Dialog box FileType Filter
    filesavedialog.Filter = "Text File|*.txt";

    //Show standard Save File Dialog
    bool? result = filesavedialog.ShowDialog();

    //Save entered text as a text file
    if (result == true)
    {
        using (StreamWriter writer = new
            StreamWriter(filesavedialog.OpenFile()))
        {
            writer.Write(SaveText.Text);
            writer.Close();
        }
    }
}
```

Note that you need to add the reference to the System.IO namespace in order to create an instance of the StreamWriter object.

▓ **Note** By default, the Silverlight application will be displayed embedded within the web browser or displayed in the out-of-browser mode. You can display the application in the full-screen mode, where the application window resizes to the current resolution of the screen. You can define the Silverlight application running mode (embedded or full-screen) using the IsFullScreen property.

OpenFileDialog and SaveFileDialog are not supported in the full-screen mode. Remember to implement the check and exit the full-screen mode before you use these classes.

ChildWindow

With the Silverlight 3 version a Silverlight Child Window template is installed as part of the default install. The ChildWindow makes it easy for developers to implement modal windows in Silverlight-based RIAs. For example, you can use the Silverlight Child Window template to get the user's attention by providing a modal window and pausing the application flow for user interaction until the child window is closed. You can also use this feature as a pop-up window to display a data data-driven report or data entry form. The child window blocks the parent window until the window is closed. The stored result in DialogResult informs the application of its status upon closing. Silverlight renders the child window with an animation sequence and renders an overlay background to ensure the user focuses on the window.

The ChildWindow class is also contained in the System.Windows.Controls namespace and is derived from System.Windows.Controls.ContentControl. Table 3-48 and 3-49 show key methods and properties of the ChildWindow class.

Table 3-48. *Key Methods of the System.Windows.Controls.SaveFileDialog Class*

Method	Description
Close	This method allows the programmer to close the child window. Calling the Close method will set the DialogResult property to false. If you want to cancel the closing of a child window, you can do so within the Closing event of the child window.
Show	This method opens the child window and returns immediately, without waiting for the child window to close. This allows ongoing activities on the parent window; however, it blocks the parent window from performing any user actions.

Table 3-49. *Key Properties of the System.Windows.Controls.ChildWindow Class*

Property	Type	Description
DialogResult	Nullable<bool>	Defines whether the user has accepted (returns true value) or cancels/closes (returns false value) the child window. The default value is null reference, which indicates that the child window is open.
HasCloseButton	bool	Defines whether the child window has a close button in the title bar. The default value is true to display the close button.
OverlayBrush	Brush	Defines the visual brush to cover the parent window when the child window is open.

OverlayOpacity	double	Defines the opacity of the overlay brush to cover the parent window when the child window is open. The default value is 1.0.
Title	Object	Defines the title of the child window.

You can add a Silverlight Child Window template by right-clicking the Silverlight application project and choosing Add New Item and then Silverlight Child Window, as shown in Figure 3-36.

Figure 3-36. Adding a Silverlight Child Window template to a Silverlight project

After successfully adding a child window, you'll see the following XAML code in the XAML view of Visual Studio. As you can see, the XAML code includes two buttons (OK and Cancel) along with related Click events. The following code snippet shows the XAML code and related code-behind. Here we just added a TextBlock to display static text.

```xml
<controls:ChildWindow x:Class="chapter3.ChildWindow1"
    xmlns="http://schemas.microsoft.com/winfx/2006/xaml/presentation"
    xmlns:x="http://schemas.microsoft.com/winfx/2006/xaml"
    xmlns:controls="clr-namespace:System.Windows.Controls;
        assembly=System.Windows.Controls"
    Width="400" Height="300"
    Title="ChildWindow1">
    <Grid x:Name="LayoutRoot" Margin="2">
        <Grid.RowDefinitions>
            <RowDefinition />
```

```
            <RowDefinition Height="Auto" />
        </Grid.RowDefinitions>
        <TextBlock Text="This is a Modal Child Window" FontSize="24"/>
        <Button x:Name="CancelButton" Content="Cancel"
            Click="CancelButton_Click" Width="75" Height="23"
            HorizontalAlignment="Right" Margin="0,12,0,0"
            Grid.Row="1" />
        <Button x:Name="OKButton" Content="OK" Click="OKButton_Click"
            Width="75" Height="23" HorizontalAlignment="Right"
            Margin="0,12,79,0" Grid.Row="1" />
    </Grid>
</controls:ChildWindow>
```

The following is the code-behind. Here the `DialogResult` property of type `Nullable<bool>` gets or sets the dialog result value. It returns true if the child window was accepted, and it returns false if the child window was cancelled.

```
namespace chapter3
{
    public partial class ChildWindow1 : ChildWindow
    {
        public ChildWindow1()
        {
            InitializeComponent();
        }

        private void OKButton_Click(object sender, RoutedEventArgs e)
        {
            this.DialogResult = true;
        }

        private void CancelButton_Click(object sender, RoutedEventArgs e)
        {
            this.DialogResult = false;
        }
    }
}
```

You can create a new instance of the add ChildWindow and display the child window by calling the `Show` method of the `ChildWindow`. In our example, upon clicking a button we will show the added child window, as shown in Figure 3-37. The following is the button click event to show the child window.

```
private void ShowChildWindowButton_Click(object sender,
    RoutedEventArgs e)
{
    var newchildwindow = new ChildWindow1();
    newchildwindow.Show();
}
```

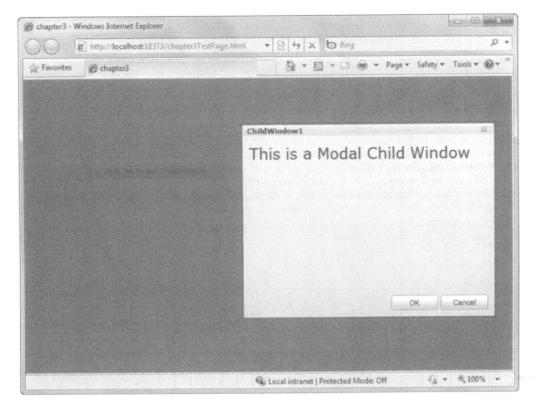

Figure 3-37. Child Window sample application

WebBrowser

Silverlight 4 introduced the WebBrowser control to host the HTML content within the Silverlight application when it runs in the Out-of-Browser (OOB) application mode. The out-of-browser mode enables a Silverlight application to run outside of the browser, as any traditional desktop application, albeit in the restricted sandbox environment. If you use the WebBrowser control within the browser (not in out-of-browser mode), then it will display a blank rectangle of the same size of the WebBrowser control.

You must define the Height and Width of the WebBrowser control, since the default value is 0. The HTML content can be hosted within the control either by calling the NavigateToString(String) method with the HTML content passed as string, or by setting the Source property of the control to the relative or fully qualified URI, or calling the Navigate(Uri) method passing the relative or fully qualified URI. The set or passed URI must be in the same domain as the Silverlight application.

For further details on the OOB feature, please visit Chapter 11.

Navigation

Silverlight 3 introduced navigation framework to connect different XAML pages together to form a complete application. While navigation brings with it the ability to move forward and backward, like we are used to in web browsers, navigation is really a broader concept that encompasses how separate XAML pages can be brought together to form an application. Silverlight 4 further enhances the navigation framework and allows developers to generate and initialize instances of pages from URIs using their own scheme, and enable scenarios such as authentication redirects, error pages, and Model-View-ViewModel Controller style navigation.

There are several important pieces of the navigation framework, including the new Frame class that is in charge of the navigation, the Page class that subjects itself to navigation, the URI mapping for simplifying page references, a journal, and, of course, integration with the host browser's forward and back buttons. We'll explore the navigation framework in depth in Chapter 11.

The navigation framework is located in the System.Windows.Navigation namespace, with supporting controls in the System.Windows.Controls namespace. They are automatically added as a reference in new Silverlight 3 and Silverlight 4 applications.

The Frame Class

The Frame class is responsible for displaying the page (actually any user control, because the Page class inherits from UserControl) that is the target of the navigation. Tables 3-50, 3-51, and 3-52 show the properties, methods, and events of the Frame class.

Table 3-50. *Properties of the System.Windows.Controls.Frame Class*

Property	Type	Description
CacheSize	int	Defines number of pages can be cached for the frame. The cached pages are reused for each navigation request. This can be used only where the NavigationCacheMode property of the Page class is Enabled.
CanGoBack	bool	Returns true if there are entries in the navigation journal previous to the currently active entry.
CanGoForward	bool	Returns true if there are entries in the navigation journal after the currently active entry.
ContentLoader	INavigation ContentLoader	Defines the responsible object for providing content that corresponds to a requested URI.
CurrentSource	Uri	Stores the URI corresponding to the content currently displayed. This property is updated only after the navigation has completed.

JournalOwnership	JournalOwnership	Controls the behavior of the journal. Possible values are Automatic (top-level frames integrate with the browser journal; otherwise, frame uses its own journal); OwnsJournal (the frame uses its own journal); and UsesParentJournal (integrates with the browser's journal; if set on a non-top-level frame, an exception is thrown).
Source	Uri	Stores the URI of the next navigation. This is distinct from CurrentSource because its value is set at the beginning of the navigation. After navigation is complete, the value of Source and CurrentSource will be the same.
UriMapper	UriMapperBase	Defines an object to manage converting a URI to another URI for this frame.

Table 3-51. Methods of the System.Windows.Controls.Frame Class

Method	Description
GoBack	Navigates to the previous journal entry if there is a journal entry previous to the currently active entry, or throws an exception if no previous entry exists.
GoForward	Navigates to the next journal entry if there is a journal entry after the currently active entry, or throws an exception if no next entry exists.
Navigate	Navigates to the specified URI. The URI can be an absolute path to XAML within the application or a URI specified in an URI mapping.
Refresh	Reloads the current page.
StopLoading	Stops the navigation request, most useful when the navigation request triggers downloading of content or lengthy creation of the XAML that is the target of the navigation.

Table 3-52. Events of the System.Windows.Controls.Frame Class

Event	Description
FragmentNavigation	Occurs at the beginning of a navigation to a content fragment (a well-formed content) request.
Navigated	Occurs after a navigation completes.
Navigating	Occurs at the beginning of a navigation request.
NavigationFailed	Occurs after an error during a navigation attempt.
NavigationStopped	Occurs after StopLoading is invoked or the current navigation is aborted via a new navigation request.

The Page Class

The Page class inherits from UserControl, so it inherits a large chunk of functionality. The reason the Page class exists is to have a navigation-aware user control. It provides event handlers that you can override to conduct custom processing based on navigation. It also exposes a Title property that you can use to show some meaningful text in the navigation history and a couple of properties that give you access to the navigation service. Tables 3-53 and 3-54 show the properties and methods of the Page class.

Table 3-53. Properties of the System.Windows.Controls.Page Class

Property	Type	Description
NavigationCacheMode	NavigationCacheMode	Defines the scope of the page to be cached or not. The NavigationCacheMode enum has three possible values: Disabled value determines no cache for that page. Each visit a new instance of the page is created. Required value determines that the page is always cached regardless of the cache size of the frame. Enabled value determines that the page will be cached only until the size of the cache for the frame exceeds the specified value.
NavigationContext	NavigationContext	Provides access to the Uri and the QueryString data.
NavigationService	NavigationService	Provides access to the NavigationService instance that the Frame is using. Exposes the same properties as Frame except for JournalOwnership. It also exposes the same events as Frame. A navigation request can be initiated from a Page via this object. Note that the NavigationService class provides methods, properties, and events to support navigation in Silverlight applications.
Title	String	The text of the Title property gets displayed in the navigation history and the browser's title bar. If this is not set, the title bar and navigation history show the URI.

Table 3-54. Key Methods of the System.Windows.Controls.Page Class

Method	Description
OnFragmentNavigation	Called when navigation to a fragment starts.
OnNavigatedFrom	Called when a page is no longer active (navigation to another page has started).
OnNavigatedTo	Called when the page is made the active page via navigation.
OnNavigatingFrom	Called before the page is no longer active (navigation to another page has started).

Between the Frame class and the Page class, there are a lot of events that provide opportunities to step into the navigation process and perform custom work. Figure 3-38 shows the order in which these events fire.

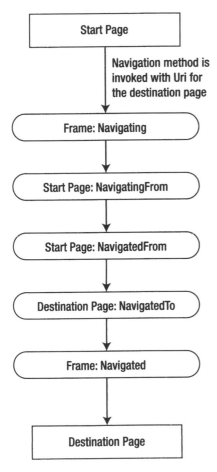

Figure 3-38. Events order during the navigation process

Summary

This chapter introduced the classes that enable the dependency property system and enable the visual dimension of Silverlight: DependencyObject, UIElement, FrameworkElement, and Control. After going over these important classes, you were exposed to many of the controls that come with Silverlight and some of the new ones introduced in Silverlight 4. This chapter concluded with a look at key classes of the navigation framework: Frame and Page. The next chapter focuses on the support of Silverlight for media integration.

PART 2

Content Integration in Silverlight Applications

■ ■ ■

CHAPTER 4

Media Integration

Ever since the debut of Silverlight 1 under its code name WPF/E, Silverlight has provided support for working with images and media (audio and video). A significant amount of Silverlight 1 applications featured smooth video integration. Subsequent versions of Silverlight (Silverlight 2, 3, and 4) continuously improved the benefits of a managed and secured environment, bringing rich support for working with images, audio, and video.

By partnering with NBC and providing more than 2,000 hours of live content and 3,500 hours of on-demand video for the China Beijing Olympic Games 2008, and repeating the same for the Winter 2010 Olympic games in Vancouver (www.nbcolympics.com), Microsoft successfully demonstrated the capabilities and power of the Microsoft Silverlight technology platform in the commercial rich-media content delivery market. The Silverlight technology, along with the adaptive video streaming, enabled NBC to develop the Control Room feature, presenting video picture-in-picture capability, and let viewers watch up to four events at the same time. You can get more details on this project by visiting the case study at www.microsoft.com/casestudies/Case_Study_Detail.aspx?CaseStudyID=4000004131.

As you've seen in the previous chapter, the Image, MultiscaleImage, and MediaElement are key controls to integrate images and media content. You can integrate media content directly from the server, or it's also possible to package images along with other media, including video files, and work with them on the client side. Microsoft has also introduced two interesting technologies to help enable rich Silverlight applications. The first is Windows Azure Platform–based Hosting and Media Delivery Services for Silverlight Applications, supporting multicast streaming. The second, Deep Zoom, is a way to efficiently handle the presentation and network transfer of a large collection of high-quality images. I'll detail these technologies in this chapter.

Media Integration Enhancements in Silverlight 4

Before we dive into the details, the following points summarize the key enhancements of the Silverlight 4 version, supporting enhanced image and media integration:

- Support to all types of PNG image formats with proper transparency.

- Support for offline DRM powered by PlayReady for OOB applications to deliver media content in the offline mode in a more protected and managed environment.

- Web Camera and Microphone integration with the set of new APIs to identify the attached audio and video devices to the computer, and play and capture the audio and video.

- Support to multicast streaming for the media files.

- Windows Azure Platform–based Hosting and Media Delivery Services for Silverlight Applications supports the multicast streaming for media files.

Images

We have already utilized the Image control in the previous chapter, but we haven't delved into the specifics. Silverlight currently supports only PNG and JPEG formats. As mentioned earlier, Silverlight 4 removed all restrictions on the PNG format support. Now all PNG image formats are supported with proper transparency.

The Image Class

As you learned in Chapter 3, the simplest way to place an image on a user interface is by using the Image control and setting its **Source** property within the XAML code:

```
<Image Source="Buddy.png"/>
```

The Image control inherits from **FrameworkElement**, so it inherits the bits from **FrameworkElement** and **UIElement**. The new properties and event introduced by the **Image** class are listed in Tables 4-1 and 4-2.

Table 4-1. Properties of the Image Class

Property	Type	Description
Source	ImageSource	Gets or sets the image source. Currently, only the **BitmapImage** class can be an image source. From XAML, you can specify a relative or an absolute URI.
Stretch	Stretch	Gets or sets how the image is sized within the width/height set on the Image control.

Table 4-2. Events of the Image Class

Event	Description
ImageOpened	Fires when the image source is downloaded and decoded with no failure. You can use this event to determine the size of an image before rendering it. If the image-decode fails for any reason, this event does not fire. Once this event fires, the **PixelHeight** and **PixelWidth** properties are guaranteed to be valid.
ImageFailed	Fires if there's a problem downloading or rendering an image. Possible causes are the image not being found at the specified address and the image format not being supported. The **EventArgs** class is **ExceptionRoutedEventArgs** and provides **ErrorException** (the thrown **Exception**) and **ErrorMessage** properties.

The specific image to display is set via the **Source** property. In XAML, you can specify the **Source** using a relative or an absolute address.

```
<Image Source="../Images/Buddy.png"/>
```

You can implement the same using code-behind to add an image as a child element of the LayoutRoot named control:

```
Image addImage = new Image();
addImage.Source = new BitmapImage(new
    Uri("Buddy.png", UriKind.RelativeOrAbsolute));
LayoutRoot.Children.Add(addImage);
```

The `Source` property is being type-converted to a `BitmapImage` that inherits from `ImageSource`. `BitmapImage` has two events, shown in Table 4-3. The specific image that `BitmapImage` represents can be a `Uri` set via a constructor or via the `UriSource` property after object creation.

Tip Images (and media) can have their Build Action set to Resource within Visual Studio in order for them to be exposed via a relative path. If you can't or don't want to do this, you can make things easy on yourself by utilizing the `Application.Current.Host.Source` property to retrieve the path where the Silverlight application is served. This can be useful when constructing image/media sources in the code-behind without needing to know the full path at compile time, such as when things change between development and production. This will be the case when you specify a relative path in the XAML; however, it's relative to the XAP location.

You can also download an image and pass the `Stream` object to the `SetSource` method. Currently, this is the only `ImageSource` inheritor, so this class handles both PNG and JPEG images.

Table 4-3. Events of `BitmapImage`

Event	Type
ImageOpened	Fires when the image source is downloaded and decoded with no failure. You can use this event to determine the size of an image before rendering it. If the image-decode fails for any reason, this event does not fire. Once this event fires, the `PixelHeight` and `PixelWidth` properties are guaranteed to be valid.
DownloadProgress	Reports the progress of the image download. The `EventArgs` class is `DownloadProgressEventArgs` and contains a `Progress` property that reports either a 0 (indicating that the image is possibly in the process of downloading) or a 1 (indicating that the image has finished downloading).
ImageFailed	Fires when the image cannot be downloaded or the image format is invalid. The event handler is passed an `ExceptionRoutedEventArgs` instance, which has `ErrorException` (the thrown `Exception`) and `ErrorMessage` properties.

If you don't specify a width or height for an image, it will display without any modifications to the image's natural width and height. The Image control has a property named `Stretch` (it is also a dependency property) that controls how an image conforms to a container. The Stretch property can have one of the following four Stretch type enum values:

None: The image maintains its original size.

Fill: The image completely fills the output area, both vertically and horizontally. The image might appear distorted because the aspect ratio is not preserved.

Uniform: The image fills the output area, both vertically and horizontally, but maintains its aspect ratio. This is the default value.

UniformToFill: The image is scaled to completely fill the output area, but its aspect ratio is maintained.

You can see the result of the various Stretch values in Figure 4-1. Reading left to right and top to bottom, Stretch takes on the values None, Fill, Uniform, and UniformToFill.

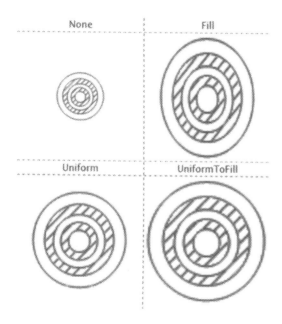

Figure 4-1. *A visual demonstration of each Stretch value*

The image is 100×80, so we can see how the image is treated in a 200×200 square area. The bounding box for the image is defined on the Image control.

```
<Image Source="target.png" Stretch="None" Height="200" Width="200"/>
```

The image is left completely unaltered when Stretch is set to None—it maintains its size of 100×80. When Stretch is set to Fill, the image appears distorted because it is taller than it is wide. For Uniform, the image now almost doubles in size. It doesn't quite fill its bounding box because it is maintaining its aspect ratio. Finally, UniformToFill is similar to Uniform but the image is scaled to the full size of the bounding box. While this specific image can still be completely seen, it is possible that the image will be cut off either horizontally or vertically in order to simultaneously fill its bounding box and maintain its aspect ratio.

Let's take a closer look at these capabilities by implementing a sample application image viewer. In this sample application, a list box will contain several ListBoxItem instances, each containing an image scaled down by setting its width/height (we're using only one source image, but for a serious image browser, you might want to store thumbnails separately due to image file size). When a specific image is clicked, the image is shown at full size. The resulting user interface is shown in Figure 4-2.

Figure 4-2. User interface for an image viewer using a list box

Here we first define the Grid control with two columns and one row, as shown here:

```
<Grid x:Name="LayoutRoot" Background="White">
    <Grid.ColumnDefinitions>
        <ColumnDefinition Width="100"/>
        <ColumnDefinition Width="*"/>
    </Grid.ColumnDefinitions>
    <Grid.RowDefinitions>
        <RowDefinition/>
```

```
        </Grid.RowDefinitions>
    </Grid>
```

Now I created a **Sample** folder under the ImageViewer project and added four JPEG images from the **Sample Pictures** folder that comes as part of Windows 7. Rename them **001.jpg** to **004.jpg** and set each image **BuildAction** property to **Resource**. Go back to the XAML code and add a list box to the first column of the Grid (using **Grid.Column**) and add these four images as **ListBoxItems** to the list box. Here notice that the **SelectionChanged** event is integrated with code-behind.

```
<ListBox x:Name="thumbnailList" Width="100" Grid.Column="0"
        SelectionChanged="thumbnailList_SelectionChanged">
    <ListBox.Items>
        <ListBoxItem>
            <Image Source="Sample/001.jpg" Width="75" Height="50" />
        </ListBoxItem>
        <ListBoxItem>
            <Image Source="Sample/002.jpg" Width="75" Height="50" />
        </ListBoxItem>
        <ListBoxItem>
            <Image Source="Sample/003.jpg" Width="75" Height="50" />
        </ListBoxItem>
        <ListBoxItem>
            <Image Source="Sample/004.jpg" Width="75" Height="50" />
        </ListBoxItem>
    </ListBox.Items>
</ListBox>
```

Add Image control to the second column of the Grid to display the full-size image with **Stretch** property **Uniform** and **Name** property set to **fullImage**, which will be referenced to set the image source to the selected image control:

```
<Image Grid.Column="1" x:Name="fullImage" Stretch="Uniform"/>
```

The following list box's **SelectionChanged** event code-behind is used to display the selected image as a uniformly-filled full-size image. Note that we can't set the source of the **fullImage** to the same source; it instead must reference a new **BitmapImage** instance.

```
private void thumbnailList_SelectionChanged(object sender,
                            SelectionChangedEventArgs e)
{
    ListBox lb = (ListBox)sender;
    ListBoxItem item = (ListBoxItem)lb.SelectedItem;
    Image img = (Image)item.Content;
    fullImage.Source = new
        BitmapImage(((BitmapImage)img.Source).UriSource);
}
```

Don't forget to add reference to the **System.Windows.Media.Imaging** namespace to create a **BitmapImage** instance.

```
using System.Windows.Media.Imaging;
```

If you build and run the project, you should see an outcome similar to that shown in Figure 4-2.

Bitmap APIs

Silverlight 3 introduced a new Bitmap API based on the `WritableBitmap` class. With the help of the Bitmap API you can achieve the following image-management features:

- Dynamic generation of bitmaps by reading/writing pixel by pixel

- Client-side manipulation of images loaded from the server or client machine

- Rendering a portion of the visual tree to a bitmap

- Creation of transforms that can be used to create reflections and similar kinds of effects

The `WritableBitmap` class is found in the `System.Windows.Media.Imaging` namespace. Tables 4-4 and 4-5 define the key methods and properties of the `WritableBitmap` class, respectively.

Table 4-4. Methods of the `WriteableBitmap` Class

Method	Type
Invalidate	Requests a draw of the entire bitmap. Call this method before `Unlock`.
Render	Renders an element within the bitmap. This can be used to create transforms like reflection, etc.

Table 4-5. Properties of the `WriteableBitmap` Class

Property	Type
Dispatcher	Inherited from the `DependencyObject`, it gets the `Dispatcher` associated with the object. Note that only the thread the `Dispatcher` was created on may access the object.
PixelHeight	Gets the height of the bitmap in pixels. It is inherited from the `BitmapSource` class, which provides a source object for properties that use a bitmap.
PixelWidth	Gets the width of the bitmap in pixels. It is inherited from the `BitmapSource` class, which provides a source object for properties that use a bitmap.
Pixels	Gets an array to represent the 2D texture of the bitmap length in pixels.

Let's create an example demonstrating the dynamic generation of the image by taking snapshots to generate thumbnails from the running video, and then create a transform to generate reflection of the generated image. We will use the `WriteableBitmap` class to achieve this functionality.

Create a regular Silverlight 4 application project MediaIntegration and add a user control named `WriteableBitmapDemonstration`. Then create a folder named `Resources` under the project, and add the Windows 7 sample video file `Wildlife.wmv` under the `Resources` folder, setting the `BuildAction` property to `Resource`. Now you are all set to use this video with your application. At the end of this exercise, you will be in a position to render the image from the running video and set the reflection using the **WriteableBitmap** class, as shown in Figure 4-3.

Figure 4-3. *Image capture from the video, generating the reflection effect using the***WriteableBitmap** *class*

Now, let us first concentrate on the XAML file, which is pretty straightforward. Change the **DesignHeight** and **DesignWidth** properties of the UserControl to **700** and **720** respectively, to make your design experience more user-friendly. Next replace the **Grid** layout control with the **StackPanel** and set **Orientation** to **Vertical**, **Margin** to **10**, **Height** to **700**, and **Background** to **Black**. Within the stack panel you need to add the **MediaElement** to play the referenced video and add the **ScrollViewer** control and **StackPanel** to create a thumbnail pane. We will add the snapshots of the running video, and, with the reflection, they will be added to this stack panel. The following is the complete XAML code.

```
<UserControl x:Class="MediaIntegration.WriteableBitmapDemonstration"
    xmlns="http://schemas.microsoft.com/winfx/2006/xaml/presentation"
    xmlns:x="http://schemas.microsoft.com/winfx/2006/xaml"
```

```
    xmlns:d="http://schemas.microsoft.com/expression/blend/2008"
    xmlns:mc="http://schemas.openxmlformats.org/markup-
    compatibility/2006"
    mc:Ignorable="d"
    d:DesignHeight="700" d:DesignWidth="720">
    <StackPanel Name="LayoutRoot" Orientation="Vertical"
        Margin="10" Height="700" Background="Black">
        <MediaElement x:Name="sourceVideo"
            Source="Resources/Wildlife.wmv"
            Height="350" Width="635" Margin="10"
            Cursor="Hand"
            MouseLeftButtonDown="sourceVideo_MouseLeftButtonDown" />
        <ScrollViewer x:Name="scrollArea"
            HorizontalScrollBarVisibility="Auto"
            VerticalScrollBarVisibility="Hidden"
            Height="200" Width="700" Margin="10,0"
            BorderBrush="{x:Null}">
            <StackPanel x:Name="thumbsPanel"
                Orientation="Horizontal" Margin="10,5,0,10" />
        </ScrollViewer>
    </StackPanel>
</UserControl>
```

Notice that using the relative path we have added the video file to the Source property of the MediaElement and the MouseLeftButtonDown event is tied to the sourceVideo_MouseLeftButtonDown code-behind event. We will discuss more about the MediaElement in the Media section of this chapter. Also, you should see that the thumbsPanel stack panel Orientation is set to Horizontal to add the snapshot images horizontally.

Next we need to finish the code-behind. Open WriteableBitmapDemonstration.xaml.cs and first add the reference to the System.Windows.Media.Imaging namespace.

```
using System.Windows.Media.Imaging;
```

To capture the snapshot from the running video, within the added sourceVideo_MouseLeftButtonDown event, you would simply use the WriteableBitmap class to render a bitmap on a per-frame basis. At the time of creating the instance of the WriteableBitmap class, just pass the MediaElement UIElement as a source to the constructor, as shown here:

```
WriteableBitmap snapShot = new WriteableBitmap(sourceVideo, null);
```

Here we have sourceVideo as the MediaElement running video and null is passed as transformation, since we do not want to apply any transform to the captured video image. The rendered bitmap can be mapped to the Image control's Source property to generate the thumbnail. The following code snippet maps the snapShot rendered bitmap source to the new created Image element with the Height set to 90 pixels.

```
Image thumbImage = new Image();
thumbImage.Height = 90;
thumbImage.Margin = new Thickness(2, 0, 2, 0);
thumbImage.Source = snapShot;
```

Now simply add this newly created thumbnail image to the `thumbsPanel` stack panel and display the latest image in the scroll viewer area by scrolling it to the very end of contained content using the `ScrollToHorizontalOffset` property, as shown here:

```
thumbsPanel.Children.Add(thumbImage);

scrollArea.UpdateLayout();
double scrollPos = thumbsPanel.ActualWidth;
scrollArea.ScrollToHorizontalOffset(scrollPos);
```

If you build and run the project, you should see the video plays automatically, and upon left-clicking on the video, that particular frame will be added as a thumbnail image to the panel without transformation.

To achieve the reflection we need to create the transform and apply it to the captured snapshot. First define the TransformGroup and LinearGradiantBrush at the `WriteableBitmapDemonstration` class level, as shown here:

```
TransformGroup imageTransform;
LinearGradientBrush lnrGradBrush;
```

Now you add a private method, `DefineImageTransform`, as shown here, to the `WriteableBitmapDemonstration` class:

```
private void DefineImageTransform()
{
    imageTransform = new TransformGroup();

    TranslateTransform TranlateImageTransform =
        new TranslateTransform();
    TranlateImageTransform.Y = -256;

    ScaleTransform ScaleImageTransform = new ScaleTransform();
    ScaleImageTransform.ScaleY = -1;

    imageTransform.Children.Add(TranlateImageTransform);
    imageTransform.Children.Add(ScaleImageTransform);
}
```

As we are going to create a reflection effect, we need to flip the image vertically. For this, set `TranslateTransform` for the y axis to -256 so the reflection of the source Image control starts right from the bottom of the image. Also, set `ScaleTransform ScaleY` to -1 to flip the scaled object but not change its vertical size. (You will learn more about the image transform in Chapter 9.)

Next add a private method, `DefineOpacityMask`, as shown here, to the `WriteableBitmapDemonstration` class. This method makes the reflected image fade out at the bottom, sets an `OpacityMask` for the target Image control, and uses a `LinearGradientBrush` with two `GradientStops` with the `Color` and `Offset` properties set appropriately. (Visit Chapter 9 to learn more about gradient brush.)

```
private void DefineOpacityMask()
{
    lnrGradBrush = new LinearGradientBrush();
```

```
lnrGradBrush.StartPoint = new Point(0.5, 0);
lnrGradBrush.EndPoint = new Point(0.5, 1);
lnrGradBrush.MappingMode =
    BrushMappingMode.RelativeToBoundingBox;

GradientStop grdStop1 = new GradientStop();
grdStop1.Color = Color.FromArgb(10, 233, 217, 217);
grdStop1.Offset = 0.6;

GradientStop grdStop2 = new GradientStop();
grdStop2.Color = Color.FromArgb(100, 0, 0, 0);
grdStop2.Offset = 0.3;

lnrGradBrush.GradientStops.Add(grdStop1);
lnrGradBrush.GradientStops.Add(grdStop2);
}
```

Define the `WriteableBitmapDemonstration_Loaded` event by placing the following line of code after calling the `InitializeComponent` method under the `WriteableBitmapDemonstration` class constructor. We would need the `Loaded` event to define the transformation and `OpacityMask` of the image to create the reflection.

```
this.Loaded += new
    RoutedEventHandler(WriteableBitmapDemonstration_Loaded);
```

Call the `DefineImageTransform` and `DefineOpacityMask` methods from the Loaded event, as shown here:

```
void WriteableBitmapDemonstration_Loaded(object sender,
    RoutedEventArgs e)
{
    DefineImageTransform();
    DefineOpacityMask();
}
```

Within the `MouseLeftButtonDown` event add a new instance of the `WriteableBitmap` class representing the reflected image, and pass the MediaElement UIElement as a source and apply the transformation to the constructor. The rendered bitmap as reflected image can be mapped to the Image control's Source property to generate the reflection. The following code snippet maps the `reflectedShot` rendered bitmap source to the newly created Image element, with the `Height` set to `90` pixels.

```
WriteableBitmap reflectedShot = new
    WriteableBitmap(sourceVideo, imageTransform);
Image reflectedImage = new Image();
reflectedImage.Height = 90;
reflectedImage.Margin = new Thickness(2, 0, 2, 0);
reflectedImage.Source = reflectedShot;
reflectedImage.OpacityMask = lnrGradBrush;
```

Note that I have also set the OpacityMask of the rendered reflected image to the defined `LinearGradientBrush`.

Now you have rendered the thumbnail image and related reflected image. What you need to do is to add them within the StackPanel control, add the stack panel to the thumbsPanel stack panel, and adjust the scroll viewer area (as explained earlier) to display the latest image with its reflection.

```
StackPanel sp = new StackPanel();

sp.Children.Add(thumbImage);
sp.Children.Add(reflectedImage);

thumbsPanel.Children.Add(sp);
```

The following is a complete code snippet of the sourceVideo_MouseLeftButtonDown event:

```
private void sourceVideo_MouseLeftButtonDown
    (object sender, MouseButtonEventArgs e)
{
    WriteableBitmap snapShot = new
        WriteableBitmap(sourceVideo, null);
    Image thumbImage = new Image();
    thumbImage.Height = 90;
    thumbImage.Margin = new Thickness(2, 0, 2, 0);
    thumbImage.Source = snapShot;

    WriteableBitmap reflectedShot = new
        WriteableBitmap(sourceVideo, imageTransform);
    Image reflectedImage = new Image();
    reflectedImage.Height = 90;
    reflectedImage.Margin = new Thickness(2, 0, 2, 0);
    reflectedImage.Source = reflectedShot;
    reflectedImage.OpacityMask = lnrGradBrush;

    StackPanel sp = new StackPanel();

    sp.Children.Add(thumbImage);
    sp.Children.Add(reflectedImage);

    thumbsPanel.Children.Add(sp);

    scrollArea.UpdateLayout();
    double scrollPos = thumbsPanel.ActualWidth;
    scrollArea.ScrollToHorizontalOffset(scrollPos);
}
```

Rebuild and run the project. Now you should be in a position to capture the frame from the playing video as an image and produce the reflection of the image at run time, as shown in Figure 4-3.

Silverlight Hardware Acceleration

Silverlight 3 and 4 leverage Graphics Processor Unit (GPU) hardware acceleration to deliver a true high-definition (HD) media experience in the in-browser and full-screen modes. In Silverlight 1 and 2, media rendering is performed by software that makes the playback of animations and video files dependent on the capabilities of the CPU of the host PC. This can cause performance issues for complex media files. With Silverlight 3 onwards, we can now fix this performance problem somewhat by taking advantage of hardware GPU acceleration, if enabled, and provide a rich and smooth media experience to users. GPU hardware acceleration allows Silverlight to use the user's video card to render portions of the user interface, which can greatly improve performance. To take advantage of the video hardware, Silverlight uses DirectX for Windows-based and OpenGL for Mac-based devices.

GPU Hardware Acceleration

GPU hardware acceleration is a manual opt-in feature on the Silverlight plug-in and thus is disabled by default. To explicitly enable GPU hardware acceleration for an HTML or ASP .NET page hosting a Silverlight plug-in, set the `EnableGPUAcceleration` parameter at the Silverlight `Object` tag level to `true`, as shown in the following code:

```
<object data="data:application/x-silverlight-2,"
    type="application/x-silverlight-2" width="100%" height="100%">
    ......
    <param name="EnableGPUAcceleration" value="true" />
    ......
</object>
```

That's it. This single line enables GPU hardware acceleration at the Silverlight plug-in level. Now you can take advantage of it in your application to enable bitmap caching at the user interface element level, which is our next topic.

Note The EnableGPUAcceleration property is a read-only property and cannot be set up through code-behind. It must be set at Silverlight plug-in level within the Silverlight application hosting page.

Bitmap Caching

The GPU hardware acceleration–enabled Silverlight application can take advantage of the improved rendering performance of applications by caching vector content, text, and controls into bitmaps. Bitmap caching can be a useful and high-performing tactic in scenarios where content needs to scale without changes being made to its internal appearance.

Bitmap caching is also a manual opt-in feature, and you need to explicitly enable it at the user interface element level within XAML code. You can enable the bitmap caching by setting the `CacheMode` attribute of the user interface element (e.g., Grid control) to `BitmapCache`. If enabled, the caching feature is applicable to that particular element and its children elements (if any). To take advantage of bitmap caching, GPU hardware acceleration must be enabled at the Silverlight plug-in level, as explained in the last section.

Once you enable GPU hardware acceleration, the following example shows bitmap caching enabled at the Grid control level.

```
<Grid CacheMode="BitmapCache" x:Name="LayoutRoot" Background="White">
    <!-- XAML Code -->
</Grid>
```

Caution Care must be taken when choosing user interface elements for hardware acceleration and bitmap caching. Choose elements in the user interface that are mostly static, like scrolling backgrounds. Items that animate, rotate, or scale can be accelerated, but if an element changes, such as through StoryBoard animation, the element will need to be re-rendered frequently and the cache will be invalidated, reducing performance. Similarly, hardware acceleration is not applicable to processes such as pixel shader effects (e.g., DropShadowEffect), PerspectiveTransform, WritableBitmap, and OpacityMask.

Cache and Frame Rate Counter Visualization

Along with GPU Hardware acceleration and bitmap caching, you can also enable cache visualization of user interface element(s), which can be useful to developers seeking to understand the scope of the bitmap caching. To achieve this, you can set up at the plug-in level by enabling the EnableCacheVisualization parameter at the Silverlight Object tag level to true (very similar to enabling GPU hardware acceleration) of the hosting ASP .NET or HTML page, as shown here:

```
<param name="EnableCacheVisualization" value="true" />
```

You can achieve the same through the code-behind:

```
Application.Current.Host.Settings.EnableCacheVisualization = true;
```

When cache visualization is enabled, objects that are cached (i.e., handled by the GPU) are displayed in their normal colors, while others are tinted in red. This feature works only in the full-screen mode on Mac machines.

Similarly, you can set up the frame rate counter either at the hosting page (HTML or ASP .NET) Silverlight plug-in level or using code-behind, as shown here:

```
<param name="EnableFramerateCounter" value="true" />
```

or

```
Application.Current.Host.Settings. EnableFramerateCounter = true;
```

The frame rate counter consists of four numbers. The first number shows the frame rate. The second number displays how many kilobytes (KB) of video memory is in use. The third number represents the total number of GPU-accelerated surfaces and the fourth number shows the total number of intermediate surfaces that are GPU-accelerated surfaces but not explicitly asked to be GPU-accelerated.

The frame rate counter will be displayed in the upper-left corner as an overlay within the Silverlight application content area (see Figure 4-4), only if both EnableGPUAcceleration and EnableFrameRateCounter are set to true.

Figure 4-4. Frame rate counter displayed on the upper-left of the Silverlight application

---

Note Your Internet Browser security setting may prevent you from displaying the scripting to the status bar and thus the frame rate counter. In that case, adjust your browser security settings appropriately. However, this security setting will not have any impact on the actual GPU hardware acceleration.

Multi-scale Images and the Deep Zoom Feature

Deep Zoom first debuted as Seadragon at the TED technology conference. The various Silverlight announcements at MIX08 included the revelation that SeaDragon is now called Deep Zoom and is a standard feature in Silverlight. The MultiScaleImage control is used to provide the deep zoom functionality in a Silverlight user interface.

Just what is Deep Zoom? It is technology that makes it easy to develop applications that can display a set of high-quality images (imagine 20MB per image or more) in a grid-style layout, allowing a user to explore the images at different zoom levels. When the user is zoomed out, the quality is not as high as when he or she is zoomed in. Because of this, the full source images don't need to be downloaded by the client; instead, lower-quality images are sent. As the user zooms in, images closer to the quality level of the original are sent, but only pieces of the images the user can see. This provides a highly optimized way to explore a collection of high-quality images. Since the images are laid out in a grid, the MultiScaleImage control also provides the ability to pan around the image collection.

You can get the gist of what Deep Zoom does to an image by consulting Figure 4-5.

Figure 4-5. The bull's-eye graphic at different zoom levels

In this figure, we revisit the image of a bull's-eye used earlier. The image stored at 100% has full detail. When we zoom out, we lose detail, but this also gives us an important advantage—less data has to be sent from the server to the client. This means that if we have a large collection of images and we're zoomed out, Silverlight won't immediately request a 100% zoom level for all the images. Instead, it will request a 50% zoom level, or 25%, or something even lower. As the user zooms into a specific image, most of the images around it disappear from view, so these don't need to be downloaded. The images still in view, however, are sent to the client—but now Silverlight requests a 50% zoom, or perhaps a 100% zoom when the user zooms all the way in. Feel free to use images with the highest resolutions you can get—the higher the resolution, the more detail there is for users to zoom in to.

The Deep Zoom Composer tool is used to create a package that Silverlight's MultiScaleImage control can use. This generated package contains versions of the images (stored at a possibly large number of different zoom levels, along with certain slices of images used to optimize partial image display) and information describing the layout as designed in the composing tool. The MultiScaleImage control is pointed to this package and then handles all the logic on the client side, such as displaying the multi-resolution images and downloading the right images at the right time to maintain a smooth user experience.

The MultiScaleImage control exposes some useful properties, methods, and events; these are shown respectively in Tables 4-6, 4-7, and 4-8.

Table 4-6. Key Properties of MultiScaleImage

Property	Type	Description
AllowDownloading	bool	Gets or sets whether downloading is permitted by this MultiScaleImage, enabling developers to control which MultiScaleImage objects are downloading data at any point in time.
AspectRatio	double	Current aspect ratio of the images (image width/image height); read-only.
BlurFactor	double	Gets or sets the extent to which data is blurred while rendering. A value of 2 means to use data that is twice as blurry (one level lower), while a value of 0.5 means to try to use data that is extra sharp (one level higher). The default value is 1.
IsDownloading	bool	Gets whether the image is still downloading. If true, requests are still outstanding. If false, then all needed tiles have been downloaded. If the image is moved, IsDownloading may become true again.
IsIdle	bool	Gets whether Deep Zoom is done downloading, decoding, blending images, and animating if springs are used. Even if AllowDownloading is false, IsIdle will be false if any images are pending.
Source	Uri	The URI to the Deep Zoom package containing the images, metadata, and so forth.
SubImages	ReadOnlyCollection <MultiScaleSubImage>	Read-only collection of the subimages used by the control. A MultiScaleSubImage exposes a read-only AspectRatio property along with Opacity (inherited from UIElement), ViewportOrigin, and ViewportWidth properties that can be used to set or discover which set of images and which layer of images are currently exposed.

UseSprings	bool	Controls spring motion (oscillating back and forth until it comes to rest) of the control. Can be set to **false** and later reset to **true** to block initial animation when the control loads.
ViewportOrigin	Point	The top-left corner of the current view as an (x,y) coordinate.
ViewportWidth	double	The width of the current viewport.

Table 4-7. Key Methods of MultiScaleImage

Method	Description
ElementToLogicalPoint	Translates a physical point (the screen) to a point located within the image currently visible beneath the physical point (values between 0 and 1).
LogicalToElementPoint	Translates a point within a currently visible image to a physical point (the screen) (values between 0 and 1).
ZoomAboutLogicalPoint	Accepts a zoom increment factor and a center (x,y) point about which to zoom. All parameters are of type **double**.

Table 4-8. Key Events of MultiScaleImage

Events	Description
ImageFailed	Fires when the image tile (part) cannot be downloaded or the image format is invalid. The event handler method is passed **ExceptionRoutedEventArgs**, which provides **ErrorException** (the thrown **Exception**) and **ErrorMessage** properties.
ImageOpenFailed	Fires when an image file cannot be opened. The event handler method is passed **ExceptionRoutedEventArgs**, which provides **ErrorException** (the thrown **Exception**) and **ErrorMessage** properties.
ImageOpenSucceeded	Fires when an image file is successfully opened. The event handler method is passed **RoutedEventHandler**.
MotionFinished	Fires when the currently ongoing motion (zoom or pan) is complete. The event handler method is passed **RoutedEventHandler**.
ViewportChanged	Fires when the viewport (the area of the image displayed) changes. The event handler method is passed **RoutedEventHandler**.

Developing an Example Using Deep Zoom Composer

The Deep Zoom Composer is a development tool that allows you to aggregate and package images for a Deep Zoom implementation. You can obtain this tool at http://download.microsoft.com by searching for Deep Zoom Composer, or go to http://silverlight.net/getstarted.

When you start the Deep Zoom Composer, you'll see a screen similar to the Expression products (Figure 4-6).

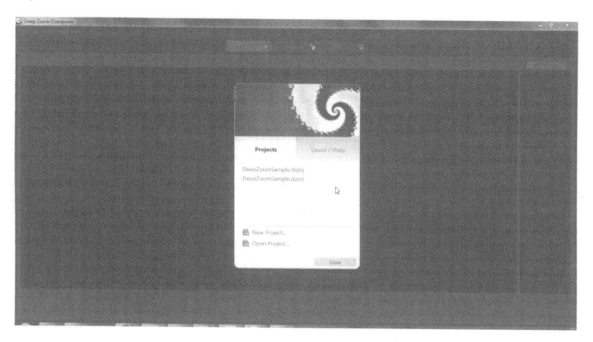

Figure 4-6. The Deep Zoom Composer's start screen

Once you open or create a new project (in our case DeepZoomSample) in Deep Zoom Composer, there are three steps (Import, Compose, and Export) to creating a new Deep Zoom package, which are clearly defined at the top of the Deep Zoom Composer interface.

1. *Import*: This is where you add the images you want to include in the project. Information about the type, dimensions, and file size of each image appear in the lower left, and the full list of added images appears to the right. You can right-click an image to remove it from the project.

2. *Compose*: The second step is where you define how the images are oriented for display, including setting their initial size and position relative to each other.

3. *Export*: The final step allows you to create a package suitable for use by the MultiScaleImage control. You can export in one of two formats: as a composition or as a collection. Optionally, you can create a new Silverlight application as a wrapper.

We will generate an example using the Deep Zoom Composer–generated Silverlight project to feature a Deep Zoom example with Windows 7 sample nature pictures. Figure 4-7 shows the nature images generated during the Compose process in DeepZoom and the default zoomed-out view when the application runs.

Figure 4-7. *Zoomed-out (default) views of the nature images*

This entire Deep Zoom example was built in the Deep Zoom Composer in a matter of a few minutes. After composing the images, as shown in Figure 4-7, you need to export them. During the Export process, within the custom tab, select the Output type as Silverlight Deep Zoom, populate the name (DeepZoomImages in our example), select the Export as a collection (multiple images) option, and select the Templates as Deep Zoom Classic + Source (see Figure 4-8).

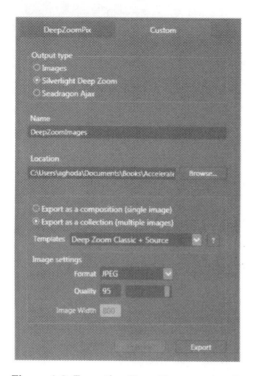

Figure 4-8. Exporting Deep Zoom project (images) as Silverlight Deep Zoom Classic project with source

Upon clicking on the Export button, you will create a traditional Silverlight project with Deep Zoom capabilities. The Deep Zoom Composer also includes, as part of the generation, all the code necessary to hook the MultiScaleImage control up to user input. Between the `MouseWheelHelper.cs` class and the event handlers in `Page.xaml.cs` (in the exported Silverlight application as the output), users can click to zoom, use the mouse wheel to zoom, and also click and drag to pan around the scene. Key items of the generated project are

- `GeneratedImages` folder under the `ClientBin` folder. This folder contains the `dzc_output.xml` file and required output images (breakout images—image parts) and output files

- `MouseWheelHelper.cs` helper class to support the mouse wheel operations for zoom-in and zoom-out functionality

- `Page.xaml` and `Page.xaml.cs` file representing the main user interface of the Deep Zoom application and key Deep Zoom code-based features implementation

- `Images` folder containing different icons to control Deep Zoom application features

Note The current version of the Deep Zoom Composer features the Silverlight 2 project, which can be migrated to Silverlight 3. However, at present there is no easy migration to the Silverlight 4 version. So what I did is the manual migration. For that I created a DeepZoomIntegration Silverlight 4 application project and added a `GeneratedImages` folder under the `ClientBin` folder and a `MouseWheelHelper.cs` file to the Silverlight project, and copied and pasted code from `Page.xaml` and `Page.xaml.cs` to `MainPage.xaml` and `MainPage.xaml.cs` files, and finally added an `images` folder to the Silverlight project.

Finally, I have just updated the MultiScaleImage element within the `MainPage.xaml` file to add Width, Height and Margin properties, as shown here in the highlighted fonts. This should provide a better user experience.

```
<MultiScaleImage x:Name="msi" Height="600" Width="800" Margin="10"/>
```

The Source attribute of the MultiScaleImage control is set to `dzc_output.xml`, either within the XAML code or under the MainPage_Loaded event, as shown here, enabling the Deep Zoom feature:

```
this.msi.Source = new DeepZoomImageTileSource(new
    Uri("GeneratedImages/dzc_output.xml", UriKind.Relative));
```

Now if you run the project you should see the Deep Zoom feature in action, as shown in Figure 4-9 (default zoomed-out view) and Figure 4-10 (zoomed-in view).

Figure 4-9. Deep Zoom application with the default zoomed-out view

Figure 4-10. Zooming in to the image

Media (Video and Audio)

Rich media integration is one of the main selling points of Silverlight. Starting with the Olympics in 2008, Microsoft has proved Silverlight's media integration capabilities, such as high-quality media integration, smooth streaming, secured media delivery, and support of offline media integration. Since then, commercial adoption of Silverlight for rich media integration, providing different types of media services, is on the rise. A few of the highlights are NFL, Netflix, and Tata Nano using the Silverlight platform to provide different levels of media-related services. The following summarizes Silverlight's key media integration features:

- High Quality Media Integration by supporting different types of media formats, such as H.264/Advanced Audio Coding (AAC)/MP4, and RAW audio/video pipeline, which supports third-party codecs, to provide HD-quality video services on a broad range of media formats.

- Smooth streaming capabilities using IIS Media Services (`www.iis.net/media`) and adaptive media streaming enable high-performing and smooth, live and on-demand, high-quality and high-definition (HD) (1080p) media streaming in the online and offline (using out of browser feature) mode with improved media synchronization, by automatically adjusting bit rates based on the network bandwidth.

- Graphic Processor Unit (GPU) hardware acceleration helps to deliver high-performing HD media experience in both in-browser and full-screen modes.

- Digital rights management (DRM) for media streaming enables protected distribution of digital media. Silverlight DRM for media streaming enables Advanced Encryption Standard (AES)–based encryption or Windows Media DRM of media files and allows protected distribution of digital media. Silverlight 4 also introduced support for offline DRM, powered by PlayReady for OOB applications, to deliver media content in offline mode in a more protected and managed environment.

You can reference a media file using either HTTP, HTTPS, or UNC protocol, or using MMS, RTSP, or RTSPT. The latter three protocols—MMS, RTSP, and RTSPT—actually will fall back to HTTP. Using the MMS protocol causes Silverlight to attempt to stream the media first; if that fails, it will attempt to download the media progressively. Other protocols work in reverse—Silverlight attempts to progressively download the media first, and if that fails, the media is streamed.

Supported Media Format

Silverlight supports a broad range of media formats. Each media format can support different media delivery methods. Table 4-9 summarizes supported media formats and possible delivery mechanisms.

Table 4-9. Supported Media Formats and Delivery Mechanisms by Silverlight

Media Format	Delivery Method
Windows Media • WMV1: Windows Media Video 7 • WMV2: Windows Media Video 8 • WMV3: Windows Media Video 9 • WMVA: Windows Media Video Advanced Profile—non-VC-1 • WVC1: Windows Media Video Advanced Profile—VC-1 • WMA Standard: Windows Media Audio 7, 8, and 9	• Progressive Download • Windows Media Streaming over HTTP • Advanced Stream Redirector (ASX) for Client-Side Playlist • Server-Side Playlist
MP3 • ISO MPEG Layer III (MP3)	• Progressive Download
MP4 • H264 (ITU-T H.264 / ISO MPEG-4 AVC) • Advanced Audio Coding (AAC-LC)	• Progressive Download • Advanced Stream Redirector (ASX) for Client-Side Playlist • PlayReady DRM

Advanced Audio Coding (AAC-LC, HE-AAC)	• Advanced Stream Redirector (ASX)
Advanced Stream Redirector (ASX), with `.asx`, `.wax`, `.wvx`, `.wmx`, or `.wpl` file extensions	• Advanced Stream Redirector (ASX)
Raw Audio/Video	• MediaStreamSource

Unsupported Media Format

The following media formats are still not supported by Silverlight 4.

- Interlaced video content
- Windows Media Screen
- Windows Media Audio Professional
- Windows Media Voice
- Combination of Windows Media Video and MP3 (WMV video + MP3 audio)
- Combination of WMV with AAC-LC
- VC-1 in MP4
- Multichannel (5.1 surround) audio content

The MediaElement Class

The `System.Windows.Controls.MediaElement` is the central media control providing media integration capability in Silverlight. We looked at the MediaElement control earlier in the Bitmap APIs section of this chapter. This section will provide more details on this class.

The key properties, methods, and events of `MediaElement` are shown in Tables 4-10, 4-11, and 4-12, respectively.

Table 4-10. Key Properties of `MediaElement`

Property	Type	Description
`Attributes`	`Dictionary` `<string,string>`	A collection of attributes; read-only.
`AudioStreamCount`	`int`	The number of audio streams in the current media file; read-only.
`AudioStreamIndex`	`int`	The index of the audio stream that is currently playing with a video.

AutoPlay	bool	If true (default state), the media will begin playing immediately after Source is set (i.e., it will transition into the Buffering state and then into the Playing state automatically). If false, the media will not start playing automatically and will remain in the Stopped state.
Balance	double	The ratio of volume across stereo speakers. The range is between -1 (100% volume to the left-side speakers) to 1 (100% volume to the right-side speakers). The default is 0, which means evenly distributed volume to right- and left-side speakers.
BufferingProgress	double	The current buffering progress, between 0 and 1. Multiply by 100 to get a percentage value; read-only.
BufferingTime	TimeSpan	The amount of time to buffer; the default is five seconds.
CanPause	bool	Returns true if the media can be paused via the Pause method; read-only.
CanSeek	bool	Returns true if the current position in the media can be set via the Seek method; read-only.
CurrentState	MediaElementState	The current state of the media. Possible states include Closed, Opening, Individualizing, AcquiringLicense, Buffering, Playing, Paused, and Stopped. It is possible for several state transitions to happen in quick succession, so you may not witness every state transition happen; read-only.
DownloadProgress	double	The current download progress, between 0 and 1. Multiply by 100 to get a percentage value; read-only.
DownloadProgressOffset	double	The offset in the media where the current download started. Used when media is progressively downloaded; read-only.
DroppedFramesPerSecond	double	Provides number of frames dropped per second by the media; read-only.
IsMuted	bool	Used to set or determine whether audio is currently muted.
LicenseAcquirer		Gets or sets the LicenseAcquirer associated with the MediaElement. LicenseAcquirer handles acquiring licenses for DRM-encrypted content.

Markers	TimelineMarker Collection	Accesses the collection of timeline markers. Although the collection itself is read-only, it is possible to dynamically add timeline markers. These are temporary since they are not saved to the media and are reset if the Source property is changed.
NaturalDuration	Duration	Duration of the currently loaded media; read-only.
NaturalVideoHeight	int	The height of the video based on what the video file itself reports; read-only.
NaturalVideoWidth	int	The width of the video based on what the video file itself reports; read-only.
Position	TimeSpan	The current position in the media file.
RenderedFramesPerSecond	double	Gets the number of frames per second being rendered by the media.
Source	Uri	Sets or retrieves the source of the current media file.
Stretch	Stretch	Gets or sets how the media fills its bounding rectangle. See the "Images" section of this chapter for a discussion of this property.
Volume	double	Gets or sets the volume of the media based on a linear scale. The value can be between 0 and 1; the default is 0.5.

Table 4-11. Key Methods of MediaElement

Method	Description
Pause	Pauses the media at the current position if it is possible to pause. If the media cannot be paused, this method does nothing.
Play	Plays the media from the current position if the media can be played.

RequestLog	Sends a request to generate a log, which will then be raised through the **LogReady** event. What this method does depends on the current state of the media. **Closed**: No operation. **Opening**: Queues the request and raises the log when the **MediaOpened** event is raised. **Individualizing**: Generates the log. **AcquiringLicense**: Generates the log. **Buffering**: Generates the log. **Playing**: Generates the log. **Paused**: Generates the log. **Stopped**: Generates the log.
SetSource	Used when you want to set the source of the media to a **Stream** object. Use the **Source** property to set the URI of the media file.
Stop	Stops the media from playing, and sets the current position to 0.

Table 4-12. Key Events of **MediaElement**

Event	Description
BufferingProgressChanged	Fires each time **BufferingProgress** changes by at least 0.05 or when it reaches 1.0.
CurrentStateChanged	Fires when the state of the media changes. If states transition quickly (such as bouncing between buffering and playing), some transitions can be lost.
DownloadProgressChanged	Fires when the progress of the downloading media changes. Use the **DownloadProgress** property to discover the current progress.
LogReady	Occurs when the log is ready. Note that this event is only raised for progressive downloads. It can be raised either by a specific request (the **RequestLog** method) or by the generation of a log due to an automatic log event such as **Seek**, **Stop**, or **SourceChanged**.
MarkerReached	Fires when a timeline marker is reached. The event handler method is passed a **TimelineMarkerRoutedEventArgs** instance, which exposes a **Marker** property of type **TimelineMarker**.
MediaEnded	Fires when the media is done playing.
MediaFailed	Fires when there is a problem with the media source (e.g., when the media can't be found or when the format is incorrect).
MediaOpened	Fires after the media file is opened and validated, and the headers are read.

Since a variety of state changes can happen to media, such as a video switching from playing to buffering when it needs to load more of the file, in most applications you will want to implement an event handler for `CurrentStateChanged`. The states and state transitions are shown in Figure 4-11. The one transition left out of this diagram is when a new source is set for `MediaElement`, the state will change to the `Opening` state, unless the source is set to null value that will result in the state changing to the `Closed` state.

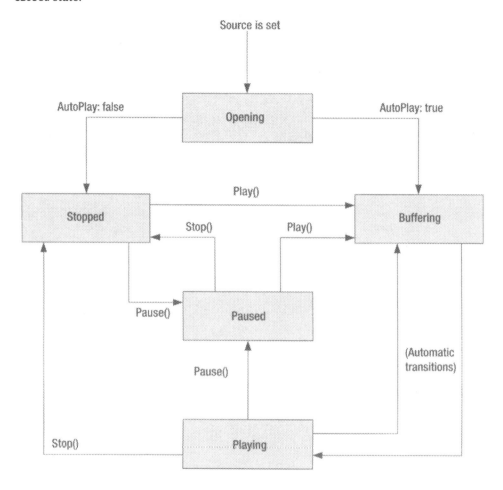

Figure 4-11. States and state transitions of `MediaElement`

Caution Avoid "not-specified" states of the media by checking the CurrentState property. As an example, avoid playing media while it's in the opening state.

While it's fairly simple to specify a source for `MediaElement`, set `AutoPlay` to `true` (which is actually the default state, so there is no need to specify specifically), and let it just go, you probably want to build something with more control for the user. Let's enhance the previous video capture example we created earlier to put more controls around the video features. Figure 4-12 shows the enhanced application outcome with additional controls (Play, Pause, Stop, and Continuous Play) around the video player.

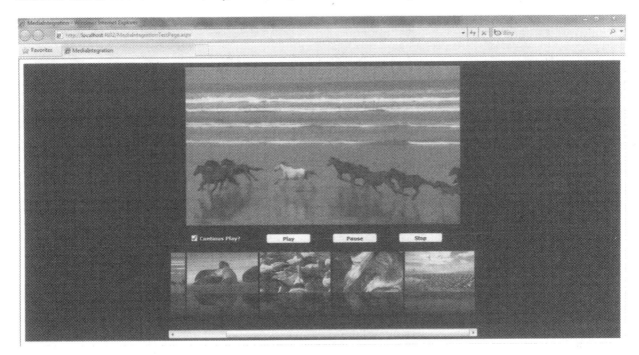

Figure 4-12. Simple video player with position indicator

Revisit the MediaIntegration project and open the `WriteableBitmapDemonstration.xaml` file to place a check box to let the user play the video continuously, as well as three buttons to control the video play—play, pause, and stop functionality. For that we will add a horizontally-aligned StackPanel control between the existing MediaElement and ScrollViewer controls. And add a CheckBox control and three Button controls, as shown here.

```
<StackPanel Name="VideoControls"
    Orientation="Horizontal" Background="DarkBlue"
    Height="30" Width="700" Margin="5">
    <CheckBox Name="ContinuousPlay"
        Background="AntiqueWhite" Content="Continuous Play?"
        Foreground="White" FontWeight="Bold"
        Margin="50,5,0,5" Width="120"/>
    <Button Name="VideoPlay"
        Background="AntiqueWhite" Content="Play"
        FontWeight="Bold" Click="VideoPlay_Click"
        Margin="50,5,0,5" Width="100"/>
    <Button Name="VideoPause"
        Background="AntiqueWhite" Content="Pause"
        FontWeight="Bold" Click="VideoPause_Click"
```

```
            Margin="50,5,0,5" Width="100"/>
        <Button Name="VideoStop"
            Background="AntiqueWhite" Content="Stop"
            FontWeight="Bold" Click="VideoStop_Click"
            Margin="50,5,0,5" Width="100" />
</StackPanel>
```

Notice that each button has the related Click event defined. Now let's write code-behind for each Click event, which is very straightforward. The basic logic will be to check the CurrentState of the MediaElement, and if the MediaElement is in the right state, perform the clicked functionality (Play, Pause, or Stop) or do nothing.

The following code-snippet shows the play button's click event, and we call the Play method of MediaElement only if the CurrentState is Paused or Stopped, or the CurrentState is not Opening.

```
private void VideoPlay_Click(object sender, RoutedEventArgs e)
{
    if
      (sourceVideo.CurrentState != MediaElementState.Opening ||
       sourceVideo.CurrentState == MediaElementState.Stopped ||
       sourceVideo.CurrentState == MediaElementState.Paused)
         sourceVideo.Play();
}
```

Similarly, implement the pause and stop button click events, as shown here:

```
private void VideoStop_Click(object sender, RoutedEventArgs e)
{
    if
      (sourceVideo.CurrentState == MediaElementState.Playing ||
       sourceVideo.CurrentState == MediaElementState.Paused)
         sourceVideo.Stop();
}

private void VideoPause_Click(object sender, RoutedEventArgs e)
{
    if (sourceVideo.CurrentState == MediaElementState.Playing)
        sourceVideo.Pause();
}
```

Go ahead and build and run the project. You should see that the video starts automatically and the Play, Pause, and Stop buttons are now working as expected. However, you will notice two things that are not working correctly. First, once the video finishes and you click on the Play button, the video will not start, since the video is finished and on the last frame. To make it work, you need to click on the Stop button and click back on the Play button. The Stop will reset the video to the first frame. Now if you click on Play, everything should work fine. Second, there is no impact if you click the Continuous Play check box, even though the video *should* start from the beginning automatically as soon as it ends. To achieve these two items automatically, you can implement the required code under the MediaEnded event of the MediaElement control. Here, I have updated the MediaElement XAML code to implement the MediaEnded event, as shown here (highlighted font).

```
<MediaElement x:Name="sourceVideo"
    Source="Resources/Wildlife.wmv" Cursor="Hand"
    Height="350" Width="635" Margin="10"
    MouseLeftButtonDown="sourceVideo_MouseLeftButtonDown"
    MediaEnded="sourceVideo_MediaEnded"/>
```

Finally, let's implement the `MediaEnded` event. As mentioned earlier, here we call the `Stop` method of the `MediaElement` to resolve the first issue (of the Play button not working once the video has ended), and then we Play the video again if the Continuous check box is selected.

```
private void sourceVideo_MediaEnded
    (object sender, RoutedEventArgs e)
{
    sourceVideo.Stop();
    if (ContinuousPlay.IsChecked == true)
        sourceVideo.Play();
}
```

There's another aspect to media players that is common for users to see: a time signature displaying the length of the video and the current position as it plays. The best approach to add the current media position to a user interface is to use a timer to poll the `Position` property of `MediaElement` and then display it. The best timer to use is `DispatcherTimer` since it works on the user interface thread, allowing you to modify user interface elements directly. (We'll take a closer look at threading and `DispatcherTimer` in Chapter 12.)

For demonstration purposes I have created the following code. If you want, go ahead and integrate it in our existing media integration project. To implement this functionality, you can use TextBlock controls to update the position, which you can also map with the Slider control (the related XAML is straightforward and is not shown).

The following code-snippet creates an instance of the timer and sets it to raise the `Tick` event every quarter of a second:

```
timer = new DispatcherTimer();
timer.Interval = new TimeSpan(0, 0, 0, 0, 250);
timer.Tick += new EventHandler(timer_Tick);
```

The `Tick` event handler calls `showCurrentPosition` to update the user interface, and the `CurrentStateChanged` event of `MediaElement` is handled in order to start/stop the timer:

```
void timer_Tick(object sender, EventArgs e)
{
    showCurrentPosition();
}

private void showCurrentPosition()
{
    currentPositionText.Text = string.Format("{0:00}:{1:00}",
        sourceVideo.Position.Minutes,
        sourceVideo.Position.Seconds);
}
```

```
private void sourceVideo_CurrentStateChanged
    (object sender, RoutedEventArgs e)
{
    MediaElementState currentState =
        ((MediaElement)sender).CurrentState;
    currentStateTextBlock.Text = currentState.ToString();
    if (currentState == MediaElementState.Paused ||
            currentState == MediaElementState.Stopped)
        timer.Stop();
    else
        timer.Start();
}
```

Note With the introduction of support to UDP multicast clients by introducing two new classes—
UdpSingleSourceMulticastClient and UdpAnySourceMulticastClient—to the System.Net.Sockets, the
Silverlight 4 MultiMedia element can support multicast streaming for the media files. We will get more details on
this topic in Chapter 5.

Timeline Markers

A timeline marker is a point of time in a media file that has metadata associated with it. A specific
timeline marker (of the System.Windows.Media.TimelineMarker class) contains three members: Text and
Type, both of type String; and Time, of type TimeSpan. Both Text and Type are arbitrary, so you can
configure these however you want. Timeline markers can be embedded in the video file either using an
editor such as Microsoft Expression Encoder or dynamically during program execution at run time.
Figure 4-13 shows the Markers pane in Expression Encoder. As shown in the Figure 4-13, I added one
timeline marker, with the value SecondClip, on the first frame of the second clip of the Wildlife.wmv
video. The video contains multiple nature clips and here I have marked each transition from one clip to
another. Select appropriate metadata to display the thumbnail and to create the key frame. If this were a
full-length nature documentary, the timeline markers could be used to initiate different audio files in
sync with events happening in the video. Let's quickly look at how you can add these markers to the
existing video step-by-step and integrate with the Silverlight application.

- First, you need to import the existing video to the project by clicking on the Import
  button available at the bottom left of the project window (see Figure 4-13).

- Next, add the marker. While you are playing the video you can click on the "+"
  icon on the Markers tab. The "+" button is available at the bottom left of the
  Markers tab (see Figure 4-13). You can see the added marker displayed with the
  metadata at the bottom right of the figure under the Markers tab.

- Each added marker is also indicated on the timeline, providing a visual position of
  the custom markers on the video.

- To update the existing marker's time to the current playhead position, you need to
  click on the icon button available at the bottom right of the Markers tab.

- To integrate with Silverlight, click on the Output tab (available next to the Markers tab), and set the template and thumbnail type in the Output tab. Once you define the Silverlight template and thumbnail type, upon encoding it will also provide you a preview and create the appropriate XAP file.

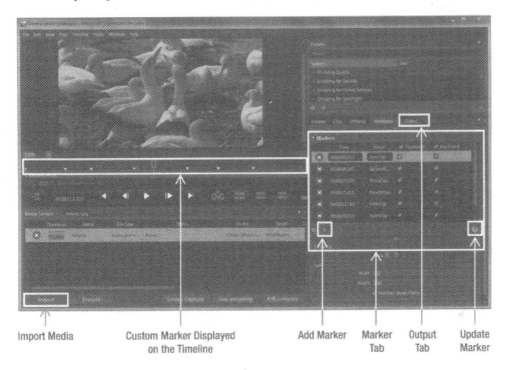

Figure 4-13. Editing the interface for timeline markers in Expression Encoder

If you define these dynamically, they are good only as long as a particular `MediaElement` exists and references the same video file. If you load a new video file into a MediaElement control, the timeline marker collection is reset.

The `Markers` property of `MediaElement` acts much like a regular collection since it implements the `IList` interface. Here's an example of creating a new `TimelineMarker` and adding it to a particular `MediaElement` named `sourceVideo`:

```
TimelineMarker mark = new TimelineMarker();
mark.Type = "Commercial Cue";
mark.Text = "First Commercial";
mark.Time = new TimeSpan(0, 5, 11);
sourceVideo.Markers.Add(mark);
```

Regardless of whether markers are defined in the media file itself or during program execution, you can use the `MarkerReached` event to perform custom processing when a specific marker is reached. The `TimelineMarkerRoutedEventArgs` class provides a `Marker` member to access the specific marker that was reached from the event handler.

Web Camera and Microphone Integration

One of the widely demanded features—web camera and microphone integration—is finally introduced in Silverlight 4, with the introduction of new set of APIs to identify the attached audio and video devices to the computer, and play and capture the audio and video. It also supports capturing raw audio and video and processing using **VideoSink** and **AudioSink** classes, which can eventually begin a new era of empowering developers to create innovative media-driven applications, including live audio and video conferencing.

The CaptureDeviceConfiguration Class

The **System.Windows.Media** namespace is in the center of achieving this functionality. To achieve the basic functionality of identifying and connecting to audio and video devices integrated with the machine, **System.Windows.Media** provides the **CaptureDeviceConfiguration** helper class, which allows programmatic access to identify and capture audio and video devices, and request client permission to access the audio and video from the available and selected devices. The static property and methods of the **CaptureDeviceConfiguration** class are shown in Table 4-13 and 4-14.

Table 4-13. Static Property of the **CaptureDeviceConfiguration** *Class*

Property	Type	Description
AllowedDeviceAccess	bool	Returns true if user has granted the device access by responding to the dialog requesting client access for the current session

Table 4-14. Static Methods of the **CaptureDeviceConfiguration** *Class*

Method	Description
GetAvailableAudioCaptureDevices	If access granted, returns a collection of AudioCaptureDevice objects providing details of available audio devices to the client machine
GetAvailableVideoCaptureDevices	If access granted, returns a collection of VideoCaptureDevice objects providing details of available video devices to the client machine
GetDefaultAudioCaptureDevice	If access granted, returns an AudioCaptureDevice object providing details of the default audio device to the client machine.
GetDefaultVideoCaptureDevice	If access granted, returns a VideoCaptureDevice object providing details of the default video device to the client machine.
RequestDeviceAccess	Requests access to all integrated audio and video devices on the client machine to capture audio and video by displaying a dialog box.

Figure 4-14 shows the consent dialog box presented to the user on every new session, to grant permission to access audio and video device(s), and capture audio and video. User has option to click on "Remember my answer" checkbox to retain the user preference for the related application. Once it is clicked, then onwards you should not receive the consent dialog box asking user permission until the settings have changed.

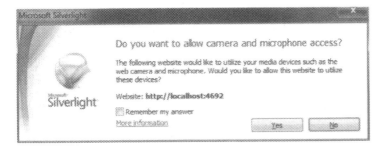

Figure 4-14. Request device access dialog box to grant permission to access and capture audio and video devices integrated with client machines

As shown in Figure 4-15, now if you look at the Silverlight configuration dialog box (by right clicking on the Silverlight application and selecting Silverlight option), you will see a Permission tab displaying permissions set for the user, which can be changed by using Allow, Remove or Deny options.

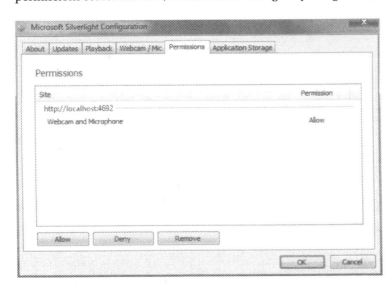

Figure 4-15. Permissions tab within the Silverlight configuration dialog box to display and change the selection of the current site settings

The CaptureDevice, AudioCaptureDevice, and VideoCaptureDevice Classes

The CaptureDevice class of System.Windows.Media provides common properties of AudioCaptureDevice and VideoCaptureDevice classes. Once the permission is granted, it basically shows which devices are connected to the application, which you can also find in the Webcam/Mic tab of the Silverlight Configuration dialog box (that you can open by right-clicking on the application and selecting the Silverlight option). Figure 4-16 shows the Webcam/Mic tab of the Silverlight configuration dialog box detailing that both default audio and video devices are selected for that given session. Manually, you can change the device selection by selecting one of the available audio and video devices in that tab.

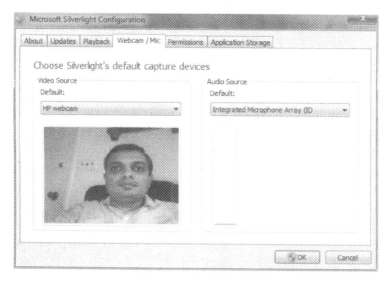

Figure 4-16. Webcam/Mic tab within the Silverlight configuration dialog box to display and change the selection of the captured audio and video devices

Key properties of the CaptureDevice class are shown in Table 4-15.

Table 4-15. Key Properties of the CaptureDevice Class

Property	Type	Description
FriendlyName	string	Provides connected captured audio/video device's friendlier UI display name
IsDefaultDevice	bool	Returns if the captured device (audio/video) is a default device or not

Inherited from the CaptureDevice class, the AudioCaptureDevice class provides further details specifically on the supported format of the captured audio device. The properties of the AudioCaptureDevice class are shown in Table 4-16.

Table 4-16. Key Properties of the AudioCaptureDevice Class

Property	Type	Description
AudioFrameSize	int	Gets or sets the audio frame size in milliseconds (default value is 1000 milliseconds). Mainly used in sampling the raw audio using the AudioSink class.
DesiredFormat	AudioFormat	Gets or sets the audio format as an AudioFormat object for the captured audio device. Default is null reference. The AudioFormat class provides the specific technical details such as BitsPerSample, Channels, SamplesPerSecond, and WaveFormat of the audio format.
SupportedFormats	AudioFormat	Returns a generic collection of the AudioFormat objects detailing supported audio formats for the captured audio device.

Inherited from the CaptureDevice class, the VideoCaptureDevice class provides further details specifically on the supported format of the captured video device. The key properties of the VideoCaptureDevice class are shown in Table 4-17.

Table 4-17. Key Properties of the VideoCaptureDevice Class

Property	Type	Description
DesiredFormat	VideoFormat	Gets or sets the video format as an AudioFormat object for the captured audio device. Default is null reference. The VideoFormat class provides the specific technical details such as FramesPerSecond, Height, PixelFormat, Stride, and Width of the video format.
SupportedFormats	VideoFormat	Returns a generic collection of the VideoFormat objects detailing supported audio formats for the captured audio device.

The CaptureSource Class

The CaptureSource class of System.Windows.Media provides a set of APIs to capture and play video and audio from the connected video device, in the online and offline (out of browser) mode, even capturing a video frame to provide a WriteableBitmap image file and convert it to a static image. The key properties, methods, and events of the CaptureSource class are shown in Tables 4-18, 4-19, and 4-20.

Table 4-18. Properties of CaptureSource Class

Property	Type	Description
AudioCaptureDevice	AudioCaptureDevice	Gets or sets the integrated audio capture device. If you want to capture only video then set AudioCaptureDevice value to null.
State	CaptureState	Returns the current capture stated of the associated audio or video devices. The CaptureState contains three members: Stopped when CaptureSource's Stop method is called and the capture is stopped and completed; Started when CaptureSource's Start method is called and capture is still active; and Failed when the requested capture has failed or no operation has started yet.
VideoCaptureDevice	VideoCaptureDevice	Gets or sets the integrated video capture device. If you want to capture only audio then set VideoCaptureDevice value to null.

Table 4-19. Method of the CaptureSource Class

Method	Description
CaptureImageAsync	Initiates an asynchronous image capture request. You can retrieve the captured image by handling CaptureImageCompleted event and by calling CaptureImageCompletedEventArgs.Result method from the event data.
Start	Starts the audio and/or video capture devices relevant to CaptureSource.
Stop	Stops the audio and/or video capture devices relevant to CaptureSource.

Table 4-20. Key Event of the CaptureSource Class

Event	Description
CaptureFailed	Raised when the capture process has failed to capture from the requested audio and/or video devices.
CaptureImageCompleted	Raised when the capture image process has completed and an image is returned. You can retrieve the captured image by calling CaptureImageCompletedEventArgs.Result method from the event data.

Developing an Example

As you might have noticed from the previous example, it should not be too difficult to develop a sample example demonstrating connection to the integrated audio and video device, capture and play video, and take a snap shot from the running live video. For that we will enhance our earlier developed Media Integration application.

Add a new Silverlight user control and name it WebCameraAndMicrophoneIntegration. Now copy the XAML and code-behind code from WriteableBitmapDemonstrationwithVideoPlayer to replicate the video player functionality with the image capture capabilities. Now we will make a few modifications in the XAML and code-behind code to replace the video player (MediaElement) with the live video from the web camera. We also need only two buttons—one to start and play capturing video and another one to stop capturing video. We will continue with the left click event to capture the image.

The following is the portion of the modified XAML code of the `WriteableBitmapDemonstrationwithVideoPlayer.xaml` file.

```
...
<Rectangle x:Name="sourceVideo" Fill="White"
    Height="350" Width = "650" Margin="10"
    MouseLeftButtonDown="sourceVideo_MouseLeftButtonDown"/>
<StackPanel Name="VideoControls" Orientation="Horizontal"
    HorizontalAlignment="Center" Background="DarkBlue"
    Height="30" Width="700" Margin="5">
    <Button Name="CaptureVideo" Background="AntiqueWhite"
        Content="Capture Web Camera" FontWeight="Bold"
        Margin="175,5,0,5" Width="150"
        Click="CaptureVideo_Click"/>
    <Button Name="VideoStop" Background="AntiqueWhite"
        Content="Stop" FontWeight="Bold"
        Margin="50,5,0,5" Width="150"
        Click="VideoStop_Click"/>
</StackPanel>
...
```

As shown, we have replaced the MediaElement with the Rectangle, which we will fill with the live video captured from the integrated webcam. Also, we removed the not-required check box and pause button and renamed the play button CaptureVideo. To align these two buttons, we changed the Margin property appropriately.

The changes in the code-behind `WriteableBitmapDemonstrationwithVideoPlayer.cs` file are also minimal. First define the `CaptureSource` class variable at the `WebCameraAndMicroPhoneIntegration` class level and create the new instance of `CaptureSource` under the Loaded event, as shown here in the highlighted fonts:

```
...
CaptureSource CapturedSource;

void WebCameraAndMicroPhoneIntegration_Loaded(object sender, RoutedEventArgs e)
{
    DefineImageTransform();
    DefineOpacityMask();
```

```
CapturedSource = new CaptureSource();
}
```

Next remove not-required events code (VideoPlay and VideoPause click events) and populate the CaptureVideo_Click event to start capturing the video through the web camera. For that you must first make sure that the video/audio device is not active and release it for our purpose by stopping it. Then set the **CaptureSource** to the default client machine's video and audio devices by using the **GetDefaultVideoCaptureDevice** and **GetDefaultAudioCaptureDevice** methods of the **CaptureDeviceConfiguration** class. We will use VideoBrush and set the captured video as a source of the VideoBrush, Finally, if access is granted to capture the audio and video, start capturing it by calling the **Start** method of **CaptureSource**. And implement **CaptureImageCompleted** event handler on the **CaptureSource** to handle still image capture. By implementing this method, you will receive the current video frame as a WriteableBitmap that we use as a BitmapSource of the image and apply the required transformation.

```
private void CaptureVideo_Click(object sender, RoutedEventArgs e)
{
    if (CapturedSource != null)
    {
        CapturedSource.Stop();

        CapturedSource.VideoCaptureDevice =
           CaptureDeviceConfiguration.GetDefaultVideoCaptureDevice();
        CapturedSource.AudioCaptureDevice =
           CaptureDeviceConfiguration.GetDefaultAudioCaptureDevice();

        VideoBrush vidBrush = new VideoBrush();
        vidBrush.SetSource(CapturedSource);
        sourceVideo.Fill = vidBrush;

        if (CaptureDeviceConfiguration.AllowedDeviceAccess ||
            CaptureDeviceConfiguration.RequestDeviceAccess())
        {
            CapturedSource.Start();

            CapturedSource.CaptureImageCompleted +=
                new EventHandler<CaptureImageCompletedEventArgs>((s, args) =>
                {
                    Image thumbImage = new Image();
                    thumbImage.Height = 90;
                    thumbImage.Margin = new Thickness(2, 0, 2, 0);
                    thumbImage.Source = args.Result;

                    Image reflectedImage = new Image();
                    reflectedImage.Height = 90;
                    reflectedImage.Margin = new Thickness(2, 0, 2, 0);
                    reflectedImage.Source = args.Result;
                    reflectedImage.OpacityMask = lnrGradBrush;
                    reflectedImage.RenderTransform = imageTransform;

                    StackPanel sp = new StackPanel();
```

```
                sp.Children.Add(thumbImage);
                sp.Children.Add(reflectedImage);

                thumbsPanel.Children.Add(sp);

                scrollArea.UpdateLayout();
                double scrollPos = thumbsPanel.ActualWidth;
                scrollArea.ScrollToHorizontalOffset(scrollPos);
            });
        }
    }
}
```

Now update the sourceVideo_MouseLeftButton event to capture the video frame as an image by calling CaptureImageAsync method of CaptuerSource. The following code snippet shows this event:

```
private void sourceVideo_MouseLeftButtonDown
    (object sender, MouseButtonEventArgs e)
{
    if (CapturedSource.State == CaptureState.Started &&
        CapturedSource != null)
    {
        CapturedSource.CaptureImageAsync();
    }
}
```

Finally, the only thing left to change is the VideoStop_Click event of the button, which is very straightforward. Just check if CaptureSource is not null and then call the Stop method of CaptureSource.

```
private void VideoStop_Click(object sender, RoutedEventArgs e)
{
    if (CapturedSource != null)
    {
        CapturedSource.Stop();
    }
}
```

Now if you build and run the project, you should see the updated application. Once you click on the Capture Web Camera button, you will get the grant access dialog box; if you grant the access, the rectangle will be filled with the captured live video and audio. If you left-click on the running video area (rectangle), the current frame should be captured with the proper transformation as a thumbnail in the thumbnail pane. If you click on the Stop button, the video capturing process should stop. Figure 4-17 shows the resulting outcome, with me sitting in my nice and small home office.

***Figure 4-17.** Demonstrating web camera and microphone capturing and taking snapshot image capabilities*

So far, so good—in terms of some basic functionalities. However, in the Silverlight 4 version, it would be a bit challenging to achieve all the desired commercial functionalities, such as processing, saving, and streaming synchronized captured video and audio in the compress format, and so forth. At present you can somewhat achieve this functionality by processing the captured uncompressed raw audio and video streams using the `AudioSink`, `VideoSink`, and `MediaStreamSources` classes. No matter what, this is still a right step in a right direction, and if you are comparing it with Adobe Flash, you will be surprised to see that Silverlight is getting closer to dominating this area.

Note There is a sample project called ManagedMediaHelpers in the MSDN Code Gallery (http://code.msdn.microsoft.com/ManagedMediaHelpers), which is provided by Larry Olson, demonstrating the MediaStreamSource capabilities and providing a set of class libraries for MP3 file streams, test projects, and sample projects to interact MediaStreamSource with MediaElement.

Windows Azure Platform–based Hosting and Media Delivery Services for Silverlight Applications

Microsoft started with a free beta Silverlight Streaming service to host and stream (progressive download) videos to Silverlight applications. It has provided 10GB of storage space free, provided each video is no longer than ten minutes (or 105MB) and is encoded at a bit rate of no more than 1.4Mbps. However, this service has been discontinued since January 31, 2010. This section provides a very brief overview of the Windows Azure Platform for Silverlight and how to publish video content for Silverlight applications. For details visit **www.microsoft.com/windowsazure**.

Subscribing to Windows Azure Platform Services

Now a user can use the Windows Azure Platform–based hosting and delivery services to host videos for Silverlight applications. However, this time it's not a free service, and you get different options for subscribing to the services (you will need Windows Azure Service for this feature—no need of SQL Azure or AppFabric services). Visit **www.microsoft.com/windowsazure/offers** to get more information on the different offers (services) available and to create a Windows Azure account. You are now all set to create services on the Windows Azure platform.

While you create the storage account, please note the primary access key and unique storage account EndPoint name. You should also enable the CDN to provide better performance on video streaming.

Publishing Silverlight Applications Video Content

Login with your Windows Live ID and create a new Storage Account Service to upload videos and content for your Silverlight applications.

Create a non-private container and use the following two options to upload the video/content for Silverlight applications:

1. Download Azure Publisher Expression Encoder Add-In from the codeplex to publish encoded video as blob to your Azure storage account directly from Expression Encoder. Visit **www.codeplex.com/AzurePublisher** to get this add-in.

2. Use the Cloud Storage Studio tool (**www.cerebrata.com/Products/CloudStorageStudio**) to upload videos and other content as blob to the Azure storage account.

This book is not focused on the Windows Azure platform and how to utilize Azure platform for Silverlight application and content publishing. Visit Microsoft site to get details on the Windows Azure platform - www.microsoft.com/windowsazure/windowsazure/. Get more details on how to publish Silverlight applications video content to the Windows Azure platform using Azure Publisher Expression Encoder Add-in, visit David Sayed's blog, http://blogs.msdn.com/david_sayed/archive/2010/01/07/hosting-videos-on-windows-azure.aspx.

Streaming Packaged Images and Media Files

While you can download images and media file by file, sometimes an application requires a collection of related images or other media before it can start. One example of this is a game that might need a number of images to display scenes, characters, and the background. You can package these resources into a single ZIP archive at design time, deploy it to the hosting server, and download it at run time. After downloading the ZIP file, using the WebClient class, you can save its stream using the StreamResourceInfo class. Use Application.GetResourceStream to stream the package. You can use this approach to store references to other media files (video/audio) and even any arbitrary data you might need to download on demand.

Visit the WebClient class section of the next chapter, which demonstrates these features by enhancing the image viewer application that will download the ZIP package of the images and display the downloaded image.

Summary

So far, we've been laying the groundwork to build a Silverlight application. This chapter covered the pieces most popularly associated with Silverlight since its 1.0 days: displaying images and media. Silverlight 3introduced more capabilities to handle images with the use of the Bitmap API, and to develop high-performing applications, by enabling GPU hardware acceleration and bitmap caching for Silverlight applications. You also saw how to manage and manipulate images, including exploring the MultiScaleImage control, which provides the Deep Zoom user experience. Next, we examined video and audio via the MediaElement control and reviewed new Silverlight 4 capabilities of Web Camera and Microphone integration. We also explored the Windows Azure Platform–based Silverlight application and content hosting and streaming capabilities. The media support is a rich and deep topic that cannot fully be explored in a single chapter, but you should have a good grasp of the possibilities when using Silverlight. As explained, Silverlight 3 and 4 include enhanced media management capabilities by supporting new media formats in a secured environment.

After explaining the media integration capabilities, in the next chapter I will cover the next major pieces of Silverlight—networking and communicating with other systems.

CHAPTER 5

■■■

Network Communication

So far, you've learned aboutXAML, Silverlight user controls, how to create user interfaces in Silverlight, and media integration capabilities of Silverlight. The next major pieces of Silverlight relate to communicating with other systems and working with data (which we'll delve into in the next chapter). The three main communication mechanisms Silverlight provides are services via Windows Communication Foundation (WCF), direct HTTP communication via the `HttpWebRequest` and `WebClient` classes, and raw communication using sockets. Silverlight 3 introduced some significant changes to WCF, including improved security and a binary binding. Two other interesting aspects related to networking were also introduced in Silverlight 3. First, Silverlight is now aware of when the network is available. This gives you the ability to gracefully handle a loss of network connectivity, perhaps queuing up what the user requested when the network comes back alive. The other new aspect is the functionality for one Silverlight application to talk directly with another Silverlight application.

Networking Enhancements in Silverlight 4

Silverlight 4 further introduces networking enhancements supporting easy and scalable implementation of line-of-business applications:

- Allowing Silverlight applications to be "trusted" out-of-browser eliminates the need of cross-domain access policy files (`ClientAccess.xml` or `CrossDomainAccess.xml`) and provides the capability to create group policies to manage the trusted applications.

- ClientHttp networking stack provides the `NetworkCredential` class, which now enables implementation of network authentication in web requests.

- Introduction of Multicast UDP for one-to-many and many-to-many communication over the network improves application performance and stability by utilizing networking resources more efficiently.

Before we get to the specifics of networking, though, it's important to understand cross-domain communication restrictions in Silverlight.

Enabling Cross-Domain Communication

Silverlight can communicate over the network via sockets or HTTP, but if a Silverlight application could communicate to any arbitrary host, then it could be leveraged for hacking into a network or participating in a denial-of-service attack. Therefore, network communication in Silverlight must be controlled. A simplistic approach is to restrict communication between a Silverlight application and the server that serves it (known as the application's site of origin), as shown in Figure 5-1.

Figure 5-1. *Communication with site of origin*

When Silverlight is communicating with its site of origin, such as contacting a web service, no restrictions are placed on the communication. Contacting any other server, however, is forbidden unless the server explicitly grants access. This permission is granted via a special property file that controls network access in specific ways. This property file is downloaded only when Silverlight determines that a network request is cross-domain. Three conditions must be met to identify a request as from the site of origin, and if any of these conditions aren't met, the request is viewed as cross-domain and triggers downloading of the cross-domain policy file. These conditions follow:

- The protocol must be the same. If the application was served over HTTP, it can communicate only over HTTP, and likewise for HTTPS.

- The port must be the same. Again, the port must match the original URL the application was downloaded from.

- The domain and path in the URL must match exactly. If the Silverlight application was downloaded from `http://www.fabrikam.com/app` and the request is made to `http://fabrikam.com/app`, the domains don't match.

■ **Caution** There are restrictions placed on what characters are considered valid in a request's URI to help prevent canonicalization attacks. The valid characters are all lowercase and uppercase letters (*A* through *Z* and *a* through *z*), all digits (0 through 9), the comma (,), the forward slash (/), the tilde (~), the semicolon (;), and the period (.), as long as there aren't two consecutive periods.

Cross-Domain Policy Files

What if Silverlight determines that a particular request is cross-domain? Before deeming the request invalid, Silverlight checks permissions on the remote server. A server that wishes to provide cross-domain permissions to Silverlight applications hosts a cross-domain policy file. There are actually two cross-domain policy files usable by Silverlight: `crossdomain.xml`, introduced by Flash, and `clientaccesspolicy.xml`, introduced by Silverlight.

■ **Note** During the lifetime of a Silverlight application, only a single request is made to a cross-domain policy file per server. This means it is safe (and suggested) to mark the cross-domain policy files as no-cache. This prevents the browser from caching the file while offering no performance penalty to Silverlight, since Silverlight will cache the file itself.

The crossdomain.xml File

The `crossdomain.xml` file is the most straightforward since it is used to opt in the entire domain. No other capabilities from this file are supported by Silverlight. You will probably continue using this approach if you want to support both Silverlight and Adobe clients using single a `crossdomain.xml` file.

In the following example, you are allowing access to all domains by setting the value * for the `domain` attribute. You can restrict the access to specific domains by defining them explicitly.

```
<?xml version="1.0"?>
<!DOCTYPE cross-domain-policy
          SYSTEM
          "http://www.macromedia.com/xml/dtds/cross-domain-policy.dtd">
<cross-domain-policy>
   <allow-access-from domain="*"/>
</cross-domain-policy>
```

■ **Caution** The cross-domain policy files must be located in the root of the server. If you are trying to enable cross-domain communication and it isn't working, ensure the file is located in the server root, not in a subpath such as `www.fabrikam.com/services`. You can use a tool such as Fiddler (`www.fiddlertool.com`), an HTTP traffic sniffer, to see the requests your Silverlight application is making. If this file is present and being downloaded successfully, check the contents of the cross-domain policy file.

The clientaccesspolicy.xml File

If you want more granular control over the allowed domains, you must use `clientaccesspolicy.xml`. This file provides the capability to restrict which domains are allowed and which paths on the server can be accessed. The domains correspond to where the Silverlight application is served, not any host information based on the client computer.

With Visual Studio 2010, an online template—the Silverlight Client Access Policy File template—is available, which you can add (using the "Add New Item" option) as a `clientaccesspolicy.xml` file template to the project. Let's take a look at the structure of this `clientaccesspolicy.xml` file, with the following example:

```
<?xml version="1.0" encoding="utf-8"?>
<access-policy>
  <cross-domain-access>
```

```
        <policy>
          <allow-from http-request-headers="CustomHeader,Mail">
            <domain uri="http://www.fabrikam.com"/>
            <domain uri="https://www.fabrikam.com"/>
          </allow-from>
          <grant-to>
            <resource path="/services" include-subpaths="false"/>
          </grant-to>
        </policy>
      </cross-domain-access>
    </access-policy>
```

The root element must appear only once; however, multiple `cross-domain-access` elements can be specified in order to link different sets of allowed domains with paths on the server.

The list of domains being granted access is located beneath the `allow-from` element. Access is granted to all Silverlight applications if you use the value * for the `domain` element. The `http-request-headers` attribute is optional, but must be specified in order to allow the sending of HTTP headers with requests from the client. It takes the form of a comma-separated list of header names. To allow all headers, set `http-request-headers` to *.

The `grant-to` element is the parent of resources (paths) local to the server that the set of domains are allowed to access. Each `resource` element has a `path` attribute used to specify the path (relative to the server root) to grant access to. The `include-subpaths` attribute is optional. Setting this to `true` is an easy way to grant access to an entire hierarchy of paths by specifying the base path in the `path` attribute. The default value for this attribute is `false`.

This file is also used to grant access to Silverlight applications communicating over sockets. The format is basically the same, but instead of using `resource` in the `grant-to` section, `socket-resource` is used.

```
<?xml version="1.0" encoding="utf-8"?>
<access-policy>
  <cross-domain-access>
    <policy>
      <allow-from>
        <domain uri="*"/>
      </allow-from>
      <grant-to>
        <socket-resource port="4502-4534" protocol="tcp"/>
      </grant-to>
    </policy>
  </cross-domain-access>
</access-policy>
```

The `port` attribute can be a range of ports or a single port. The only ports Silverlight can use are between 4502 and 4534, inclusive. Currently, the only supported protocol is TCP and thus the `protocol` attribute must be set to `tcp`.

The need for this policy file is placed on all communication, including client proxies generated for services, the `System.Net.WebClient` class, and the `System.Net.HttpWebRequest` class.

In the case of the `ClientHttp` stack, to allow methods other than `GET` and `POST` (such as `PUT` and `DELETE`), you need to specify the allow-from tag as a wildcard entry, as shown in following code snippet:

```
<allow-from http-methods="*" >
    <domain uri="*"/>
</allow-from>
```

Note that if the web server is going to support clients of Silverlight 2 and later versions, then the policy file should contain two policy sections. This is because the previously defined allow-from section will allow only custom requests other than GET and POST requests to be used by the client HTTP handler. The allow-from http-methods policy element was added for Silverlight 3 and supported in Silverlight 3 and 4 only. So the other policy section for Silverlight 2 clients can be set as follows:

```
<allow-from >
    <domain uri="*"/>
</allow-from>
```

Visit Microsoft MSDN site - http://msdn.microsoft.com/en-us/library/cc645032(VS.96).aspx – to get more understanding on network security access restrictions in Silverlight and role of cross-domain policy files.

Trusted Applications

Silverlight 4 out-of-browser (OOB) applications can be "trusted" by setting the ElevatedPermissions property to Required in the OutOfBrowserSettings.xml file. The trusted Silverlight OOB-mode applications have elevated privileges that allow an application to call native code outside of the sandbox environment on the client machine, which we will further cover in Chapter 11. In addition to that, running trusted Silverlight applications in OOB mode also eliminates the need of cross-domain access policy files (clientaccesspolicy.xml or crossdomain.xml) for cross-domain network communication.

You must select the "Enable running application out of browser" option in the Silverlight tab of the project properties tab and the "Require elevated trust when running outside the browser" option in the out-of-browser tab, as shown in Figures 5-2 and 5-3, to make the Silverlight application trusted in OOB mode.

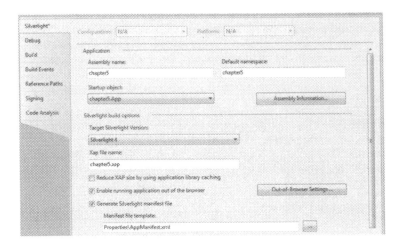

Figure 5-2. Enabling a Silverlight application in out-of-browser mode

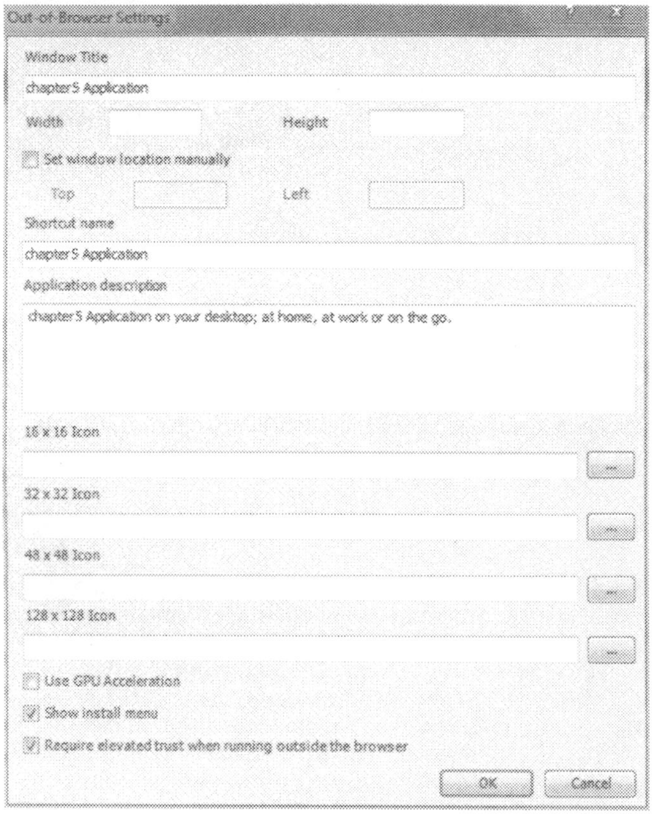

Figure 5-3. Making a Silverlight application a trusted application in OOB mode

The OutofBrowserSettings.xml file should be added under the Properties tab of the Silverlight application project. If you open this XML file, you should see that the ElevatedPermissions property of SecuritySettings is set to Required (as shown here in the highlighted bold fonts) to make the application trusted in OOB mode.

```
<OutOfBrowserSettings ShortName="chapter5 Application"
    EnableGPUAcceleration="False" ShowInstallMenuItem="True">
    <OutOfBrowserSettings.Blurb>chapter5 Application on your desktop;
        at home, at work or on the go.</OutOfBrowserSettings.Blurb>
    <OutOfBrowserSettings.WindowSettings>
        <WindowSettings Title="chapter5 Application" />
    </OutOfBrowserSettings.WindowSettings>
    <OutOfBrowserSettings.SecuritySettings>
        <SecuritySettings ElevatedPermissions="Required" />
    </OutOfBrowserSettings.SecuritySettings>
    <OutOfBrowserSettings.Icons />
</OutOfBrowserSettings>
```

Now that we've gone over the network security restrictions placed on communication in Silverlight, let's take a closer look at all the ways Silverlight can communicate with other systems.

Network-Aware Applications

Silverlight 3 introduced the capability for a Silverlight application to detect changes in the local network. This can prove especially useful for a Silverlight application deployed to the desktop. If it requires the network, such as invoking web services, a loss of network connectivity might trigger the queuing of work that will get done when the application detects the network is available again.

The `System.Net.NetworkInformation` namespace in the System.Net assembly provides two classes useful for detecting changes in the network. The first, `NetworkChange`, exposes the `NetworkAddressChanged` event. Since a loss of network connectivity has the effect of losing the IP address, this event fires.

```
NetworkChange.NetworkAddressChanged +=
        new NetworkAddressChangedEventHandler
          (NetworkChange_NetworkAddressChanged);
```

The other class, `NetworkInterface`, provides the `GetIsNetworkAvailable` static method that can be called in the network address–changed event handler. The following code-snippet will fill the ellipse with green if you are connected to the network; otherwise it will be filled with red.

```
void NetworkChange_NetworkAddressChanged(object sender, EventArgs e)
{
    if (NetworkInterface.GetIsNetworkAvailable())
    {
        statusEllipse.Fill = new SolidColorBrush(Colors.Green);
    }
    else
    {
        statusEllipse.Fill = new SolidColorBrush(Colors.Red);
    }
}
```

You can register for this event in `App.xaml.cs` to control application logic based on the status of the network. We will cover this topic in more detail with a real example in Chapter 11.

Consuming Web Services with WCF

Windows Communication Foundation (WCF) is a communication stack introduced in .NET 3.0 that separates the implementation of a service from how it communicates. The details of the communication can be configured after deployment by modifying the application's configuration file. This makes it easy to change the service from HTTP to HTTPS or to change whether data is sent in a textual or a binary format. The fundamental aspects of WCF services are known as the ABCs. These letters stand for address, binding, and contract. The address specifies the location of the service. Bindings are used to control the nature of the communication channel, such as encodings, transports, and time-outs. Contracts specify the operations that a particular service implements. Together, these aspects combine to form an endpoint for a service. These endpoints are configured both on the service side and the client side in the configuration files.

In this section we will discuss the WCF services in the context of Silverlight. Windows Communication Foundation (WCF) is much broader than this section, and a complete discussion of WCF is beyond the scope of this book. If you need to know more about WCF, I recommend a book from Apress titled *Pro WCF: Practical Microsoft SOA Implementation* (http://apress.com/book/view/1590597028).

Creating a WCF Service Consumable by Silverlight

Let's write a simple web service that will be used by a Silverlight application. This web service will retrieve book-related information.

First, create a Silverlight application project named chapter5, and add a `BookInfo` class under the web project. This class details the book profile and a list of chapters, as shown in the following code snippet:

```
public class BookInfo
{
    public string Title;
    public string Author;
    public string ISBN;
    public List<string> Chapters;
}
```

The service must use `basicHttpBinding` as this is the only binding Silverlight can use. While you can create a WCF service and change the binding, you can shortcut this by creating a new "Silverlight-enabled WCF Service," as shown in Figure 5-4. You can add the Silverlight-enabled WCF service by selecting "Add New Item" in Solution Explorer.

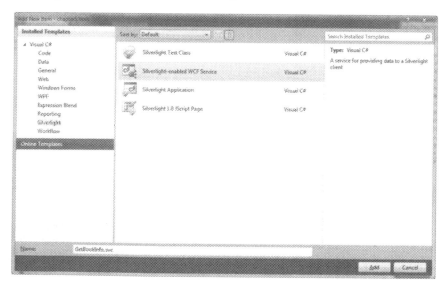

Figure 5-4. Creating a new Silverlight-enabled WCF service in Visual Studio 2010

The service is located in the `GetBookInfo.svc` file. The code-behind contains only the service class, decorated with two attributes, `ServiceContract` and `AspNetCompatibilityRequirements`. We will add three simple methods—`initBooks`, `GetByTitle`, and `GetAllTitle`—to the code-behind file `GetBookInfo.svc.cs`. The `initBooks` method will initialize the sample `BookInfo` object array, and `GetByTitle` and `GetAllTitle` will query this `BookInfo` object array. The following code snippet is for `GetBookInfo.svc.cs`:

```
using System;
using System.Collections.Generic;
using System.Linq;
using System.Runtime.Serialization;
using System.ServiceModel;
using System.ServiceModel.Activation;

namespace chapter5.Web
{
  [ServiceContract(Namespace = "")]
  [AspNetCompatibilityRequirements(RequirementsMode =
    AspNetCompatibilityRequirementsMode.Allowed)]
  public class GetBookInfo
  {
    //Sample book data array
    private BookInfo[] books = new BookInfo[3];

    //initialize the books object
    private void initBooks()
    {
    if (books != null)
    {
        books[0] = new BookInfo();
        books[0].Title = "Pro Silverlight for the Enterprise";
        books[0].Author = "Ashish Ghoda";
        books[0].Chapters = new List<string>
        { "Chapter 1- Understanding Silverlight",
        "Chapter 2-Developing a Simple Silverlight Application",
        "Chapter 3-Silverlight: An Enterprise-Ready Technology
            Platform",
        "Chapter 4-Silverlight and Service-Oriented Architecture",
        "Chapter 5-Developing a Service-Oriented Enterpise RIA"};
        books[0].ISBN = "978-1-4302-1867-8";

        books[1] = new BookInfo();
        books[1].Title = "Accelerated Silverlight 3";
        books[1].Author = "Ashish Ghoda and Jeff Scanlon";
        books[1].Chapters = new List<string>
        { "Chapter 1-Introducing Silverlight",
        "Chapter 2-Getting to Know XAML",
        "Chapter 3-Creating User Interfaces",
        "Chapter 4-Network Communication",
        "Chapter 5-Working with Data"};
        books[1].ISBN = "978-1-4302-2430-3";
```

```
            books[2] = new BookInfo();
            books[2].Title = "Introducing Silverlight 4";
            books[2].Author = "Ashish Ghoda";
            books[2].Chapters = new List<string>
            { "Chapter 1-Introducing Silverlight",
            "Chapter 2-Silverlight Concepts",
            "Chapter 3-Silverlight User Interface Controls",
            "Chapter 4-Media Integration",
            "Chapter 5-Data Integration"};
            books[2].ISBN = "978-1-4302-2991-9";
            }
        }

        //Get books by title
        [OperationContract]
        public BookInfo GetByTitle(string Title)
        {
            initBooks();
            foreach (var item in books)
            {
                if (item.Title.ToUpper() == Title.ToUpper())
                    return item;
            }
            return null;
        }

        //Get all book titles
        [OperationContract]
        public List<string> GetAllTitle()
        {
            initBooks();
            List<string> allTitles= new List<string>();
            foreach (var item in books)
            {
                    allTitles.Add(item.Title);
            }
            return allTitles;
        }
    }
}
```

While WCF services are generally separated into an interface (the contract) and the service implementation (that implements the interface), it's possible to use the ServiceContract attribute on the service implementation class. The OperationContract attribute specifies which methods form the operations of the service for the service contract.

Every WCF service must have a host. In classic ASMX web services, the host was ASP.NET itself. The way a client contacts ASP.NET for web pages is the same way a client invokes a web service. Using WCF, the host is outside the HTTP pipeline of ASP.NET. By using the AspNetCompatibilityRequirements attribute, you can ensure a service will be consumable by Silverlight. By setting the RequirementMode property of the attribute to AspNetCompatibilityRequirementsMode.Allowed you ensure that ASP.NET compatibility can be turned on in the application configuration file within the system.serviceModel section. Since this service is part of an ASP.NET web application, the configuration details are located in web.config in the system.serviceModel section. There are four significant elements in this section: behaviors, bindings, serviceHostingEnvironment, and services.

```
<system.serviceModel>
    <behaviors>
        <serviceBehaviors>
            <behavior name="">
                <serviceMetadata httpGetEnabled="true" />
                <serviceDebug
                    includeExceptionDetailInFaults="false" />
            </behavior>
        </serviceBehaviors>
    </behaviors>
    <bindings>
        <customBinding>
            <binding name="chapter5.Web.GetBookInfo.customBinding0">
                <binaryMessageEncoding />
                <httpTransport />
            </binding>
        </customBinding>
    </bindings>
    <serviceHostingEnvironment aspNetCompatibilityEnabled="true"
        multipleSiteBindingsEnabled="true" />
    <services>
        <service name="chapter5.Web.GetBookInfo">
            <endpoint address="" binding="customBinding"
                bindingConfiguration=
                  "chapter5.Web.GetBookInfo.customBinding0"
                contract="chapter5.Web.GetBookInfo" />
            <endpoint address="mex" binding="mexHttpBinding"
                contract="IMetadataExchange" />
        </service>
    </services>
</system.serviceModel>
```

We must build the service now so it can be readily available to the other operations in our Silverlight project that will consume the service.

XAML to Consume Information

Next, define the MainPage.xaml UserControl to display the user-entered, title-based book information. Call the web service through the button-click event code-behind to get the book information related to the user-entered title. You bind the returned book data, based on the BookInfo class object, to UserControl. (We will learn more about data binding in the next chapter.) The following is the related XAML code:

```
<StackPanel x:Name="LayoutRoot" Background="White">
    <TextBlock Text="Insert Book Title"/>
    <TextBox x:Name="txtTitle"/>
```

```
<Button x:Name="getDetail" Content="Get Book detail"
        Click="getDetail_Click" Width="150"/>
<StackPanel x:Name="InfoPanel">
    <TextBlock x:Name="title" Text="{Binding Title}"/>
    <TextBlock x:Name="author" Text="{Binding Author}"/>
    <TextBlock x:Name="ISBN" Text="{Binding ISBN}"/>
    <ListBox x:Name="chapters" ItemsSource="{Binding Chapters}"/>
</StackPanel>
</StackPanel>
```

Invoking Services from Silverlight

Before Silverlight can consume a web service, it must know what the available operations on the service are and also have relevant type information, such as the **BookInfo** type, shown previously. There are two ways to generate this proxy. The first is using the Add Service Reference functionality in Visual Studio 2010, and the other is using a Silverlight tool named **SLsvcUtil.exe** (Silverlight Service Utility).

Figure 5-5 shows what the Add Service Reference dialog looks like after contacting the **GetBookInfo** service.

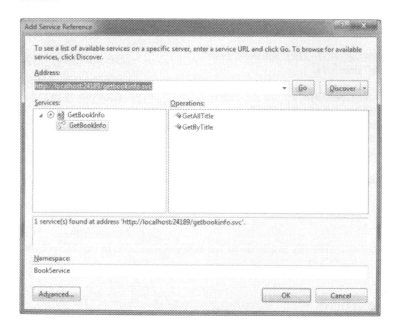

Figure 5-5. *Add Service Reference dialog*

After adding a service reference, the **ServiceReferences.ClientConfig** file gets created in the Silverlight project. The configuration file has a **system.serviceModel** section that's similar to the **web.config** file we discussed earlier, but now it has a **client** element along with the **bindings** element. We will discuss each option of this file when we create a similar file using the new Silverlight Service Utility tool.

Silverlight Service Utility Tool

The Silverlight Service Utility tool, SlSvcUtil.exe, is part of the Silverlight 4 SDK and can be found under C:\Program Files\Microsoft SDKs\Silverlight\v4.0\Tools in a 32-bit environment; in a 64-bit environment, the tool can be found under C:\Program Files (x86)\Microsoft SDKs\Silverlight\v4.0\Tools.

This tool provides a large number of options. The default operation of the tool creates the client service configuration file (ServiceReferences.ClientConfig) and the necessary proxy code to contact the web service and handle any required types. Table 5-1 describes a number of the most useful options of this tool.

Table 5-1. Command-Line Options for SlSvcUtil.exe

Option	Description	Short Form
/directory:<directory>	Specifies the output directory	/d
/config:<fileName>	File name to use for the configuration file	--
/out:<fileName>	File name for the generated code	/o
/enableDataBinding	Implements INotifyPropertyChanged on all data contract types for data binding	/edb
/collectionType:<type>	Fully qualified or assembly-qualified name of the data type used for collections	/ct
/reference:<path>	Referenced types that contain types used by metadata	/r
/noConfig	No configuration file is generated	--
/mergeConfig	Configuration file changes are merged into an existing file instead of being put into a new one.	
/serializer:<serializer>	Specifies which serializer to use; possible values are Auto, DataContractSerializer, and XmlSerializer.	

For demonstration purposes, we created the GetBookInfo service proxy using the Add Service Reference option. Delete the created BookService proxy and ServiceReferences.ClientConfig. Now let's create the GetBookInfo service proxy using SLsvcUtil.exe. Open a command prompt and navigate to C:\Program Files\Microsoft SDKs\Silverlight\v4.0\Tools for a 32-bit environment or C:\Program Files (x86)\Microsoft SDKs\Silverlight\v4.0\Tools for a 64-bit environment. As we are going to generate a proxy on the running service, make sure that the GetBookInfo.svc service is running. Then, issue the following command to generate the service proxy:

```
slsvcutil.exe http://localhost:14278/GetBookInfo.svc
```

Note that in the previous command, the port value may differ on your machine. If you are using an IIS server, there will not be a port value; in that case, replace/remove the port value as appropriate.

After the successful completion of the previous command, navigate to the directory where SlSvcUtil.exe resides. You will see a service proxy and configuration files ServiceReferences.ClientConfig and GetBookInfo.cs created under that folder. Copy both files to the chapter5 Silverlight project. As mentioned earlier, the configuration file contains a system.serviceModel section that's similar to the web.config file, but it now has a client element along with the bindings element.

```
<configuration>
    <system.serviceModel>
        <bindings>
            <customBinding>
                <binding name="CustomBinding_GetBookInfo">
                    <binaryMessageEncoding />
                    <httpTransport
                        maxReceivedMessageSize="2147483647"
                        maxBufferSize="2147483647">
                        <extendedProtectionPolicy
                            policyEnforcement="Never" />
                    </httpTransport>
                </binding>
            </customBinding>
        </bindings>
        <client>
            <endpoint address="http://localhost:14278/GetBookInfo.svc"
                binding="customBinding"
                bindingConfiguration="CustomBinding_GetBookInfo"
                contract="GetBookInfo"
                name="CustomBinding_GetBookInfo" />
        </client>
        <extensions />
    </system.serviceModel>
</configuration>
```

In the ServiceReferences.ClientConfig file, the address of the endpoint specifies where the service is located. Remember that if you are crossing a domain boundary, the cross-domain policy file must be located one directory above chapter5.Web on the server. The binding matches that of the service, specifically using HTTP and the binary message encoding. The default configuration file supplies values for the maximum buffer size and maximum received message size, two configuration options not specified in the services configuration section. The GetBookInfo.cs file contains the BookInfo class (as derived from the metadata of the service) and the GetBookInfo interface.

When you want to invoke the service, using the default constructor is the easiest approach. Other constructors on the service provide a way to specify the endpoint to use (provided multiple endpoints are specified in the configuration file) by creating a binding and an endpoint programmatically as follows. Note that for this approach, you need to add the namespace System.ServiceModel:

```
GetBookInfoClient GetBook = new
    GetBookInfoClient(new BasicHttpBinding(),
        new EndpointAddress("http://localhost:14278/GetBookInfo.svc"));
```

Asynchronous Communication

The proxy supports two asynchronous mechanisms to invoke the service. The first, slightly easier method is to provide a `Completed` event handler along with the operations of the service, followed by `Async`. The other method uses `IAsyncResult` with `Begin`/`End` methods for each operation of the service. The key difference between these two is that the first approach is available directly on the client proxy and executes on the foreground thread, so it will block the user interface while contacting the service, but it makes connecting the data to the user interface much easier. The second approach runs in the background thread and will not block the user interface while contacting the service.

Let's look at the first approach. The code for the `MainPage.xaml.cs` button-click event is as follows:

```
private void getDetail_Click(object sender, RoutedEventArgs e)
{
    GetBookInfoClient GetBook = new GetBookInfoClient();
    GetBook.GetByTitleCompleted += new
    EventHandler<GetByTitleCompletedEventArgs>
        (GetBook_GetByTitleCompleted);
    if (txtTitle.Text != string.Empty)
        GetBook.GetByTitleAsync(txtTitle.Text);
    Else
    {
        //Call GetAllTitle using IAsyncResult
        //Detailed later in this section
    }
}
```

A new instance of the `GetBook` proxy is created when you click the `getDetail` button with the default constructor, so the endpoint in `ServiceReferences.ClientConfig` is populated. Before invoking the `GetByTitleAsync` method, the corresponding `Completed` event is connected to an event handler. The event handler simply connects the result of the call to a StackPanel `InfoPanel` on the user interface via data binding.

```
void GetBook_GetByTitleCompleted(object sender,
  GetByTitleCompletedEventArgs e)
{
   InfoPanel.DataContext = e.Result;
}
```

If you run the project, enter "Pro Silverlight for the Enterprise" in the text box, and click the button, the result should be similar to what's shown in Figure 5-6 showing book details.

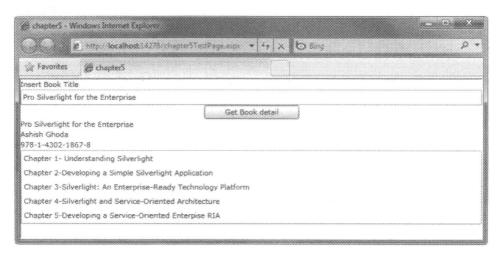

Figure 5-6. Book details retrieved over the WCF service

The `EventArgs` instances for these service calls always have a set of useful properties, which are described in Table 5-2.

Table 5-2. Properties of Client Proxy Operation EventArgs classes

Property	Type	Description
Cancelled	bool	True when the asynchronous operation was cancelled.
Error	Exception	The Exception instance if an exception happened during the operation.
Result	Varies, depending on the data	The data type corresponding to the data returned from the service operation
UserState	object	The `Async` methods for the service operations include a second constructor, providing a way to pass arbitrary data from the call of the service operation to the completed event handler. If this parameter was used, `UserState` stores that data.

While we will take a closer look at data binding in Chapter 6, the data returned from the service operations is suitable for data binding. When non-array types are used, they are wrapped in an `ObservableCollection` and implement the `INotifyPropertyChanged` interface in order to support two-way data binding (that is, automatically updating when the underlying data source changes).

Now let's look at the second approach. In order to use the `Begin`/`End` methods for invoking service operations, the client proxy instance must be cast to its interface. The interface for the `GetBookInfo` service looks like the following in the `GetBookInfo.cs` file:

```
[System.CodeDom.Compiler.GeneratedCodeAttribute("System.ServiceModel", "3.0.0.0")]
[System.ServiceModel.ServiceContractAttribute(Namespace="", ↵
 ConfigurationName="GetBookInfo")]
public interface GetBookInfo
{
    [System.ServiceModel.OperationContractAttribute
      (AsyncPattern=true, Action="urn:GetBookInfo/GetByTitle",
        ReplyAction="urn:GetBookInfo/GetByTitleResponse")]

    System.IAsyncResult BeginGetByTitle(string Title,
      System.AsyncCallback callback, object asyncState);

    chapter4.Web.BookInfo EndGetByTitle(System.IAsyncResult result);

    [System.ServiceModel.OperationContractAttribute
      (AsyncPattern=true, Action="urn:GetBookInfo/GetAllTitle",
        ReplyAction="urn:GetBookInfo/GetAllTitleResponse")]
    System.IAsyncResult BeginGetAllTitle
      (System.AsyncCallback callback, object asyncState);

    string[] EndGetAllTitle(System.IAsyncResult result);
}
```

If you've worked with the asynchronous programming model on .NET, these method signatures should be no surprise. This time, invocation of a service operation is slightly different since the Dispatcher must be used to update the user interface since the asynchronous callback happens on a background thread. To demonstrate, invoke GetAllTitle by calling BeginGetAllTitle within the getDetail_Click method else section, as follows:

```
else
{
    //Call GetAllTitle using IAsyncResult
    GetBookInfo GetBook1 = (GetBookInfo)GetBook;
    GetBook1.BeginGetAllTitle
      (new AsyncCallback(GetAllTitle_AsyncCallBack), GetBook1);
}
```

Next, the asynchronous callback method calls EndGetAllTitle to get the result of the operation and then binds it to the Chapters list box on the user interface.

```
void GetAllTitle_AsyncCallBack(IAsyncResult ar)
{
    string [] items =
        (((GetBookInfo)ar.AsyncState).EndGetAllTitle(ar)).ToArray();

    Dispatcher.BeginInvoke(delegate()
    {
        chapters.ItemsSource = items;
    });
}
```

Run the project. When you click the Get Book detail button, you should see the book titles displayed, as shown in Figure 5-7.

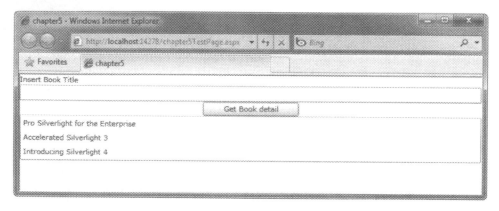

Figure 5-7. *Invoking* `GetAllTitle` *using* `Async` *callback*

Here you may wonder which mechanism to choose—subscribing to the `completed` event or using the `Async` callback. It very much depends upon your needs. Asynchronous callbacks are very similar to events in terms of what they do. They both provide a mechanism for one piece of code to say to another, "Do this job and when you are done, let me know." The difference here is that with a completed event, many pieces of code can be notified when the event occurs, whereas with an `Async` callback, only the caller can be notified. This is because essentially an event is a wrapper around a set of callbacks. You use the `+=` operator to subscribe to the callback that is, in turn, the event handler onto the event object. The event class handles the work of invoking all the subscribed callbacks when the event is raised. But a method that takes an explicit callback parameter (such as `BeginInvoke` in our previous example) doesn't support any mechanism for handling a set of callbacks. They remember only the callback that was passed to them as a parameter (`Async` callback `GetAllTitle` in our case), and then invoke that when they're finished.

So to be straight, use `Async` callbacks if you need to notify only the code that called of completion, and use `Events` for a multi-threading scenario in which you want to enable more than one piece of code to be notified.

Handling Errors

If you use the previous approach to invoke a service and an exception happens in the service, Silverlight will receive only limited information about the exception. You can check for the exception in the `Result` property of the `EventArgs` class or by wrapping the `End` method in a `try/catch` block. If something goes wrong in the service, the browser will get an HTTP 500 error message from the server. Unfortunately, Silverlight can't access the details of the exception, so you must modify the WCF service by augmenting the endpoint to ensure the fault data is sent via an HTTP 200 error message, rather than an HTTP 500 error message. This is accomplished using a custom `IDispatchMessageInspector` method and a custom `IEndpointBehavior` method on the service side. The custom `IDispatchMessageInspector` method simply changes the HTTP status code to 200 (OK) when the message that passes through it is a fault.

Let's create a class named `SilverlightFaultBehavior.cs` in the `chapter5.Web` project and add the following code:

```
public class SilverlightFaultProcessor : IDispatchMessageInspector
{
    #region IDispatchMessageInspector Members

    public object AfterReceiveRequest(
        ref System.ServiceModel.Channels.Message request,
        System.ServiceModel.IClientChannel channel,
        System.ServiceModel.InstanceContext instanceContext)
    {
        return (null);
    }

    public void BeforeSendReply(
      ref System.ServiceModel.Channels.Message reply,
      object correlationState)
    {
        if (reply.IsFault)
        {
            // If it's a fault, change the status code
            // to 200 so Silverlight can receive the
            // details of the fault

            HttpResponseMessageProperty responseProperty =
                new HttpResponseMessageProperty();

            responseProperty.StatusCode =
                    System.Net.HttpStatusCode.OK;

            reply.Properties[HttpResponseMessageProperty.Name]
                = responseProperty;
        }
    }

    #endregion
}
```

The custom IEndpointBehavior method also inherits from BehaviorExtensionElement so the behavior can be used in the configuration file. Methods from interfaces that do not have implementations are not shown here in the interest of space.

```
public class SilverlightFaultBehavior : BehaviorExtensionElement,
                            IEndpointBehavior, IServiceBehavior
{
    public override Type BehaviorType
    {
        get { return (typeof(SilverlightFaultBehavior)); }
    }

    protected override object CreateBehavior()
    {
        return (new SilverlightFaultBehavior());
```

```
    }
    #region IEndpointBehavior Members

    public void ApplyDispatchBehavior(ServiceEndpoint endpoint,
            System.ServiceModel.Dispatcher.EndpointDispatcher
            endpointDispatcher)
    {
        SilverlightFaultProcessor processor =
            new SilverlightFaultProcessor();

        endpointDispatcher.DispatchRuntime.
            MessageInspectors.Add(processor);
    }
}
```

All that's left is to change the Web.config configuration file to add this behavior to the service's endpoint. This requires adding the behavior extension under a new element, extensions, and then using it in the behavior (the added/updated items are shown in bold in the following snippet):

```
<system.serviceModel>
  <extensions>
    <behaviorExtensions>
      <add name="silverlightFaults"
          type="SilverlightFaultBehavior, chapter5.Web,
                Version=1.0.0.0,
                Culture=neutral, PublicKeyToken=null"/>
    </behaviorExtensions>
  </extensions>
  <behaviors>
    <endpointBehaviors>
      <behavior name="SilverlightFaultBehavior">
        <silverlightFaults />
      </behavior>
    </endpointBehaviors>
    <serviceBehaviors>
     <behavior name="chapter5.Web.GetBookInfoBehavior">
     <serviceMetadata httpGetEnabled="true" />
     <serviceDebug includeExceptionDetailInFaults="false" />
     </behavior>
    </serviceBehaviors>
  </behaviors>
```

▓ **Caution** Note that at the time of finishing this chapter, there is a known bug in specifying behaviorExtensions's type. You must write the type in one line without a line break or it will throw an exception that the SilverlightFaultBehavior type is not found. Visit the link to get more information on the defect: http://connect.microsoft.com/wcf/feedback/ViewFeedback.aspx?FeedbackID=216431.

The revised service element includes the `behaviorConfiguration` attribute (shown in bold in the following snippet) in order to make the new Silverlight fault behavior work:

```
<services>
  <service behaviorConfiguration=
      "chapter5.Web.GetBookInfoBehavior"
    name="chapter5.Web.GetBookInfo">
    <endpoint address="" binding="customBinding"
      behaviorConfiguration="SilverlightFaultBehavior"
      bindingConfiguration="chapter5.Web.GetBookInfo.customBinding0"
      contract="chapter5.Web.GetBookInfo" />
    <endpoint address="mex" binding="mexHttpBinding"
      contract="IMetadataExchange" />
  </service>
</services>
```

Now the Silverlight application can receive faults from the service. Let's augment the `GetByTitle` operation with a fault contract. A *fault contract* states certain faults are expected by the application, such as placing an order for too many supplies.

```
[OperationContract]
[FaultContract(typeof(BookNotFound))]
public BookInfo GetByTitle(string Title)
{
    initBooks();
    …
    …
}
```

`BookNotFound` is a simple class that contains a custom message.

```
public class BookNotFound
{
    public string NotFoundMessage { get; set; }
}
```

There are two types of faults a service client might receive from the service. The first are unhandled faults, and the details of these faults should be communicated back to the client only in test/debug scenarios. The second are violations of application logic and thus are expected and can be safely communicated back to the client (in this case, Silverlight) for a graceful application operation. If you are developing a Silverlight application and want to configure the service to send the full details of the unhandled faults to Silverlight, you can set the `includeExceptionDetailInFaults` attribute to `true` in the `serviceDebug` element of a behavior.

```
<behavior name="chapter5.Web.GetBookInfoBehavior">
  <serviceMetadata httpGetEnabled="true" />
  <serviceDebug includeExceptionDetailInFaults="true" />
</behavior>
```

░ **Note** From a security prospective, the `includeExceptionDetailInFaults="true"` WCF configuration should never be deployed in production environments. It exposes sensitive server-side data such as the exception type and stack trace, which present a security risk.

Finally, in the `GetBookInfo.svc.cs` service code-behind file, we add the following lines of code to throw a fault of type `BookNotFound` in the case where the entered title does not match any of the titles in our books array object.

```
BookNotFound fault = new BookNotFound();
fault.NotFoundMessage= "Book not found";
    throw new FaultException<BookNotFound>
      (fault, new FaultReason
        ("Reason: Book not found fault occurred."));
```

Note that here we supplied the custom `FaultReason` message, otherwise `FaultException` will say that "The creator of this fault did not specify a reason." It is good practice to supply a proper reason to identify the type of fault that has occurred, when you can have multiple fault types.

As we modified the `GetBookInfo` service, similarly we need to update the proxy class. At this point, you need to regenerate a `GetBookInfo.cs` proxy class file using **slsvcutil.exe** (or within Visual Studio 2010, adding it by Add/Update Service Reference), as described previously, and replace the existing file with this new one in the chapter5 Silverlight project. While generating a proxy class to the `GetBookInfo` service, it will generate code for the `BookNotFound` class since it was exposed in the service metadata. This enables the class to be used inside the Silverlight client and drive the programming logic.

Now we need to add reference by adding **using chapter5.Web** in the namespace section of `MainPage.xaml.cs` and modifying the `GetBook_GetByTitleCompleted` event handler as shown here.

```
void GetBook_GetByTitleCompleted
    (object sender, GetByTitleCompletedEventArgs e)
{
    if (e.Error==null)
    {
        InfoPanel.DataContext = e.Result;
    }
    else if (e.Error is FaultException<GetBookInfoBookNotFound >)
    {
        FaultException<GetBookInfoBookNotFound> fault = e.Error as
            FaultException<GetBookInfoBookNotFound>;
        MessageBox.Show
            (fault.Detail.NotFoundMessage,"Error has occurred",0);
    }
}
```

Here we place an *if* condition to check whether `GetByTitleCompletedEventArgs e` contains any `Error`. If it contains an error and if it is `FaultException` of type `GetBookInfoBookNotFound`, then we cast the `e.Error` to `GetBookInfoBookNotFound` object fault and show the `MessageBox` box with the message set to `NotFoundMessage` fault object.

Rebuild the solution and press F5 (or Ctrl + F5 if you don't want Visual Studio to break on FaultException) and enter some string that does not match the title of any book we previously stored in the books array and press the Get Book detail button. Notice that this time a custom fault occurred at the GetBookInfo WCF service level, and a custom "Book not found" message is displayed rather than the default "Not found" message.

■ **Note** Get more details on creating and handling faults in Silverlight by visiting the Microsoft MSDN web site at http://msdn.microsoft.com/en-us/library/dd470096(VS.96).aspx.

Communicating Directly over HTTP

Two classes are provided to support direct communication over HTTP: System.Net.WebClient and System.Net.HttpWebRequest. WebClient is simpler but exposes only simplified access to the GET and POST methods of HTTP. WebClient is most useful for easily downloading resources. The HttpWebRequest class provides greater control over HTTP communication.

The WebClient Class

The WebClient class provides simplified access to communicating over HTTP (it is located in the System.Net assembly). Its most important members are listed in Table 5-3.

Table 5-3. Members of the System.Net.WebClient Class

Name	Type	Description
DownloadStringAsync	Method	Asynchronously downloads data and returns it as a string.
DownloadStringCompleted	Event	Occurs when DownloadStringAsync is complete.
UploadStringAsync	Method	Asynchronously uploads a string to a specified URI.
UploadStringCompleted	Event	Occurs when UploadStringAsync is complete.
OpenReadAsync	Method	Asynchronously downloads data and returns it as a Stream.
OpenReadCompleted	Event	Occurs when OpenReadAsync is complete.
DownloadProgressChanged	Event	Occurs when some/all data is transferred. This is useful for building a status indicator such as a download progress bar.
UploadProgressChanged	Event	Occurs when some/all data is uploaded. This is useful for building a status indicator such as an upload progress bar.
CancelAsync	Method	Used to cancel an already-issued asynchronous operation.

BaseAddress	Property (URI)	Gets/sets the base address. This is useful for using relative addresses in multiple operations with a single WebClient.
IsBusy	Property (bool)	Indicates whether an asynchronous operation is in progress.

One aspect of Silverlight that is really useful is its support of archived media. You can store images, audio, and video in a ZIP file, download it to the client via WebClient, and then use MediaElement's or BitmapImage's SetSource method to connect the visual element to the media content within the archive. Let's take a look at a simple Silverlight application to download and display images as shown in Figure 5-8. We'll also implement the DownloadProgressChanged event for showing a simple progress indicator.

Figure 5-8. *Demonstrating the use of the WebClient class*

The following is the XAML code snippet for this example.

```xml
<Grid x:Name="LayoutRoot" Background="White">
    <Button Content="Download" Height="25" HorizontalAlignment="Left"
        Margin="12,21,0,0" Name="downloadButton"
        VerticalAlignment="Top" Width="107"
        Click="downloadButton_Click" />
    <ListBox Name="imageListBox" Height="234"
        HorizontalAlignment="Left" Margin="12,54,0,0"
        VerticalAlignment="Top" Width="135"
        SelectionChanged="imageListBox_SelectionChanged"
        Visibility="Collapsed"/>
    <Image Height="234" HorizontalAlignment="Left" Margin="164,54,0,0"
        Name="image" Stretch="Fill"
        VerticalAlignment="Top" Width="224" />
    <TextBlock Height="25" HorizontalAlignment="Left"
        Margin="135,21,0,0" Name="progressTextBox"
        VerticalAlignment="Top" Width="120" />
</Grid>
```

The code-behind would need additional reference to the following namespaces.

```
using System.Windows.Resources;
using System.Windows.Media.Imaging;
```

We need a `System.Windows.Resources.StreamResourceInfo` object in the code-behind to store the result of the download (i.e., the archive of images).

```
private StreamResourceInfo imageArchive;
```

Next, we'll implement the click event on the button to initiate the download. We are using the `OpenReadAsync` method to download a stream of data and thus implement an `OpenReadCompleted` event handler to handle the data when it is finished downloading. We also will implement the `DownloadProgressChanged` event handler to notify UI (`progressTextBox.Text`) about the download progress of the file.

```
private void downloadButton_Click(object sender, RoutedEventArgs e)
{
    WebClient wc = new WebClient();
    wc.OpenReadCompleted +=
            new OpenReadCompletedEventHandler(wc_OpenReadCompleted);
    wc.DownloadProgressChanged += new
        DownloadProgressChangedEventHandler
          (wc_DownloadProgressChanged);
    wc.OpenReadAsync(new Uri
        ("/ImageBrowser/renaissance.zip", UriKind.Relative));
}
```

The `OpenReadCompleted` event handler is straightforward: we'll check for an error or a cancel and make our list box of image names visible (we're cheating here—the image names are hard-coded in a `String`-type array). We could add a metadata file to the ZIP archive that the Silverlight application can access and then cache the downloaded image archive for later use (in our case it is `renaissance.zip`).

```
private void wc_OpenReadCompleted
    (object sender, OpenReadCompletedEventArgs e)
{
    if ((e.Error == null) && (e.Cancelled == false))
    {
        imageListBox.Visibility = Visibility.Visible;
        imageArchive = new StreamResourceInfo(e.Result, null);
    }
}
```

The download progress indicator is simply a percentage value displayed in a TextBlock. `DownloadProgressChangedEventArgs` contains several useful properties (listed in Table 5-4), including the percentage progress, so we don't have to calculate percentage completion.

```
private void wc_DownloadProgressChanged
    (object sender,DownloadProgressChangedEventArgs e)
{
    progressTextBox.Text = e.ProgressPercentage + "%";
}
```

Table 5-4. Members of the DownloadProgressChangedEventArgs Class

Name	Type	Description
BytesReceived	long	A count of the bytes received so far.
ProgressPercentage	int	A number from 0 to 100 representing the percentage of bytes downloaded; equates to the formula (BytesReceived / TotalBytesToReceive) * 100.
TotalBytesToReceive	long	Corresponds to the file size of the file requested.
UserState	object	Corresponds to the optional data passed to the OpenReadAsync or DownloadStringAsync method.

Now that we have the image archive cached in the class, we can access an image inside when the user selects a different image in the list box.

```
private void imageListBox_SelectionChanged(object sender,
    SelectionChangedEventArgs e)
{
    BitmapImage bitmapImageSource = new BitmapImage();
    StreamResourceInfo imageResourceInfo =
        Application.GetResourceStream(imageArchive,
            new Uri(imageListBox.SelectedItem.ToString(),
                UriKind.Relative));
    bitmapImageSource.SetSource(imageResourceInfo.Stream);
    image.Source = bitmapImageSource;
}
```

First, we need to get access to the specific image inside the archive. We use the Application.GetResourceStream to access the specific image we want. GetResourceStream has two overloads: one to access resources stored in the application, and the other to access resources within an arbitrary ZIP stream. The resource to access is specified by a Uri object. The images in the ZIP archive are referenced relative to the path within the ZIP—the path to the Silverlight application has no relation to the paths of images inside the archive. The only other remarkable thing about this piece of code is that the BitmapImage class is needed to get a source for the Image object. The DownloadStringAsync method works just like the OpenReadAsync method. The only difference is that the Result property of the DownloadStringCompletedEventArgs class is of type String instead of Stream. This method makes it easy to download content such as XML documents for parsing by the XML classes. We will be utilizing DownloadStringAsync in the next chapter.

The WebClient class provides only basic communication support. Downloading files, either as a String or a Stream, is done via the GET method of HTTP. The HTTP POST method is supported via the UploadStringAsync method. There are three overloads of this method. One version takes a Uri and the string to upload. A second version takes the Uri, a string specifying the HTTP method to use (it defaults to POST if this parameter is null), and the string to upload. The final variant includes a user token that is passed to the asynchronous response handler.

If we want to utilize HTTP in more complex ways, manipulate cookies, or communicate securely, we need something more powerful. This power is provided by the System.Net. HttpWebRequest class.

The HttpWebRequest Class

The HttpWebRequest is a specialization of the WebRequest class designed to communicate over the HTTP and HTTPS protocols. It also supports the GET and POST methods. Generally, if the host browser can do it, the HttpWebRequest can do it too, since this class leverages the host browser's networking.

An instance of HttpWebRequest cannot be created directly. The WebRequest class contains a factory method named Create that returns an appropriate instance of a WebRequest inheritor, based on the protocol specified in the URI. Silverlight supports only the HTTP and HTTPS protocols, and both cause Create to return an instance of HttpWebRequest (actually, since HttpWebRequest is also abstract, a concrete implementation of HttpWebRequest is created; however, for all intents and purposes, it is an HttpWebRequest). For example,

```
Uri uri = new Uri("http://www.technologyopinion.com");
HttpWebRequest myHttpWebRequest1=
    (HttpWebRequest)WebRequest.Create(uri);
```

The HttpWebRequest class works in concert with HttpWebResponse to handle the data sent back from the server. The nature of communication using HttpWebRequest is also asynchronous; however, it utilizes the BeginXXX/EndXXX pattern that you may be familiar with from .NET. Tables 5-5 and 5-6 describe the key methods and properties of this class, respectively.

Table 5-5. Key Methods of the System.Net.HttpWebRequest Class

Name	Description
BeginGetRequestStream	Begins an asynchronous request to obtain a Stream to write data.
EndGetRequestStream	Returns a Stream. Use this in the asynchronous callback method passed to BeginGetRequestStream to get the Stream to write your request to.
BeginGetResponse	Begins an asynchronous request to communicate with a server.
EndGetResponse	Returns a WebResponse; provides access to a Stream containing the data downloaded from the server.
Abort	Cancels an executing asynchronous operation.

Table 5-6. Key Properties of the System.Net.HttpWebRequest Class

Name	Description
ContentType	Corresponds to the Content-Type HTTP header.
HaveResponse	true if a response has been received; false otherwise.
Headers	A collection containing the HTTP headers.
Method	Corresponds to the method used in the request. Currently, it can be only GET or POST.
RequestUri	The URI of the request.

The EndGetResponse of the HttpWebRequest class returns a WebResponse. Much like the WebRequest, the WebResponse is abstract and actually requires us to look one level deeper in the hierarchy, so let's take a look at the HttpWebResponse class.

The HttpWebResponse class provides access to the data sent by the server to Silverlight. Its most important method is GetResponseStream, inherited from the WebResponse class. This method gives you a Stream containing the data sent by the server. When you are done with the response, make sure you call its Close method since the connection to the server remains open in the meantime. Tables 5-7 and 5-8 describe the key methods and properties of this class, respectively.

Table 5-7. Methods of the System.Net.HttpWebResponse Class

Name	Description
Close	Closes the stream and releases the connection to the server.
GetResponseStream	Returns a Stream. Use this to access the data sent by the server to Silverlight.

Table 5-8. Properties of the System.Net.HttpWebResponse Class

Name	Description
ContentLength	Length of the data sent to Silverlight.
ContentType	MIME type of the content sent, if available.
ResponseUri	URI of the server that sent the response.

One way to use the HttpWebRequest class is to retrieve data from a server. In this case, we can go straight to using the BeginGetResponse method, since all we care about is retrieving data from a server, not sending data. The following code demonstrates that, based on the user-entered address to connect to the server to download data, such as downloading an HTML file from our site of origin.

```
HttpWebRequest request = (HttpWebRequest)HttpWebRequest.Create(
    new Uri(addressTB.Text));
request.BeginGetResponse(new AsyncCallback(responseHandler), request);
```

The implementation of the response handler is where we read the response from the server.

```
void responseHandler(IAsyncResult asyncResult)
{
    try
    {
        HttpWebRequest request = (HttpWebRequest)asyncResult.AsyncState;
        HttpWebResponse response =
            (HttpWebResponse)request.EndGetResponse(asyncResult);
        StreamReader reader = new
            StreamReader(response.GetResponseStream());
        string line;
        outputTB.Text = "";
```

```
        while ((line = reader.ReadLine()) != null)
        {
            outputTB.Text += line;
        }
    }
    catch (Exception ex)
    {
        outputTB.Text = ex.Message;
    }
}
```

In the response handler, we grab the request object via the `AsyncState` parameter, and then get the `Stream` from `GetResponseStream`. This is the equivalent of the HTTP `GET` method.

Sending data to a server is similar to initiating an asynchronous operation for retrieving the response. `BeginGetRequestStream` starts the operation, and then `EndGetRequestStream` gives us the `Stream` in the asynchronous callback method passed to `BeginGetRequestStream`. This is equivalent to the HTTP `POST` method.

Communicating via Sockets

While most applications will use either the service proxy or one of the classes for downloading via HTTP/HTTPS, some applications will need a raw communication channel. Performance is the chief reason for using sockets for communication, since less data is sent between the client and server, but there's also the potential for needing to interoperate with existing systems that communicate via sockets. Silverlight places severe restrictions on socket communication, and just like communicating over HTTP, a client access policy file must be obtained.

Controlling Client Access via a Socket Policy Server

Since there is no web server that Silverlight can automatically obtain the client access policy from, this policy file must be supplied by some other means. This other means is a socket policy server listening on port 943, located on the same machine that the Silverlight application will use to communicate via sockets. The details of the socket policy server are straightforward. It listens on TCP port 943 and waits for a connection. If it receives the string `<policy-file-request/>` from the client, it sends the contents of the `clientaccesspolicy.xml` file back to the Silverlight application. The details of the client access policy were shown earlier in this chapter, but as a refresher, this file looks like the following for sockets:

```xml
<?xml version="1.0" encoding="utf-8"?>
<access-policy>
  <cross-domain-access>
    <policy>
      <allow-from>
        <domain uri="*"/>
      </allow-from>
      <grant-to>
        <socket-resource port="4502-4534" protocol="tcp"/>
      </grant-to>
    </policy>
```

```
        </cross-domain-access>
      </access-policy>
```

As shown, Silverlight supports a full valid range (from 4502 to 4534) of ports with the use of the TCP protocol. Based on the settings of the **domain** element, the communication can be made between the same domains, all domains, or specific domains. Further details are provided in the "Enabling Cross-Domain Communication" section of this chapter.

The System.Net Namespace

The **System.Net** namespace provides a programming interface for the network communication using different protocols. Several key classes are used in the course of communicating over sockets. The **System.Net.Sockets.Socket** class contains the core functionality for socket communication. The **System.Net.Sockets.SocketAsyncEventArgs** class is used to pass parameters to a socket operation and also to handle the result of a socket operation, such as receiving data. The **System.Net.DnsEndPoint** class specifies an endpoint as a combination of a hostname and port number, while **System.Net.IPEndPoint** specifies the endpoint as an IP address and port number. An endpoint must be specified when executing a socket operation.

The Socket Class

The **Socket** class has three socket operations: connecting (**ConnectAsync**), sending data (**SendAsync**), and receiving data (**ReceiveAsync**). The socket must first connect to a remote endpoint, described by either the **IPEndPoint** or **DnsEndPoint** class. The former is used to connect to an IP address, and the latter is used to connect to a hostname. Tables 5-9 and 5-10 display the key methods and properties of the **Socket** class, respectively.

Table 5-9. Key Methods of the System.Net.Sockets.Socket Class

Name	Description
ConnectAsync	Static method initiates a connection to a remote host. A nonstatic version takes only a **SocketAsyncEventArgs**, while a static version takes a **SocketType**, a **ProtocolType**, and a **SocketAsyncEventArgs**. It returns **true** if the operation is pending, and **false** if the operation has completed.
CancelConnectAsync	Used to cancel a pending connection. It must pass the **SocketAsyncEventArgs** used in the **ConnectAsync** method.
SendAsync	Sends data specified in a **SocketAsyncEventArgs**. It returns **true** if the operation is pending, and **false** if the operation has completed.
ReceiveAsync	Receives data from the open socket. It returns **true** if the operation is pending, and **false** if the operation has completed. The **SocketAsyncEventArgs.Completed** event on the **SocketAsyncEventArgs** object passed in the **e** parameter will be raised upon completion of the operation.

Shutdown	Shuts down sending, receiving, or both on the socket. It ensures that pending data is sent/received before shutting down a channel, so you should call this before you call Close.
Close	Closes the socket, releasing all resources.
Dispose	Releases unmanaged (and optionally managed) resources used by Socket.

You should always call the Shutdown method before Close to ensure that data is finished sending/receiving on the open socket.

Table 5-10. Properties of the System.Net.Socket Class

Name	Description
AddressFamily	Addressing scheme used to resolve addresses. Valid values from the AddressFamily enumeration are Unknown, Unspecified, InterNetwork (for IPv4), and InterNetworkV6 (for IPv6). AddressFamily is initially specified when a socket is created.
Connected	.Gets a value that indicates whether a Socket is connected to a remote host as of the last operation. Returns true if the Socket was connected to a remote resource as of the most recent operation; otherwise, false.
NoDelay	Gets or sets a Boolean value that specifies whether the Socket is using the Nagle algorithm. Returns false if the Socket uses the Nagle algorithm; otherwise, true. The default is false. The Nagle algorithm reduces network traffic by causing the socket to buffer packets for up to 200 milliseconds and then combines and sends them in one packet.
OSSupportsIPv4	Static property; indicates whether IPv4 addressing is supported on the current host.
OSSupportsIPv6	Static property; indicates whether IPv6 addressing is supported on the current host.
ProtocolType	Defines the protocol used by Socket. At present it supports only TCP. Possible values are Tcp, Unspecified, and Unknown.
ReceiveBufferSize	The size of the socket's receive buffer.
RemoteEndPoint	The endpoint of the remote server.
SendBufferSize	The size of the socket's send buffer.
Ttl	The time-to-live value for IP packets.

The SocketAsyncEventArgs Class

The **SocketAsyncEventArgs** class is possibly the most important class for socket communication, since it is used as a way to both pass data/configuration asynchronously to the three socket operation methods and pass access status information/data after an asynchronous call completes. Table 5-11 lists its key members.

Table 5-11. Key Members of the **System.Net.SocketAsyncEventArgs** *Class*

Name	Type	Description
SetBuffer	Method	Initializes the data buffer for an asynchronous operation. One overload sets only the **Count** and **Offset** properties (**Buffer** is set to **null**) while the other also sets the **Buffer** property to an array of bytes.
Buffer	Property (**byte[]**)	Accesses the data buffer. This property is read-only—use the **SetBuffer** method to initialize and possibly place data into this buffer.
BufferList	Property (**IList<ArraySegment<byte>>**)	Specifies an array of data buffers for use by **ReceiveAsync** and **SendAsync**. This property has precedence over the **Buffer** property.
BytesTransferred	Property (**int**)	Number of bytes transferred in socket operation. After a read operation, if this property is **0**, it indicates that the remote service has closed the connection.
ConnectSocket	Property (**Socket**)	Socket related to this operation.
Count	Property (**int**)	Maximum number of bytes to send/receive. This property is read-only—use the **SetBuffer** method to initialize and possibly place data into this buffer.
LastOperation	Property (**SocketAsyncOperation**)	Valid values from **SocketAsyncOperation** enumeration are **None**, **Connect**, **Receive**, and **Send**. This is set to **None** before one of the asynchronous methods is invoked, and then it is set to the value corresponding to the asynchronous operation.
Offset	Property (**int**)	The offset, in bytes, into the **Buffer** property. This is set via the **SetBuffer** method.
RemoteEndPoint	Property (**EndPoint**)	Specifies the remote endpoint used for the **ConnectAsync** method. This can be **IPEndPoint** or **DNSEndPoint**. It supports both IPv4 and IPv6 addressing.

SocketError	Property (SocketError)	Corresponds to a socket error from the most recent socket operation (Connect, Send, or Receive). There are a large number of error codes; however, SocketError.Success is the only code representing success. Check against this to ensure that the most recent operation succeeded.
UserToken	Property (object)	Arbitrary object used to pass data from the invocation of an asynchronous method to the Completed event handler.
Completed	Event	Used to specify an event handler that is invoked when the asynchronous operation is complete.

Building a Socket-Based Sample Text Chat Application

On Windows, the best approach to implement this server is as a Windows service. An implementation of a socket policy server is included in the source code for this book. It is a standard Silverlight application project with the name chapter5Socket, with two Windows Service projects (in C#) named PolicyServer and MessengerServer. The policy server's functionality resides in two key custom-created classes in this project. The first class, SocketPolicyServer, is responsible for waiting and listening for connections. When a connection is received, it's handed over to a new instance of the second class, SocketPolicyConnection, which then sends the policy file. This implementation of the policy server should fulfill the requirements for most policy servers, but if not, it offers a great base to start with. Figure 5-9 shows the sample text chat application project (chapter5Socket) solution structure in the Visual Studio Solution Explorer.

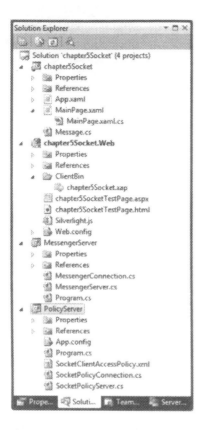

Figure 5-9. *Project structure for a sample chapter5Socket solution enabling text chat*

In this chapter, we are not going to detail the full implementation of the text chat application project, so I will assume that you have gone through the provided source code of the chapter5Socket project. It is recommended that you open the project as a reference for the remainder of this chapter.

The PolicyServer Windows Service Project

The PolicyServer project includes two custom classes, `SocketPolicyServer.cs` and `SocketPolicyConnection.cs`, and a `SocketClientAccessPolicy.xml` file, as shown in Figure 5-9.

The SocketPolicyServer Class

The following is an overall skeleton of the `SocketPolicyServer` class:

```
//additional references
using System.IO;
using System.Net;
using System.Net.Sockets;
```

```
namespace PolicyServer
{
    class SocketPolicyServer
    {

        private TcpListener Listener;
        private byte[] Policy;

        // Path to an XML file containing the
         //socket policy as a parameter
        public SocketPolicyServer(string PathToPolicyFile)
        {

        }
        // This method gets called when we receive
         //a connection from a client
        public void OnConnection(IAsyncResult ar)
        {

        }

        //This method gets called upon shutting down
         //the policy server
        public void Close()
        {

        }
    }
}
```

The constructor of the **SocketPolicyServer** class of the PolicyServer Windows service contains a path to the cross-domain policy file as a parameter. The constructor reads the contents of the policy file and caches it in a byte array. The implementation of the **SocketPolicyServer** class constructor is as follows:

```
// Path to an XML file containing the socket policy as a parameter
public SocketPolicyServer(string PathToPolicyFile)
{
  // Load the policy file in a FileStream object
  FileStream PStream = new
     FileStream(PathToPolicyFile, FileMode.Open);
  Policy = new byte[PStream.Length];
  PStream.Read(Policy, 0, Policy.Length);
  PStream.Close();

  // Port 943 is the default listener port in Silverlight
  Listener = new TcpListener(IPAddress.Any,943);
  Listener.Start();
  Listener.BeginAcceptTcpClient
    (new AsyncCallback(OnConnection), null);
}
```

As shown in the previous code snippet, the constructor invokes the OnConnection method with the callback. The OnConnection method reads the data sent from the client, converts the raw bytes to a string, and, if the string matches <policy-file-request/>, sends the data to the client.

```
// This method gets called when we receive a connection from a client
public void OnConnection(IAsyncResult ar)
{
  TcpClient Client = null;
  try
  {
    Client = Listener.EndAcceptTcpClient(ar);
  }
  catch (SocketException)
  {
    return;
  }
  // handle this policy request with a SocketPolicyConnection
  SocketPolicyConnection PCon = new
    SocketPolicyConnection(Client, Policy);

  // Then look for other connections
  Listener.BeginAcceptTcpClient
    (new AsyncCallback(OnConnection), null);
}
```

Notice that the end of the OnConnection method effectively loops back on itself, instructing the Listener instance to wait for another connection (this isn't recursion since the method isn't being invoked directly). This is essentially all there is to a socket policy server. Fortunately, it's not tricky to implement.

Now that you can grant a Silverlight application permission to communicate via sockets, let's explore exactly how to do just that. There are several key classes used in the course of communicating over sockets. The Socket class contains the core functionality for socket communication. The SocketAsyncEventArgs class is used to pass parameters to a socket operation and also to handle the result of a socket operation, such as receiving data. The DnsEndPoint class specifies an endpoint as a combination of a hostname and port number, while IPEndPoint specifies the endpoint as an IP address and port number. An endpoint must be specified when executing a socket operation.

The SocketPolicyConnection Class

The following is an overall skeleton of the SocketPolicyConnection class. An instance of this class stores a reference to the policy file data. When the OnConnection method is called, the instance accesses the network stream for the new connection and attempts to read from it. If everything goes well, after reading the string containing the text <policy-file-request/>, the instance sends policy data to that client, and closes the connection. For the full implementation of this class, you need to look at the SocketPolicyConnection.cs file under the PolicyServer Windows service project:

```
//additional references
using System.Net.Sockets;

namespace PolicyServer
```

```
{
  class SocketPolicyConnection
  {
    private TcpClient Connection;

    // Buffer to receive client request
    private byte[] Buffer;
    private int Received;

    // The policy to return
    private byte[] Policy;

    //The request string that is expected from the client
    private static string PolicyRequestString =
      "<policy-file-request/>";

    public SocketPolicyConnection(TcpClient client, byte[] policy)
    {

    }

    // Called when we receive data from the client
    private void OnReceive(IAsyncResult res)
    {

    }

    // Called after sending the policy and
    //closes the connection
    public void OnSend(IAsyncResult ar)
    {

    }
  }
}
```

The SocketPolicyConnection class constructor stores a reference to the policy file data and starts receiving the request from the client.

```
public SocketPolicyConnection(TcpClient client, byte[] policy)
{
  Connection = client;
  Policy = policy;
  Buffer = new byte[PolicyRequestString.Length];
  Received = 0;
  try
  {
    // receive the request from the client
    Connection.Client.BeginReceive(Buffer, 0,
      PolicyRequestString.Length, SocketFlags.None,
    new AsyncCallback(OnReceive), null);
```

```
    }
    catch (SocketException)
    {
      Connection.Close();
    }
  }
}
```

The OnReceive method checks for the valid PolicyRequestString and sends back the policy file to the client. This method also makes a call to the OnSend method, which simply closes the connection upon successful delivery of the policy file.

```
private void OnReceive(IAsyncResult res)
{
  try
  {
    Received += Connection.Client.EndReceive(res);
    // Make sure that we received a full request or
     //try to receive again
    if (Received < PolicyRequestString.Length)
    {
      Connection.Client.BeginReceive(Buffer, Received,
        PolicyRequestString.Length - Received,SocketFlags.None,
        new AsyncCallback(OnReceive), null);
      return;
    }
    // Make sure the request is valid by
    //comparing with PolicyRequestString
    string request = System.Text.Encoding.UTF8.
      GetString(Buffer, 0, Received);
    if (StringComparer.InvariantCultureIgnoreCase.
      Compare(request, PolicyRequestString) != 0)
    {
      Connection.Close();
      return;
    }
    // Now send the policy
    Console.Write("Sending the policy...\n");
    Connection.Client.BeginSend(Policy, 0, Policy.Length,
      SocketFlags.None, new AsyncCallback(OnSend), null);
  }
  catch (SocketException)
  {
    Connection.Close();
  }
}
```

The SocketClientAccessPolicy.xml Policy File

Add the following SocketClientAccessPolicy.xml policy file to allow access to all domains and define socket communication using port 4530 and the TCP protocol:

```xml
<?xml version="1.0" encoding="utf-8"?>
<access-policy>
  <cross-domain-access>
    <policy>
      <allow-from>
        <domain uri="*" />
      </allow-from>
      <grant-to>
        <socket-resource port="4530" protocol="tcp" />
      </grant-to>
    </policy>
  </cross-domain-access>
</access-policy>
```

The MessengerServer Windows Service Project

In the chapter5Socket solution, we have added MessengerServer as a separate Windows service project. Like the PolicyServer project, the MessengerServer project contains two classes: MessengerServer, which listens for requests and tracks clients, and MessengerConnection, which handles the interaction of a single client.

The MessengerServer Class

The following is an overall skeleton of the MessengerServer class:

```csharp
//added
using System.Net.Sockets;
using System.Threading;
using System.Net;

namespace MessengerServer
{
  public class MessengerServer
  {
    private Socket Listener;
    private int ClientNo;
    private List<MessengerConnection> Clients = new
      List<MessengerConnection>();
    private bool isRunning;

    public void Start()
    {

    }

    private void OnConnection(IAsyncResult ar)
    {

    }
```

```
    public void Close()
    {

    }

    public void DeliverMessage(byte[] message, int bytesRead)
    {

    }
  }
}
```

As shown in the following code, the Start method of the MessengerServer class listens on port 4530 and invokes the OnConnection method with the callback. Here the IPAddress.Any read-only field provides an IPv4 address that indicates that a server must listen for client activity on all network interfaces for IPv4. The Any field is equivalent to 0.0.0.0 in dotted-decimal notation for IPv4:

```
public void Start()
{
    Listener = new Socket
     (AddressFamily.InterNetwork, SocketType.Stream,
        ProtocolType.Tcp);
    Listener.SetSocketOption(SocketOptionLevel.Tcp,
     (SocketOptionName)SocketOptionName.NoDelay, 0);
    // The allowed port range in Silverlight is 4502 to 4534.
    Listener.Bind(new IPEndPoint(IPAddress.Any, 4530));
    // Waiting on connection request
    Listener.Listen(10);
    Listener.BeginAccept
      (new AsyncCallback(OnConnection), null);
    isRunning = true;
}
```

When the MessengerServer receives a connection request, it performs two tasks. First, it creates an instance of a MessengerConnection class to handle the communication. Next, it adds the client to a collection so it can keep track of all the connected clients. This is the only way to achieve interaction between these clients. So the collection here performs the tracking, and we give each new client a different identifying number. The following is a code snippet of the OnConnection method:

```
private void OnConnection(IAsyncResult ar)
{
  if (isRunning==false)
    return;
  ClientNo++;
  // Look for other connections
  Listener.BeginAccept
   (new AsyncCallback(OnConnection), null);
  Console.WriteLine("Messenger client No: " +
   ClientNo.ToString() + " is connected.");
  Socket Client = Listener.EndAccept(ar);
```

```
  // Handle the current connection
  MessengerConnection NewClient = new
    MessengerConnection(Client, "Client " +
    ClientNo.ToString(), this);
  NewClient.Start();

  lock (Clients)
  {
    Clients.Add(NewClient);
  }
}
```

When the message is received, the MessengerConnection class's OnMsgReceived method calls the DeliverMessage method of the MessengerServer class to send the message to all clients that are currently connected with MessengerServer. The DeliverMessage method also checks for disconnected clients and removes them from the tracking collection of connected clients to avoid future attempts to send a message.

```
public void DeliverMessage(byte[] message, int bytesRead)
{
  Console.WriteLine("Delivering the message...");
  // Duplication of connection to prevent cross-threading issues
  MessengerConnection[] ClientsConnected;
  lock (Clients)
  {
    ClientsConnected = Clients.ToArray();
  }

  foreach (MessengerConnection cnt in ClientsConnected)
  {
    try
    {
      cnt.ReceiveMessage(message, bytesRead);
    }
    catch
    {
      // Remove disconnected clients
      lock (Clients)
      {
        Clients.Remove(cnt);
      }
      cnt.Close();
    }
  }
}
```

The MessengerConnection Class

The following is an overall skeleton of the MessengerConnection class:

```
//added
using System.Net.Sockets;
using System.IO;

namespace MessengerServer
{
  public class MessengerConnection
  {
    private Socket Client;
    private string ID;
    private MessengerServer MServer;

    public MessengerConnection(Socket Client, string ID,
      MessengerServer server)
    {

    }

    private byte[] Message = new byte[1024];

    public void Start()
    {

    }

    public void OnMsgReceived(IAsyncResult ar)
    {

    }

    public void Close()
    {

    }

    public void ReceiveMessage(byte[] data, int bytesRead)
    {

    }
  }
}
```

The MessengerConnection class constructor sets the reference to the current client and MessengerServer server class.

```
public MessengerConnection(Socket Client, string ID,
  MessengerServer server)
{
  this.Client = Client;
  this.ID = ID;
  this.MServer = server;
}
```

The Start method prepares the connection to listen for messages. This method also makes an Async callback to the OnMsgReceived method, as shown in the following code snippet:

```csharp
public void Start()
{
  try
  {
    // Listen for messages
    Client.BeginReceive(Message, 0, Message.Length, SocketFlags.None,
      new AsyncCallback(OnMsgReceived), null);
  }
  catch (SocketException se)
  {
    Console.WriteLine(se.Message);
  }
}
```

The OnMsgReceived method calls the DeliverMessage method of the MessengerServer class to send the message to all clients that are currently connected with MessengerServer by utilizing the stored reference to the message server. After delivering the message, the OnMsgReceived method prepares the connection to listen for the next message, as shown in the following code snippet:

```csharp
public void OnMsgReceived(IAsyncResult ar)
{
  try
  {
    int bytesRead = Client.EndReceive(ar);
    if (bytesRead > 0)
    {
      //Send message to all connected clients
      MServer.DeliverMessage(Message, bytesRead);

      // Listen for next message
      Client.BeginReceive(Message, 0, Message.Length,
        SocketFlags.None, new AsyncCallback(OnMsgReceived), null);
    }
  }
  catch (Exception err)
  {
    Console.WriteLine(err.Message);
  }
}
```

The ReceiveMessage method simply sends the message data to this client.

```csharp
public void ReceiveMessage(byte[] data, int bytesRead)
{
  Client.Send(data, 0, bytesRead,SocketFlags.None);
}
```

The Message.cs File

This **Message** class represents a simple chat message, as follows:

```
public class Message
{
    public string MsgText { get; set; }
    public string Sender { get; set; }
    public DateTime SendTime { get; set; }

    public Message(string text, string sender)
    {
        MsgText = text;
        Sender = sender;
        SendTime = DateTime.Now;
    }
    public Message()
    {
    }
}
```

The MainPage.xaml File

Let's build a simple user interface for the Silverlight text chat application. First, put the following self-explanatory XAML in the MainPage.xaml file:

```
<UserControl x:Class="chapter5Socket.MainPage"
    xmlns="http://schemas.microsoft.com/winfx/2006/xaml/presentation"
    xmlns:x="http://schemas.microsoft.com/winfx/2006/xaml"
    xmlns:d="http://schemas.microsoft.com/expression/blend/2008"
    xmlns:mc="http://schemas.openxmlformats.org/
        markup-compatibility/2006"
    mc:Ignorable="d"
    d:DesignHeight="300" d:DesignWidth="400">
    <StackPanel x:Name="LayoutRoot" Background="White">
        <ScrollViewer  x:Name="Scroller" Height="200">
            <TextBlock x:Name="Messages" TextWrapping="Wrap"/>
        </ScrollViewer>
        <StackPanel Orientation="Horizontal">
            <TextBlock Text="Enter your name: " />
            <TextBox x:Name="txtName" MaxLength="20" Width="200"/>
            <Button x:Name="btnConnect" Width="100"
                Content="Connect" Click="btnConnect_Click"/>
        </StackPanel>
        <StackPanel Orientation="Horizontal" Margin="0,10,0,0" >
            <TextBox x:Name="txtMessage" MaxLength="200"
                Height="100" Width="300"/>
            <Button x:Name="btnSend" Width="100"
                Click="btnSend_Click" Content="Send"/>
        </StackPanel>
```

```
    </StackPanel>
</UserControl>
```

Here we have wired up the `Click` event handler for the `btnConnect` button and the `btnSend` button controls. You will see the implementation of this event handler in the next section when we construct the code-behind.

The MainPage.xaml.cs Code-Behind File

Before we start anything, first you need to add the reference to the `System.Xml.Serialization` assembly to the project, which is part of Silverlight SDK and resides under the `..\Microsoft SDKs\Silverlight\v4.0\Libraries\Client` folder. Also add the following four additional assembly references to the `MainPage` class:

```
using System.Net.Sockets;
using System.IO;
using System.Text;
using System.Xml.Serialization;
```

Next, declare the `Socket` object type variable at the `MainPage` class level to define the primary socket-based connection, as follows:

```
// The MSocket for the connection
private Socket MSocket;
```

Now let's implement the `Click` event for the `btnConnect` button control.

```
private void btnConnect_Click(object sender, RoutedEventArgs e)
{
  try
  {
    if ((MSocket != null) && (MSocket.Connected == true))
      MSocket.Close();
  }
  catch (Exception err)
  {
    AddMessage("ERROR: " + err.Message);
  }
  DnsEndPoint endPoint = new
    DnsEndPoint(Application.Current.Host.Source.DnsSafeHost, 4530);
  MSocket = new Socket(AddressFamily.InterNetwork,
    SocketType.Stream, ProtocolType.Tcp);
  SocketAsyncEventArgs SocketArgs = new SocketAsyncEventArgs();
  SocketArgs.UserToken = MSocket;
  SocketArgs.RemoteEndPoint = endPoint;
  SocketArgs.Completed += new
    EventHandler<SocketAsyncEventArgs>(SocketArgs_Completed);
  MSocket.ConnectAsync(SocketArgs);
}
```

The previous code snippet is self-explanatory. Before creating a new socket-based connection, first check if the socket is already open. If the socket is already open, close the connection. Then, an object of type DnsEndPoint is created to identify the location of the remote host. In this case, the location of the removed host is the web server that hosts the Silverlight page, and the port number is 4530. Finally, the code creates SocketAsyncEventArgs, and attaches the SocketArgs_Completed event handler to the Completed event. Note that the catch block calls the AddMessage method, as shown in the following code:

```
private void AddMessage(string message)
{
  //Separate thread
  Dispatcher.BeginInvoke(
    delegate()
    {
      Messages.Text += message + "\n";
      Scroller.ScrollToVerticalOffset(Scroller.ScrollableHeight);
    });
}
```

Here, to implement typical Windows chat message behavior, the Scroller ScrollViewer automatically scrolls to the bottom of each message and is added to the Messages TextBlock.

The send button performs the sending and receiving of the text message and then appends the response to the main text box that shows the chat conversation.

```
private void btnSend_Click(object sender, RoutedEventArgs e)
{
  SocketAsyncEventArgs Args = new SocketAsyncEventArgs();
  // Prepare the message.
  XmlSerializer serializer = new
    XmlSerializer(typeof(Message));
  MemoryStream ms = new MemoryStream();
  serializer.Serialize(ms, new
    Message(txtMessage.Text, txtName.Text));
  byte[] messageData = ms.ToArray();
  List<ArraySegment<byte>> bufferList = new
    List<ArraySegment<byte>>();
  bufferList.Add(new ArraySegment<byte>(messageData));
  Args.BufferList = bufferList;
  // Send the message.
  MSocket.SendAsync(Args);
  //clear the text box
  txtMessage.Text = string.Empty;
}
```

Executing the Text Chat Application

While you are in development mode, before you open the application, visit C:\book\examples\ chapter5Socket\PolicyServer\bin\Debug to start the PolicyServer console application and double-click the PolicyServer.exe file to run it. Similarly, visit C:\book\examples\chapter5Socket\MessengerServer \bin\Debug to start the MessengerServer console application and double-click the MessengerServer.exe file to run it. (Note that these paths may differ, based on where you set up the application.) Two command shell windows should open, indicating that both console applications are running, as shown in Figure 5-10.

Figure 5-10. PolicyServer and MessengerServer console applications started

Now you are all set to run the project. Go to the Solution Explorer of the open chapter5Socket project in Visual Studio. Select `chapter5SocketTestPage.html` or `chapter5SocketTestPage.aspx` to open the project in the browser. You should see the socket client text-chat application default user interface before connecting to a remote service, as shown in Figure 5-11.

Figure 5-11. Socket client text-chat application before connecting to a remote service

As you can see, we need to provide a name and click the Connect button to join the chat room. Upon successful connection to the server, the message "Connected to server" is appended to the message box. Figure 5-12 shows two chat clients connected to the MessengerServer using two browser windows, and the message history between them is shown with the date and time appended after each message.

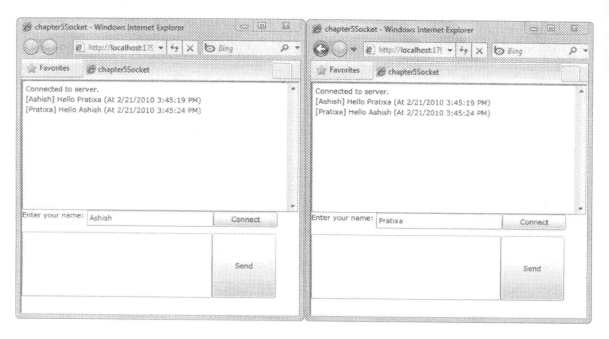

Figure 5-12. Socket client example after connecting and sending data

UDP Multicast

In the digital age, most of the multimedia features such as video streaming and conferencing face a bandwidth constraint in supporting a rich and high-performing media experience. The Unicast network provides a message stream for each user by creating one-to-one communication. This will cause a heavy network load, as well as impact the overall performance. But if the network supports multicast communication, by implementing IP multicast you can establish many-to-many and one-to-many communication to deliver one data package to all users (nodes), reducing overall network overhead. User Datagram Protocol (UDP) is used for the IP multicast.

Silverlight 3 introduced a third party plug-in—Starlight plug-in (projectstarlight.codeplex.com)—to support the UDP multicast. With Silverlight 4, the `System.Net.Sockets` namespace introduced two new UDP multicast client classes—**UdpAnySourceMulticastClient** and `UdpMultiSourceMulticastClient`—to support UDP multicast networking using IPv4 and IPv6.

The UdpAnySourceMulticastClient Class

The `UdpAnySourceMulticastClient` class enables implementation of many-to-many communication, allowing multiple sources from the same group to send data packets to group clients, which is also known as Any Source Multicast (ASM) or Internet Standard Multicast (ISM). You can implement server-less multicast streaming by having any peer(s) as the source to implement peer-to-peer communication. ASM is used for the group conferencing feature. Since multiple senders are sending packets at the same time, the quality of service may be compromised due to possible data stream interference. Using this class, you can also enable unicast communication or one-to-one communication, so that the receiver can send the datagrams back to the specific sender.

Tables 5-12 and 5-13 display the key methods and properties of the UdpAnySourceMulticastClient class, respectively.

Table 5-12. Key Methods of the System.Net.Socket.UdpAnySourceMulticastClient Class

Name	Description
BeginJoinGroup	Binds a UDP multicast socket to a local port and joins a multicast group to receive data packets from the **any** multicast group participant. Here the UDP port and multicast group are defined as part of the UdpAnySourceMulticastClient class constructor. You can also define the policies to allow/not allow a client to access the multicast group for communication. SocketException This is thrown if the access is not allowed. If the client has already joined the group, you will receive the InvalidOperationException.
BeginReceiveFromGroup	Once a client joins the multicast group, he can begin receiving data packets from any group member using this method. It invokes the specified callback once the data packet has arrived from the **any** sender. You can identify the sender source by getting address of the received packets.
BeginSendTo	Once you join the multicast group and send a multicast packet to the receiver client at least once, the receiver can begin the operation to send unicast data packets back to the sender. The destination address and UDP port are defined as remoteEndPoint parameters. You should not define the UDP port less than 1024.
BeginSendToGroup	Once you join the multicast group, you can begin sending data packets to group members using this method. It invokes the specified callback once the data packet has been sent to the group.
BlockSource	Once you join the multicast group, you can block sent packets from a specific source. The sourceAddress parameter contains the IPv4 or IPv6 address matching the address family of the multicast group.
Dispose	Using this method, you can leave the multicast group and release all resources used by the current instance of the UdpAnySourceMulticastClient class and the underlying socket.
EndJoinGroup	Completes an asynchronous join group operation to a multicast group.
EndReceiveFromGroup	Completes an asynchronous operation of receiving a multicast packet from one of the sources of the joined multicast group and provides access to the received information.
EndSendTo	Completes an asynchronous operation to send a unicast packet to a specified destination.

| EndSendToGroup | Completes an asynchronous operation of sending a multicast packet to a multicast group. |
| UnblockSource | You can unblock the specific source to receive the sent packets from that specific source. The **sourceAddress** parameter contains the IPv4 or IPv6 address matching the address family of the multicast group. The source must be blocked earlier using the **BlockSource** method. |

Table 5-13. Properties of the System.Net.Socket.UdpAnySourceMulticastClient Class

Property	Type	Description
MulticastLoopback	bool	True when the outgoing packets are delivered to the sending application.
ReceiveBufferSize	int	Defines the receive buffer size of the **Socket** used for the receive multicast operations. It defines the buffer size for the packets received before calling the **BeginReceiveFromGroup** method. If the buffer is full before the **BeginReceiveFromGroup** and **EndReceiveFromGroup** methods are called, the older packets will be dropped. The buffer size is defined in bytes and the default is 8,192 bytes for Windows.
SendBufferSize	int	Defines the send buffer size of the **Socket** used for sending multicast operations. The buffer size is defined in bytes and the default is 8,192 bytes for Windows.

The UdpSingleSourceMulticastClient Class

In contrast to the **UdpAnySourceMulticastClient** class, the **UdpSingleSourceMulticastClient** enables implementation of one-to-many communication, allowing a receiver to receive the multicast UDP packets from a specific single source, which is also known as Specific-Source Multicast (SSM). SSM produces the managed secured traffic, and thus the quality of service is much better than ASM communication. Using this class, you can also enable unicast communication or one-to-one communication, so that the receiver can send the datagrams back to the specific sender.

Tables 5-14 and 5-15 display the key methods and properties of the **UdpSingleSourceMulticastClient** class, respectively.

Table 5-14. Key Methods of the System.Net.Socket.UdpSingleSourceMulticastClient Class

Name	Description
BeginJoinGroup	Binds a UDP multicast socket to a local port and joins a multicast group to receive data packets from the single multicast group source. Here the UDP port, multicast group, and sender source address are defined as part of the **UdpSingleSourceMulticastClient** class constructor. You can also define the policies to allow/not allow a client to access the multicast group for communication. **SocketException** is thrown if the access is not allowed. If the client has already joined the group, you will receive the **InvalidOperationException**.

BeginReceiveFromSource	Once a client joins the multicast group, he can begin receiving data packets from a single group member using this method. It invokes the specified callback once the data packet has arrived from the single sender.
BeginSendToSource	Once you join the multicast group and send a multicast packet to the receiver client from the specified source at least once, the receiver can begin an operation to send unicast data packets back to the sender. The destination address and UDP port are defined as remoteEndPoint parameters. You should not define the UDP port less than 1024.
Dispose	Using this method, you can leave the multicast group and release all resources used by the current instance of the UdpSingleSourceMulticastClient class and the underlying Socket.
EndJoinGroup	Completes the asynchronous join group operation to a multicast group.
EndReceiveFromSource	Completes an asynchronous operation of receiving a multicast packet from a specific source of the joined multicast group and provides access to the received information.
EndSendToSource	Completes an asynchronous operation to send a unicast packet to a specified single source.

Table 5-15. Properties of the System.Net.Socket.UdpSingleSourceMulticastClient Class

Property	Type	Description
ReceiveBufferSize	int	Defines the receive buffer size of the socket used for the receive multicast operations. It defines the buffer size for the packets received before calling the BeginReceiveFromSource method. If the buffer is full before the BeginReceiveFromSource and EndReceiveFromSource methods are called, the older packets will be dropped. The buffer size is defined in bytes and the default is 8,192 bytes for Windows.
SendBufferSize	int	Defines the send buffer size of the socket used for sending multicast operations. The buffer size is defined in bytes and the default is 8,192 bytes for Windows.

An excellent article is available on MSDN demonstrating key components of the multicast network for Silverlight applications. Visit http://msdn.microsoft.com/en-us/library/ee707325(VS.96).aspx to access the article.

You need a multicast policy server to authorize Silverlight multicast clients. You can also enhance the previously-developed chat application to use the many-to-many multicast communication. Silverlight SDK provides these samples (Multicast Policy Server and Peer-to-Peer Chat application using many-to-many multicast communication). Instead of rewriting the code, you can download the source code of these sample applications by visiting http://code.msdn.microsoft.com/silverlightsdk.

Considerations for Using Networking

So far, you have seen two ways to communicate over HTTP: using proxy classes (for communicating with SOAP, WCF, and ASP.NET services) and making HTTP requests using WebClient and HttpWebRequest. We also looked at how to communicate over sockets in Silverlight. Great questions to ask at this point are "How do these approaches compare to each other?" and "When should I use which?"

Generating a client proxy for a service is the easiest approach from a development standpoint. It's also easy to use a different endpoint when constructing an instance of the client proxy. Using a generated proxy is the easiest and best way to call services exposed on the World Wide Web. If the service changes, you can simply update the proxy. If there are multiple endpoints exposed, you will see these in the ClientConfig and can choose which to use. It is also important to note that this approach uses SOAP 1.1 as a way to communicate with objects over HTTP.

The easiest way to download a resource from a site is to use the System.Net.WebClient class. The two biggest resources are files (e.g., the archived media in the example earlier in this chapter) and text files (such as syndication feeds in XML format). The WebClient class provides a way to download data via a Stream or as a String, making the access of resources quite easy.

Although the WebClient class provides both the HTTP GET and POST methods, it is impossible to send more complicated requests to a server. The System.Net.HttpWebRequest class supports both GET and POST, and also supports both the HTTP and HTTPS protocols. The other major benefit of the HttpWebRequest class is that capabilities provided by the browser, such as authentication and cookies, are supported.

Finally, the socket support exists to directly communicate with an exposed TCP service. Whereas HTTP is an application layer protocol, socket communication has no application layer protocol. A communication protocol must be previously agreed on between a service and the Silverlight application. The major benefit to socket communication is performance—a well-designed TCP service can have less overhead than communication directly over HTTP/SOAP.

By implementing UDP protocol–based IP multicast you can now establish many-to-many and one-to-many communication to deliver one data package to all users (nodes), reducing overall network overhead.

Summary

Silverlight exists in a connected world. Its network support is primarily focused on communication over HTTP(S), which enables it to easily invoke services on the World Wide Web and download documents such as syndication feeds. In this chapter, you've learned about the support for HTTP(S) communication provided by the WebClient and HttpWebRequest classes. Silverlight also supports raw socket communication, albeit with severe restrictions. The support for UDP multicast opens up many avenues to effectively implement video conferencing and video gaming applications with the use of network resources. The next chapter will utilize the networking support built into Silverlight to retrieve data for consumption by Silverlight.

CHAPTER 6

■ ■ ■

Working with Data

Data can take many forms, from simple types passed back from web services to complex formats such as XML. In the previous chapter, you saw how to consume web services from Silverlight and connect to various servers, including ones that live outside your application's host domain and others that communicate over sockets. Once you have data, though, you must process it and/or display it to users. Silverlight provides a DataGrid control, a data binding architecture to connect data to user interface elements, and even item templates for controls like the ListBox to specifically define how each item should appear. On the data-processing side, Silverlight provides a number of classes for working with XML, including Language Integrated Query (LINQ). Another important aspect to data is how to save data on the client. While you can use cookies, Silverlight provides something called *isolated storage* that provides file system semantics for saving and loading data. Let's dig into all this support Silverlight provides for working with data.

Enhancements in Silverlight 4

To support the development of enterprise-level and data-driven line-of-business applications, Silverlight 4 introduces numerous enhancements in the area of data binding. The following is the list of these enhancements, which we will see in detail in this chapter.

- Drag-and-drop data binding is now possible with Silverlight 3 or later using Visual Studio 2010 with intelligent tooling support.

- Support for the IDataErrorInfo interface (similar to WPF) that allows you to validate property values without throwing exceptions at the client side.

- Complex, multi-property validation of bound objects that implement the IDataErrorInfo (for synchronous validation) or INotifyDataErrorInfo (for asynchronous validation) interface.

- Binding to the DependencyObject instances and String indexers.

- Ability to specify String formatting options through the StringFormat property and specify default display values through the FallbackValue and TargetNullValue properties in the data binding system.

- Minor enhancements in the DataGrid control, such as row-level copy and auto-sizing columns features.

- Ability to group collection items through the GroupDescriptions property of the CollectionViewSource class.

- Support to data binding with Silverlight controls using WCF Data Service using the DataServiceCollection(T) class.

- Enhanced isolated storage capabilities for better file management.

Displaying Data

Explanation of the data templates and the Binding markup extension was given in Chapter 2. In Chapter 3, you were introduced to a number of controls, including a brief introduction to data integration and manipulation controls such as ListBox and DataGrid. Controls such as ListBox enable you to connect a user interface element to a data source and automatically display data. The DataGrid control is specifically designed for displaying data in rows and columns. It provides a lot of flexibility for displaying the data and the column headers and footers. We'll take a detailed look at data controls in this section.

Data Binding

Data binding is the connection of a data source to a user interface element such as a TextBlock, TextBox, or ListBox. It is possible to do one-way data binding where data is simply displayed in the user interface, and two-way data binding where any changes a user makes within the user interface elements get reflected in the underlying data source. Data sources in Silverlight are generally objects or collections of objects with properties that can be accessed.

Before we can take a closer look at data binding, we need to examine what makes it happen: the Binding markup extension. This can be used either in XAML or in the code-behind. It's not possible to bind directly to basic data types such as Int32 and string, so we need at least one containing class, such as WebDeveloper, shown here:

```
public class WebDeveloper
{
    public string FirstName { get; set; }
    public string LastName { get; set; }
    public string Email { get; set; }
    public string Website { get; set; }
}
```

This class contains several properties that will be used in the data binding. If we have a TextBlock control and want to display the FirstName property, we first bind the Text property of the TextBlock control to the FirstName property.

```
<TextBlock x:Name="nameTextBlock" Text="{Binding FirstName}"/>
```

This gets us halfway there. The other step is to set the DataContext property of the TextBlock control to the WebDeveloper object. This step is necessary only when it isn't possible to set the data context in XAML, and a simple object like this is one of those cases. The Binding markup extension provides support for three modes of operation: OneTime, OneWay, and TwoWay. These modes of operation control how data is bound and controls the flow between the data source and user interface elements. The following list describes each of these modes:

OneTime: The data binding happens exactly once, meaning that any changes to the data source after the initial binding will not be reflected in the user interface.

OneWay. The data flows only from the data source to the user interface. Any time the data source is updated, the user interface will reflect the changes. This is the default mode.

TwoWay. The data flows from the data source to the user interface and also from the user interface to the data source. Any changes on either side will automatically be reflected in the other side.

After showing it in Chapter 3, it is worth it to show Table 6-1 again, which displays various valid XAML syntaxes for the Binding markup extension.

Table 6-1. *Valid Syntax for the Binding Markup Extension*

Syntax	Description
{Binding}	This signals data binding. The mode of operation is OneWay. This is most commonly used with item templates for controls such as ListBox.
{Binding *path*}	This signals data binding and specifies which property will supply the data. The path takes the form of object properties separated by dots, allowing you to drill down into an object.
{Binding *properties*}	This signals data binding but provides the ability to set data binding configuration properties using a *name=value* syntax.
{Binding *path, properties*}	This combines the previous two formats, allowing you to specify which object property supplies the data and also configure the data binding.

There are a number of properties that help control how data binding behaves, such as controlling how errors during data binding are handled. The full list of properties is shown in Table 6-2.

Table 6-2. *Properties of the System.Windows.Data.Binding Class*

Name	Type	Description
BindsDirectlyToSource	bool	Defines whether the binding binds to the data source by ignoring ICollectionView settings on the data source. The default value is false.
Converter	IValueConverter	This is used to easily perform a custom conversion of the data on its way to or from the data source. This is useful for changing how data appears in the user interface while still maintaining proper data format for the data source.
ConverterCulture	CultureInfo	This is used to specify the culture the converter uses. If the value is null reference, then the culture is determined by the FrameworkElement.Language property.

ConverterParameter	object	This is a custom parameter for use in the converter. The default value is a null reference.
ElementName	String	This specifies the name of the element to use as the binding source object. The default value is a null reference.
Mode	BindingMode	The binding mode specifies how and where data flows between the data source and user interface. The valid modes are OneWay, OneTime, and TwoWay. The default value is set to OneWay binding.
NotifyOnValidatonError	bool	When set to true, the data binding system will raise a BindingValidationError event if validation fails when committing changes to the data source in TwoWay data binding. If false (default value), validation errors will be ignored.
Path	string	This specifies the target property path of the data binding source. To set the data source using the Binding.Source property, keep the path value to an empty string ("").
RelativeSource	RelativeSource	This specifies the binding source by specifying its location relative to the position of the binding target. The default value is a null reference.
Source	object	This specifies the source object for data binding. This overrides the DataContext set on containing elements within the visual tree.
UpdateSourceTrigger	UpdateSourceTrigger	Defines a value determining when the binding source is updated for two-way bindings. The default value is Default, which determines that the binding source is updated automatically upon value change in the binding target. The other possible value is Explicit, which disables automatic update. You need to explicitly call the BindingExpression.UpdateSource method to update the binding source.
ValidatesOnDataErrors	bool	Defines whether the binding engine will report IDataErrorInfo validation errors. The default value is false. This is a new property in Silverlight 4.

ValidatesOnExceptions	bool	When this and NotifyOnValidationError are true, any exceptions generated from the source object's setters or the binding engine's type converters will be reported by raising BindingValidationError. If this is false, or if it's true and NotifyOnValidationError is false, your application will not be aware of exceptions generated by the data binding system. This applies only in TwoWay binding when the data source is updated. The default value is false.
ValidatesOnNotifyData Errors	bool	Defines whether the binding engine will report INotifyDataErrorInfo validation errors. The default value is true. This is a new property in Silverlight 4.

Now let's take a closer look at data binding using a WebDeveloper object. This will be a TwoWay data binding scenario, where changes done to the user interface will be reflected in the data source and vice versa. Figure 6-1 shows an interface where the same data is shown twice.

Figure 6-1. *TwoWay data binding example*

In the top half, the user interface elements (in this case, text boxes) are bound to the data source. Any changes made to these text boxes are reflected in the data source. You can verify this by clicking the Show Data Source Contents button after modifying a value. The lower half lets you change the data source directly. When you click the Update Data Source button, the values in the data source will be updated directly and the corresponding fields in the top half will automatically change. The following XAML shows how the upper half of the user interface is put together and how the Binding markup extension is used on several of the user interface elements in the lower half of the user interface.

```
<UserControl  x:Class="chapter6.TwoWayDataBindingDemo"
    xmlns="http://schemas.microsoft.com/winfx/2006/xaml/presentation"
    xmlns:x="http://schemas.microsoft.com/winfx/2006/xaml"
    xmlns:d="http://schemas.microsoft.com/expression/blend/2008"
    xmlns:mc="http://schemas.openxmlformats.org/markup-compatibility/2006"
    mc:Ignorable="d"
    d:DesignHeight="300" d:DesignWidth="400">
```

```xml
        <StackPanel  x:Name="LayoutRoot" Background="White">
            <Border BorderBrush="Black" BorderThickness="2" Grid.Row="1">
                <StackPanel Orientation="Vertical">
                    <TextBlock Text="User Interface" FontSize="16" ↵
    HorizontalAlignment="Center"/>
                    <StackPanel Orientation="Horizontal" HorizontalAlignment="Center">
                        <TextBlock Text="First Name:"/>
                        <TextBox x:Name="firstNameTextBox"
                            Text="{Binding FirstName, Mode=TwoWay}" Width="140"/>
                    </StackPanel>
                    <StackPanel Orientation="Horizontal" HorizontalAlignment="Center">
                        <TextBlock Text="Last Name:"/>
                        <TextBox x:Name="lastNameTextBox" Width="140"
                            Text="{Binding LastName, Mode=TwoWay}"/>
                    </StackPanel>
                    <StackPanel Orientation="Horizontal" HorizontalAlignment="Center">
                        <TextBlock Text="Email:"/>
                        <TextBox x:Name="emailTextBox" Width="140"
                            Text="{Binding Email, Mode=TwoWay}"/>
                    </StackPanel>
                    <StackPanel Orientation="Horizontal" HorizontalAlignment="Center">
                        <TextBlock Text="Website:"/>
                        <TextBox x:Name="websiteTextBox" Width="140" />
                    </StackPanel>
                    <Button x:Name="btnViewDataSourceButton" Margin="5" Width="155"
                            Content="Show Data Source Contents" ↵
    Click="btnViewDataSourceButton_Click"/>
                </StackPanel>
            </Border>
            <StackPanel Orientation="Vertical">
                <StackPanel Orientation="Horizontal" HorizontalAlignment="Center">
                    <TextBlock Text="First Name:"/>
                    <TextBox x:Name="dsFirstNameTextBox" Width="140"/>
                </StackPanel>
                <StackPanel Orientation="Horizontal" HorizontalAlignment="Center">
                    <TextBlock Text="Last Name:"/>
                    <TextBox x:Name="dsLastNameTextBox" Width="140" />
                </StackPanel>
                <StackPanel Orientation="Horizontal" HorizontalAlignment="Center">
                    <TextBlock Text="Email:"/>
                    <TextBox x:Name="dsEmailTextBox" Width="140" />
                </StackPanel>
                <StackPanel Orientation="Horizontal" HorizontalAlignment="Center">
                    <TextBlock Text="Website:"/>
                    <TextBox x:Name="dsWebsiteTextBox" Width="140" />
                </StackPanel>
                <Button x:Name="btnUpdateDataSource" Margin="5" Width="155"
                        Content="Update Data Source " Click="btnUpdateDataSource_Click"/>
            </StackPanel>
        </StackPanel>
    </UserControl>
```

The lower half of the user interface is similar but uses no data binding. An instance of WebDeveloper wd is created at the class level of this page and then connected when the page loads via the Loaded event handler.

```
void TwoWayDataBindingDemo_Loaded(object sender, RoutedEventArgs e)
{
    wd.FirstName = "Ashish";
    wd.LastName = "Ghoda";
    wd.Email = "aghoda@TechnologyOpinion.com";
    wd.Website = "www.TechnologyOpinion.com";
    LayoutRoot.DataContext = wd;

    //Binding in code-behind
    Binding dataBinding = new Binding("Website");
    dataBinding.Source = wd;
    dataBinding.Mode = BindingMode.TwoWay;
    websiteTextBox.SetBinding(TextBox.TextProperty, dataBinding);

    //lower half controls
    dsFirstNameTextBox.Text = wd.FirstName;
    dsLastNameTextBox.Text = wd.LastName;
    dsEmailTextBox.Text = wd.Email;
    dsWebsiteTextBox.Text = wd.Website;
}
```

Note that here we demonstrated how to create the data binding completely code-behind. If you look at the XAML again, you'll notice that the websiteTextBox doesn't use the Binding markup extension. Instead, the property name is set in the Binding constructor, the data source is linked, and then the data is bound by setting the TextProperty dependency property to the Binding instance. This is almost everything we need to completely enable TwoWay data binding.

Enabling Data Change Notification

If you assemble the code as is, you'll discover that direct changes to the data source are not reflected immediately in the user interface. This is because the data binding system isn't aware that the data source changed. In order to provide this notification, the object being used as the data source must implement the INotifyPropertyChanged interface. This interface defines a single event—PropertyChanged—that must be provided. Let's modify the WebDeveloper class to implement this interface.

```
public class WebDeveloper: INotifyPropertyChanged
{
    private string firstName;
    private string lastName;
    private string email;
    private string website;

    public string FirstName
    {
        get
```

```
        {
            return firstName;
        }
        set
        {
            firstName = value;
            RaisePropertyChanged("FirstName");
        }
    }
    public string LastName
    {
        get
        {
            return lastName;
        }
        set
        {
            lastName = value;
            RaisePropertyChanged("LastName");
        }
    }
    public string Email
    {
        get
        {
            return email;
        }
        set
        {
            email= value;
            RaisePropertyChanged("Email");
        }
    }
    public string Website
    {
        get
        {
            return website;
        }
        set
        {
            website = value;
            RaisePropertyChanged("Website");
        }
    }

    public event PropertyChangedEventHandler PropertyChanged;

    public void RaisePropertyChanged(string propertyName)
    {
        if (PropertyChanged!=null)
        {
```

```
        PropertyChanged(this, new PropertyChangedEventArgs(propertyName));
      }
    }
}
```

Each time the FirstName property is updated, the PropertyChanged event will be raised and the data binding system will be notified. This is the mechanism that will cause the user interface elements (the top half of our demonstration interface) to change immediately after clicking the button to update the data source directly. At this point, run the project, click the Update Data Source button, and you will immediately see the changes made to the Website property. The code for the btnUpdateDataSource_Click event is here:

```
private void btnUpdateDataSource_Click(object sender, RoutedEventArgs e)
{
    //updating data source
    wd.Website = "www.SilverlightStuff.net";
}
```

Rich Data Binding Support in Visual Studio 2010

With Visual Studio 2010, the designer surface is again back with full tooling support for Silverlight 3 and Silverlight 4. Now the designer surface allows drag-and-drop data binding support and automatically creates data-bound controls such as ListBox and DataGrid for the data source. You can create data-bound controls for different services, custom business objects, and SharePoint objects by dragging them from the Data Sources window to the Silverlight Designer surface. Figure 6-2 shows how the tooling screen looks for the DataGrid control.

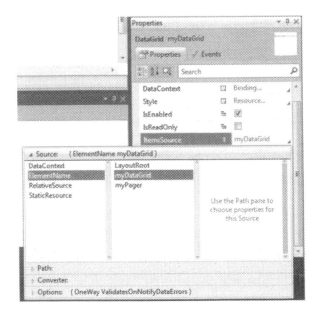

Figure 6-2. *Tooling feature for data binding in Visual Studio 2010*

Data Validation

Data validation plays an important role in any line-of-business application. Data validation confirms the validity of the stored data and also provides proper guidance to users to perform valid data entry. There are plenty of mechanisms in client-side technologies to perform validation of the data entered by the user. In the case of Silverlight, it is obviously related with the data-binding system allowing automatic flow of data and validation logic between the user interface and the server-based data source.

When the data source throws an exception in the Silverlight data binding system, the exception is simply ignored. The exception can be about property setters or incorrect data types. So if your Silverlight application runs into these kinds of errors, it is likely to be missed and there would be no visual indication of the error from the data binding system to the user interface. So the incorrect value will remain in the bound control and never gets applied to the bound object. The only way to avoid this is to notify the user about the incorrect values. You can deal with this by using either two properties of the Binding object, ValidatesOnExceptions and NotifyOnValidationError, or the newly introduced IDataErrorInfo interface in Silverlight 4 to enable reporting of the validation errors that the user interface can bind to. We will see both approaches here.

So let us start with the two properties of the Binding object, ValidatesOnExceptions and NotifyOnValidationError. First consider the following simple class, Choice, implementing the INotifyPropertyChanged interface:

```
public class Choice : INotifyPropertyChanged
{
    private double _answerValue;
    public double AnswerValue
    {
        get { return _answerValue; }
        set
        {
            if (value < 0 || value > 1)
            {
                throw new ArgumentException("Can't be less than 0 or greater than 1");
            }
            _answerValue = value;
            if (PropertyChanged!=null)
            {
                this.PropertyChanged(this, new PropertyChangedEventArgs("AnswerValue"));
            }
        }
    }
    public event PropertyChangedEventHandler PropertyChanged;
}
```

Here, the possible value that the AnswerValue property can be set to is either 0 or 1. For any other value, it will raise the ArgumentException with the message that we supply in property setter.

Binding.ValidatesOnExceptions Property

To demonstrate the Binding.ValidatesOnExceptions property, we will build a very simple user interface, a caption/title with a text box. We set the Binding for Text property of the txtAnswer TextBox. Here we set ValidateOnExceptions to True so that the binding system will watch for any exception in the property setter or incorrect data types for the bound control. The following is the related code snippet:

```
<UserControl x:Class="chapter6.SimpleDataValidationDemo"
    xmlns="http://schemas.microsoft.com/winfx/2006/xaml/presentation"
    xmlns:x="http://schemas.microsoft.com/winfx/2006/xaml"
    xmlns:d="http://schemas.microsoft.com/expression/blend/2008"
    xmlns:mc="http://schemas.openxmlformats.org/markup-compatibility/2006"
    mc:Ignorable="d"
    d:DesignHeight="300" d:DesignWidth="400">
    <StackPanel   x:Name="LayoutRoot" Background="White">
        <TextBlock Height="23" HorizontalAlignment="Left" Text="Enter Value:"
            VerticalAlignment="Top" Width="120" />
        <TextBox x:Name="txtAnswer" Height="23" HorizontalAlignment="Left"
            VerticalAlignment="Top" Width="120" >
            <TextBox.Text>
                <Binding Mode="TwoWay" Path="AnswerValue" ValidatesOnExceptions="True" />
            </TextBox.Text>
        </TextBox>
    </StackPanel>
</UserControl>
```

In the code-behind, we need to set the DataContext property of the LayoutRoot StackPanel control to the instance of the Choice class.

```
Choice ch = new Choice();
LayoutRoot.DataContext = ch;
```

You can place this code in either the Loaded event or in the default UserControl constructor. Now run the sample and enter any invalid value (not between 0 and 1) in the text box, such as -5 or "abc," and press the TAB key. You will see the red border around the TextBox txtAnswer with an error-notification icon in the upper-right corner in an unfocused state. In the focused state, or if you move the mouse over that red icon, the exception message appears in a pop-up as a red alert balloon. Figure 6-3 shows both of these states. Note that if your Visual Studio is set to break on all exceptions, Visual Studio will notify you when the ArgumentException is thrown and will switch into break mode. At this point, simply click the Continue button or press shortcut key F5 to get similar results.

Figure 6-3. Using the DataBinding.ValidatesOnExceptions property to display data validation errors

As you have seen, simply by using the ValidatesOnExceptions property and setting it to true, you can enable your application to catch and display data validation errors. You can apply this property to the controls of the ValidationState group of control states, such as TextBox, PasswordBox, and controls derived from the ItemsControl class.

Binding.NotifyOnValidationError Property and FrameworkElement.BindingValidationError Event

Extending the simple data validation process, as we saw in the last section, to perform some additional actions when the value entered in the bound control raises an exception, you can set `NotifyOnValidationError` to true, along with `ValidatesOnExceptions` also set to true. Turning both properties to true will fire the `FrameworkElement.BindingValidationError` event when the data is not entered correctly.

The `FrameworkElement.BindingValidationError` event is a routed bubbling event. So it can be handled either at the control that raises this or can be bubble up to each successive parent control level, such as the layout container of that control, like `Grid` or `StackPanel`. In an n-tier Silverlight application scenario with pattern implementation such as Model-View-View-Model (MVVM), if you catch such exceptions at the boundary of that particular layer (at a higher level), it will give you an opportunity to use the same logic to handle different kinds of errors raised by various controls. However, if you want more precise error handling for particular types of errors, you should catch such errors where they happen and not at the boundary of that layer.

To demonstrate this, let's extend our previous example and add one TextBlock as a last element and a `NotifyOnValidationError` event handler as shown in the following code snippet. Note that the updated part of the code is in bold font.

```
<StackPanel  x:Name="LayoutRoot" Background="White">
    <TextBlock Height="23" HorizontalAlignment="Left" Text="Enter Value:"
        VerticalAlignment="Top" Width="120" />
    <TextBox x:Name="txtAnswer" Height="23" HorizontalAlignment="Left"
        VerticalAlignment="Top" Width="120" >
        <TextBox.Text>
            <Binding Mode="TwoWay" Path="AnswerValue" ValidatesOnExceptions="True"
                NotifyOnValidationError="True" />
        </TextBox.Text>
    </TextBox>
    <TextBlock x:Name="errMessage" />
</StackPanel >
```

Here our idea is to display that error message in the errMessage TextBlock control. So in the BindingValidationError event handler, we will set errMessage's Text property to the content of the error message. Of course, as a better approach, you may want to use the Label control here instead, as we discussed in Chapter 3. Here we used TextBlock for keeping things simple for demonstration purposes. Note that here we defined the BindingValidationError event at the User Control level. To do that, in the UserControl constructor we wired this event handler as shown here:

```
this.BindingValidationError += new EventHandler<ValidationErrorEventArgs>
    (SimpleDataValidationDemo_BindingValidationError);
```

And the corresponding method—SimpleDataValidationDemo_BindingValidationError—is implemented as follows, which basically populates the added newly added TextBlock with the error message:

```
void SimpleDataValidationDemo_BindingValidationError
    (object sender, ValidationErrorEventArgs e)
{
```

```
        errMessage.Text = e.Error.ErrorContent.ToString();
}
```

We are all set now to run the sample. Input invalid data to cause the data error. You will see the additional error message right beneath the TextBox in the errMessage TextBlock control, as shown in Figure 6-4:

Figure 6-4. *Using* `DataBinding.ValidatesOnExceptions` *and* `DataBinding.NofifyOnValidationError` *properties with the* `FrameworkElement.BindingValidationError` *event to display a data validation error*

IDataErrorInfo Interface for Client-Side Validation

If you have ever worked with WPF applications, you will find that it provides validation infrastructure for binding scenarios through the IDataErrorInfo interface. Silverlight 3 introduced support for validation by throwing exceptions, and you can catch them and convey the appropriate error message to the end user, which we covered in the previous section. With Silverlight 4 there is now support for the IDataErrorInfo interface (similar to WPF) that allows you to validate property values without throwing exceptions. The IDataErrorInfo interface enables client-side validation logic implementation reporting validation errors so that a user interface can bind to them. Table 6-3 shows the properties of this interface.

Table 6-3. *Properties of the* `IDataErrorInfo` *Interface*

Property	Type	Description
Error	string	Gets a message that describes any client-side validation error on the object. It contains a null reference or is Empty if no error is reported.
Item	string	Gets a message that describes a single validation error message for a specified property or column name. The message can represent multiple errors. If you want to display individual messages for each error, use INotifyDataErrorInfo instead.

As described in Table 6-3, the IDataErrorInfo interface exposes an Error property and a string indexer Item. The Error property should return an error message explaining the error with the object. The indexer should return the error message for the property with the given name passed to the indexer. Let's extend our previous example again to use it with the IDataErrorInfo interface. We will update the existing Choice class with implementation of the IDataErrorInfo interface as follows.

```
public class Choice : INotifyPropertyChanged, IDataErrorInfo
{
    private double _answerValue;
    public double AnswerValue
    {
        get { return _answerValue; }
```

```
        set
        {
            _answerValue = value;
            if (PropertyChanged != null)
            {
                this.PropertyChanged(this, new PropertyChangedEventArgs("AnswerValue"));
            }
        }
    }
}

public event PropertyChangedEventHandler PropertyChanged;

string errors = null;
public string Error
{
    get { return errors; }
}

public string this[string columnName]
{
    get
    {
        string result = null;
        if (columnName == "AnswerValue")
        {
            if (AnswerValue < 0 || AnswerValue > 1)
                result = "Can't be less than 0 or greater than 1";
        }
        return result;
    }
}
}
```

As you can see, we have removed the property validation from the AnswerValue property setter and moved that custom validation logic to the String indexer method of the IDataErrorInfo interface (shown in highlighted fonts).

In terms of the XAML code, it would be similar to that in the section of Binding.ValidationOnExceptions, except replace the ValidationOnExceptions property of the txtAnswer text box with the new property in Silverlight 4, ValidationOnDataErrors, and set it to true (shown in highlighted fonts).

```
<TextBox x:Name="txtAnswer" Height="23" HorizontalAlignment="Left"
    VerticalAlignment="Top" Width="120" >
    <TextBox.Text>
        <Binding Mode="TwoWay" Path="AnswerValue" ValidatesOnDataErrors="True" />
    </TextBox.Text>
</TextBox>
```

And we set the DataContext the same way that we did previously:

```
Choice ch = new Choice();
this.DataContext = ch;
```

Run the project and enter some negative or value greater than 1. As soon as you enter the value and press the TAB key, an error-notification icon in the upper-right corner of the txtAnswer text box gets displayed. The cool thing is that this time Visual Studio does not go into break mode and you silently see this validation state change. You will get results similar to those shown in Figure 6-3.

You might be wondering why we need to press the TAB key to invoke these various types of validations. The thing is that this happens only when the value is changed and the edit is committed. So in our case of the TextBox control, this does happen only after we press the TAB key—thus TextBox loses focus. So if you want to instantly catch when the user enters the value, you should use the BindingExpression.UpdateSource() method to achieve immediate validation and notification as the user starts typing for the value. You can get more details on the BindingExpression.UpdateSource() method by visiting http://msdn.microsoft.com/en-us/library/system.windows.data.bindingexpression.update source.aspx.

INotifyDataErrorInfo Interface for Asynchronous Server-Side Validation

By this time, you may have realized that the IDataErrorInfo interface is limited to validate on a per-property basis and is used primarily for simple data validation logic that runs on the client side. This is because the IDataErrorInfo interface was originally designed for pure client environments, such as WPF, and thus it has limitations in client-server technology, such as Silverlight, to perform server-side data validation. If you need to access server-side data validation logic, the INotifyDataErrorInfo interface, introduced in Silverlight 4, is the right choice. It enables data entity classes to implement custom validation rules and exposure of the validation results to the user interface. For example, you may want to check for the value that the user has entered against the stored value in the backend database to make sure it will not create any duplicates. Often in Silverlight-based line-of-business applications, user-entered data needs to be validated on a server asynchronously, rather than on the client side.

INotifyDataErrorInfo contains one property, one method, and one event. It has a HasErrors property of type bool that allows you to check whether an entity has any error. So it is useful to determine the validation state of an entire entity in one go. The GetErrors method allows retrieval of the custom error object rather than just the string (error message) and, more importantly, a property can have more than just one validation error at the same time. The ErrorsChanged event allows notification of the user interface if the validation errors change. It is very useful in asynchronous validation scenarios (e.g., validation over web service or webclient call) or validation that requires some long running process.

Note that ValidatesOnNotifyDataErrors needs to be set to true on the bound control to enable the data binding system to listen for the ErrorsChanged event, and thus display any errors if they are added or changed later on. We will create an example of checking the validity of email and website URLs in order to better understand the INotifyDataErrorInfo interface and demonstrate the use of all three members of the interface.

For that I created a new folder INotifyDataErrorInfoDemo under the existing chapter6 solution. I will try to keep things as simple as possible so you can better focus on the main feature and, at the same time, I will recommend better approaches and advanced usage scenarios at particular places as we go through the code. We will develop one asp.net web service, ValidationService.asmx, one business class named Consultant, implementing the interface, and a simple UI in XAML with a little bit of code-behind.

Developing an ASP .NET Validation Web Service

First create a classic ASP.NET web service (ASMX) named `ValidationService` that will do validation for a few properties of the `Consultant` class that we will develop next. As described in Chapter 5, we need to add this web service to the `chapter6.Web` ASP.NET web project. We need to add the following namespaces to develop validation logic.

```
using System.Net;
using System.Net.Sockets;
using System.Text.RegularExpressions;
```

The web service will expose two methods, named `ValidateUrl` and `ValidateEmail`. The `ValidateUrl` method accepts one string parameter and it validates whether the string supplied is a valid link to web resource. Here is the code for the `ValidateUrl` method.

```
[WebMethod]
public bool ValidateUrl(string URL)
{
    bool isValid = false;
    try
    {
        Dns.GetHostEntry (URL);
        isValid = true;
    }
    catch ( SocketException se)
    {
        isValid = false;
    }
    return isValid;
}
```

As shown in the code snippet, the `Dns` class with the method `GetHostEntry` that provides simple domain-name resolution functionality is used to determine the validity of the supplied string URL. If the resource supplied in the URL does not exist or is incorrect, it will raise an exception of the type `SocketException`. We have a catch block to catch this exception and, according to the validity of the string URL, we set the value for the Boolean flag to `isValid` and return it.

Here is the code for the `ValidateEmail` method.

```
[WebMethod]
public string ValidateEmail(string Email)
{
    string strRegex = @"^([a-zA-Z0-9_\-\.]+)@((\[[0-9]{1,3}" +
        @"\.[0-9]{1,3}\.[0-9]{1,3}\.)|(([a-zA-Z0-9\-]+\." +
        @".)+))([a-zA-Z]{2,4}|[0-9]{1,3})(\]?)$";

    Regex re = new Regex(strRegex);

    if (re.IsMatch(Email) == false)
    {
        return ("E501");
    }
```

```
        else if (Email.Substring(Email.IndexOf("@") + 1 ) == "example.com")
        {
            return ("E502");
        }
        return null;
}
```

As shown, this method uses a regular expression to validate the format of the supplied string as an email. If it is not a valid email, it returns string value E501, which is an error code for our custom error object that we will develop next. And just for an idea, there is another validation rule to put a ban on email for the domain example.com. If the supplied string email has the example.com domain, the string value E502 as an error code will be returned to the calling environment.

At this point, you may be wondering why we used web service to implement this simple validation for email! This validation can also be possible on the client side using the IDataErrorInfo interface. The only reason is to demonstrate asynchronous validation over web service and the use of a custom error object with this interface. In a real usage scenario, you would be using an SMTP network connection and SMTP handshakes to check validity for an email. We avoid such implementation to keep things focused more on the interface itself. This is all required code for the ValidationService web service. To consume this web service, you need to add a service reference of it named ValidationServiceReference in your chapter6 Silverlight application project.

Adding Consultant.cs Class to Implement INotifyDataErrorInfo Interface

Now create a new class named Consultant that will implement the INotifyDataErrorInfo interface. Make sure that you add this class to the previously created folder INotifyDataErrorInfoDemo in the chapter6 Silverlight project, to keep the same structure as described here.

We need to add the following namespaces:

```
using System.ComponentModel;
using System.Collections.Generic;
using System.Linq;
```

For the ease of understanding, we will divide the code into regions (#region). So let us start with the region private members (#region private members). As you can see in the code snippet, there is a ValidationService soap client proxy vds created and some private string objects to use with public properties that we will develop next.

```
#region private members
    private ValidationServiceReference.ValidationServiceSoapClient vds = new
        ValidationServiceReference.ValidationServiceSoapClient();
    private string name;
    private string email;
    private string websiteurl;
#endregion
```

Our custom error class is called ErrorInfo, with public properties and an override version of the ToString method, as shown here. Here we override the default ToString() method to a more meaningful method that outputs ErrorMessage with ErrorCode.

```
public class ErrorInfo
{
    public ErrorInfo(string Code, String Message)
    {
        this.ErrorCode = Code;
        this.ErrorMessage = Message;
    }
    public string ErrorCode { get; set; }
    public string ErrorMessage { get; set; }
    public override string ToString()
    {
        return ErrorCode + ": " + ErrorMessage;
    }
}
```

In the region public members (#region public members), a Dictionary object is used to store the validation errors as a property name key and error value pair. Here is the code for it.

```
#region public members
    public Dictionary<string, List<ErrorInfo>> Errors = new
        Dictionary<string, List<ErrorInfo>>();
#endregion
```

Now it's time to implement three required members of the INotifyDataErrorInfo interface in the region INotifyDataErrorInfo Members (#region INotifyDataErrorInfo Members).

```
#region INotifyDataErrorInfo Members
    public event EventHandler<DataErrorsChangedEventArgs> ErrorsChanged;

    public System.Collections.IEnumerable GetErrors(string propertyName)
    {
        if (string.IsNullOrEmpty(propertyName))//retrieve errors for entire entity
        {
            return Errors.Values;
        }
        else
        {
            if (Errors.ContainsKey(propertyName))
                return Errors[propertyName];
            return null;
        }
    }

    public bool HasErrors
    {
        get
        {
            if (Errors.Count == 0)
                return false;
            return true;
        }
```

```
    }
#endregion
```

Here the GetErrors method returns a possible collection of errors for the supplied property name. If the property name is omitted, it will return the entire collection of errors for the given entity. The value of HasErrors will determine the validation state of an entity.

To keep track of validation errors per property, we will implement two methods, addError and removeError. As the name suggests, addError will add an entry in the Errors Dictionary object with the property name to which the error belongs. The one property can have more than one error at the same time, and it can be stored as a value of the type ErrorInfo in the list of type <ErrorInfo> in the Errors Dictionary object. The following is the code snippet of the addError method in the region Error add/remove (#region Error add/remove).

```
private void  addError(string propertyName,ErrorInfo error)
{
    if (Errors.ContainsKey(propertyName)==true)
    {
        var list = Errors[propertyName];
        list.Add(error);
    }
    else// adding the error to the already existing list
    {
        Errors.Add(propertyName, new List<ErrorInfo>() { error });
    }
    if (ErrorsChanged != null)
        ErrorsChanged(this, new DataErrorsChangedEventArgs(propertyName));
}
```

As we add the validation error to the Errors Dictionary, we raise the ErrorsChanged event to make sure that the binding system will listen for the validation errors that happen afterwards and also errors that change.

Now look at the second method, the removeError method in the region Error add/remove (#region Error add/remove). It will remove a validation error for a specified property with the supplied error code for that error.

```
private void removeError(string propertyName, string errorCode)
{
    if (Errors.ContainsKey(propertyName))
    {
        var Error = Errors[propertyName].Where<ErrorInfo>
            (e => e.ErrorCode == errorCode).FirstOrDefault();
        var list = Errors[propertyName];
        list.Remove(Error);

        if (list.Count == 0)//no more errors for this property
        {
            Errors.Remove(propertyName);
        }

        if (ErrorsChanged != null)
            ErrorsChanged(this, new DataErrorsChangedEventArgs(propertyName));
```

```
    }
}
```

In the code snippet, we used the Where clause for the var Error object. It is the LINQ to query for the supplied error code! That is why we added the namespace System.Linq.

Now we jump back to the code for public properties for the class to which the user interface control can bind. In the existing region public members (#region public members) we add the following code for the public Name property.

```
public string Name
{
    get { return name; }
    set
    {
        name = value;
        if (value==string.Empty)
        {
            //Add error
            ErrorInfo er = new ErrorInfo("N501", "Name is required.");
            addError("Name", er);
        }
        else
        {
            //Remove error
            removeError("Name", "N501");
        }
        if (ErrorsChanged != null)
            ErrorsChanged(this, new DataErrorsChangedEventArgs("Name"));
    }
}
```

In the code snippet, we simply check for the name string and if the name is empty, a validation error of the type ErrorInfo is created and added to the Error dictionary object using the addError method. If this validation error is corrected in bound control, then the removeError method will invoke to remove this validation error from the property error list. In both cases the ErrorsChanged event is raised to keep the user interface bound control updating.

The code for the other two public properties, Websiteurl and Email, is shown here.

```
public string Websiteurl
{
    get { return websiteurl; }
    set
    {
        websiteurl = value;
        vds.ValidateUrlAsync(value);
    }
}

public string Email
{
    get { return email; }
```

```
    set
    {
        email = value;
        vds.ValidateEmailAsync(value);
    }
}
```

Here we used the proxy vds of ValidationService to call to appropriate validation methods for the property. As this is an asynchronous call, we need to define an asynchronous operation completed event handler for both methods. The best place to define them is in constructor of the Consultant class, as shown here.

```
vds.ValidateEmailCompleted += new
    EventHandler<ValidationServiceReference.ValidateEmailCompletedEventArgs>
    (vds_ValidateEmailCompleted);

vds.ValidateUrlCompleted += new
    EventHandler<ValidationServiceReference.ValidateUrlCompletedEventArgs>
    (vds_ValidateUrlCompleted);
```

However, in validation methods, where we are using the ValidationService web service proxy directly, you should create a service agent class that is responsible for making calls from Silverlight to remote services. The task of the service agent can be the initialization of the service call, capturing the data that's returned and forwarding the data back to the calling environment. By doing this you can offload the data gathering responsibilities to the service agent. So a service agent can also be re-used across multiple classes as needed.

The last part of this class is the region validation methods (#region Validation methods), where we will create the ErrorInfo object with proper error messages set for the property. The code for vds_ValidateEmailCompleted is:

```
#region Validation methods

    void vds_ValidateEmailCompleted(object sender,
        ValidationServiceReference.ValidateEmailCompletedEventArgs e)
    {
        if (e.Result=="E501")
        {
            //Add error
            ErrorInfo er = new ErrorInfo("E501", "Email format is Invalid.");
            addError("Email",er);
        }
        else
        {
            //Remove error
            removeError("Email","E501");
        }

        if (e.Result=="E502")
        {
            //Add error
            ErrorInfo er = new ErrorInfo("E502", "Email provider is not supported.");
```

```
            addError("Email",er);
        }
        else
        {
            //Remove error
            removeError("Email", "E502");
        }
    }
#endregion
```

Here we either add or remove validation errors for the Email property based on the retrieved error code from the validation method ValidateEmail on the web service. And there is the same kind of approach for the vds_ValidateUrlCompleted method.

```
void vds_ValidateUrlCompleted(object sender,
    ValidationServiceReference.ValidateUrlCompletedEventArgs e)
{
    if (e.Result)
    {
        //Remove the error
        removeError("Websiteurl", "W501");
    }
    else
    {
        //add the error
        ErrorInfo er = new ErrorInfo("W501", "Website does not exist.");
        addError("Websiteurl", er);
    }
}
```

Here, based on retrieved bool value, we add or remove one validation error for the Websiteurl property. With this Consultant class, implementing INotifyDataErrorInfo is now complete. Next we need to quickly set up the user interface to make use of this class.

AsyncValidationDemo.xaml and Code-Behind

Let's add a Silverlight user control named AsyncValidationDemo.xaml and set the Width property of the user control to 600 in XAML. The following code snippet shows the implementation of the user interface.

```
<Grid x:Name="LayoutRoot" Background="White" HorizontalAlignment="Left"
    BindingValidationError="LayoutRoot_BindingValidationError" >
    <StackPanel Width="300">
        <TextBlock Text="Enter Name:"/>
        <TextBox x:Name="txtName" Text="{Binding Path=Name,Mode=TwoWay,
            ValidatesOnNotifyDataErrors=True, NotifyOnValidationError=True}"/>
        <TextBlock Text="Enter Website URL:" Margin="0,10,0,0"/>
        <TextBox x:Name="txtWebsite" Text="{Binding Path=Websiteurl,Mode=TwoWay,
            ValidatesOnNotifyDataErrors=True, NotifyOnValidationError=True}"/>
        <TextBlock Text="Enter Email:" Margin="0,10,0,0"/>
        <TextBox x:Name="txtEmail" Text="{Binding Path=Email,Mode=TwoWay,
            ValidatesOnNotifyDataErrors=True, NotifyOnValidationError=True}"/>
```

```
        <Button Content="Submit" x:Name="btnSubmit" Width="100" Margin="10"/>
    </StackPanel>
</Grid>
```

Here, for each TextBox control, we set ValidatesOnNotifyDataErrors and NotifyOnValidationError to true. ValidatesOnNotifyDataErrors will tell the binding system to listen for the ErrorChanged event of the interface and the controls will go into the appropriate validation state for the value violating the validation rule. The NotifyOnValidationError set to true will fire BindingValidationError when a validation error occurs. So we defined the BindingValidationError event handler at a higher level in Grid LayoutRoot. Based on the validation errors, we will either enable or disable the Submit button. But we will do this in code-behind, as shown in the following code snippet of the entire code-behind.

```
namespace chapter6.INotifyDataErrorInfoDemo
{
    public partial class AsyncValidationDemo : UserControl
    {
        private Consultant cs;

        public AsyncValidationDemo()
        {
            InitializeComponent();
            this.Loaded += new
                RoutedEventHandler(AsyncValidationDemo_Loaded);
        }

        void AsyncValidationDemo_
            Loaded(object sender, RoutedEventArgs e)
        {
            cs = new Consultant();
            this.DataContext = cs;
        }

        private void LayoutRoot_BindingValidationError
            (object sender, ValidationErrorEventArgs e)
        {
            if (cs.HasErrors)
            {
                btnSubmit.IsEnabled = false;
            }
            else
            {
                btnSubmit.IsEnabled = true;
            }
        }
    }
}
```

In the LayoutRoot_BindingValidationError method, the value of HasErrors is used to enable or disable the Submit button. As a better approach, you can also implement the INotifyPropertyChanged interface and bind btnSubmit Button's isEnabled property to HasErrors, thus avoiding any code in the code-behind file. This can be a better utilization of the rich data binding system in Silverlight. In the Loaded event of the user control, we set the DataContext to an instance of the Consultant class.

Now run the project and enter some invalid values in the txtWebsite and txtEmail text boxes that can cause validation error. You will see both textboxes go into a validation state, as shown in Figure 6-5.

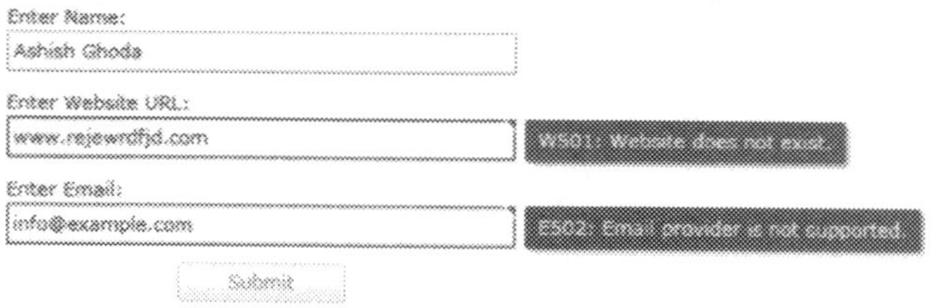

Figure 6-5. *Using* INotifyDataErrorInfo *for showing custom validation errors*

In Figure 6-5, you can see both error messages with corresponding error code. This is because of our override version of the ToString method that we created in the ErrorInfo class.

XAML Element Data Binding / Element-to-Element Binding

Unlike WPF-based rich client applications, until Silverlight 3 you needed to develop code to implement XAML-based element-to-element binding, which allowed two user interface components to integrate through properties. As an example, if you wanted to set the Volume of a MediaElement using a Slider control, some code was needed to pull the value of the slider and change the volume according to the slider's value.

Silverlight 3 made the developer community happy by introducing XAML element property data binding to Common Language Runtime (CLR) objects and other user interface components. This allowed you to bind elements' properties to each other so the value/behavior of the bound element changed based on the element's changes. You can achieve element-to-element data binding by adding the ElementName property in the binding expression. The following example binds the TextBlock control's Text property to the mySlider control's Value property, as follows:

```
Text="{Binding Value, ElementName=mySlider}">
```

Now let's look at this example's complete code snippet.

```
<UserControl x:Class="chapter6.ElementBindingDemo"
    xmlns="http://schemas.microsoft.com/winfx/2006/xaml/presentation"
    xmlns:x="http://schemas.microsoft.com/winfx/2006/xaml"
    xmlns:d="http://schemas.microsoft.com/expression/blend/2008"
    xmlns:mc="http://schemas.openxmlformats.org/markup-compatibility/2006"
    mc:Ignorable="d"
    d:DesignHeight="300" d:DesignWidth="400">
    <StackPanel x:Name="LayoutRoot" Background="White">
        <TextBlock x:Name="myValue" Height="32" Width="auto" FontSize="14"
            Text="{Binding Value, Mode=OneWay, ElementName=mySlider}" />
        <Slider x:Name="mySlider" Maximum="100" Minimum="1" Value="5" />
    </StackPanel>
</UserControl>
```

As shown in Figure 6-6, the text value is now set to the default value 5. This value will change as you move the mySlider control to the left or right. If you move the control to the right, the value will increase (the maximum value is set to 100); if you move the control to the left, the value will decrease (the minimum value is set to 1).

17.9794344473008

Figure 6-6. XAML element data binding between Slider and TextBlock controls

DependencyObject Binding

Before Silverlight 4, data binding support was limited to objects derived from the FrameworkElement class, and thus missed some key objects, including transformations. The Silverlight 4 binding system now supports binding of properties on a DependencyObject and not just on FrameworkElements. This new ability opens up the possibility of user interface interactions through the use of only XAML. For example, now in Silverlight 4 you can bind the rotation angle of a RotateTransform of an Image control to a Slider control, using the ElementName property in the binding expression, as shown in the following XAML.

```
<StackPanel  x:Name="LayoutRoot" Background="White">
    <Image x:Name="myImage" Source="Games.png" Stretch="None"
        Margin="0,120,0,5" >
        <Image.RenderTransform>
            <RotateTransform Angle="{Binding ElementName=mySlider,
                Path=Value}" />
        </Image.RenderTransform>
    </Image>
    <TextBlock Text="{Binding ElementName=mySlider, Path=Value}"
        Width="200" />
    <Slider x:Name="mySlider" Minimum="0" Maximum="360" Width="200"/>
</StackPanel>
```

In the code snippet, we bind the myImage Image control's RotateTransform angle to a Slider control named mySlider. And to see the current value for the rotation angle, we did an element binding of mySlider with the TextBlock control. Upon running this sample and moving the slider, you will see what's shown in Figure 6-7.

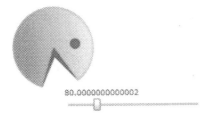

80.0000000000002

Figure 6-7. DependencyObject binding of Image's RotateTransform to Slider control

Silverlight 4 also includes a DependencyObjectCollection that provides a way for third parties to define collection properties that contain DependencyObjects and have properties on those DependencyObjects in binding operations. Get more information by visiting http://msdn.microsoft.com/en-us/library/ee652772(VS.96).aspx.

Type Converters

There are certain cases where you want to show values in data-bound control with some symbol, such as currency data. Silverlight provides something called a type converter that can be used by the data binding system to conduct custom conversion as the data flows from the data source to the user interface or vice versa. A custom type converter implements the IValueConverter interface, providing the Convert and ConvertBack methods for handling the conversion. So let us add one more property called Fees to our existing WebDeveloper class, as shown in the following code snippet.

```
private double fees;
public double Fees
{
    get
    {
        return fees;
    }
    set
    {
        fees = value;
        RaisePropertyChanged("Fees");
    }
}
```

And we also need to update the existing user interface in the page TwoWayDataBindingDemo.xaml to add a feesTextBox control in the upper half-section and just below the websiteTextBox.

```
<StackPanel Orientation="Horizontal" HorizontalAlignment="Center">
    <TextBlock Text="Fees:"/>
    <TextBox x:Name="feesTextBox" Width="140" />
</StackPanel>
```

And here's the implementation of a type converter used for formatting the currency for fees. Just in case this type converter is used in a TwoWay data binding scenario, the ConvertBack method is also implemented.

```
public class FeesConverter : IValueConverter
{
    public object Convert(object value, Type targetType,
        object parameter,
        System.Globalization.CultureInfo culture)
    {
        return (String.Format("{0:C}", (double)value));
    }

    public object ConvertBack(object value, Type targetType,
```

```
      object parameter,
      System.Globalization.CultureInfo culture)
   {
      string fees = (string)value;
      return(System.Convert.ToDouble(fees.Replace("$", "").Replace(",", "")));
   }
}
```

The type converter must be registered as a resource and assigned an x:Key value before it can be used in the XAML. Here's what this registration looks like in the TwoWayDataBindingDemo.xaml page (with updated code in the highlighted fonts):

```
<UserControl x:Class="chapter6.TwoWayDataBindingDemo"
    xmlns="http://schemas.microsoft.com/winfx/2006/xaml/presentation"
    xmlns:x="http://schemas.microsoft.com/winfx/2006/xaml"
    xmlns:d="http://schemas.microsoft.com/expression/blend/2008"
    xmlns:mc="http://schemas.openxmlformats.org/markup-compatibility/2006"
    mc:Ignorable="d"
    xmlns:me="clr-namespace:chapter6"
    d:DesignHeight="300" d:DesignWidth="400">
    <UserControl.Resources>
        <me:FeesConverter x:Key="feeConverter"/>
    </UserControl.Resources>
    ......
</UserControl>
```

Binding syntax for feesTextBox will look like the following:

```
<TextBox x:Name="feesTextBox" Text="{Binding Fees,
    Mode=TwoWay, Converter={StaticResource feeConverter}}" Width="140" />
```

This gives us information on consulting fees in a nice format without having to exert too much effort. You can see the result in Figure 6-8.

Figure 6-8. *Using a type converter to format data for the user interface*

StringFormat

Though a type converter is quite handy for simple formatting needs in data binding, the use of type converters is not suitable for all scenarios. It is a repetitive task, as you have to create an IValueConverter class for different types of property with different formatting to display. It would be really good if you could do such formatting directly in the data binding.

Now Silverlight 4 adds this ability, providing a more simplified and straightforward way of formatting data back and forth. The good thing is it also uses the format to perform parsing for the two-way data binding mode. The newly introduced `BindingBase.StringFormat` property enables formatting a value using either a predefined format or a custom format without the need for a converter class. It is effectively the equivalent of the `String.Format()` method.

So if you want to display some value in bound control as a percentage you can implement it like the following, using the `StringFormat` property within the Binding expression:

```
<TextBox Text="{Binding Path=TotalAggregate, Mode=TwoWay, StringFormat=P}"/>
```

It's the same if you want to display value with some currency formatting—you can use `StringFormat=C`. Custom formats are also supported, so you can display the `Website` property of `WebDeveloper` class with custom formatting like the following:

```
<TextBlock Text="{Binding Path=Website,StringFormat=Visit my site: {0}}" />
```

BindingBase.FallbackValue and BindingBase.TargetNullValue Properties

There are certain cases when you want to show some value in bound control. There might be cases where the value is `Null` or the binding system fails to load the value. For such situations, Silverlight 4 has introduced `BindingBase.TargetNullValue` and `BindingBase.FallbackValue` properties.

There can be a number of reasons for which it might not be possible to get the data from the bound object to the user interface. There might be an exception in the property getter or any binding operation failure. The `FallbackValue` property provides a mechanism for specifying a fallback value when the binding is unable to return a value.

Taking the existing `WebDeveloper` class in account, we will change the `FirstName` property getter to what's shown here:

```
get
{
    throw new NotImplementedException("exception occurred.");
}
```

So this code will raise an exception, and the fall-back value that we provide will be shown as per the code snippet here:

```
<TextBlock x:Name="firstNameTextBox"
    Text="{Binding Path=FirstName, Mode=TwoWay, FallbackValue=None}" Width="140" />
```

The `TargetNullValue` binding extension property applies its value to the target when the source value of the binding operation is `null`. The following code will display `None` when the source value of the binding operation is `null`.

```
<TextBlock x:Name="firstNameTextBox"
    Text="{Binding Path=FirstName, Mode=TwoWay, TargetNullValue=None}" Width="140" />
```

The only difference between the `TargetNullValue` and `FallbackValue` markup extensions is that if the bound value is null then `TargetNullValue` will show the specified value. `FallbackValue` works much the same way, but its value is shown when the value cannot be loaded through data binding, such as when `DataContext` is null or binding fails to find the property on a bound object.

Binding to String Indexers

If you have ever developed a class that allows you to define custom sets of properties, then you have likely used string indexers. And binding that class's properties in Silverlight 3 and earlier versions, you've found that these indexers are breaking the data binding. The good news is that in Silverlight 4 there is new syntax that enables binding to string indexers. For a better understanding of this feature, consider the following Book class snippet.

```
public class Book
{
    public Dictionary<string, object> extraFields { get; set; }
    public string Title { get; set; }
    public string Author { get; set; }

    public Book()
    {
        extraFields = new Dictionary<string, object>();
    }

    public object this[string indexer]
    {
        get
        {
            return (extraFields[indexer]);
        }
        set
        {
            extraFields[indexer] = value;
        }
    }
}
```

In the preceding code snippet, each entry in the `extraFields` dictionary represents a custom property. The key in the dictionary describes the name of the property, and the value corresponding to that key represents the value of that property.

We will add a custom property named `ISBN` and `PreviewUrl` to it as shown in the following code snippet:

```
Book b = new Book();
b.Title = "Introducing Silverlight 4";
b.Author = "Ashish Ghoda";
b.extraFields.Add("ISBN", "978-1-4302-2991-9");
b.extraFields.Add("PreviewUrl", @"http://apress.com/book/view/9781430229919");
LayoutRoot.DataContext = b;
```

As shown in the code snippet, we added two custom properties to the extraFields dictionary and set the DataContext property of the LayoutRoot StackPanel that contains four TextBlock controls, as shown in the following XAML code snippet:

```
<StackPanel  x:Name="LayoutRoot" Background="White">
    <TextBlock Text="{Binding Path=Title}"/>
    <TextBlock Text="{Binding Path=Author}"/>
    <TextBlock Text="{Binding Path=[ISBN]}"/>
    <TextBlock Text="{Binding Path=[PreviewUrl]}"/>
</StackPanel >
```

Note the syntax of using the indexer in the data binding system in the last two text blocks, where square brackets [] indicate that it binds indexer to access an item of the defined property. Now if you run the project, the output screen will look like Figure 6-9:

Introducing Silverlight 4
Ashish Ghoda
978-1-4302-2991-9
http://apress.com/book/view/9781430229919

Figure 6-9. Binding to String indexer

The DataGrid Control

The DataGrid control is useful for displaying data in a tabular format with rows and columns. As we learned in Chapter 3, it isn't part of the core Silverlight installation, so you must download the Silverlight SDK and distribute the System.Windows.Controls.Data assembly with your application. In order to use DataGrid in XAML, you must make its namespace visible.

```
<UserControl x:Class=" chapter6.DataGridDemo"
    xmlns="http://schemas.microsoft.com/winfx/2006/xaml/presentation"
    xmlns:x="http://schemas.microsoft.com/winfx/2006/xaml"
    xmlns:d="http://schemas.microsoft.com/expression/blend/2008"
    xmlns:mc="http://schemas.openxmlformats.org/
        markup-compatibility/2006"
    xmlns:data="clr-namespace:System.Windows.Controls;
        assembly=System.Windows.Controls.Data">
    mc:Ignorable="d"
    d:DesignHeight="300" d:DesignWidth="400">
    <Grid x:Name="LayoutRoot" Background="White">
        <data:DataGrid x:Name="accountsDataGrid"/>
    </Grid>
</UserControl>
```

Note You will learn in the next Chapter 7 that Silverlight 4 supports the `XmlnsDefinition` attribute to declare the namespace for custom assemblies. To utilize the DataGrid control, which is part of the Silverlight SDK, you just need to define the namespace `xmlns:sdk="http://schemas.microsoft.com/winfx/2006/xaml/presentation/toolkit"` at the user control level to use any SDK control, rather than adding the specific assembly as we added here, `xmlns:data="clr-namespace:System.Windows.Controls;assembly=System.Windows.Controls.Data"` for the DataGrid control.

You then connect the DataGrid to a data source using the `ItemsSource` property. By default, the DataGrid automatically generates column headings. The appearance of the default DataGrid after connecting it to the sample data is shown in Figure 6-10.

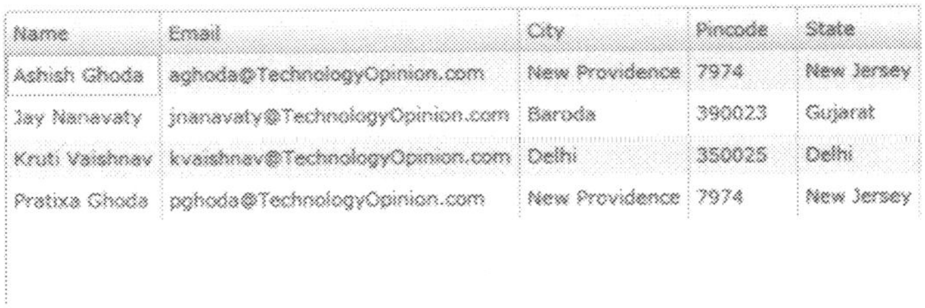

Name	Email	City	Pincode	State
Ashish Ghoda	aghoda@TechnologyOpinion.com	New Providence	7974	New Jersey
Jay Nanavaty	jnanavaty@TechnologyOpinion.com	Baroda	390023	Gujarat
Kruti Vaishnav	kvaishnav@TechnologyOpinion.com	Delhi	350025	Delhi
Pratixa Ghoda	pghoda@TechnologyOpinion.com	New Providence	7974	New Jersey

Figure 6-10. The default DataGrid control

The DataGrid provides a lot of functionality. You can change the style of rows, alternate rows, and column/row headers. The DataGrid can be configured to permit or prevent the reordering of columns, enable row selection, and enable in-place editing of data. It also provides a number of events to give you plenty of opportunity to transform or otherwise handle data. Silverlight 3 introduced the enhanced DataGrid control features such as RowGrouping, additional events, and cell- and row-level data validation. Silverlight 4 also introduces minor enhancements such as row level copy and auto-sizing columns features.

Implementing Grouping, Sorting, Filtering, and Paging

Grouping, sorting, filtering, and paging are the basic functionalities that are required in any Silverlight line-of-business application that uses data-bound controls such as the DataGrid control. The `PagedCollectionView` class, residing in the `System.Windows.Data` namespace, represents a view for grouping, sorting, filtering, and navigating a paged data collection before it appears in the data-bound control such as the DataGrid control. We also need to add the namespace `System.ComponentModel` for `SortDescriptionCollection`, representing a collection of `SortDescription` objects. Let's implement each of these functionalities one by one.

Grouping

The grouping support for the DataGrid introduced in Silverlight version 3 allows you to organize rows together into a logical group. You just need to select a property to use for grouping so objects with the same value will be organized in a single logical group that can be collapsed and expanded in the DataGrid. To demonstrate this in our example, we include an Employee class with some common employee-related properties, and we will define the PagedCollectionView object to display these employees in a DataGrid control grouped by the State property. As shown here, the Employee class includes the string type properties Name, Email, City, State, and Pincode.

```
public class Employee
{
    public string Name { get; set; }
    public string Email { get; set; }
    public string City { get; set; }
    public string State { get; set; }
    public int Pincode { get; set; }
}
```

The user interface is very simple, with one DataGrid having four columns bound to properties of the Employee class, as shown in the following XAML code snippet:

```
<UserControl x:Class="chapter6.PagedCollectionViewDemo"
    xmlns="http://schemas.microsoft.com/winfx/2006/xaml/presentation"
    xmlns:x="http://schemas.microsoft.com/winfx/2006/xaml"
    xmlns:d="http://schemas.microsoft.com/expression/blend/2008"
    xmlns:mc="http://schemas.openxmlformats.org/
        markup-compatibility/2006"
    mc:Ignorable="d"
    d:DesignHeight="300" d:DesignWidth="400"
    xmlns:data="clr-namespace:System.Windows.Controls;
        assembly=System.Windows.Controls.Data">
    <Grid x:Name="LayoutRoot" Background="White"
        Width="400" Height="300">
        <data:DataGrid x:Name="myDataGrid" AutoGenerateColumns="False" >
            <data:DataGrid.Columns>
                <data:DataGridTextColumn Binding="{Binding Name}"
                    Header="Name"  />
                <data:DataGridTextColumn Binding="{Binding Email}"
                    Header="Email"  />
                <data:DataGridTextColumn Binding="{Binding City}"
                    Header="City"  />
                <data:DataGridTextColumn Binding="{Binding Pincode}"
                    Header="Pin Code"  />
            </data:DataGrid.Columns>
        </data:DataGrid>
    </Grid>
</UserControl>
```

In the code-behind class, create the Employee class-related array, populate it, and create a PagedCollectionView object pgn based on this emps array. To achieve row-grouping for the State property, we set the GroupDescriptions property to the State property. And finally, bind the pgn object to the DataGrid control's ItemsSource property in the Loaded event of the class. The following is the code-behind class code snippet:

```
void PagedCollectionViewDemo_Loaded(object sender, RoutedEventArgs e)
{
    Employee[] emps = new Employee[10];

    emps[0] = new Employee();
    emps[0].Name = "Ashish Ghoda";
    emps[0].Email = "aghoda@TechnologyOpinion.com";
    emps[0].City = "New Providence";
    emps[0].Pincode = 07974;
    emps[0].State = "New Jersey";

    emps[1] = new Employee();
    emps[1].Name = "Jay Nanavaty";
    emps[1].Email = "jnanavaty@TechnologyOpinion.com";
    emps[1].City = "Baroda";
    emps[1].Pincode = 390023;
    emps[1].State = "Gujarat";

    emps[2] = new Employee();
    emps[2].Name = "Kruti Vaishnav";
    emps[2].Email = "kvaishnav@TechnologyOpinion.com";
    emps[2].City = "Delhi";
    emps[2].Pincode = 350025;
    emps[2].State = "Delhi";

    emps[3] = new Employee();
    emps[3].Name = "Pratixa Ghoda";
    emps[3].Email = "pghoda@TechnologyOpinion.com";
    emps[3].City = "New Providence";
    emps[3].Pincode = 07974;
    emps[3].State = "New Jersey";

    //PagedCollectionView
    //Grouping
    PagedCollectionView pgn = new PagedCollectionView(emps);
    pgn.GroupDescriptions.Add(new PropertyGroupDescription("State"));
    //Binding to the DataGrid
    myDataGrid.ItemsSource = pgn;
}
```

Now, if you run the project, you should see all the added employee information displayed in the DataGrid control grouped by state, as shown in Figure 6-11.

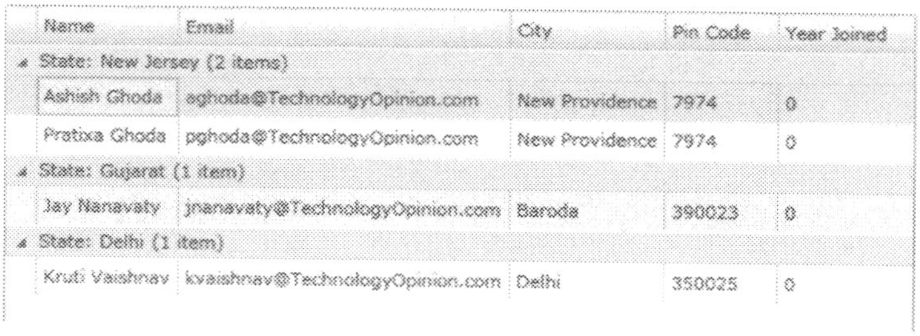

Name	Email	City	Pin Code	Year Joined
▲ State: New Jersey (2 items)				
Ashish Ghoda	aghoda@TechnologyOpinion.com	New Providence	7974	0
Pratixa Ghoda	pghoda@TechnologyOpinion.com	New Providence	7974	0
▲ State: Gujarat (1 item)				
Jay Nanavaty	jnanavaty@TechnologyOpinion.com	Baroda	390023	0
▲ State: Delhi (1 item)				
Kruti Vaishnav	kvaishnav@TechnologyOpinion.com	Delhi	350025	0

Figure 6-11. DataGrid grouped by state

Just now you created one-level grouping by adding one property in GroupDescriptions. You can achieve multilevel grouping very easily: just add more than one property in GroupDescriptions. Using the previous example, let's group by the State and then the City property. The order of grouping is from top to bottom, according to the order in which properties are added using GroupDescriptions. So, to group by State and then by City, just add the following code under the previously set GroupDescriptions property:

```
pgn.GroupDescriptions.Add(new PropertyGroupDescription("City"));
```

Figure 6-12 shows the DataGrid grouped by the State and then the City property.

Name	Email	City	Pin Code	Year Joined
▲ State: New Jersey (2 items)				
▲ City: New Providence (2 items)				
Ashish Ghoda	aghoda@TechnologyOpinion.com	New Providence	7974	0
Pratixa Ghoda	pghoda@TechnologyOpinion.com	New Providence	7974	0
▲ State: Gujarat (1 item)				
▲ City: Baroda (1 item)				
Jay Nanavaty	jnanavaty@TechnologyOpinion.com	Baroda	390023	0
▲ State: Delhi (1 item)				
▲ City: Delhi (1 item)				
Kruti Vaishnav	kvaishnav@TechnologyOpinion.com	Delhi	350025	0

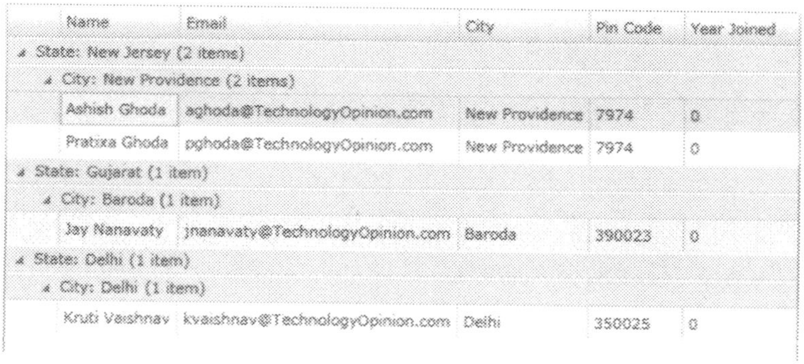

Figure 6-12. Multilevel DataGrid grouping, grouped by State and City

Sorting

The DataGrid by default provides the sorting feature by just clicking the column. To specify how items are sorted in a DataGrid through code-behind, the SortDescription type is used. So we create a SortDescription on the Name property and define the ListSortDirection enumeration (Ascending or Descending) and add the SortDescription to the pgn collection.

```
//Sorting
pgn.SortDescriptions.Add(new SortDescription("Name",
    ListSortDirection.Ascending));
```

Filtering

The PagedCollectionView.Filter property provides filtering where you need to set a callback. A callback will check whether each row satisfies the filtering condition and should be hidden or displayed. The following code snippet shows only employee(s) living in New Jersey (in our case it will be two employees).

```
//Filtering
pgn.Filter = delegate(object fo)
{
    Employee emp = (Employee)fo;
    return (emp.State == "New Jersey");
};
```

Paging using the DataPager Control

Data paging is critical in the scenarios where you need to show a large amount of data to the user in a managed fashion so that the user can navigate through the data page by page. The PagedCollectionView provides paging support to split the data into pages, where each page has a fixed number of rows. There are two properties of PagedCollectionView that enable use of paging, PageSize and PageIndex.

The PageSize property gets or sets the number of items to display on a page. By default it is set to 0 so we need to set it explicitly to a desired value to enable paging.

The PageIndex property gets the zero-based index of the current page. So the first page would have a 0 index value, the second page would have 1, and so on.

The DataPager Control

To ease down this paging task offered by PagedCollectionView, Silverlight has one dedicated control—the DataPager control—that does exactly the same task. The DataPager resides in the System.Windows.Controls namespace in the System.Windows.Controls.Data.dll assembly. Table 6-4 lists properties of the DataPager control.

Table 6-4. Properties of the DataPager Control

Property	Type	Description
AutoEllipsis	bool	Determines whether to use an ellipsis as the last numeric button. When true the last numeric page button is replaced with an ellipsis for any DisplayMode that shows numeric page buttons. The default value is false.
CanChangePage	bool	Determines if the user can move (set to true) to another page or not (set to false). The default value is false. Note that this property cannot be set by the user—it is modified when a Source is specified.

CanMoveToFirstPage	bool	Determines if the user can move (set to true) to the first page or not (set to false). The default value is false. Note that this property cannot be set by the user—it is modified when a Source is specified. CanMoveToFirstPage is true when CanChangePage is true and the first page is not the current page.
CanMoveToLastPage	bool	Determines if the user can move (set to true) to the last page or not (set to false). The default value is false. Note that this property cannot be set by the user—it is modified when a Source is specified. CanMoveToLastPage is true when CanChangePage is true and the last page is not the current page.
CanMoveToNextPage	bool	Determines if the user can move (set to true) to the next page or not (set to false). The default value is false. Note that this property cannot be set by the user—it is modified when a Source is specified. If IsTotalItemCountFixed is true, CanMoveToNextPage is true when CanChangePage is true and the current page is not the last page. If IsTotalItemCountFixed is false, CanMoveToNextPage is always true.
CanMoveToPreviousPage	bool	Determines if the user can move (set to true) to the previous page or not (set to false). The default value is false. Note that this property cannot be set by the user—it is modified when a Source is specified.
DisplayMode	PagerDisplayMode	Gets or sets a value that indicates how the DataPager user interface is displayed. The possible values are FirstLastNumeric, FirstLastPreviousNext, FirstLastPreviousNextNumeric, Numeric, PreviousNext, and PreviousNextNumeric. When the AutoEllipsis property is true, the last numeric page button is replaced with an ellipsis for any DisplayMode that shows numeric page buttons.
IsTotalItemCountFixed	bool	Determines if the total number of items in the collection is fixed (true) or not (false).
ItemCount	int	Gets the current number of known items in the source data collection.
NumericButtonCount	int	Gets or sets a value that indicates the number of page buttons shown on the DataPager user interface.
NumericButtonStyle	Style	Gets or sets the style that will be used for the numeric buttons.

PageCount	int	Gets or sets the PageCount property of PagedCollectionView the control is bound to; otherwise it is set to 1.
PageIndex	int	Gets or sets the index of the current page when the source is IPagedCollectionView, otherwise it is 0. The default value is -1. If Source is a null reference or if PageSize is 0, PageInedex must be set to -1. In other cases, it must be 0 or more.
PageSize	int	Gets or sets a value defining the number of items displayed on the current page when the source is IPagedCollectionView, otherwise DataPager ignores the PageSize value.
Source	IEnumerable	Gets or sets the data collection that the DataPager controls paging for.

To use the DataPager, you simply need to add it to your page, set a few properties, and then link it to PagedCollectionView as shown in the following code snippet.

```
<data:DataPager x:Name="myPager" PageSize="2" DisplayMode="FirstLastNumeric" />
```

And in the code-behind, you just need to set the DataPager Source property to PagedCollectionView, as shown here.

```
myPager.Source = pgn;
```

Now run the project and you will see the DataPager control displayed just below the DataGrid, as shown in Figure 6-13.

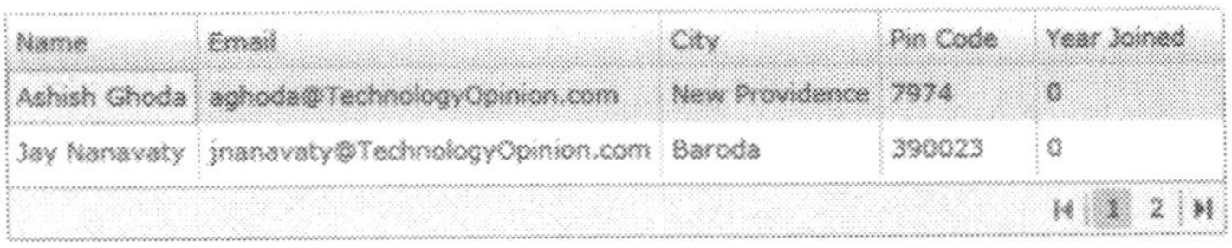

Name	Email	City	Pin Code	Year Joined
Ashish Ghoda	aghoda@TechnologyOpinion.com	New Providence	7974	0
Jay Nanavaty	jnanavaty@TechnologyOpinion.com	Baroda	390023	0
				I◀ 1 2 ▶I

Figure 6-13. Paging in DataGrid using the DataPager control

DataGrid Editing Events

With support for explicit binding, Silverlight 3 and Silverlight 4 support the DataGrid editing events CellEditEnding, CellEditEnded, RowEditEnding, and RowEditEnded. With the use of these events, the DataGrid can properly raise cancellable editing events and ended notifications, as in the following code snippet:

```
public event EventHandler<DataGridCellEditEndingEventArgs>
    CellEditEnding;
public event EventHandler<DataGridCellEditEndedEventArgs>
```

```
    CellEditEnded;
public event EventHandler<DataGridRowEditEndingEventArgs>
    RowEditEnding;
public event EventHandler<DataGridRowEditEndedEventArgs>
    RowEditEnded;
```

You can cancel these CellEditEnding and RowEditEnding events by setting the Cancel property of the e argument to true in the event handler. If the CellEditEnding or RowEditEnding event is not canceled, the specified EditAction will be performed to commit or cancel the edit. After the edit has been successfully committed or canceled, the CellEditEnded or RowEditEnded event occurs accordingly.

DataGrid Column Sizing

Silverlight 4 introduces support for auto-sizing the columns in the DataGrid. Auto-sizing allows columns to share the remaining width of a DataGrid. This is similar to star sizing of the Grid control that you have seen in Chapter 3 by using the asterisk (*) sign, while setting the Width property. The DataGridLengthUnitType enumeration (Auto, Pixel, SizeToCells, SizeToHeader, and Star) defines constants that describe how DataGrid elements, such as columns, are sized. When you are working with a Silverlight 4 DataGrid with Visual Studio 2010 in Design mode, you'll find new options for the Width of a column in the Properties window, as shown in Figure 6-14.

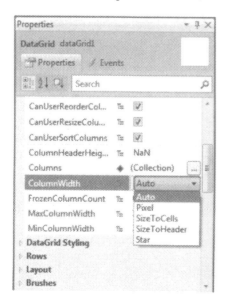

Figure 6-14. DataGrid ColumnWidth sizing values in the Properties window in Visual Studio 2010

Table 6-5. The DataGridLengthUnitType *Enumeration*

Enum Name	Description
Auto	The unit of measure is based on the size of the cells and the column header.
Pixel	The unit of measure is expressed in pixels.
SizeToCells	The unit of measure is based on the size of the cells.
SizeToHeader	The unit of measure is based on the size of the column header.
Star	The unit of measure is a weighted proportion of the available space.

To demonstrate this, we will use the previously created emps Employee class array object and, rather than applying sizing in XAML, we will do it in the code-behind on the button's click event so changes made to the column at runtime will give you a better idea about this feature.

The user interface will have one DataGrid control, five button controls, and one TextBox as shown here:

```
<StackPanel  x:Name="LayoutRoot" Background="White" Width="400">
    <data:DataGrid Height="300" Name="dataGrid1" Width="400" />
    <TextBox x:Name="txtUnitValue" Width="50"/>
    <StackPanel Orientation="Horizontal" >
        <Button Width="80" Content="Auto" Click="UpdateSizing"/>
        <Button Width="80" Content="Pixel" Click="UpdateSizing"/>
        <Button Width="80" Content="SizeToCells"
            Click="UpdateSizing"/>
        <Button Width="80" Content="SizeToHeader"
            Click="UpdateSizing"/>
        <Button Width="80" Content="Star" Click="UpdateSizing"/>
    </StackPanel>
</StackPanel>
```

We will enter a numeric value in the txtUnitValue TextBox, select any cell for which we want to change the column width, and then click to any of the button controls that will raise the UpdateSizing event, which will set the Width of the current column as per the provided value and unit type. The code for the UpdateSizing method is here:

```
private void UpdateSizing(object sender, RoutedEventArgs e)
{
    double unitValue;
    Button b=sender as Button;
    if (txtUnitValue.Text != string.Empty)
    {
        unitValue = double.Parse(txtUnitValue.Text);
    }
    else
    {
```

```
            unitValue = 1;
        }

        switch (b.Content.ToString())
        {
            case "Auto":
                SetColumnSize(unitValue ,DataGridLengthUnitType.Auto );
                break;
            case "Pixel":
                SetColumnSize(unitValue, DataGridLengthUnitType.Pixel );
                break;
            case "SizeToCells":
                SetColumnSize(unitValue,
                    DataGridLengthUnitType.SizeToCells );
                break;
            case "SizeToHeader":
                SetColumnSize(unitValue,
                    DataGridLengthUnitType.SizeToHeader );
                break;
            case "Star":
                SetColumnSize(unitValue, DataGridLengthUnitType.Star);
                break;
        }
}
```

As shown, the UpdateSizing method contains a switch case on the Button's Content property that has raised the event, and, based on the Content property value, we call another method named SetColumnSize to set the Width with the parameter unitValue and a DataGridLengthUnitType enum value. Code for the SetColumnSize method is here:

```
private void SetColumnSize(double value,
    DataGridLengthUnitType unitType)
{
    DataGridColumn dc = dataGrid1.CurrentColumn as DataGridColumn;
    dc.Width = new DataGridLength(value, unitType);
}
```

You are all set to run the sample. Try selecting the different cells, entering different values, and clicking any of the buttons to see how DataGrid column sizing works.

Clipboard Support

Silverlight 4 introduces support to copy and paste content for the DataGrid at row level. This means you can copy a row of a DataGrid to the clipboard and then paste it to another program such as Notepad or Excel. This is as simple as selecting some rows and pressing Ctrl+ C (for copy) and then Ctrl + V (for paste) on Windows, or Command + C (for copy) and then Command + V (for paste) on Mac. The contents are copied to the clipboard as a tab delimited string.

The value of the DataGrid.ClipboardCopyMode property controls how the data is copied to the clipboard. If set to DataGridClipboardCopyMode.None, content cannot be copied to the clipboard from the DataGrid control. If set to DataGridClipboardCopyMode.ExcludeHeader, content can be copied to the clipboard from the DataGrid control. However, it does not include the column headers. If set to `DataGridClipboardCopyMode.IncludeHeader`, content can be copied to the clipboard from the DataGrid control including column headers.

You can also control what is being copied for a particular column by using the `DataGridBoundColumn.ClipboardContentBinding` property to point to different data if the cell contents aren't what you want to have copied. In addition to this, the DataGrid now also provides a `DataGrid.CopyingRowClipboardContent` event that you can handle. This event occurs when the row is prepared for a clipboard copy operation.

Cell-Level Data Validation

From Silverlight 3, the DataGrid control supports framework validation at the cell level by default. Developers do not have to write a single line of code or set any property to perform basic framework, data-level validation of each cell.

To demonstrate cell-level validation, I added an additional `int` type property, `YearJoined`, to the `Employee` class and changed the XAML code appropriately to display it in the DataGrid. As you can see in Figure 6-15, I entered "Text" instead of any integer value for the Year Joined column, and automatically the DataGrid raised a type conversion error at the time of binding the value. The message in the red box is displayed automatically, and the row background color changes to pink.

Figure 6-15. Default cell validation in the Silverlight DataGrid control

Row-Level Data Validation

You saw how easy it is to implement cell-level validation; now, with some minor custom coding, let's implement row-level validation when you commit a particular row or entity in the DataGrid.

Row-level validation uses the features of `System.ComponentModel.DataAnnotations`. You decorate the class with the `CustomValidation` attribute, specifying the validation class and the method to be used for validation. Row-level validation errors show at the bottom of the DataGrid in an error ListBox. If you implement custom validation for more than one property and you have more than one error, all errors are displayed at the bottom of the DataGrid in the ListBox. If you click the error in the ListBox, focus goes to the cell where the error occurred. When the error is resolved, the error entry is removed from the ListBox automatically.

Using our previous example, let's implement row-level validation for the `Email` attribute. First, include a reference to the `ComponentModel` and `DataAnnotations` assemblies to the class, as shown in the following code:

```
using System.ComponentModel;
using System.ComponentModel.DataAnnotations;
```

Now let's implement the `ValidateEmployee` validation class to validate if the Email field in the DataGrid is empty. If the Email field is empty, a customized message is displayed.

277

```
public static ValidationResult EmailNotNull(Employee emp)
{
    if (emp.Email == null)
    {
        return (new ValidationResult("Email cannot be empty"));
    }
    else
    {
        return (ValidationResult.Success);
    }
}
```

Now add the CustomValidation attribute to define ValidateEmployee as the validation class and EmailNotNull as the validation method at the Employee class level.

```
[CustomValidation(typeof(ValidateEmployee), "EmailNotNull")]
```

Finally, the Employee class has to implement the INotifyPropertyChanged interface to get notified about property changes. For that, first modify the signature of the Employee class as follows:

```
public class Employee : INotifyPropertyChanged
```

As you implement INotifyPropertyChanged, you must implement the PropertyChanged event.

```
public event PropertyChangedEventHandler PropertyChanged;
```

Now NotifyPropertyChanged will raise the PropertyChanged event, passing the source property that is being changed, as follows:

```
private void NotifyPropertyChanged(String changedproperty)
{
    if (PropertyChanged != null)
    {
        PropertyChanged(this, new
          PropertyChangedEventArgs(changedproperty));
    }
}
```

In the end, you need to call NotifyPropertyChanged when the Email property is being changed by updating the code as follows:

```
public string email;
[Required]
public string Email
{
    get { return email; }
    set
    {
        if (value != email)
        {
            email = value;
```

```
            NotifyPropertyChanged("email");
      }
    }
}
```

Note that here I have added the [Required] attribute is added to implement the CustomValidation we implemented earlier. Run the project, as you can see in Figure 6-16, if you keep the Email field empty, the message is displayed at the end of the DataGrid in the ListBox and the row background color changes to pink.

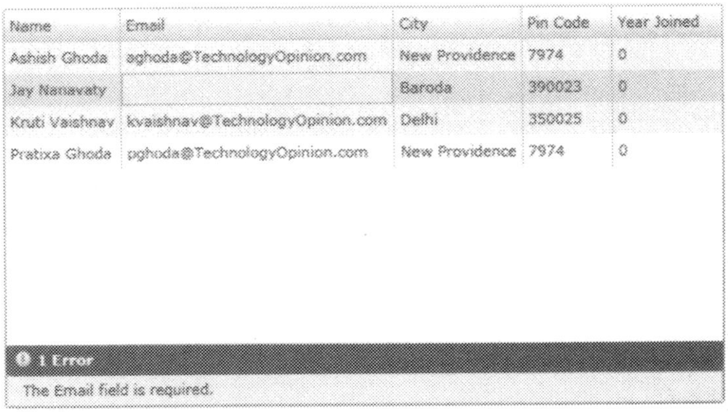

Name	Email	City	Pin Code	Year Joined
Ashish Ghoda	aghoda@TechnologyOpinion.com	New Providence	7974	0
Jay Nanavaty		Baroda	390023	0
Kruti Vaishnav	kvaishnav@TechnologyOpinion.com	Delhi	350025	0
Pratixa Ghoda	pghoda@TechnologyOpinion.com	New Providence	7974	0

① 1 Error
The Email field is required.

Figure 6-16. Row custom validation in the Silverlight DataGrid control

The DataForm Control

The DataForm control was introduced in Silverlight 3 as part of the Silverlight Toolkit, which empowers designers and developers to implement enterprise-level and data-driven form-based applications in an agile mode. The DataForm control can be bound to the data and allows you to present and perform data operations including data validation very easily. You can easily extend the integration of the DataForm control with Silverlight's code-behind capabilities, such as integration with LINQ and Windows Communication Foundation (WCF) services (discussed in Chapter 5), to develop enterprise-level, complex, data-driven, and service-oriented multitier applications. Let's jump into understanding the DataForm control without wasting further time.

For any DataForm control-based application with data validation, you need to add the following four assemblies as a reference to the Silverlight project:

```
System.ComponentModel
System.ComponentModel.DataAnnotations
System.Windows.Controls.Data
System.Windows.Controls.Data.DataForm
```

There are two ways to bind the DataForm control. The first is by creating a resource to the current UserControl with a set of properties in the corresponding class, and the second approach is by creating ObservableCollection.

For the first approach, create a simple `Consultant` class with the `FirstName`, `LastName`, `Email`, and `Website` properties of the `string` type, as shown in the following code. Note that the implementation of this class is different than the one that we created with the same name for the `INotifyDataErrorInfo` section discussed earlier in this chapter:

```
public class Consultant
{
    public string FirstName { get; set; }
    public string LastName { get; set; }
    public string Email { get; set; }
    public string Website { get; set; }
}
```

Now in the XAML code, define the DataForm XML namespace `DF` in the UserControl. This allows the DataForm control in the layout and local namespace to set a reference to the project itself so we can use the `Consultant` class, as in the following code:

```
<UserControl x:Class="chapter6.DataFormDemo"
    xmlns="http://schemas.microsoft.com/winfx/2006/xaml/presentation"
    xmlns:x="http://schemas.microsoft.com/winfx/2006/xaml"
    xmlns:d="http://schemas.microsoft.com/expression/blend/2008"
    xmlns:mc="http://schemas.openxmlformats.org/
        markup-compatibility/2006"
    mc:Ignorable="d"
    xmlns:local="clr-namespace:chapter6"
    xmlns:DF="clr-namespace:System.Windows.Controls;assembly=
        System.Windows.Controls.Data.DataForm.Toolkit"
    d:DesignHeight="300" d:DesignWidth="400">
```

Next, define the local resource by adding `UserControl.Resources` and `local:Consultant` with the defined Key, as follows:

```
<UserControl.Resources>
    <local:Consultant x:Key="C1"
            FirstName="Ashish"
            LastName="Ghoda"
            Email="aghoda@TechnologyOpinion.com"
            Website="TechnologyOpinion.com" >
    </local:Consultant>
</UserControl.Resources>
```

Now you are all set to add the DataForm control to the project. Add the DataForm control instance, and use the `ItemsSource` property to bind to the local resource C1 (defined in the previous code snippet). Also, set the other properties as follows:

```
<Grid x:Name="LayoutRoot" Background="White">
    <DF:DataForm  ItemsSource="{Binding C1}"
        Header="TechnologyOpinion.com -
            Strive for the Strategic Excellence"
        Background="Gray"
        LabelPosition="Auto">
```

```
    </DF:DataForm>
</Grid>
```

Now you are all set to run your first DataForm control project. Are you thrilled? I am! Run the project, and you should see a DataForm displaying the fields associated with the `Consultant` class properties populated with the local data resource, as shown in Figure 6-17.

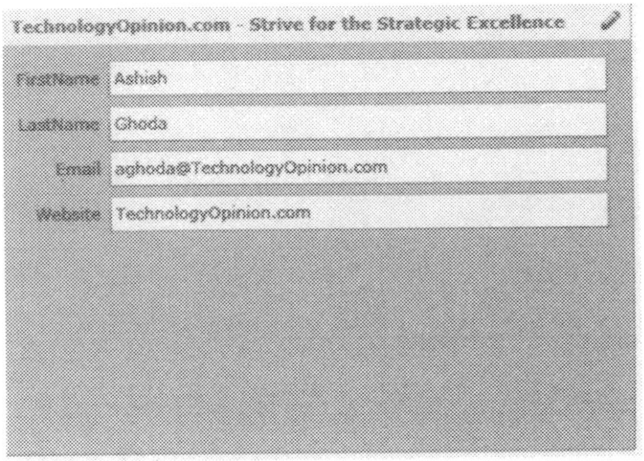

Figure 6-17. The DataForm control in action

Take a look at the top-right corner of Figure 6-17. The pencil symbol allows you to change the mode of the DataForm to Edit mode. The `Binding` markup extension set on the fields determines whether you can modify the fields. At present, we have not set up any `Binding` markup extension, so by default the `BindingDirection` is set to `TwoWay` for all fields. If you click the pencil symbol once, all fields become editable and the Save button becomes available, as shown in Figure 6-18.

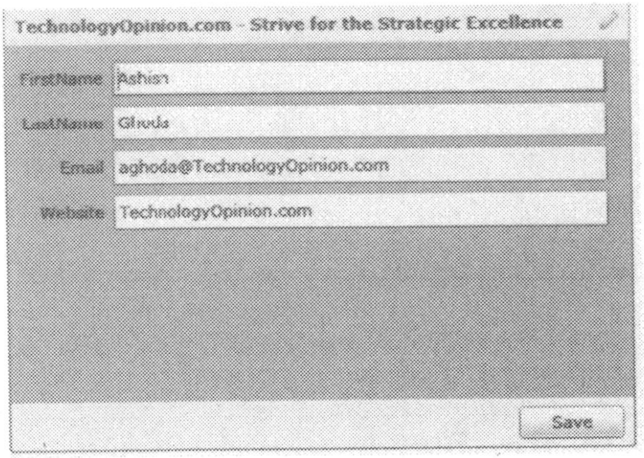

Figure 6-18. DataForm in Edit mode

IEditableObject Interface Implementation

You can also apply the IEditableObject interface implementation to the Consultant class to get more custom control with the BeginEdit, CancelEdit, and EndEdit methods, as demonstrated in the following code:

```
public class Consultant : IEditableObject
{
   public string FirstName { get; set; }
   public string LastName { get; set; }
   public string Email { get; set; }
   public string Website { get; set; }

   public void BeginEdit()
   {
     //Implement code here
   }

   public void CancelEdit()
   {
     //Implement code here
   }

   public void EndEdit()
   {
     //Implement code here
   }
}
```

This implementation gives you more control over the DataForm. The key change is the availability of the Save and Cancel buttons in Edit mode.

Customized Display of DataForm Fields

You can customize an individual field's attributes, such as Name, Description, Order, GroupName, Prompt, ResourceType, ShortName, etc. The following code demonstrates the customized names, descriptions, and order of the Consultant class attributes:

```
public class Consultant
{
    [Display(Name = "First Name :",
            Description = "Enter Your First Name", Order = 1)]
    public string FirstName { get; set; }
    [Display(Name = "Last Name :",
            Description = "Enter Your Last Name", Order = 2)]
    public string LastName { get; set; }
    [Display(Name = "Email :", Description = "Enter Your Email",
        Order = 4)]
    public string Email { get; set; }
    [Display(Name = "Website :",
```

```
            Description = "Enter Your Website Url", Order = 3)]
    public string Website { get; set; }
}
```

Change the `Binding` attribute of the DataForm control in the XAML code to `Consultants`, as shown in the following code:

```
<DF:DataForm ItemsSource="{Binding Consultants}"
    Header="TechnologyOpinion.com -
      Strive for the Strategic Excellence"
    Background="Cyan"
    FieldLabelPosition="Auto">
</DF:DataForm>
```

Run the project, and you should see the customized names for the fields. Also, the Email and Website fields are reordered, and an information button is available for each field. Highlighting the information button displays the field description, as shown in Figure 6-19.

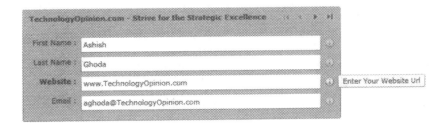

Figure 6-19. Customized DataForm with display attributes applied to fields

Field-Level Validation

You can use these different approaches based on field types to perform validation:

- Apply the `[Required (ErrorMessage = "This field cannot be blank")]` attribute to any attribute to force it to be a required field. If the user does not enter a value, the defined error message is displayed to the field upon validation.

- Apply different attributes for different types of validation:

  For an int type field, use the `[Range(1, 200, ErrorMessage="Over Value")]` attribute.

  For a string type field, use the `[StringLength(40, ErrorMessage="Exceed number of characters")]` attribute.

  For other field types, use the `RegularExpression` attribute.

In our sample application, apply the `Required` attribute (as shown) to the `Email` property and run the application. If you do not populate the Email field, you will get an error message at the bottom of the DataForm and the respective field will be highlighted in red, as shown in Figure 6-20.

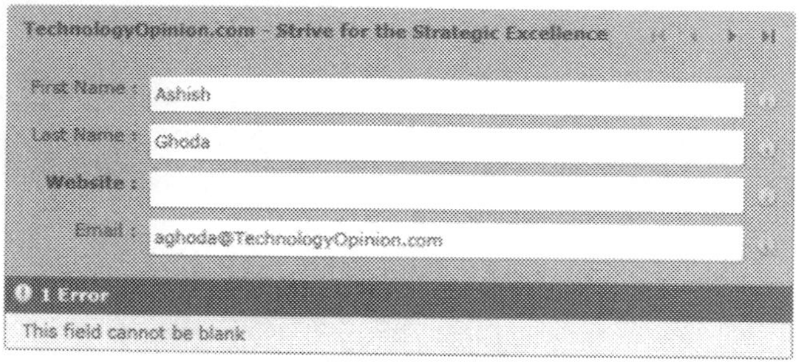

Figure 6-20. Custom field validation in the DataForm control

The CollectionViewSource

The PagedCollectionView, about which we just learned, does not provide a declarative way for binding in XAML as it has no default constructor. If you are following any design pattern such as MVVM for your application, you are likely to do bind data in XAML as much as possible, instead of doing it in code-behind. In such a scenario, the System.Windows.Data.CollectionViewSource comes to the rescue. Basically it provides the same functionality that we saw for PagedCollectionView, but we can use it in XAML in a declarative way. So CollectionView is a XAML proxy of a collection view class. CollectionViewSource has a View property that holds the actual view and a Source property that holds the source collection. Visit http://msdn.microsoft.com/en-us/library/system.windows.data.collectionviewsource.aspx to get more information on CollectionViewSource.

You can think of a collection view as the mediator between the binding source collection and the XAML user interface of data bound controls, which allows you to navigate and display the collection based on sort, filter, and grouping queries, without having to manipulate the underlying source collection itself. If the source collection implements the INotifyCollectionChanged interface, the changes raised by the CollectionChanged event are propagated to the views.

The interesting scenario is that when CollectionViewSource is used as the ItemsSource of both a Silverlight DataForm and a DataGrid, the data manipulation performed by DataForm to the collection are conveyed to the DataGrid. Both the DataGrid and DataForm perform entity-level validations whenever CommitEdit() is called, generating immediate feedback to the user. So CollectionViewSource keeps in synchronization with the DataForm and DataGrid.

WCF Data Services

WCF Data Services (formerly known as ADO.NET Data Services) is a platform built on patterns and provides a set of libraries to develop and consume flexible data services for the web. WCF Data Services is part of the .NET Framework, so both Visual Studio and the .NET Framework provide you with the necessary tools and technologies to begin developing.

WCF Data Services uses Open Data Protocol (OData) for addressing and updating the resources, thus enabling access from any client that can parse and access data that is transmitted over standard HTTP protocol. This facilitates requesting and writing data operations to resources by using well-known transfer formats like JavaScript Object Notation (JSON), a text-based data exchange format widely used in AJAX application, and Atom, a set of standards for exchanging and updating data as XML format. The great feature of WCF Data Services is that it exposes the entity data model without having to write any service methods. It exposes the data model by a series of unique URIs that are mapped to the domain entities. Figure 6-21 provides an architectural overview of WCF Data Services integration to your application.

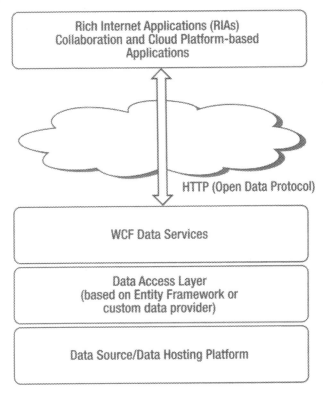

Figure 6-21. Architectural overview of WCF Data Services integration

A complete discussion of WCF Data Services is beyond the scope of this book. Refer to the Microsoft WCF Service site at http://msdn.microsoft.com/en-us/data/bb931106.aspx to get more details and samples for WCF Data Services. You should also visit www.odata.org to get more details on the Open Data Protocol.

Entity Data Model (EDM)

WCF Data Services exposes data, represented as Entity Data Model (EDM) objects, via web services accessed over HTTP. The data can be addressed using a REST-like URI and provides features to account for authorization, business logic, and custom service operations. The EDM represents the data in terms of data entities and relationships between these entities. It can be created based on the Microsoft ADO .NET Entity Framework or custom implementation. The entity data model can be anything as long as it is exposed as IQueryable. The IQueryable interface resides in the System.Linq namespace in the System.Core.dll assembly. The IQueryable interface provides functionality to evaluate queries against a specific data source wherein the type of the data is not specified and it is typically implemented by the query provider.

Silverlight Client Library for WCF Data Services

Silverlight provides a client library to work with WCF Data Services, which allows you to write LINQ queries to operate on the entities using the LINQ query syntax. This query is examined by the client library and turned into the standard URI / HTTP web request. To support all CRUD data operations, WCF Data Services maps the four basic data-access operations to the four basic HTTP verbs as shown in Table 6-6:

Table 6-6. WCF Data Services Mapping of Data-Access Verbs to HTTP Verbs

Data-Access Verbs	HTTP Verb
Create	POST
Read	GET
Update	PUT
Delete	DELETE

The Silverlight client library for WCF Data Services resides in the System.Data.Services.Client namespace. Let's take a brief look at three important members of this library: DataServiceContext, DataServiceQuery, and DataServiceCollection.

The DataServiceContext Class

The DataServiceContext class represents the runtime context of WCF Data Services. While WCF Data Services is stateless, DataServiceContext does not exist in order to support features such as update management. Tables 6-7 and 6-8 lists some key methods and properties of this class respectively:

Table 6-7. Key Methods of the System.Data.Services.Client.DataServiceContext Class

Method	Description
AddLink	This method adds the specified link to the set of objects DataServiceContext is tracking.
AddObject	This method adds the specified object to the set of objects that the DataServiceContext is tracking. Each object must be added by making a separate call to AddObject.
AddRelatedObject	This method adds a related object to the context and creates the link that defines the relationship between the two objects in a single request. This is a new method in Silverlight 4.
AttachLink	Notifies the DataServiceContext to start tracking the specified link between the source and the specified target entity.

AttachTo	Notifies the DataServiceContext to start tracking the specified resource and supplies the location of the resource within the specified resource set.
BeginExecute(T)	Asynchronously sends the request so that this call does not block processing while waiting for the results from the service.
BeginSaveChanges	Asynchronously submits the pending changes to the data service collected by the DataServiceContext since the last time changes were saved.
DeleteLink	Changes the state of the link to Deleted in the list of links being tracked by the DataServiceContext.
DeleteObject	Changes the state of the specified object to Deleted in the DataServiceContext.
Detach	Removes the entity from the list of entities that the DataServiceContext is tracking.
DetachLink	Removes the specified link from the list of links being tracked by DataServiceContext.
EndExecute(T)	It is called to complete the BeginExecute(T) async call.
EndSaveChanges	It is called to complete the BeginSaveChanges operation.
SetLink	This method notifies DataServiceContext that a new link exists between the objects specified and that the link is represented by the property specified by the sourceProperty parameter.
SetSaveStream	Sets a new data stream as the binary property of an entity. This is a new method in Silverlight 4.
UpdateObject	This method changes the state of the specified object in DataServiceContext to Modified.

Table 6-8. Key Properties of the System.Data.Services.Client.DataServiceContext Class

Property	Type	Description
ApplyingChanges	bool	Gets a value that indicates whether DataServiceContext is currently applying changes to tracked objects. This is a new property in Silverlight 4.
BaseUri	Uri	Gets the absolute URI identifying the root of the target WCF Data Service.

Credentials	ICredentials	Provides a base authentication interface to retrieve credentials for Web client authentication. This is a new property in Silverlight 4.
DataNamespace	string	Defines the XML namespace for data items of a payload in the Atom format. The default value is the default WCF Data Services namespace, `http://schemas.microsoft.com/ado/2007/08/dataservices`.
Entities	ReadOnlyCollection (EntityDescriptor)	Gets a list of all the resources currently being tracked by `DataServiceContext`.
HttpStack	HttpStack	Gets a value that indicates the type of HTTP implementation to use when accessing the data service. The default value is `Auto`, which is used for the HTTP implementation. You can also set to `ClientHttp` to use Silverlight client HTTP implementation and set to `XmlHttp` to use XMLHTTP implementation. This is a new property in Silverlight 4.
MergeOption	MergeOption	Gets or sets the synchronization option for receiving entities from a data service.
SaveChanges DefaultOptions	SaveChanges DefaultOptions	Gets or sets the `SaveChangesOptions` values used by the `BeginSaveChanges` method.
UseDefaultCredentials	bool	Defines whether to use default credentials of the currently logged-in user (`true` value) or not (`false` value).

The DataServiceQuery Class

The DataServiceQuery class represents a single query request to a data service. The query can be a LINQ query.

As Silverlight allows only asynchronous Web requests, we need to cast this query into a DataServiceQuery<T> object and then explicitly call the BeginExecute method to start the asynchronous execution of the query. You call the EndExecute method to complete the asynchronous operation of executing the query. Table 6-9 shows the properties of this class:

Table 6-9. Properties of the `System.Data.Services.Client.DataServiceQuery` *Class*

Property	Type	Description
Expression	Expression	Defines an expression that contains the query to the data service.
Provider	System.Linq.IQueryProvider	Defines the query provider instance.

The DataServiceCollection (T) Class

To support data binding with Silverlight controls using WCF Data Services is a new functionality introduced in Silverlight 4, which can be achieved using the DataServiceCollection(T) class. It represents a dynamic entity collection that provides notifications when items get added or removed, or when the list is refreshed. This class inherits from the ObservableCollection class to automatically update bound data when there are changes to data in bound controls. Using this class you can enable rich two-way data binding by implementing automatic change tracking on client-side objects created using the WCF Data Services client library. Table 6-10 defines the methods of this class:

Table 6-10. Methods of the System.Data.Services.Client.DataServiceCollection Class

Method	Description
Add	Adds a new item to the end of the Collection (T).
Clear(bool)	Removes all elements from the Collection (T) and detaches all items from the DataServiceContext when true is passed.
Detach	Disables DataServiceContext tracking of all items in the root collection.
Load(T) or Load(IEnumerable<T>)	Loads a single entity object or a collection of entity objects into the collection.
LoadAsync	Asynchronously loads items into the collection.
LoadNextPartialSetAsync	Loads the next page of data into the collection.

The DataServiceCollection(T) class contains a property called Continuation, which gets a continuation object that is used to return the next set of paged results. The LoadCompleted event of the DataServiceCollection(T) class occurs when an asynchronous load operation completes.

Silverlight Application using WCF Data Service

Let's build a simple Silverlight application that will consume the WCF Data Services. Later we will discover some of the enhancements in this area based on the developed example.

To start Silverlight application development with WCF Data Services, there are some prerequisites:

- .NET Framework 4.0

- Entity Data Model tools, included in Visual Studio 2010

- Microsoft SQL Server 2008 Express

- Microsoft SQL Server 2008 Management Studio Express

- For our example, a sample ApressBooks database supplied with the source code of this chapter

Once all of these prerequisites are met, next you need to attach the ApressBooks database to your SQL Server 2008 Express instance using the management console. The SQL Express instance is usually named <your computer name>\SQLEXPRESS. If you are unsure how to do this, you should follow this link on MSDN: http://msdn.microsoft.com/en-us/library/ms190209.aspx.

Now start with the Silverlight application project named WCFDataServiceDemo and follow steps described in the following sub-sections.

Create ADO .NET Entity Data Model

Before creating an entity data model, consider Figure 6-22, which shows a diagram of the ApressBooks database having two tables and one association between them:

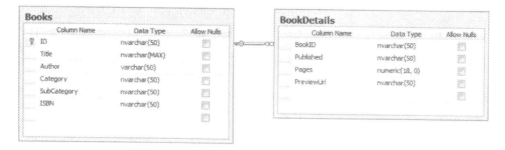

Figure 6-22. Relationship diagram of Books and BookDetails tables of the ApressBooks database

Next add a new item ADO.NET Entity Data Model to your WCFDataServiceDemo.Web project and name it to DataModel.edmx, as shown in Figure 6-23.

Figure 6-23. Adding an ADO.NET Entity Data Model item to the project

As you press Add, the Entity Data Model Wizard will appear. I will list settings/values for each screen of the wizard along with the title of the wizard steps:

1. *Choose Model Content*: Select Generate from Database

2. *Choose Your Data Connection*: Here create a new connection for the ApressBooks database. Name this connection setting ApressBooksEntities in the text box at bottom of this wizard screen.

3. *Choose Your Database Objects*: Here choose both Books and BookDetails tables and set Model Namespace to ApressBooksModel and click the Finish button.

When you click Finish, you will be presented with a class diagram of the DataModel.edmx entity just created, as shown in Figure 6-24.

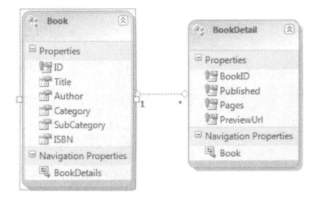

Figure 6-24. *The class diagram of an ADO.NET Entity Data Model related to the ApressBooks database*

Note that in Figure 6-24, there is a section called *Navigation Properties* in each entity set. The Navigation Properties section describes navigable paths between associations. In our case, it describes the association between both tables for Book.ID and BookDetails.BookID fields (see Figure 6-22). For example, in an association between Book and BookDetail entities, the Book entity can declare a NavigationProperty named BookDetails to represent the BookDetail instances associated with that particular Book instance. Navigation properties are very useful and we will make use of them while loading related entities in the later part of this topic.

Create WCF Data Service

Right-click the WCFDataServiceDemo.Web project, add a new item, WCF Data Service, and name it to DBService.svc, as shown in Figure 6-25:

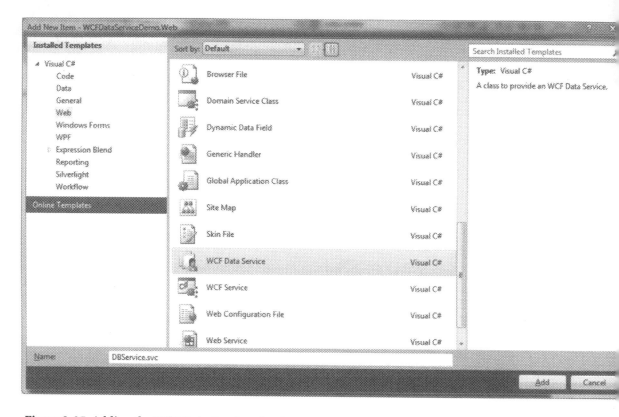

Figure 6-25. *Adding the WCF Data Services database*

Now, open the `DBService.svc.cs` file and change the text for the main entry point class from

```
DataService< /* TODO: put your data source class name here */ >
```

to

```
DataService< ApressBooksEntities>.
```

Next, set the rules of data service operations and entity access in the `InitializeService` method by adding the two lines, as shown in the following code snippet.

```
config.SetEntitySetAccessRule("*", EntitySetRights.All);
config.SetServiceOperationAccessRule("*", ServiceOperationRights.All);
```

In the first line, we are setting access rules to `EntitySetRights.All` allowing any Read and Write operation for all the entities, specified by the asterisk (*) sign. Here we have Books and BookDetails entities. If you want to specify access rules per entity base, then define the name of the entity rather than using an asterisk (*). Table 6-11 lists possible access rule (EntitySetRights) enumeration values that can be set for the entity.

Table 6-11. Enum Values of EntitySetRights Enumeration

Enum	Value	Description
None	0	This denies all rights to access data.
ReadSingle	1	This enables authorization to read single data items.
ReadMultiple	2	This enables authorization to read sets of data.
AllRead	3	This enables authorization to read data (including single data items and sets of data).
WriteAppend	4	This enables authorization to create new data items in data sets.
WriteReplace	8	This enables authorization to replace data.
WriteDelete	16	This enables authorization to delete data items from data sets.
WriteMerge	32	This enables authorization to merge data.
AllWrite	60	This enables authorization to write data (including creating new and deleting existing data items in data sets, and replacing and merging data.
All	63	This enables authorization to create, read, update, and delete data.

Setting appropriate access rules per entity is critical and it prevents accidental modification of an entity to create robust data services. This will help you implementing secure and error-free data access operations (CRUD operations) to database.

The second line sets all rights access to the service operation.

At this point, if you run the service, the output would be something similar to Figure 6-26.

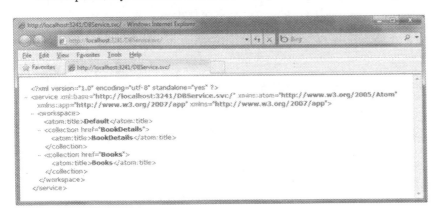

Figure 6-26. Running DBService.svc WCF Data Services

Caution When developing your service, you might run into some issues, motivating you to debug your service. Imagine that you are inserting data into the store using data service and you start getting DataServiceExceptions in your client code. The normal error message would be "An error occurred while processing this request." While debugging the service, you would need more information than just this generic error message. So, to switch to a more detailed error mode for the development environment, you can set `UseVerboseErrors` to `true` in the ServiceConfiguration in the `InitializeService` method.

Create WCF Data Services Proxy and Retrieve the Records

To create a `DBService.svc` WCF Data Services proxy, right-click the WCFDataServiceDemo Silverlight project and choose the Add Service Reference... option to add service reference for the `DBService.svc` service and define a namespace to DSProxy.

Now let us jump to building the UI of our simple application. For that just drop the DataGrid control from the toolbox to `MainPage.xaml` and name it `BookDataGrid`. We will also place one button to query the entity model. Here is the complete XAML of the usercontrol:

```xml
<UserControl
    x:Class="WCFDataServiceDemo.MainPage"
    xmlns="http://schemas.microsoft.com/winfx/2006/xaml/presentation"
    xmlns:x="http://schemas.microsoft.com/winfx/2006/xaml"
    xmlns:d="http://schemas.microsoft.com/expression/blend/2008"
    xmlns:mc="http://schemas.openxmlformats.org/
        markup-compatibility/2006"
    xmlns:my="clr-namespace:System.Windows.Controls;assembly=
        System.Windows.Controls.Data"
    mc:Ignorable="d"
    d:DesignHeight="300" d:DesignWidth="600">
    <StackPanel x:Name="LayoutRoot" Background="White">
        <my:DataGrid x:Name="BookDataGrid" Height="200" Width="600" />
        <Button x:Name="btnGetData" Width="120" Height="26" Content="Get data"
            Click="btnGetData_Click"/>
    </StackPanel>
</UserControl>
```

In the code-behind file `MainPage.xaml.cs`, add the following additional namespaces to enable the use of the data service proxy and Silverlight client WCF Data Services library.

```csharp
using WCFDataServiceDemo.DSProxy.ApressBooksModel;
using System.Data.Services.Client;
```

Now in the `btnGetData` Click event, we create the data context and query the database for retrieving all records using LINQ. Here we will use the newly introduced (in Silverlight 4) `DataServiceCollection` dynamic collection. The code for `MainPage.xaml.cs` at this point is as follows:

```csharp
public partial class MainPage : UserControl
{
```

```
//Dynamic Data context creation
DataServiceCollection<Book> books = new
    DataServiceCollection<Book>();

//Entity context
ApressBooksEntities context = new ApressBooksEntities
    (new Uri("DBService.svc", UriKind.Relative));

public MainPage()
{
    InitializeComponent();

     //Appropriate merge option set for context
    context.MergeOption = MergeOption.PreserveChanges;
}

private void btnGetData_Click(object sender, RoutedEventArgs e)
{
    //LINQ to ADO.NET Data Service
    var q = (from c in context.Books select c );

    //Async call to load data
    books.LoadAsync(q);

    //Async load completed event
    books.LoadCompleted += new
        EventHandler<LoadCompletedEventArgs>(books_LoadCompleted);
}

void books_LoadCompleted(object sender, LoadCompletedEventArgs e)
{
    if (e.Error==null)
    {
        BookDataGrid.ItemsSource = books;
    }
}
}
```

As you can see, we set ItemSource of the BookDataGrid to the query result retrieved using the LoadAsync method on the DataServiceCollection books. The result is shown in Figure 6-27.

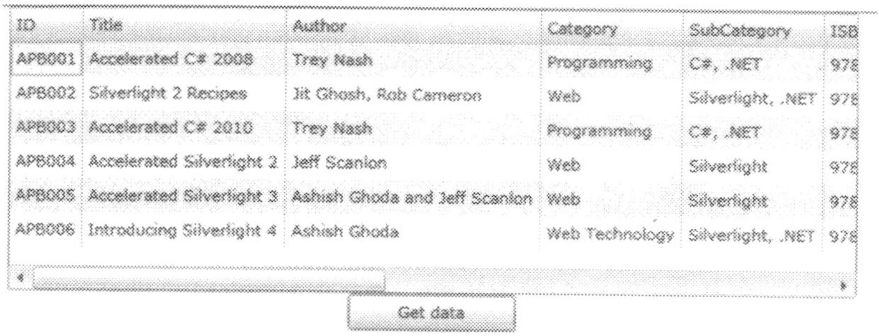

Figure 6-27. DataGrid showing the result of LINQ to WCF Data Services Query

Using this example, let us learn about some of the enhancements in this area introduced in Silverlight 4.

Two-Way Binding with DataServiceCollection Class

So far we have set up a data service, created a Silverlight client, and one-way bound the result of a LINQ query to the data service to a DataGrid control. The DataServiceCollection also supports two-way binding. This means that any changes made to the collection or items in the collection will propagate to the service when a call to BeginSaveChanges is made on the context.

To achieve two-way binding in our example, let's add a button just under existing btnGetData button and name it to btnAddItem. On the Click event of the btnAddItem, a book object will be added to the collection of books, issuing BeginSaveChanges on context, thus taking advantage of two-way binding to have those changes propagate to the service and the backing ApressBooks database.

The additional button's XAML code is as follows:

```
<Button x:Name="btnAddItem" Content="Add item" Width="120"
    Click="btnAddItem_Click"/>
```

And here is the code-behind for the Click event of btnAddItem:

```
private void btnAddItem_Click(object sender, RoutedEventArgs e)
{
    //Adding new item of type Book
    Book b1 = new Book();
    b1.ID = "APB006";
    b1.Title = "Introducing Silverlight 4";
    b1.Author = "Ashish Ghoda";
    b1.Category = "Web Technology";
    b1.SubCategory = "Silverlight, .NET";
    b1.ISBN = "978-1-4302-2991-9";

    // Adding new item to context, AddObject can also be used instead.
    context.AddToBooks(b1);

    // Async save changes request to context
    context.BeginSaveChanges(SaveChangesOptions.Batch, (asyncResult) =>
```

```
    {
        context.EndSaveChanges(asyncResult);
    }, null);
}
```

Here we have called the `DataServiceContext.BeginSaveChanges` method on the context `DataServiceContext` to asynchronously submit the added item to the data service and save it in a single batch request by using the `SavechangesOptions.Batch` option. We have called the `DataServiceContext.EndSaveChanges` method to complete the BeginSaveChanges operation.

Run the project, click the Add item button, and then click the Get data button to see the newly added book object.

Imagine that you are building a spreadsheet kind of application in Silverlight and there you need to deal with lots of data records. In such an application, you can use the DataGrid control along with WCF Data Services and `DataServiceCollection` dynamic collections to mimic an Excel type of spreadsheet behavior. You can perform CRUD operations by using the DataGrid's editing events such as `BeginningEdit`, `CellEditEnding`, `RowEditEnding`, etc. to achieve the desired functionality.

Handling Deferred Content

In this example so far, we queried the Books entity and bound the result to the DataGrid control. Doing it this way does not load the related `BookDetail` entity. This is because, by default, WCF Data Services limits the amount of data a query can return. However, you can explicitly enable loading of additional data including related entities, paged response data (if paging limits are set on data service), and binary streams, too.

The WCF Data Services client library in Silverlight 4 has been updated to load objects associated with an object already in the `DataServiceContext`. For example, we can extend our current example where selecting a book in `BookDataGrid` will display related details about that book in another `BookDetailsDataGrid`. You can load related entities in two ways, eager loading and on-demand (lazy) loading.

Eager Loading

Eager loading is the mechanism to load the full objects tree in one query request. This loads multiple related objects with a single `SELECT` statement rather using multiple `SELECT` statements. Therefore, in some situations, implementing eager loading can also improve the performance and responsiveness of the application to the end user by reducing the number of times of accessing the database. It is advisable to use eager loading when you know that the related information is needed for every object.

To facilitate eager loading, the `DataServiceQuery` class (context.Books in the example shown here) supports the `Expand` extension method. This method allows you to specify the name of the navigation property with paths to load when the query executes. The `Expand` extension method is used in the `From` clause of the LINQ query to tell the provider to attempt to load those related entities. So in our example, to achieve eager loading of the `BookDetails` related entity, include the `Expand` extension method in our LINQ query in the `btnGetData_Click` method and assign an event handler to the `SelectionChanged` event of the BookDataGrid. We also need to add one more DataGrid control just under `BookDataGrid` and name it `BookDetailsDataGrid`. Then when a book is selected, the event handler will query the context for the `BookDetails` property for the selected book in `BookDataGrid`. The updated code for dataGrid1 and the new DataGrid XAML code are highlighted in the following code snippet:

```xml
<my:DataGrid x:Name="BookDataGrid" Height="200" Width="600"
    SelectionChanged="BookDataGrid_SelectionChanged" />
<my:DataGrid x:Name="BookDetailsDataGrid" Height="100" Width="600" />
```

And the highlighted updated LINQ query code in the btnGetData_Click method is shown here:

```
//LINQ to Entity with Eager loading using Expand
var q = (from c in context.Books.Expand("BookDetails") select c);
```

The code for BookDataGrid_SelectionChanged method is as follows:

```csharp
private void BookDataGrid_SelectionChanged(object sender,
    SelectionChangedEventArgs e)
{
    //Getting reference to current selected book
    Book currentBook = BookDataGrid.SelectedItem as Book;

    //LINQ to get details for the selected book
    var q = from bd in context.Books where bd.ID ==
        currentBook.ID select bd;
    var dsq = (DataServiceQuery<Book>)q;
    //Async execution of the query
    dsq.BeginExecute(result =>
        {
            BookDetailsDataGrid.ItemsSource =
                dsq.EndExecute(result).FirstOrDefault().
                    BookDetail.ToList();
        }, null);
}
```

As Silverlight follows asynchronous models for such operations, we need to cast LINQ query q to DataServiceQuery and start an asynchronous execution of the query using the BeginExecute/EndExecute method pair as shown in the previous code snippet. Finally we bind the result of the asynchronous query to BookDetailsDataGrid. At this point you can run the project, press the Get data button, and click any of the books in BookDataGrid, and the result will be similar to the one shown in Figure 6-28.

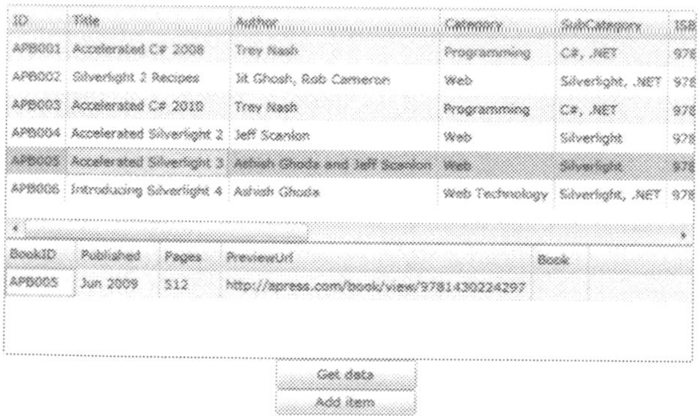

Figure 6-28. Demonstrating eager loading using LINQ

On-Demand Loading (Lazy Loading)

On-demand loading is the mechanism to load objects as they are required by the application by making separate query requests to the data source for each object. The main objective for such a mechanism is to dedicate memory resources only when necessary by loading and instantiating an object only at the point when it is absolutely needed. This approach is advisable when you need to load the data for a few entities and the volume of the data is large.

To facilitate loading on demand, the DataServiceContext class has a BeginLoadProperty method, which follows the same asynchronous model where you specify the source entity, the name of the property, and a callback, as shown in the BeginLoadProperty method signature here:

```
public IAsyncResult BeginLoadProperty(
    Object entity,
    string propertyName,
    AsyncCallback callback,
    Object state
)
```

So let's implement this approach in our example by adding the following line of code in the BookDataGrid_SelectionChanged method.

```
//Explicit loading (Lazy loading) using BeginLoadPropety
context.BeginLoadProperty(currentBook , "BookDetails", PropertyLoadCompleted, null);
```

The callback method PropertyLoadCompleted is as follows:

```
private void PropertyLoadCompleted(IAsyncResult result)
{
    context.EndLoadProperty(result);
    //Getting reference to current selected book
    Book currentBook = BookDataGrid.SelectedItem as Book;
    if (currentBook == null) return;
    var query = (from bd in currentBook.BookDetails select bd);
    BookDetailsDataGrid.ItemsSource = query.ToList();
}
```

So, as per the code snippet, once the EndLoadProperty is called, the property has been properly loaded with the related entity, so we can access the related entity BookDetail through the navigation property BookDetails to bind to our BookDetailsDataGrid control.

Processing XML Data

You've seen how to connect data directly to the user interface. This data can be retrieved in a number of ways, including directly downloading it via WebClient or HttpWebRequest/Response, and having it returned from a web service call. The sample code for this chapter has a simple implementation of a web search utilizing Microsoft's Bing web service. The ListBox is configured with bindings to properties in the result set from Bing.

```
<ListBox Grid.Row="3" x:Name="resultsListBox">
    <ListBox.ItemTemplate>
```

```
<DataTemplate>
    <StackPanel Orientation="Vertical">
        <TextBlock FontFamily="Arial" Text="{Binding Title}"/>
        <TextBlock FontSize="10" Text="{Binding Url}"/>
        <TextBlock Text="{Binding Description}"
            FontSize="10" />
    </StackPanel>
</DataTemplate>
    </ListBox.ItemTemplate>
</ListBox>
```

Invoking the web service is done according to the Bing API documentation available on MSDN (http://msdn.microsoft.com/en-us/library/dd900818.aspx), the code for which is shown here:

```
MSNSearchPortTypeClient client = new MSNSearchPortTypeClient();
client.SearchCompleted += new
    EventHandler<SearchCompletedEventArgs>
        (client_SearchCompleted);
SearchRequest req = new SearchRequest();
SourceRequest[] sourceReq = new SourceRequest[1];
sourceReq[0] = new SourceRequest();
sourceReq[0].Source = SourceType.Web;
req.Query = searchTerms.Text;
req.Requests = sourceReq;
req.AppID = /* enter your AppID here!! */
req.CultureInfo = "en-US";
client.SearchAsync(req);
```

The asynchronous callback simply sets ItemsSource to the data source, provided no error has occurred:

```
resultsListBox.ItemsSource = e.Result.Responses[0].Results;
```

This demonstrates how easy it can be to hook up data returned from web services to the user interface. The services infrastructure within Silverlight handles the serialization/deserialization of data for communication purposes, so your application can focus on the objects that can serve as data sources. Of course, sometimes you'll retrieve data directly, such as by downloading XML data files specific to your application. Silverlight provides a rich set of XML classes for reading/writing/processing XML files. Since version 3, it provides support for LINQ, a technology that provides syntax roughly similar to SQL for working with data directly within C# or VB .NET.

Parsing XML

The System.Xml.XmlReader class provides the ability to parse XML documents from a variety of sources, such as a stream or a string. It also provides the ability to directly access an XML file contained in the XAP file. These various approaches to handling an XML file are accessed through the many overloads of the XmlReader.Create method. Let's use the WebDeveloper class again, this time stored in an XML file.

```
<?xml version="1.0" encoding="utf-8" ?>
<WebDevelopers>
```

```
<WebDeveloper>
    <FirstName>Ashish</FirstName>
    <LastName>Ghoda</LastName>
    <Email>aghoda@technologyopinion.com</Email>
    <Website>www.TechnologyOpinion.com</Website>
</WebDeveloper>
<WebDeveloper>
    <FirstName>Jay</FirstName>
    <LastName>Nanavaty</LastName>
    <Email>jnanavaty@technologyopinion.com</Email>
    <Website>www.TechnologyOpinion.com</Website>
</WebDeveloper>
</WebDevelopers>
```

You use XmlReaderSettings to configure the behavior of XmlReader. In this case, we'll instruct XmlReader to ignore whitespace. If we didn't do this, it would take more code to advance to the correct nodes within the XML file.

```
List<WebDeveloper> WebDevelopers = new List< WebDeveloper>();

XmlReaderSettings settings = new XmlReaderSettings();
settings.IgnoreWhitespace = true;
XmlReader xmlReader = XmlReader.Create("WebDevelopers.xml", settings);

while (xmlReader.ReadToFollowing("WebDeveloper"))
{
    WebDeveloper wd = new WebDeveloper();
    xmlReader.ReadToDescendant("FirstName");
    wd.FirstName = xmlReader.
        ReadElementContentAsString("FirstName","");
    wd.LastName = xmlReader.
        ReadElementContentAsString ("LastName","");
    wd.Email = xmlReader.ReadElementContentAsString ("Email","");
    wd.Website = xmlReader.ReadElementContentAsString ("Website","");

    WebDevelopers.Add(wd);
}
```

Silverlight also provides an XmlWriter class that you can use to write data to isolated storage—essentially a secure, private file system for your Silverlight applications.

Serializing XML

Sometimes you'll need to use XmlReader to parse XML files directly, such as when you want to extract only certain details. If you're saving/loading business objects manually (i.e., not leveraging the automatic serialization provided by web services), then you can use serialization directly. The System.Xml.Serialization namespace, which you will need to add as a reference to the project, provides the XmlSerializer class that you can use to easily save and load objects to any stream. XmlSerializer also supports working directly with XmlReader and TextReader.

This is how you can serialize the List<WebDeveloper> collection to isolated storage. Using serialization with isolated storage is an easy way to save a collection of objects to a special permanent storage area on the client.

```
XmlSerializer ser = new XmlSerializer(typeof(List<WebDeveloper>));
using (IsolatedStorageFile rootStore =
    IsolatedStorageFile.GetUserStoreForApplication())
{
    using (IsolatedStorageFileStream fs =
        new IsolatedStorageFileStream("WebDevelopers.xml",
          FileMode.Create, rootStore))
    {
        ser.Serialize(fs, WebDevelopers);
    }
}
```

After serializing the list to isolated storage, you can verify that the file is created and even view its contents. When you want to turn the file within isolated storage back into objects, you follow a similar pattern, but invoke Deserialize.

```
List< WebDeveloper > wds = new List< WebDeveloper >();
XmlSerializer ser = new XmlSerializer(typeof(List< WebDeveloper >));
using (IsolatedStorageFile rootStore =
    IsolatedStorageFile.GetUserStoreForApplication())
{
    using (IsolatedStorageFileStream fs =
        new IsolatedStorageFileStream("WebDevelopers.xml",
          FileMode.Open, rootStore))
    {
        wds = (List< WebDeveloper>)ser.Deserialize(fs);
    }
}
```

Serialization is by far the easiest way to save business objects to XML files and load them from sources such as isolated storage, or download them via the Web using a class like WebClient.

Using LINQ

LINQ is a language-level technology that makes working with data such as collections of objects and XML documents much easier. While it looks like SQL in some regards, and uses relational model thinking, it has many differences. One similarity, though, is that you can use LINQ to query XML. The System.Xml.Linq namespace (as part of the .NET Framework library) contains the classes for LINQ to XML. Note that you need to add the reference to this namespace to utilize the LINQ to XML feature. We have seen usage of the LINQ query in previous topics of this chapter while working with WCF Data Services and querying the entities. Revisiting the WebDeveloper class, this time we'll download the WebDevelopers.xml file put within the XAP file. Then we can use LINQ to easily process the data and load it into an array.

```
void wc_DownloadStringCompleted(object sender,
    DownloadStringCompletedEventArgs e)
```

```
{
    XDocument xmlDocument = XDocument.Parse(e.Result);
    var  wdsdata = from b in xmlDocument.Descendants("WebDeveloper")
    select new WebDeveloper
    {
        FirstName = b.Element("FirstName").Value,
        LastName = b.Element("LastName").Value,
        Email = b.Element("Email").Value,
        Website = b.Element("Website").Value,
    };
    outputTextBox.Text = "";
    int count = 1;
    foreach (WebDeveloper wd in wdsdata)
    {
        outputTextBox.Text += "Record #" + count + "\r\n";
        outputTextBox.Text += "----------\r\n";
        outputTextBox.Text += "First Name: " + wd.FirstName + "\r\n";
        outputTextBox.Text += "Last Name: " + wd.LastName + "\r\n";
        outputTextBox.Text += "Email: " +
        string.Format("{0:C}", wd.Email) +"\r\n";
        outputTextBox.Text += "Website: " + wd.Website + "\r\n";
        outputTextBox.Text += "\r\n";
        count++;
    }
}
```

The var keyword is a LINQ-ism that can be viewed as a way to hold a reference to an unknown type. It provides an easy way to obtain an IEnumerable from the LINQ query—in this case, the WebDeveloper objects. The var keyword here could easily be replaced with IEnumerable<WebDeveloper> since we know the query will return a collection of WebDeveloper objects. The call to Descendents is used to get a hold of all the WebDeveloper nodes. Next, a new WebDeveloper is used to signal the creation of new WebDeveloper objects, which the data we "select" will fill. The compound statement specifies exactly where the properties of WebDeveloper get their values from—specifically the values of the three elements within each WebDeveloper element.

LINQ is a huge topic that can't satisfactorily be covered in this chapter. If you want to learn more about LINQ, consult *Pro LINQ: Language Integrated Query in C# 2010* by Joseph C. Ratz, Jr. (to be published). If you want to learn more about the differences between LINQ in .NET 3.5/4.0 and Silverlight, consult the MSDN online documentation at http://msdn.microsoft.com/en-us/library/cc189074(VS.96).aspx.

Saving State on the Client

There are two ways to store data on the client: through cookies and through isolated storage. The most direct method to save and access cookies is through the HtmlPage. Document class.

```
HtmlPage.Document.Cookies = "name=value; expires=Monday, 1-Nov-2010 12:00:00 GMT";
```

I won't go into too much detail on working with cookies. Isolated storage, however, is much more interesting. It is a mechanism provided by Silverlight to cache data or store user-specific data on the client. The isolated storage support in Silverlight is based on the isolated storage support in .NET, so you may already be familiar with this topic. Besides granting the ability to persist information on the client, the two biggest advantages to isolated storage are safety and ease of use. Each Silverlight application has its own dedicated storage area on disk, but the application isn't aware of the actual disk usage since it is managed by the runtime. This ensures safety because each application can use only its own dedicated storage area, and there is isolation between the application and the actual disk, mediated by the runtime. Different users on the same computer using the same Silverlight application will each have their own isolated store for the application, ensuring any data stored for one user is safe from other users since each user's store is private and isolated.

The other advantage is ease of use. While access to the underlying disk is prevented, nonetheless, file/directory semantics are used for saving and accessing data in isolated storage. The runtime transparently handles the translation of isolated storage paths to physical paths on the computer.

In Silverlight, the isolated storage area is linked to a Silverlight application via the application's address—including its full path. For example, if you use a Silverlight application at http://www.fabrikam.com/productbrowser, each time you visit this address, the application served will access the same isolated storage area. By default, for each in-browser Silverlight application, the isolated storage is limited to 1MB of storage. However, for a partial or elevated-trusted out-of-browser application, the default storage size is 25MB (visit Chapter 11 to get more details on out-of-browser applications).This limit can be increased; however, it requires the user to explicitly grant permission. When a Silverlight application attempts to grow its reserved space in isolated storage, a pop-up like the one shown in Figure 6-29 will ask the user for permission.

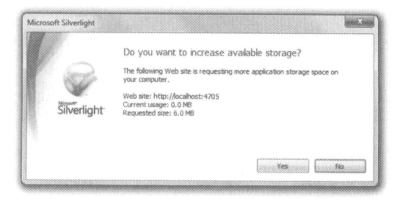

Figure 6-29. Confirmation dialog shown when an application attempts to increase space

The two significant classes used when working with isolated storage are IsolatedStorageFile and IsolatedStorageFileStream. These can be found in the mscorlib assembly in the System.IO.IsolatedStorage namespace. The IsolatedStorageFile class contains methods for working with directories and files, and querying and increasing allocated space. Tables 6-12 and 6-13 show properties and methods of this class. All methods will throw an IsolatedStorageException if the store has been removed (through IsolatedStorageFile.Remove) or if there's an isolated storage–related error. They also will throw an ObjectDisposedException if you attempt an operation on an IsolatedStorageFile instance that has been disposed.

Table 6-12. Properties of the System.IO.IsolatedStorageFile Class

Name	Type	Description
AvailableFreeSpace	long	The free isolated storage space, in bytes, for the current application; read-only property.
IsEnabled	bool	A static property defines whether the isolated storage is enabled. Note that isolated storage for full .NET application is always enabled. This is a new read-only property in Silverlight 4.
Quota	long	The maximum space allocated, in bytes, for the current application; read-only property.
UsedSize	long	Provides total used isolated storage, in bytes. This is a new read-only property in Silverlight 4.

Table 6-13. Key Methods of the System.IO.IsolatedStorageFile Class

Name	Description
CopyFile	Copy an existing file to a new file (or optionally overwrite an existing file). This is a new method in Silverlight 4.
CreateDirectory	Attempts to create a directory based on the string path passed in. It can create a tree of directories by passing in a path such as \root\data.
CreateFile	Attempts to create a file at the specified string path. If successful, it returns an instance of the IsolatedStorageFileStream class.
DeleteDirectory	Attempts to remove a directory from isolated storage. The directory must be empty for the delete to succeed.
DeleteFile	Attempts to delete a specific file from isolated storage.
DirectoryExists	Returns true if the specified directory exists, and false otherwise.
Dispose	Implements IDisposable.Dispose() to release all resources used by the IsolatedStorageFile.
FileExists	Returns true if the specified file exists, and false otherwise.
GetCreationTime	Returns the date and time of a specified file or directory when created.

GetDirectoryNames	Overloaded. The parameter-less version returns a string array of directory names from the root of the store. The overload accepts a string search expression to search subdirectories and also uses wildcards: the ? matches a single character and the * matches multiple characters. If no results are found, the Length property of the returned array will be 0.
GetFileNames	Overloaded. The parameter-less version returns a string array of files in the root of the store. The overload accepts a string search expression to search subdirectories and also uses wildcards: the ? matches a single character and the * matches multiple characters. If no results are found, the Length property of the returned array will be 0.
GetLastAccessTime	Provides the date and time when the file or directory was last accessed. This is a new property in Silverlight 4.
GetLastWriteTime	Provides the date and time when the file or directory was last written to. This is a new property in Silverlight 4.
GetUserStoreFor Application	Static method. Used to get a reference to the isolated storage for the current user and application.
IncreaseQuotaTo	Enables an application to increase the quota to a certain size, specified in bytes. Expanding the size of an isolated store causes a confirmation dialog to appear for user confirmation. It returns true if the new quota is accepted by the user, and false otherwise.
MoveDirectory	Moves a specified directory and its content to a new specified location. This is a new property in Silverlight 4.
MoveFile	Moves a specified file to a new specified location with or without rename. This is a new property in Silverlight 4.
OpenFile	Overloaded. Opens a specified file from the store using the requested FileMode and, optionally, FileAccess and FileShare options. If successful, it returns an instance of the IsolatedStorageFileStream class.
Remove	Removes all contents from the isolated storage and the store itself.

The System.IO.FileMode enumeration, a required parameter of all of the OpenFile overloads, contains the following options.

Append: Appends to an existing file or creates the file if it does not exist.

Create: Creates a file if one doesn't exist. If a file does exist, OpenFile will fail.

CreateNew: Creates a file if one doesn't exist, and re-creates it if it does exist (use with caution).

Open: Opens a file. Unless Append is specified, it also sets the file pointer at the beginning of the file.

OpenOrCreate: Opens the file if it exists, and creates it otherwise.

Truncate: Removes all contents from the file.

The System.IO.FileAccess enumeration contains the following options. It is used to specify the type of access requested to the file.

Read: Allows only reading from the file.

ReadWrite: Allows reading from and writing to the file.

Write: Allows only writing to the file.

The System.IO.FileShare enumeration contains the following options. It is used to specify the type of access concurrently granted to other FileStream objects.

Delete: Allows the file to be deleted by others.

Inheritable: Allows the file handle to be inherited by others.

None: Disallows shared access.

Read: Allows others to read from but not write to the file.

ReadWrite: Allows others to read from and write to the file.

Write: Allows others to write to the file but not read from it.

To get more ideas about various isolated storage tasks regarding creating, reading, updating, and deleting files, visit http://msdn.microsoft.com/en-us/library/8dzkff1s.aspx.

To get an IsolatedStoreFile object to work with isolated storage you need to use the IsolatedStoreFile.GetUserStoreForApplication static method. Following best practices in .NET, it's a good idea to always wrap this in a using statement so that Dispose is automatically called.

```
using (IsolatedStorageFile rootStore =
    IsolatedStorageFile.GetUserStoreForApplication())
{
    // can now interact with isolated storage files/directories/etc.
}
```

The XmlReader example uses isolated storage to store an object in XML format. The IsolatedStorageFileStream inherits from System.IO.FileStream, so we can use it directly with the Serialize method since it can write to any Stream.

```
XmlSerializer ser = new XmlSerializer(typeof(List<WebDeveloper>));
using (IsolatedStorageFile rootStore =
    IsolatedStorageFile.GetUserStoreForApplication())
{
    using (IsolatedStorageFileStream fs =
        new IsolatedStorageFileStream("WebDevelopers.xml", FileMode.Create, rootStore))
    {
        ser.Serialize(fs, WebDevelopers);
    }
}
```

When successful, the OpenFile and CreateFile methods return an instance of the IsolatedStorageFileStream class. Its public properties are listed in Table 6-14, and its public methods are listed in Table 6-15.

Table 6-14. Properties of the System.IO.IsolatedStorageFileStream Class

Name	Type	Description
CanRead	bool	Returns true if reading from the file is allowed, and false otherwise; read-only. Overrides FileStream.CanRead.
CanSeek	bool	Returns true if the position of the file pointer can be changed, and false otherwise; read-only. Overrides FileStream.CanSeek.
CanWrite	bool	Returns true if writing is allowed, and false otherwise; read-only. Overrides FileStream.CanWrite.
Length	long	Specifies the length of the file in bytes; read-only. Overrides FileStream.Length.
Position	long	Specifies the current position of the file pointer. Overrides FileStream.Position.

Table 6-15. Methods of the System.IO.IsolatedStorageFileStream Class

Name	Description
BeginRead	Asynchronous method to begin a read operation. Accepts a byte array buffer along with an offset into the array to start writing to, and the maximum number of bytes to read. Overrides FileStream.BeginRead().
BeginWrite	Asynchronous method to begin a write operation. Accepts a byte array buffer along with an offset into the array to start reading, and the number of bytes to write. Overrides FileStream.BeginWrite().
EndRead	Used when the read operation ends. Returns an int specifying the number of bytes read. Overrides FileStream.EndRead().
EndWrite	Used when the write operation ends. Overrides FileStream.EndWrite().
Flush	Flushes any pending data from the internal buffer to disk. Overrides FileStream.Flush().
Read	Synchronous read operation. Accepts a byte array buffer along with an offset into the array to start writing to, and the maximum number of bytes to read. Returns the number of bytes actually read. Overrides FileStream.Read().
ReadByte	Synchronously reads a single byte from the stream and returns it. Overrides FileStream.ReadByte().

Seek	Moves the stream pointer to the specified offset, modified by the SeekOrigin option specified. SeekOrigin.Begin treats the offset as an absolute offset from the beginning of the file. SeekOrigin.Current treats the offset as a relative offset from the current position. SeekOrigin.End treats the offset as relative from the end of the file. Overrides FileStream.Seek().
SetLength	Attempts to set the length of the file to the passed-in value. Overrides FileStream.SetLength().
Write	Synchronous write operation. Accepts a byte array buffer along with an offset into the array to start reading, and the number of bytes to write. Overrides FileStream.Write().
WriteByte	Synchronously writes a single byte to the stream. Overrides FileStream.WriteByte().

Summary

This chapter discussed how Silverlight is getting into the main stream by providing data-driven RIAs. Connecting data to the user interface and synchronizing the interface with data sources is now easy to implement and very efficient, thanks to an enhanced DataGrid control, element-to-element data binding, new editing events, RowGrouping, row- and cell-level data validation capabilities, and DataForm and DataPager controls. With the use of WCF Data Services, you can implement efficient data-driven line-of-business applications. This chapter also covered support for working with XML documents, including the System.Xml classes and LINQ. It closed with a discussion of how to save state on the client using isolated storage.

The next chapter is focused solely on demonstrating key features and capabilities introduced in Silverlight 4, such as drag-and-drop functionality, clipboard access, printing functionality, and support to right-click and mouse-wheel functions. In addition I will also introduce enhanced XAML features introduced in Silverlight 4.

PART 3

Improving User Experience

■ ■ ■

CHAPTER 7

Extending User Experience of LoB Applications

So far we have learned about the basics of the Silverlight technology platform and core capabilities of Silverlight for media and data integration and networking. This chapter is solely focused on new and extended features and capabilities provided in Silverlight 4. New features and capabilities of Silverlight 4 extend the user interface and functionalities by providing an opportunity to developers to develop true line-of-business (LoB) applications and thus improve the user experience significantly.

Enhancements in Silverlight 4

Silverlight 4 introduces the following key enhancements, enabling the development of LoB applications and providing a better and more familiar user experience:

- One of the widely implemented features for any LoB application is drag-and-drop functionality. Silverlight 4 allows `UIElement`s as a drop target and thus enables the implementation of drag-and-drop functionality by introducing the `UIElement.AllowDrop` property and related drag-and-drop events.

- Silverlight 4 extends the `UIElement.MouseWheel` event implementation through the managed code, which allows mouse-wheel support in full-screen mode as well as in an application running in out-of-browser mode.

- Like drag-and-drop functionality, right-click functionality is also a popular feature for any LoB application. With Silverlight 4, two new `MouseRightButtonDown` and `MouseRightButtonUp` events for `UIElement` are introduced to handle the right-click functionality and implement required custom features.

- Another critical feature of any LoB application is printing capability. Silverlight 4 introduces this capability and enables you to print either the existing visual tree or a custom virtual visual tree, using `PrintDocument` class. The printing functionality can be implemented in both in-browser and out-of-browser modes.

- Silverlight 4 also introduces the `System.Windows.Clipboard` class to provide access to the system clipboard to copy and paste data.

- Silverlight 4 extends the capabilities by supporting bi-directional text and adding support to many more languages, including right-to-left languages. This is critical for developing global aware applications.

313

- Silverlight 4 brings the Silverlight version of the XAML parser one step closer to the regular WPF parser. We will take a look at key enhancements before ending this chapter.

Drag-and-Drop Functionality

Drag-and-drop functionality is always a favorite feature for developers to implement and it also brings a great end-user experience. Silverlight 4 allows Silverlight UIElements as a drop target and thus enables the implementation of the drag-and-drop functionality for partially trusted in-browser and out-of-browser (OOB) applications, as well as elevated-trusted OOB applications.

We already looked at a brief example of drag-and-drop functionality in Chapter 1, and we learned about key property and events of UIElement, enabling drag-and-drop functionality, in Chapter 3. Let's revisit the properties and events of UIElement that are required to enable the drag-and-drop functionality.

Properties of UIElement to Enable Drag-and-Drop Functionality

The `System.Windows.UIElement` class contains two properties—`AllowDrop` and `Visibility`—that need to be enabled for the user control to make it a drop target.

The `AllowDrop` dependency property is the key property to enable drag-and-drop functionality, which is introduced in Silverlight 4. Set it to `true` if you want to allow that specific UIElement to be a drop target. The default value of `AllowDrop` property is `false`.

Along with the `AllowDrop` property setting of `true`, the `Visibility` property of that specific UIElement must be set to `Visibility.Visible`, to make the control visible and allow it to be a drop target. Note that `Visibility.Visible` is the default value of the UIElement, so you do not need to explicitly mention that.

Events of UIElement to Enable Drag-and-Drop Functionality

The `System.Windows.UIElement` class contains four new events—`DragEnter`, `DragLeave`, `DragOver`, and `Drop`—in Silverlight 4 that can be implemented to enable drag-and-drop functionality. The `AllowDrop` property must be set to `true` in order to raise these events. If you set the `AllowDrop` property to `false`, even if these events are implemented, they will not be raised. Table 7-1 details these properties of the `System.Windows.UIElement` class.

Table 7-1. Events of the `System.Windows.UIElement` Class

Event	Description
DragEnter	Fires when the input system reports an underlying drag event with the specific event as the target. The event occurs only if the `AllowDrop` property of that element is set to `true`. Event args class: `DragEventHandler`. New event in Silverlight 4.
DragLeave	Fires when the input system reports an underlying drag event with the specific event as the origin. The event occurs only if the `AllowDrop` property of that element is set to `true`. Event args class: `DragEventHandler`. New event in Silverlight 4.

DragOver	Fires when the input system reports an underlying drag event with the specific event as the potential drop target. The event occurs only if the AllowDrop property of that element is set to true. Event args class: DragEventHandler. New event in Silverlight 4.
Drop	Fires when the input system reports an underlying drag event with the specific event as the drop target. The event occurs only if the AllowDrop property of that element is set to true. The Drop event is a bubbling event allowing multiple Drop events received by each object in a parent-child relationship in the object tree. Event args class: DragEventHandler. New event in Silverlight 4.

Processing Dropped File(s)

Silverlight 4's drag-and-drop feature supports only the processing of the dropped (one or more) files. The data object containing the dropped file(s) is accessible through the DragEventArgs.Data value from the drag-and-drop event. It implements the IDataObject, which provides a general interface for transferring data. For Silverlight, the only supported data object is of DataFormat.FileDrop format. You use the DataObject.GetData(DataFormat.FileDrop) method to retrieve the dropped file(s). Depending on the number files selected and dropped, it will return a FileInfo type array containing a one-item data set (for a single dropped file) or a multi-item data set (for more than one dropped file). You use the FileInfo.OpenRead or FileInfo.OpenText methods to access the file content.

Only the Drop event provides a dropped data object through the DragEventArgs.Data that can be processed to access the content of the file(s). DragEnter, DragLeave, and DragOver events also use the DragEventArgs with the DragEventArgs.Data value as null, which will cause the SecurityException if you try to attempt accessing data using the IDataObject APIs.

Developing an Example

We will build an image-viewer application enabling drag-and-drop functionality to drop PNG- and JPG-type images from the local system to the specific area (dropping zone) of the application. Valid dropped images will be inserted to the application, which can be viewed with a larger view by clicking the inserted image.

Defining User Control

The following XAML code of the DragnDropDemo user control is self-explanatory. Notice the highlighted AllowDrop property and drag-and-drop feature-related events set for DropZoneCanvas Canvas control determining the dropping zone of the application.

```
<UserControl x:Class="chapter7.DragnDropDemo"
    xmlns="http://schemas.microsoft.com/winfx/2006/xaml/presentation"
    xmlns:x="http://schemas.microsoft.com/winfx/2006/xaml"
    xmlns:d="http://schemas.microsoft.com/expression/blend/2008"
    xmlns:mc="http://schemas.openxmlformats.org/
        markup-compatibility/2006"
    xmlns:toolkit="http://schemas.microsoft.com/winfx/2006/
        xaml/presentation/toolkit"
```

```
        mc:Ignorable="d"
        d:DesignHeight="300" d:DesignWidth="400">

    <Grid x:Name="LayoutRoot" Background="White">
        <Grid.RowDefinitions>
            <RowDefinition Height="110"/>
            <RowDefinition Height="30"/>
            <RowDefinition Height="*"/>
        </Grid.RowDefinitions>

        <Border Grid.Row="0" BorderThickness="3"
            BorderBrush="DarkBlue" >
            <Canvas x:Name="DropZoneCanvas"
                Background="Cyan" Height="104" AllowDrop="True"
                Drop="DropZoneCanvas_Drop"
                DragOver="DropZoneCanvas_DragOver"
                DragLeave="DropZoneCanvas_DragLeave" >
                <TextBlock HorizontalAlignment="Center"
                    FontWeight="Bold" FontSize="14"
                    Canvas.Top="40" Canvas.Left="30" >
                    |Drop images here |</TextBlock>
            </Canvas>
        </Border>

        <TextBlock Grid.Row="1" FontSize="12" Height="26" Margin="8">
            Click on thumbnails for larger size</TextBlock>

        <ScrollViewer Grid.Row="2" Height="450">
            <toolkit:WrapPanel x:Name="ImageBox"
                Orientation="Horizontal"
                ScrollViewer.HorizontalScrollBarVisibility="Auto"/>
        </ScrollViewer>
    </Grid>
</UserControl>
```

As highlighted in the code, to enable drag-and-drop functionality, the `AllowDrop` property of the `DropZoneCanvas` Canvas layout control is set to true. You also need to implement at least the `Drop` event for this control to enable drag-and-drop files. As highlighted in the code, in addition to the `Drop` event, we have wired `DragOver` and `DragLeave` events to the Canvas control. Visual Studio will add the related event handlers automatically.

Also notice that we have used the WrapPanel control to display the inserted images, which is part of the Silverlight toolkit. Traditionally, if you are using Silverlight 3 or 2, you need to reference the Silverlight Toolkit in the XAML by declaring the `xmlns` and providing definition per namespace and assembly. Silverlight 4 supports the `XmlnsDefinition` attribute to declare the namespace for custom assemblies. Silverlight SDK and Toolkit now support the `XmlnsDefinition` attribute and you do not need to define all referenced assemblies and namespaces explicitly (see the preceding highlighted code to declare the Silverlight toolkit).

We completed the XAML implementation—now let us switch our focus to the code-behind of `DragnDrop` user control. The `Drop` event, for the `DropZoneCanvas` control, will retrieve one or more dragged and dropped files from the local system. Then it will validate whether each file is of the right image file type (PNG or JPG). It will insert all valid image files within the WrapPanel and notify users about any invalid files. To demonstrate the use of **DragOver** and **DragLeave** events, we will display a pop-up with a message, in the context of the mouse movement when the mouse is on and is moving within the **DropZoneCanvas** control area.

Implementing Code-Behind of the User Control

Now that you have a high-level understanding of the functionality, let us look at the **DragnDrop.xaml.cs** code-behind step-by-step.

First you need to add references to the following assemblies to allow file processing (read and write image files and obtain basic file profile information), process bitmap images, and display the pop-up message.

```
using System.IO;
using System.Windows.Media.Imaging;
using System.Windows.Controls.Primitives;
```

Declare the image collection to store the retrieved images at the class level.

```
List<Image> imgs = new List<Image>();
```

Implement the **Drop** event—**DropZoneCanvas_Drop** event—of the **DropZoneCanvas** control, as shown here:

```
private void DropZoneCanvas_Drop(object sender, DragEventArgs e)
{
    if (e.Data == null)
        return;

    IDataObject data = e.Data;
    FileInfo[] files = (FileInfo[])data.GetData(DataFormats.FileDrop);

    foreach (FileInfo file in files)
    {
        if (file.Extension == ".png" || file.Extension == ".jpg")
        {
            FileStream fs = file.OpenRead();
            BitmapImage bitmap = new BitmapImage();
            bitmap.SetSource(fs);
            Image img = new Image();
            img.Source = bitmap;
            img.Height = 120;
            img.Width = 120;
            img.Margin = new Thickness(5);
            img.Stretch = Stretch.Uniform;
            ImageBox.Children.Add(img);
        }
        else
        {
            MessageBox.Show(file.Name +
                " is not suppored image file.");
```

317

```
            }
        }
    }
```

As shown in this **Drop** event, each dropped file is represented as a **FileInfo** object. The **FileInfo** object will allow opening and reading of the file and also provide a file profile. Before processing the JPG and PNG image files, you need to check whether each dropped file is a valid type of file. We used the **Extension** property of the **FileInfo** object to get the extension of the file to validate the file type. Each dropped JPG and PNG file is streamed and set as the source of a **BitmapImage**, which is then used as a source of the **Image** object. The image objects will be added as children to the **ImageBox** WrapPanel. Now you are all set to handle the dragged and dropped image files. At this point, if you run the project, you will be in a position to drop JPG and PNG image file(s) on the dropping zone of the application. All valid files will be inserted to the WrapPanel, as shown in Figure 7-1. If you have tried to drop any invalid file (any file type except JPG or PNG file type), you will receive a notification for each invalid dropped file, as shown in Figure 7-2.

Figure 7-1. Drag-and-drop example

Figure 7-2. Invalid file notification

Now let us demonstrate the DragOver and DragLeave events. For that we will implement functionality to show a pop-up menu displaying a tip message, as you drag the file(s) over the dropping zone. Once you either drop the dragged files on the dropping zone or leave the dropping zone area, the pop-up message will be hidden.

First we need to declare Popup control at the class level, as shown here.

```
Popup tipPopup;
```

Next, implement the DropZoneCanvas_DragOver event, as shown here.

```
private void DropZoneCanvas_DragOver(object sender, DragEventArgs e)
{
    //If popup not created, create it.
    if (tipPopup == null)
    {
        tipPopup = new Popup();
        string message = "Drag and Drop PNG and JPG types images";

        Border border = new Border();
        border.BorderBrush = new SolidColorBrush(Colors.Green);
        border.BorderThickness = new Thickness(2.0);
        border.Background = new SolidColorBrush(Colors.White);
```

```
        TextBlock textblock1 = new TextBlock();
        textblock1.Text = message;
        textblock1.Margin = new Thickness(2);
        border.Child = textblock1;
        tipPopup.Child = border;
    }

    //if popup created already above, just update its postion
    tipPopup.VerticalOffset = e.GetPosition(null).Y;
    tipPopup.HorizontalOffset = e.GetPosition(null).X;
    tipPopup.IsOpen = true;
}
```

The `DragOver` event handler simply checks whether `tipPopup` is `null`. If it is `null`, it will create a pop-up with the appropriate message. The position of the pop-up message is determined by setting `VerticalOffset` and `HorizontalOffset` properties of the pop-up based on the current position of the mouse, which you can get using the `DragEventArgs.GetPosition` method. It reuses the pop-up if it is already created, and, in that case, it simply updates the position of the pop-up as the cursor moves.

The `DropZoneCanvas_DragLeave` event will make the pop-up hidden, using the `IsOpen` property of the Popup control, as shown here.

```
private void DropZoneCanvas_DragLeave(object sender, DragEventArgs e)
{
    if (tipPopup.IsOpen == true)
        tipPopup.IsOpen = false;
}
```

Run the project. You will notice that a pop-up will be displayed as soon as you drag the files to the defined dropping zone of the application (see Figure 7-3). The pop-up will be hidden when you drop the file(s) on the dropping zone or leave the dropping zone area of the application.

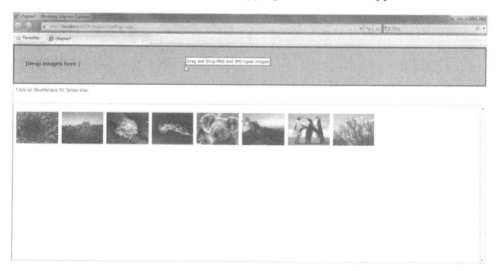

Figure 7-3. Demonstrating `DragOver` and `DragLeave` events

■ **Note** Silverlight 4 does not support the drag-and-drop functionality if the application is running in full-screen mode (for Windows and Mac platform) or windowless mode (for Windows platform). Visit Microsoft MSDN library (http://msdn.microsoft.com/en-us/library/cc838156(VS.96).aspx) to get more information on the windowless mode.

Adding ChildWindow as an Image Viewer

To provide a larger preview of the clicked image, we will use a ChildWindow control. Add a new ChildWindow control to the project and name it ImageWindow.xaml. Open the ImageWindow.xaml file and set its Width to 800 and Height to 600 and Title to Larger Preview. The following is a complete XAML code for the added ChildWindow.

```
<controls:ChildWindow x:Class="chapter7.ImageWindow"
    xmlns="http://schemas.microsoft.com/winfx/2006/xaml/presentation"
    xmlns:x="http://schemas.microsoft.com/winfx/2006/xaml"
    xmlns:controls="clr-namespace:System.Windows.Controls;assembly=
        System.Windows.Controls"
    Width="800" Height="600"
    Title="Larger Preview">
    <Grid x:Name="LayoutRoot" Margin="2">
        <Grid.RowDefinitions>
            <RowDefinition Height="26"/>
            <RowDefinition />
            <RowDefinition Height="Auto" />
        </Grid.RowDefinitions>
        <TextBlock
            Text="Use Mouse wheel to zoom in or out"
            Grid.Row="0">
        </TextBlock>
        <Image x:Name="ImageStage" Grid.Row="1" />
        <StackPanel Grid.Row="2"
            HorizontalAlignment="Right"  Orientation="Horizontal" >
            <Button x:Name="btnReset" Content="Reset Zoom"
                Width="75" Height="23" HorizontalAlignment="Right"
                Margin="10" Click="btnReset_Click"/>
            <Button x:Name="btnClose" Content="Close"
                Click="btnClose_Click" Width="75" Height="23"
                HorizontalAlignment="Right" />
        </StackPanel>
    </Grid>
</controls:ChildWindow>
```

The XAML markup is fairly simple, with one Image control to display the clicked image on ImageBox, StackPanel, and a Close button to close the ImageWindow ChildWindow with the btnClose_Click event defined.

Notice that I have also added an extra TextBlock describing the zoom-in and zoom-out features, and an additional Reset Zoom button, which we will implement to set the image back to the normal view.

This is part of the preparation of implementing zoom-in and zoom-out functionality for the image, demonstrating the MouseWheel support introduced in Silverlight 4, which we will implement in the next section of this chapter.

In the code-behind of the ChildWindow, we need to define one private property of type ImageSource at the class level to set the ImageStage.Source property when the ChildWindow loads.

We supply the imgSource ImageSource property in the MouseLeftButtonDown event handler of dropped images to the ImageWindow ChildWindow instance. To supply this using the default constructor, we added one parameter of type ImageSource to the ImageWindow default constructor. See the following code snippet.

```
private ImageSource imgSource {get; set;}

public ImageWindow(ImageSource source)
{
    InitializeComponent();
    imgSource = source;
    this.Loaded+=new RoutedEventHandler(ImageWindow_Loaded);
}

void ImageWindow_Loaded(object sender, RoutedEventArgs e)
{
    ImageStage.Source = imgSource;
}
```

Now implement the btnClose_Click event and set the DialogResult property of the ChildWindow to false to close the child window.

```
private void btnClose_Click(object sender, RoutedEventArgs e)
{
    this.DialogResult = false;
}
```

Now you need to revisit the DragnDropDemo user control and implement the img_MouseLeftButtonDown event, as shown here (see the highlighted bold fonts).

```
private void DropZoneCanvas_Drop(object sender, DragEventArgs e)
{
    if (e.Data == null)
        return;

    IDataObject data = e.Data;
    FileInfo[] files = (FileInfo[])data.GetData(DataFormats.FileDrop);

    foreach (FileInfo file in files)
    {
        if (file.Extension == ".png" || file.Extension == ".jpg")
        {
            FileStream fs = file.OpenRead();
            BitmapImage bitmap = new BitmapImage();
            bitmap.SetSource(fs);
            Image img = new Image();
```

```
        img.Source = bitmap;
        img.Height = 120;
        img.Width = 120;
        img.Margin = new Thickness(5);
        img.Stretch = Stretch.Uniform;
        //attaching MouseLeftButtonDown so uplon click
          //on image will show image in ImageWindow
        img.MouseLeftButtonDown += new
            MouseButtonEventHandler(img_MouseLeftButtonDown);
        ImageBox.Children.Add(img);
    }
    else
    {
        MessageBox.Show(file.Name +
            " is not suppored image file.");
    }
  }
}

void img_MouseLeftButtonDown(object sender, MouseButtonEventArgs e)
{
    ImageWindow iw = new ImageWindow(((Image)sender).Source);
    iw.Show();
}
```

Here I simply cast the sender object to Image and supply its Source (which is of the ImageSource type) as a parameter of the constructor of ImageWindow. Next you need to call the Show method to display the ImageWindow ChildWindow showing a larger preview of the clicked image.

Now run this sample. Drop some images on the dropping zone of the application to insert them to the application. Click any of the images to see a larger preview in the child ImageWindow, as shown in Figure 7-4.

Figure 7-4. Image previewer using a ChildWindow control

Mouse-Wheel Support

Originally Silverlight 3 added support for the UIElement.MouseWheel event. However, the controls in Silverlight 3 didn't generally respond well to the mouse-wheel event and you needed to implement some workarounds to achieve proper functionality to support mouse-wheel input. As a workaround, we could use the HTML DOM mouse-wheel events, and we needed to wire up logic in managed code to do so. However, this workaround did not support the following two scenarios:

- Application displayed in full-screen mode

- Application deployed and running in out-of-browser mode, where you cannot host an HTML page to handle DOM events

Silverlight 4 addresses this issue, and now controls can handle the MouseWheel event as expected with the managed code. The managed MouseWheel event helps to overcome these two limitations. It is recommended that you use the MouseWheel event instead of DOM events.

Developing an Example

To demonstrate this feature, let's extend the previous image viewer example and add zoom-in and zoom-out functionality on the mouse-wheel scroll to the existing ImageWindow ChildWindow.

In the previous section, we already prepared the user interface related to the zoom-in and zoom-out functionality on the mouse-wheel scroll by adding an instruction TextBlock and Reset Zoom Button in the ImageWindow ChildWindow. So let us implement the required code-behind.

Revisit and open the ImageWindow.xmal.cs file and create a MouseWheel event handler within the ImageWindow class constructor, as shown here:

```
this.MouseWheel += new MouseWheelEventHandler(ImageWindow_MouseWheel);
```

We need to apply ScaleTransform to the ImageStage.RenderTransform property to create zoom-in/out. You will learn more about the various types of transforms in Chapter 9, but here, I will quickly show you the code to implement ScaleTransform to achieve the desired zoom feature. For this, first define ScaleTransform at the ImageWindow class level as follows:

```
ScaleTransform zoomTransform = new ScaleTransform();
```

Apply the ScaleTransform to the ImageStage Image control by setting the RenderTransform property in the constructor of the ImageWindow class as follows:

```
ImageStage.RenderTransform = zoomTransform;
```

Next, implement the ImageWindow_MouseWheel event handler as described here:

```
void ImageWindow_MouseWheel(object sender, MouseWheelEventArgs e)
{
    //Following two lines ensures that it will center zoom
    //the image portion where cursor is
    zoomTransform.CenterX = e.GetPosition(null).X;
    zoomTransform.CenterY = e.GetPosition(null).Y;

    if (e.Delta > 0)
```

```
{
    zoomTransform.ScaleX += 0.05;
    zoomTransform.ScaleY += 0.05;
}
else
{
    zoomTransform.ScaleX -= 0.05;
    zoomTransform.ScaleY -= 0.05;
}
}
```

Note that the `MouseWheelEventArgs.Delta` property provides value indicating the amount that the mouse wheel rotated relative to its starting state or to the last occurrence of the event. Based on this value, we either increase or decrease the `ScaleX` and `ScaleY` to stretch or shrink the `ImageStage` object. To zoom into or out of the portion by keeping the current location of the cursor as the center point, we also set `CenterX` and `CenterY` to the current location of the cursor using the `GetPosition` property that we implemented for the `tipPopup` earlier.

We also need to provide a way to reset the image to its original rendered size in the `ImageStage` control. We use the previously-added reset zoom button and implement the `Click` event of this button, as shown here:

```
private void btnReset_Click(object sender, RoutedEventArgs e)
{
    zoomTransform.ScaleX = 1;
    zoomTransform.ScaleY = 1;
}
```

Now hit F5, drag and drop some images, and click any inserted image. A child window will open with the clicked image. Now use your mouse wheel to zoom into and out of the image. If you click the Reset Zoom button, the size of the image will be reset to the original size. Figure 7-5 shows the child window with the zoomed-in image.

Figure 7-5. Demonstrating mouse-wheel support

Limitations

Support to the `MouseWheel` event is platform-specific. This feature is supported only on the Microsoft Windows operating system, in Internet Explorer and Firefox web browsers in the in-browser or out-of-browser mode, and in the full-screen mode. It is not supported in the windowless mode in Firefox on Mac, or other web browsers. Table 7-2 details the supported/not-supported platform.

Table 7-2. Platform-Specific `MouseWheel` Support

Platform	MouseWheel Support
Windows, In-Browser Mode, Internet Explorer and Firefox	Yes
Windows, Out-of-Browser Mode, Internet Explorer and Firefox	Yes
Windows, Full-Screen Mode, Internet Explorer	Yes
Windows, Windowless Mode, Firefox	No
Macintosh	No

Right-Click Context Menu Support

One of the core features of most LoB applications is the support of right-click context menu-based features.

By default, a Silverlight application provides a right-click context menu with the "Silverlight" menu option. Upon clicking that, you will get a pop-up displaying the details about the Silverlight plug-in itself, including the version information, update configuration, DRM configuration, and isolated storage configuration. If you have OOB mode enabled for the application, you will also get a second option to install or remove the application in OOB mode. However, Silverlight 3 and prior versions did not provide an option to build custom right-click context menus to implement application specific features.

With Silverlight 4, this is still the default behavior for the right mouse button. However, as we learned in Chapter 3, there are two new `MouseRightButtonDown` and `MouseRightButtonUp` events for UIElement that are introduced to handle the right mouse click and implement required custom features. As these new events are introduced on the `UIElement` class, they work in a similar manner as the existing `MouseLeftButtonDown` and `MouseLeftButtonUp` events and are routed events as well.

To demonstrate the right-click context menu feature, we will extend the previous application and implement the right-click Print feature for the image previewer child window. In this section, we will implement the right-click Print context menu and in the next section, we will implement the Print functionality.

Revisit the `ImageWindow.xaml` file of the project. Here we will implement the right-click capability at the Grid control level by adding the `MouseRightButtonDown` and `MouseRightButtonUp` events to the as shown here (in the highlighted text).

```
<Grid x:Name="LayoutRoot" Margin="2"
    MouseRightButtonDown="LayoutRoot_MouseRightButtonDown"
    MouseRightButtonUp="LayoutRoot_MouseRightButtonUp">
```

This would enable you to have custom right-click features on any controls that are part of the Grid control. However, if you run the project you will notice that you are still getting the default Silverlight option upon right-clicking. The first step is to remove that. You need to set `MouseButtonEventArgs.Handled` to `true` of the `MouseRightButtonDown` event, as shown here. Run the project and you will notice that if you click any Grid control (Image, TextBlock, or Buttons), the default Silverlight right-mouse context menu will not be displayed. However, if you click anywhere else on the opened child window, you will still get the default Silverlight right-mouse context menu.

```
private void LayoutRoot_MouseRightButtonDown
    (object sender, MouseButtonEventArgs e)
{
    e.Handled = true;
}
```

Now define `Popup contextMenu = new Popup();` at the class level and then add the following the code snippet for the `LayoutRoot_MouseRightButtonUp` event.

```
private void LayoutRoot_MouseRightButtonUp
    (object sender, MouseButtonEventArgs e)
{
    Border border = new Border();
    border.BorderBrush = new SolidColorBrush(Colors.Green);
    border.BorderThickness = new Thickness(3);
    border.Background = new SolidColorBrush(Colors.White);

    StackPanel panel1 = new StackPanel();
    panel1.Background = new SolidColorBrush(Colors.LightGray);

    //Print Screen Button
    Button printscreenbutton = new Button();
    printscreenbutton.Content = "Print Screen";
    printscreenbutton.Width = 100;
    printscreenbutton.Margin = new Thickness(3);
    //Click event to provide print functionality
    printscreenbutton.Click += new
        RoutedEventHandler(printscreen_Click);

    //Print Image Button
    Button printimagebutton = new Button();
    printimagebutton.Content = "Print Image";
    printimagebutton.Width = 100;
    printimagebutton.Margin = new Thickness(3);
    //Click event to provide print functionality
    printimagebutton.Click += new
        RoutedEventHandler(printimage_Click);

    //Custom Print Button
    Button printcustombutton = new Button();
    printcustombutton.Content = "Custom Print";
    printcustombutton.Width = 100;
    printcustombutton.Margin = new Thickness(3);
```

```
        //Click event to provide print functionality
        printcustombutton.Click += new
            RoutedEventHandler(printcustom_Click);

        panel1.Children.Add(printscreenbutton);
        panel1.Children.Add(printimagebutton);
        panel1.Children.Add(printcustombutton);

        border.Child = panel1;

        contextMenu.Child = border;
        //set display location to current cursor
        contextMenu.VerticalOffset = e.GetPosition(null).Y;
        contextMenu.HorizontalOffset = e.GetPosition(null).X;
        //show the context print menu
        contextMenu.IsOpen = true;
}
```

As you can see here, we have added three buttons as part of the pop-up context menu window and made it visible. The position of the pop-up context menu is determined by setting `VerticalOffset` and `HorizontalOffset` properties of the pop-up based on the current position of the mouse, which you can get using the `MouseButtonEventArgs.GetPosition` method. Notice that each button has implemented a `Click` event to perform the required actions. In this section, we will just display a message box and close the context menu as shown here. In the next section we will implement the actual Printing capability.

```
private void printscreen_Click(object sender, RoutedEventArgs e)
{
    MessageBox.Show("Print Screen Functionality Goes Here..");
    contextMenu.IsOpen = false;
}

private void printimage_Click(object sender, RoutedEventArgs e)
{
    MessageBox.Show("Print Image Functionality Goes Here..");
    contextMenu.IsOpen = false;
}

private void printcustom_Click(object sender, RoutedEventArgs e)
{
    MessageBox.Show("Custom Print Functionality Goes Here..");
    contextMenu.IsOpen = false;
}
```

If you run the project at this point, you will notice that the Print context menu is displayed upon right-clicking. If you click one of the Print buttons, you will get an appropriate message as shown in Figure 7-6 and close the context menu. However, if you do not click any of the context menu buttons, the context menu will still be visible.

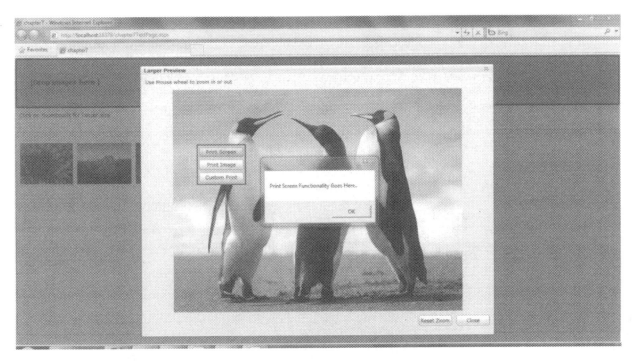

Figure 7-6. Demonstrating Right-Click Context Menu Feature

Usually the default behavior is that you can close the context menu upon the left-click event. Let's implement the `LayoutRoot_MouseLeftButtonDown` event to close the visible context menu pop-up. See the following appropriate XAML code update (in highlighted text) to the Grid control and related code-behind.

```
<Grid x:Name="LayoutRoot" Margin="2"
    MouseRightButtonDown="LayoutRoot_MouseRightButtonDown"
    MouseRightButtonUp="LayoutRoot_MouseRightButtonUp"
    MouseLeftButtonDown="LayoutRoot_MouseLeftButtonDown">

private void LayoutRoot_MouseLeftButtonDown
    (object sender, MouseButtonEventArgs e)
{
    contextMenu.IsOpen = false;
}
```

Printing Capabilities

One of the most widely requested features for Silverlight is support to the Printing feature. Silverlight 4 introduces this capability and enables you to either print the existing visual tree or create a custom virtual visual tree. The printing functionality can be implemented in both in-browser and out-of-browser modes.

PrintDocument Class

The **PrintDocument** class is the core class that provides printing APIs for Silverlight 4 applications. It resides in the **System.Windows.Printing** namespace in the **System.Windows** assembly. This class contains only one method, the **Print** method, which you will call to open the default Print dialog box to start the printing process for the specified document. You can pass the document name as a string to the **Print** method, which will be displayed as a document name to the active printer dialog box displaying the document submitted for the printing.

The **PrintDocument** class also has one property, the **PrintedPageCount** property, that returns the number of pages that have printed. Table 7-3 shows the events of this class, which control the printing process.

Table 7-3. Events of the System.Windows.Printing.PrintDocument Class

Event	Description
BeginPrint	Occurs after the **Print** method is called and the print dialog box successfully returns, but before the **PrintPage** event is raised. If the user cancels the Print dialog box, this event will not raise. You can use this event to handle any activity (showing the printing progress indicator, for example) before the printing starts. The **BeginPrintEventArgs** provides data for the **BeginPrint** event.
EndPrint	Occurs when the printing operation is completed successfully or the print operation is cancelled by the user. If the user cancels the Print dialog box, this event will not raise. You can use this event to handle any print operation–ending activity (making the printing progress indicator invisible, for example) or perform any clean-up operation after the printing finishes. If any error occurs during the printing operation, you can use the **EndPrintEventArgs.Error** property to get the error information. The default value of **EndPrintEventArgs.Error** is null.
PrintPage	Occurs when each page is printing. After the **PrintPage** event occurs, the specified **PrintPageEventArgs.PageVisual** will be sent to the printer to be printed. You set up the **PrintPageEventArgs.PageVisual** to the layout root element to print the entire screen, or to a specific element to print specific information within the screen. Or you can develop a virtual visual tree and set it up to the virtual tree to print custom developed information. If **PrintPageEventArgs.HasMorePages** is true, the **PrintPage** event will occur again. The default value of **PrintPageEventArgs.HasMorePages** is false.

PrintPageEventArgs Class

You probably have already predicted from the preceding table that the **PrintPageEventArgs** class plays a critical role in the printing operation. It provides data for the **PrintPage** event. Table 7-4 shows properties of this class.

Table 7-4. Properties of the System.Windows.Printing.PrintPageEventArgs Class

Property	Type	Description
HasMorePages	bool	Defines if there are more pages to print. If the value is true, it means there are additional pages to print. The default value is false.
PageMargins	System.Windows.Thickness	Read-only property. Gets the margins to the current printing page.
PageVisual	System.Windows.UIElement	Defines the scope of the printing operation by setting PrintPageEventArgs.PageVisual. You set up the PrintPageEventArgs.PageVisual to the layout root element to print the entire screen, or to a specific element to print specific information within the screen, or develop a virtual visual tree and set it up to the virtual tree to print custom developed information. The default value is null.
PrintableArea	System.Windows.Size	Read-only property. Gets the size of the printable area. Silverlight provides the conversion between the device pixels and screen pixels so that the PrintableArea property value can represent the printable area, which is smaller than the actual page size. If the size is greater than the actual page size, then the printed content is clipped.

Implementing the Printing Function

Let's extend the Print button click events we implemented in our previous section to enable the printing functionality. Revisit ImageWindow.xaml.cs and add the System.Windows.Printing namespace as shown here.

```
using System.Windows.Printing;
```

Now let's implement each Print button click event one by one, demonstrating the different printing capabilities—printing complete screens, printing only the displayed image, and custom printing.

Printing the Application Screen

Remove the MessageBox and implement the print screen functionality for the **printscreen_Click** event as shown here (see highlighted text).

```
private void printscreen_Click(object sender, RoutedEventArgs e)
{
    contextMenu.IsOpen = false;
    PrintDocument pdoc = new PrintDocument();
```

```
// Set the printable area
pdoc.PrintPage += (s, args) =>
{
    args.PageVisual  = LayoutRoot;
};

// Print the document
pdoc.Print("Printing Application Screen");
}
```

Here we create the instance of the `PrintDocument`, implement the `PrintPage` event and then set `PrintPageEventArgs.PageVisual` to the LayoutRoot Grid control to include all controls included in the grid control defining the print scope. Call the `PrintDocument.Print` method and pass "Printing Application Screen" as the document name that will be displayed in the print spooler.

Now run the project, drag and drop images, and click one of the images to view in the image viewer window. Right-click the image and select the Print Screen button—you will get the Print dialog box when the `Print` method is called (see Figure 7-7).

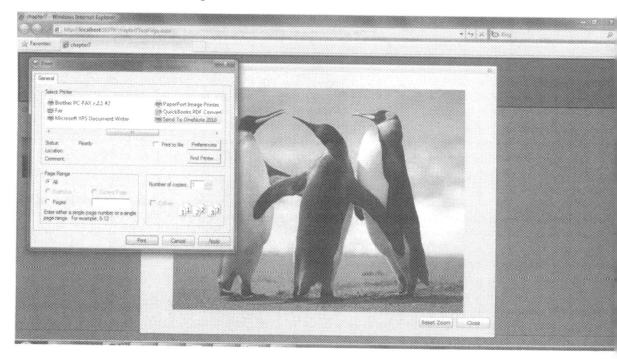

Figure 7-7. *Print dialog box opened after calling the* `PrintDocument.Print` *method*

For demonstration purposes, I have selected the Send To OneNote 2010 option to insert the print document output within the OneNote, as shown in Figure 7-8. You can see that the TextBlock control, Image control, and two Button controls, which are within the `LayoutRoot` Grid control, are added to the OneNote.

Figure 7-8. The whole screen is inserted as print output to the OneNote.

If you select a regular printer, then the passed document name to the `Print` method is displayed in the active printer window, as shown in Figure 7-9.

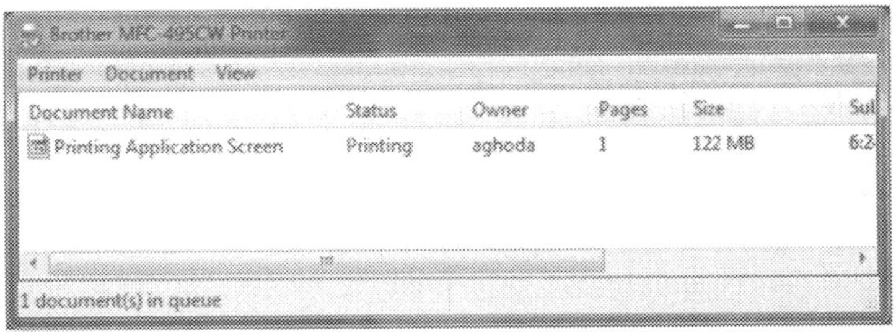

Figure 7-9. Displaying printing document name in the active printing window

Printing Selected Control

Similarly remove the MessageBox and implement the print image functionality for the `printimage_Click` event, as shown here. Note that we set `PageVisual` to the `ImageStage` control (see highlighted text) to print only the displayed image and also pass the appropriate document name to the `Print` method.

```
private void printimage_Click(object sender, RoutedEventArgs e)
{
    contextMenu.IsOpen = false;
    PrintDocument pdoc = new PrintDocument();

    // Set the printable area
```

```
        pdoc.PrintPage += (s, args) =>
        {
            args.PageVisual  = ImageStage;
        };

        // Print the document
        pdoc.Print("Printing Image");
}
```

Now run the project and select the Print Image option, and select the OneNote 2010 option to print to OneNote. As shown in Figure 7-10, only the image will be inserted to the OneNote page as print output.

Figure 7-10. Only the image is inserted as print output to the OneNote.

Custom Printing

Here we will remove the MessageBox, and then we will define the custom user interface in memory and send that as a printing document. In this example, we will add a TextBlock control displaying text, and clip the image using `EllipseGeometry`. Refer to Chapter 9 to learn in detail about the graphics capabilities of Silverlight.

Now add both controls to the StackPanel and set `PageVisual` to StackPanel to provide the custom output. Call the `Print` method and pass the appropriate document name. The following is a complete code snippet of `PrintCustom_Click`.

```
private void printcustom_Click(object sender, RoutedEventArgs e)
{
    contextMenu.IsOpen = false;
```

```
    //Define custom print output
    StackPanel panel1 = new StackPanel();
    panel1.Background = new SolidColorBrush(Colors.White);

    TextBlock textblock = new TextBlock();

    textblock.Text = "Custom Print Example";
    textblock.FontWeight = FontWeights.Bold;
    textblock.FontSize = 12;

    Image image = new Image();
    image.Source = imgSource;
    image.Width = 300;
    image.Height = 300;

    Point point = new Point(150, 150);
    EllipseGeometry eg = new EllipseGeometry();
    eg.RadiusX = 100;
    eg.RadiusY = 100;
    eg.Center = point;

    image.Clip = eg;

    panel1.Children.Add(textblock);
    panel1.Children.Add(image);

    PrintDocument pdoc = new PrintDocument();

    // Set the printable area
    pdoc.PrintPage += (s, args) =>
    {
        args.PageVisual = panel1;
    };

    // Print the document
    pdoc.Print("Custom Printing");
}
```

Now run the project and select the Print Custom option, and select the OneNote 2010 option to print to OneNote. As shown in Figure 7-11, the custom output—text and clipped image—is inserted to the OneNote page as print output.

Figure 7-11. *Custom runtime-created content inserted as print output to the OneNote*

Clipboard Access

Silverlight 4 introduced the `System.Windows.Clipboard` class to provide access to the system clipboard to copy and paste data. Note that Silverlight 4 supports only Unicode text access to and from the system clipboard. The access to the clipboard can be implemented in both in-browser and out-of-browser modes.

The `Clipboard` class provides three static methods to perform the data transfer operations to and from the clipboard system. Table 7-5 details these methods.

Table 7-5. *Static Methods of the* `System.Windows.Clipboard` *Class*

Method	Description
ContainsText	Returns `true` if the data in the UnicodeText format is available in the system clipboard; otherwise it returns `false`.
GetText	Returns UnicodeText format data from the system clipboard; otherwise it returns empty string.
SetText	Stores the UnicodeText format data to the system clipboard.

Let's quickly build an example to demonstrate this functionality by adding a `ClipDemo` user control to the existing project. Here we will create a Scratch Pad using the RichTextBox, and we will add two Buttons to perform a copy from Scratch Pad and paste to Scratch Pad functionalities. The following is a self-explanatory XAML code of the control.

```xml
<UserControl x:Class="chapter7.ClipDemo"
    xmlns="http://schemas.microsoft.com/winfx/2006/xaml/presentation"
    xmlns:x="http://schemas.microsoft.com/winfx/2006/xaml"
    xmlns:d="http://schemas.microsoft.com/expression/blend/2008"
    xmlns:mc="http://schemas.openxmlformats.org/
        markup-compatibility/2006"
    mc:Ignorable="d"
    d:DesignHeight="600" d:DesignWidth="600">
    <StackPanel HorizontalAlignment="Center">
        <Border BorderBrush="Black" BorderThickness="2"
            Height="600" Width="600" Margin="2">
            <StackPanel x:Name="stp2"  Height="600" Width="500">
                <TextBlock Text="Scratch Pad"
                    HorizontalAlignment="Center"
                    FontWeight="Bold" FontSize="14" Margin="2"/>
                <StackPanel Orientation="Horizontal"
                    HorizontalAlignment="Center">
                    <Button x:Name="btnCopy"
                        Content="Copy from Scratch Pad"
                        Margin="10" Height="25" Width="150"
                        Click="btnCopy_Click"/>
                    <Button x:Name="btnPaste"
                        Content="Paste to Scratch Pad"
                        Margin="10" Height="25" Width="150"
                        Click="btnPaste_Click"/>
                </StackPanel>
                <RichTextBox
                    Name="richTextArea"
                    Background="WhiteSmoke"
                    Cursor="Stylus"
                    FontFamily="Portable User Interface"
                    TextWrapping="Wrap"
                    VerticalScrollBarVisibility="Auto"
                    HorizontalScrollBarVisibility="Auto"
                    MinHeight="500" MaxHeight="500"
                    MinWidth="500" MaxWidth="500" />
            </StackPanel>
        </Border>
    </StackPanel>
</UserControl>
```

▪ **Note** Note that RichTextBox control has in-built functionality to support the copy/paste functionality. You can use Ctrl + C to copy information and Ctrl + V to paste the copied information. In this section we are just demonstrating the Clipboard APIs by implementing the custom Copy/Paste functionality.

Now quickly implement the Click events in the code-behind for both buttons, as shown here.

```
private void btnCopy_Click(object sender, RoutedEventArgs e)
{
    if (!String.IsNullOrEmpty(richTextArea.Selection.Text))
        Clipboard.SetText(richTextArea.Selection.Text);
    else
        MessageBox.Show("No Text is selected to copy");
}

private void btnPaste_Click(object sender, RoutedEventArgs e)
{
    if (Clipboard.ContainsText())
    {
        Run insertText = new Run();
        insertText.Text = Clipboard.GetText();
        richTextArea.Selection.Insert(insertText);
    }
    else
        MessageBox.Show("No Text available to paste");
}
```

As shown in the **btnCopy_Click** event, first we check whether any text is selected in the RichTextBox control. If selected, the text will be stored in the system clipboard using the **Clipboard.SetText** method. If no text is selected, it informs the user using the MessageBox.

In the **btnPaste_Click** event, first we check whether any UniCodeText format text is available in the system clipboard by using the **Clipboard.ContainsText** method. If there is text available, it will get the text using the **Clipboard.GetText** method and insert it to the current cursor location.

Now, if you run the project, you should be in a position to copy selected text to the system clipboard, which can be pasted back to the scratch pad or any other application such as Notepad or Microsoft Word. Similarly copied text from any external application or from this application to the system clipboard can be inserted to the scratch pad.

Globalization and Localization of Silverlight Applications

Implementation of globalization and localization plays a critical role in the success of any enterprise-level global line-of-business applications. Silverlight has supported the globalization and localization of applications since Silverlight 2. Silverlight 4 extends the capabilities by supporting bi-directional text and adding support to many more languages, including right-to-left languages. During the design, development, and deployment of Silverlight applications, enterprises must consider the localization factor.

Globalization

Any global application must support requirements of global and diversified user groups with different culture and requirements. Globalization is the application design and development process that incorporates local culture-specific requirements, such as local language support, in the user interface design and support for local numbers, currency, and date formats in the data representation.

■ **Note** This section will cover the key essence of the globalization. You may want to refer to the Microsoft MSDN website, `http://msdn.microsoft.com/en-us/library/cc853414(VS.96).aspx`, to get more details on how to create globally-aware Silverlight applications.

CultureInfo Class

Silverlight supports globalization features using traditional .NET Framework techniques. We can use the `CultureInfo` class of the `System.Globalization` namespace to retrieve information about the specific culture. The `CultureInfo` class provides culture-specific information such as languageCode-regionCode (e.g., en-US for English language and US region), character set, currency symbol, and number and date (calendar) format.

Table 7-6 details key properties of the `CultureInfo` class.

Table 7-6. Key Properties of the System.Globalization.CultureInfo Class

Property	Type	Description
Calendar	System.Globalization.Calendar	Gets the default calendar used by the culture.
CurrentCulture	System.Globalization.CultureInfo	Gets the CultureInfo object representing the culture used by the current thread.
CurrentUICulture	System.Globalization.CultureInfo	Gets the CultureInfo object that represents the current culture used by the Resource Manager to look up culture-specific resources at runtime.
DateTimeFormat	System.Globalization.DateTimeFormatInfo	Defines the DateTimeFormatInfo object detailing the culturally appropriate format for converting dates and times to strings.
DisplayName	string	Gets the culture name in the format "language (country/region)" in the language of the localized version of .NET Framework.
EnglishName	string	Gets the culture name in the format "language (country/region)" in English. As an example, culture "en-US" displays "English (United States)" as EnglishName.
InvariantCulture	System.Globalization.CultureInfo	Gets the CultureInfo that is culture-independent (invariant).
Name	string	Gets the culture name in the format "languagecode-country/regioncode". As an example, culture "en-US" represents "en-US" as Name.

NativeName	string	Gets the culture's native name, which consists of the language, the country/region, and the optional script, that the culture is set to display.
NumberFormat	System.Globalization .NumberFormatInfo	Defines a NumberFormatInfo object that defines the culturally appropriate format for converting numbers, currency values, and percentages to strings.
Parent	System.Globalization .CultureInfo	Gets the CultureInfo that represents the parent culture of the current CultureInfo. As an example, zh-Hant culture (Chinese culture) is the parent culture of zh-HK (Chinese Hong Kong S.A.R.), zh-MO (Chinese Macao S.A.R.), and zh-TW (Chinese Taiwan) cultures.

Developing an Example

I created a new user control name CultureInfoDemo in the existing project to retrieve and display the current culture, UI culture, and Invariant culture information of the local machine. In the XAML code I have added one TextBlock control to display the retrieved culture information. The code-behind is also very simple, as shown here.

```
public CultureInfoDemo()
{
    InitializeComponent();
    GetCultureInfo();
}

private void GetCultureInfo()
{
    string s;

    CultureInfo cul = CultureInfo.CurrentCulture;

    s = "Current Culture Information " + cul.Name + "\n";
    s += String.Format("   Name: {0}\n", cul.Name);
    s += String.Format("   Display Name: {0}\n", cul.DisplayName);
    s += String.Format("   Native Name: {0}\n", cul.NativeName);
    s += String.Format("   English Name: {0}\n", cul.EnglishName);
    s += String.Format("   Parent Culture Name: {0}\n",
        cul.Parent.Name);
    s += String.Format("   Calendar: {0}\n", cul.Calendar.ToString());
    s += String.Format("   Is read-only: {0}\n",
        cul.Calendar.IsReadOnly);

    CultureInfo culUI = CultureInfo.CurrentUICulture;

    s += "\nCurrent UI Culture Information " + culUI.Name + "\n";
    s += String.Format("   Name: {0}\n", culUI.Name);
    s += String.Format("   Display Name: {0}\n", culUI.DisplayName);
```

```
s += String.Format("   Native Name: {0}\n", culUI.NativeName);
s += String.Format("   English Name: {0}\n", culUI.EnglishName);
s += String.Format("   Parent Culture Name: {0}\n",
    culUI.Parent.Name);
s += String.Format("   Calendar: {0}\n",
    culUI.Calendar.ToString());
s += String.Format("   Is read-only: {0}\n",
    culUI.Calendar.IsReadOnly);

CultureInfo culInvariant = CultureInfo.CurrentUICulture;

s += "\nCurrent Invariant Culture Information " +
    culInvariant.Name + "\n";
s += String.Format("   Name: {0}\n", culInvariant.Name);
s += String.Format("   Display Name: {0}\n",
    culInvariant.DisplayName);
s += String.Format("   Native Name: {0}\n",
    culInvariant.NativeName);
s += String.Format("   English Name: {0}\n",
    culInvariant.EnglishName);
s += String.Format("   Parent Culture Name: {0}\n",
    culInvariant.Parent.Name);
s += String.Format("   Calendar: {0}\n",
    culInvariant.Calendar.ToString());
s += String.Format("   Is read-only: {0}\n",
    culInvariant.Calendar.IsReadOnly);

current.Text = s;
}
```

Note that you need to add a reference to System.Globalization, as shown here.

```
using System.Globalization;
```

I ran the project and retrieved the results shown in Figure 7-12, which can be further used to determine the user machine's culture information and adjust the application accordingly based on the localization capabilities of the application.

```
Current Culture Information en-US
   Name: en-US
   Display Name: English (United States)
   Native Name: English (United States)
   English Name: English (United States)
   Parent Culture Name: en
   Calendar: System.Globalization.GregorianCalendar
   Is read-only: True

Current UI Culture Information en-US
   Name: en-US
   Display Name: English (United States)
   Native Name: English (United States)
   English Name: English (United States)
   Parent Culture Name: en
   Calendar: System.Globalization.GregorianCalendar
   Is read-only: True

Current Invariant Culture Information en-US
   Name: en-US
   Display Name: English (United States)
   Native Name: English (United States)
   English Name: English (United States)
   Parent Culture Name: en
   Calendar: System.Globalization.GregorianCalendar
   Is read-only: True
```

Figure 7-12. Retrieving culture information from the local machine

Localization

Based on the design concepts implemented as part of the globalization process, localization is the physical process of implementing culture-specific language requirements, which mainly involves the process of translating text and images into the local language to provide a localized presentation layer. For Silverlight applications, one of the standard ways of implementing localization is to develop culture- or locale-specific resource files, including translated text and images.

▪ **Note** This section will cover the key essence of the localization. You may want to refer to the Microsoft MSDN website, `http://msdn.microsoft.com/en-us/library/cc838238(VS.96).aspx`, to get more details on how to localize Silverlight applications.

Hub-and-Spoke Model

The .NET Framework uses satellite assemblies to package and deploy resources, and it uses the traditional hub-and-spoke model to locate the appropriate resources in those satellite assemblies at runtime, based on the user's locale-specific culture information. The hub is the main application assembly containing the executable application and the neutral culture or default culture. The neutral or default culture assembly refers to only the default language (e.g., **en** for English) and is not associated with any region (e.g., US or UK).

Each satellite assembly is a spoke and contains resources for one specific culture. This concept also allows enterprises to deploy additional culture-specific satellite assemblies even after they have deployed the Silverlight application without recompiling and redeploying the whole application.

As mentioned earlier, with the hub-and-spoke model concept, the .NET Framework resource manager follows a structured pattern to load the proper resource file based on the client locale and deployed satellite assemblies for that application. Figure 7-13 demonstrates the structured execution path of the resource manager to identify and load the appropriate resource file.

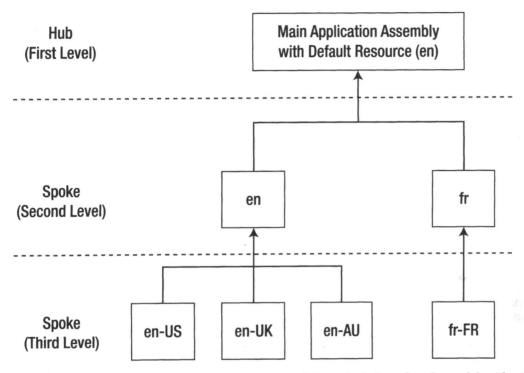

Figure 7-13. The .NET Framework Resource Manager follows the hub-and-spoke model to identify and load the appropriate satellite assembly.

As shown in Figure 7-13, if we go from top to bottom, the first level is the hub, which is a main application assembly containing the neutral/default culture resource assembly (in this example, the default resource assembly is for the English language—en). The spoke is the next two levels. The second level contains one or more neutral language-specific resource assemblies and no region (similar to the hub resource assembly file). In this example, the second level contains neutral resource assemblies for English (en) and French (fr). The third level, which contains the culture-specific assemblies, would have resources associated with the language and region. In this example, for the English language, we have assemblies specific to the US region (en-US), UK region (en-UK), and Australia region (en-AU), and for the French language we have assemblies specific to the France region (fr-FR).

The resource management execution model follows the bottom-up approach. Based on the retrieved cultural information of the client, it will start to find the appropriate satellite assembly starting from culture-specific (third level), to neutral language-specific (second level), to the default assembly (first level), and load the appropriate resources. If no specific match is found, it will load the default resources. Here are three examples to help you understand the concept:

- For the culture specific to the English language (en) and US region (US), in this example the resource manager will identify and load the culture-specific satellite assembly (third level—en-US).

- For the culture specific to the French language (fr) and Canada region (CA), in this example, the resource manager will identify and load the neutral French language–specific satellite assembly (second level—fr), since the application does not have any French language and Canada region–specific satellite assemblies available.

- For the culture specific to the German language (de) and Germany region (DE), in this example, the resource manager will identify and load the default resource assembly (first level—en), since the application does not have any German culture–specific satellite assemblies available.

Implementing an Example

Let us extend the existing drag-and-drop application that we developed earlier in this chapter, to display the user interface in three languages—English, French, and Hebrew. For that we first add a drop-down to the user interface for the language selection. Based on the language selection, a related resource file will be selected, and based on the translated text available in the associated resource file, the XAML user interface will display the text. Also keep in mind that English and French are left-to-right languages, whereas Hebrew is a right-to-left language.

Adding Culture-Specific Resource Files

First you need to develop resource files providing translated text for the XAML user interface that can be displayed at runtime based on the language selection. We will keep English as the default language at start-up time.

Visual Studio provides a Resource Designer tool that enables you to manage project-specific resources such as strings, images, videos, and icons that will be used for localization purposes. For more information on the how to manage resources, visit Microsoft MSDN, http://msdn.microsoft.com/en-us/library/t69a74ty.aspx.

Create a new Resources folder at the chapter7 Silverlight application project level. Right-click the Resources folder and add a new item of type Resources File and name it to Strings.resx file, as shown in Figure 7-14.

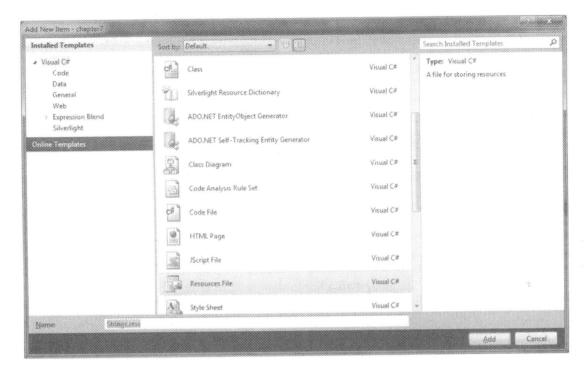

Figure 7-14. Adding a Resource File to the Silverilght application project

It should add two files: **Strings.resx** and **Strings.Designer.cs**. The **Strings.resx** file stores the resource designer information, and code for the resources is stored in the **Strings.Designer.cs** file.

If you double-click the **Strings.resx** file, it opens a resource designer. Change the Access Modifier to **Public** from **Internal** (default value) to allow access to the resources and settings that we have added to the class libraries (**.dll** files). Now add a meaningful name and value pair for each string resource (for English language) for our application, as shown in Figure 7-15.

Name	Value	Comment
CloseButtonContent	Close	
DropMessage	¦ Drop images here ¦	
FD	LeftToRight	
ImageWindowTitle	Larger Preview	
MouseWheelZoomMessage	Use Mouse wheel to zoom in or out	
PrintButtonContent	Print	
ResetZoomButtonContent	Reset Zoom	
ThumbnailMessage	Click on thumbnails for larger size	

Figure 7-15. Resource Designer Interface in Visual Studio 2010 helps to maintain resources.

Note that there is an existing problem with the code-generation tool for Resource files. It makes everything **Public** except the constructor for the **Strings** class. So you need to open **Strings.Designer.cs** and manually change the constructor to **public** from **internal**, every time you modify or add a new entry to the **Strings.resx** file. To do so, look for the line in the **Strings.Designer.cs** file:

```
internal  Strings() {
    }
```

and change it to

```
public  Strings() {
    }
```

We need to add two more resource files to support French and Hebrew cultures. The culture-specific resource file follows the **<resource file name>.<Culture Code>.resx** file format. Here our resource file name is **Strings**, the culture code for French culture is **fr-fr**, and the culture code for Hebrew culture is **he**. So add two resource files (follow Figure 7-14) with the names **Strings.fr-fr.resx** and **Strings.he.resx** under the **Resources** folder.

You can visit the Microsoft MSDN link at http://msdn.microsoft.com/en-us/library/system.globalization.cultureinfo(VS.96).aspx to get a complete list of culture codes.

To provide local culture–specific values for the XAML user interface, open each culture-specific **.resx** file and keep the same **Name** column value, as we kept in the **Strings.resx** file, but change the **Value** column value with the translated text. For simplicity and demonstration purposes, you can use any online translator to translate English to French and Hebrew. Figure 7-16 shows the resource designer view for the French and Hebrew culture-related **.resx** files.

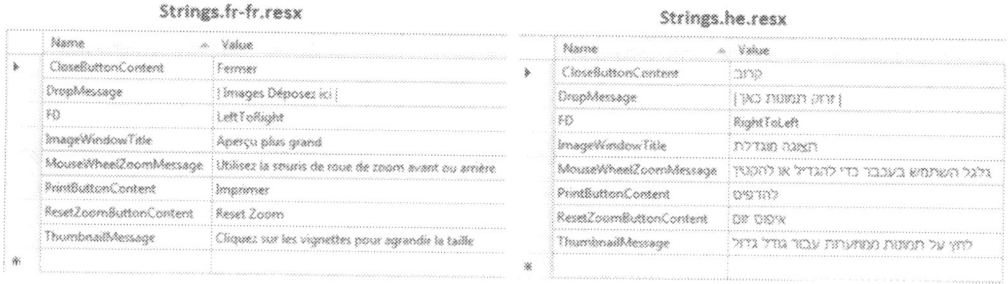

Figure 7-16. Translated French and Hebrew culture-specific .resx files

Note that for **Strings.fr-fr.resx** and **Strings.he.resx** files you need to change **Access Modifier** to **No code generation**, since we do not need any code generation other than the default **Strings.resx** file.

Adding Helper Class to Support Dynamic Culture-Specific Change in User Interface

Next, to support dynamic change in the UI based on the culture/language selection, we need to have one helper class that implements the **INotifyPropertyChanged** interface to inform the bound UI controls to update the bound property. As we learned in Chapter 6, here we will use two-way binding.

Right-click the chapter7 Silverlight application project to add a new class named **LocalizedStrings.cs**. In this class, we will create an instance of the **Strings** class (this class has the name **chapter7** in the **Strings.resx** file), and we will use the **PropertyChanged** event to notify the bound UI

Controls about culture changes. Note that to enable support for the `INotifyPropertyChanged` interface, you need to add the `System.ComponentModel` namespace, as follows:

```
using System.ComponentModel;
```

The following is the code-snippet of the `LocalizedStrings.cs` class. Refer to Chapter 6 to get more details on the following class:

```
namespace chapter7
{
    public class LocalizedStrings : INotifyPropertyChanged
    {
        public LocalizedStrings()
        {
        }

        private static Resources.Strings resource =
            new Resources.Strings();

        public Resources.Strings Resource {
            get
            {
                return resource;
            }
            set
            {
                resource = value;
                if (this.PropertyChanged!=null )
                {
                    PropertyChanged(this,
                        new PropertyChangedEventArgs("Resource"));
                }
            }
        }

        public event PropertyChangedEventHandler PropertyChanged;
    }
}
```

Now we need to define the application-level resource for `LocalizedStrings` in `App.xaml`. For that, add the namespace as shown here in the highlighted fonts.

```
<Application
    xmlns="http://schemas.microsoft.com/winfx/2006/xaml/presentation"
    xmlns:x="http://schemas.microsoft.com/winfx/2006/xaml"
    x:Class="chapter7.App"
    xmlns:local="clr-namespace:chapter7.Resources"
    xmlns:c="clr-namespace:chapter7">
```

And then, within the `<Application.Resources>` tag, define the resource as follows, with the key name set to `LocalizedStrings`.

```xml
<Application.Resources>
    <c:LocalizedStrings x:Key="LocalizedStrings" />
</Application.Resources>
```

Bind XAML Controls with Culture-Specific Resource Files

Now our string resources are ready to bind to XAML controls to make the user interface localizable based on the language selection.

For that, revisit the `DragnDropDemo.xaml` page. Here we will data-bind Content/Text properties of XAML controls to resources in `Strings.resx`, to set up the default as the English language. Also we need to add a ComboBox control to let the user select English, French, or Hebrew culture.

The following is the updated XAML code with changes shown in the highlighted fonts.

```xml
<UserControl x:Class="chapter7.DragnDropDemo"
    xmlns="http://schemas.microsoft.com/winfx/2006/xaml/presentation"
    xmlns:x="http://schemas.microsoft.com/winfx/2006/xaml"
    xmlns:d="http://schemas.microsoft.com/expression/blend/2008"
    xmlns:mc="http://schemas.openxmlformats.org/
        markup-compatibility/2006"
    mc:Ignorable="d"
    d:DesignHeight="300" d:DesignWidth="400"
    xmlns:toolkit="http://schemas.microsoft.com/winfx/2006/
        xaml/presentation/toolkit"
    FlowDirection="{Binding Source=
        {StaticResource LocalizedStrings}, Path=Resource.FD}">

    <Grid x:Name="LayoutRoot" Background="White">
        <Grid.RowDefinitions>
            <RowDefinition Height="150"/>
            <RowDefinition Height="30"/>
            <RowDefinition Height="*"/>
        </Grid.RowDefinitions>
        <StackPanel Grid.Row="0">
            <StackPanel Orientation="Horizontal">
                <TextBlock Text="Select UI Culture"
                    Margin="10,10,0,0" FontWeight="Bold"/>
                <ComboBox Height="23" x:Name="CultureList" Width="150"
                    SelectionChanged="CultureList_SelectionChanged"
                    Margin="5,10,0,5">
                    <ComboBoxItem Content="en-US" />
                    <ComboBoxItem Content="fr-fr" />
                    <ComboBoxItem Content="he" />
                </ComboBox>
            </StackPanel>
        </StackPanel>
        <Border BorderThickness="3" BorderBrush="DarkBlue" >
            <Canvas x:Name="DropZoneCanvas"
                AllowDrop="True"
                Drop="DropZoneCanvas_Drop"
                DragOver="DropZoneCanvas_DragOver"
                DragLeave="DropZoneCanvas_DragLeave"
```

```
                    Background="Cyan" Height="103" >
                    <TextBlock
                        Text="{Binding Source={StaticResource
                            LocalizedStrings},
                            Path=Resource.DropMessage}"
                            HorizontalAlignment="Center"
                            FontWeight="Bold" FontSize="14"
                            Canvas.Top="65" Canvas.Left="10"/>
                </Canvas>
            </Border>
        </StackPanel>
        <TextBlock
            Text="{Binding Source={StaticResource
                LocalizedStrings}, Path=Resource.ThumbnailMessage}"
                Grid.Row="1" FontSize="12" Height="26" Margin="8"/>
        <ScrollViewer Grid.Row="2" >
            <c:WrapPanel  x:Name="ImageBox"    />
        </ScrollViewer>
    </Grid>
</UserControl>
```

As shown previously, we bind **FlowDirection** to **Resource.FD** to update the direction of flow for our language resource **he** (Hebrew) with required text flow direction as right-to-left. Similarly, we bound the Text property of two TextBlocks to the proper name of the resources. Also we added a ComboBox control named **CultureList** to provide the option to select UI culture. Notice that we have defined the **SelectionChanged** event of the **CultureList** ComboBox to load the culture-specific UI resources dynamically based on the user selection of the UI culture.

Go ahead and apply the similar binding to the image viewer child window, **ImageWindow.xaml**. The mechanism is the same, which is why it is not shown here. However, as always, you can download the code from the Apress web site and refer to it.

Next let's implement the **CultureList_SelectionChanged** event handler in the **DragnDrop.xaml.cs** file. Here we will determine the selected UI culture by the user and accordingly change the UI culture of the current running thread to update the resource as per the new culture. We will update the application-level defined resource **LocalizedStrings** as shown in following code snippet.

```
private void CultureList_SelectionChanged
    (object sender, SelectionChangedEventArgs e)
{
    ComboBoxItem item = CultureList.SelectedItem as ComboBoxItem;

    Thread.CurrentThread.CurrentCulture = new
        System.Globalization.CultureInfo(item.Content.ToString());

    Thread.CurrentThread.CurrentUICulture = new
        System.Globalization.CultureInfo(item.Content.ToString());

    ((LocalizedStrings)App.Current.Resources["LocalizedStrings"]).
        Resource = new chapter7.Resources.Strings();
}
```

Note that you need to add a reference to `System.Threading` to make this work.

Making the Project Aware of Localization Capabilities

The final and important step is to make the Silverlight project aware of the application's localization capabilities (i.e., edit the `chapter7.csproj` file to define supported cultures). You can make this change unloading the Silverlight project and editing the project properties to define supported cultures by adding a `SupportedCultures` tag and comma-separated cultures. After that, you can reload the Silverlight project again. You can achieve this by following these steps:

1. Right-click the Silverlight project and select the Unload Project option. This will unload the project from Solution Explorer.

2. Right-click the unloaded project and select the Edit `chapter7.csproj` option. You will see the project file properties in editable mode.

3. In the Project node and under `PropertyGroup`, find the `SupportedCultures` tag. If it is not available, add it.

4. Add comma-separated cultures that need to be supported by the Silverlight project. In our case it will be `en-en,fr-fr,he`. The tag should look like `<SupportedCultures>en-en,fr-fr,he</SupportedCultures>`.

5. Save the file, right-click the project, and choose "Reload the project."

We are all set to hit F5 and run the project. Drop some photos, change the UI culture from `CultureList` ComboBox, and see that all of the UI control's string changes to the currently selected culture. You can also click the image and see a larger preview in ImageWindow, where our currently selected culture is applied. See Figure 7-17, which shows snapshots of the application in the French and Hebrew languages. Notice the right-to-left direction of the UI and text for the Hebrew language.

Application running in French (fr-fr) culture

Application running in Hebrew (he) culture

Figure 7-17. Localized drag-and-drop application in French and Hebrew languages

Preparing for Global Silverlight Application

Now you are all set to deploy the Silverlight application as a global application supporting different cultures. Upon compiling the project, the default culture (the `Strings.resx` file) becomes part of the main application assembly. The main application assembly with the default resources and other added satellite assemblies will be inserted into the Silverlight XAP file. Each satellite assembly is defined under the `Deployment.Parts` section of the `AppMainifest.xml` file.

The main disadvantage of this approach is that all satellite assembly files are part of the default Silverlight XAP file and thus will be downloaded at start-up. A Silverlight application with many defined cultures will increase the XAP package file size and thus degrade the application start-up performance. Also, if your application is running in the out-of-browser mode, you will want to provide a culture-specific satellite assembly.

Silverlight also allows us to develop a localized, culture-specific application package for each culture. The approach will reduce the XAP package size and thus improve the application's start-up performance. The Visual Studio Configuration Manager is used to define and create localized application packages.

■ **Note** To get more details on how to deploy a targeted localized application, refer to the Microsoft MSDN website, `http://msdn.microsoft.com/en-us/library/cc838238(VS.96).aspx`. To get more details on how to localize information about an out-of-browser application, refer to the Microsoft MSDN website, `http://msdn.microsoft.com/en-us/library/dd772170(VS.96).aspx`.

Enhancements in XAML Features

As we discussed in Chapter 2, the Silverlight XAML parser is different than the regular WPF XAML parser and has limited features. Silverlight 4 brings the Silverlight version of the XAML parser one step closer to the regular WPF parser. Originally, I would have covered this topic in Chapter 2, however, by the time XAML enhancements were introduced in Silverlight 4 RC, Chapter 2 of this book was already finalized. Before we end this chapter, we will cover key XAML features enhancements introduced in Silverlight 4.

■ **Note** To get a complete overview of the XAML processing differences between Silverlight 3 and Silverlight 4, visit the Microsoft MSDN library at `http://msdn.microsoft.com/en-us/library/ff457753(VS.96).aspx`.

Flexible Root XAML Namespace

In Silverlight 3 and prior versions you must use the root XAML namespace as `xmlns="http://schemas.microsoft.com/winfx/2006/xaml/presentation"`. Silverlight 4 introduced flexibility in defining the root XAML namespace; now you can use a custom XAML namespace as per your requirement.

XmlnsDefinitionAttribute

As we learned earlier in the discussion of the drag-and-drop functionality, Silverlight 4 supports the `XmlnsDefinition` attribute to declare the namespace for custom assemblies. As a result, Silverlight SDK and Toolkit now support the `XmlnsDefinition` attribute, and you do not need to define all referenced assemblies and namespaces explicitly.

As you saw in the example we created to demonstrate drag-and-drop functionality, to utilize the WrapPanel control, which is part of the Silverlight Toolkit, you just need to define the namespace `xmlns:toolkit="http://schemas.microsoft.com/winfx/2006/xaml/presentation/toolkit"` at the user-control level to use any toolkit controls, rather than adding the specific assembly as `xmlns:c="clr-namespace:System.Windows.Controls;assembly=System.Windows.Controls.Toolkit"`.

Direct Content

WPF developers will be relieved that the Silverlight 4 parser now allows you to apply direct content to XAML controls. As an example, you can set the Button content as follows, which is very WPF-like:

```
<Button>I am a Button</Button>
```

If you use Silverlight 3, you have to use the Content attribute of the Button, as follows:

```
<Button Content="I am a Button"/>
```

Whitespace Handling

Silverlight 3 and prior versions preserve extra whitespace as is. For example, the following XAML will result in "This is" and "new line" text appearing in two separate lines:

```
<TextBlock>
    <TextBlock.Text>This is
        new line
    </TextBlock.Text>
</TextBlock>
```

If you run the same XAML code in Silverlight 4, it will discard extra CRLF whitespaces and will result in "This is new line" text output in a single line.

Similar to WPF, in Silverlight 4 you use `xml:space="preserve"` to preserve the CRLF whitespaces. As an example, the following XAML with `xml:space="preserve"` will result in "This is" and "new line" text appearing in two separate lines by keeping the whitespace:

```
<TextBlock xml:space="preserve">
    <TextBlock.Text>This is
        new line
    </TextBlock.Text>
</TextBlock>
```

Custom IDictionary Support

In Silverlight 4 you are not limited to implementing a dictionary and adding items using the **x:Key** attribute within the **ResourceDictionary**. It extends the **x:Key** usage to any XAML element that can implement the **IDictionary** to implement a custom dictionary and add items within it.

■ **Note** To support the backward compatibility, Silverlight 4 core libraries include Silverlight 3 and 4 XAML parsers side-by-side. It means that if you are running any Silverlight 3 (compiled) application using Silverlight 4 runtime, you should see no problem. However, if you are opening a Silverlight 3 project for Silverlight 4 migration in Visual Studio, you need to make all necessary corrections.

Summary

This chapter provided a detailed overview of key capabilities introduced in Silverlight 4, such as drag-and-drop, right-click, and printing, to implement critical features of any line-of-business application. We also looked at the key aspect of any LoB application, support to localize applications, making them country- and culture-specific. In the end, we had a brief overview of the enhancements made to the XAML parser.

Silverlight provides the capability to easily style elements of user interfaces and alter the appearance (separate from the behavior) of controls. In the next chapter, we will extend the user interface topic discussion. We will cover styling (including implicit styling introduced in Silverlight 4) and templating to provide user-interface customization capabilities to designers and developers for Silverlight applications and to develop consistent branding across LoB applications.

■ ■ ■

CHAPTER 8

Styling and Templating

Silverlight provides the capability to easily style elements of user interfaces and alter the appearance (separate from the behavior) of controls. Styling is similar in spirit to how CSS properties work: user interface elements can reuse fonts, colors, and sizes that are specified as a style by applying a specific style to a `FrameworkElement`. Templating, however, is limited to `Control`-based classes and is used to completely change how controls are rendered visually. This mechanism works because what the control does (its behavior) is separate from how it looks. These two capabilities provide a significant amount of user interface customization to designers and developers when working with Silverlight.

Enhancements in Silverlight 4

One of the missing features prior to Silverlight 4 was the ability to define a consistent style/theme of a specific control that is applicable to all instances of that control across the application. With Silverlight 4, the implicit styling feature allows one to define styles as a resource and target them to specific types of UIElement implicitly. This would allow you to categorize the theme based on the control type to provide a consistent look and feel of specific types of controls across the application.

Using Styles

If you're building a simple application that has just a few user interface screens, it probably makes sense to set properties such as `FontSize` and colors on user interface elements themselves. If you're building a larger application, though, you can quickly find yourself replicating the same property values on page after page. A *style*, in Silverlight, is a group of properties and specific values that you can reuse within a page or even across the whole application. A specific style is given a name and stored within a resource dictionary, so a style can be scoped to the page or application level. It's possible to place a style within any resource dictionary, but in practice, styles are rarely seen outside the page or application level since the benefit of a style is in the reuse of sets of attribute values. Figure 8-1 shows a layout that many web sites follow.

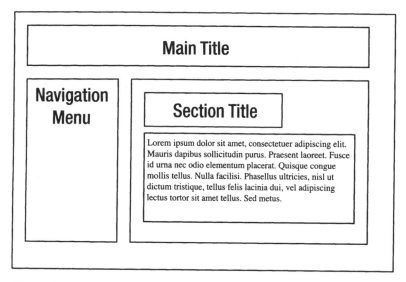

Figure 8-1. Common design layout for a web site

The main title and the navigation menu are omnipresent as the user navigates from one page to another. The part of the interface that changes, however, features the content from an individual page. In ASP.NET, the navigation menu and main title go into something called a *master page*, which separates the common parts of the site from the page-specific parts. Figure 8-1 shows a section title and some example text that might appear in a specific page of a Silverlight application. The section title and page text will change from one page to the next. In fact, there might be many elements used by different pages, such as hyperlinks and other text. Before you can effectively use styles, you must understand the different user interface elements used throughout your application.

Two of these elements are visible in Figure 8-1: the section title and the page-specific text. Some other possible elements are bylines (for blogs or news articles), image captions, and hyperlinks. Once you have a list of the common user interface elements, though, you have to determine exactly which properties you want to apply across your application. The properties you choose to group into styles correspond to the properties from various Silverlight controls. Both the section header and the page text from Figure 8-1 could be displayed using TextBlock. Some properties of TextBlock that are great for use in a style are `FontSize`, `Foreground`, `FontWeight`, `FontFamily`, `Margin`, and `TextWrapping`. All of these properties control how the text is presented.

Figure 8-2 shows this master page/content page relationship in a theoretical online bookstore. The navigation menu at the left and the title at the top are present regardless of which section of the site a user visits.

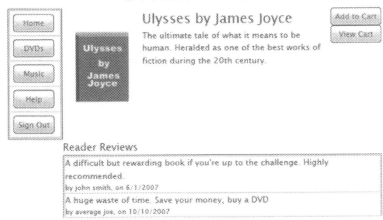

Figure 8-2. *Potential user interface for an online bookstore*

Here's the XAML used for the section title (book name), page content (book description), and the navigation menu without using styles:

```xaml
<Grid.ColumnDefinitions>
    <ColumnDefinition Width="85"/>
    <ColumnDefinition Width="75"/>
    <ColumnDefinition />
</Grid.ColumnDefinitions>
<StackPanel Grid.Row="1" Grid.Column="0">
    <ListBox>
        <ListBoxItem>
            <Button Content="Home" Width="60" Margin="5"/>
        </ListBoxItem>
        <ListBoxItem>
            <Button Content="DVDs" Width="60" Margin="5"/>
        </ListBoxItem>
        <ListBoxItem>
            <Button Content="Music" Width="60" Margin="5"/>
        </ListBoxItem>
        <ListBoxItem>
            <Button Content="Help" Width="60" Margin="5"/>
        </ListBoxItem>
        <ListBoxItem>
            <Button Content="Sign Out" Width="60" Margin="5"/>
        </ListBoxItem>
    </ListBox>
</StackPanel>
<StackPanel Grid.Row="1" Grid.Column="2" VerticalAlignment="Top">
    <TextBlock FontSize="20">Ulysses by James Joyce</TextBlock>
    <TextBlock FontSize="12" TextWrapping="Wrap">
```

```
    The ultimate tale of what it means to be human. Heralded as one
    of the best works of fiction during the 20th century.
  </TextBlock>
</StackPanel>
```

You can see the duplication of the Width and Margin properties in the navigation buttons. Also, the properties used for the content of a page wouldn't necessarily be the same as other content pages (e.g., DVDs and music), since the values must manually be kept consistent. These are two of the biggest issues that styles solve. These properties will be pulled out and grouped into three styles: one for the navigation buttons, one for the page header, and one for the page content.

The System.Windows namespace provides framework classes for the Silverlight client and provides many Silverlight base classes that have different presentation features. The Style class is derived from System.Windows.DependencyObject and contains different property setters that can be applied to instances of similar types of UI elements. Table 8-1 defines properties of the Style class.

Table 8-1. Properties of the System.Windows.DependencyObject Style Class

Property	Type	Description
BasedOn	Style	This property gets or sets a defined style that is the basis of the current style. Each style supports only one BasedOn style. The BasedOn style cannot be changed when a style is sealed. The TargetType property of a BasedOn style must match or be derived from the TargetType of a style.
IsSealed	bool	This property returns true if the style is read-only and cannot be changed.
Setters	SetterBaseCollection	This property gets a collection of Setter objects. Each Setter object has a Property and a Value. The Property contains the name of the property of the element to which the style is applied. The Value defines the values that will be applied to the element's property.
TargetType	Type	This property gets or sets the type for which the style is intended. It's a mandatory property to define the style.

There are two components to a style: where it is applied and what it does. In order to specify where a style is applied, you must give it a unique key (except implicit styling, which we learn about later in the Implicit Styling section of this chapter) and a target type. This target type is the name of a class that will use the style. This target type must match directly—the style will not automatically apply to descendents of the specified class. This makes styling a user interface predictable since a derived type won't take on a specific style set for its parent class. Since these user interface elements apply to the entire Silverlight application, the styles will go into the application's resource dictionary in the App.xaml file.

```
<Application xmlns="http://schemas.microsoft.com/winfx/2006/xaml/presentation"
             xmlns:x="http://schemas.microsoft.com/winfx/2006/xaml"
             x:Class="chapter8.App">
  <Application.Resources>
    <Style x:Key="ContentHeader" TargetType="TextBlock">
      <Setter Property="FontSize" Value="20"/>
```

```
        </Style>
        <Style x:Key="ContentDescription" TargetType="TextBlock">
            <Setter Property="FontSize" Value="12"/>
            <Setter Property="TextWrapping" Value="Wrap"/>
        </Style>
        <Style x:Key="NavigationButton" TargetType="Button">
            <Setter Property="Width" Value="60"/>
            <Setter Property="Margin" Value="5"/>
        </Style>
    </Application.Resources>
</Application>
```

You can set `Style` on any UI element that is derived from the `FrameworkElement`. Each style is given an `x:Key` attribute that serves as the key for the resource dictionary and also the key used when applying a style to a user interface element. The `TargetType` is set to `TextBlock` for the page content header and page content and to `Button` for the navigation buttons. These properties, grouped in styles and then placed in the application's resource dictionary, provide the consistency and ease of maintenance for your application's look and feel.

Applying the styles is a simple matter of using the `StaticResource` markup extension referencing to `x:Key` in the `Style` attribute of a user interface element of the corresponding type. Here's the updated XAML (shown in bold) that makes up the navigation menu and the page content using styles:

```
<StackPanel Grid.Row="1" Grid.Column="0">
    <ListBox>
        <ListBoxItem>
            <Button Content="Home" Style="{StaticResource NavigationButton}"/>
        </ListBoxItem>
        <ListBoxItem>
            <Button Content="DVDs" Style="{StaticResource NavigationButton}"/>
        </ListBoxItem>
        <ListBoxItem>
            <Button Content="Music" Style="{StaticResource NavigationButton}"/>
        </ListBoxItem>
        <ListBoxItem>
            <Button Content="Help" Style="{StaticResource NavigationButton}"/>
        </ListBoxItem>
        <ListBoxItem>
            <Button Content="Sign Out" Style="{StaticResource NavigationButton}"/>
        </ListBoxItem>
    </ListBox>
</StackPanel>
<StackPanel Grid.Row="1" Grid.Column="2" VerticalAlignment="Top">
  <TextBlock Style="{StaticResource ContentHeader}">
        Ulysses by James Joyce
  </TextBlock>
  <TextBlock Style="{StaticResource ContentDescription}">
    The ultimate tale of what it means to be human. Heralded
    as one of the best works of fiction during the 20th century.
  </TextBlock>
</StackPanel>
```

Silverlight 3 introduced enhanced styling features, such as style inheritance (which means you can have cascading styles by basing them on each other), style override, style resetting (for dynamic styling and skinning), and merged resource dictionaries. Silverlight 4 introduces implicit styling, allowing styles to be defined as a resource, which can be targeted to specific types of UIElement implicitly. We'll discuss them one by one.

Style Inheritance/Style Cascading

Style inheritance, also known as *style cascading* or *based-on styles*, is one of the most widely used features in WPF-based applications. Most developers have used Cascading Style Sheets (CSS) when working with HTML pages, and style inheritance in Silverlight is very similar. Having this feature incorporated in Silverlight makes Silverlight application development more versatile. This feature can be extremely useful; for example, say you need to create several different buttons that share the same control template and several style properties, but then you want to change a minor detail like the background and foreground color. Broadly speaking, you can also use style inheritance to standardize fonts and colors throughout an application. The style inheritance is accomplished by using the BasedOn attribute of the Style class.

Consider the following XAML code:

```
<Grid x:Name="LayoutRoot" Background="White">
    <Grid.Resources>
      <ResourceDictionary>
        <Style x:Name="Title" TargetType="TextBlock">
            <Setter Property="FontFamily" Value="Arial" />
            <Setter Property="FontSize" Value="15" />
            <Setter Property="FontWeight" Value="Bold"/>
        </Style>

        <Style x:Name="MainTitle" TargetType="TextBlock"
          BasedOn="{StaticResource Title}">
            <Setter Property="Foreground" Value="Blue" />
        </Style>

        <Style x:Name="SubTitle" TargetType="TextBlock"
          BasedOn="{StaticResource Title}">
            <Setter Property="FontSize" Value="12" />
        </Style>
      </ResourceDictionary>
    </Grid.Resources>
    <StackPanel>
       <TextBlock Text="Title" Style="{StaticResource Title}" Margin="5"/>
       <TextBlock Text="Main Title" Style="{StaticResource MainTitle}" Margin="5"/>
       <TextBlock Text="Sub Title" Style="{StaticResource SubTitle}" Margin="5"/>
    </StackPanel>
</Grid>
```

The previous code snippet has the base style Title that targets TextBlock elements and defines the values for the FontFamily, FontSize, and FontWeight properties. The code also contains another style, called MainTitle, that, again, targets TextBlock elements. Note the additional attribute BasedOn. By using it, we are basing this style on the style defined by its value—Title—in this example. Here we set the Foreground property of the TextBlock to Blue.

When we use the MainTitle style on a TextBlock, we are going to have both of the values set in the Title style (FontFamily, FontSize, and FontWeight) and those set in MainTitle (Foreground).

Another style, SubTitle, is also based on the Title style, but this time it overrides the base value set for FontSize. Now, when we use the SubTitle on a TextBlock, we can see that it appears in font family Arial but in font size 12.

▪ **Note** Silverlight includes about 11 built-in fonts that can be set using the FontFamily property. If you are not using the built-in Silverlight font as the FontFamily property, it will not be displayed to end-users within the Silverlight application. For instance, in the preceding example we used Arial font (available as a built-in Silverlight font) for text block control, which will be displayed properly. However, you cannot display Calibri font (as an example) without a custom additional step, since it's not part of the built-in fonts. In the case of using a non-built-in font in your application, you can either install the font on your computer and use Express Blend to embed the font to the Silverlight project, or add the font files to the Silverlight project.

Figure 8-3 shows the outcome of the previous XAML code.

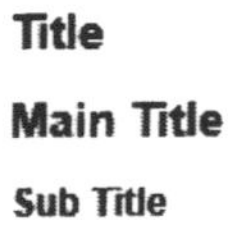

Title

Main Title

Sub Title

Figure 8-3. Style inheritance using BasedOn style

Style Override/Style Resetting

Silverlight 3 eliminated the limitation of the write-once quality of the Style property. You can now override/reset the default style multiple times by setting the Style property at runtime. This feature makes it easy to implement the skinning of your application. As an example, with the style override capabilities, you can style your application using a set of different styles for different color schemes by basing all of your graphics' and controls' skin colors on style values. They will then automatically update when you change the style.

To demonstrate style resetting, we will add one more style with the name DynamicTitle to our previous style inheritance example. And upon clicking a button, we toggle style to show resetting of style multiple times. So, first we have defined the style as follows:

```
<Style x:Name="DynamicTitle" TargetType="TextBlock"
  BasedOn="{StaticResource Title}">
    <Setter Property="FontSize" Value="20" />
    <Setter Property="Foreground" Value="Green"/>
</Style>
```

Now to dynamically change the styles of UI elements at runtime, we add a Button control with the Click event (as the last control) in the existing StackPanel, as shown here.

```
<Button x:Name="ToggleButton" Click="ToggleButton_Click"
    Content="Toggle Style" Width="150"
    HorizontalAlignment="Left" Margin="5"/>
```

Now to identify one of the existing TextBlock controls in the code-behind, we name the Main Title-related TextBlock control as tbMainTitle, and change the text to show what style is applicable (Main Title or Dynamic Title style) as shown here (in bold fonts):

```
<TextBlock x:Name="tbMainTitle" Text="Main Title (with MainTitle style)"
    Style="{StaticResource MainTitle}" Margin="5"/>
```

The following is the corresponding code-behind that toggles the style of the tbMainTitle control between the DynamicTitle and MainTitle style definitions:

```
private void ToggleButton_Click(object sender, RoutedEventArgs e)
{
    if (isToggle==false)
    {
        tbMainTitle.Style = LayoutRoot.Resources["DynamicTitle"] as Style;
        tbMainTitle.Text = "Main Title (with DynamicTitle style)";
    }
    else
    {
        tbMainTitle.Style = LayoutRoot.Resources["MainTitle"] as Style;
        tbMainTitle.Text = "Main Title (with MainTitle style)";
    }
    isToggle =! isToggle;
}
```

Once you run this sample, you can toggle styles by clicking the button. Here, as explained earlier, for demonstration purposes I have also changed the Main Title-related TextBlock text to display which style is used to display text. Note that in the previous code snippet the isToggle variable needs to be defined at class level as bool.

Figure 8-4 shows the outcome of style overriding.

Figure 8-4. Style overriding example

In this example, we defined styles in Grid.Resources. However, it is best practice to define global styles at the application level by defining them in App.xaml. In that case, the code to reference such styles will look like this:

```
tbMainTitle.Style = Application.Current.Resources["DynamicTitle"] as Style;
```

Merged Resource Dictionaries

Earlier in Chapter 2, we covered the merged resource dictionary, a feature introduced in Silverlight 3. However, it is worth revisiting these dictionaries in this chapter in the context of styles.

The merged resource dictionaries feature allows you to use externally defined resources. A widely used scenario here is to share the same resources between different applications. The merged resource dictionaries provide a way to define and split resources into separate files. This feature can be helpful in custom control development.

Until the Silverlight 3 version, resources could not be divided into separate files, which leads to a large App.xaml file having application-shared resources. The same problem exists while developing custom controls. All default style keys must be specified in Themes/Generic.xaml, which again tends to create a very large file. The merged resource dictionaries resolve these issues. They enable you to split style definitions and other resources into manageable pieces, making them easy to localize and revise. To demonstrate this feature, let's extend the previous example and add one more resource to Grid.Resources under ResourceDictionary:

```xaml
<ResourceDictionary.MergedDictionaries>
    <ResourceDictionary Source="external.xaml" />
</ResourceDictionary.MergedDictionaries>
```

In the previous example, a style used in the resource dictionary is defined external to the MainPage.xaml file by defining them in the external external.xaml file. Note that the Source attribute of the ResourceDictionary element is set to the external.xaml file. You also need to add a new file named external.xaml to your Silverlight project to achieve this functionality successfully. Set its Build Action property to Resource, and define an external style with the name LargeTitle, as shown in the following XAML code:

```xaml
<ResourceDictionary
  xmlns="http://schemas.microsoft.com/winfx/2006/xaml/presentation"
  xmlns:x="http://schemas.microsoft.com/winfx/2006/xaml">
    <Style x:Key="LargeTitle" TargetType="TextBlock">
            <Setter Property="FontFamily" Value="Verdana" />
            <Setter Property="FontSize" Value="20" />
    </Style>
</ResourceDictionary>
```

You can use the same markup to apply the externally defined style that we used to apply local styles, as shown here:

```xaml
<TextBlock Text="Sub Title" Style="{StaticResource LargeTitle}" Margin="5"/>
```

Upon running this, as shown in Figure 8-5, the subtitle text is displayed with the LargeTitle style definition:

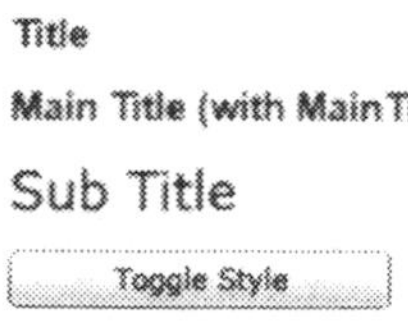

Title

Main Title (with Main Title style)

Sub Title

[Toggle Style]

Figure 8-5. Applying style defined in merged resource dictionaries

Implicit Styling

Prior to Silverlight 4, one of the features missing from Silverlight was the definition of a consistent style/theme of a specific control that is applicable to all instances of that control across the application. This feature is required to develop a line of business applications following consistent branding across the enterprise. The implicit styling is available in WPF and now in Silverlight with version 4, which allows defining styles as a resource, targeted to specific types of UIElement implicitly.

The definition of implicit styling is pretty straightforward. Upon defining the style as a resource, you do not define the x:Key attribute to provide a unique name of the style, but only define the TargetType representing the UIElement. The following code snippet shows the definition of implicit styling at the UserControl level for the Button control. All buttons within that page will follow the defined implicit styles without mentioning the Style attribute to button control.

```
<UserControl.Resources>
    <Style TargetType="Button">
        <Setter Property="Background" Value="#FF065293"/>
        <Setter Property="Foreground" Value="#FF296C1E"/>
        <Setter Property="FontSize" Value="14"/>
        <Setter Property="FontWeight" Value="Bold"/>
        <Setter Property="RenderTransformOrigin" Value="0.5,0.5" />
        <Setter Property="Effect">
            <Setter.Value>
                <DropShadowEffect/>
            </Setter.Value>
        </Setter>
    </Style>
</UserControl.Resources>

<StackPanel x:Name="LayoutRoot" Background="White">
        <Button Content="Button1 follows implicit style"
            HorizontalAlignment="Left"
            Height="35" Margin="5" Width="300"/>
        <Button Content="Button2 follows implicit style"
            HorizontalAlignment="Left"
            Height="35" Margin="5" Width="300"/>
        <Button Content="Button3 overrides implicit style"
            HorizontalAlignment="Left"
            Height="35" Margin="5" Width="300"
            FontSize="10" Foreground="Red"/>
        <Button Content="Button4 does not follow implicit style"
            HorizontalAlignment="Left"
```

```
            Height="35" Margin="5" Width="300"
            Style="{x:Null}"/>
</StackPanel>
```

Note that for the third button, we have defined the `FontSize` and `Foreground` properties (bolded in the preceding snippet) to the button, which will override the implicit defined styles, whereas the last button forces that no styles are applied by adding the Style value to x:Null.

As shown in Figure 8-6, in our example we demonstrate the definition of the implicit styles for a button at the UserControl level. Out of four added buttons, the first two follow the implicit style, the third button has `FontSize` and `Foreground` properties
different than the defined implicit style, and the fourth button does not follow implicit style at all.

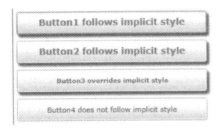

Figure 8-6. Demonstrating implicit styling feature

Style Setter

In the style, the setter is used to set a property to a specific value. Property element syntax is also supported when setting the value of a property. One example of using property element syntax is to set a control template, which can completely change the look and feel of a control. We'll examine control templates in more detail in the Using Control Templates section of this chapter. Setting a control template in a style looks like this:

```
<Style ...>
    <Setter Property="Template">
        <Setter.Value>
            <ControlTemplate ...>
        </Setter.Value>
    </Setter>
</Style>
```

What if a property is defined in a style and also defined locally? As detailed in Chapter 2 (Figure 2-5, which is shown again as Figure 8-7), you'll see that the style setter actually has rather low precedence. The property values from style setters can be overridden by values from many sources, and, as you can see, the local value has a relatively high precedence. If you use a style setter and it doesn't appear to work, look at these other sources for property values, since something is most likely overriding the property value.

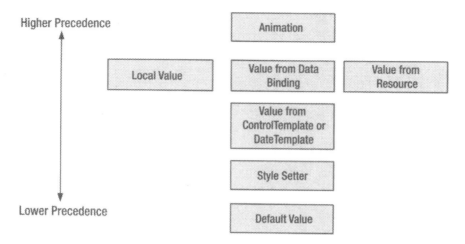

Figure 8-7. *Precedence for sources of dependency property values*

There is one significant drawback to using styles. The feature supported in WPF but not in Silverlight is *conditional styling* (known as *property triggers*). Conditional styling is useful for applying styles to framework elements based on conditions such as a user hovering over the element. Although it would be nice to have this directly supported in the styling system, you can accomplish this behavior using control templates, which we'll look at next.

Using Control Templates

One of the biggest advantages to the control architecture in Silverlight is that the behavior of the standard controls is separated from their visual appearance. A control template is a mechanism used to specify how a control looks but not how it behaves. This core behavior can most simply be viewed as what makes a particular control the control that it is. For example, what is a button? Loosely defined, it is a control that can be clicked. There are specializations of buttons, such as repeat buttons—but these specializations provide a different core behavior.

Each control can exist in a number of possible states, such as disabled, having input focus, a mouse hovering over it, and so on. A control template provides the ability to define what the control looks like in each of these states. Sometimes this is referred to as changing the "look and feel" of the control, since changing the visual appearance of each state can alter how a user sees and experiences a control in different states.

Creating a Control Template

The simplest control template contains a root layout control with a visual representation. Let's take a look at a diamond-shaped button with a gradient to color the top and bottom. You can see the result in Figure 8-8.

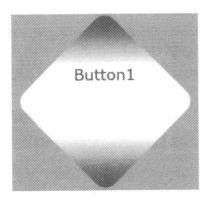

Figure 8-8. A fancy button using a rotate transform and gradient brush

The control template is defined as the property value for the **Template** property of the **Control** class. For ease of illustration, the style that contains the control template is stored in the StackPanel's resource dictionary. The button control sets its style and automatically picks up the control template, completely changing its appearance.

```
<StackPanel Background="#FFAAAAAA">
  <StackPanel.Resources>
    <Style x:Key="buttonStyle" TargetType="Button">
      <Setter Property="Template">
        <Setter.Value>
          <ControlTemplate TargetType="Button">
            <Grid>
              <Rectangle Width="200" Height="200" RadiusX="20" RadiusY="20">
                <Rectangle.Fill>
                  <LinearGradientBrush>
                    <GradientStop Color="Blue" Offset="0"/>
                    <GradientStop Color="White" Offset="0.3"/>
                    <GradientStop Color="White" Offset="0.7"/>
                    <GradientStop Color="Blue" Offset="1"/>
                  </LinearGradientBrush>
                </Rectangle.Fill>
                <Rectangle.RenderTransform>
                  <TransformGroup>
                    <RotateTransform Angle="45"/>
                    <TranslateTransform X="100"/>
                  </TransformGroup>
                </Rectangle.RenderTransform>
              </Rectangle>
              <TextBlock HorizontalAlignment="Center"
                         VerticalAlignment="Center"
                         FontSize="20" Text="BUTTON TEXT"/>
            </Grid>
          </ControlTemplate>
        </Setter.Value>
      </Setter>
```

```
    </Style>
  </StackPanel.Resources>
  <Button Content="Button1" FontSize="24" Style="{StaticResource buttonStyle}"/>
</StackPanel>
```

A button that uses this style takes on the diamond shape, but the button's text is forced to display the text "BUTTON TEXT." This isn't useful as a general control template since using this approach requires a new control template defined for each text you would want to display. This problem is solved by the `TemplateBinding` markup extension. This markup extension exists to connect properties used by a control template to properties defined on a specific control, and therefore it can be used only in conjunction with control templates. The first revision we will make to the preceding control template is to make `TemplateBinding` use the same content as that specified on a particular button.

⬛ **Note** The `TemplateBinding` markup extension is one of the few cases where an aspect of XAML does not have a backing class. Since this is a XAML-only construct, there is no way to utilize a `TemplateBinding` in the code-behind. This also means that control templates are XAML-only, since their purpose is to replace the visual appearance of controls. Fortunately, there are tools such as Expression Blend to make working with control templates quite easy.

In order to use the `TemplateBinding` markup extension with a button, a special class called `ContentPresenter` must be used. This class provides the capability of displaying the wide range of content options possible with Button and other controls' `Content` property. We can revisit the control template included in the preceding style and replace the TextBlock that displays "BUTTON TEXT" with the following `ContentPresenter`:

```
<ContentPresenter HorizontalAlignment="Center"
                  VerticalAlignment="Center"
                  Content="{TemplateBinding Content}"/>
```

In the preceding example, we used `ContentPresenter` to carry over `Content` property to define a Button control. If a property such as `FontSize` property is not specified, the default value is used. Thus in general, while a template can reference one or all properties, it doesn't mandate that these properties are set in the control utilizing the template.

Visual State Manager (VSM)

If you build an application using this control template and attempt to use the button, you will observe that the button doesn't do anything. Actually, it does something—the events still work on the button—but there is no visual feedback communicated to the user reflecting the various states a Button control can have.

Defining different visual appearances based on the different states a control can be in is accomplished using something called the *Visual State Manager* (VSM). Each control declaratively defines a set of visual state groups and visual states. The states within a group are mutually exclusive, but the control can exist in multiple states if multiple groups are defined. Figure 8-9 shows the two state groups and the valid states within each group for the Button control.

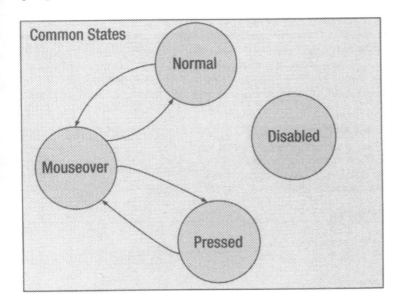

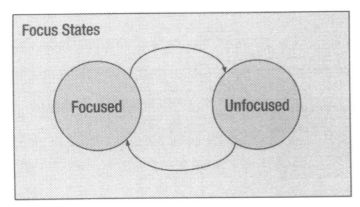

Figure 8-9. The visual state groups and states of the Button control

The groups and states are defined declaratively by the control's author. The states and groups shown in Figure 8-9 are defined on the Button class using attributes. We'll take a look at these attributes shortly in the context of creating a new control that supports control templates.

The control template must then specify the appearance of the control in each state. Since a control can exist in different states simultaneously (one per visual group), you must be careful to define visual appearances that can be combined. For example, the color of a button's border might change based on whether it has focus, but the contents of the rectangle change based on whether the button is pressed, disabled, moused over, or none of the above (normal). This is the approach that the default Button takes.

Fortunately, Expression Blend makes defining control templates easy. We'll first take a look at defining a new control template for the Button control and then take a closer look at the XAML generated.

Create or open a project in Expression Blend. Create a new button onto the design surface. Right-click the button and navigate to Edit Template, and you'll see two options. You can edit a copy of the button's current control template or create an empty one by choosing Create Empty. Here, when you click Create Empty option (Figure 8-10), the visual appearance of the button would disappear from the design surface, and the generated XAML would be the minimum needed for the button's control template, as shown. This approach creates a control template resource in the UserControl with the key you specify.

```xaml
<UserControl x:Class="Chapter8.CTWithExpressionBlendDemo"
    xmlns="http://schemas.microsoft.com/winfx/2006/xaml/presentation"
    xmlns:x="http://schemas.microsoft.com/winfx/2006/xaml"
    xmlns:d="http://schemas.microsoft.com/expression/blend/2008"
    xmlns:mc="http://schemas.openxmlformats.org/markup-compatibility/2006"
    mc:Ignorable="d"
    d:DesignHeight="300" d:DesignWidth="400">
    <UserControl.Resources>
        <ControlTemplate x:Key="ButtonControlTemplate1"
            TargetType="Button">
            <Grid/>
        </ControlTemplate>
    </UserControl.Resources>

    <Grid x:Name="LayoutRoot" Background="White">
        <Button Content="Button" Margin="64,73,168,0" Height="50"
            VerticalAlignment="Top"
            Template="{StaticResource ButtonControlTemplate1}"/>
    </Grid>
</UserControl>
```

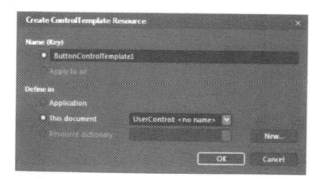

Figure 8-10. *Creating empty control template resource for the Button at UserControl level*

When you click Edit a Copy and enter a name for the style in the dialog (as shown in Figure 8-11), the full default control template is placed into the XAML. The default control template for Silverlight's controls is part of a style because other properties of controls are also set, such as Background, Foreground, and padding. These styled properties apply to every visual state of a control.

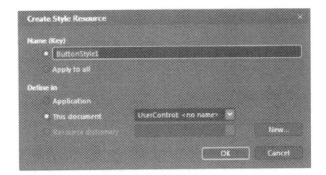

Figure 8-11. Creating a style resource that contains a control template

While at this point you could edit the XAML directly to change the appearance of the button in each state, Expression Blend makes it easy to modify each state and state transition without needing to drop down to the XAML. This is facilitated by the States pane (available on the left side of the window) in Expression Blend. Figure 8-12 shows what this looks like for the default control template for the Button class, while you are in the designer and have the template selected in the control tree.

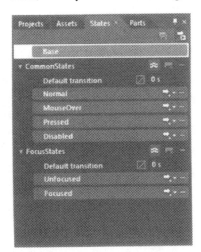

Figure 8-12. The States pane for the Button control

There are several important aspects to this pane. It lists all the states that are defined for the control and also provides capabilities for specifying state transitions. The arrow on the states makes it easy to handle specifying transitioning from any state to this state.

Let's take a closer look at the copy of the default control template (by selecting Edit a Copy option) for the Button control before replacing it with our own. The style containing the default control template, now located in the XAML file, starts off with five simple style property setters:

```
<UserControl.Resources>
    <Style x:Key="ButtonStyle1" TargetType="Button">
```

```xml
<Setter Property="Background" Value="#FF1F3B53"/>
<Setter Property="Foreground" Value="#FF000000"/>
<Setter Property="Padding" Value="3"/>
<Setter Property="BorderThickness" Value="1"/>
<Setter Property="BorderBrush">
    <Setter.Value>
        <LinearGradientBrush EndPoint="0.5,1" StartPoint="0.5,0">
            <GradientStop Color="#FFA3AEB9" Offset="0"/>
            <GradientStop Color="#FF8399A9" Offset="0.375"/>
            <GradientStop Color="#FF718597" Offset="0.375"/>
            <GradientStop Color="#FF617584" Offset="1"/>
        </LinearGradientBrush>
    </Setter.Value>
</Setter>
...
```

The sixth style setter is the control template.

```xml
<Setter Property="Template">
    <Setter.Value>
        <ControlTemplate TargetType="Button">
            <Grid>
                ...
            </Grid>
        </ControlTemplate>
    </Setter.Value>
</Setter>
```

The Grid is the layout container for the various parts of the button. The first child element of the Grid is VisualStateGroups, the attached property of VisualStateManager. As shown here, the Common states visual state group includes common visual states of the button control. They are Normal, MouseOver, Pressed, and Disabled. It also includes the FocusStates visual state group, containing Focused and Unfocused visual states:

```xml
<vsm:VisualStateManager.VisualStateGroups>
    <vsm:VisualStateGroup x:Name="CommonStates">
        <vsm:VisualState x:Name="Normal"/>
        <vsm:VisualState x:Name="MouseOver">
            <!-- changes background gradient to reflect mouse over state -->
        </vsm:VisualState>
        <vsm:VisualState x:Name="Pressed">
            <!-- changes background gradient to reflect pressed and changes
                 opacity of the DownStroke visual element -->
        </vsm:VisualState>
        <vsm:VisualState x:Name="Disabled">
            <!-- changes opacity of DisabledVisual -->
        </vsm:VisualState>
    </vsm:VisualStateGroup>
    <vsm:VisualStateGroup x:Name="FocusStates">
        <vsm:VisualState x:Name="Focused">
            <!-- makes FocusVisual visible -->
```

```
    </vsm:VisualState>
    <vsm:VisualState x:Name="Unfocused">
      <!-- hides FocusVisual -->
    </vsm:VisualState>
  </vsm:VisualStateGroup>
</vsm:VisualStateManager.VisualStateGroups>
```

The `VisualStateTransition` class defines the control's visual behavior during the transition from one state to another. Each VisualState includes the default visual transition for each state (in our case for the button control). The state transition duration represents the length of time it takes to transition from one state to another. For example, if you set the `MouseOver` state duration (currently zero seconds) to five seconds (by adding * to MouseOver transition), the animation to reflect the moused-over state will take a lot longer. The following is the corresponding XAML code:

```
<VisualStateGroup x:Name="CommonStates">
    <VisualStateGroup.Transitions>
        <VisualTransition GeneratedDuration="0:0:5" To="MouseOver"/>
    </VisualStateGroup.Transitions>

    ...

</VisualStateGroup>
```

The `VisualTransition` class has four properties that can specify the duration and behavior of state transitions. Its properties are described in Table 8-2.

Table 8-2. Properties of System.Windows.VisualTransition

Property	Type	Description
GeneratedDuration	TimeSpan	Gets or sets the length of time the specified state transition takes. This duration will affect the **Storyboard** specified in the **VisualState** if none is specified here.
GeneratedEasingFunction	IEasingFunction	Defines the easing function applied to the generated animations.
From	string	Gets or sets the starting state. If this property is not specified, the transition will be from any state within the state group to the state specified in the **To** property.
To	string	Gets or sets the name of the state to transition to.
Storyboard	string	Gets or sets the name of the storyboard that describes the behavior of the state transition. If no storyboard is specified, the **Storyboard** property of the **VisualState** class describes the behavior.

The rest of the control template consists of a number of visual elements that, when combined, create the full appearance of a default button. You can edit these visual elements directly using

Expression Blend. Figure 8-13 shows each element in the Objects and Timeline pane (available on the left side of the window).

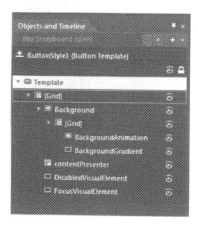

Figure 8-13. The visual elements that make up the Button control

These various visual elements are stored next to each other. Each state contains something called a Storyboard, which alters the appearance of different visual elements. We'll take a closer look at what the Storyboard class provides and how to use it in the next chapter. For now, the important thing to note about the Storyboard is that it provides the capability to change the value of any dependency property over a specified length of time.

Custom Button Control using Control Template

Let's now create a new button that looks like a jagged-lined bubble you might see in a comic book. This could be useful for a comic-related site, an online store or modeling program, or any site that's on the whimsical side. The outline of the button is created in Expression Design using the PolyLine. Figure 8-14 shows the outline of the button.

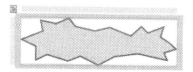

Figure 8-14. Jagged outline for the new button skin using the Path object

You can convert the drawn jagged outline path to the Button-type control by right-clicking on it and selecting the *Make Into Control* option. You need to select the Button control as control type and name the key CustomButton. It will define the following CustomButton named (x:Key value) template with the TargetType set to Button. This custom skinned template for the Button type controls will be added as a resource of the UserControl. See the following code snippet:

```
<UserControl.Resources>
    <Style x:Key="CustomButton" TargetType="Button">
        <Setter Property="Template">
            <Setter.Value>
                <ControlTemplate TargetType="Button">
                    <Grid>
                        <Path x:Name="path" Data="M121,39 L153,46
                            L177,40 L210,53 L226,38 L236,48 L261,38
                            L256,54 L270,63 L281,73 L262,79 L267,91
                            L221,81 L185,86 L159,100 L130,86 L110,94
                            L77,84 L59,93 L59,71 L36,60 L70,47 L66,30
                            L91,35 L111,26 z" Stretch="Fill"
                            UseLayoutRounding="False"
                            StrokeThickness="2" Fill="#FFD2D2E0"
                            Stroke="Black"/>
                        <ContentPresenter HorizontalAlignment=
                            "{TemplateBinding HorizontalContentAlignment}"
                            VerticalAlignment=
                            "{TemplateBinding VerticalContentAlignment}"/>
                    </Grid>
                </ControlTemplate>
            </Setter.Value>
        </Setter>
    </Style>
</UserControl.Resources>
```

The approach we will take for this button is to have different visual appearances of the custom skinned button for Normal, MouseOver, and Pressed states. For simplicity, we have not added the Disabled common state and Focused and Unfocused states. We'll use a thin stroke for the default appearance, the mouseover will change the filled background color, and when the button is pressed we will keep the same changed filled background but thicken the border. When the button is moused over, the border and fill will change back to the normal state. Figure 8-15 shows a default button in Silverlight, the new button as it appears normally, and the new button as it appears when pressed.

Skinned Button in Normal State

Skinned Button in MouseOver State

Skinned Button in Pressed State

Figure 8-15. *A custom skinned button in Normal, MouseOver, and Pressed States*

As shown here, using Expression Blend you will record animations for MouseOver and Pressed states to change the Fill color and the stroke thickness. Again, we'll delve deeper into animation (including how to record animations) in Chapter 10.

```xml
<VisualStateManager.VisualStateGroups>
    <VisualStateGroup x:Name="CommonStates">
        <VisualStateGroup.Transitions>
            <VisualTransition GeneratedDuration="0" To="MouseOver"/>
        </VisualStateGroup.Transitions>
        <VisualState x:Name="Normal"/>
        <VisualState x:Name="Pressed">
            <Storyboard>
                <DoubleAnimationUsingKeyFrames
                    Storyboard.TargetProperty="(Shape.StrokeThickness)"
                    Storyboard.TargetName="path">
                    <EasingDoubleKeyFrame KeyTime="0" Value="4"/>
                </DoubleAnimationUsingKeyFrames>
                <ColorAnimationUsingKeyFrames
                    Storyboard.TargetProperty=
                      "(Shape.Fill).(SolidColorBrush.Color)"
                    Storyboard.TargetName="path">
                    <EasingColorKeyFrame
                        KeyTime="0" Value="#FF8585A9"/>
                </ColorAnimationUsingKeyFrames>
            </Storyboard>
        </VisualState>
        <VisualState x:Name="Disabled"/>
        <VisualState x:Name="MouseOver">
            <Storyboard>
                <ColorAnimationUsingKeyFrames
                    Storyboard.TargetProperty=
```

```
                    "(Shape.Fill).(SolidColorBrush.Color)"
                    Storyboard.TargetName="path">
                    <EasingColorKeyFrame
                        KeyTime="0" Value="#FF8585A9"/>
                </ColorAnimationUsingKeyFrames>
            </Storyboard>
        </VisualState>
    </VisualStateGroup>
</VisualStateManager.VisualStateGroups>
```

Now you can apply the created CustomButton template to any button (using **Style** property) within that UserControl, as shown here:

```
<Button Content="Button" Height="75" Width="300" Margin="10"
    Style="{StaticResource CustomButton}" VerticalAlignment="Top"/>
```

Control Templates for Other Controls

The following key controls provide the ability to customize their control template:

Button: The common states (CommonStates) are normal, pressed, moused over, and disabled. The focus states (FocusStates) are focused and unfocused.

Calendar: The validation states are invalid focused, invalid unfocused, and valid. The Calendar uses the CalendarButton, **CalendarDayButton**, and **CalendarItemStyle** controls. The CalendarButton has five state groups: common (normal, disabled, moused over, and pressed); selection (selected and unselected); focus states (focused and not focused); active states (active and inactive); and CalendarButtonFocusStates (CalendarButtonFocused and CalendarButtonUnfocused). The **CalendarDayButton** shares similar states as **CalendarButton** control, but also includes additional two state groups: Day states (RegularDay and Today), and BlackoutDay states (NormalDay and BlackoutDay). The CalendarItemStyle includes normal and disabled common states.

CheckBox: The common states are normal, moused over, pressed, and disabled. The focus states (focused and unfocused. The check states are checked, unchecked, and indeterminate. The validation states are valid, invalid unfocused, and invalid focused.

DataGrid: The DataGrid provides common states, normal and disabled, and validation states (invalid and valid). It also includes different states for Cell Style, Column Header Style, Drag Indicator Style, Drop Location Indicator Style, Row Details Template, Row Header Style, and Row Style.

DatePicker: The common states are normal and disabled. The Validate states are invalid focus, invalid not focused, and valid. The DatePicker uses CalendarStyle, which also includes the similar validation states.

GridSplitter: The common states are normal, moused over, and disabled. The focus states are focused and unfocused.

HyperlinkButton: The common states are normal, moused over, and pressed, and disabled. The focus states are focused and unfocused.

ListBox: The ListBox control has validation states (valid, invalid unfocused, and invalid focused). The control uses a ScrollViewer and the **ListBoxItem** classes. The **ListBoxItem** defines 11 states:

common states (normal, moused over, and disabled); focus states (focused and unfocused); selection states (selected, unselected, and selected, but not focus); and Layout states (Before loaded, loaded, and unloaded).

PasswordBox: The common states are normal, moused over, and disabled. The focused states are focused and unfocused. The validation states are valid, invalid unfocused, and invalid focused.

ProgressBar: The common states are determinate and indeterminate.

RadioButton: The common states are normal, moused over, disabled, and pressed. The focus states are focused and unfocused. The checked states are checked, unchecked, and indeterminate. The validation states are valid, invalid not focused, and invalid focused.

RepeatButton: The common states are normal, moused over, pressed, and disabled. The focus states are focused and unfocused.

RichTextArea: The common states are normal, moused over, disabled, and read-only. The focus states are focused and unfocused. The validation states are valid, invalid not focused, and invalid focused.

ScrollBar: The ScrollBar itself only has common states (normal, moused over, and disabled). It consists of two sets of a template, two repeat buttons, and a thumb control. One set is for vertically-oriented scrollbars and the other is for horizontally-oriented scrollbars. The `Thumb` control includes the `ThumbStyle`, which has common states (normal, mouse over, pressed, and disabled) and focus states (unfocused and focused).

ScrollViewer: This has no states, but consists of a horizontal scrollbar, a vertical scrollbar, and a content presenter class (`ScrollContentPresenter`).

Slider: The common states are normal, moused over, and disabled. The focus states are focused and unfocused. Much like the ScrollBar, the Slider consists of two sets of templates (one set for vertical orientation and the other for horizontal). Each set consists of two repeat buttons and a thumb.

TabControl: The common states are normal and disabled. The tab control consists of TabItem instances, each of which has common states (normal, moused over, and disabled); focus states (focused and unfocused); and selection states (selected and unselected).

TextBox: The common states are normal, moused over, disabled, and read-only. The focused states are focused and unfocused. The validation states are valid, invalid unfocused, and invalid focused.

ToggleButton: The common states are normal, moused over, pressed, and disabled. The focus states are focused and unfocused. The check states are checked, unchecked, and indeterminate.

Developing a Templated Control

If you want to create your own control, it's a good idea to also make it compatible with control templates. There are really only two things you must do: use the `TemplateVisualState` attribute to specify state groups and states, and use the `VisualStateManager` class within the control's code to handle switching from one state to the next. Since you should be quite familiar with the Button control, let's look at the definition of the `Button` class:

```
[TemplateVisualState(Name = "Normal", GroupName = "CommonStates")]
 [TemplateVisualState(Name = "Pressed", GroupName = "CommonStates")]
[TemplateVisualState(Name = "Disabled", GroupName = "CommonStates")]
```

```
[TemplateVisualState(Name = "Unfocused", GroupName = "FocusStates")]
[TemplateVisualState(Name = "Focused", GroupName = "FocusStates")]
[TemplateVisualState(Name = "MouseOver", GroupName = "CommonStates")]

public class Button : Control
{
    // class implementation
}
```

The two properties of the `TemplateVisualState` attributes `GroupName` and `Name` are used here. The `GroupName` attribute defines the name of the state group and `Name` defines the state related to the group. The groups and states you specify define the behavior of the control. Try to use as few states as possible that still completely define the behavior of your new control. Once these states are defined, the other requirement is for your new control to switch states at the right time.

Some controls consist of other controls, such as the ScrollBar using the RepeatButton control for its increasing/decreasing visual element.

```
[TemplatePartAttribute(Name = "HorizontalThumb", Type = typeof(Thumb))]
[TemplatePartAttribute(Name = "VerticalSmallIncrease", Type = typeof(RepeatButton))]
[TemplatePartAttribute(Name = "VerticalSmallDecrease", Type = typeof(RepeatButton))]
[TemplateVisualStateAttribute(Name = "Disabled", GroupName = "CommonStates")]
[TemplatePartAttribute(Name = "HorizontalLargeIncrease",
    Type = typeof(RepeatButton))]
[TemplatePartAttribute(Name = "HorizontalLargeDecrease",
    Type = typeof(RepeatButton))]
[TemplatePartAttribute(Name = "HorizontalSmallDecrease",
    Type = typeof(RepeatButton))]
[TemplatePartAttribute(Name = "HorizontalSmallIncrease",
    Type = typeof(RepeatButton))]
[TemplatePartAttribute(Name = "VerticalRoot", Type = typeof(FrameworkElement))]
[TemplatePartAttribute(Name = "VerticalLargeIncrease", Type = typeof(RepeatButton))]
[TemplatePartAttribute(Name = "VerticalLargeDecrease", Type = typeof(RepeatButton))]
[TemplatePartAttribute(Name = "HorizontalRoot", Type = typeof(FrameworkElement))]
[TemplatePartAttribute(Name = "VerticalThumb", Type = typeof(Thumb))]
[TemplateVisualStateAttribute(Name = "Normal", GroupName = "CommonStates")]
[TemplateVisualStateAttribute(Name = "MouseOver", GroupName = "CommonStates")]
public sealed class ScrollBar : RangeBase
```

When you edit the control template of a control with template parts in Expression Blend (via Edit a Copy), the control templates for each of the template parts are added as a resource to the root layout container of the main control's control template. The ScrollBar causes the following XAML to be generated (most of the details are left out for brevity). Notice the series of `ControlTemplate` elements added to the Grid's resource dictionary.

```
<ControlTemplate TargetType="ScrollBar">
    <Grid x:Name="Root">
        <Grid.Resources>
            <ControlTemplate x:Key="RepeatButtonTemplate" TargetType="RepeatButton">
                <Grid x:Name="Root" Background="Transparent">
                    <vsm:VisualStateManager.VisualStateGroups>
                        <vsm:VisualStateGroup x:Name="CommonStates">
```

```xml
                    <vsm:VisualState x:Name="Normal"/>
                </vsm:VisualStateGroup>
            </vsm:VisualStateManager.VisualStateGroups>
        </Grid>
    </ControlTemplate>
    <ControlTemplate x:Key="HorizontalIncrementTemplate"
                                TargetType="RepeatButton">
    </ControlTemplate>
    <ControlTemplate x:Key="HorizontalDecrementTemplate"
                                TargetType="RepeatButton">
    </ControlTemplate>
    <ControlTemplate x:Key="VerticalIncrementTemplate"
                                TargetType="RepeatButton">
    </ControlTemplate>
    <ControlTemplate x:Key="VerticalDecrementTemplate"
                                TargetType="RepeatButton">
    </ControlTemplate>
    <ControlTemplate x:Key="VerticalThumbTemplate" TargetType="Thumb">
    </ControlTemplate>
    <ControlTemplate x:Key="HorizontalThumbTemplate" TargetType="Thumb">
    </ControlTemplate>
</Grid.Resources>
<vsm:VisualStateManager.VisualStateGroups>
    <vsm:VisualStateGroup x:Name="CommonStates">
        <vsm:VisualState x:Name="Normal"/>
        <vsm:VisualState x:Name="MouseOver"/>
        <vsm:VisualState x:Name="Disabled">
            <Storyboard>
                <DoubleAnimationUsingKeyFrames
                            Storyboard.TargetName="Root"
                            Storyboard.TargetProperty="(UIElement.Opacity)">
                    <SplineDoubleKeyFrame KeyTime="00:00:00" Value="0.5"/>
                </DoubleAnimationUsingKeyFrames>
            </Storyboard>
        </vsm:VisualState>
    </vsm:VisualStateGroup>
</vsm:VisualStateManager.VisualStateGroups>
<Grid x:Name="HorizontalRoot">
    <!-- Grid definition and main controls -->
    <RepeatButton x:Name="HorizontalSmallDecrease" ...>
    <RepeatButton x:Name="HorizontalLargeDecrease" ...>
    <Thumb MinWidth="10" x:Name="HorizontalThumb" ...>
    <RepeatButton x:Name="HorizontalLargeIncrease" ...>
    <RepeatButton x:Name="HorizontalSmallIncrease" ...>
</Grid>
<Grid x:Name="VerticalRoot" Visibility="Collapsed">
    <!-- vertical appearance of ScrollBar -->
</Grid>
    </Grid>
</ControlTemplate>
```

When you develop a control, the state changes are accomplished using the `VisualStateManager`'s `GoToState` method. This method takes three parameters: a reference to a control, the name of the state to transition to, and a `bool` value specifying whether to use the visual transition specified by the `Storyboard` in the control template. For example, in the Button control, when the button handles the `MouseOver` event, it triggers a state transition, accomplished by invoking the `VisualStateManager`.

```
VisualStateManager.GoToState(this, "MouseOver", true);
```

By using the two attributes, `TemplateVisualState` and `TemplatePart`, and handling the state transitions within your custom control via the `GoToState` method of the `VisualStateManager`, you can easily create a control that isolates its behavior and allows designers and developers to completely change the look of your control. Of course, if you create a new control that supports control templates, you must create a default control template if you expect others to consume the control.

Summary

This chapter covered styles and control templates. Styles make reusing properties easy, throughout a single page or an entire application, depending on which resource dictionary contains the styles. In this chapter we also covered the enhanced styling features of Silverlight 3 and Silverlight 4 Control templates are a mechanism to completely change the visual appearance of a control. This chapter also briefly covered developing custom controls to utilize a control template, and using the `Storyboard` class, a vital part of animation and the topic for the next chapter.

In the next chapter, we'll look at the Silverlight graphics capabilities. We'll explore more aspects of building user interfaces, such as 2D and 3D drawing and brush support in Silverlight. We will also cover ImageBrush and VideoBrush, which provide the ability to use images and videos in even more interesting ways than you have seen so far.

CHAPTER 9

Graphics

We've covered a lot of ground so far demonstrating Silverlight's capabilities to build rich user interfaces. 2D and 3D graphics play a vital role in developing rich user interfaces providing different effects. Silverlight provides a rich set of classes to perform 2D drawing, including lines, Bezier curves, and various geometrical figures such as ellipses and rectangles. We'll take a look at transformations and brushes, both of which provide a great deal of control in how elements are presented on an interface. Any element inheriting from UIElement can have a transform or a composite transform (introduced in Silverlight 4) applied to it—you can create some interesting video presentations, for example, by skewing or growing/shrinking a video. Silverlight 3 introduced development of 3D effects using perspective transforms. We'll also take a look at the support for brushes in Silverlight. You can use specific brushes to fill surfaces with images or video and other effects such as gradients.

Enhancements in Silverlight 4

Silverlight 4 introduces the following key enhancements in the graphics and transformation areas supporting wider types of graphics file format and simplifying the transformation implementation.

- True transparency support to display all PNG image formats, which we covered earlier in Chapter 4.

- A new transform type named CompositeTransform is introduced, which simplifies the coding. Now you can apply multiple transforms using the single CompositeTransform XAML node, which we will cover later in this chapter.

2D Graphics

Silverlight provides two categories of classes for two dimensional graphics: shapes and geometries. The System.Windows.Shapes.Shape class forms the base for all shape-related classes. The Shape class inherits directly from FrameworkElement, so it gains all that is provided by the UIElement and FrameworkElement classes. The System.Windows.Media.Geometry class, however, inherits directly from DependencyObject, not from UIElement or FrameworkElement. There are similarities between the two categories, but the difference is what they are designed for. The Geometry-based classes provide more flexibility and focus more on the behavior of the geometric shapes (and are actually used by some of the Shape-based classes). The Shape-derived classes, however, are meant for easily adding 2D shapes to a Silverlight user interface. The hierarchy of 2D classes we will look at is shown in Figure 9-1.

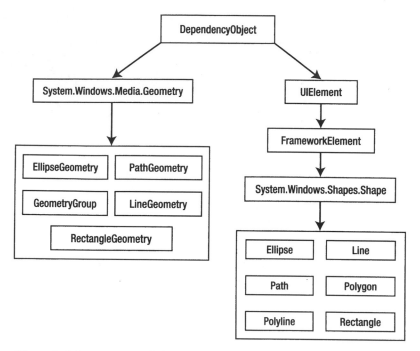

Figure 9-1. Geometry- and Shape-based classes

Using Geometries

We'll take a look at the Geometry-based classes first since these provide more versatility. The UIElement class uses a Geometry object to define a region used to clip what's shown, and the Path class derives from the Shape class, which uses a Geometry object to know what to draw. The Shapes.Path class is the mechanism to use if you want to draw a Geometry-derived class on a user interface, since the Geometry classes on their own can't do this.

Simple Geometries

The LineGeometry, RectangleGeometry, and EllipseGeometry classes represent basic geometrical figures. These classes cover the basic shapes, including lines, rectangles, and ellipses. These geometries are shown in Figure 9-2.

Figure 9-2. *Line, rectangle, and ellipse geometries*

LineGeometry

The LineGeometry class represents a single line with a start point and endpoint. Its two properties are shown in Table 9-1.

Table 9-1. *Properties of the System.Windows.Media.LineGeometry Class*

Property	Type	Description
StartPoint	Point	The (x,y) point of the start of the line
EndPoint	Point	The (x,y) point of the end of the line

Since the Geometry-based classes can't be shown directly, they must be shown using the Path class. Let's draw a line using the LineGeometry class in XAML:

```
<Path Stroke="Red" StrokeThickness="5">
    <Path.Data>
        <LineGeometry StartPoint="10,10" EndPoint="20,20"/>
    </Path.Data>
</Path>
```

RectangleGeometry

The RectangleGeometry class is used for representing rectangles (and squares, of course). Its properties are shown in Table 9-2. The RadiusX and RadiusY properties are used to round the corners. Combined, these properties represent an ellipse that is used to control the degree to which the corners are rounded. If you set these sufficiently high, the rectangle will not disappear, but instead will render as an ellipse or a circle.

Table 9-2. Properties of the System.Windows.Media.RectangleGeometry Class

Property	Type	Description
RadiusX	double	Gets or sets the x radius of the ellipse used for rounding the rectangle's corners.
RadiusY	double	Gets or sets the y radius of the ellipse used for rounding the rectangle's corners.
Rect	System.Windows.Rect	Gets or sets the rectangle's dimensions. The Rect class has x, y origin point and width, height dimensions properties, each of type double.

Let's draw a rectangle on the screen again using the Path class:

```
<Path Stroke="Red" StrokeThickness="5">
  <Path.Data>
    <RectangleGeometry Rect="10,10,40,40" RadiusX="5" RadiusY="5"/>
  </Path.Data>
</Path>
```

EllipseGeometry

The EllipseGeometry class represents an ellipse defined by a center point and two radii, one for the top and bottom of the ellipse and the other for the sides. Its properties are shown in Table 9-3.

Table 9-3. Properties of the System.Windows.Media.EllipseGeometry Class

Property	Type	Description
RadiusX	double	Gets or sets the x radius of the ellipse used for defining the ellipse's sides.
RadiusY	double	Gets or sets the y radius of the ellipse used for defining the ellipse's top and bottom.
Center	Point	Gets or sets the center point (x, y coordinates) of the ellipse.

Yet again, we use the Path class to display EllipseGeometry on the screen:

```
<Path Stroke="Red" StrokeThickness="5">
  <Path.Data>
    <EllipseGeometry Center="50,50" RadiusX="50" RadiusY="20"/>
  </Path.Data>
</Path>
```

Path Geometries

The `PathGeometry` class, inherited from the `Geometry` class, is where the geometries get interesting. The `PathGeometry` class is used to represent an arbitrary geometrical shape made up of lines and/or curves. `PathGeometry` contains one or more `PathFigure` objects. Each `PathFigure` object contains one or more `PathSegment` objects. The various segments are connected automatically within each `PathFigure` object by each segment's start point, starting at the previous segment's endpoint. There are seven segment classes you can use to construct figures, as shown in Table 9-4. Since using these segments to construct geometrical shapes can be unwieldy, there is a special syntax used with the `Path` class for drawing multiple segments. We'll take a closer look at this in the next section when we look at the various `Shape`-related classes.

Table 9-4. Segment Classes Derived from `PathSegment` Used in a `PathFigure`

Class	Description
`ArcSegment`	Elliptical arc between two points
`BezierSegment`	Cubic Bezier curve between two points
`LineSegment`	Straight line between two points
`PolyBezierSegment`	Represents a series of cubic Bezier curves
`PolyLineSegment`	Represents a series of lines
`PolyQuadraticBezierSegment`	Represents a series of quadratic Bezier curves
`QuadraticBezierSegment`	Quadratic Bezier curve between two points

Before we go over the specific properties of each segment, let's take a look at piecing together a rectangle. You can see what the rectangle looks like in Figure 9-3; its XAML code is also shown.

▓ **Caution** If you use a `StrokeThickness` larger than 1, the final segment will leave a gap. Keep this in mind when manually piecing together segments. The final segment might need an adjustment to go far enough to fill in the visual gap left by the difference between the endpoint and the stroke thickness.

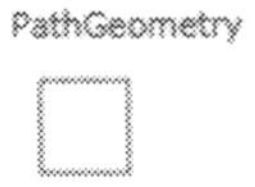

Figure 9-3. Rectangle drawn using PathGeometry

```
<Path Stroke="Red" StrokeThickness="1">
    <Path.Data>
        <PathGeometry>
            <PathGeometry.Figures>
                <PathFigure StartPoint="10,10">
                    <PathFigure.Segments>
                        <LineSegment Point="10,40"/>
                        <LineSegment Point="40,40"/>
                        <LineSegment Point="40,10"/>
                        <LineSegment Point="10,10"/>
                    </PathFigure.Segments>
                </PathFigure>
            </PathGeometry.Figures>
        </PathGeometry>
    </Path.Data>
</Path>
```

Let's take a look at what each segment describes and its properties briefly here, and later we will discuss the Bezier curve in detail in the context of implementing animation.

ArcSegment

This segment draws an elliptical segment between the end of the previous segment (or the figure's start point) and the specified destination point. Since the elliptical segment only has two points, there must be a way to define how the arc is drawn since there are multiple candidate arcs. The IsLargeArc and SweepDirection properties exist for this purpose. Table 9-5 shows the properties of ArcSegment.

Table 9-5. Properties of the System.Windows.Media.ArcSegment Class

Property	Type	Description
IsLargeArc	bool	If true, the arc drawn is greater than 180 degrees. This is one of the two properties required to define how the arc is drawn.
Point	System.Windows.Point	This defines the endpoint of the arc.
RotationAngle	double	This specifies the rotation angle (in degrees) of the arc around the *x* axis. It defaults to 0.
Size	System.Windows.Size	This specifies the x and y radii of the arc.
SweepDirection	System.Windows .Media.SweepDirection	This defines which direction the arc is drawn in. It can be set to Clockwise or Counterclockwise. The use of this property with IsLargeArc fully specifies the type of arc drawn.

BezierSegment

This segment represents a Bezier curve, which is a curve defined by a start point, an endpoint, and two control points. The line is bent toward each control point, so if the control points are placed on opposite sides of the line, the line appears to have a hill and a valley along its length. This class provides three properties, all of type `System.Windows.Point`, used to specify the Bezier segment's control points and ending point.

- `Point1`: Defines the first control point
- `Point2`: Defines the second control point
- `Point3`: Defines the endpoint of the curve

LineSegment

This segment represents a straight line. It has a single property, `Point`, which defines the endpoint of the line.

QuadraticBezierSegment

A quadratic Bezier segment is a Bezier curve with only a single control point. It defines a single control point and an endpoint.

- `Point1`: Defines the control point
- `Point2`: Defines the endpoint of the curve

PolyBezierSegment

This segment is similar to `BezierSegment` but provides an easy way to combine multiple Bezier curves. Each curve is defined by three points and automatically connects to the endpoint of the previous line (or previous segment if it's the first line in the series). This class contains one property, `Points`, of type `System.Windows.Media.PointCollection,` containing control points and endpoints defining Bezier curves.

PolyLineSegment

Similar in spirit to `PolyBezierSegment`, this segment allows you to easily combine multiple straight lines in a series. It also exposes a property, `Points`, of type `System.Windows.Media.PointCollection`. Each line is automatically connected to the endpoint of the previous line/segment, so for each new line, all you need to do is add one new point.

PolyQuadraticBezierSegment

This segment combines multiple quadratic Bezier segments together. Each segment is defined by two points: the control point and the endpoint. These are stored in the `Points` property, similar to the other poly segments.

Grouping Geometries

The GeometryGroup class is used to group multiple geometries together that are derived from the Geometry class. Since it is possible for multiple geometrical shapes to intersect, the GeometryGroup class exposes a FillRule property to specify how the intersections of geometries are treated to judge whether points within the intersection are in the combined geometry. The FillRule property can take on one of two possible values:

- EvenOdd: A point is judged within the fill region if the number of path segment rays drawn in every direction away from the point ultimately cross an odd number of segments. This is the default value.

- Nonzero: A point is judged within the fill region if the number of crossings of segments across rays drawn from a point is greater than zero.

In addition to the FillRule property, the GeometryGroup class includes other properties, such as Bounds (inherited from the Geometry class), to get a Rect (structure defining the width, height, and point of origin of a rectangle) specifying the axis-aligned bounding box of the Geometry class; Children, to define the GeometryCollection that contains the objects defining the GeometryGroup class, and Transform (inherited from the Geometry class), to define the Transform object applied to the Geometry class.

Clipping with Geometries

Geometries are also used to set the Clip property of any UIElement, such as images and videos (see Chapter 3), to crop an object by cutting out the display area of an object based on the defined shape of geometric. The Clip property gets or sets the Geometry used to define the outline of the contents of a UIElement. The Clip property takes a Geometry type that can be a line, rectangle, ellipse, or group geometry.

If you set the clip property of an image to an EllipseGeometry and set the RadiusX, RadiusY, and Center properties of the geometry as shown here in the code snippet, you will receive the clipped image shown in Figure 9-4.

```
<Image Source="Penguins.jpg" Width="300" Height="300">
    <Image.Clip>
        <EllipseGeometry
            RadiusX="100"
            RadiusY="100"
            Center="150,150"/>
    </Image.Clip>
</Image>
```

Normal Image

Image with Clipping

Figure 9-4. Image clipping using EllipseGeometry

Using Shapes

The `System.Windows.Shapes.Shape` class forms the base for classes that represent geometrical figures that have the ability to draw themselves on the screen. There are classes for drawing lines, rectangles, ellipses, and polygons, all deriving from `Shape`. The most interesting `Shape`-derived class is `Path`. The `Path` class is what we used in the previous section—it has the ability to draw `Geometry`-based objects on the screen, and it can also process a specialized syntax for piecing together `Path`-based geometries. Some of the most useful properties of the `Shape` class are shown in Table 9-6.

Table 9-6. Properties of the System.Windows.Shapes.Shape Class

Property	Type	Description
Fill	Brush	The brush used to fill the interior of the shape.
Stretch	Stretch	The value from the **Stretch** enumeration; controls how the shape fills its bounding space. **None**, **Fill**, **Uniform**, and **UniformToFill** are possible values. The default value is based on the type of the **Shape**.
Stroke	Brush	The brush used to paint the outline of the shape.
StrokeDashArray	DoubleCollection	Collection of **double** values specifying the dash pattern to use in outlining the shape
StrokeThickness	double	The thickness of the outline of the shape.

Let's briefly look at some of the simple **Shape**-based classes before moving on to the more complicated **Path** class. The results of the XAML for each of these shapes are shown in Figure 9-5.

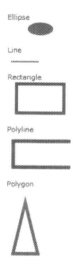

Figure 9-5. Appearance of the Shape-based classes

Ellipse

The **Ellipse** class exposes **Height** and **Width** properties that define what the ellipse looks like. Unlike the **Geometry** class, where you specify a center point and x and y radius values, the **Ellipse** class only needs to know its bounding box as defined by its **Height** and **Width** properties. This provides more flexibility in visual presentation, since a **Shape** can have different stretch behaviors and can be affected by the width of its outline and other properties. You can specify an ellipse in XAML by using the following:

```
<Ellipse Fill="Red" Height="20" Width="40"/>
```

Line

The **Line** class has two properties to define the start point of the line: **X1** and **Y1**. The **X2** and **Y2** properties are used to define the endpoint of the line. Drawing a line is accomplished using the following XAML:

```
<Line X1="5" Y1="10" X2="50" Y2="10" Stroke="Red" StrokeThickness="2" />
```

Rectangle

The **Rectangle** class defines **Height** and **Width** properties, specifying the dimensions of the rectangle. The following XAML draws a rectangle:

```
<Rectangle Width="80" Height="50" Fill="White" Stroke="Black" StrokeThickness="5" />
```

Polyline

The **Polyline** class is used to draw multiple connected straight lines. A polyline does not need to be a closed shape, like a polygon (explained next). The **Points** property contains the set of points (x and y values separated by a space) defining the lines. The following XAML draws the letter *C*:

```
<Polyline Points="100,10 10,10 10,50 100,50" Stroke="Black" StrokeThickness="5" />
```

Polygon

A polygon is a set of two or more points that form a filled and closed shape. If two points are specified and **StrokeThickness** and **Stroke** are defined, a line will be drawn. A set of points is specified in the **Polygon**'s **Points** property (same format as **Polyline**). The following XAML draws a red triangle on the screen. Four points are specified in order to connect the edges back to the triangle's starting point. The shape formed must be a closed shape, or it will be auto-closed.

```
<Polygon Points="30,20 50,100 10,100 30,20" Stroke="Red" StrokeThickness="5" />
```

Path

The **Path** class is by far the most versatile **Shape**-based class. This class can display any **Geometry** object by setting its **Data** property to the object. While this can be used to show complex **Path**-based geometries using **PathGeometry**, there is also a special syntax supported in XAML to specify **Path**-based geometries in a more terse string form. This syntax is utilized by Expression Media when constructing **Path**-based geometries and when specifying the value for the **Data** property of the **Path** class.

The string starts with specifying the fill rule, which is optional. If you want to specify a `FillRule` enumeration, it must come first. You can use the string `F0` to specify `EvenOdd` (the default value) or `F1` to specify `Nonzero` for the fill rule.

After the fill rule (if you specify one) comes one or more figure descriptions. A figure description is made up of a move command, a draw command, and optionally a close command. Each point in this string can take the form *x y* or *x,y*, and whitespace is ignored.

The move command is marked by either a capital `M` or a lowercase `m`, and then one or more points. The capital `M` represents a move to an absolute position, and the lowercase `m` means that the point specified is relative to the previous point. Generally, only one point will be specified, since if multiple points are specified, move operations will be combined with draw operations to draw lines. If only a single point is specified, the behavior of the move command is less ambiguous.

The draw command can be used to draw eight possible shapes. Each command is either a capital letter (for absolute positioning) or a lowercase letter (for relative positioning). Table 9-7 lists the possible draw commands. For simplicity each command is shown only in its capital letter form.

Table 9-7. Valid Draw Commands

Command	Description
L endPoint	Draws a line starting at the current point and ending at endPoint.
H x	Draws a horizontal line from the current point to the specified x coordinate.
V y	Draws a vertical line from the current point to the specified y coordinate.
C point1 point2 endPoint	Draws a cubic Bezier curve, with **point1** and **point2** representing the control points and **endPoint** representing the endpoint of the curve.
Q point1 endPoint	Draws a quadratic Bezier curve using **point1** as the control point and ending at the point specified by **endPoint**.
S point2 endPoint	Draws a smooth cubic Bezier curve. The first control point is a reflection of **point2** relative to the current point. The curve ends at **endPoint**.
T point1 endPoint	Draws a smooth quadratic Bezier curve.
A size rotationAngle isLargeArcFlag sweepDirectionFlag endPoint	Draws an elliptical arc. See the "EllipseGeometry" section earlier in the chapter for a description of each parameter. You can set the flag to **0** to turn it off and **1** to turn it on.

The close command is optional. If specified, the current figure is automatically closed by connecting the current point to the starting point of the figure using a line. The close command is specified using either a capital or lowercase `Z`. The close command is not case-sensitive.

The star shape shown in Figure 9-6 is drawn using a `Path` with a solid fill.

Figure 9-6. *Star shape drawn using a* Path

The Path in XAML used to make the star looks like this:

```
<Path Stretch="Fill"
        StrokeThickness="2"
        StrokeLineJoin="Round"
        Stroke="Blue"
        Data="F1 M 0,100 L 150,100 L 200,0 L 250,100 L 400,100
                    L 266, 150 L 300,300 L 200,170 L 110,300 L 133,150 Z ">
    <Path.Fill>
        <SolidColorBrush Color="#FFAACCEE"/>
    </Path.Fill>
</Path>
```

Transforms

Transforms are used to alter an element's coordinate system, so applying a transform to a root element causes it and all child content to uniformly alter in appearance. The benefit of a transform is that the underlying elements need no knowledge of the transform—they act as if the coordinate system is unaltered. Silverlight supports transforms for scaling, skewing, and rotating. Scaling makes it easy to shrink or grow an element; skewing can rotate x and y coordinates independently; and rotating causes the entire element to rotate around a center, defaulting to the element's top-left corner. Silverlight also supports a matrix transform, which provides more flexibility in transforms in case you want to do something that isn't a scale, skew, or rotation. Technically, there is one more transform, TransformGroup. This is used to group multiple transformations together and is in itself a Transform.

Many visual elements in Silverlight are eligible for transforming. The Geometry base class has a Transform property that can be set to any of the Transform inheritors. The Brush base class has both a Transform property and a RelativeTransform property. A relative transform is most useful when you don't know the size of the element being transformed—we'll briefly look at this in the next section when we discuss brushes. The UIElement base class has a RenderTransform property that can also be set to any of the Transform inheritors. Let's take a closer look at the transforms represented by classes in Silverlight.

Translation

A translation transform changes the position of an element. This is a simple operation of moving the top left of the element horizontally and/or vertically. A constant value is added to the x and/or y coordinates to reposition the entire element. These values are specified in the X and Y properties of the TranslateTransform class. The following XAML is used to translate a rectangle. Figure 9-7 shows the rectangle translated in both a positive and a negative direction. Translating an element, such as this rectangle, in XAML is a simple matter of specifying its RenderTransform.

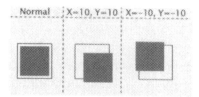

Figure 9-7. Translating a rectangle diagonally down and up

```
<Rectangle Stroke="Black" Width="60" Height="60"/>
   <Rectangle Stroke="Crimson" Fill="Crimson" Width="50" Height="50">
      <Rectangle.RenderTransform>
         <TranslateTransform X="10" Y="10"/>
      </Rectangle.RenderTransform>
</Rectangle>
```

Rotation

The RotateTransform class is used to rotate the entire element undergoing transformation. This transform has three important properties for specifying how the rotation is performed: Angle, CenterX, and CenterY. The CenterX and CenterY properties specify which point the rotation is done around. The top left of an element is (0,0), as illustrated in Figure 9-8, and it is around this point that rotation is done by default.

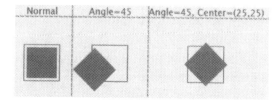

Figure 9-8. Rotating a rectangle about its default center and true center

You can rotate in a clockwise direction by using a positive angle (in degrees) between 0 and 360. If you want to rotate counterclockwise, you can specify a negative angle. Angles greater than 360 or less than –360 are valid, but they wrap around the circle. For example, a rotation by 405 degrees has the same result as rotating by 45 degrees, since 405 is equal to 360 (one full rotation) plus 45.

Again, we specify the rectangle's RenderTransform. We will rotate the rectangle on the screen by 45 degrees.

```
<Rectangle Height="50" Width="50" Fill="Crimson">
   <Rectangle.RenderTransform>
      <RotateTransform CenterX="0" CenterY="0" Angle="45"/>
   </Rectangle.RenderTransform>
</Rectangle>
```

Since our center point is at (0,0), the rotation is done around the top-left corner of the rectangle. If you want to rotate the rectangle around its true center, make sure you set CenterX and CenterY appropriately. In this case, we'd set the center to the point (25,25). From left to right, Figure 9-8 shows what our rectangle looks like normally, rotated by 45 degrees around its top-left corner, (0,0), and rotated 45 degrees around its true center, (25,25).

Skewing

A skew transformation stretches the coordinate space in either the x or y direction (or both). This is sometimes called a shear transformation. The angle controls how the corresponding coordinate plane is stretched.

The SkewTransform.AngleX property defines the x-axis skew angle defined in degrees counterclockwise from the y axis if there is a positive value and anticlockwise from the y axis if there is a negative value.

The SkewTransform.AngleY property defines the y-axis skew angle defined in degrees counterclockwise from the x axis if there is a positive value and anticlockwise from the x axis if there is a negative value. The values can be between -360 and 360. The values less than -360 or greater than 360 will treated with the mod(360) formula applied.

For example, if you specify an AngleX of 45 degrees, the x and y planes will form a 45 degree angle with each other. You can see this in Figure 9-9 (first row, second column). As the y values increase (remember, top left of the rectangle is 0,0), the x values are shifted over until the bottom of the rectangle is reached, forming the 45 degree angle at the bottom. The third column shows a skewing transformation done using the AngleY property. Similar to rotation, you can control the center point around which skewing is performed. The second row of Figure 9-9 shows the same skewing transformations, but with the center of the rectangle, (25,25), as the center point.

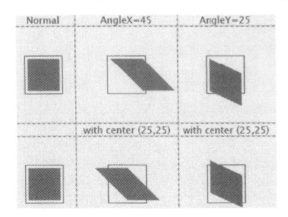

Figure 9-9. Skewing a rectangle about its default center and true center

```
<Rectangle Stroke="Crimson" Fill="Crimson" Width="50" Height="50">
    <Rectangle.RenderTransform>
        <SkewTransform AngleX="45"/>
    </Rectangle.RenderTransform>
</Rectangle>
```

Scaling

A scaling transformation uniformly increases or decreases the size of an element. You can zoom into an element by scaling it up, and zoom out (e.g., as a cheap way to show thumbnails) by scaling the element down. The `ScaleTransform.ScaleX` and `ScaleTransform.ScaleY` properties are used to specify how much to scale the element by.

The `ScaleTransform.ScaleX` defines the scale factor in the x axis. The default is 1, which means no scale in the x-direction. Values between 0 and 1 decrease the width of the scaled object. A value greater than 1 will increase the width of the scaled object. A negative value flips the scaled object horizontally. Values between 0 and -1 will flip the object horizontally and decrease the width of the scaled object. Values less than -1 flip the object horizontally and increase the width of the scaled object.

The `ScaleTransform.ScaleY` defines the scale factor in the y axis. The default is 1, which means no scale in the y-direction. Values between 0 and 1 decrease the height of the scaled object. A value greater than 1 will increase the height of the scaled object. A negative value flips the scaled object vertically. Values between 0 and -1 will flip the object vertically and decrease the height of the scaled object. Values less than -1 flip the object vertically and increase the height of the scaled object.

This transformation also has a `CenterX` and `CenterY` point. This point specifies which point will stay constant in the scaling. Figure 9-10 shows our normal rectangle again in the top left, and the first row shows a scale-up and a scale-down using the default, (0,0), as the center point. Notice how the top-left corner is unmoved. If we specify (25,25) as the center point, as is done in the second row, the rectangle completely overtakes its bounding box when scaled up and is centered within its bounding box when scaled down. This behavior is important to note when you utilize the scaling transformation. If you think about how some menu animation has the menu expanding while its top-left corner stays intact, you can see how using the top-left corner as the anchor point could prove useful. If this were a button, though, and you wanted its size to change when a user hovered over it, it would be better to scale the button up with its true center as the anchor so that it would grow/shrink in a more expected manner for the user.

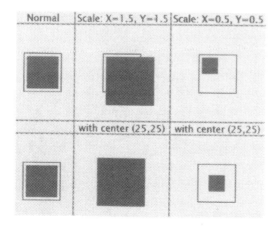

Figure 9-10. Scaling a rectangle up and down based on its default center and true center

Here's the XAML used for scaling the rectangle up and down in the second row of Figure 9-10.

```
<Rectangle Stroke="Crimson" Fill="Crimson" Width="50" Height="50">
    <Rectangle.RenderTransform>
        <ScaleTransform ScaleX="1.5" ScaleY="1.5"/>
    </Rectangle.RenderTransform>
</Rectangle>
```

Arbitrary Linear Transforms

The final transformation class that Silverlight provides is the matrix transformation. This can be used when the other transformations don't give you what you want, or when you want to combine multiple transformations into a single transformation (although you could also use TransformGroup to group several). Each of the other transformations can be represented by a 3~TMS3 matrix. Let's dust off our linear algebra textbooks and revisit the basics of matrix math to see how a matrix can give us the other transformations, and even combine multiple transformations into a single operation.

The 3~TMS3 matrix that Silverlight uses looks like Figure 9-11.

M11	M12	0
M21	M22	0
offsetX	offsetY	1

Figure 9-11. The transformation matrix used by Silverlight

The final column will always be (0,0,1) because Silverlight supports only affine transformations. In reality, the transformation matrix is 2~TMS2, but it includes within its structure translation values for the x and y coordinates (in the third row). An affine transformation is essentially a linear transformation. Any three points that were on a line before the transformation continue to be on a line after the transformation. We won't trouble ourselves with proving this, since this isn't a math textbook, but if you look at a side of a rectangle in the preceding rotation and skewing figures, you'll see that three arbitrary points along this line are still on a line after the transformation (not the same line obviously, but *a* line nonetheless).

The bottom row of the 3~TMS3 matrix contains values for the x and y offsets. These offsets are used for translation. The M11, M12, M21, and M22 properties of the MatrixTransform class are used to specify the custom transformation. Projection and reflection are two examples of affine transformations not supported directly by Silverlight with a class of their own.

The simplest transformation is the translation. It allows you to specify only OffsetX and/or OffsetY to perform a translation without having to worry about an unexpected transformation happening if the M values are all 0 (actually, if they are all 0, the element undergoing transformation might disappear!) By setting M11 and M22 to 1, M12 and M21 to 0, the OffsetX property to 10, and the OffsetY property to 0, the transformation will shift the entire element being transformed ten units to the right. The transformed points are calculated by multiplying each point (x,y) in the element being transformed by the matrix shown in Figure 9-12.

$$\begin{bmatrix} 1 & 0 & 0 \\ 0 & 1 & 0 \\ 10 & 0 & 1 \end{bmatrix}$$

Figure 9-12. Transformation matrix to translate ten units to the right

In general, the result of multiplying a point (technically a vector) by the matrix is (x * M11 + y * M12 + offsetX), (x * M21 + y * M22 + offsetY). There is a special matrix, known as the *identity matrix*, where M11 = 1, M12 = 0, M21 = 0, and M22 = 1, and OffsetX and OffsetY are 0. If you multiply any (x,y) point by the identity matrix, you'll get the same point again, provided that OffsetX and OffsetY are 0. (Go ahead and try this on a piece of paper.) This identity matrix is important because it is the default configuration of the matrix. We can skew both coordinates and translate the element at the same time by specifying OffsetX and the M12 and M21 properties as follows:

```
<Rectangle Stroke="Crimson" Fill="Crimson" Width="50" Height="50">
    <Rectangle.RenderTransform>
        <MatrixTransform>
            <MatrixTransform.Matrix>
                <Matrix OffsetX="-10" M12="0.5" M21="0.5"/>
            </MatrixTransform.Matrix>
        </MatrixTransform>
    </Rectangle.RenderTransform>
</Rectangle>
```

From left to right, Figure 9-13 shows our normal rectangle, the rectangle translated right using a matrix, and the rectangle skewed and translated at the same time.

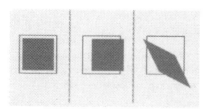

Figure 9-13. Using MatrixTransform to translate and skew/translate

Combining Multiple Transformations

While you could use the `MatrixTransform` class to combine multiple transformations into a single transformation, if you want to combine two or more of the directly supported transformations (such as a rotation and a scale), you can use the `TransformGroup` transform. Figure 9-14 shows the result of combining a `ScaleTransform` and a `RotateTransform` together inside a `TransformGroup`.

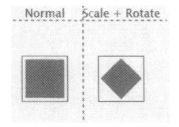

Figure 9-14. Combining transforms using TransformGroup

```
<Rectangle Stroke="Crimson" Fill="Crimson" Width="50" Height="50">
   <Rectangle.RenderTransform>
      <TransformGroup>
         <ScaleTransform ScaleX="0.75" ScaleY="0.75" CenterX="25" CenterY="25"/>
         <RotateTransform Angle="45" CenterX="25" CenterY="25"/>
      </TransformGroup>
   </Rectangle.RenderTransform>
</Rectangle>
```

The `TransformGroup` class is used in this code to apply multiple transformations simultaneously.

Composite Transformation

Silverlight 4 simplifies the code development to implement multiple transforms to an object by adding a `CompositeTransform` class. The `CompositeTransform` class provides a simpler way to transform an element, by simply offering a single object to instantiate rather than a group of transforms made for specific transforms.

In the previous example, we used the `TransformGroup` class to combine scale and rotate transformations to the rectangle. Using the single `CompositeTransform` XAML node (or code-behind), now you can combine scale, skew, rotate, and translate transformation all together. This simplifies the code and makes it more concise, user-friendly, and readable. There is one restriction to apply the composite transformation—it follows scale, skew, rotate, and translate transformation order to apply multiple transformations. If you have to follow a different order then you need to use the `TransformGroup` class.

Table 9-8 lists key properties of the `CompositeTransform` class.

Table 9-8. Key Properties of the `System.Windows.Media.CompositeTransform` *class*

Property	Type	Description
CenterX	double	Defines x-coordinate of the center point for all transforms specified by CompositeTransform.
CenterY	double	Defines y-coordinate of the center point for all transforms specified by the CompositeTransform.
Rotation	double	Defines angle for clockwise rotation (in degrees). The default value is 0.
ScaleX	double	Defines the *x*-axis scale factor for stretching or shrinking an object horizontally. The default value is 1 (the object is not scaled in horizontally). A 0 to 1 value decreases the width of the scaled object. A value set to more than 1 increases the width of the scaled object. 0 to -1 value flips the scale object horizontally and decreases its width. -1 value flips the scaled object but does not change the horizontal size. A value less than -1 flips the scale object and increases its width.
ScaleY	double	Defines the *y*-axis scale factor for stretching or shrinking an object vertically. The default value is 1 (the object is not scaled vertically). A 0 to 1 value decreases the height of the scaled object. A value set to more than 1 increases the height of the scaled object. A 0 to -1 value flips the scale object and decreases its height. A -1 value flips the scaled object but does not change the vertical size. A value less than -1 flips the scale object and increases its height.
SkewX	double	Defines the *x*-axis skew angle, which is measured in degrees counterclockwise from the *y* axis. A skew transform can be useful for creating the illusion of three-dimensional depth in a two-dimensional object. The default value is 0. Positive value results in the counterclockwise skew. Negative value results in the clockwise skew.
SkewY	double	Gets or sets the *y*-axis skew angle, which is measured in degrees counterclockwise from the *x* axis. A skew transform can be useful for creating the illusion of three-dimensional depth in a two-dimensional object. The default value is 0. Positive value results in the counterclockwise skew. Negative value results in the clockwise skew.
TranslateX	double	Defines the distance to translate along the *x* axis (in pixels). The default value is 0. Positive value moves the object to the right and negative moves it to the left.
TranslateY	double	Defines the distance to translate (move) an object along the *y* axis (in pixels). The default value is 0. Positive value moves the object down and negative moves it up.

If you rewrite the previous example using the `CompositeTransform`, the code will be concise, as shown here, and provide the same transformation as shown in Figure 9-14.

```
<Rectangle Stroke="Crimson" Fill="Crimson" Width="50" Height="50">
    <Rectangle.RenderTransform>
        <CompositeTransform ScaleX="0.75" ScaleY="0.75" Rotation="45"
            CenterX="25" CenterY="25" />
    </Rectangle.RenderTransform>
</Rectangle>
```

So far we have used the XAML code to apply the transforms to the objects at design time. You can apply transforms dynamically using code-behind. Just to demonstrate code-behind capability, you can apply the similar multiple transformation at runtime using the `CompositeTransform` class in code-behind. See the following self-explanatory code snippet.

```
CompositeTransform ct = new CompositeTransform();
ct.ScaleX = 0.75;
ct.ScaleY = 0.75;
ct.Rotation = 45;
ct.CenterX = 25;
ct.CenterY = 25;

rec.RenderTransform = ct;
```

3D Effects Using Perspective Transforms

Silverlight 3 introduced the capability to create 3D effects by using perspective transforms. This feature does not produce true 3D content since it does not support 3D mesh models, shading, hidden line removal, and so on; however, you can simulate live content rotation in the 3D space by applying perspective transforms to XAML elements. Another common scenario for using the perspective transforms is to arrange objects in relation to one another to create a 3D effect. You can apply perspective transforms to any XAML element such as a `DataGrid` or a `TextBox`.

To apply a perspective transform to a `UIElement`, you need to set the `UIElement` object's `Projection` property to `PlaneProjection`. The `PlaneProjection` class defines how the transform is rendered in space. Table 9-9 displays the key properties of the `PlaneProjection` class.

Table 9-9. Common Properties of the `System.Windows.Media.PlaneProjection` *Class*

Property	Type	Description
CenterOfRotationX	Double	Defines the x coordinate of the center of rotation of the object you rotate. The default value is 0.5 (center of object). Value range is between 0 and 1; 0 represents one edge of the object, and 1 represents the opposite edge.
CenterOfRotationY	Double	Defines the y coordinate of the center of rotation of the object you rotate. The default value is 0.5 (center of object). Value range is between 0 to 1; 0 represents one edge of the object, and 1 represents the opposite edge.

CenterOfRotationZ	Double	Defines the z coordinate of the center of rotation of the object you rotate. The default value is 0. A value greater than 0 corresponds to coordinates out from the plane of the object, while a negative value represents coordinates behind the plane of the object.
GlobalOffsetX	Double	Defines the distance the object is translated along the *x* axis of the screen.
GlobalOffsetY	Double	Defines the distance the object is translated along the *y* axis of the screen.
GlobalOffsetZ	Double	Defines the distance the object is translated along the *z* axis of the screen.
LocalOffsetX	Double	Defines the distance the object is translated along the *x* axis of the plane of the object.
LocalOffsetY	Double	Defines the distance the object is translated along the *y* axis of the plane of the object.
LocalOffsetZ	Double	Defines the distance the object is translated along the *z* axis of the plane of the object.
ProjectionMatrix	PlaneProjection	Gets the projection matrix on the PlaneProjection. The default value is a null reference.
RotationX	Double	Defines the number of degrees to rotate the object around the *x* axis of rotation. The default value is 0.
RotationY	Double	Defines the number of degrees to rotate the object around the *y* axis of rotation. The default value is 0.
RotationZ	Double	Defines the number of degrees to rotate the object around the *z* axis of rotation. The default value is 0.

Here is a simple example of rotating an image on the *y* axis with a slider by using element binding:

```xml
<UserControl x:Class="chapter9.PlanetProjectionDemo"
    xmlns="http://schemas.microsoft.com/winfx/2006/xaml/presentation"
    xmlns:x="http://schemas.microsoft.com/winfx/2006/xaml"
    xmlns:d="http://schemas.microsoft.com/expression/blend/2008"
    xmlns:mc="http://schemas.openxmlformats.org/markup-compatibility/2006"
    mc:Ignorable="d"
    d:DesignHeight="300" d:DesignWidth="400">

    <Grid x:Name="LayoutRoot" Background="White">
        <StackPanel>
```

```
            <Image x:Name="image1" Source="true.png" Stretch="None">
                <Image.Projection>
                    <PlaneProjection x:Name="Rotate" RotationY="45"></PlaneProjection>
                </Image.Projection>
            </Image>
            <Slider Value="{Binding RotationY, Mode=TwoWay, ElementName=Rotate}"↵
  Minimum="0" Maximum="360" ></Slider>
        </StackPanel>
    </Grid>
</UserControl>
```

Now when you run the project, you should see the check mark image set to 45 degrees by default, as shown in Figure 9-15. The image will rotate from 0 degrees on the left to 360 degrees on the right.

Figure 9-15. 3D effect by applying perspective transform

Pixel Shaders

Pixel shader effects drive the visual behavior of the graphical content. Pixel shaders are a set of software instructions that are used to calculate the color of individual pictures onscreen.

Pixel shader effects are introduced in Silverlight 3. By default, Silverlight 3 and 4 support drop-down and blur effects. You can create custom effects by using Microsoft's High-Level Shading Language (HLSL) and the DirectX SDK. However, in Silverlight, pixel shaders are rendered using a software-based algorithm and not on the GPU. Thus, pixel shader effects in Silverlight aren't nearly as fast as they might be using the GPU.

The `System.Windows.Media.Effects` library contains built-in pixel shaders for blurring and drop shadowing, and they can be added to an `Image` or `TextBlock` element using that element's `Effect` property in XAML or in the code-behind. In Chapter 1, we demonstrated the `DropShadowEffect` property using a TextBlock control. Here we will demonstrate the blur and drop shadow effects for an image using an Image control, and we will show how to set the `Effect` property of the Image control to the `BlurEffect` and `DropShadowEffect` effects:

```
<UserControl x:Class="chapter9.PixelShadderDemo"
    xmlns="http://schemas.microsoft.com/winfx/2006/xaml/presentation"
```

```
        xmlns:x="http://schemas.microsoft.com/winfx/2006/xaml"
        xmlns:d="http://schemas.microsoft.com/expression/blend/2008"
        xmlns:mc="http://schemas.openxmlformats.org/markup-compatibility/2006"
        mc:Ignorable="d"
        d:DesignHeight="300" d:DesignWidth="400">

    <StackPanel x:Name="LayoutRoot" Background="White"
        Orientation="Horizontal" >
        <StackPanel>
            <TextBlock Text="Blurr Effect" FontSize="12"
                Margin="15,0,0,0"/>
            <Image Source="lcd.png" Stretch="None" Margin="15,0,0,0" >
                <Image.Effect>
                    <BlurEffect Radius="5" />
                </Image.Effect>
            </Image>
        </StackPanel>
        <StackPanel>
            <TextBlock Text="DropShadow Effect" FontSize="12"
                Margin="40,0,0,0"/>
            <Image Source="lcd.png" Stretch="None" Margin="40,0,0,0" >
                <Image.Effect>
                    <DropShadowEffect ShadowDepth="8"/>
                </Image.Effect>
            </Image>
        </StackPanel>
    </StackPanel>
</UserControl>
```

Now when you run the project, you should see two images. The first image is blurred, and the second one has the drop shadow effect (see Figure 9-16).

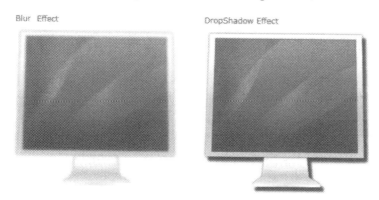

Figure 9-16. Blur and drop shadow effects for the Image control

▓ **Note** Windows Presentation Foundation Pixel Shader Effects Library (WPFSLFx) with sample HLSL effects for WPF and Silverlight applications is available on the codeplex site. You can get more details and download the sample, documentation, and library by visiting `http://wpffx.codeplex.com/`. However, it may not support Silverlight 4 as is.

Brushes

Throughout this book, brushes have been applied several times (generally, any time an element has been filled with a solid color). For filling with a solid color, the `SolidColorBrush` class is used. Silverlight also provides several other brushes, including an image brush, a video brush, and several gradient brushes. As you can probably surmise, combining a video brush with a geometric shape such as an ellipse or polygon (and perhaps even a transform) provides a staggering degree of flexibility in how content is presented in Silverlight. The hierarchy of brushes is shown in Figure 9-17.

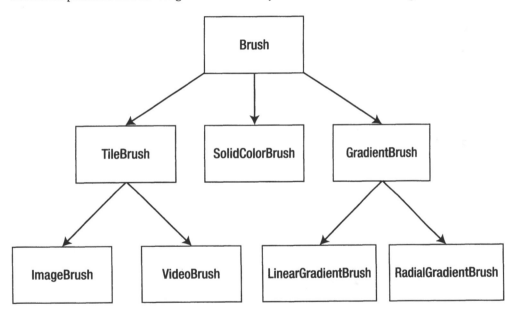

Figure 9-17. Inheritance hierarchy of Brush*-related classes*

The `System.Windows.Media.Brush` class forms the base of all the brushes in Silverlight. This class inherits directly from `DependencyObject`. Its properties are listed in Table 9-10.

Table 9-10. Properties of the `System.Windows.Media.Brush` *Class*

Property	Type	Description
Opacity	double	Gets or sets the opacity of the brush. A value of 0 specifies a fully transparent brush, and a value of 1 specifies a fully opaque brush. The default value is 1.
RelativeTransform	Transform	Applies a transform using relative coordinates. This is useful for applying a transform when the size of the surface being filled isn't known. The default value is null.
Transform	Transform	Applies a single transform using absolute coordinates. Use to apply scale, skew, rotate, translate, and transform group transformations.

The SolidColorBrush

The simplest brush you can use is the solid color brush. This inherits directly from **Brush** and thus does not share functionality with other brush types. The solid color brush has a single property, **Color**. In XAML, this can be set to the name of a color (see the **Brushes** class in the MSDN documentation online (`http://msdn.microsoft.com/en-us/library/system.windows.media.brushes.aspx`) for a full list of the colors, or use IntelliSense while editing the XAML in Visual Studio) or an ARGB value by using the hexadecimal value syntax (e.g., **#FFFF0000** for Red color). Filling a rectangle with a solid color (Crimson) can be accomplished with the following XAML:

```
<Rectangle Width="50" Height="50">
   <Rectangle.Fill>
      <SolidColorBrush Color="Crimson"/>
   </Rectangle.Fill>
</Rectangle>
```

The Tile Brushes

The parent of both **ImageBrush** and **VideoBrush** is **TileBrush**. This class cannot be instantiated on its own—it exists to provide tiling behavior to inheriting classes. There are four properties supported by the **TileBrush** class, listed in Table 9-11. Each is also a dependency property.

Table 9-11. Properties of the `System.Windows.Media.TileBrush` *Class*

Property	Type	Description
AlignmentX	AlignmentX	Horizontal alignment used for positioning. This can be set to Left, Center, or Right. The default value is Center.
AlignmentY	AlignmentY	Vertical alignment used for positioning. This can be set to Top, Center, or Bottom. The default value is Center.

Stretch	Stretch	Specifies how the contents of the brush fill the bounding space. Possible values are None, Uniform, UniformToFill, and Fill. The default value is Fill.

The ImageBrush

The ImageBrush is a type of TileBrush, which defines its content as an image. Earlier we drew a star using the Path class and filled it with the solid color brush. Instead you can fill up the image by using the image brush as shown in Figure 9-18.

Figure 9-18. Example of image brush

The following code snippet shows the related XAML:

```
<Path Stretch="Fill"
    StrokeThickness="2"
    StrokeLineJoin="Round"
    Stroke="Blue"
    Data="F1 M 0,100 L 150,100 L 200,0 L 250,100 L 400,100
        L 266, 150 L 300,300 L 200,170 L 110,300 L 133,150 Z ">
    <Path.Fill>
        <ImageBrush ImageSource="penguins.jpg"/>
    </Path.Fill>
</Path>
```

The Video Brush

The video brush works much like the image brush, but uses a video instead of an image. The VideoBrush class provides methods to play, pause, stop, and seek a different position in the video. The SourceName property of the VideoBrush class must be set to the name of a MediaElement specified in your XAML. You need to set the opacity of the media element to 0 to avoid displaying a media element–related video file. Mute the audio of the video file by setting the IsMuted property to true. The following XAML gives an example:

```
<MediaElement x:Name="videoMediaElement" Source="Wildlife.wmv" Opacity="0" />
<Rectangle Width="300" Height="250" Stroke="Red" StrokeThickness="2">
   <Rectangle.Fill>
      <VideoBrush SourceName="videoMediaElement" />
   </Rectangle.Fill>
</Rectangle>
```

The Gradient Brushes

There are two gradient brushes that are used to paint with a gradient of colors. The first is the linear gradient brush, used to paint a gradient along a straight line. The second is the radial gradient brush, used to spread colors across an elliptical surface. Both brushes utilize a gradient specified by one or more gradient stops. What a gradient looks like depends on the values of control parameters and gradient stops. *Gradient stops* specify the color at which a particular gradient ends. It's possible to paint multiple gradients within a surface by using multiple gradient stops. The `GradientBrush` class forms the base of both the linear and radial gradient brushes. The properties provided by `GradientBrush` are shown in Table 9-12.

Table 9-12. Properties of the `System.Windows.Media.GradientBrush` Class

Property	Type	Description
ColorInterpolationMode	ColorInterpolationMode	Specifies the color space to use when interpolating colors. Set it to `ScRgbLinearInterpolation` to use the scRGB space (visit http://en.wikipedia.org/wiki/ScRGB for more details) or `SRgbLinearInterpolation` to use the sRGB space (visit http://en.wikipedia.org/wiki/SRGB for more details).
GradientStops	GradientStopCollection	The collection of gradient stops defining how colors are spread in the surface being filled.
MappingMode	BrushMappingMode	Gets or sets the coordinate system used by the brush. Set this to `Absolute` for coordinates to be interpreted in local space, and set it to `RelativeToBoundingBox` to use coordinates relative to the bounding box (0 corresponds to 0 percent of the box, and 1 corresponds to 100 percent, so 0.5 would be interpreted as the center point). The default value is `RelativeToBoundingBox`. It does not affect offset values of gradient brushes.
SpreadMethod	GradientSpreadMethod	Gets or sets how the gradient is spread. Valid values are `Pad` (the default), `Reflect`, and `Repeat`.

The LinearGradientBrush

A linear gradient brush spreads a color gradient across a straight line. This straight line can be any straight line through the surface being painted, and is described by the StartPoint and EndPoint properties of the LinearGradientBrush class. The top-left corner is (0,0) and the bottom-right corner is (1,1). Using 0 and 1 for the start point and endpoint of each coordinate plane allows you to use this brush without worrying about the actual size of the surface being painted. It is through this line that the gradient spreads by default, starting from the top left and ending at the bottom right. You can see this default behavior in the first column of Figure 9-19.

If you specify only a single gradient stop, the linear gradient brush paints a solid color. If you use two gradient stops—for example, starting at black (#FF000000) and ending in red (#FFFF0000)—the gradient starts at black and the color spreads evenly from black to red along the length of the surface being painted, until the end of the surface is reached. Multiple gradient stops can be specified along a gradient line from 0.0 to 1.0 by using the Offset property of gradient stop.

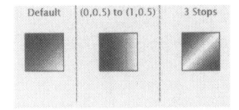

Figure 9-19. Different configurations of the linear gradient brush

Figure 9-19 shows the behavior of several different options for the linear gradient brush. The default behavior is shown first, spreading from black to white. Here's the XAML for this gradient:

```
<Rectangle Stroke="Black" Width="60" Height="60">
   <Rectangle.Fill>
      <LinearGradientBrush>
         <GradientStop Color="#FF000000" Offset="0.0"/>
         <GradientStop Color="#FFFFFFFF" Offset="1.0"/>
      </LinearGradientBrush>
   </Rectangle.Fill>
</Rectangle>
```

The following code shows how to spread the gradient horizontally instead of diagonally:

```
<Rectangle Stroke="Black" Width="60" Height="60">
   <Rectangle.Fill>
      <LinearGradientBrush StartPoint="0,0.5" EndPoint="1,0.5">
         <GradientStop Color="#FF000000" Offset="0.0"/>
         <GradientStop Color="#FFFFFFFF" Offset="1.0"/>
      </LinearGradientBrush>
   </Rectangle.Fill>
</Rectangle>
```

The next code block creates a gradient that spreads to the center point of the gradient line and a second gradient that spreads from the center point to fill up the other half of the surface:

```
<Rectangle Stroke="Black" Width="60" Height="60">
   <Rectangle.Fill>
      <LinearGradientBrush>
         <GradientStop Color="#FF000000" Offset="0.0"/>
         <GradientStop Color="#FFFFFFFF" Offset="0.5"/>
         <GradientStop Color="#FF000000" Offset="1.0"/>
      </LinearGradientBrush>
   </Rectangle.Fill>
</Rectangle>
```

The RadialGradientBrush

The radial gradient brush spreads a color gradient from a point outward in an elliptical pattern. The Center property specifies the center of the ellipse, and the RadiusX and RadiusY properties control how the ellipse is shaped. If RadiusX and RadiusY are equal, the resulting ellipse is a circle. The GradientOrigin property specifies the point at which the gradient starts. The gradient spreads outward from this point until it completely fills the bounding ellipse.

Figure 9-20 shows various radial gradients.

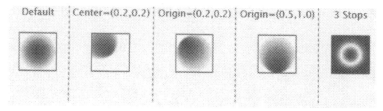

Figure 9-20. Different configurations of the radial gradient brush

The left-hand image in Figure 9-20 shows the default radial gradient, with the center at (0.5,0.5) and the gradient going from black to white. Here's the XAML for this first radial gradient example:

```
<Rectangle Stroke="Black" Width="60" Height="60">
   <Rectangle.Fill>
      <RadialGradientBrush>
         <GradientStop Color="#FF000000" Offset="0.0"/>
         <GradientStop Color="#FFFFFFFF" Offset="1.0"/>
      </RadialGradientBrush>
   </Rectangle.Fill>
</Rectangle>
```

The first two examples use different gradient origins, and the final one uses gradient stops.

Transparency and Opacity Masks

Silverlight supports true transparency for all UI Elements. So if you create layer of controls on top of one another and set their Opacity property to varying value, you can see through controls visual. So you can think of using this feature to create a background that "shows through" the controls that you place on top of it. With Silverlight 4, now all PNG formats are supported with proper transparency. There are several ways you can set the transparency of an element.

- *Setting Opacity property.* Opacity of given UIElement can be set to any fractional value from 0 to 1, where 1 is completely solid (the default value) and 0 is completely transparent.

- *Using brushes.* Various Brush classes that you just learned about have an Opacity property that can be set properly to make their fill transparent.

- *Using semitransparent color.* Setting the Alpha value to less than 255 makes the color semitransparent. You can set the Alpha value right in the Properties pane of the given control in Visual Studio 2010, as shown in the Figure 9-21.

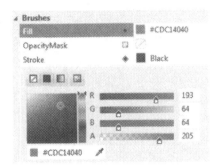

Figure 9-21. Setting the Alpha value of UI control in Visual Studio 2010

- *Using OpacityMask property.* The OpacityMask property enables you to make a specific region of an element partially transparent. It can be set to any brush object. As stated earlier, the Alpha channel of the brush will determine the offset of the transparency. The following code snippet shows how to set OpacityMask to RadialGradientBrush for Rectangle element (the resultant outcome is shown in Figure 9-22).

```
<Rectangle Height="100" HorizontalAlignment="Left" Width="200"
    Fill="Red">
    <Rectangle.OpacityMask>
        <RadialGradientBrush>
            <GradientStop Color="White" Offset="0.538" />
            <GradientStop Color="#23FFFFFF" Offset="1" />
        </RadialGradientBrush>
    </Rectangle.OpacityMask>
</Rectangle>
```

Figure 9-22. Using OpacityMask on Rectangle element

413

Summary

This chapter has covered much more of the support Silverlight provides for building user interfaces. First, it covered the support Silverlight provides for 2D drawing, including the **Geometry**- and **Shape**-based classes. Then it covered the various transformations (including the newly introduced composite transformation) used to alter how elements are rendered, such as applying a rotation.

You also learned about creating 3D effects using perspective transforms, pixel shaders, and the existing brush capability in Silverlight that provides flexibility in how content is drawn within bounding elements. You can achieve some interesting effects when you animate the properties of a brush. In the next chapter, we will cover animation, and by combining transformations with animation, you can perform interesting effects such as setting something spinning by continually altering its rotational angle.

CHAPTER 10

■ ■ ■

Animation

When it comes to making user interfaces that make people go "wow," you have many of the pieces of the puzzle: media (video/audio/images), brushes to easily create interesting surfaces, and a set of controls that can be completely re-skinned. There's one final big piece of the user interface support in Silverlight: animation. Silverlight makes it easy to make elements of user interfaces move, and when you put together the various components into a full application, you end up with something quite interesting. Any dependency property can potentially be influenced by animation. If you give some thought to the various properties discussed throughout this book, such as transforms and brushes, it's possible to start coming up with a variety of creative effects to jazz up a user interface. For example, by shifting offsets in gradient stops, a gradient can appear to move from one side of the surface it is filling to the other side, creating a shimmer effect. This chapter will delve into how to use animation and also discuss the support Expression Blend provides for working with animation.

Introduction to Silverlight Animation

At its most basic, animation is the modification of a property value over time. Since we generally want animation to cause a visual effect, such as a moving object on the screen, the properties you'll animate are sizes, positions, transforms, etc. If you place a rectangle on a canvas and set its `Canvas.Left` property to the width of the canvas (so it sits just off the right side), and then decrement the `Canvas.Left` property until it reaches zero, the rectangle will seem like it is suddenly appearing and moving until it settles at the far left of the canvas. The animation is made up of one logical frame (in reality, many more actual frames are involved) per change to the `Canvas.Left` property, but because the rectangle is re-positioned and updated quickly, it seems to the human eye like the rectangle is moving smoothly from one side to the other. This is the illusion of animation that we are witness to on a daily basis when we watch television or movies, or play video games.

Silverlight provides two animation mechanisms: from/to/by animation (a.k.a. basic animation) and keyframe animation. While from/to/by is a somewhat awkward name, it also explicitly describes what it is. The "from" part specifies the initial value of a particular property, the "to" is the final value of the property, and "by" is how much that value should change for each step during the animation. With the from/to/by animation type, the property value varies smoothly and continuously over the duration of the animation. Three animation classes of Silverlight are applicable to the from/to/by animation type, `DoubleAnimation`, `PointAnimation`, and `ColorAnimation`. The keyframe animation provides far more flexibility. Instead of specifying the from/to/by type, you specify what the value of the property should be at specific times. With keyframe animation, values can jump abruptly from one value to another, or they can combine jumps and periods of linear interpolation. Silverlight animation classes—`ColorAnimationUsingKeyFrames`, `DoubleAnimationUsingKeyFrames`, `PointAnimationUsingKeyFrames`, and `ObjectAnimationUsingKeyFrames`—are applicable to keyframe animation. Since only property values and their coinciding times are specified, the property must know how to change. This is accomplished via interpolation, and there are many ways you can specify this interpolation, such as using the new animation-easing functions introduced in Silverlight 3 to easily create a bouncing effect. Whether you use from/to/by animation or keyframe animation, the actual animation is controlled by a storyboard. The storyboard contains a specific animation, such as moving our rectangle from the right to the left using a from/to/by animation. Before we delve into the specifics of storyboards and animation techniques, it's important to understand how time is used by the animation system in Silverlight.

Timelines

In Silverlight, the System.Windows.Media.Animation.Timeline class represents a timeline and forms the base class for the various types of animations (shown in Figure 10-1). The two types of animation Silverlight provides are *from/to/by* and *keyframe*. From/to/by animations make it easy to specify the start and end values for a property. Keyframe animations, however, provide much more control because each keyframe specifies a property's value at a specific time. All animations happen over a length of time. The base Timeline class provides time-related behavior to inheritors, featuring a number of properties controlling duration, repeat behavior, and the speed at which time elapses.

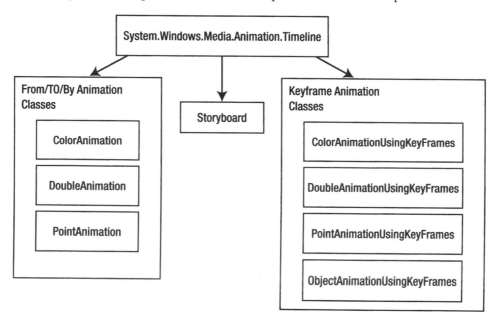

Figure 10-1. Timeline-related animation classes

The Timeline class defines six properties that influence how time is represented and manipulated. These properties are listed in Table 10-1.

Table 10-1. Properties of System.Windows.Media.Animation.Timeline

Property	Type	Description
AutoReverse	Bool	If True, the animation will happen once and then repeat once in the reverse direction. For more than a single reverse, also use RepeatBehavior.
BeginTime	Nullable<TimeSpan>	If this property is null, it indicates there is no BeginTime. This property can be used to stack animations back to back, so if one animation takes two seconds, the BeginTime of the second animation can be set to 2s so that it starts immediately after the first.
Duration	Duration	This represents the duration of a single sequence of the animation.
FillBehavior	Animation.FillBehavior	This specifies what happens when an animation hits its end. Set this to HoldEnd to make the animation maintain its final value until the end of its parent's active period, or to Stop to make the animation stop when it reaches its end, even if its parent is inside its active period.
RepeatBehavior	Animation.RepeatBehavior	This specifies how many times the timeline repeats (or if it should repeat forever) and the total length of time.
SpeedRatio	Double	This specifies the rate of time at which the current timeline elapses relative to its parent. The default value is 1.

Let us consider the SpeedRatio property in detail. If the SpeedRatio is set to three, then the animation completes three times faster. If you decrease it, the animation is slowed down (for example, if SpeedRatio is set to 0.5 then the animation takes twice as long). Although the overall effect is the same as changing the Duration property of your animation, setting SpeedRatio makes it easier to control how simultaneous animations overlap.

The following snapshot describes the DoubleAnimation of the from/to/by type with the SpeedRatio property set to two. This will cause the fade-in effect on the Image1 Image control to be completed in 0.5 seconds.

```
<Storyboard x:Name="fadeIn">
    <DoubleAnimation From="0" To="1"
        Storyboard.TargetName="Image1"
        Storyboard.TargetProperty="Opacity"
        SpeedRatio="2">
    </DoubleAnimation>
</Storyboard>
```

The Timeline class also provides a single event, Completed, that fires when the timeline has reached its end. Timeline's properties provide a wide range of capabilities of how time is managed and consequently how animation occurs. There are some subtleties in how the properties work together and how a parent timeline can affect a child timeline, so we need to dig deeper into how these properties work.

AutoReverse

The AutoReverse property causes the animation to happen in reverse after the animation reaches its end, much like rewinding a tape in a VCR while it is still playing. Figure 10-2 shows what using this property by itself does to a timeline. Note that the forward iteration happens once, the reverse iteration happens once, and then the timeline stops.

Consider the following XAML code snippet:

```
<UserControl x:Class="chapter10.AutoReverseDemo"
    xmlns="http://schemas.microsoft.com/winfx/2006/xaml/presentation"
    xmlns:x="http://schemas.microsoft.com/winfx/2006/xaml"
    xmlns:d="http://schemas.microsoft.com/expression/blend/2008"
    xmlns:mc="http://schemas.openxmlformats.org/markup-compatibility/2006"
    mc:Ignorable="d"
    d:DesignHeight="300" d:DesignWidth="400">
    <Grid x:Name="LayoutRoot" Background="White">
        <Grid.Resources>
            <Storyboard x:Name="Grow" AutoReverse="True" >
                <DoubleAnimation Storyboard.TargetName="btnGrow"
                    Storyboard.TargetProperty="Width"
                    From="150" To="300" Duration="0:0:5">
                </DoubleAnimation>
            </Storyboard>
        </Grid.Resources>
        <Button x:Name="btnGrow" Width="150" Height="150"
            Content="This button grows" SizeChanged="btnGrow_SizeChanged" />
    </Grid>
</UserControl>
```

In the previous XAML code, we defined one simple Storyboard, "Grow," as having the AutoReverse property set to True, so the animation will grow the Width of the Button "btnGrow" to 300 from 150 in five seconds. Here you describe the format of Duration in Hours:Minutes:Seconds, so 0:0:5 represents five seconds. As AutoReverse is set to True, the reverse iteration will happen and the button will be set to its original Width after forward iteration completes. So this animation will cause the button to grow in width from 150px to 300px and then shrink from 300px to 150px.

As shown in the following code-behind, we will start the Grow storyboard first in the Loaded event. With the help of the SizeChanged event, when the Width of the Button control reaches 300px, the text changes to "This button now shrinks" and the button will shrink, since AutoReverse is set to True.

```
public AutoReverseDemo()
{
    InitializeComponent();
    this.Loaded += new RoutedEventHandler(AutoReverseDemo_Loaded);
}
void AutoReverseDemo_Loaded(object sender, RoutedEventArgs e)
{
```

```
    Grow.Begin();
}

void btnGrow_SizeChanged(object sender, SizeChangedEventArgs e)
{
    if (btnGrow.ActualWidth == 300)
    {
        btnGrow.Content = "This button now shrinks";
    }
}
```

Figure 10-2 shows the Button "btnGrow" in the forward and reverse iteration stages.

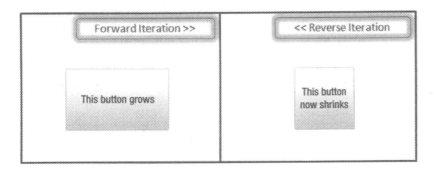

Figure 10-2. An example of the AutoReverse property

BeginTime

The BeginTime property is used to delay the start of the timeline. When the timeline is started (such as by starting an animation), the current value of this property is used, so this can be changed after a timeline is stopped but before it is restarted. Figure 10-3 illustrates the BeginTime property.

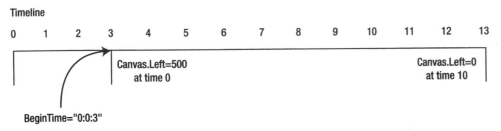

Figure 10-3. Illustration of BeginTime's effect on a timeline

---

Note The BeginTime property is of type TimeSpan. This type specifies a length of time measured in days, hours, minutes, seconds, and fractions of a second. The XAML syntax to specify a TimeSpan takes the form of [*days.*]*hours:minutes:seconds*[*.fractional seconds*]. The days and fractional seconds are optional and are separated from their nearest neighbor by a period instead of a colon. Hours, minutes, and seconds, however, are mandatory.

Again, we have a 10-second timeline, but there is a 3-second delay. The timeline automatically lengthens by the addition of BeginTime and the timeline's Duration. In this case, a 10-second timeline becomes a 13-second timeline. Since the timeline is used for animation, you can see the begin time as a measure of time to delay before the animation starts. This makes it possible to place timelines back to back and cause them to execute in sequence by setting the BeginTime of the next timeline to the length of time it takes for all previous timelines to complete.

It is also possible to specify a negative BeginTime. Doing this provides a way to start the animation at a specified point later in the timeline than its true beginning. For example, a 10-second timeline with a BeginTime of 0:0:-2 starts the timeline at two seconds, as if the timeline started at the specified time in the past. This would cause the 10-second timeline to be active for only eight seconds.

Duration

The Duration property represents the timeline of a single iteration. This property is of the special type System.Windows.Duration. While the Duration type can represent a time span (and uses the same syntax as any property of type TimeSpan when specified in markup), you can also set a property of this type to the special value Automatic. The effects of using Automatic differ depending on whether this property is used on a Storyboard (a Storyboard contains one or more animations, and will be discussed shortly) or on a specific animation. When set on a Storyboard, Automatic causes Duration to be set to the length of time for all the animations it contains put together. For animations, Automatic causes Duration to be set to one second (0:0:1). The 1-second default ensures that the animation does something, despite its brevity. You'll rarely if ever use the Automatic value on animations directly. Figure 10-4 highlights the Duration section of the previous timeline.

Caution The value Forever can also be specified for properties of type Duration, but this property value is deprecated; do not use it. See the "RepeatBehavior" section of this chapter for details on how to cause an animation to run continuously.

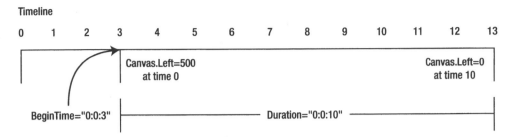

Figure 10-4. Illustration of Duration *combined with* BeginTime

FillBehavior

An animation's *active period*—also known as the animation's *fill period*—is the time during which the animation is happening. The FillBehavior property specifies what happens when the end of the fill period is reached. It can be set to two values: Stop and HoldEnd. When set to HoldEnd, the animation appears to freeze in its final state. For our original moving rectangle example, this means that the rectangle would stop at the left side of the screen, holding its final property value from the animation. The value Stop, however, causes the animation to freeze in its initial state instead of its final state. For our rectangle, this means that after the rectangle reaches the left side, it disappears (since it started completely off the right side of the canvas).

RepeatBehavior

RepeatBehavior, as its name implies, controls how the timeline repeats. It can take one of three forms: a time span, an iteration count, or the special property value Forever (which causes the repetition to happen continuously). The RepeatBehavior property is of the type Animation.RepeatBehavior, which has two properties that specify the exact repeat behavior: Count and Duration. The Count property is of type double and specifies the number of times the timeline should repeat. Since this is a double property, it's possible to repeat a fraction of the timeline by specifying a value (e.g., 1.5). To specify the Count property in XAML, the property value must be followed by x (e.g., 1.5x) to indicate that the timeline repeats a full iteration and a half. There is also a boolean property, HasCount, which is set to True if the RepeatBehavior represents a Count.

The Duration property is the other means used to specify a repeat behavior. This property is of type Duration and is used to specify the total time to run the animation. If the Duration of the repeat is longer than the Duration of the timeline, the timeline will continue for the length of the RepeatBehavior's duration. If the repeat's duration is shorter, however, the timeline will stop before reaching its end. For example, if the Duration of the RepeatBehavior property is set to 0:0:5 and the timeline's duration is 0:0:2, the timeline will repeat one and a half times.

There is also a HasDuration property that is set to true when the Duration is specified. It is also possible to set RepeatBehavior to Forever, which represents an animation that continuously repeats.

SpeedRatio

The SpeedRatio property is used to increase or decrease the rate at which time elapses within a timeline. When this value is greater than 1.0 (its default value), the time elapses faster. Likewise, values less than 1.0 cause the timeline to elongate. See Figure 10-5 for a representation of our 10-second timeline sped up and slowed down. The total length of time for a timeline with this property set (and the other properties set to their defaults) is its Duration multiplied by the SpeedRatio.

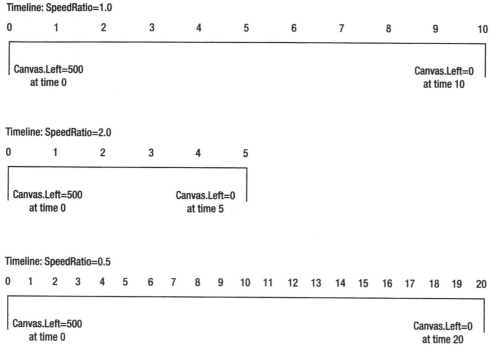

Timeline: SpeedRatio=1.0

| 0 | 1 | 2 | 3 | 4 | 5 | 6 | 7 | 8 | 9 | 10 |

Canvas.Left=500 at time 0

Canvas.Left=0 at time 10

Timeline: SpeedRatio=2.0

| 0 | 1 | 2 | 3 | 4 | 5 |

Canvas.Left=500 at time 0

Canvas.Left=0 at time 5

Timeline: SpeedRatio=0.5

| 0 | 1 | 2 | 3 | 4 | 5 | 6 | 7 | 8 | 9 | 10 | 11 | 12 | 13 | 14 | 15 | 16 | 17 | 18 | 19 | 20 |

Canvas.Left=500 at time 0

Canvas.Left=0 at time 20

Figure 10-5. Illustration of different SpeedRatio values

If we put all these properties together (disregarding a RepeatBehavior set to Forever), the total time it takes for an animation is described by the formula shown in Figure 10-6.

$$\text{Total Timeline Duration} + \text{Begin Time} + \frac{\text{RepeatBehavior}}{\text{(as a TimeSpan)}} + \frac{\text{Duration} \times (\text{AutoReverse ? 2 : 1})}{\text{SpeedRatio}} \times \frac{\text{RepeatBehavior}}{\text{(as a double)}}$$

Figure 10-6. Formula describing total time span of a timeline

Now that you're familiar with how timelines can be represented and manipulated, it's time to see exactly what the animation classes bring to the table beyond the inherited timeline support.

Storyboards and Animation

The Storyboard class also inherits from Timeline. This is a special class used as a container for other animations. Its timeline represents a length of time corresponding to the combination of all the timelines in animations stored in the storyboard (if left unspecified) or a length of time that constrains the total animation runtime. The most important aspects of this class are its methods to begin, stop, pause, and resume the animation. These, along with the other methods of the class, are described in Table 10-2.

Table 10-2. Methods of System.Windows.Media.Animation.Storyboard

Method	Description
Begin	Starts the animation with the first timeline in the storyboard.
GetCurrentState	Returns a ClockState enumeration value. Possible states are Active (the animation is active and is changing in direct relation to its parent timeline), Filling (the animation is active but not changing in direct relation to its parent—e.g., it might be paused), and Stopped.
GetCurrentTime	Returns a TimeSpan value corresponding to the current time in the storyboard's timeline.
Pause	Pauses the current storyboard's timeline. Call Resume to unpause the timeline.
Resume	Resumes the current storyboard's timeline.
Seek	Accepts a TimeSpan value corresponding to the time in the storyboard's timeline to move to. This can be done while an animation is active or inactive. The seek operation happens on the next clock tick.
SeekAlignedToLastTick	Same as Seek, but the seek operation happens relative to the last clock tick.
SkipToFill	Changes the frame of the animation to the end of the storyboard's active period. If AutoReverse is True, the end of the active period is the initial frame of the animation. If RepeatBehavior is Forever, using this method throws an InvalidOperation exception.
Stop	Stops the animation.

Since the Storyboard class isn't particularly interesting by itself, you'll see it in action when we take a closer look at the animation classes.

From/To/By Animations

The simplest form of animation is generally referred to as from/to/by because of its nature. As explained earlier, three animation classes of Silverlight are applicable to the from/to/by animation type—

DoubleAnimation, PointAnimation, and ColorAnimation. The From and To in its name refer to the fact that these animations modify a target property's value starting at the From value and ending at the To value (not taking into account different configurations of the timeline). The By property provides a relative offset controlling where the animation ends, and it is ignored if combined with the To property. Each of these properties can be used by themselves. Table 10-3 describes these properties and how they control the timeline when we use them by themselves.

Table 10-3. Usages of From/To/By Properties

Property	Description
From	This specifies the starting value of the property to animate. The animation stops at the base value of the target property or at the final value of the target property from a previous animation.
To	The target property's value starts at its base value or its final value from a previous animation. It finishes at the value specified in the To property.
By	The target property's value starts at its base value or its final value from a previous animation. The final value of the target property is its initial value added to the value specified in the By property.

The combination of the From/To properties specify the initial (From) and final (To) values of the target Storyboard. The combination of From/By specifies the initial value of the target Storyboard and an offset value used to calculate the target's final value (From + By); however, if you also specify To, it will override the By value.

Foreground Animation: An Example

Since we've been using From/To properties often in our applications, let's take a look at how the moving rectangle is animated using XAML. Nothing interesting is going on with the rectangle itself. We give it a name, a position, a size, and a fill with a storyboard named *rectAnimation* as shown in the following code snippet:

```
<Canvas x:Name="LayoutRoot" Background="White">
    <Canvas.Resources>
        <Storyboard x:Name="rectAnimation">
            <DoubleAnimation Storyboard.TargetName="rect" Duration="0:0:2"
                Storyboard.TargetProperty="(Canvas.Left)" From="370" To="5" />
        </Storyboard>
    </Canvas.Resources>
    <Rectangle x:Name="rect" Width="25" Height="25"
        Canvas.Left="370" Canvas.Top="270" Fill="Black"/>
</Canvas>
```

DoubleAnimation is a type of animation used to modify properties of type double. The other two from/to/by animation classes exist to animate points (PointAnimation) and colors (ColorAnimation). Nothing particularly complicated is going on in this example—Storyboard.TargetName refers to the object to animate and Storyboard.TargetProperty is the property to animate. You should be familiar with Duration, From, and To.

Caution If you set a Duration on a storyboard that is less than the length of time of the animations the storyboard contains, the animations will not have a chance to run to completion. While this should come as no surprise, it has repercussions when you don't specify the Duration on the animations within the storyboard. Individual animations default to one second, so a storyboard with a Duration of less than one second will cause behavior that might be unexpected if you're unprepared.

Attempting to animate a single target property using multiple animations within a single storyboard will cause the animation to fail (and possibly your application to crash if you don't handle the exception). This happens even if you stagger the animations using the BeginTime property. If you want to stagger animations of a specific property, place them in different storyboards and handle the Completed event to transition to the next storyboard automatically. For example, assume that we have created three storyboards named "SB1," "SB2," and "SB3." If we want to start these storyboards one after another in the order SB1, SB2, SB3, we need to wire up the Completed event as shown in the following code snippet.

```
SB1.Completed += new EventHandler(SB1_Completed);
SB2.Completed += new EventHandler(SB2_Completed);

void SB1_Completed(object sender, EventArgs e)
{
  SB2.Begin();
}

void SB2_Completed(object sender, EventArgs e)
{
  SB3.Begin();
}
```

You should take note of how the TargetProperty adheres to the property path syntax. The simplest property path is the name of a dependency property on the object specified in TargetName. Take, for example, the Width property:

```
TargetProperty = "Width"
```

If you want to specify an attached property (described in Chapter 2), it must be surrounded by parentheses. This was shown earlier with the Canvas.Left property:

```
TargetProperty = "(Canvas.Left)"
```

The object to the left of the dot can be qualified with an XML namespace prefix if the class is not located in the default XML namespace. The property to the right of the dot must be a dependency property. If you want to access a subproperty, you can use the parentheses to surround a *Type.Property* string before accessing the subproperty. For example, if you want to use a `ColorAnimation` to change the background of our moving rectangle, you can specify it using either of the following syntaxes for `TargetProperty`:

```
TargetProperty = "(Rectangle.Fill).Color"
TargetProperty = "(Rectangle.Fill).(SolidColorBrush.Color)"
```

The second syntax simply adds the extra qualification to the `Color` property. This syntax illustrates how to specify other subproperties if they are needed. A final syntax for property paths is required for animating elements such as gradient stops that require indexing:

```
TargetProperty = "GradientStops[0].Offset"
```

As previously shown, the three types of properties you can animate with from/to/by animations are `doubles`, `Points`, and `Colors`. None of these classes provide any specific properties unique to them, and having seen XAML throughout this book, you should be familiar with the property syntaxes for these types. The important thing to keep in mind is that from/to/by animations provide a linear interpolation of values, meaning that the rate at which animation happens is the difference between the initial and final property values during a single iteration, divided by the duration of a single iteration. That is, the rate of change is constant throughout the entire duration of the animation. If you want more control over the animation or the possibility of differing rates of change, Silverlight provides something called a *keyframe animation*, which is discussed in the next section.

Let's make the rectangle animation a little more complicated. In the next example, the rectangle will make a circuit around its host canvas and slowly spin as it goes around. While this implies two logical animations, it requires five actual animations (one for each side of the canvas and one for the rotation) and three storyboards (two for the circuit, since we can't animate the same property twice within a storyboard, and one for the rotation). Each animation is controlled by its own start/stop and pause/resume button.

Note Many of the animation examples use the `Canvas.Left` and `Canvas.Top` attached properties to change an object's position during animation. In more complete applications, this is a poor approach because it assumes the object being animated is within a Canvas and that the position uses absolute coordinates. A much better approach to animating the position and size of objects is to animate the `TranslateTransform` and `ScaleTransform` properties that belong to the object being animated.

The following is the complete XAML code:

```
<UserControl x:Class="chapter10.FromToAnimationDemo"
    xmlns="http://schemas.microsoft.com/winfx/2006/xaml/presentation"
    xmlns:x="http://schemas.microsoft.com/winfx/2006/xaml"
    xmlns:d="http://schemas.microsoft.com/expression/blend/2008"
    xmlns:mc="http://schemas.openxmlformats.org/markup-compatibility/2006"
```

```xml
        mc:Ignorable="d"
        d:DesignHeight="300" d:DesignWidth="400">

    <StackPanel Orientation="Vertical" x:Name="LayoutRoot" Background="White">
        <StackPanel Orientation="Horizontal" Grid.Row="0" Grid.Column="0"↵
Background="White">
            <StackPanel Orientation="Vertical">
                <TextBlock FontSize="14">Movement Animation</TextBlock>
                <StackPanel Orientation="Horizontal" Margin="15 0 0 0">
                    <Button Content="Start" x:Name="movementStartStopButton" Margin="2"↵
Width="40"
                        Click="movementStartStopButton_Click"/>
                    <Button Content="Pause" x:Name="movementPauseResumeButton" Margin="2"
                        Width="60" Click="movementPauseResumeButton_Click"/>
                </StackPanel>
            </StackPanel>
            <StackPanel Orientation="Vertical" Margin="15 0 0 0">
                <TextBlock FontSize="14">Rotation Animation</TextBlock>
                <StackPanel Orientation="Horizontal" Margin="10 0 0 0">
                    <Button Content="Start" x:Name="rotationStartStopButton" Margin="2"↵
Width="40"
                        Click="rotationStartStopButton_Click" />
                    <Button Content="Pause" x:Name="rotationPauseResumeButton" Margin="2"↵
Width="60"
                        Click="rotationPauseResumeButton_Click"/>
                </StackPanel>
            </StackPanel>
        </StackPanel>
        <Canvas>
            <Canvas.Resources>
                <Storyboard x:Name="rectAnimation" Completed="rectAnimation_Completed">
                    <DoubleAnimation Storyboard.TargetName="rect" Duration="0:0:2"
                        Storyboard.TargetProperty="(Canvas.Left)" From="370" To="5"  />
                </Storyboard>
                <Storyboard x:Name="rectAnimBottomLeft"↵
Completed="rectAnimBottomLeft_Completed">
                    <DoubleAnimation Storyboard.TargetName="rect"
                        Storyboard.TargetProperty="(Canvas.Top)" From="270" To="5"
                        Duration="0:0:2" BeginTime="0:0:2"/>
                </Storyboard>
                <Storyboard x:Name="rectAnimTopRight">
                    <DoubleAnimation Storyboard.TargetName="rect"
                        Storyboard.TargetProperty="(Canvas.Left)"  From="5" To="370"↵
Duration="0:0:2"/>
                    <DoubleAnimation Storyboard.TargetName="rect"
                        Storyboard.TargetProperty="(Canvas.Top)" From="5" To="270"
                        Duration="0:0:2" BeginTime="0:0:2" />
                </Storyboard>
                <Storyboard x:Name="rectRotationAnim">
                    <DoubleAnimation Storyboard.TargetName="rect"
                        Storyboard.TargetProperty=
```

```
                               "(UIElement.RenderTransform).(TransformGroup.Children)[0]↵
         .(RotateTransform.Angle)"
                               From="0" To="360" RepeatBehavior="Forever" Duration="0:0:4" />
                </Storyboard>
            </Canvas.Resources>
            <Rectangle x:Name="rect" Width="25" Height="25"
                    Canvas.Left="370" Canvas.Top="270" Fill="Black">
                <Rectangle.RenderTransform>
                    <TransformGroup>
                        <RotateTransform Angle="0">
                        </RotateTransform>
                    </TransformGroup>
                </Rectangle.RenderTransform>
            </Rectangle>
        </Canvas>
    </StackPanel>
</UserControl>
```

We define the Completed event handlers in order to track which of the movement animations is currently executing, as well Click event handlers to control the animation (start, pause, and stop animation).

Caution Never invoke the Begin method in a constructor to start animation when the page is loaded. The animation will not start and you will not get any feedback detailing why. Instead, handle the Loaded event of the UserControl or a layout container, and then invoke Begin.

```
private void rectAnimBottomLeft_Completed(object sender, EventArgs e)
{
    //current is a reference of Storyboard
      //that is used for Pause/Resume
    current = rectAnimTopRight;
    rectAnimTopRight.Begin();
}
private void rectAnimTopRight_Completed(object sender, EventArgs e)
{
    current = rectAnimBottomLeft;
    rectAnimBottomLeft.Begin();
}
```

The start/stop and pause/resume functionalities for each animation are similar. Here's the pause/resume button click handler. We need to check whether the animation is running and whether it's paused (in order to build the expected behavior into the buttons).

```
private void movementPauseResumeButton_Click(object sender, RoutedEventArgs e)
{
    if(current.GetCurrentState() != ClockState.Stopped && !movementPaused)
    {
```

```
        current.Pause();
        movementPauseResumeButton.Content = "Resume";
        movementPaused = true;
    }
    else
    {
        current.Resume();
        movementPauseResumeButton.Content = "Pause";
        movementPaused = false;
    }
}
```

You should get the controlled rectangle animation (movement and rotation animation) if you run the program now. Figure 10-7 shows the animated rectangle at different times.

Rectangle with no animation – Initial Position

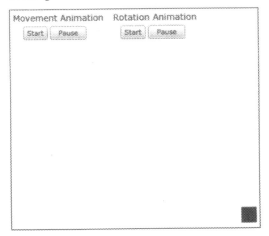

Rectangle with Movement Animation

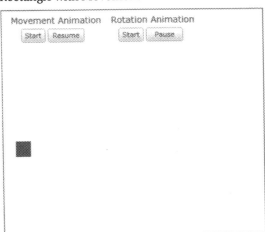

Rectangle with Movement and Rotation Animation

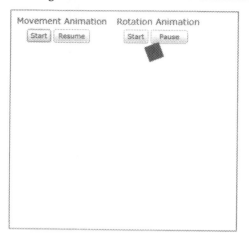

Figure 10-7. *Animated rectangle example demonstrating foreground animation*

Shimmering Effect for Background Animation: An Example

Animation does not need to always happen in the foreground. Let us construct a quick example to create a shimmering effect in the background by changing gradient offsets in a linear gradient brush that is used as the background for a Canvas. We will also handle the Loaded event of the Canvas in order to start the animation. We add a rectangle to demonstrate background animation clearly. Next we need to create a storyboard named shimmer to create animation that changes the offsets for each gradient stop evenly over the duration of the animation (one second). The storyboard's duration is set to five seconds so that the shimmering effect doesn't immediately repeat. If it did, it would make the shimmering effect far less effective. The following is a complete XAML code.

```
<UserControl x:Class="chapter10.BackgroundAnimationDemo"
    xmlns="http://schemas.microsoft.com/winfx/2006/xaml/presentation"
    xmlns:x="http://schemas.microsoft.com/winfx/2006/xaml"
    xmlns:d="http://schemas.microsoft.com/expression/blend/2008"
    xmlns:mc="http://schemas.openxmlformats.org/markup-compatibility/2006"
    mc:Ignorable="d"
    d:DesignHeight="300" d:DesignWidth="400">

    <Canvas x:Name="LayoutRoot" Loaded="LayoutRoot_Loaded" Width="500" Height="400">
        <Canvas.Resources>
            <Storyboard x:Name="shimmer" Duration="0:0:5" RepeatBehavior="Forever">
                <DoubleAnimation Storyboard.TargetName="background"
                    Storyboard.TargetProperty="GradientStops[0].Offset"
                    From="-0.2" To="1.0" Duration="0:0:1" />
                <DoubleAnimation Storyboard.TargetName="background"
                    Storyboard.TargetProperty="GradientStops[1].Offset"
                    From="-0.1" To="1.1" Duration="0:0:1" />
                <DoubleAnimation Storyboard.TargetName="background"
                    Storyboard.TargetProperty="GradientStops[2].Offset"
```

```
                    From="0" To="1.2" Duration="0:0:1" />
            </Storyboard>
        </Canvas.Resources>

        <Canvas.Background>
            <LinearGradientBrush x:Name="background" StartPoint="0,1" EndPoint="1,0">
                <GradientStop Color="#FF000000"/>
                <GradientStop Color="#FFAAAAAA"/>
                <GradientStop Color="#FF000000"/>
            </LinearGradientBrush>
        </Canvas.Background>
        <Rectangle Width="350" Height="250" Canvas.Left="25" Canvas.Top="25" Fill="Beige"/>
    </Canvas>
</UserControl>
```

Now use the Begin method of the Storyboard class to initiate the animation related to the defined shimmer named Storyboard under the LayoutRoot_Loaded, as shown here.

```
private void LayoutRoot_Loaded(object sender, RoutedEventArgs e)
{
    shimmer.Begin();
}
```

Figure 10-8 shows the developed shimmering effect in the background that changes the gradient offsets in a linear gradient brush that is used as the background for a Canvas.

Figure 10-8. *Shimmering effect for the background animation*

Keyframe Animations

Keyframe animations provide significant capabilities over the simpler from/to/by animations. Instead of specifying a starting and ending value and letting the animation smoothly change the target property's value over the animation's duration, keyframe animations instead specify the desired value at two or more points in time. Each specification of a property value is known as a *keyframe*: a moment in time when you want a property to take on a certain value. The way the value changes during each keyframe is called *interpolation*. Keyframe animation supports interpolations that are more complicated than the linear interpolations used by from/to/by animations. Keyframe animations also have another important advantage: from/to/by animations can animate only `Points`, `doubles`, and `Colors`, while keyframe animations can animate arbitrary properties using the `ObjectAnimationUsingKeyFrames` class.

A keyframe is a snapshot of a particular property at a specific moment in time. Instead of specifying the starting and ending values of a property using a single animation class, you specify each value of the property you want within a keyframe class. The specific keyframe classes correspond to the property type and interpolation method, which we will discuss shortly. Taking our rectangle from earlier, let's animate it so it moves in a straight line up and down. Figure 10-9 shows what each keyframe looks like.

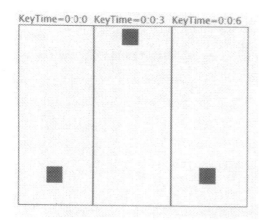

Figure 10-9. Snapshots of the three keyframes for animating the rectangle

The following is the related XAML code:

```
<UserControl x:Class="chapter10.KeyFrameAnimationDemo"
    xmlns="http://schemas.microsoft.com/winfx/2006/xaml/presentation"
    xmlns:x="http://schemas.microsoft.com/winfx/2006/xaml"
    xmlns:d="http://schemas.microsoft.com/expression/blend/2008"
    xmlns:mc="http://schemas.openxmlformats.org/markup-compatibility/2006"
    mc:Ignorable="d"
    d:DesignHeight="300" d:DesignWidth="400">
    <Canvas x:Name="LayoutRoot" Background="White">
        <Canvas.Resources>
            <Storyboard x:Name="rectAnimation">
                <DoubleAnimationUsingKeyFrames Storyboard.TargetName="rect"
                    Storyboard.TargetProperty="(Canvas.Top)" RepeatBehavior="Forever">
                    <LinearDoubleKeyFrame Value="240" KeyTime="0:0:0"/>
                    <LinearDoubleKeyFrame Value="25" KeyTime="0:0:3"/>
                    <LinearDoubleKeyFrame Value="240" KeyTime="0:0:6"/>
                </DoubleAnimationUsingKeyFrames>
            </Storyboard>
        </Canvas.Resources>
        <Rectangle x:Name="rect" Width="25" Height="25"
```

```
          Canvas.Left="370" Canvas.Top="270" Fill="Black">
          <Rectangle.RenderTransform>
              <TransformGroup>
                  <RotateTransform Angle="0">
                  </RotateTransform>
              </TransformGroup>
          </Rectangle.RenderTransform>
      </Rectangle>
   </Canvas>
</UserControl>
```

Here, as shown in the bolded fonts, the DoubleAnimationUsingKeyFrames class acts as a container for keyframes. LinearDoubleKeyFrame uses linear interpolation while it is active. Each keyframe specifies the value of the target property at the time specified in the KeyTime property. Since the KeyTime is 0:0:0 in the first keyframe, the target property is set to 240 when the animation begins. If a keyframe is not specified with a KeyTime of 0, the target property uses whatever its current value is, which might be the result of a previous animation or the property's local value. In the code-behind, we need to start the storyboard in the Loaded event of the user control, as follows:

```
rectAnimation.Begin();
```

Interpolation

Interpolation is the process of calculating the set of property values between two known values. As the timeline advances, the property changes to a value within this set. There are three types of interpolation available for use with keyframe animation: *linear*, *discrete*, and *spline*. The way interpolation works is by using a function that describes a line/curve from (0,0) to (1,1).

Linear Interpolation

Linear interpolation uses a diagonal line, as shown in Figure 10-10. If you think back to freshman-level calculus, you'll recall that the derivative of a function describes its rate of change. The linear interpolation function is $y = C \times f(x)$, where C is a constant and the derivative is a horizontal line, also shown in Figure 10-10. Unsurprisingly, this describes a constant rate of change. The coordinate space, although it runs from 0 to 1 in both axes, maps to any timeline/property value range. For example, if a timeline has a duration of ten seconds, five seconds corresponds to x = 0.5 on the graph, and ten seconds corresponds to x=1. This coordinate space will be useful when we look at spline interpolation.

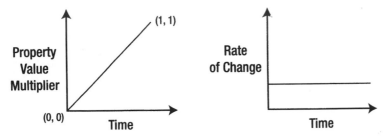

Figure 10-10. Graph of linear interpolation and its rate of change

You have already seen linear interpolation in action, since it is the only interpolation supported in from/to/by animations.

Discrete Interpolation

Discrete interpolation is even simpler than linear interpolation. The property value can have one of two values: its initial or its final value. As long as the current keyframe is active, the property has its initial value. The target property immediately changes to its final value when the end of the keyframe is reached. This might seem useless at first, since if a property can assume only one of two values, where's the animation? However, there are two main advantages to using discrete interpolation: it's a convenient way to hold a specific value for a length of time, and it's the only way to animate properties of types other than Point, double, and Color.

Let's use ObjectAnimationUsingKeyFrames to change an image used in an animation. This will change the Visibility property of two images to show only one image at a time. The two images are animated simultaneously to make it easy to switch between them simply by changing the Visibility. The following is the complete XAML code of the example, and Figure 10-11 shows the related output:

```xml
<UserControl x:Class="chapter10.InterpolationDemo"
    xmlns="http://schemas.microsoft.com/winfx/2006/xaml/presentation"
    xmlns:x="http://schemas.microsoft.com/winfx/2006/xaml"
    xmlns:d="http://schemas.microsoft.com/expression/blend/2008"
    xmlns:mc="http://schemas.openxmlformats.org/markup-compatibility/2006"
    mc:Ignorable="d"
    d:DesignHeight="300" d:DesignWidth="400">

    <Canvas x:Name="LayoutRoot" Background="White">
        <Canvas.Resources>
            <Storyboard x:Name="BallUpDown" RepeatBehavior="Forever">
                <DoubleAnimationUsingKeyFrames
                    Storyboard.TargetName="ballImageUp"
                    Storyboard.TargetProperty="(Canvas.Top)">
                <LinearDoubleKeyFrame Value="300" KeyTime="0:0:0"/>
                <LinearDoubleKeyFrame Value="25" KeyTime="0:0:1"/>
                <LinearDoubleKeyFrame Value="300" KeyTime="0:0:2"/>
                </DoubleAnimationUsingKeyFrames>
                <DoubleAnimationUsingKeyFrames
                    Storyboard.TargetName="ballImageDown"
                    Storyboard.TargetProperty="(Canvas.Top)">
                <LinearDoubleKeyFrame Value="300" KeyTime="0:0:0"/>
                <LinearDoubleKeyFrame Value="25" KeyTime="0:0:1"/>
                <LinearDoubleKeyFrame Value="300" KeyTime="0:0:2"/>
                </DoubleAnimationUsingKeyFrames>
                <ObjectAnimationUsingKeyFrames
                    Storyboard.TargetName="ballImageUp"
                    Storyboard.TargetProperty="Visibility">
                <DiscreteObjectKeyFrame KeyTime="0:0:0">
                    <DiscreteObjectKeyFrame.Value>
                        <Visibility>Visible</Visibility>
                    </DiscreteObjectKeyFrame.Value>
                </DiscreteObjectKeyFrame>
                <DiscreteObjectKeyFrame KeyTime="0:0:1">
```

```
                    <DiscreteObjectKeyFrame.Value>
                        <Visibility>Collapsed</Visibility>
                    </DiscreteObjectKeyFrame.Value>
                </DiscreteObjectKeyFrame>
                <DiscreteObjectKeyFrame KeyTime="0:0:2">
                    <DiscreteObjectKeyFrame.Value>
                        <Visibility>Visible</Visibility>
                    </DiscreteObjectKeyFrame.Value>
                </DiscreteObjectKeyFrame>
            </ObjectAnimationUsingKeyFrames>
        </Storyboard>
    </Canvas.Resources>
    <Image x:Name="ballImageUp" Canvas.Left="10" Canvas.Top="10" Height="56"↵
 Stretch="None"
            Width="51" Source="/chapter10;component/res/ball.png" />
    <Image x:Name="ballImageDown" Canvas.Left="10" Canvas.Top="10" Height="56"
            Stretch="None" Width="51" Source="/chapter10;component/res/ball.png" />
    </Canvas>
</UserControl>
```

The animation for the other image is similar, but the Visibility values are opposite to those used in this XAML. The property element syntax for this keyframe's Value is used to animate different property types.

In the code-behind, we need to start the storyboard in the Loaded event of the user control, as follows:

```
BallUpDown.Begin();
```

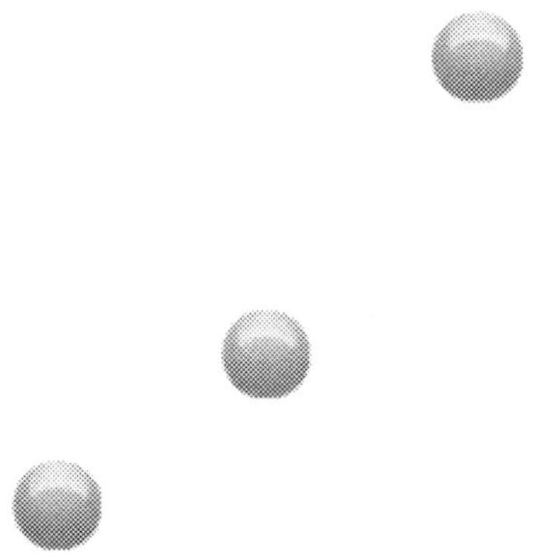

Figure 10-11. Example of discrete interpolation

Spline Interpolation

The final interpolation method is the most complex. Spline interpolation provides a mechanism to alter the rate at which the property value changes at different points during the time a keyframe is active. This means that Silverlight makes it easy to create some sophisticated animations, such as an object that starts out moving slowly and increases its speed over the length of the animation. Let's look at one example of modeling an object that changes its velocity over the course of its total movement. Imagine a single car in motion between two stoplights, as shown in Figure 10-12.

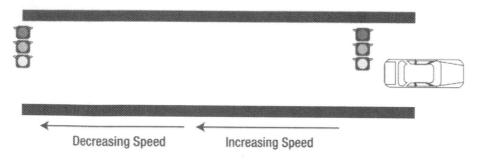

Figure 10-12. *Illustration of a car's acceleration and deceleration segments*

The car begins at a full stop and then the first light turns green. The car's speed increases for a while, but as it approaches the second stoplight, the car must slow down before finally coming to a full stop again. The car's speed can be modeled using the Bezier curve shown in Figure 10-13.

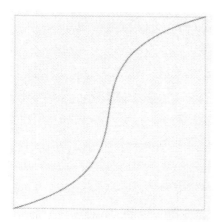

Figure 10-13. *Bezier curve describing the acceleration and deceleration of the car*

A Bezier curve is what the spline interpolation process uses to describe the varying rate of change. Keep in mind this curve describes the values of the property over time. Bezier curves were briefly mentioned in Chapter 9, but let's take a closer look at how they work so it's clear how spline interpolation can be used. The type of Bezier curve used by spline interpolation is a cubic Bezier with two control points, so the cubic Bezier curve is defined by four points, including the endpoints. If P1 and P4 are the endpoints, and P2 and P3 are the control points, the Bezier curve is a line that connects P1 to P4 but is pulled toward P2 and P3 in order to create the curve. The control points are not necessarily touched by the curve. If you set P2 and P3 to points along the line from P1 to P4, such as setting them to (0.25,0.25) and (0.75,0.75), the Bezier curve is a straight line and the animation is effectively using linear interpolation.

The Bezier curve modeling the car in Figure 10-13 used the control points (0.9,0.25) (0.1,0.75). The code in this chapter with the name SplineDemo includes a plot of the Bezier curve, along with our famous rectangle moving in a straight line (on top of a line that marks the full path of the rectangle).

Figure 10-14 shows the curve and the rectangle in its starting position. You can divide this Bezier curve into two regions: the first curvy segment (from x = 0 to x = 0.5) and the second curvy segment (from x = 0.5 to x = 1). The first segment starts out with a subtle curve that corresponds to a slowly increasing rate of movement (it's not quite straight along a diagonal, so the rate is not constant). After the bend, the curve is quite steep up to the center point, corresponding to a fast rate of change. The second curvy segment is the mirror opposite of this: the movement continues quickly and suddenly starts slowing down before coming to a complete stop (when the final value of the property is reached).

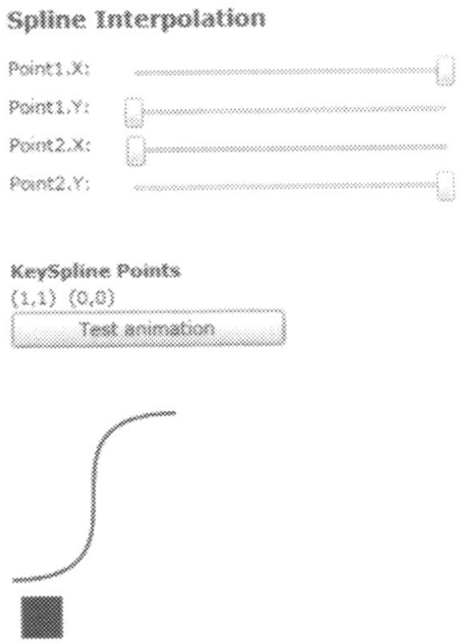

Figure 10-14. Rectangle animated using spline interpolation, and the curve plotted

If you want to figure out the curve that describes the animation you desire, you have several options. There are tools online that can assist, since Bezier curves are a popular approach to modeling animation. You can experiment using the code in this chapter by plugging in control points using sliders to preview the animation curve. You can also take out the trusty pen and paper and draw a curve that you think will work, roughly determine the control points, and then experiment. (The derivative for Bezier curves to show the rate of change, while interesting, is left as an exercise for the reader.)

Animation Easing

When it comes to using keyframe animations and attempting to define an interpolation function to model the effect you desire, you might spend a while getting it just right (unless you know the formula to use ahead of time). Silverlight 3 introduced a stock set of easing functions that control the change of property values over the duration of the animation. Two of these easing functions are bouncing and springing effects, and you can also define your own custom easing function with the use of the IEasingFunction interface. The full set of easing functions that come with Silverlight are shown in Table 10-4.

Table 10-4. Stock Animation-Easing Functions

Easing Function	Description
BackEase	The property value is first "backed up" a little before animating to its end. For example, a property value animating from 10 to 90 might go from 10 to 5 first and then from 5 to 90. This function has one double property, Amplitude, which controls the animation.
BounceEase	The property bounces before stopping at its final value. The number of bounces is specified by the integer property Bounces.
CircleEase	Uses a circular function to control the animation.
CubicEase	Uses the function f(t) = t^3.
ElasticEase	Property oscillates back and forth as if on a spring, slowing down until it comes to rest.
ExponentialEase	Uses an exponential function.
PowerEase	Uses an arbitrary power (specified by the double Power property). This is a general form of the cubic, quadratic, quartic, and quintic easing functions.
QuadraticEase	Uses the function f(t) = t^2.
QuarticEase	Uses the function f(t) = t^4.
QuinticEase	Uses the function f(t) = t^5.
SineEase	Uses a sine formula.

The easing functions that come with Silverlight inherit from the base class EasingFunctionBase. This base class provides an additional property, EasingMode, which makes it easy to invert the easing function or to run it inverted for half the time and then normal for the other half. The EasingMode enums are as follows:

- EaseOut: This mode of interpolation follows 100 percent interpolation minus the output of the formula associated with the easing function.

- EaseIn: This mode of interpolation follows the mathematical formula associated with the easing function.

- EaseInOut: This mode of interpolation uses EaseIn for the first half of the animation and EaseOut for the second half.

Using an easing function in XAML starts with an Easing keyframe corresponding to the type you want to animate, such as EasingDoubleKeyFrame and EasingColorKeyFrame. Then the easing function is applied and the animation is ready to go. The following XAML defines animation to make a circle appear to fall down and bounce repeatedly, like a rubber ball.

```xml
<Storyboard x:Name="myStoryboard">
    <DoubleAnimationUsingKeyFrames x:Name="doubleAnimation"
        Storyboard.TargetProperty="(Canvas.Top)"
        Storyboard.TargetName="ball">
        <EasingDoubleKeyFrame Value="170" KeyTime="00:00:06">
            <EasingDoubleKeyFrame.EasingFunction>
                <BounceEase Bounces="5" EasingMode="EaseOut"/>
            </EasingDoubleKeyFrame.EasingFunction>
        </EasingDoubleKeyFrame>
    </DoubleAnimationUsingKeyFrames>
</Storyboard>
```

The `EasingMode` is set to `EaseOut` to cause the bounce to happen at the end of the animation. If this was set to `EaseIn`, the bounce would happen off the ceiling and then the ball would drop and come to rest.

Understanding Animation-Easing Functions

Each animation-easing function, unsurprisingly, has a mathematical function behind it. Functions for bouncing, elasticity, etc. are more complicated, so let's take a closer look at one of the mathematically simpler easing functions. The quadratic easing function uses the formula $f(t) = t^2$ where t is the time. Figure 10-15 shows what this looks like visually.

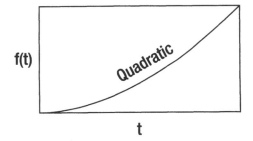

Figure 10-15. *Plot of the quadratic formula*

Easing functions use normalized time, so the beginning of the animation is always at time = 0 and the end is time = 1. The output of this function is the progress of the animation. Let's animate a `Canvas.Top` that starts at 0 and ends at 100 (to keep the math simple). The values for this property, sampled every 0.1 seconds, are shown in Table 10-5.

Table 10-5. Animation Progress Every 0.1 Seconds Using Quadratic Easing

Normalized Time	Quadratic Animation Progress	Property Value
0	0	0
0.1	0.01	1
0.2	0.04	4
0.3	0.09	9
0.4	0.16	16
0.5	0.25	25
0.6	0.36	36
0.7	0.49	49
0.8	0.64	64
0.9	0.81	81
1	1	100

The third column is arrived at using the formula shown in Figure 10-16. $V_{initial}$ is the initial value of the property and V_{final} is the final value.

$$V_{initial} + f(t) \cdot (V_{final} - V_{initial})$$

Figure 10-16. Formula used with easing function to get property value

Ease-out and ease-in/out are manipulations of the core easing function and thus can be derived from the ease-in function. Easing out inverts both the domain and the range, as shown in Figure 10-17. Easing in and out is an ease-in for half the time of the animation followed by an ease-out, forming one continuous function. It is described by the function shown in Figure 10-18.

$$1.0 - f(1 - t)$$

Figure 10-17. Formula used to modify easing function to ease out

For t=0 to 0.5:

   $f(t \cdot 2) / 2$

For t=0.5 to 1:

   $0.5 + (1 - f(2 - 2 \cdot t)) / 2$

Figure 10-18. Formula used to modify easing function to ease in then ease out

If you want to create your own easing function, all you need to do is implement the `IEasingFunction` interface. This interface defines a single method, `Ease`, which takes the normalized time as a `double` and returns the progress of the animation as a `double`. This is precisely where you define your own f(t). Since the ease-out and ease-in/out variants are provided by a separate class (`EasingFunctionBase`), implementing directly from the `IEasingFunction` interface allows you only a single easing. This should be fine, though, since your own easing function needs only a single implementation. If you need more capability, you can define your own properties and even your own implementation of the `EasingMode` property.

Procedural Animation

So far we have used a declarative approach for defining animation. This means that we defined the animation in XAML (and not in code-behind) and controlled the animation code-behind. It is very likely that in real-world applications you need to define and control the animation dynamically at runtime, and thus you end up doing *procedural animation*. In this case you will define the different types of animations we discussed earlier and target them dynamically at runtime using code-behind capabilities.

To demonstrate procedural animation, let's develop a more complex example. We will develop a bubbles animation, where bubbles originate from bottom of the screen and go upwards. We will use `Canvas` and will animate `Canvas.Left` and `Canvas.Top` attached properties of the bubble element to achieve this animation. Of course, you can enhance it more by using `TranslateTransform`, but to keep more focused on how to do procedural animation, we will use `Canvas` instead.

Here I have created a new folder named `ProceduralAnimationDemo` in this chapter's `chapter10` Silverlight project. Now first we will create a definition of the bubble, which essentially will also determine the size and color of the bubble. Then we will create hosting control, where we will create bubbles and will attach them to dynamically-created animations and storyboards.

Bubble User Control

Add a new user control named `Bubble.xaml` that will represent a simple vector bubble graphic. I used Expression Design 3 to create the vector bubble graphic. The related XAML that creates the bubble graphic is shown here:

```
<UserControl x:Class="chapter10.ProceduralAnimationDemo.Bubble"
    xmlns="http://schemas.microsoft.com/winfx/2006/xaml/presentation"
    xmlns:x="http://schemas.microsoft.com/winfx/2006/xaml"
    xmlns:d="http://schemas.microsoft.com/expression/blend/2008"
    xmlns:mc="http://schemas.openxmlformats.org/markup-compatibility/2006"
    mc:Ignorable="d" >
    <Canvas xmlns="http://schemas.microsoft.com/winfx/2006/xaml/presentation"
```

```
      xmlns:x="http://schemas.microsoft.com/winfx/2006/xaml"
      Width="68" Height="62" Clip="F1 M 0,0L 800,0L 800,600L 0,600L 0,0"
      UseLayoutRounding="False">
      <!--We will set this in code behind to create different sized bubbles-->
      <Canvas.RenderTransform>
          <ScaleTransform x:Name="BubbleScaleTransform" ScaleX="1" ScaleY="1" />
      </Canvas.RenderTransform>

      <Canvas Width="66" Height="64" Canvas.Left="0" Canvas.Top="0">
          <Path x:Name="Path" Width="60.9533" Height="60.952" Canvas.Left="0"↵
Canvas.Top="0"
              Stretch="Fill" Data="F1 M 0,30.476C 0,47.3067 13.6453,60.952 30.4773,60.952L
                  30.4773,60.952C 47.308,60.952 60.9533,47.3067 60.9533,30.476L↵
60.9533,30.476C
                  60.9533,13.6453 47.308,0 30.4773,0L 30.4773,0C 13.6453,0 0,13.6453↵
0,30.476 Z ">
              <Path.Fill>
                  <RadialGradientBrush RadiusX="0.925305" RadiusY="0.925325"
                      Center="0.493919,0.925275" GradientOrigin="0.493919,0.925275">
                      <RadialGradientBrush.GradientStops>
                          <GradientStop  Color="#FFFFFFFF" Offset="0"/>
                          <!--Gradient fill stop; we will change the color value in↵
code behind to create different
                              colored bubbles-->
                          <GradientStop x:Name="ColorStop" Color="#FFBABABA" Offset="1"/>
                      </RadialGradientBrush.GradientStops>
                      <RadialGradientBrush.RelativeTransform>
                          <TransformGroup/>
                      </RadialGradientBrush.RelativeTransform>
                  </RadialGradientBrush>
              </Path.Fill>
          </Path>
          <Path Width="40.9973" Height="34.4693" Canvas.Left="8.9524" Fill="White"↵
Opacity="0.5"
              Canvas.Top="0.242859" Stretch="Fill" Data="F1 M 49.9497,17.4761C↵
49.9497,26.9962
                  40.7711,34.7122 29.4511,34.7122C 18.1284,34.7122 8.9524,26.9962↵
8.9524,17.4761C
                  8.9524,7.95746 18.1284,0.242859 29.4511,0.242859C 40.7711,0.242859↵
49.9497,7.95746
                  49.9497,17.4761 Z ">
          </Path>
      </Canvas>
  </Canvas>
</UserControl>
```

Note that there are two named elements in the preceding code that are highlighted in bold. The first is BubbleScaleTransform, which is a ScaleTransform, and we will handle its ScaleX and ScaleY property in code-behind when creating new bubbles of different sizes. The second is ColorStop of type GradientStop, which is used to set different colors for bubbles.

The code-behind is straightforward, as it just does the work of setting new colors and sizes of bubbles in the Loaded event of the UserControl, as shown in the following code snippet:

```
using System;
using System.Collections.Generic;
using System.Linq;
using System.Net;
using System.Windows;
using System.Windows.Controls;
using System.Windows.Documents;
using System.Windows.Input;
using System.Windows.Media;
using System.Windows.Media.Animation;
using System.Windows.Shapes;

namespace chapter10.ProceduralAnimationDemo
{
    public partial class Bubble : UserControl
    {
        public Color BubbleColor { get; set; }
        public double BubbleSize { get; set; }

        public Bubble()
        {
            InitializeComponent();
            this.Loaded += new RoutedEventHandler(Bubble_Loaded);
        }

        void Bubble_Loaded(object sender, RoutedEventArgs e)
        {
            //set bubble color
            ColorStop.Color = BubbleColor;

            //set bubble size through ScaleTransform defined in Xaml
            BubbleScaleTransform.ScaleX = BubbleSize;
            BubbleScaleTransform.ScaleY = BubbleSize;
        }
    }
}
```

DemoPage User Control

Now add a new DemoPage user control that will act as a sky where the bubbles will fly. This page holds canvas control with RadialGradientBrush as its background. The following is the XAML code:

```
<UserControl x:Class="chapter10.ProceduralAnimationDemo.DemoPage"
    xmlns="http://schemas.microsoft.com/winfx/2006/xaml/presentation"
    xmlns:x="http://schemas.microsoft.com/winfx/2006/xaml"
    xmlns:d="http://schemas.microsoft.com/expression/blend/2008"
    xmlns:mc="http://schemas.openxmlformats.org/markup-compatibility/2006"
    mc:Ignorable="d"
```

```
        d:DesignHeight="600" d:DesignWidth="600">
        <Canvas  x:Name="LayoutRoot" Height="600" Width="600" >
            <Canvas.Background>
                <RadialGradientBrush>
                    <GradientStop Color="White" Offset="0" />
                    <GradientStop Color="#FF479BFC" Offset="1" />
                </RadialGradientBrush>
            </Canvas.Background>
        </Canvas >
</UserControl>
```

The code-behind of this control is where we put all the required logic of creating instances of bubbles and attaching them to dynamically-created animations and storyboards. We use the Random class object to create differently-sized bubbles on the fly, and thus we need to define it at the class level, as follows:

```
private Random rnd = new Random();
```

We also need to remove the bubbles that have finished moving from the bottom to the top of the canvas. For that, we need to track information about each bubble. To achieve this, we use a simple Dictionary object that will store the Bubble instance with the associated storyboard, as shown here:

```
private Dictionary<Storyboard, Bubble> BubblesTracker = new Dictionary<Storyboard,↵
  Bubble>();
```

Now create a central method CreateBubble of the project, as shown next. This method will create instances of Bubble user control and apply random sizes and randomly chosen colors with transparency to them. Here we also create goUpBubble and swayBubble animations, both of type DoubleAnimation. The swayBubble animation will animate bubbles sideways while they float to the top. To do so, we will use the ElasticEase easing function. The following code snippet contains proper comments to explain various areas.

```
private void CreateBubble()
{
    Duration duration;

    //Random size for new bubble
    double sizeFactor = (double)(rnd.Next(100, 1000)) / 1000;

    // New color for each bubble using random variable and fromargb method
    Color color = Color.FromArgb((byte)(255 - (byte)(100 * sizeFactor)),↵
(byte)(rnd.Next(0, 255)),
        (byte)(rnd.Next(0, 255)), (byte)(rnd.Next(0, 255)));

    //bubble transparency by setting Alpha channel of the color
    color.A = (byte)(255 - (byte)(100 * sizeFactor));

    // create a new bubble
    Bubble bubble = new Bubble();

    //Apply size and color created above
```

```
bubble.BubbleColor = color;
bubble.BubbleSize = sizeFactor;

//Left position setting of bubble
double left = rnd.Next(0, (int)(LayoutRoot.ActualWidth - bubble.ActualWidth));
//Top position setting of bubble
double top = LayoutRoot.ActualHeight;

//Apply position to bubble
bubble.SetValue(Canvas.LeftProperty, left);
bubble.SetValue(Canvas.TopProperty, top);

// To make bubble look near, set higher z-index
bubble.SetValue(Canvas.ZIndexProperty, (int)(sizeFactor * 100));

// Moving closer bubbles faster
duration = new Duration(TimeSpan.FromSeconds((int)(60 - 50 * sizeFactor)));

// bubble Storyboard
Storyboard bubblesStoryboard = new Storyboard();

//This animates bubble from down to up
DoubleAnimation goUpBubble = new DoubleAnimation();
goUpBubble.From = top;
goUpBubble.To = 0 - bubble.ActualHeight;
goUpBubble.Duration = duration;

//This animates bubble sideways using EasingFunction
DoubleAnimation swayBubble = new DoubleAnimation();
swayBubble.From = left;
swayBubble.To = left + 100;
swayBubble.Duration = duration;
ElasticEase es = new ElasticEase();
es.Springiness = 3;
es.Oscillations = 6;
swayBubble.EasingFunction = es;

//Setting Canvas.Top as a target property of goUpBubble double animation
Storyboard.SetTarget(goUpBubble, bubble);
Storyboard.SetTargetProperty(goUpBubble, new PropertyPath(Canvas.TopProperty));

//Setting Canvas.Left as a target property of swayBubble double animation
Storyboard.SetTarget(swayBubble, bubble);
Storyboard.SetTargetProperty(swayBubble, new PropertyPath(Canvas.LeftProperty));

//Adding both animation to storyboard
bubblesStoryboard.Children.Add(goUpBubble);
bubblesStoryboard.Children.Add(swayBubble);

// add the bubble to the LayoutRoot canvas
LayoutRoot.Children.Add(bubble);
```

```
    // bubbles tracker dictionary object to remove bubbles from canvas later on↵
as they reach top in
    //completed event.
    BubblesTracker.Add(bubblesStoryboard, bubble);

    //storyboard set up
    bubblesStoryboard.Duration = duration;
    bubblesStoryboard.Completed += new EventHandler(bubblesStoryboard_Completed);
    //starting storyboard
    bubblesStoryboard.Begin();
}
```

To create bubbles (by calling the CreateBubble method) at regular intervals of time, we will use the DispatcherTimer object (that you will learn about in depth in Chapter 12). Note that to make use of this class, you need to add a namespace, System.Windows.Threading. We create a timer object in the Loaded event of UserControl, as shown in following code snippet:

```
void DemoPage_Loaded(object sender, RoutedEventArgs e)
{
    DispatcherTimer timer = new DispatcherTimer();

    timer.Interval = TimeSpan.FromSeconds(0.6);
    timer.Tick += new EventHandler(timer_Tick);
    timer.Start();
}

void timer_Tick(object sender, EventArgs e)
{
    CreateBubble();
}
```

If you run the project at this stage, you will see that nice-looking bubbles are floating up in the sky, as shown in Figure 10-19.

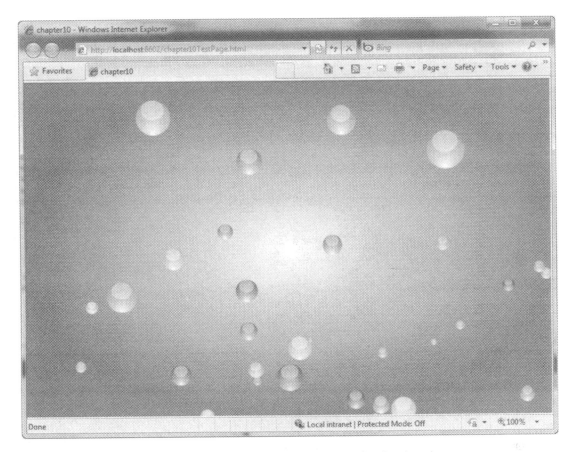

Figure 10-19. Creating bubble elements dynamically using procedural animation

Animating with Expression Blend

Expression Blend makes it easy to create animation using its built-in timeline editor. You may have noticed the Timeline part of the Objects and Timeline section, and now you know exactly what it means.

In Expression Blend, let's animate another rectangle. Create a new UserControl and place a rectangle on the design surface. Next, click the plus sign next to the "(No Storyboard open)" text, as shown in Figure 10-20.

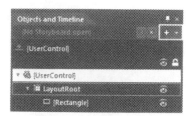

Figure 10-20. The Objects and Timeline pane in Expression Blend

Once you click the plus sign, a dialog appears asking for a name for the storyboard. Give it the name rectangleAnimation. The user interface will change in several ways. First, a red outline will surround the design surface and the text "Timeline recording is on" will appear. Next, the timeline editor will open, as shown in Figure 10-21.

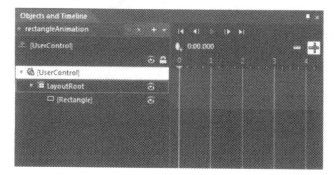

Figure 10-21. The timeline editor in Expression Blend

The reason the object hierarchy and timeline editing are combined within the same pane is that each object has a corresponding line in the timeline. The control bar at the top of the timeline editor has buttons to change the current frame to the first frame, the previous frame, the next frame, or the last frame. The center button is the play button and runs the animation on the design surface. The only type of animation Expression Blend supports is keyframe, which is reflected in the organization of the timeline editor. The default interpolation used is spline, with the default control points set to effectively create linear interpolation.

Make sure the rectangle object is highlighted in gray in the object hierarchy, and then click the small plus button next to the time signature. This creates a keyframe with the rectangle in its current position at time 0:0:0. A small white oval appears under the 0-second vertical, showing that a keyframe exists at this time for the corresponding object. Next, click the 1 on top of the timeline's 1-second vertical. This moves the yellow marker to the 1-second line. Next, after ensuring that the rectangle is currently highlighted on the design surface, hold down the Shift key and press the right arrow key to move the rectangle quickly along a straight horizontal line. Stop somewhere close to the right edge of the design surface. As soon as you start moving the rectangle, a new keyframe is created at the 1-second line, shown with another gray oval. The keyframe's target property is set to whatever value corresponds to where you complete the movement. Figure 10-22 shows what the timeline looks like after moving the rectangle to a new position at the 1-second mark.

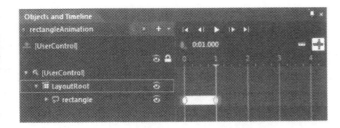

Figure 10-22. The timeline editor with a keyframe recorded at the 0- and 1-second marks

Look at the XAML, and notice that the rectangle contains an empty version of the CompositeTransform, highlighted in bold, which Silverlight provides:

```
<Grid x:Name="LayoutRoot" Background="White">
    <Rectangle x:Name="rectangle" Fill="#FFF4F4F5" HorizontalAlignment="Left" Height="108"
        Margin="28,22,0,0" Stroke="Black" VerticalAlignment="Top" Width="109"
        RenderTransformOrigin="0.5,0.5">
        <Rectangle.RenderTransform>
            <CompositeTransform/>
        </Rectangle.RenderTransform>
    </Rectangle>
</Grid>
```

An empty transform does nothing to the object being transformed. However, it makes it easy for the animation to affect a specific transform, such as this example does to the TranslateX property of the CompositeTransform:

```
<Storyboard x:Name="rectangleAnimation">
    <DoubleAnimationUsingKeyFrames
        Storyboard.TargetProperty="(UIElement.RenderTransform)↵
.(CompositeTransform.TranslateX)"
        Storyboard.TargetName="rectangle">
        <EasingDoubleKeyFrame KeyTime="0" Value="0"/>
        <EasingDoubleKeyFrame KeyTime="0:0:1" Value="205"/>
    </DoubleAnimationUsingKeyFrames>
</Storyboard>
```

You can change the interpolation for a specific keyframe. The ease-in percentage controls how the property value changes as time advances toward the selected keyframe. The higher the ease-in value, the faster this keyframe is approached as the closer time gets to it. The ease-out functionality is similar, except it controls how the property value changes as time advances away from the current keyframe. The ease-in and ease-out percentages alter the control points for the KeySpline, for which Expression Blend offers a full-blown editor if you click the Properties tab while a keyframe is selected. The KeySpline editor is shown in Figure 10-23.

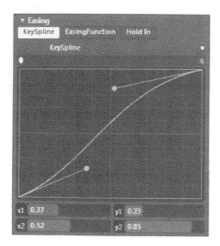

Figure 10-23. *The KeySpline editor in Expression Blend*

The yellow dots correspond to the control points, which are set to the control points used earlier in the car example. You can click and drag these yellow dots, or change the points by using the sliders (hold the mouse on the x1, y1, x2, and y2 points area and move it left or right) or entering the numbers by hand after clicking one of the sliders. This editor is likely the best option for exploring KeySplines and discovering which control points will accomplish what you are aiming for.

If you want to change the repeat count of the animation, you need to drill down into the specific target property being animated. You can do this when in timeline recording mode by repeatedly clicking the arrow button on the left of each object until you arrive at a series of highlighted objects, as shown in Figure 10-24.

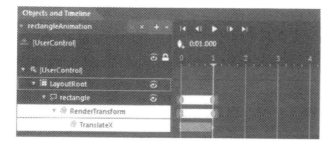

Figure 10-24. *Right-clicking the drilled-down object to modify the repeat count*

Figure 10-24 also shows the context menu when you right-click the target property (X in this case). This context menu also appears if you right-click the time span for the X property. When you select the Edit Repeat Count option, the Edit Repeat dialog appears, as shown in Figure 10-25.

Figure 10-25. Setting the repeat count using Expression Blend

You can set a repeat count or click the infinity sign to the right of the text entry to set the repeat count to forever. Expression Blend provides other capabilities as well, such as creating a motion path and converting it to a timeline, and manipulating keyframes in a variety of ways. This section has introduced what Expression Blend can do to make creating animations easier for you.

3D Animation

As we just learned in the previous chapter, perspective transforms, which were introduced in Silverlight 3, are the next step towards developing 3D Silverlight RIAs. In previous versions of Silverlight, transforms were processed in the *x* and *y* axes using the UIElement's RenderTransform property. Starting with the Silverlight 3 version, you can use the PlaneProjection class to render 3D-like effects. All elements that derive from UIElement have the Projection property, which allows the element to simulate transformation in a 3D space. In the following XAML code, we have a simple example of a rotating image using PlaneProjection that simulates 3D-like animation:

```
<Grid x:Name="LayoutRoot" Background="Black">
    <Grid.Resources>
        <Storyboard x:Name="Rotate" >
            <DoubleAnimation
                From="0" To="360" Storyboard.TargetName="p1"
                Storyboard.TargetProperty="RotationY"
                RepeatBehavior="Forever" Duration="0:0:5">
            </DoubleAnimation>
        </Storyboard>
    </Grid.Resources>
    <Image x:Name="image1" Source="CD.png" Stretch="None">
        <Image.Projection>
            <PlaneProjection x:Name="p1"/>
        </Image.Projection>
    </Image>
</Grid>
```

In the previous XAML code, I have defined the Storyboard "Rotate" with DoubleAnimation having its RepeatBehavior set to Forever. The only image control that image1 has is its Projection property, set to PlaneProjection x:Name property to p1.

In the code-behind, we need to start the storyboard in the Loaded event of the user control, as follows:

```
Rotate.Begin();
```

451

Run the project and you should see a continuously rotating compact disc in 3D space. Figure 10-26 shows two positions of the rotating disc.

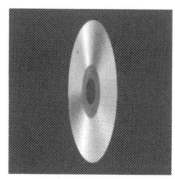

Figure 10-26. An example of 3D animation: rotating compact disc in 3D space

Summary

This chapter covered the animation support that comes with Silverlight. Timelines are central to the animation support, and the Timeline class provides several properties to control how time advances, possibly repeating or even reversing. The simplest form of animation is the from/to/by type, and several applications of it were demonstrated. Next, you learned about the most powerful animation support in Silverlight: keyframe animation. This provides the capability to alter how property values change by supporting different interpolation methods—specifically linear, discrete, and spline. The keyframe animation also supports modifying properties of types other than double, Point, and Color. Finally, you got a taste of the animation support built into Expression Blend, an invaluable tool for working with animation in both WPF and Silverlight, along with the newly introduced animation feature—3D animation.

In the next chapter, we will look at advanced Silverlight features, such as the navigation framework and out-of-browser capabilities.

■ ■ ■

CHAPTER 11

Advanced Silverlight Features

Although this book has covered a significant amount of Silverlight, there is much more to Silverlight. This chapter aims to provide information on some of the more advanced topics of Silverlight. Silverlight 3 introduced some very strategic features to help you develop enterprise-level rich Internet applications (RIAs), and Silverlight 4 enhanced these features to further develop line-of-business applications. In this chapter, we will cover Silverlight navigation framework and out-of-browser functionality with extended support to local file systems, integration with COM applications, and Notification API in Silverlight 4. We will also discuss deep linking and search engine optimization (SEO) and extended commanding support to support the MVVM design pattern. We'll end the chapter by demonstrating how to implement communication across different Silverlight applications.

Silverlight Navigation Framework

Basic web-based application features such as support to browsing from one XAML-based page to another, maintaining browser-level history, enabling the default browser's back and forward functionalities, and implementing search engine–friendly pages are key features of any line-of-business rich Internet application (RIA). Silverlight 3 introduced the Silverlight Navigation Framework, which added support for all of these features.

As mentioned in Chapter 1, when you create a Silverlight 4 project using Visual Studio 2010, the Silverlight Navigation Application template is available. Let's walk through an example. Create a project based on the Silverlight Navigation Application template, and name it AdvanceFeaturesDemoApp. You will get a sample application with a predefined set of view pages. The MainPage.xaml page behaves as a central or start-up page, and the pages About.xaml, ErrorWindow.xaml and Home.xaml are available in the Views folder, as shown in Figure 11-1.

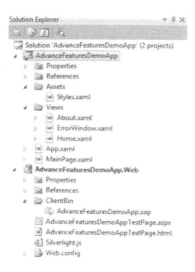

Figure 11-1. *Master and view pages of the project based on the Silverlight Navigation Application template*

If you run the project, you will see most of the functionality available by default. The About.xaml and Home.xaml pages are hosted on the MainPage.xaml master page. The browser header displays the page-specific customized title defined using the Title property in the Page property. The application maintains the browser history, and you can use the browser's default back and forward buttons. Figure 11-2 shows the default navigation framework–based Silverlight application.

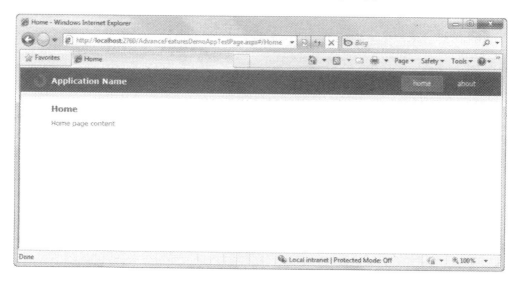

Figure 11-2. *Default view of the navigation framework–based Silverlight application*

Understanding the Navigation Framework

Now we'll help you understand some key components of the framework, such as Frame, UserControl, and Page. Frame is the core component of the navigation framework; it mainly behaves as the master start-up page/container and also performs validation. The following XAML code showing the Frame tag is added by default in the MainPage.xaml page; it declares the container for the application:

```
<navigation:Frame
    x:Name="ContentFrame"
    Style="{StaticResource ContentFrameStyle}"
    Source="/Home"
    Navigated="ContentFrame_Navigated"
    NavigationFailed="ContentFrame_NavigationFailed">
```

The Source property defines the page that will be loaded as a start-up page of the application. By default Home.xaml is the start-up page of the navigation framework–based Silverlight application. You can change it appropriately to suit your requirements. There are two event handlers defined by default: Navigated event as ContentFrame_Navigated and NavigationFailed event as ContentFrame_NavigationFailed, which we will discuss shortly. Before that, let's take a look at key methods, events, and properties of the Frame class.

The Frame Class

The System.Windows.Controls.Frame class represents a control supporting navigation to and from Silverlight Page controls. You can create one or more Silverlight Page controls with a unique URI for each page to navigate to and from. Tables 11-1, 11-2, and 11-3 show methods, events, and properties of this class respectively.

Table 11-1. Methods of the System.Windows.Controls.Frame Class

Method	Description
GoBack	Navigates to the most recent entry in the back navigation history, or throws an exception if no entry exists in the back navigation applied. You can use the CanGoBack property to determine if backward navigation history exists.
GoForward	Navigates to the most recent entry in the forward navigation history, or throws an exception if no entry exists in forward navigation. You can use the CanGoForward property to determine if forward navigation history exists.
Navigate	Navigates to the content specified by the uniform resource identifier (URI). It returns true if the navigation started properly, otherwise it returns false.
Refresh	Reloads the current page. By default, navigation to the current URI will not reload the content. However, you can use this method to force the content to reload. This method is useful only when you set the ContentLoader property to an INavigationContentLoader implementation that can produce different page contents upon reload. See the "Implementing Custom Navigation" section for more details.
StopLoading	Stops asynchronous navigations that have not yet been processed.

Table 11-2. Events of the System.Windows.Controls.Frame Class

Event	Description
FragmentNavigation	Occurs when the navigation to a content fragment begins. Note that the fragment portion of the URI is the text contained after the fragment marker (#).
Navigated	Occurs when the content that is being navigated to has been found and is available.
Navigating	Occurs when a new navigation is requested.
NavigationFailed	Occurs when an error is encountered while navigating to the requested content.
NavigationStopped	Occurs when navigation is terminated by either calling the StopLoading method, or requesting a new navigation while the current navigation is in progress.

Table 11-3. Properties of the System.Windows.Controls.Frame Class

Property	Type	Description
CacheSize	int	Defines the number of pages that can be cached for the frame. Default value is 10.
CanGoBack	bool	Determines if backward navigation history is available (one or more returns true value), or not (false value).
CanGoForward	bool	Determines if forward navigation history is available (one or more returns true value), or not (false value).
ContentLoader	INavigationContentLoader	Gets or sets the object responsible for providing the content that corresponds to a requested URI. This is a new property introduced in Silverlight 4.
CurrentSource	Uri	Gets the uniform resource identifier (URI) of the content that is currently displayed.

JournalOwnership	JournalOwnership	Gets or sets whether a frame is responsible for managing its own navigation history or it integrates with the Web browser journal. By default, it is set to Automatic, which automatically records navigation history to the browser journal (if allowed). Otherwise, it will be recorded only in the Frame control journal. You can set the value of the JournalOwnership property to OwnsJournal to store history only in the Frame control journal. If set to UsesParentJournal, then the Frame control will follow the settings of the parent Frame control's JournalOwnership property. If there is no parent Frame control, then the navigation history will be stored in the browser journal.
Source	Uri	Gets or sets the uniform resource identifier (URI) of the current content or the content that is being navigated to.
UriMapper	UriMapperBase	Gets or sets the object to manage converting a uniform resource identifier (URI) to another URI for this frame.

Start-Up Page and Application Navigation Features

The MainPage.xaml file's UserControl control includes a reference to the System.Windows.Controls.Navigation assembly (see highlighted bold fonts). The Grid control NavigationGrid contains two HyperlinkButtons for page navigation and the TextBlock showing the application name, placed inside the Border and StackPanel controls—one group for the hyperlink buttons and the other group for the branding. Many controls are defined using the style defined in the Styles.xaml file under the Assets directory of the project (see Figure 11-1). The following is the complete default XAML code of the MainPage.xaml file:

```
<UserControl
    x:Class="AdvanceFeaturesDemoApp.MainPage"
    xmlns="http://schemas.microsoft.com/winfx/2006/xaml/presentation"
    xmlns:x="http://schemas.microsoft.com/winfx/2006/xaml"
    xmlns:navigation="clr-namespace:System.Windows.Controls;
        assembly=System.Windows.Controls.Navigation"
    xmlns:uriMapper="clr-namespace:System.Windows.Navigation;
        assembly=System.Windows.Controls.Navigation"
    xmlns:d="http://schemas.microsoft.com/expression/blend/2008"
    xmlns:mc="http://schemas.openxmlformats.org/
        markup-compatibility/2006"
    mc:Ignorable="d" d:DesignWidth="640" d:DesignHeight="480">
    <Grid x:Name="LayoutRoot" Style=
        "{StaticResource   LayoutRootGridStyle}">
        <Border x:Name="ContentBorder"
            Style="{StaticResource ContentBorderStyle}">
            <navigation:Frame x:Name="ContentFrame"
                Style="{StaticResource ContentFrameStyle}"
```

```
                    Source="/Home" Navigated="ContentFrame_Navigated"
                    NavigationFailed="ContentFrame_NavigationFailed">
                    <navigation:Frame.UriMapper>
                      <uriMapper:UriMapper>
                        <uriMapper:UriMapping Uri=""
                            MappedUri="/Views/Home.xaml"/>
                        <uriMapper:UriMapping Uri="/{pageName}"
                            MappedUri="/Views/{pageName}.xaml"/>
                      </uriMapper:UriMapper>
                    </navigation:Frame.UriMapper>
                </navigation:Frame>
            </Border>
            <Grid x:Name="NavigationGrid"
                Style="{StaticResource NavigationGridStyle}">
                <Border x:Name="BrandingBorder"
                    Style="{StaticResource BrandingBorderStyle}">
                    <StackPanel x:Name="BrandingStackPanel"
                        Style="{StaticResource BrandingStackPanelStyle}">
                        <ContentControl
                            Style="{StaticResource LogoIcon}"/>
                        <TextBlock x:Name="ApplicationNameTextBlock"
                            Style="{StaticResource ApplicationNameStyle}"
                            Text="Application Name"/>
                    </StackPanel>
                </Border>
                <Border x:Name="LinksBorder"
                    Style="{StaticResource LinksBorderStyle}">
                    <StackPanel x:Name="LinksStackPanel"
                        Style="{StaticResource LinksStackPanelStyle}">
                        <HyperlinkButton x:Name="Link1"
                            Style="{StaticResource LinkStyle}"
                            NavigateUri="/Home"
                            TargetName="ContentFrame" Content="home" />
                        <Rectangle x:Name="Divider1"
                            Style="{StaticResource DividerStyle}"/>
                        <HyperlinkButton x:Name="Link2"
                            Style="{StaticResource LinkStyle}"
                            NavigateUri="/About"
                            TargetName="ContentFrame" Content="about"/>
                    </StackPanel>
                </Border>
            </Grid>
        </Grid>
    </UserControl>
```

The navigation framework project represents a consistent set of styles across the Silverlight application. For that, the App.xaml file of the project defines a reference to ResourceDictionary Styles.xaml. The Styles.xaml file resides in the Assets directory of the project (see Figure 11-1) containing styles for the main page and content pages. The styles for the main page include primary color brushes, as well as a navigation container style, navigation border style, navigation panel style, page link style, branding border style, branding panel style, branding text highlight style, branding text normal style, frame container style, and frame inner board style. The styles for the content pages include a header text style, content text style, hyperlink button style, and content text panel style. As you can see in the previous code XAML code snippets, these defined styles are referenced across the project, which provides a consistent look and feel.

Navigation to Pages

The start-up page includes two default HyperlinkButtons, called home and about, with the NavigateUri property set to facilitate navigation to different pages. The NavigateUri property of both HyperlinkButtons is set to a URI—"/Home" and "/About"—respectively mapping to a page. Note that here you have not defined the TargetName property of the HyperlinkButtons since both HyperlinkButtons reside within the frame. If they have been residing outside of the frame, then you also need to set the TargetName property to the value of the x:Name of the frame.

User-Friendly URIs

Note the use of UriMapping to map to pages by pageName that are inside the Views directory in <navigation:Frame.UriMapper>. The UriMapping class defines the pattern for converting a requested uniform resource identifier (URI) into a new user-friendly URI. Here UriMapping converts the user-friendly URI to the physical location of a page file residing in the Views directory (i.e., /Views/Home.xaml is set to /Home and /Views/About.xaml to /About). I will further cover this topic later in the "Deep Linking" section of this chapter.

The following code is added to the MainPage.xaml.cs code-behind file by default and defines the Navigated and NavigationFailed event handlers for ContentFrame:

```
// After the Frame navigates, ensure
// the HyperlinkButton representing the current page is selected
private void ContentFrame_Navigated
    (object sender, NavigationEventArgs e)
{
    foreach (UIElement child in LinksStackPanel.Children)
    {
        HyperlinkButton hb = child as HyperlinkButton;
        if (hb != null && hb.NavigateUri != null)
        {
            If (hb.NavigateUri.ToString().Equals(e.Uri.ToString()))
            {
                VisualStateManager.GoToState(hb, "ActiveLink", true);
            }
            else
            {
            VisualStateManager.GoToState(hb, "InactiveLink", true);
            }
        }
    }
}

// If an error occurs during navigation, show an error window
private void ContentFrame_NavigationFailed
    (object sender, NavigationFailedEventArgs e)
```

```
{
    e.Handled = true;
    ChildWindow errorWin = new ErrorWindow(e.Uri);
    errorWin.Show();
}
```

Here the `ContentFrame_Navigated` event is critical. With the use of the `foreach` loop, it iterates through the Children collection of the LinksStackPanel and casts each child as a HyperlinkButton. It then checks for the `NavigateUri` property and matches it to the received argument e.Uri of the `NavigationEventArgs e` object. If it matches, the State change happens for that matching HyperlinkButton to ensure the HyperlinkButton representing the current page is selected using VisualStateManager. The `ContentFrame_NavigationFailed` event simply handles the error occurring during the navigation and shows an error window.

Navigation Pages

The Silverlight navigation pages are defined as follows under the Views folder (refer to Figure 11-1). The `Title` attribute of the `Page` class defines the page-specific title that will be displayed as the browser heading when a user visits that particular page.

```
<navigation:Page x:Class="AdvanceFeaturesDemoApp.Home"
    xmlns="http://schemas.microsoft.com/winfx/2006/xaml/presentation"
    xmlns:x="http://schemas.microsoft.com/winfx/2006/xaml"
    xmlns:d="http://schemas.microsoft.com/expression/blend/2008"
    xmlns:mc="http://schemas.openxmlformats.org/
        markup-compatibility/2006"
    xmlns:navigation="clr-namespace:System.Windows.Controls;
        assembly=System.Windows.Controls.Navigation"
    mc:Ignorable="d" d:DesignWidth="640" d:DesignHeight="480"
    Title="Home"
    Style="{StaticResource PageStyle}">
```

Note that rest of the XAML file of Silverlight navigation pages is just like a normal XAML page.

Navigation History and Integration with Browser

You can add the `JournalOwnership` property to the `Frame` object in the `MainPage.xaml` file, which defines a frame either as being responsible for managing its own navigation history, or integrating with the Web browser journal. By default, it is set to `Automatic`, which automatically records navigation history to the browser journal, allowing navigation integrated with the browser. In this case, now you can use the back and forward buttons to navigate pages within the Silverlight application.

You can set the value of the `JournalOwnership` property to `OwnsJournal` to store history only in the Frame control journal. If set to `UsesParentJournal`, then the Frame control will follow the settings of the parent Frame control's `JournalOwnership` property. If there is no parent Frame control, then the navigation history will be stored in the browser journal. Note that if you are running an out-of-browser application, you cannot implement the navigation integrated with the browser. It will always run in the OwnsJournal mode while running in the out-of-browser mode.

You also need to add an iframe named _sl_historyFrame to the page hosting the Silverlight application plug-in, which is already added as part of the hosting pages (ASPX and HTML) created as part of the Silverlight application. In the custom hosting page, if you are using anything other than OwnsJournal mode, you must add the following code to the Silverlight application hosting page, to support navigation history.

```
<iframe id="_sl_historyFrame"
  style="visibility:hidden;height:0px;width:0px;border:0px"></iframe>
```

Implementing Custom Navigation

The Silverlight navigation framework is not only about simplifying the navigation across the Silverlight application. Silverlight 4 adds a public ContentLoader property (see Table 11-3) to the Frame control and introduces the INavigationContentLoader interface. The INavigationContentLoader interface defines methods for loading content that corresponds to a URI. Together this allows developers to develop pluggable custom navigation using their own scheme and allows loading of arbitrary content in conjunction with the Silverlight navigation enabling scenarios, such as authentication redirects, custom error pages, and MVC-style navigation. This way you can have control over Frame about turning URIs into content.

The INavigationContentLoader Interface

The INavigationContentLoader interface resides in the namespace System.Windows.Navigation in the System.Windows.Controls.Navigation assembly. The PageResourceContentLoader class is the only INavigationContentLoader implementation in the Silverlight 4 framework. By default the ContentLoader property is set to an instance of this class when it is not explicitly set on the Frame.

Table 11-4 shows the methods provided by the INavigationContentLoader interface.

Table 11-4. Methods Provided by the INavigationContentLoader Interface

Method	Description
BeginLoad	Begins asynchronous loading of the content for the specified target URI.
CancelLoad	Attempts to cancel content loading for the specified asynchronous operation.
CanLoad	Gets a value that indicates whether the specified URI can be loaded.
EndLoad	Completes the asynchronous content loading operation.

The BeginLoad Method

The signature of the INavigationContentLoader.BeginLoad method is as follows:

```
IAsyncResult BeginLoad(
    Uri targetUri,
    Uri currentUri,
    AsyncCallback userCallback,
    Object asyncState
)
```

The return type of the BeginLoad method is an IAsyncResult object that stores information about the asynchronous operation. The targetUri parameter is the URI to load content for, and currentUri is the URI that is currently loaded. userCallback is the method called when the content finishes loading. And finally the last parameter asyncState is of type Object for storing custom state information. This method is called by the navigation system to begin loading the content that corresponds to the targetUri value.

The CancelLoad Method

The signature of the INavigationContentLoader.CancelLoad method is as follows:

```
void CancelLoad(IAsyncResult asyncResult)
```

The parameter asyncResult identifies the asynchronous operation to cancel. Usually this method is called by the navigation system, to cancel the load request, when either the Frame.StopLoading or NavigationService.StopLoading methods are called, or a new navigation occurs before the previous one is completed. The CancelLoad method does not ensure that the asynchronous operation will be canceled. You need to check whether the EndMethod returns value to determine if the operation was really cancelled.

The CanLoad Method

The signature of the INavigationContentLoader.CanLoad method is as follows:

```
bool CanLoad(
    Uri targetUri,
    Uri currentUri
)
```

This method is called by the navigation system to check whether a particular URI is available for navigation. You can use this method to validate the correct format of the URI before loading it. The targetUri parameter represents the URI to test and the currentUri parameter represents the URI that is currently loaded. The method returns true if the passed URI as targetUri can be loaded, otherwise it returns false.

The EndLoad Method

The signature of the INavigationContentLoader.EndLoad method is as follows:

```
LoadResult EndLoad(IAsyncResult asyncResult)
```

The EndLoad method returns the System.Windows.Navigation.LoadResult object providing access to the loaded content or to a redirection URI. Usually this method is called by the navigation system from the userCallback delegate passed to the BeginLoad method (see the signature of the BeginLoad method) to retrieve the loaded content or a redirection URI. So the argument passed to the userCallback method is passed to the EndLoad method. You can also pass the userCallback parameter of the BeginLoad method as a null reference to call the EndLoad value and pass the returned value of the BeginLoad method. Here, the EndLoad method will block until the operation completes.

Summarizing How to Use the INavigationContentLoader Interface

The following steps summarize the use of the INavigationContentLoader interface with the Frame control and NavigationService:

1. Frame or NavigationService receives a request to navigate to an URI and so it uses its UriMapper to map the URI it was given.

2. Frame or NavigationService passes the current URI and the target URI to the content loader by calling the BeginLoad method.

3. Frame or NavigationService waits for an AsyncCallback (userCallback) from the content loader. Meanwhile, if the StopLoading method is called either on Frame or NavigationService, the CancelLoad method is called.

4. When called back, Frame or NavigationService calls the EndLoad method on the content loader and receives a LoadResult object.

5. If the LoadResult object contains a redirect Uri, the new load operation is begun with the new URI as the target by Frame or NavigationService. Otherwise, Frame or NavigationService displays the content retrieved as the LoadResult object.

Extending the Example

We will develop a class called CustomAuthContentLoader, implementing INavigationContentLoader, but we will make use of PageResourceContentLoader to avoid full implementation of the interface to save on code and time, to remain within the scope of this book. The custom content loader will load the login screen when we try to navigate to a page that requires authentication. So let's start by creating a simple login screen first.

Before we start to design a login page, open App.xaml.cs and create an application-level boolean flag called IsLoggedIn, which will determine whether the user is logged in.

```
public static bool IsLoggedIn { get; set; }
```

Now right-click the Views folder in the AdvanceFeaturesDemoApp Silverlight project, add a new item of type Silverlight Page, and name it LoginPage.xaml. The complete XAML markup for this page is as follows. Note that I have highlighted the added code markup in bold.

```
<navigation:Page x:Class="AdvanceFeaturesDemoApp.Views.LoginPage"
    xmlns="http://schemas.microsoft.com/winfx/2006/xaml/presentation"
    xmlns:x="http://schemas.microsoft.com/winfx/2006/xaml"
    xmlns:d="http://schemas.microsoft.com/expression/blend/2008"
    xmlns:mc="http://schemas.openxmlformats.org/
        markup-compatibility/2006"
    mc:Ignorable="d"
    xmlns:sdk="http://schemas.microsoft.com/winfx/2006/xaml/
        presentation/sdk"
    xmlns:navigation="clr-namespace:System.Windows.Controls;
        assembly=System.Windows.Controls.Navigation"
    Height="140" Width="210"
    Title="LoginPage Page" >
```

```xml
<StackPanel x:Name="LayoutRoot" HorizontalAlignment="Left"
    Background="Aqua" Width="210">
    <sdk:Label Height="28" Content="UserID"
        FontWeight="Bold"  Width="200" />
    <TextBox x:Name="txtUserID" Height="23" Width="200" />
    <sdk:Label Height="28" Content="Password"
        FontWeight="Bold" Width="200" />
    <PasswordBox x:Name="txtPassword" Height="23"  Width="200"/>
    <Button x:Name="btnLogin" Content="Login" Height="23"
        Width="75" HorizontalAlignment="Left" Margin="5"
        Click="btnLogin_Click" />
</StackPanel>
</navigation:Page>
```

First add a reference to System.Windows.Controls.Data.Input to the project. Now the code for btnLogin_Click is self-explanatory, as follows.

```csharp
private void btnLogin_Click(object sender, RoutedEventArgs e)
{
    //call your WCF authentication service here and validate
    //the user set application level boolean flag as per result
    //received from the service
    //For demo purpose, I am only checking the supplied
    //credentials against string
    if (txtUserID.Text == "Ashish" && txtPassword.Password=="123456")
    {
        App.IsLoggedIn = true;
        this.NavigationService.Navigate
            (new Uri("/Home", UriKind.Relative));
    }
    else
    {
        ErrorWindow ew = new ErrorWindow("Incorrect Login",
            "The login credentials you supplied are not correct.
            Please try again");
        ew.Title = "Login error";
        ew.IntroductoryText.Text = "";
        ew.Show();
    }
}
```

For simplicity, the user name and password are hardcoded. However, in real practice, you will probably call a WCF service–based authentication service. As just shown, if you enter correct credentials, the Home.xaml page will be shown, and on passing incorrect credentials, an error window will pop up, showing the custom error message and details.

Next let's implement the custom ContentLoader. Right-click the AdvanceFeaturesDemoApp Silverlight project and create a folder called CustomContentLoader. From now on we will add the class files to this folder. So let's add a new class named CustomAuthContentLoader and add the following required namespace.

```
using System.Windows.Navigation;
using System.Threading;
```

The AuthLoaderAsyncResult Class

First within the CustomAuthContentLoader class file, we will create a new class called AuthLoaderAsyncResult that inherits IAsyncResults. IAsyncResults is implemented by a class whose method operates asynchronously, and it is the return type of such methods. In our case the method is the BeginLoad method that will return an object of this class to the calling Frame or NavigationService.

Create a class called AuthLoaderAsyncResult that inherits the IAsyncResult.

```
public class AuthLoaderAsyncResult : IAsyncResult
```

The quick way to implement all the members of this interface is using IntelliSense, provided by Visual Studio 2010. Using IntelliSense, after you type the name of an interface in a class declaration (or you place the cursor over the interface name for some time), a smart tag is displayed. The smart tag gives you the option to implement the interface automatically, using explicit or implicit naming. In our case, choose implicit, as shown in Figure 11-3.

Figure 11-3. *IntelliSense in Visual Studio showing options for automatic implementation of the interface*

Now delete all the lines that throw the NotImplementedException exception from all the properties. Since AsyncState and IsCompleted do simple getting and setting operations, we can omit the body implementation for them by using the automatic properties feature in C# in the following way.

```
public object AsyncState { get; private set; }
public bool IsCompleted { get; private set; }
```

The code for the other two properties for our requirement will go like this:

```
public WaitHandle AsyncWaitHandle
{
    get { return null; }
}

public bool CompletedSynchronously
{
    get { return false; }
}
```

As for the internal working of the class, we need the following three properties as well when we initialize through the constructor.

```
internal Uri Uri { get; set; }
internal Uri RedirectUri { get; set; }
internal object Content { get; set; }
```

The following is the implementation of the constructor.

```
public AuthLoaderAsyncResult(Uri uri, object asyncState)
{
    this.AsyncState = asyncState;
    this.Uri = uri;
}
```

The CustomAuthContentLoader Class

Now it's time to develop the CustomAuthContentLoader class inheriting the INavigationContentLoader interface.

```
public class CustomAuthContentLoader : INavigationContentLoader
```

Implement the interface members the same way we did for the AuthLoaderAsyncResult class. As I mentioned earlier, we will use the PageResourceContentLoader object to load pages that correspond to a given URI.

```
PageResourceContentLoader Loader = new PageResourceContentLoader();
```

The complete code for the BeginLoad method is as follows:

```
public IAsyncResult BeginLoad(Uri targetUri, Uri currentUri,
    AsyncCallback userCallback, object asyncState)
{
    AuthLoaderAsyncResult result = new
        AuthLoaderAsyncResult(currentUri, asyncState);

    if (targetUri.Equals(new Uri
        ("/Views/Home.xaml", UriKind.Relative)))
    {
        if (App.IsLoggedIn)
        {
            result.Content = new Home();
        }
        else
        {
            result.RedirectUri = new
                Uri("/LoginPage", UriKind.Relative);
        }

        if (userCallback != null)
        {
            userCallback(result);
        }
```

```
        return result;
    }

    return Loader.BeginLoad
        (targetUri, currentUri, userCallback, asyncState);
}
```

Before loading the requested URI, this method will check whether the user is logged in by checking the value of the IsLoggedIn Boolean flag. If the user is not logged in, it will redirect the request to LoginPage.xaml and return the result to the calling NavigationService or Frame. For a page other than Home.xaml, there is no authentication needed, so it will simply call Loader.BeginLoad for that.

The complete code for the EndLoad method is as follows:

```
public LoadResult EndLoad(IAsyncResult asyncResult)
{
    AuthLoaderAsyncResult result = asyncResult
        as AuthLoaderAsyncResult;

    if (result == null)
    {
        return Loader.EndLoad(asyncResult);
    }
    elseif (result.Content != null)
    {
        return new LoadResult(result.Content);
    }
    else
    {
        return new LoadResult(result.RedirectUri);
    }
}
```

As mentioned earlier, this method gets called by NavigationService or Frame on the Callback function because by that time the operation has already completed, and so LoadResult is available to return to the calling environment.

The code for the CanLoad method is as simple as the following:

```
public bool CanLoad(Uri targetUri, Uri currentUri)
{
    if (targetUri.Equals(new Uri("/Views/Home.xaml",
        UriKind.Relative)))
    {
        return true;
    }

    return Loader.CanLoad(targetUri, currentUri);
}
```

And finally, the code for the last method, CancelLoad, is as follows.

```
public void CancelLoad(IAsyncResult asyncResult)
{
    Loader.CancelLoad(asyncResult);
}
```

Now our custom content loader class is completed. Next jump back to `MainPage.xaml` and add the following XML namespace.

```
xmlns:local="clr-namespace:AdvanceFeaturesDemoApp.CustomContentLoader"
```

And set the `ContentLoader` property of the navigation:Frame named ContentFrame to our CustomAuthContentLoader.

```
<navigation:Frame.ContentLoader>
    <local:CustomAuthContentLoader />
</navigation:Frame.ContentLoader>
```

Now run the project by pressing F5. Upon running the project, the login page will be shown in center of the screen, which requires you to log in before viewing the `Home.xaml` page (see Figure 11-4). At this point, if you click the "About page" link, the login page will disappear and you can view the "About" page. And, again, if you click the Home page link, the login page appears again. If you supply incorrect credentials, the ErrorWindow will come up, showing the error details. Once you log in with Ashish and password 123456, it will show the `Home.xaml` page.

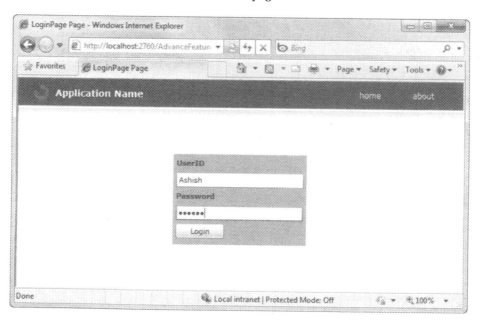

Figure 11-4. Implementation of the custom content loader showing the login page

Deep Linking

If you take a closer look at Figure 11-2, you will notice that the browser address bar includes the page-specific URL, which is `http://localhost:2760/AdvanceFeaturesDemoAppTestPage.aspx#/Home`.

When you switch from one page to another page, the Frame control generates the page-specific URL and query string that can be used to go directly to that particular page. As explained earlier, with the use of the Source property of the `navigation:Frame` tag, you can have the default page displayed as the start-up page of the application. Thus, by leveraging the navigation framework, Silverlight supports *deep linking*, which helps the user bookmark the page and supports SEO.

The URL can expose the real XAML page name or you can customize the page URL to make it user-friendly by using the UriMapper control (as we learned earlier in the "User-Friendly URIs" section of this chapter). As explained in Tim Heuer's video available on Silverlight.net (`www.silverlight.net/learn/learnvideo.aspx?video=187319`), you can define the UriMapper control at the frame level or the application resource level. You can see the available `uriMapper` namespace containing the UriMapper control in the `MainPage.xaml` file, as shown here:

```
xmlns:uriMapper="clr-namespace:System.Windows.Navigation;
    assembly=System.Windows.Controls.Navigation"
```

Now you can define the UriMapper control of the navigation framework. The UriMapper control can contain one or more UriMapping controls defining the mapping of specific pages. As shown in the following example, the `Uri` property defines the URL that is displayed by the browser, whereas the `MappedUri` attribute defines the actual page URL:

```
<uriMapper:UriMapper>
    <uriMapper:UriMapping Uri=""
        MappedUri="/Views/Home.xaml"/>
    <uriMapper:UriMapping Uri="/{pageName}"
        MappedUri="/Views/{pageName}.xaml"/>
</uriMapper:UriMapper>
```

Please note that here the URI mapping operation is based on the page of the name as specified by pageName in the URI of UriMapper.

Search Engine Optimization

A single topic in the book is not sufficient to understand and cover the subject of search engine optimization (SEO). There are many areas of search engine optimization, from how search engines work to how a search engine–friendly web page is designed. At a high-level summary, SEO can be thought as the science of customizing elements of your web site to achieve the best possible search engine ranking. This section of the book will address SEO in the context of Silverlight RIAs.

Silverlight RIAs work dynamically. This means that when you load the page, you do not see static content but a desktop-like application, and you can work with the application almost in the same way you work with a desktop application. The single key problem is that the search engine (Google, Yahoo, Bing, or others) cannot see what is inside these RIAs, simply because they cannot read them. Their search robots cannot understand JavaScript, CSS, or Silverlight content. In fact, often the HTML page simply becomes a container of "Silverlight embed tags" and doesn't contain the meaningful data that needs to be indexed. So the daunting task here is how to tell the search robot what is inside your Silverlight RIA so the search engine can analyze and index it for the search keywords that target your RIA.

Let's visit the Silverlight embed tag in the application test HTML web page:

```
<div id="silverlightControlHost">
    <object data="data:application/x-silverlight-2,"
        type="application/x-silverlight-2"
        width="100%" height="100%">
        <param name="source"
            value="ClientBin/AdvanceFeaturesDemoApp.xap"/>
        <param name="onError" value="onSilverlightError" />
        <param name="background" value="white" />
        <param name="minRuntimeVersion" value="4.0.50401.0" />
        <param name="autoUpgrade" value="true" />
        <a href="http://go.microsoft.com/fwlink/?LinkID=
            149156&v=4.0.50401.0" style="text-decoration:none">
            <img src="http://go.microsoft.com/fwlink/?LinkId=161376"
                alt="Get Microsoft Silverlight"
                style="border-style:none"/>
        </a>
    </object>
    <iframe id="_sl_historyFrame"
        style="visibility:hidden;height:0px;width:0px;border:0px">
    </iframe>
</div>
```

Here the highlighted bold line is what the search engine robots see when they visit the web page that hosts a Silverlight application. And you can see that the "Get Microsoft Silverlight" message has nothing to do with your original Silverlight RIA contents and keywords.

There is no single silver bullet to make your Silverlight RIA search engine–friendly. The reality is that not only are application development platforms and the community exploring all possible alternative techniques to make the application search engine–friendly, but search engines also are continuously fine-tuning their approach to avoid information overload and help end-users to provide the right information at the right time.

You can check the search engine friendliness of the developed Silverlight RIA using free services, such as those provided by www.seo-browser.com (provided by commerx). Figure 11-5 shows a screen shot of the advanced SEO analysis report generated by www.seo-browser.com for the quince.infragistics.com site, which is developed in Silverlight 3.

Figure 11-5. seo-browser.com showing an SEO analysis of the quince.infragistics.com web site in the advanced mode

In the preceding example, the HTML meta tag is used with description and keyword attributes to provide information about the Silverlight application. You can see the implementation by clicking on the Source Code option provided by the web site. Similarly you can also use the title tag and other techniques, such as extracting text from XAML and indexing it.

Additional References

As stated earlier, there is no single silver bullet to make your Silverlight RIA search engine–friendly.

- Ashish Shetty published a document describing the best practices to implement SEO techniques to make Silverlight RIAs search engine–friendly: www.silverlight.net/learn/whitepapers/seo-for-silverlight/.

- Visit www.silverlightshow.net/items/Silverlight-SEO.aspx to get an overview of Silverlight SEO.

- An open-source project called Silverlight SEO on Codeplex (http://silverlightseo.codeplex.com/) is available, which simplifies configuring sites that host Silverlight navigation applications for search engine optimization. It can provide HTML content to search engine crawlers and Silverlight to users with the plug-in installed.

Out-of-Browser Functionality

Globalization has broken the physical boundaries between organizations and end-users and has introduced the concept of virtual organizations and virtual communities (as part of social networking). As a result, enterprise mobility has become a strategic initiative for any organization in defining next-generation RIAs that support virtual organizations and collaborative virtual community needs. Therefore, to support the mobile workforce and a diversified and distributed user community, you need to consider available connectivity, signal strength, available bandwidth, and support for disconnected mode aspects of enterprise mobility while designing and developing any RIA. Support for disconnected mode (i.e., offline mode) makes any RIA a complete solution.

Silverlight 3 introduced out-of-browser Silverlight application capabilities, as well as new networking APIs (to detect the connected and disconnected modes and changes in the network connection state) and new offline APIs (to detect the application running mode and version updates). These features meant that Silverlight applications could be installed on user machines and be running in disconnected and connected modes as rich client applications in the out-of-browser mode.

The out-of-browser application is installed on the local machine, so you do not need any additional plug-ins (other than Silverlight plug-in) to work offline. While running in out-of-browser mode, the application runs as a Windows application but in the Silverlight sandbox environment, and you can utilize an isolated cache to perform any offline operations (including file management). The isolated storage quota for applications running in the out-of-browser mode is increased to 25MB from 1 MB. You can save the data in the isolated cache, and the next time you're connected, you can synchronize the updated data back to the central database system with your custom implementation.

■ **Note** A sandbox is a security-enabled environment for separating running programs and often used to execute untested code, or untrusted programs from unverified third-parties, suppliers, and untrusted users. The sandbox environment typically provides a tightly-controlled set of resources for guest programs to run in, such as isolated space on disk and memory. Network access, the ability to inspect the host system or read from input devices are usually disallowed or heavily restricted in the sandbox.

With Silverlight 4, out-of-browser applications come in two types: sandboxed (partially trusted) and trusted (with elevated trust). The default is sandboxed. Silverlight 4 introduces the new type, trusted. The trusted out-of-browser applications have greater access to local machine resources and devices compared to the sandboxed partially-trusted applications such as:

- Native integration with the host operating system such as automation support via COM (Windows platform only).

- Ability to read and write files on the local disk and not restricted to just isolated storage.

- Cross-domain networking and sockets are allowed without the need of policy files.

However, it does not mean that trusted applications have completely unrestricted access to the local resources. The trusted applications must be installed and run in the out-of-browser mode. For more details on partially-trusted and elevated-trusted applications, visit Chapter 12.

■ **Note** Silverlight has been developed entirely under Microsoft's Secure Development Lifecycle (SDL), a methodology that includes threat modeling of designs, fuzz testing file formats and network interfaces, penetration testing, and static analysis tools. See `www.microsoft.com/security/sdl/default.aspx` for more information about the Secure Development Lifecycle.

We'll now show how easy it is to make any Silverlight application capable of supporting out-of-browser capabilities by updating the Silverlight navigation project we created earlier in this chapter. Then we will also see enhancements made to the out-of-browser model in Silverlight 4.

Enabling the Out-of-Browser Functionality

All Silverlight applications come with the basics of out-of-browser functionality, but by default the option is not enabled. So, you'll need to enable the functionality.

To enable the out-of-browser functionality, right-click the AdvanceFeaturesDemoApp Silverlight project and choose Properties from the menu. Within the Silverlight tab, under the "Silverlight build options" section, you will see check box "Enable running application out of browser." At a minimum, to enable Silverlight 4 applications in the out-of-browser mode, you need to check this check box. When you do so, the Out-of-Browser Settings… button gets enabled and you can click it to open a window to set up various parameters and settings for the out-of-browser application, such as shortcut name, application description, and application icons for different screen resolutions, as shown in Figure 11-6.

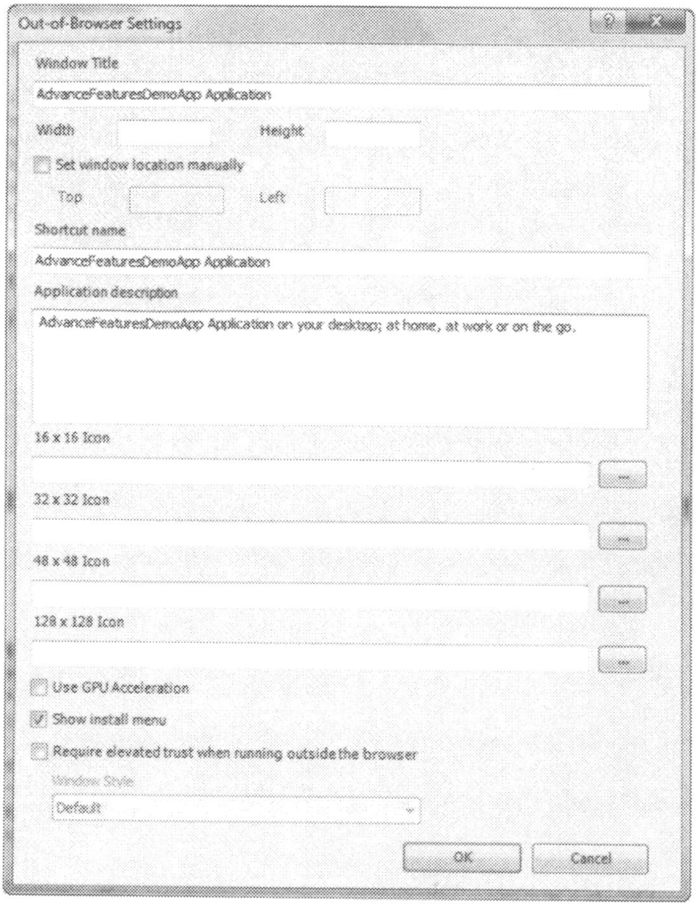

Figure 11-6. Silverlight 4 out-of-browser settings window

An OutOfBrowserSettings.xml file is automatically added in the Properties folder of the AdvanceFeaturesDemoApp, as shown here. It includes all the settings we made so far (see Figure 11-6).

```
<OutOfBrowserSettings ShortName="AdvanceFeaturesDemoApp Application"
    EnableGPUAcceleration="False" ShowInstallMenuItem="True">
  <OutOfBrowserSettings.Blurb>
      AdvanceFeaturesDemoApp Application on your desktop;
      at home, at work or on the go.
  </OutOfBrowserSettings.Blurb>
  <OutOfBrowserSettings.WindowSettings>
      <WindowSettings Title="AdvanceFeaturesDemoApp Application" />
  </OutOfBrowserSettings.WindowSettings>
  <OutOfBrowserSettings.Icons />
</OutOfBrowserSettings>
```

Installing Out-of-Browser Applications

There are two ways you can perform installation of the out-of-browser–enabled Silverlight applications: in-browser install (default of custom installation) and silent install.

In-Browser Install: Default Option

You have to take no extra steps to use the default in-browser installation capability to set up a Silverlight application in the out-of-browser mode. Once you enable the application for out-of-browser mode, just run the project and right-click the application running in the browser. You should see an additional option available (in addition to Silverlight) to enable installation of the application to run in the out-of-browser mode (see Figure 11-7).

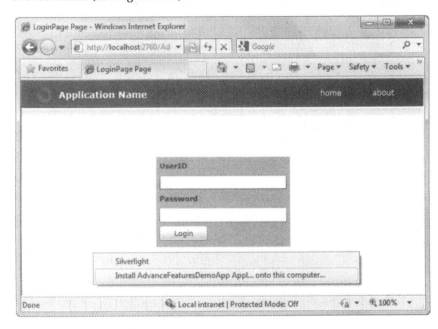

Figure 11-7. *Option to install the Silverlight application onto the computer to enable out-of-browser functionality*

Next, select the option to install the Silverlight application, and you will see a pop-up user consent window with a default icon image with options to create shortcuts on the desktop and Start menu, as shown in Figure 11-8.

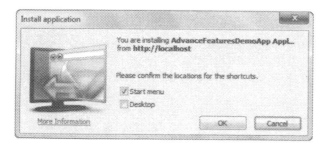

Figure 11-8. Installing the Silverlight application with the appropriate shortcuts

You can select or deselect the option to create shortcuts and click OK to install the application. The application will be installed onto your desktop, the appropriate shortcuts with default icons will be created based on your selection to your machine, and the application will be opened in out-of-browser mode, as shown in Figure 11-9. The application contains the default application icon and also shows the window title with the text you populated in the Title property of the ApplicationIdentity section of the AppManifest.xml file.

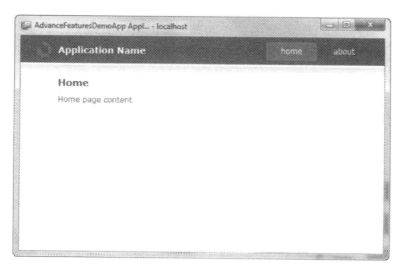

Figure 11-9. Silverlight application running in out-of-browser mode

In-Browser Install: Custom Developed Option

The custom out-of-browser application installation option in addition to the default right-click option is a useful way to improve the user experience. It is also very straightforward to implement.

You can determine whether the application in the out-of-browser mode is installed by using the Application.InstallState property. It actually returns the out-of-browser application installation state and can have four possible states. System.Windows.InstallState.NotInstalled means that the application is not installed in the out-of-browser mode. The Installing state means the installation process is in progress. The Installed state means the application has been installed as an out-of-browser application.

And the InstallFailed state means the application could not install successfully to run in the out-of-browser mode.

You can also use the `Application.IsRunningOutOfBrowser` property to determine if the application is running in the out-of-browser mode (returns a `true` value) or running in the in-browser mode (returns a `false` value). You can also use this property to provide unique application mode (in-browser vs. out-of-browser mode) specific functionalities.

Finally you use the `Application.Install()` method, which can be called from the user-initiated event, to install the application to enable the out-of-browser mode. Note that you will receive a similar user consent pop-up window (see Figure 11-8) asking for user permission to install. If installation fails, it will throw an `InvalidOperationException` exception.

Silent Install

Until Silverlight 3, you had to use an in-browser session to install the out-of-browser application. In some cases where you want to distribute and deploy the application via a managed desktop software installer, CD-ROM, or Network share, you can use the silent installation approach introduced in Silverlight 4. With the silent install approach you don't need to start the in-browser session to install the application.

The `sllauncher.exe` utility tool is used to enable the silent installation. This tool gets installed with the Silverlight plug-in and is located at `%Program Files%\Microsoft Silverlight` on 32-bit OS or `%Program Files(x86)%\Microsoft Silverlight` on 64-bit OS.

To develop a silent install approach, there are two prerequisites; first you should have the copy of the XAP file that you want to install, and secondly you must ensure that the proper version of the Silverlight plug-in is installed. The `sllauncher.exe` tool provides the following parameters for installation.

- */install:"path to xap file"*:This is the first and required option and points to the XAP file you want to install. As said earlier, it can be on a local machine, network share, or on the CD.

- */origin:"Uri to origin of the xap file"*: Required option specifies the origin of the XAP. Even though you might not be using auto-update features, it is advisable to provide a real origin for the XAP you are installing.

- */shortcut:desktop+startmenu*: This is an optional option but it is advisable to choose both the desktop as well as the Start menu for the shortcut location. You can specify desktop, Start menu, or desktop+Start menu for this option.

- */overwrite*: This option confirms that the version of the XAP file you are installing will overwrite any existing version currently installed. This is optional but it is good practice to include this in the install command.

- */emulate:"path to xap file"*: This option provides a way to start an out-of-browser application in emulation mode without the need of installing it.

Let's install the application that we just enabled for out-of-browser mode. Open the command prompt and navigate to the `ClientBin` folder of the project (the path will be different based on where you have set up the project in your machine) and run the install command. Note that the following install command is for the 64-bit OS and must be typed in a single line:

```
"%ProgramFiles(x86)%\Microsoft Silverlight\sllauncher.exe"
/install:"AdvanceFeaturesDemoApp.xap"
/origin:"http://localhost:2760/ClientBin/AdvanceFeaturesDemoApp.xap"
/shortcut:desktop+startmenu
/overwrite
```

Note that here I am providing full absolute URI to the XAP package for the origin option. Upon successful completion of the preceding command, you should see shortcuts for AdvanceFeaturesDemoApp Appl... are created in Start menu->All Programs and on the desktop.

The emulate option provides a way to launch the application without installing it. But behind the scenes, the application gets installed at a random location on the disk and then launched immediately. For consistent behavior, it is best to provide an overwrite option when using this option. This option can be useful while developing a CD/DVD auto-run scenario. The command for our application will go something like this in one line.

```
"%ProgramFiles(x86)%\Microsoft Silverlight\sllauncher.exe"
/emulate:"AdvanceFeaturesDemoApp.xap" /origin:"http://localhost:2760/ClientBin/↵
AdvanceFeaturesDemoApp.xap" /overwrite
```

Upon successful completion of that command, the application will start immediately in out-of-browser mode.

This topic is covered in more depth in Chapter 17.

▦ **Caution** The silent install is currently available for Windows machines only.

Uninstalling Out-of-Browser Applications

There are two ways you can uninstall out-of-browser Silverlight applications—the default right-click option and silent uninstall.

The Default Option

There is no extra effort involved to use the default uninstallation option to uninstall existing Silverlight applications in the OOB mode. Once the application is installed, either running in the in-browser or out-of-browser mode, just right-click the running application. This time you should see an additional option available (in addition to Silverlight) to uninstall the out-of-browser Silverlight application.

The Silent Uninstall Option

In silent install, there is also automation for performing an uninstall of the application using the sllauncher.exe utility. As shown, simply issue the origin command in one line to uninstall the application that we just installed:

```
"%ProgramFiles(x86)%\Microsoft Silverlight\sllauncher.exe"
/uninstall
/origin:"http://localhost:2760/ClientBin/AdvanceFeaturesDemoApp.xap"
```

This command will silently uninstall the application, and you will see that the application shortcuts are removed from the desktop as well from the Start menu.

Trusted Out-of-Browser Applications

So far we have learned how to make Silverlight applications run out of the browser and install them. The application is still a sandboxed partially-trusted application with the same set of restrictions, just like in the in-browser mode. Let's make this application trusted with elevated trust, so we can have access to special features in OOB mode.

In order to request elevated permissions while installing the out-of-browser application, OutOfBrowserSettings.xml must have SecuritySettings with ElevatedPermissions set to Required to enable elevated trust. You can select the option by selecting the "Require elevated trust when running outside the browser" option in the out-of-browser setting window (revisit Figure 11-6). This adds a new section to the OutOfBrowserSettings.xml file:

```
<OutOfBrowserSettings.SecuritySettings>
    <SecuritySettings ElevatedPermissions="Required" />
</OutOfBrowserSettings.SecuritySettings>
```

When you make the application trusted, the install prompt is changed to one that is shown in Figure 11-10 (compare to Figure 11-8).

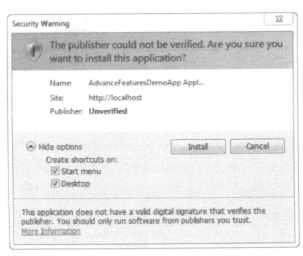

Figure 11-10. Silverlight out-of-browser trusted application install prompt

---

▓ **Note** Visit Chapter 15 to get more details on configuring a Silverlight application to run with elevated trust in the out-of-browser mode and how to sign the XAP file digitally using a digital certificate.

By making the application trusted, we can have access to special features (in out-of-browser mode) such as Silverlight OOB window manipulation, cross-domain network access without policy file check, getting a full file path from the Open/Save file dialog, access to user folders, like Documents and Pictures, and COM Interoperability. We will learn these features as we go through this chapter.

Customizing Out-of-Browser Applications

Right from Silverlight 3, the out-of-browser application model tends to reassemble the flavor of desktop applications as much as possible. Silverlight 3 introduced the out-of-browser mode with the ability to supply custom icons for the application shortcuts. The Silverlight 4 release introduces a new set of APIs to programmatically resize the out-of-browser windows and control its position on the screen. For trusted OOB applications, you can choose from various window styles. Let's take a look at these features one by one.

Custom Icons

You can change the default icons for the installation window, out-of-browser application window, desktop, and Start menu icons by adding <Icon/> in the <OutOfBrowserSettings.Icons> node in the file OutofBrowserSettings.xml and adding the appropriate size of <Icon> nodes. You can use the Size attributes 16x16, 32x32, 48x48, and 128x128 to cover all the possibilities. You can also set custom icons from the out-of-browser settings window as shown in Figure 11-6. Then you need to the add the appropriate icon files in PNG format to your application and change the BuildAction property from Resource to Content for each icon image file. Then add the appropriate path for each Icon node. The following is a sample code snippet demonstrating incorporating custom icons, where required. Different sizes of images are available in the Icons folder with the following names.

```
<OutOfBrowserSettings.Icons>
    <Icon Size="16,16">Assets/icons/16x.png</Icon>
    <Icon Size="32,32">Assets/icons/32x.png</Icon>
    <Icon Size="48,48">Assets/icons/64x.png</Icon>
    <Icon Size="128,128">Assets/icons/128x.png</Icon>
</OutOfBrowserSettings.Icons>
```

If you run the application now, you should see custom-added icons for the application download window, out-of-browser application window, and shortcuts. The operating system chooses the most appropriate icon to display for the installation window, out-of-browser application window, desktop, and Start menu icons. You need to consider the following three issues to make sure the application installs and runs without error:

- Icon files must be of the PNG file type.

- The added icon files' BuildAction property must be set to Content.

- Icon files must be added correctly, and you must have all four mentioned (i.e., no icon should be missing). Otherwise, the installation process will fail.

Window Manipulation and Customization

New Windowing APIs in Silverlight 4 enable you to programmatically control the top and left positions of the out-of-browser window, bring it to the foreground (if not active), check if the window is topmost, and define its width and height. So this way you can modify the out-of-browser application window at runtime. For example, you can also handle the Closing event, which you can cancel except when the computer is shutting down or the user is logging off. The Closing event enables you to perform actions such as displaying a warning that the user has unsaved changes in the application data.

All of these features are being exposed by the MainWindow object of the application, as shown in Figure 11-11.

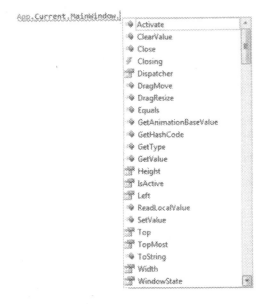

Figure 11-11. Application.MainWindow providing different properties for controlling the position of applications running in out-of-browser mode

Trusted applications can hide the title bar and border of the out-of-browser application window in order to provide a completely customized user interface. The Window class provides APIs that trusted applications can use to replace the title bar buttons and enable mouse-dragging to move or resize the window. To apply a window style, you need to select styles from the Window Style drop-down list that is placed last in the Out-of-Browser Settings window (See Figure 11-6).

Figure 11-12 shows this drop-down list expanded.

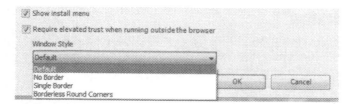

Figure 11-12. *Drop-down list showing possible window styles for the OOB trusted application window*

Basically these windows styles control how the title bar and border should appear in the window. If you choose No Border or Borderless Round Corners options, you will lose the title bar, and thus the default minimize, maximize, and close buttons along with default drag/move behavior. In that case you need to provide custom buttons as well drag/move behavior for your application.

As an example, to code for the custom Close button, you can use the Close method (see Figure 11-11) of the MainWindow object as shown in following code snippet.

```
if (Application.Current.IsRunningOutOfBrowser)
{
    Application.Current.MainWindow.Close();
}
```

And for drag/move behavior, you can code in MainPage.xaml.cs as follows.

```
bool isDragging = false;

private void MainPage_MouseLeftButtonDown
    (object sender, MouseButtonEventArgs e)
{
    if (Application.Current.IsRunningOutOfBrowser && ! isDragging)
        isDragging = true;
}

private void MainPage_MouseLeftButtonUp
    (object sender, MouseButtonEventArgs e)
{
    if (Application.Current.IsRunningOutOfBrowser && isDragging)
        isDragging = false;
}

private void MainPage_MouseMove(object sender, MouseEventArgs e)
{
    if (isDragging)
        Application.Current.MainWindow.DragMove();
}
```

Working with the Networking and Offline APIs

Now let's take a brief look at the networking APIs and offline APIs by incorporating them into the sample application.

First remove the TextBlock with the name ApplicationNameTextBlock from the XAML code, and then add the following lines of code to represent the application connectivity status (Connected/Disconnected) and application running mode (In Browser/Out of Browser):

```
<StackPanel>
    <TextBlock FontWeight="Bold" Foreground="White" >
        Connectivity Status</TextBlock>
    <TextBlock x:Name="txtNWStatus" FontSize="14"  >
    </TextBlock>
 </StackPanel>

<StackPanel Margin="15,0,0,0">
    <TextBlock FontWeight="Bold" Foreground="White" >
        Application Mode</TextBlock>
    <TextBlock x:Name="txtAppMode" FontSize="14"  >
    </TextBlock>
</StackPanel>
```

To get the application network connectivity status, add the System.Net.NetworkInformation namespace to the MainPage.xaml code-behind class:

```
using System.Net.NetworkInformation;
```

Then create a private UpdateNetworkConnectivityStatus method to get the network connection status, update the status TextBlock tag's Text property to Connected or Disconnected, and change the TextBlock tag's Foreground to Cyan or Red. Here you call the NetworkInterface.GetIsNetworkAvailable method to get the network connectivity status. The following code snippet demonstrates this method:

```
private void UpdateNetworkConnectivityStatus()
{
    if (NetworkInterface.GetIsNetworkAvailable())
    {
        txtNWStatus.Text = "Connected";
        txtNWStatus.Foreground = new
            SolidColorBrush(Colors.Cyan);
    }
    else
    {
        txtNWStatus.Text = "Disconnected";
        txtNWStatus.Foreground = new
            SolidColorBrush(Colors.Red);
    }
}
```

Now under the MainPage constructor, add the Loaded and NetworkAddressChange event handlers to raise the event when the page is loaded and to report the status of the network connection upon a change in the network connectivity state, as shown in the following code snippet:

```
this.Loaded += new RoutedEventHandler(MainPage_Loaded);
NetworkChange.NetworkAddressChanged += new
```

```
NetworkAddressChangedEventHandler
  (NetworkChange_NetworkAddressChanged);
```

Now define both event handlers, and call the UpdateNetworkConnectivityStatus method, as shown in the following code snippet:

```
void MainPage_Loaded(object sender, RoutedEventArgs e)
{
    UpdateNetworkConnectivityStatus();
}

void NetworkChange_NetworkAddressChanged(object sender, EventArgs e)
{
    UpdateNetworkConnectivityStatus();
}
```

Save, build, and then run the application. You should see the start-up connected or disconnected status with cyan or red fonts in the browser. When you change the network connectivity state while running the application, the connectivity state will be automatically reflected in the application. If you install the application as an out-of-browser application and run it, you should see the same network connectivity status update behavior! Isn't it amazing?

Now let's update the application running status with the use of the ApplicationServiceContext.IsRunningOutOfBrowser property. Add a new UpdateApplicationModeStatus method, as shown here, which will utilize the ApplicationServiceContext.IsRunningOutOfBrowser property:

```
private void UpdateApplicationModeStatus()
{
    if (App.Current.IsRunningOutOfBrowser)
    {
        txtAppMode.Text = "Out of Browser";
        txtAppMode.Foreground = new SolidColorBrush(Colors.Yellow);
    }
    else
    {
        txtAppMode.Text = "In Browser";
        txtAppMode.Foreground = new SolidColorBrush(Colors.Yellow);
    }
}
```

Now call this method from the existing Loaded event of the MainPage to update the application mode.

If you run the application, you will see that the status is updated based on the network connection and application mode. Figure 11-13 shows the application running in in-browser mode with different versions for the network connection status.

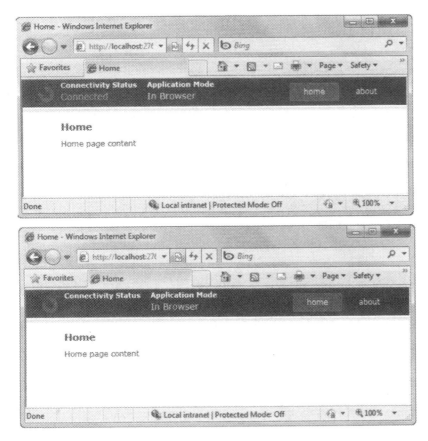

Figure 11-13. Silverlight application running in in-browser mode with different versions for the network connectivity states

Figure 11-14 shows the application running in out-of-browser mode with different versions for the network connection status.

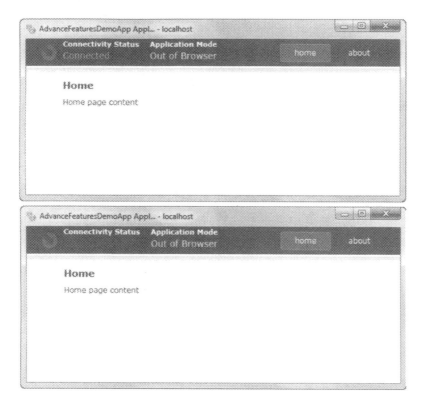

Figure 11-14. Silverlight application running in out-of-browser mode with different versions for the network connectivity states

Incorporating an Updated Version

The next logical question that may come to your mind is, "If the application is updated and you are running in out-of-browser mode, how would the user be notified of the availability of the new version of the application?" Here you can use CheckAndDownloadUpdateAsync, which basically checks for and retrieves the available update for the installed out-of-browser application. You can then handle the Application.CheckAndDownloadUpdateCompleted event. In the event handler the UpdateAvailable property value is true if a newer version of your application is discovered and successfully downloaded. In this case, you can alert the user to restart in order to load the update.

In the case where an application update requires a newer version of Silverlight than the currently installed version on the client machine, the update will not be downloaded. Partially trusted applications will not be updated when an update requires elevated trust. In both cases, the UpdateAvailable property value is false, and the Error property value is an Exception instance. With a Silverlight version change, the exception is a PlatformNotSupportedException instance. With a security change, the exception is a SecurityException instance. When this happens, you can alert the user to open the application's host web site and reinstall the application from there.

In the case of trusted out-of-browser applications, this update mechanism will not work unless the application and the update have both been signed with the same valid, code-signing certificate (see

Chapter 15). To update a trusted application that does not have a valid signature, users must uninstall the old version and install the new version manually.

Let's add a button just after the txtAppMode textblock in MainPage.xaml (see Figure 11-15) to demonstrate the application update process.

```
<Button Height="26" Margin="15,0,0,0" x:Name="btnCheckUpdate"
    Click="btnCheckUpdate_Click">Check for Update</Button>
```

The code for the btnCheckUpdate_Click event handler is as follows:

```
private void btnCheckUpdate_Click(object sender, RoutedEventArgs e)
{
    App.Current.CheckAndDownloadUpdateCompleted += new
        CheckAndDownloadUpdateCompletedEventHandler
            (Current_CheckAndDownloadUpdateCompleted);
    App.Current.CheckAndDownloadUpdateAsync();
}
```

The code for the CheckAndDownloadUpdateCompleted event handler is simple and just notifies the user about the update status of the application.

```
void Current_CheckAndDownloadUpdateCompleted
    (object sender, CheckAndDownloadUpdateCompletedEventArgs e)
{
    if (e.UpdateAvailable)
    {
        MessageBox.Show("An application update has been downloaded. "
            + "Restart the application to run the new version.");
    }
    else if (e.Error !=
        null && e.Error is PlatformNotSupportedException)
    {
        MessageBox.Show("An application update is available, " +
            "but it requires a new version of Silverlight. " +
            "Visit the application home page to upgrade.");
    }
    else
    {
        MessageBox.Show("There is no update available.");
    }
}
```

Figure 11-15 shows the resultant output with the custom application update availability option.

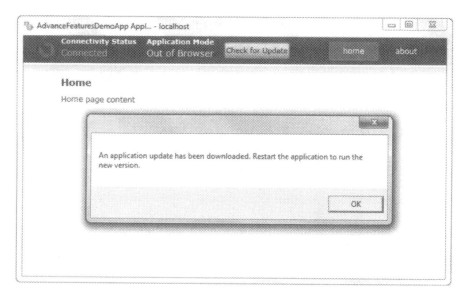

Figure 11-15. *Silverlight application running in out-of-browser mode and getting a message about the availability of the updated version on the server side*

Note that from now onwards, as example menu items increase, I have made the page navigation bar vertical and made some changes to the UI. You can view the supplied source code for this chapter for that. And from now on, I will assume that this sample application is in OOB mode with elevated privileges.

Files Management

Silverlight out-of-browser trusted applications have access to the user file system. For that, System.IO and related types are available to use. This enables you to access user files directly without using the OpenFileDialog and SaveFileDialog classes. However, you can access only files in user folders, specifically the MyDocuments, MyMusic, MyPictures, and MyVideos folders (on Windows OS) and similarly appropriate folders for Mac.

To demonstrate this feature, we will extend the application to enable browsing the My Pictures folder and sub folders (if any) for image files (JPG and PNG type). We will use Chapter 7's ImageWindow control for larger previews of images in this folder. So first add that control in the Views folder and change the namespace in XAML and code-behind from chapter7 to AdvanceFeaturesDemoApp. Add a new Silverlight page in the Views folder and name it LocalFileAccessDemo.xaml. Now open the XAML file and define a simplified user interface.

```
<navigation:Page
    x:Class="AdvanceFeaturesDemoApp.Views.LocalFileAccessDemo"
    xmlns="http://schemas.microsoft.com/winfx/2006/xaml/presentation"
    xmlns:x="http://schemas.microsoft.com/winfx/2006/xaml"
    xmlns:d="http://schemas.microsoft.com/expression/blend/2008"
    xmlns:mc="http://schemas.openxmlformats.org/markup-
        compatibility/2006"
```

```
    mc:Ignorable="d"
    xmlns:ms="clr-namespace:Microsoft.Windows;assembly=
        System.Windows.Controls.Toolkit"
    xmlns:navigation="clr-namespace:System.Windows.Controls;assembly=
        System.Windows.Controls.Navigation"
    d:DesignWidth="640" d:DesignHeight="480"
    Title="LocalFileAccessDemo Page"
    xmlns:sdk="http://schemas.microsoft.com/winfx/2006/xaml/
        presentation/sdk"
    xmlns:toolkit="http://schemas.microsoft.com/winfx/2006/
        xaml/presentation/toolkit">
    <Grid x:Name="LayoutRoot" Background="White" Loaded="LocalFileAccessDemo_Loaded">
        <Grid.ColumnDefinitions>
            <ColumnDefinition Width="230"></ColumnDefinition>
            <ColumnDefinition Width="*" > </ColumnDefinition>
        </Grid.ColumnDefinitions>
        <StackPanel Width="200" HorizontalAlignment="Left" >
            <TextBlock  Text="My Pictures"
                FontWeight="Bold" FontSize="14"/>
            <sdk:TreeView x:Name="treeDir"
                 SelectedItemChanged="treeDir_SelectedItemChanged">
            </sdk:TreeView>
        </StackPanel>
        <ScrollViewer Grid.Column="1" >
            <toolkit:WrapPanel x:Name="ImageBox" />
        </ScrollViewer>
    </Grid>
</navigation:Page>
```

The UI is simple enough as it has a treeDir TreeView control for showing folders and subfolders under the My Pictures folder. Then there is an ImageBox WrapPanel control to display the image files of selected folders in treeDir as small thumbnails.

Now in the code-behind, first add two namespaces:

```
using System.IO;
using System.Windows.Media.Imaging;
```

At the class level, define one List collection to hold an absolute path for the image files residing in the folder under My Pictures.

```
List<string> imageFileList = new List<string>();
```

Now in the Loaded event of the page, we will populate treeDir with folders under My Pictures as shown here:

```
void LocalFileAccessDemo_Loaded(object sender, RoutedEventArgs e)
{
    //If running with elevated permissions, populate the TreeView
    if (Application.Current.HasElevatedPermissions)
    {
```

```
        string path = Environment.GetFolderPath
            (Environment.SpecialFolder.MyPictures);

        foreach (string dir in Directory.EnumerateDirectories(path))
        {
            TreeViewItem item = new TreeViewItem();
            item.Header = dir.Substring(dir.LastIndexOf('\\') + 1);
            treeDir.Items.Add(item);
            GetDir(dir, item.Items);
        }
    }
}
```

Note the use of the Environment.Specialfolder enumeration, which specifies enumerated constants used to retrieve directory paths to system special folders. For more details, visit http://msdn.microsoft.com/en-us/library/system.environment.specialfolder.aspx.

The GetDir method that is called in foreach loop gets the subdirectories under the current directory:

```
private void GetDir(string path, ItemCollection items)
{
    foreach (string dir in Directory.EnumerateDirectories(path))
    {
        TreeViewItem item = new TreeViewItem();
        item.Header = dir.Substring(dir.LastIndexOf('\\') + 1);
        items.Add(item);
        GetDir(dir, item.Items);
    }
}
```

Next implement the SelectedItemChanged event handler for treeDir TreeView. Here we will get the full absolute path for image files for the selected directory item in treeDir. We will store this path information in the previously defined imageFileList List object.

```
private void treeDir_SelectedItemChanged
    (object sender, RoutedPropertyChangedEventArgs<object> e)
{
    // Get the path to the selected folder
    TreeView tv = (TreeView)sender;
    string path = Environment.GetFolderPath
        (Environment.SpecialFolder.MyPictures);
    foreach (KeyValuePair<object, TreeViewItem> node
        in tv.GetSelectedPath())
        path += "\\" + node.Value.Header.ToString();
    // Remove existing items from imageFileList and ImageBox
    ImageBox.Children.Clear();
    imageFileList.Clear();
    // Add new items to the imageFileList for processing later on
    foreach ( string  file in Directory.EnumerateFiles(path))
    {
        string name = file.ToLower();
        if (name.EndsWith(".png") || name.EndsWith(".jpg") ||
```

```
            name.EndsWith(".jpeg"))
            imageFileList.Add(file);
    }
    foreach (var item in imageFileList)
    {
        CreateThumbnail(item);
    }
}
```

The CreateThumbnail method called in the preceding foreach loop is responsible for creating small Image instances and adding them to ImageBox.

```
private void CreateThumbnail(string file)
{
    using (FileStream stream = File.Open(file, FileMode.Open))
    {
        // Decode the image bits
        BitmapImage bi = null;
        bi = new BitmapImage();
        bi.SetSource(stream);
        Image img = new Image();
        img.Source = bi;
        img.Margin = new Thickness(5);
        img.Width = 120;
        img.MouseLeftButtonDown += img_MouseLeftButtonDown;
        img.Stretch = Stretch.Uniform;
        ImageBox.Children.Add(img);
    }
}
```

And the MouseLeftButtonDown for each generated thumbnail Image is

```
void img_MouseLeftButtonDown(object sender, MouseButtonEventArgs e)
{
    ImageWindow iw = new ImageWindow(((Image)sender).Source);
    iw.Show();
}
```

Run the sample and you can browse the images under My Pictures as shown in Figure 11-16. Also, if you click on any image, you will see the child window (developed in Chapter 7) displayed with the clicked image as an image viewer.

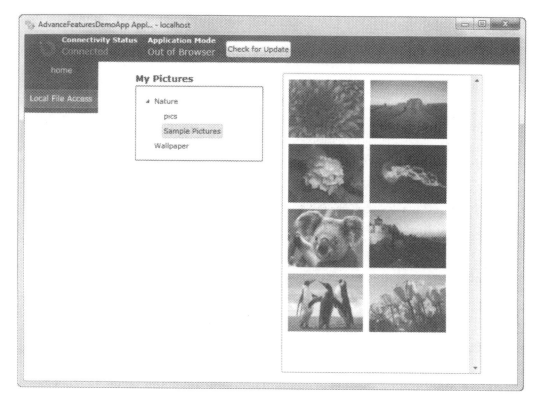

Figure 11-16. Files management example in an elevated-trusted OOB application

Notification API

In Silverlight 4, applications that are running out-of-browser have the ability to raise notification messages in the bottom right corner of the screen similar to a new mail message notification you receive for Outlook or Live Messenger/Yahoo messenger contacts sign-in messages. To provide notification service, Silverlight 4 introduces a new NotificationWindow class. This new class is simple to use as it has a single Content property of type FrameworkElement and you can assign almost any content, like UserControl. Then calling the Show method displays the notification for the specified duration of time that we supplied as a parameter when calling the Show method. As usual, there can be only one notification window displayed at a time, and the application should be running in OOB mode.

Let's see a quick example of it by adding notification support to our previous Local File Access example, where a notification message will display the total number of images in the selected folder in treeDir TreeView.

Right-click the Views folder, add a new Silverlight UserControl, and name it NotifyContent.xaml. The code highlighted in bold is changed or added.

```
<UserControl x:Class="AdvanceFeaturesDemoApp.Views.NotifyContent"
    xmlns="http://schemas.microsoft.com/winfx/2006/xaml/presentation"
    xmlns:x="http://schemas.microsoft.com/winfx/2006/xaml"
```

```xml
xmlns:d="http://schemas.microsoft.com/expression/blend/2008"
xmlns:mc="http://schemas.openxmlformats.org/
    markup-compatibility/2006"
mc:Ignorable="d" Height="50" Width="200">

<StackPanel x:Name="LayoutRoot" Background="Aqua" >
    <TextBlock FontSize="14">Total image files:</TextBlock>
    <TextBlock FontSize="14" FontWeight="Bold"
        Foreground="Blue" Text="{Binding Count}"></TextBlock>
</StackPanel>
</UserControl>
```

And the following is the code for the code-behind NotifyContent.xaml.cs.

```csharp
//added namespace
using System.ComponentModel;

namespace AdvanceFeaturesDemoApp.Views
{
    public partial class NotifyContent :
        UserControl, INotifyPropertyChanged
    {
        private int _count;
        public int Count
        {
            get
            {
                return _count;
            }
            set
            {
                count = value;
                if (PropertyChanged!=null)
                {
                    PropertyChanged(this,
                      new PropertyChangedEventArgs("Count"));
                }
            }
        }

        public NotifyContent()
        {
            InitializeComponent();
            this.DataContext = this;
        }

        public event PropertyChangedEventHandler PropertyChanged;
    }
}
```

We will set the Count property in the treeDir_SelectedItemChanged event handler. So jump to this event handler in LocalFileAccessDemo.xaml.cs and add the following lines of code at the end of the existing code in the event handler.

```
//display notification window
NotificationWindow notify = new NotificationWindow();
var content = new NotifyContent();
content.Count = imageFileList.Count();
notify.Height = content.Height;
notify.Width = content.Width;
notify.Content = content;
notify.Show(2000);
```

As you can see, we simply created an instance of the NotificationWindow class and set its various properties. You can visit http://msdn.microsoft.com/en-us/library/system.windows.notification window.aspx to get more details about members of the NotificationWindow class.

Upon running the example, when you click any item in treeDir TreeView, a notification window will pop up, showing the total number of images in the selected folder, as shown in Figure 11-17.

Figure 11-17. Notification window showing the total number of images in the selected folder in treeDir TreeView

COM Automation

Silverlight 4 elevated-trusted OOB applications can integrate with some native functionality of the host operating system. You can interoperate with applications and platforms that expose a COM interface on the Windows platform only. This opens up a new possibility for LoB Silverlight applications, where it can integrate with an installed Windows application such as Microsoft Word or Outlook, or it can integrate with famous accounting software like QuickBooks.

The `AutomationFactory` class resides in the `System.Runtime.InteropServices.Automation` namespace in the `System.Windows` assembly, enabling access to registered automation servers. To access a registered COM object, you should first check the `static IsAvailable` property of this class. This property returns true only for trusted applications running outside the browser on Windows. If it is available, you can use the static `CreateObject` or `GetObject` method to retrieve a late-bound reference to a COM object. To use the reference as a late-bound object, you must assign it to a variable type dynamic in C#. Note that to enable use of a dynamic keyword, your Silverlight application must reference the `Microsoft.CSharp.dll` assembly. In a Windows 7 64-bit environment, this assembly can be found at `c:\Program Files (x86)\Microsoft SDKs\Silverlight\v4.0\Libraries\Client`.

To demonstrate this feature, let's extend the application that can export contents of DataGrid to Excel and Word applications.

First, to generate some meaningful data that we can bind to DataGrid, add a new class to the Silverlight project and name it `BookInfo`. This class simply defines a Book object and the static method `GetBooks` will return the IEnumerable collection of the Book array objects. Note that we need to add the `System.Collections` namespace to support the IEnumerable collection. The complete code for this class is as follows.

```
//added
using System.Collections;

public class BookInfo
{
    public string Title { get; set; }
    public string Author { get; set; }
    public string isbn { get; set; }
    public string Url { get; set; }
}

public class BookData
{
    public static IEnumerable GetBooks()
    {
        BookInfo[] books = new BookInfo[4];
        books[0] = new BookInfo ();
        books[0].Title = "Accelerated Silverlight 2";
        books[0].Author = "Jeff Scanlon";
        books[0].isbn = "978-1-4302-1076-4";
        books[0].Url =
            @"http://apress.com/book/view/9781430210764";

        books[1] = new BookInfo ();
        books[1].Title = "Accelerated Silverlight 3";
        books[1].Author = "Ashish Ghoda, Jeff Scanlon";
        books[1].isbn = "978-1-4302-2429-7";
```

```
        books[1].Url =
            @"http://apress.com/book/view/9781430224297";

        books[2] = new BookInfo ();
        books[2].Title = "Introducing Silverlight 4";
        books[2].Author = "Ashish Ghoda";
        books[2].isbn = "978-1-4302-2991-9";
        books[2].Url =
            @"http://apress.com/book/view/9781430229919";

        books[3] = new BookInfo();
        books[3].Title = "Silverlight 2 Recipes";
        books[3].Author = "Jit Ghosh, Rob Cameron";
        books[3].isbn = "978-1-59059-977-8";
        books[3].Url =
            @"http://apress.com/book/view/9781590599778";

        return books;
    }
}
```

To build the supporting user interface, right-click the Views folder, add a new Page control, and name it to COMAccessDemo.xaml. Open the file and place the following code replacing the default LayoutRoot Grid code that basically adds two buttons to perform Excel and Word integration.

```
<StackPanel x:Name="LayoutRoot" Loaded="COMAccessDemo_Loaded" >
    <sdk:DataGrid x:Name="BooksGrid" HorizontalAlignment="Left"
        VerticalAlignment="Top" Width="700" />
    <StackPanel Orientation="Horizontal" VerticalAlignment="Top"  >
        <Button x:Name="btnExportExcel" Content="Export to Excel"
            Click="btnExportExcel_Click"
            Height="23" Width="120" Margin="10" />
        <Button x:Name="btnExportWord" Content="Export to Word"
            Click="btnExportWord_Click" Height="23" Width="120" />
    </StackPanel>
</StackPanel>
```

Note that for DataGrid, I choose to drag it from the toolbox and drop it on the designer surface. This way it creates the following XML namespace for me. If you choose to type instead, you need to manually write this namespace and add a project reference to the SDK dlls.

```
xmlns:sdk="http://schemas.microsoft.com/winfx/2006/
    xaml/presentation/sdk"
```

Now open the code-behind file and, in the Loaded event of the page, we set the ItemsSource for the BookGrid DataGrid to display the added books information.

```
void COMAccessDemo_Loaded(object sender, RoutedEventArgs e)
{
    BooksGrid.ItemsSource = BookData.GetBooks();
}
```

Now upon clicking the Export to Excel button, a visible instance of the Microsoft Excel application will be created with the workbook added to it. Then using the foreach loop, contents of BooksGrid will populate this workbook. The following is the self-explanatory code (with proper comments) for the btnExportExcel_Click event handler.

```
private void btnExportExcel_Click(object sender, RoutedEventArgs e)
{
    // create an instance of excel
    dynamic excel = AutomationFactory.
        CreateObject("Excel.Application");
    // make it visible to the user.
    excel.Visible = true;
    // add a workbook to the instance
    dynamic workbook = excel.workbooks.Add();
    // get the active sheet
    dynamic sheet = excel.ActiveSheet;
    dynamic cell = null;

    int i = 1;
    // iterate through our data source and populate
    //the excel spreadsheet
    foreach (BookInfo item in BooksGrid.ItemsSource)
    {
        cell = sheet.Cells[i, 1]; // row, column
        cell.Value = item.Title;
        cell.ColumnWidth = 25;

        cell = sheet.Cells[i, 2];
        cell.Value = item.Author;

        cell = sheet.Cells[i, 3];
        cell.Value = item.isbn;

        cell = sheet.Cells[i, 4];
        cell.Value = item.Url;

        i++;
    }
}
```

Similarly, the btnExportWord_Click event handler will populate the word table with the contents of BooksGrid.

```
private void btnExportWord_Click(object sender, RoutedEventArgs e)
{
    // create an instance of excel
    dynamic word = AutomationFactory.
        CreateObject("Word.Application");
    // make it visible to the user.
    word.Visible = true;
    // add a new Document to the instance
```

```
dynamic wordDocument = word.Documents.Add();
//setting up some properties for the Document
dynamic range = wordDocument.Range(0, 0);
dynamic table = wordDocument.Tables.Add(range, 5, 4);

//some property setting on table
table.ApplyStyleHeadingRows = true;
table.AllowAutoFit = true;

//setting header
table.Cell(1, 1).Range.Text = "Title";
table.Cell(1, 2).Range.Text = "Author";
table.Cell(1, 3).Range.Text = "ISBN";
table.Cell(1, 4).Range.Text = "URL";

int j = 2;
foreach (BookInfo item in BooksGrid.ItemsSource)
{
    table.Cell(j, 1).Range.Text= item.Title;
    table.Cell(j, 2).Range.Text = item.Author;
    table.Cell(j, 3).Range.Text = item.isbn;
    table.Cell(j, 4).Range.Text = item.Url;
    j++;
}
}
```

Note that as you type code, you won't get IntelliSense support. However, Visual Studio Object Browser can bring help in this situation. You can create separate a Windows Application project and then add reference to Microsoft Word 14.0 Object Library and Microsoft Excel 14.0 Object Library using the COM tab in the Add Reference dialog box. Note that I am using Office 2010, so the library version may differ for your system. Now you can see various members of the added Office library using Object Browser, which will help you to develop code for COM access in your Silverlight application. Run the project.

Figure 11-18 shows the screen when I choose Export to Excel, and Figure 11-19 shows the screen when Export to Word is clicked.

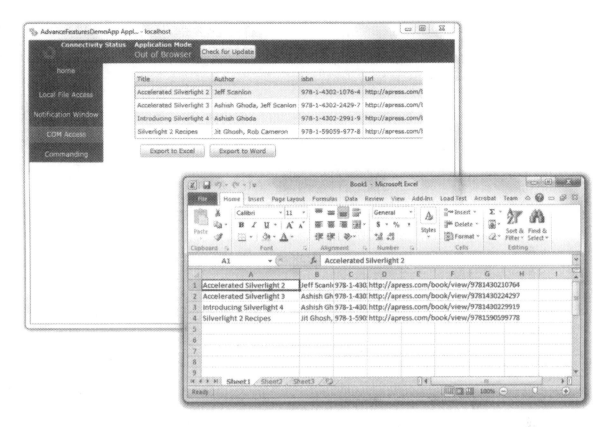

Figure 11-18. Microsoft Excel automation in a Silverlight OOB trusted application

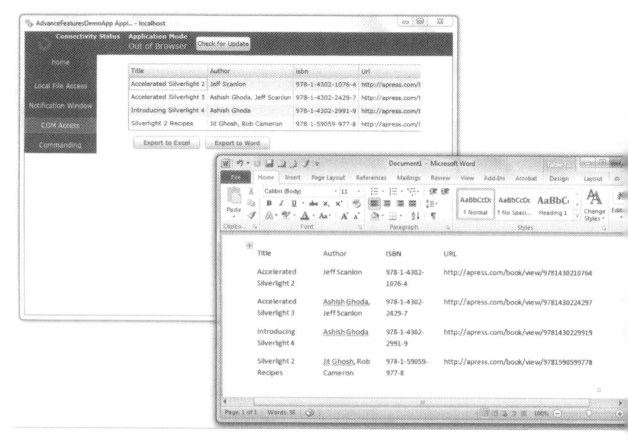

Figure 11-19. Microsoft Word automation in a Silverlight OOB trusted application

Commanding Support

You can follow standard design patterns like MVC (Model View Controller) and MVP (Model View Presenter) when it comes to implementing separation of business logic from the main user interface/presentation. The MVVM (Model-View-ViewModel) is a more suitable pattern among Silverlight LoBs. One of the most important aspects of implementing the MVVM pattern in WPF and Silverlight is the ability for the UI layer to bind directly to the commands in the ViewModel. Commanding allows designers/developers to specify, in XAML, events that fire back into the ViewModel. The ViewModel is nothing but a presentation of the view but as a class. The reason to use a ViewModel is the separation of concerns, as we do not have to add logic to the view, i.e., the user interface.

Commanding can be used only on controls derived from the `ButtonBase` class at the moment, and will be executed only by the `Click` event. The `ButtonBase` class represents the base class for all button controls, such as Button, RepeatButton, and HyperlinkButton, which we saw in Chapter 3. To define the contract for commanding for ButtonBase controls, it uses the same contract ICommand from the `System.Windows.Input` namespace as used in WPF. But the Silverlight command infrastructure is limited compared to the WPF command infrastructure. Beyond ButtonBase, the ICommand interface exists for compatibility purposes and is helpful in a scenario of migrating existing WPF code-defined or particularly markup-defined command bindings for a Silverlight implementation of the same.

Table 11-5 describes the properties that enable support for commanding in the ButtonBase class.

Table 11-5. Key Properties to Enable Support for Commanding in the ButtonBase Class

Property	Type	Description
Command	ICommand	This property gets or sets the command to invoke when this button is pressed.
CommandParameter	Object	This property gets or sets the parameter to pass to the Command property. The default is null.

■ **Note** Complete coverage of the MVVM pattern for Silverlight is outside the scope of this book. There is a well-explained article on the MVVM pattern in Silverlight by Shawn Wildermuth in the March 2009 issue of *MSDN Magazine*. You can review it by visiting http://msdn.microsoft.com/en-us/magazine/dd458800.aspx.

The contract for commanding is defined by implementing the ICommand interface. The following code snippet shows the interface signature with its members.

```
public interface ICommand
{
    bool CanExecute(
        Object parameter
    )

    void Execute(
        Object parameter
    )

    event EventHandler CanExecuteChanged
}
```

The CanExecute method determines whether the command can execute in its current state. The only parameter is the Object data that is used by the command. If the command does not require data to be passed, this object can be set to null. The Execute method defines the method or logic that is called when the command is invoked. And the event CanExecuteChanged occurs when changes occur that affect whether the command should execute.

To understand this feature, let's turn our COM Automation into an MVVM example with commanding support for Word and Excel export buttons. So add a new folder called MVVM under the Views folder. Add two new classes named Model.cs and ViewModel.cs and one Silverlight Page control named View.xaml.

The Model Class

The Model class serves as a data model that provides methods and data classes. We will reuse the code in BookInfo.cs for Model.cs. So we just need to copy and paste the code for the Book and BookData classes into the Model.cs file, replacing the empty Model class code.

Note that you also need to add the following namespace:

```
using System.Collections;
```

The ViewModel Class

The ViewModel class will provide public properties so our View can bind to them. In our case the View is View.xaml. ViewModel typically implements the INotifyPropertyChanged interface to keep the View updated about the changes made in the ViewModel properties. In our case, it is not required, so I am not going to implement this interface. If you want to extend this example where the user can modify or add new entries in BooksGrid, then you should implement this interface. In our case, only the implementation of ICommand for our custom commanding class is required with some public properties. Start with adding the required additional namespaces.

```
using System.Runtime.InteropServices.Automation;
using System.Collections;
```

Now create one public property of type IEnumerable and name it Books. This will call the static GetBooks method of the Model class.

```
public IEnumerable Books
{
    get{
        //call to GetBooks of Model class
        return BookData.GetBooks();
    }
}
```

Next create a method named WordExport with the method signature as:

```
public void WordExport()
```

Copy and paste code from the btnExportWord_Click event handler from COMAccessDemo.xaml.cs into this method body and then change the line of the foreach loop,

```
foreach (Book item in BooksGrid.ItemsSource)
```

to

```
foreach (Book item in Books)
```

Similarly, create a method named ExcelExport by performing similar steps as you did for the WordExport method.

Now we implement the class COMCommand in ViewModel implementing ICommand as follows:

```
public class COMCommand : ICommand
{
    private ViewModel _vm;

    public COMCommand(ViewModel vm)
    {
        _vm = vm;
    }

    public bool CanExecute(object parameter)
    {
        return true;
    }

    public event EventHandler CanExecuteChanged;

    public void Execute(object parameter)
    {
        if (parameter.ToString()=="Word") //it is Word export button clicked
        {
            _vm.WordExport();
        }
        else //it is Excel export button clicked
        {
            _vm.ExcelExport();
        }
    }
}
```

Here, the constructor of this class takes one parameter of type ViewModel and assigns this to the private _vm instance of the ViewModel class. Then the Execute method simply checks the string value of the supplied parameter and, based on that value, it invokes either the WordExport or ExcelExport method.

For the View's UI Button controls that we implement next (in View.xaml), we need to provide the public property of type ICommand so their Command property can bind to this property. The following is the code for the public COMCommand property.

```
public ICommand COMCommand
{
    get {return new COMCommand(this);}
}
```

The View.xaml File

To define the user interface, just copy code for the container StackPanel LayoutRoot from COMAccessDemo.xaml and paste it to View.xaml replacing the default Grid LayoutRoot control. The following code shows the final markup for this, with added/modified entries highlighted in bold.

```
<navigation:Page x:Class="AdvanceFeaturesDemoApp.Views.MVVM.View"
    xmlns="http://schemas.microsoft.com/winfx/2006/xaml/presentation"
```

```
    xmlns:x="http://schemas.microsoft.com/winfx/2006/xaml"
    xmlns:d="http://schemas.microsoft.com/expression/blend/2008"
    xmlns:mc="http://schemas.openxmlformats.org/
        markup-compatibility/2006"
    mc:Ignorable="d"
    xmlns:navigation="clr-namespace:System.Windows.Controls;
        assembly=System.Windows.Controls.Navigation"
    d:DesignWidth="640" d:DesignHeight="480"
    xmlns:vm="clr-namespace:AdvanceFeaturesDemoApp.Views.MVVM"
    xmlns:sdk="http://schemas.microsoft.com/winfx/2006/xaml/
        presentation/sdk"
    Title="View Page">
    <UserControl.Resources>
        <vm:ViewModel x:Name="myViewModel"/>
    </UserControl.Resources>
    <StackPanel x:Name="LayoutRoot"
        DataContext="{StaticResource myViewModel}">
        <sdk:DataGrid x:Name="BooksGrid" HorizontalAlignment="Left"
            VerticalAlignment="Top" Width="700"
            ItemsSource="{Binding Books}" />
        <StackPanel Orientation="Horizontal" VerticalAlignment="Top">
            <Button x:Name="btnExportExcel" Content="Export to Excel"
                Command="{Binding COMCommand}" CommandParameter="Excel"
                Height="23" Width="120" Margin="10" />
            <Button x:Name="btnExportWord" Content="Export to Word"
                Command="{Binding COMCommand}" CommandParameter="Word"
                Height="23" Width="120" />
        </StackPanel>
    </StackPanel>
</navigation:Page>
```

Here we first added an XML namespace to create an instance of the ViewModel class declaratively in XAML as UserControl.Resources named myViewModel. Then we set the DataContext of the container StackPanel LayoutRoot to myViewModel. Next, to fill up the grid, we bind ItemSource to the Books public property of the ViewModel class. And finally, both buttons have their Command property bind to the COMCommand property of the ViewModel class. We supply an appropriate CommandParameter so the Execute method of the COMCommand class can determine which method to invoke.

The beauty of the MVVM pattern is that there is no code in the View.xaml code-behind, and we did everything by doing simple data binding in a declarative way in View.xaml. Now, if you run the sample, the result is similar to the earlier COM automation sample (see Figures 11-18 and 11-19) but everything is happening here with the support of Silverlight's rich data binding system, enabling the MVVM pattern with Command support.

Cross-Silverlight Application Communication

The Silverlight local messaging feature allows Silverlight applications to communicate across different Silverlight plug-ins/applications. These Silverlight plug-ins/applications can be hosted on the same page, on different browser tabs, in different browsers, or in the out-of-browser application. To establish a local connection and perform communications between Silverlight applications executed on the client side only, no server-side round-trips are required.

Figure 11-20 explains the communication process between Silverlight applications through a flow diagram.

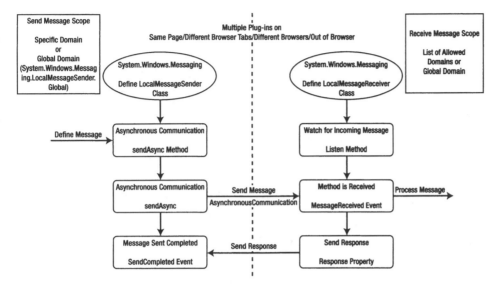

Figure 11-20. Cross-application communication process

Using the System.Windows.Messaging Namespace

As shown in Figure 11-20, the System.Windows.Messaging namespace, which is a Microsoft .NET Framework library component for Silverlight, facilitates local messaging between two Silverlight applications.

The System.Windows.Messaging namespace provides the required set of classes to support local messaging between two Silverlight applications on the client side. Table 11-6 describes the key classes of this namespace.

Table 11-6. Classes of the System.Windows.Messaging Namespace

Class	Details
LocalMessageSender	Used on the sender's Silverlight application side to send messages to the local Silverlight application receiver/listener.
LocalMessageReceiver	Used on the receiver's Silverlight application side to receive messages.
MessageReceivedEventArgs	Provides data for the LocalMessageReceiver.MessageReceived event.
SendCompletedEventArgs	Provides data for the LocalMessageSender.SendCompleted event.
ListenFailedException	Occurs when a LocalMessageReceiver fails to receive a message.
SendFailedException	Occurs when a LocalMessageSender fails to send a message.

Table 11-7 provides details on the key members of the `LocalMessageSender` class.

Table 11-7. Key Members of the `LocalMessageSender` *Class*

Member	Details
SendAsync	This method sends a message to the receiver in asynchronous mode.
ReceiverDomain	This property gets the domain information of the `LocalMessageReceiver` for sending messages.
ReceiverName	This property gets the name of the `LocalMessageReceiver` for sending messages.
SendCompleted	This event is raised when the message is successfully sent to the `LocalMessageReceiver`.

Table 11-8 provides details on the key members of the `LocalMessageReceiver` class.

Table 11-8. Key Members of the `LocalMessageReceiver` *Class*

Member	Details
AllowedSenderDomains	This property gets the domain from where the receiver can receive messages.
ReceiverName	This property gets the receiver name of the `LocalMessageReceiver`.
MessageReceived	This event is raised when a message is successfully received from the `LocalMessageSender`. This event will not occur until after you have called the `Listen` method.

Seeing an Example in Action

Let's develop an example demonstrating cross-communication between two Silverlight applications hosted on the same page and on the same domain. Similarly, you can establish communication between Silverlight applications that are deployed on different domains by deploying the proper cross-domain policy files.

First create a Silverlight application project solution named chapter11. Then delete the chapter11 Silverlight application project from the chapter11 solution, and add two new Silverlight application projects to the chapter11 solution named SenderApp and ReceiverApp. Remove the extra test pages from the chapter11.web project: chapter11TestPage.aspx, chapter11TestPage.html, ReceiverAppTestPage.aspx, ReceiverAppTestPage.html, SenderAppTestPage.aspx, and SenderAppTestPage.html. Figure 11-21 shows these two newly created Silverlight application projects and the related test pages in Visual Studio Solution Explorer.

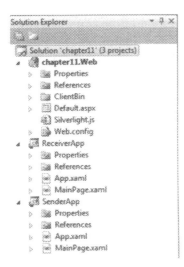

Figure 11-21. SenderApp and ReceiverApp Silverlight applications

Creating the Sender Silverlight Application

In this section, you'll create a very simple sender Silverlight application containing three RadioButton controls, each related to one color (red, green, and blue), and a Button control to submit the RadioButton-related color selection to the receiver application.

The following is the XAML code for the SenderApp MainPage.xaml file to achieve this simple UI:

```
<UserControl x:Class="SenderApp.MainPage"
    xmlns="http://schemas.microsoft.com/winfx/2006/xaml/presentation"
    xmlns:x="http://schemas.microsoft.com/winfx/2006/xaml"
    xmlns:d="http://schemas.microsoft.com/expression/blend/2008"
    xmlns:mc="http://schemas.openxmlformats.org/
        markup-compatibility/2006"
    mc:Ignorable="d" Height="300" Width="400">
    <StackPanel x:Name="LayoutRoot" Background="White">
        <TextBlock Text="Select Color and Press Submit"></TextBlock>
        <RadioButton Foreground="Red" IsChecked="true" Content="Red"
            Checked="Color_Checked" ></RadioButton>
        <RadioButton Foreground="Blue" Content="Blue"
            Checked="Color_Checked"></RadioButton>
        <RadioButton Foreground="Green" Content="Green"
            Checked="Color_Checked" ></RadioButton>
        <Button x:Name="btnSubmit" Width="100" Height="32"
            Content="Submit" Click="btnSubmit_Click" ></Button>
    </StackPanel>
</UserControl>
```

As you can see from the previous XAML code, by default the Red RadioButton control is selected by setting the IsChecked property to true. We also have integrated all the RadioButton controls' Checked events to the same Color_Checked event handler and the Button control's Click event to the btnSubmit_Click event handler. Before we implement them, first include the Systems.Windows.Messaging reference, as shown here:

```
using System.Windows.Messaging;
```

Next declare the following three private string variables at the MainPage class level:

```
private const string SenderAppName = "Sender1";
private const string ReceiverAppName = "Receiver1";
private string message = "Red";
```

Now define the RadioButton controls' Checked event handler. Based on the RadioButton control selection, set the message to the selected RadioButton control's Content property representing the corresponding selected color—red, green, or blue—as shown here:

```
private void Color_Checked(object sender, RoutedEventArgs e)
{
    RadioButton rbtn = sender as RadioButton;
    message = rbtn.Content.ToString();
}
```

Finally, define the submit Button control's Click event handler. First you need to create a new instance of the LocalMessageSender class to establish a communication channel between two Silverlight-based applications, where the SenderApp application is representing the sending end. Then asynchronously send the message to the receiver application using the SendAsync method only if the message is not null or empty. The following is the related code snippet:

```
private void btnSubmit_Click(object sender, RoutedEventArgs e)
{
    LocalMessageSender msgSender = new
      LocalMessageSender(ReceiverAppName);

    if(message ! =null || message != string.Empty)
      msgSender.SendAsync(message);
}
```

Build the project successfully. You are all set with the sender application. Now it's time to develop the receiver application.

Creating the Receiver Silverlight Application

The receiver Silverlight application is simpler than the sender Silverlight application. Here you will have only one Rectangle control, which will be filled with the color that is received from the sender application based on the color-specific RadioButton control selection on the sending end.

The following is the XAML code for the ReceiverApp MainPage.xaml file to achieve this simple UI:

```
<UserControl x:Class="ReceiverApp.MainPage"
    xmlns="http://schemas.microsoft.com/winfx/2006/xaml/presentation"
    xmlns:x="http://schemas.microsoft.com/winfx/2006/xaml"
```

```
    xmlns:d="http://schemas.microsoft.com/expression/blend/2008"
    xmlns:mc="http://schemas.openxmlformats.org/
        markup-compatibility/2006"
    mc:Ignorable="d" Height="300" Width="400">
    <StackPanel x:Name="LayoutRoot" Background="White">
        <TextBlock Text="Selected Color in SenderApp..."></TextBlock>
        <Rectangle x:Name="rect" Height="25"></Rectangle>
    </StackPanel>
</UserControl>
```

Here also you need to include the Systems.Windows.Messaging reference:

```
using System.Windows.Messaging;
```

Next declare the following two private string variables at the MainPage class level:

```
private const string SenderAppName = "Sender1";
private const string ReceiverAppName = "Receiver1";
```

In the MainPage constructor, first you need to create a new instance of the LocalMessageReceiver class to establish a communication channel between two Silverlight-based applications, where the ReceiverApp application is representing the receiving end. Next, based on the MessageReceived event of the msgReceiver object, you apply the switch case on the Message parameter of MessageReceivedEventArgs e to set the Rectangle control's Fill property with the received color information. At last, call the msgReceiver.Listen() method to listen for messages from a LocalMessageSender, which is SenderApp in this case. The following is the related code snippet:

```
public MainPage()
{
    InitializeComponent();

    LocalMessageReceiver msgReceiver = new
        LocalMessageReceiver(SenderAppName);
    msgReceiver.MessageReceived += (object sender,
        MessageReceivedEventArgs e) =>
    {
        switch (e.Message)
        {
            case "Red":
            {
                rect.Fill = new SolidColorBrush(Colors.Red);
                break;
            }

            case "Green":
            {
                rect.Fill = new SolidColorBrush(Colors.Green);
                break;
            }
```

```
        case "Blue":
        {
            rect.Fill = new SolidColorBrush(Colors.Blue);
            break;
        }

    }
};

msgReceiver.Listen();
}
```

Build the project successfully. You are all set with the receiver application also. Next let's host the sender and receiver applications on the same page.

Hosting the Sender and Receiver Applications on the Same Page

Because you need to host both the sender and receiver Silverlight applications on the same page, you will use the Default.aspx file in the chapter11.web ASP.NET web application project. For that, host the SenderApp and ReceiverApp Silverlight applications using the HTML object tag within the body section of the Default.aspx page:

```
<html xmlns="http://www.w3.org/1999/xhtml">
<head runat="server">
    <title></title>
    <style type="text/css" >
      #leftcolumn {
          margin: 5px;
          float: left;
          width: 350px;
      }
      #rightcolumn {
          margin: 5px;
          float: left;
          width: 350px;
      }
    </style>
</head>
<body>
    <form id="form1" runat="server">
    <div id="leftcolumn">
    <h3>Sender App...</h3>
    <object data="data:application/x-silverlight-2,"
        type="application/x-silverlight-2" width="100%" height="100%">
        <param name="source" value="ClientBin/SenderApp.xap"/>
        <param name="onError" value="onSilverlightError" />
        <param name="background" value="white" />
        <param name="minRuntimeVersion" value="4.0.50401.0" />
        <param name="autoUpgrade" value="true" />
        <a href="http://go.microsoft.com/fwlink/
```

```
            ?LinkID=149156&v=4.0.50401.0"
                style="text-decoration:none">
            <img src="http://go.microsoft.com/fwlink/?LinkId=161376"
                alt="Get Microsoft Silverlight"
                style="border-style:none"/>
        </a>
    </object>
    </div>
    <div id="rightcolumn" >
    <h3>Receiver App...</h3>
    <object data="data:application/x-silverlight-2,"
        type="application/x-silverlight-2" width="100%" height="100%">
        <param name="source" value="ClientBin/ReceiverApp.xap"/>
        <param name="onError" value="onSilverlightError" />
        <param name="background" value="white" />
        <param name="minRuntimeVersion" value="4.0.50401.0" />
        <param name="autoUpgrade" value="true" />
        <a href="http://go.microsoft.com/fwlink/
            ?LinkID=149156&v=4.0.50401.0"
                style="text-decoration:none">
            <img src="http://go.microsoft.com/fwlink/?LinkId=161376"
                alt="Get Microsoft Silverlight"
                style="border-style:none"/>
        </a>
    </object>
    </div>
    </form>
</body>
</html>
```

Set the Default.aspx page as a start-up page, and you are all set to run the cross plug-in Silverlight communication sample! You should see the receiver Rectangle control is filled with the appropriate color based on the color-specific RadioButton control selected on the sending end when the user clicks the Submit button. Figure 11-22 shows the Blue RadioButton control selected on the sending end and the blue color applied to the Rectangle control on the receiving end. This black-and-white book doesn't really illustrate the point, so you should try it out to see for yourself!

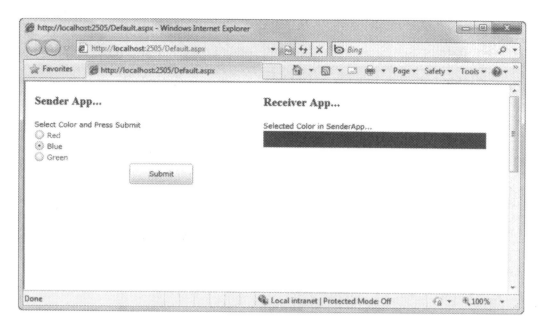

Figure 11-22. Same-page-hosted cross-Silverlight applications communication in action

Summary

This chapter delved into some of the advanced aspects of Silverlight 4. You probably won't use these features in every application, but when you need to develop a true enterprise-level line-of-business application, they will now be familiar to you. This chapter demonstrated the enterprise-level capabilities of Silverlight as an RIA development technology platform.

We started by demonstrating the navigation framework, which can help organizations implement the reusability and standardization features. With the out-of-browser functionality, you can develop a truly rich Internet application that supports connected and disconnected modes and the integration between them. With elevated-trusted out-of-browser applications, Silverlight 4 extends support to truly develop a desktop-like application by supporting local file system access, COM automation, and development of notification windows. We also discussed the client-side local messaging capabilities across Silverlight applications within the page, across browser tabs, across browsers, and in out-of-browser mode in a same-domain or cross-domain deployment scenario. Chapter 12 will cover an even more advanced topic, multithreading.

CHAPTER 12

Threading in Silverlight

In the previous chapter, we covered advanced Silverlight support (along with enhanced support in Silverlight 4) for enterprise-level design concepts and features. Another advanced topic is the multithreading support that Silverlight provides, which we will cover in this chapter. Used properly, threading is a great way to provide a smooth user experience by doing work such as lengthy calculations or downloading files while the user interface remains responsive. Another useful technique for certain applications is the use of a `Timer`—a way to execute some code on a certain periodic schedule (such as every ten seconds).

■ **Note** This chapter does not include complete code of developed samples, but the code is straightforward. I recommend you download the source code and review the code while you review this chapter.

Using Threading

Silverlight is a *multi-threaded* environment, which means multiple sequences of code can execute simultaneously. You've already encountered this in the asynchronous nature of network communication. The main application thread makes a call to the **BeginGetResponse** method of **HttpWebRequest**, and then your code doesn't need to sit around waiting for a response. The actual network communication happens on a different thread, and when a response from the server is received, the method specified as the asynchronous callback is invoked. In Silverlight, this specific callback actually happens on a thread other than the main application thread, referred to as the *worker thread*. The main application thread is usually referred to as the *user interface thread*, since this is the thread where all user interface–related code lives (for example, code that creates the user interface, code for handling events, and so on). You cannot directly access user interface elements from the callback thread. You must use the Dispatcher object and its **BeginInvoke** method to perform cross-thread communication. Figure 12-1 shows an illustration of two threads of execution: the user interface thread and a worker thread that is used for the network communication. The worker thread representation is shifted down to illustrate the time when the worker thread is created.

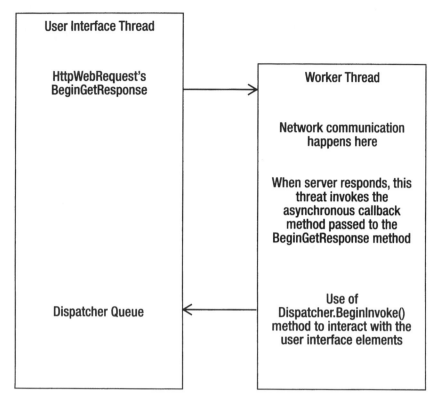

Figure 12-1. *Illustration of user interface thread and worker thread*

If you build web applications solely using technologies such as HTML, JScript, and Ajax, you can't take advantage of threading in the underlying operating system. Using multiple threads allows you to build more complex applications that have a high degree of responsiveness to users. With multiple cores and multiple processors in computers these days, it would be surprising if Silverlight did not provide support for using threads. Of course, using threads introduces new sets of problems for developers. First, you want to be careful to not overuse threads. Since ultimately each thread is backed by an operating system thread, there are a limited number of threads you can use, because each thread requires memory and costs CPU time. Another significant problem occurs any time several threads want to access the same data. If two threads want to modify a shared piece of data, such as an integer variable, it's possible to see unexpected behavior if one thread modifies the variable while the other thread is in the middle of a modification operation. This is known as a *race condition*, since both threads are in a race to access the shared data and it's unpredictable which will "win." Race conditions are only one type of potential threading issue. If you need to use threads in your Silverlight application, use them carefully. Of course, the benefit of threads can outweigh the inherent problems when used properly.

The Thread Class

The `System.Threading.Thread` class is the managed class that wraps a thread in the underlying operating system. This is the class you use when you manually create threads or when you want to do something like put a thread to sleep. Table 12-1 shows the properties of the `Thread` class.

Table 12-1. Properties of the System.Threading. Thread Class

Property	Type	Description
CurrentCulture	CultureInfo	Gets/sets the culture for the current thread.
CurrentThread	static Thread	Gets the currently active thread.
CurrentUICulture	CultureInfo	Gets/sets the culture used by the resource manager when accessing culture-specific resources at runtime.
IsAlive	bool	**true** if the thread is currently running normally and not aborted/stopped.
IsBackground	bool	**true** if the thread is a background thread. Background threads do not prevent the Silverlight runtime from shutting down; therefore, they may be killed abruptly without completing.
ManagedThreadId	Int32	Unique identifier assigned to the managed thread.
Name	string	Gets/sets the name of the thread.
ThreadState	System.Threading.ThreadState	Gets the current execution state of the thread. Possible states are **Running**, **StopRequested**, **SuspendRequested**, **Background**, **Unstarted**, **Stopped**, **WaitSleepJoin**, **Suspended**, **AbortRequested**, and **Aborted**. The initial value is **Unstarted**. See Figure 12-2 for more details on state transition during the thread execution.

Table 12-2 describes the most useful methods of the **Thread** class.

Table 12-2. Key Methods of the System.Threading. Thread Class

Method	Description
Abort	Causes a **ThreadAbortException** to occur in the thread. The thread will usually terminate. It will transition to the **AbortRequested** state and ultimately to the **Aborted** state.
GetDomain	A static method, which returns the current domain in which the current thread is running.
Join	Blocks the calling thread until the thread that **Join** is invoked on is finished. This is useful when the calling thread must wait for results or other events to complete before proceeding.
Sleep	Static method. Puts the calling thread to sleep for a specified time span or number of milliseconds. While sleeping, the thread will not consume any processor time.
Start	Starts the thread. You can optionally pass an object to the **Start** method that the thread's work method will use.

A thread can be in one of several states, as shown in Table 12-3. Note that the **Background** state is not mutually exclusive to the other states. It's possible for a thread to be a background thread and to be running, for example. Both of these states can be discovered by consulting the **ThreadState** property of a thread.

Table 12-3. Execution States of System.Threading.ThreadState

State	Description
Background	Thread is running in background. You can control the thread scope (background or foreground) by using **Thread.IsBackground** property.
UnStarted	The thread is created within CLR, is not in the Aborted state and still the **Thread.Start** method is not invoked.
Running	Thread has started and is executing (not blocked) and there is no pending **System.Threading.ThreadAbortException**.
WaitSleepJoin	Thread is being blocked by using **Thread.Sleep** or **Thread.Join**.
StopRequested	For internal use only. Thread is being requested to stop.
Stopped	The thread is stopped.
SuspendRequested	Thread is marked for the suspension.
Suspended	The thread is suspended.

AbortRequested	The thread is requested to abort using **Thread.Abort** method. However, **System.Threading.ThreadAbortException** is still pending.
Aborted	The thread is dead and in the **AbortRequested** state. However, its state has not changed to **Stopped**.

Creating and Managing Threads

If you want to execute some code on an alternate thread, you can place the code to execute in its own method and then pass this method to the **Thread** class's constructor (by wrapping the method in a **ThreadStart** object). Note that to make use of this class, you need to add the namespace **System.Windows.Threading**. We'll use the following method to simulate some work:

```
public void doSomething()
{
    Thread.Sleep(5000); // 5 seconds
    Dispatcher.BeginInvoke(delegate() { statusText.Text = "Work done."; });
}
```

The code for this chapter contains a simple interface with a button control that is used to start a thread executing the **doSomething** method.

You can repeatedly click the **startThreadButton**-named button to see the current state of the thread. You should see the state go from **Running** to **WaitSleepJoin** and finally to **Stopped** after the five-second sleep period is over. Here's the event handler for the **startThreadButton**-named button that creates and starts the thread:

```
private void startThreadButton_Click(object sender, RoutedEventArgs e)
{
    currentThread = new Thread(new ThreadStart(doSomething));
    currentThread.Start();
    statusText.Text = "Thread created and started";
    threadStateText.Text = currentThread.ThreadState.ToString();
}
```

The **Thread** constructor uses the **ThreadStart** class to wrap the method that does the work. There is an alternate class, **ParameterizedThreadStart**, which is used when you want to pass an object to the method that performs the work. This object gets passed to the **Start** method, which subsequently passes it to the method wrapped by **ParameterizedThreadStart**. A method suitable for use with **ParameterizedThreadStart** takes a single object as a parameter.

```
public void gotoSleep(object time)
{
    int timeToSleep = (int)time;
    Thread.Sleep(timeToSleep);
}
```

Starting the thread is accomplished using code similar to the nonparameterized **ThreadStart** class, but with the **ParameterizedThreadStart** delegate passed to the constructor, as shown here:

```
currentThread = new Thread(new
    ParameterizedThreadStart(delegate { gotoSleep(7500);}));
```

Although this is an effective way to create a thread to do some processing, it has several problems. The main problem is that creating a thread is expensive, and if you continue to create threads like this, your application's performance might be impacted, since the environment handles the creation and eventually the cleanup of threads. To address this problem, you should use something called the *thread pool*, which contains a number of already created threads ready to jump into action and do some work.

The thread pool automatically handles the allocation, creation, and cleanup of threads. If your application requires a larger number of threads than the thread pool already has, then new threads are created and added to the pool. If your application requires fewer threads than the pool has, however, your application won't incur the cost of creation of new threads, since they are already available in the pool. Another advantage to the thread pool is that if at one point your application requires a large number of threads, but later it doesn't, the unused threads will automatically clean themselves up until the pool contains a number of threads closer to what your application currently requires. You interact with the thread pool using the `System.Threading.ThreadPool` class. You never create an instance of the thread pool, since it is completely managed by the environment (the Silverlight plug-in), so all methods are static. The `ThreadPool` class provides methods to get and set the minimum and maximum number of threads, but you'll usually leave this up to the thread pool itself. The vast majority of the time the thread pool will better manage thread counts than you can. The most useful method to you is the `QueueUserWorkItem` method, which places the method in a queue for the execution. The method will be executed once a thread in the thread pool is available.

The simplest way to use `QueueUserWorkItem` is to pass it a method that does the work. This is similar to passing a method to a `ThreadStart` class constructor, but it requires less work and frees you from having to interact with the thread directly.

```
private void startThreadButton_Click(object sender, RoutedEventArgs e)
{
    ThreadPool.QueueUserWorkItem(delegate () { doSomething(); });;
    statusText.Text = "Work queued for a thread pool thread";
}
```

Although this code functions similarly to manually creating and using a thread, you can't get state information about the thread since there is no `Thread` object. The work is sent to a background thread, and then the application just carries on.

Let's say you have a user interface with a TextBox, named `resultTextBox`, that displays the contents of something you download using `HttpWebRequest`. Error handling and details of reading the response stream are left out for simplicity since they aren't needed for this illustration.

```
void responseHandler(IAsyncResult asyncResult)
{
    HttpWebResponse response = (HttpWebResponse)request.EndGetResponse(asyncResult);
    StreamReader reader = new StreamReader(response.GetResponseStream());
    string result = "";
    // read and process file
    resultTextBox.Text = result;
}
```

If you attempt to run this code, you'll get an error about cross-thread access not being allowed. This problem with modifying `resultTextBox` directly from the response handler happens because the response handler is executing on a different thread. Only the main user interface thread can modify user interface elements. What you need, then, is a way to get the user interface thread to make the user interface modification. This happens using something called the **Dispatcher**. We have already seen the use of **Dispatcher.BeginInvoke** earlier in this chapter to access the user interface elements.

The Dispatcher

The **DependencyObject** class acts as the base object for many classes in Silverlight. One important aspect of this class, however, is its single property, **Dispatcher**. Objects can be modified only on the thread they are created on. Each object, therefore, has a **Dispatcher** property that provides two important pieces of functionality. For starters, you can test whether an object can be modified from the current thread by calling the **CheckAccess** method. If the current thread is the same as the one the **Dispatcher** belongs to, **CheckAccess** will return **true**. The other important functionality is the ability to queue some code to execute on the **Dispatcher**'s thread. This is how you go about solving the cross-thread access problem when modifying user interface objects. The method used to execute some code on the **Dispatcher**'s thread is called **BeginInvoke**. Figure 12-2 shows the relationship of two threads and the **Dispatcher** object.

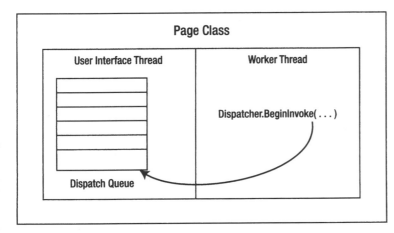

*Figure 12-2. A worker thread using the **Dispatcher** to queue code to execute on the main thread*

Let's rewrite the **responseHandler** to properly interact with the user interface by using the **Dispatcher** property (bolded fonts):

```
void responseHandler(IAsyncResult asyncResult)
{
    HttpWebResponse response = (HttpWebResponse)request.EndGetResponse(asyncResult);
    StreamReader reader = new StreamReader(response.GetResponseStream());
    string result = "";
    // read and process file
    Dispatcher.BeginInvoke(delegate() { resultTextBox.Text = result; });
}
```

This usage of **BeginInvoke** creates an anonymous, zero-parameter method by using the **delegate** keyword. You can also execute a method that has parameters by using the alternate form of **BeginInvoke**, which takes an array of parameters as its second parameter. In this case, we call **BeginInvoke** directly because part of the defined behavior of **HttpWebResponse** is that the response handler is invoked on a thread other than the original calling thread. If you're in a situation where the invoking thread might be the user interface thread or a different thread, you can use **CheckAccess** combined with **BeginInvoke** in order to modify the user interface:

```
void modifyUserInterface()
{
    if(Dispatcher.CheckAccess())
    {
        resultTextBox.Text = "modified from UI thread";
    } else {
        Dispatcher.BeginInvoke(
            delegate() {
                resultTextBox.Text = "modified from non-UI thread";
            }
        );
    }
}
```

Of course, although you'll primarily use the **Dispatcher** to modify the user interface, it is also useful for modifying any data that is associated with a different thread. As illustrated in Figure 12-2, each thread has a dispatch queue. This is where the code you specify in a **BeginInvoke** method goes. Each call to **BeginInvoke** adds a unit of work to the dispatch queue.

The BackgroundWorker Class

If you need to perform work on a separate thread, the easiest way to do this is by using the **BackgroundWorker** class, which is available in the **System.ComponentModel** namespace. This class makes it easy to do work (such as a long download) on a separate background thread, running operation in the background, so your user interface stays responsive. This class also provides events for reporting the progress of the work. Table 12-4 describes its properties.

Table 12-4. Properties of the System.ComponentModel.BackgroundWorker Class

Property	Type	Description
CancellationPending	bool	true when the application attempts to cancel the BackgroundWorker via a call to the CancelAsync method.
IsBusy	bool	true when the BackgroundWorker's task is in progress (after the call to RunWorkerAsync, and as long as the task isn't complete or cancelled).
WorkerReportsProgress	bool	true when the BackgroundWorker is configured to report progress via the ProgressChanged event handler.
WorkerSupportsCancellation	bool	true when the BackgroundWorker is capable of being cancelled via CancelAsync.

The **BackgroundWorker** has three events: **DoWork, ProgressChanged**, and **RunWorkerCompleted**. Normally, a method you register with an event is invoked when the event is raised. This same mechanism, however, is used by the **DoWork** event. In this case, what is normally an event handler instead contains code that makes up the work that will be performed by the **BackgroundWorker**. **ProgressChanged** is used to register a method that can handle progress change notification—most useful for displaying a status indicator on the user interface, since the method call happens on the initiating thread (most commonly the user interface thread). The **RunWorkerCompleted** event is raised when the work is complete.

■ **Note** Avoid updating the user interface within the **DoWork** event; use **ProgressChanged** and **RunWorkerCompleted** events instead to update the user interface.

Let's explore just how the **BackgroundWorker** operates. Figure 12-3 shows a demonstration with three buttons. Clicking each button will start a new **BackgroundWorker** configured with some information to tell it how long to execute, as well as where to send data (the TextBlock next to the button) as it executes and when it completes.

Figure 12-3. BackgroundWorker demonstration

Before you can use **BackgroundWorker**, you must define a method that encapsulates the work that you want done on a background thread. This method supports cancellation and takes an integer argument (contained in the **CustomWorkerArgs** instance that is passed in via the **DoWorkEventArgs** object) that controls how long the method takes to execute. The long-running operation is simulated via **Thread.Sleep**:

```
public void performLengthyOperation(object sender, DoWorkEventArgs e)
{
    BackgroundWorker bw = (BackgroundWorker)sender;
    CustomWorkerArgs args = (CustomWorkerArgs)e.Argument;
    e.Result = args;
    for (int i = 1; i <= 10; i++)
    {
        if (bw.CancellationPending)
        {
            e.Cancel = true;
            break;
        }
        else
        {
            Thread.Sleep(args.sleepTime / 10);
            bw.ReportProgress(i * 10, args);
```

```
        }
    }
}
```

The `DoWorkEventArgs` object defines several useful properties: `Argument`, which contains an arbitrary object that was passed to `RunWorkerAsync`; `Cancel`, which you set to `true` to cancel the work (generally done when `CancellationPending` is set to `true`); and `Result`, which is used to store an object that can be processed by the `RunWorkerCompleted` event handler. Since this configuration of `BackgroundWorker` supports cancellation (something we must explicitly implement in the method that performs work), the `CancellationPending` property is checked, and the loop aborts prematurely if it is `true`. The `ReportProgress` method takes two parameters: an integer representing percentage completion and optionally a user state, used to communicate some form of information to the progress event handler.

The `CustomWorkerArgs` class simply holds an integer representing an index (so we can easily access the button/text block associated with `BackgroundWorker`) and an integer for `sleepTime` (the total time the worker method should take to execute). Using a class like this is how you can communicate as much information as needed to `BackgroundWorker`.

```
class CustomWorkerArgs
{
    public int index;
    public int sleepTime;
}
```

Since the various event handlers for `BackgroundWorker` include a sender (the `BackgroundWorker` instance), you can hold a reference to this worker at the class level and compare the instances instead of passing the index via `CustomWorkerArgs`. In fact, in one case (when the worker is cancelled or throws an exception), this is mandated. However, this information is included in the `CustomWorkerArgs` class in order to show where information can be accessed and used in the `BackgroundWorker`'s event handlers. You can keep an array of `BackgroundWorker` instances at the class level, along with an array of Buttons and an array of TextBlocks. The Button, in XAML, stores the appropriate index in the `Tag` attribute. A single Button event handler is used to start `BackgroundWorker`.

```
private void buttonTask_Click(object sender, RoutedEventArgs e)
{
    // Tag used to get index for button/text blocks
    int index = Convert.ToInt32(((Button)sender).Tag);
    if (workers[index] != null)
    {
        resultBoxes[index].Text = "Cancelling...";
        workers[index].CancelAsync();
        bwButtons[index].Content = "Start";
    }
    else
    {
        BackgroundWorker worker = new BackgroundWorker();
        worker.WorkerReportsProgress = true;
        worker.WorkerSupportsCancellation = true;
        worker.ProgressChanged +=
                new ProgressChangedEventHandler(worker_ProgressChanged);
        worker.RunWorkerCompleted +=
                new RunWorkerCompletedEventHandler(worker_RunWorkerCompleted);
```

```
        worker.DoWork += new DoWorkEventHandler(performLengthyOperation);
        CustomWorkerArgs args = new CustomWorkerArgs();
        args.index = index;
        args.sleepTime = 25000;
        bwButtons[index].Content = "Cancel";
        resultBoxes[index].Text = "Starting...";
        workers[index] = worker;
        worker.RunWorkerAsync(args);
    }
}
```

The index is retrieved via the **Tag** attribute, and then the corresponding **worker** entry in the **workers** array is checked. This entry is set to **null** when **BackgroundWorker** completes (or errors or is cancelled), so if you find it not **null**, then the worker is active and working. Otherwise, a new **BackgroundWorker** is created. This is where we set **WorkReportsProgress** and **WorkerSupportsCancellation** to **true**. Again, these properties should be set to **true** only when you construct the method that does work to explicitly handle the cancel condition and to report progress.

Next, the event handlers are registered. Let's take a closer look at these. **DoWork** is registered with the method that actually does the work. In this case, this is the **performLengthyOperation** that you already implemented. The rest of this method creates a **CustomWorkerArgs** instance, configures it, and passes it to the **BackgroundWorker** in the **RunWorkerAsync** method. **RunWorkerAsync** is what starts the actual work, provided **DoWork** is registered with the work method.

The progress handler is straightforward. The **UserState** property of **ProgressChangedEventArgs** contains the object originally passed to **RunWorkerAsync**. The source of this property, however, is the second (optional) parameter to the **ReportProgress** method of **BackgroundWorker**. If you need to pass something custom specifically to the progress report handler, you can do it using the **UserState** property.

```
void worker_ProgressChanged(object sender, ProgressChangedEventArgs e)
{
    int index = ((CustomWorkerArgs)e.UserState).index;
    resultBoxes[index].Text = "In progress: " + e.ProgressPercentage + "%";
}
```

The **RunWorkerCompleted** event handler is much more interesting. Here, you must check whether the background worker was cancelled or if it had an error. If either of these conditions is true, you can't use the **Result** property of the **RunWorkerCompletedEventArgs**, or else your code will throw an exception.

```
void worker_RunWorkerCompleted(object sender, RunWorkerCompletedEventArgs e)
{
    BackgroundWorker bw = (BackgroundWorker)sender;
    int index;
    if (e.Error != null || e.Cancelled)
    {
        // if there's an Error or this worker was cancelled,
        // we can't access Result without throwing an exception
        if (bw == workers[0])
            index = 0;
        else if (bw == workers[1])
            index = 1;
        else
```

```
            index = 2;
        if (e.Error != null)
            resultBoxes[index].Text = "Exception: " + e.Error.Message;
        else
            resultBoxes[index].Text = "Cancelled";
    }
    else
    {
        index = ((CustomWorkerArgs)e.Result).index;
        resultBoxes[index].Text = "Completed";
    }
    bwButtons[index].Content = "Start";
    workers[index] = null;
}
```

If there is no error and the worker was not cancelled, the Result property can be accessed. The else block illustrates accessing Result, providing a quick way to arrive at the right text block.

Remember that all of these event handlers happen in the thread that created the BackgroundWorker. Since these workers were created on the user interface thread, it's possible to directly access the various text blocks to set their Text property to something appropriate. There are two big advantages to using the BackgroundWorker. First, it makes it easy to do work on a background thread without needing to worry about manually creating and managing a thread. Second, the various event handlers happen on the calling thread, making modification of a user interface easy without needing to use a Dispatcher.

Working with Shared Data

One of the trickiest problems when it comes to working with multiple threads is using shared resources—typically, shared memory in the form of objects or primitive types. When it comes to shared data, one potential issue is known as a *race condition*. Figure 12-4 illustrates two threads attempting to increment a single integer variable named value. However, a simple increment is split into smaller operations behind the scenes: the value of the variable is read, incremented, and stored back into the variable.

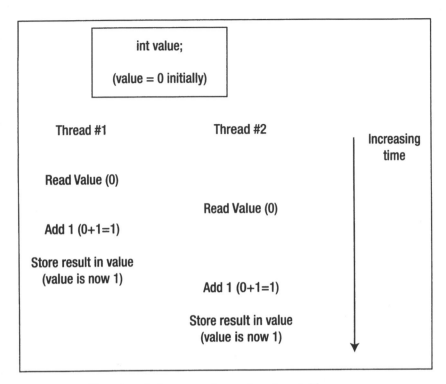

Figure 12-4. Two threads incrementing a shared variable

After each thread is done executing, you would expect the value of the integer variable to be 2, not 1. Unfortunately, while the second thread did read the value, the read happened before the first thread was done with its increment. This means both threads think the value was 0 and increment it to 1. The second thread clobbers the increment done by the first thread.

What you want is a way to ensure that all the tiny pieces of the increment (the read, the increment, and the write-back) work as a single unit. This increment then acts as an atomic operation—an operation (or sequence of operations) that works together and isn't preempted by another thread. This atomicity is achieved by using synchronization mechanisms. Actually, the increment and decrement are such common operations that the Silverlight base class framework provides a specialized increment and decrement that are guaranteed to happen without another thread preempting them. These convenience operations, and a few others, are provided by the **System.Threading.Interlocked** class. Table 12-5 describes the methods of **Interlocked**. All methods are static.

Table 12-5. Static Methods of the System.Threading.Interlocked Class

Method	Description
Add	Adds two 32-bit or two 64-bit integers and stores the result in the memory location of the first integer (pass first integer by reference).
CompareExchange	Compares two values (integers or arbitrary types via a generic version) and replaces the value in the memory location of the first parameter with the second parameter if the first parameter is equal to the third parameter (a value used in comparison with first parameter).
Decrement	Decrements a 32-bit or 64-bit integer by 1.
Exchange	Exchanges two values (32-bit or 64-bit integers, or arbitrary types via a generic version). The exchange occurs by setting the memory of the first parameter to the value of the second parameter, and then the original value stored at the memory of the first parameter is returned from the method.
Increment	Increments a 32-bit or 64-bit integer by 1.

The Interlocked class can be extremely useful if you are performing atomic operations. You don't need to do anything other than invoke Interlocked.Increment(ref number) if you want to add 1 to an integer variable without worrying about other threads getting in the way. If you want to do something beyond a simple increment, add, or comparison, you need a mechanism to turn an arbitrary set of operations into an atomic operation that can't be affected by other threads.

This atomicity is achieved by using a *synchronization mechanism.* A synchronization mechanism is a way for a thread to gain exclusive access to something (possibly one or more resources), locking out all other threads. When a thread is done with its work, it sends a signal essentially saying "I'm done" and letting other threads then obtain access to the shared resources.

One of these synchronization mechanisms is known as a *monitor.* Every object instance has a monitor associated with it. You can view a monitor as a token that only a single thread can own at any given time. If there are multiple threads attempting to gain access to a monitor, only the first thread that successfully requests it gets it. Other threads then line up, waiting for the first thread to release the monitor. The C# language provides a keyword, lock, that makes it easy to obtain a lock on an object's monitor.

If you need to control access to resources within a class, it's recommended you create a private object instance to use as a lock. This solves several problems with the design of the monitors in the CLR, including ensuring that the lock cannot be obtained by an outside class. If you were to obtain a lock on the current object instance via this, an outside class could also request a lock on the same instance. In practice, this looks like the following if you attempt to write a simple list (that uses an array internally). Here is a simple list without error handling to illustrate how to use this synchronization functionality.

```
class ThreadSafeList
{
    private Object m_lock = new Object();
    private int[] listItems;
    private int count;
```

```
public ThreadSafeList()
{
    listItems = new int[100];
    count = 0;
}
public void Add(int num)
{
    lock(m_lock)
    {
        // if list is full, allocate more space
        // otherwise, just add to end...
        listItems[count] = num;
        count++;
    }
}
public void RemoveAt(int index)
{
    lock(m_lock)
    {
        for(int i=index; i<count; i++)
        {
            listItems[i] = listItems[i+1];
        }
        count--;
    }
}
}
```

Using the lock keyword ensures that only a single thread has access to the internals of the list (the listItems array and the count variable) at any given time. If you removed the lock requests and let several threads add items to and remove items from the list, it probably won't take long for something to go wrong, such as phantom values showing up in the list or the count variable not accurately reflecting the proper size of the list.

Using Timers

Timing can be quite useful in applications, such as to execute time code, influence animations (such as when a certain animation starts), or perform other application-specific functions, such as using a stage timer in a game. The two most useful timer classes in Silverlight are DispatcherTimer, a timer integrated with the dispatch queue, and Timer, from the System.Threading namespace. The major difference between these two timers is where the work method that occurs periodically is executed. The Timer class executes the work method on a separate thread, leaving the user interface responsive, but requiring use of the Dispatcher to change the user interface. The DispatcherTimer, however, does not have this restriction since it executes on the same thread. This makes it much easier to use. Figure 12-5 shows an interface used to experiment with both of these timers.

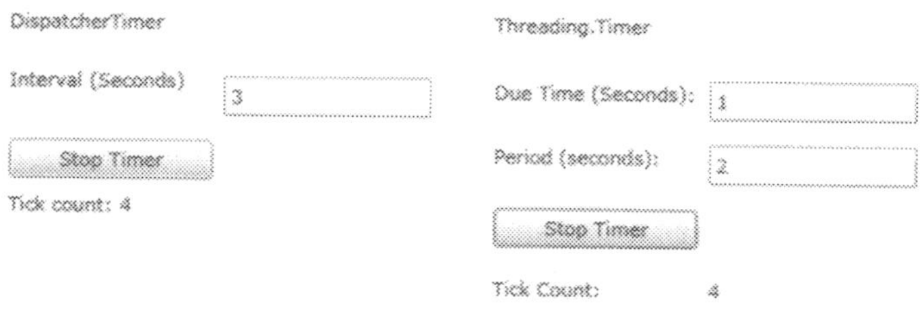

Figure 12-5. DispatcherTimer and Timer class demonstrations

Using the DispatcherTimer

The DispatcherTimer works by hooking its Tick event up to a method that will be called on a periodic basis. You specify how often the Tick event is raised by passing a TimeSpan to the DispatcherTimer constructor or by setting the Interval property to the TimeSpan. The timer is then started via the Start method and stopped via the Stop method. Here's code that counts to 20 in one-second intervals, displaying each number on the user interface:

```
private int count = 0;
DispatcherTimer timer;

private void startTimer_Click(object sender, RoutedEventArgs e)
{
    if (startTimer.Content.ToString()=="Start Timer")
    {
        timer = new DispatcherTimer();
        timer.Interval = new TimeSpan(0, 0, int.Parse(intervalTimeTextBox.Text));
        timer.Tick += new EventHandler(timer_Tick);
        timer.Start();
        startTimer.Content = "Stop Timer";
    }
    else
    {
        timer.Stop();
        startTimer.Content = "Start Timer";
    }
}

void timer_Tick(object sender, EventArgs e)
{
    count++;
    outputText.Text = "Tick count: " + count;
    if (count == 20)
        ((DispatcherTimer)sender).Stop();
}
```

Using the System.Threading Timer

The `Timer` in the `System.Threading` namespace does basically the same thing, but the work (in the form of a callback method passed to `Timer`) is done on a thread from the thread pool. The method that does work on a periodic basis is specified as a parameter to the `Timer` constructor. There are five overloads of this constructor, each providing a different way to specify how often the work method is invoked. You can also optionally pass extra state information. The most important parameter to each constructor is `TimerCallback`, used to wrap the method that does the work. The **dueTime** parameter is used to specify delay before the timer starts, and the **period** parameter is used to specify delay between each subsequent invocation of the callback. If **dueTime** or **period** is set to infinite, each is effectively disabled (an infinite due time, for example, causes the timer to never start). A due time of zero causes the timer to start immediately, and a period of zero causes the work method to get invoked only once.

`Timer(TimerCallback)`: Creates a timer with an infinite due time and infinite period, preventing the timer from invoking the callback. Use the `Change` method to set a new due time/period. The state object is the `Timer` itself.

`Timer(TimerCallback, object state, Int32 dueTime, Int32 period)`: Creates a timer with a custom state object (useful for passing information to the work method), and a due time and period in milliseconds.

`Timer(TimerCallback, object state, Int64 dueTime, Int64 period)`: Same as the `Int32` version, but provides the ability to specify lengths of time that can't be represented in a 32-bit integer.

`Timer(TimerCallback, object state, TimeSpan dueTime, TimeSpan period)`: Same as the `Int32` version, but uses a `TimeSpan` to make it easier to specify lengths of time such as seconds or minutes.

`Timer(TimerCallback, object state, UInt32 dueTime, UInt32 period)`: Same as the `Int32` version, but instead uses unsigned integers to represent the due time and period.

▓ **Caution** Each time the Timer's period elapses, the work method passed to the TimerCallback is invoked. This work is then executed by a thread from the thread pool. If the work method takes longer to execute than the period, it is likely that the work method will be executed by two threads from the thread pool at the same time. You must ensure that the work method can tolerate this scenario. This can also happen if the threads in the pool are exhausted and the work method is queued multiple times, waiting for threads from the pool to become available.

There is only one useful method on the `Timer` class: `Change`. The `Change` method is used to change the due time and interval of the timer and has four overloads that match the four ways to specify due time and period in the constructor. The work method takes a single object parameter that corresponds to the **state** parameter passed to the constructor (or the `Timer` object itself if the first form of the constructor was used).

```
private void doSomething(object state)
{
    Dispatcher.BeginInvoke(
        delegate() {
            timerOutputText.Text =
```

```
                                    (Convert.ToInt32(timerOutputText.Text) + 1).ToString();
        });
}
```

Since the work method happens on a different thread, the **Dispatcher** must be used to make changes to the user interface. A button on the user interface is again hooked up to a method that starts/stops the timer:

```
private void timerButton_Click(object sender, RoutedEventArgs e)
{
    if (threadTimer != null)
    {
        threadTimer.Change(0, Timeout.Infinite);
        timerButton.Content = "Start Timer";
    }
    else
    {
        if (threadTimer != null)
            threadTimer.Change(Convert.ToInt32(dueTimeTextBox.Text) * 1000,
                                    Convert.ToInt32(periodTextBox.Text) * 1000);
        else
            threadTimer = new Timer(new TimerCallback(doSomething), null,
                                    Convert.ToInt32(dueTimeTextBox.Text) * 1000,
                                    Convert.ToInt32(periodTextBox.Text) * 1000);
        timerButton.Content = "Stop Timer";
    }
}
```

You instruct the timer to stop by setting the period to **Timeout.Infinite**. The **Change** method is used to restart the timer also. This is the only way to interact with the **Timer** after it has been created, except for destroying it via **Dispose**.

Summary

When the .NET Framework is a back-end platform for Silverlight, the multi-threading support is provided by Silverlight. Although you can manually create and use threads, it's much better to either leverage the thread pool or use the **BackgroundWorker** class to do work on a thread other than the main application thread. You also saw two timers provided by Silverlight: the **DispatcherTimer** and the **Timer** from the **System.Threading** namespace. In the next chapter, we will look at the Silverlight support for dynamic languages such as IronRuby and IronPython.

CHAPTER 13

WCF RIA Services and Silverlight for Mobile

The Silverlight platform is meant to provide a technology platform to develop and deploy platform- and device-agnostic and enterprise-level line-of-business rich Internet applications. So far you have learned basic and advanced features and capabilities to develop Silverlight RIAs. This chapter provides you with the following:

- A high-level overview of the newly introduced capabilities in Silverlight 4, including WCF RIA Services (previously known as .NET RIA Services) to truly develop n-tier enterprise-level business applications

- Extended support of Silverlight on the Windows Mobile 7 platform to develop Silverlight-based applications for Windows mobile devices

Note that one chapter is not sufficient to cover all aspects of WCF RIA Services for Silverlight and Silverlight for the Windows Mobile 7 platform in detail. This chapter is intended to introduce these capabilities at a very basic level to give you a quick start.

WCF RIA Services for Silverlight

Usually business applications are data-driven and need to support different types of business logic supporting CRUD operations in a secured role-based application environment. It is also important to keep the application logic independent to the data platform and application presentation layer. Efficient coordination of application logic between client and server sides, for any n-tier RIA application, is critical to avoid redundancy of the application logic at the client side (presentation layer level) and the server side.

In Chapter 11, we learned about the Model View ViewModel (MVVM) design pattern and demonstrated how ViewModel (in the MVVM pattern) can encapsulate the application behavior independent to View, and how to leverage data-binding and commanding to bind the View to its ViewModel.

WCF RIA Services is intended to provide framework components and services as building blocks, and design and development tools and templates (for Visual Studio) to develop the server-side application logic, and, based on the implemented server-side application logic, manage and maintain the Silverlight client-side application logic without you maintaining it manually. With the help of WCF RIA Services and Visual Studio, you can develop a single solution containing the server- and client-side projects and generate and maintain the application logic code for the RIA client automatically based on the implemented middle-tier server-side application logic. WCF RIA Services also provides out-of-the-box common security services for form-based authentication, roles, and profile management. Figure 13-1 provides a high-level overview of an n-tier rich Internet application and the role of WCF RIA Services.

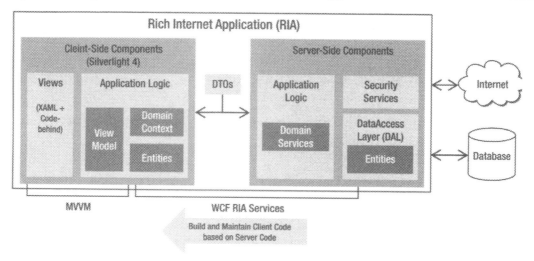

Figure 13-1. *Overview of n-tier application and role of WCF RIA Services and MVVM*

Setting Up a Development Environment

WCF RIA Services is available for Silverlight 4 and Silverlight 3 and it is also supported on Visual Studio 2010 and Visual Studio 2008 (for Silverlight 3 only).

The WCF RIA services 1.0 release is available for Visual Studio 2010 and Silverlight 4. You can visit www.silverlight.net/getstarted/riaservices/ and select WCF RIA Services 1.0 to download. Note that if you have already installed Microsoft Silverlight 4 Tools for Visual Studio 2010, you do not need to install WCF RIA Services 1.0 separately. The WCF RIA Services tool kit is also available, which extends the WCF RIA Services framework by providing LinqToSql DomainService, ASP.NET DomainDataSource control to integrate ASP .NET application with the domain service, JSON and SOAP endpoints that can be exposed to the domain service, and WCF client proxy auto generation/updating for WCF Core Service.

You will use WCF RIA Services Beta for Visual Studio 2008 and Silverlight 3. Visit www.silverlight.net/getstarted/riaservices/ to get more information.

As we learned in Chapter 1, installing WCF RIA Services 1.0, you will get two additional Visual Studio 2010 templates (see Figure 13-2). The Silverlight Business Application template by default integrates core components and services of WCF RIA Services within the navigation framework to develop line-of-business applications. The WCF RIA Services Class Library template enables you to develop a WCR RIA Services reusable class library that can be used by one or more Silverlight applications.

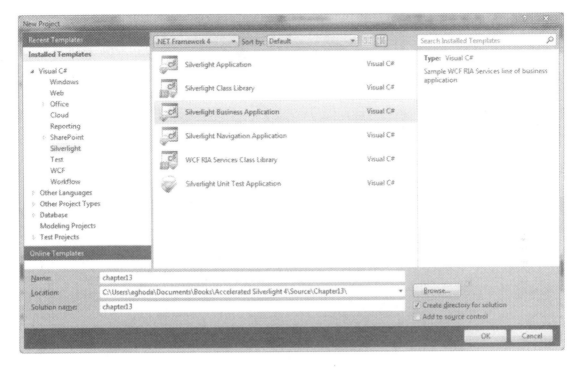

Figure 13-2. Additional WCR RIA Services Silverlight 4 project templates in Visual Studio 2010

Introducing Silverlight Business Application Template

As shown in Figure 13-2, create a new Silverlight application using the Silverlight Business Application project template. Name the project chapter13. Like other Silverlight projects, it will include a Silverlight project and web project, however, it will contain more than just an empty project. However, as you might have noticed, it does not ask you how to host the application as well as whether to enable WCF RIA Services as a separate dialog window during your new project creation process. The reason is the Silverlight Business Application project template automatically selects ASP .NET Web Application as the hosting project and also selects the Enable WCR RIA Services option and creates the project directly. You can verify it by going to chapter13's project properties. You will notice that the WCR RIA Services link is set to the chapter13.Web project as a server-side project.

If you look at the project solution explorer, you will notice that the Silverlight Business Application project implemented a navigation framework with default pages under the Views folder and resources and styles under the Assets folder. In addition, the Controls folder contains custom controls, the Helpers folder contains data binding extension, resource wrapper, and value converter helper classes, and the Models folder contains the data objects to use with an out-of-the box supplied authentication service and login system as part of the WCF RIA Services implementation. See Figure 13-3 for the details.

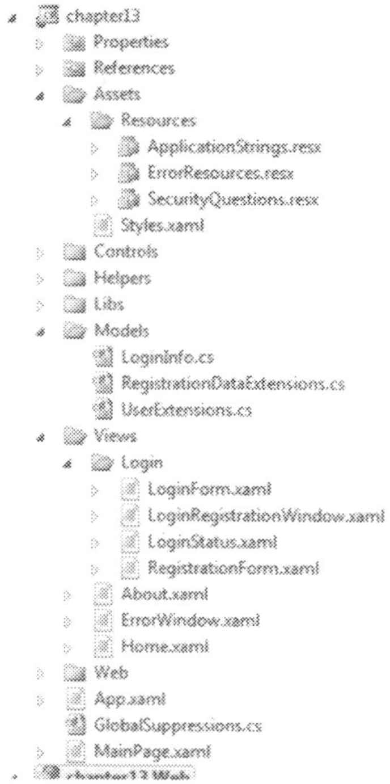

Figure 13-3. Default files of a Silverlight Business Application project

The Silverlight Business Application project implements a web project with authentication and user registration RIA services and related data models. The Services folder contains authentication and registration WCF services, the Models folder contains related classes, and the Resources folder keeps related resources. See Figure 13-4 for the details.

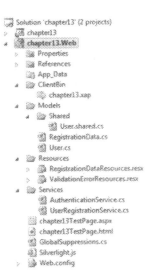

Figure 13-4. *Default files of a Silverlight Business Application web project*

Running the Default Project

Now, if you run the project, you will get the usual default Navigation template-based Silverlight application output with the addition of the login option near the top right corner, as shown in Figure 13-5.

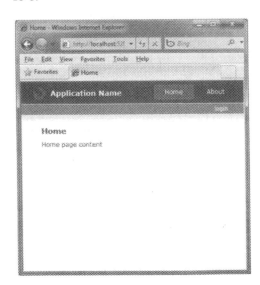

Figure 13-5. *Default Silverlight Business Application with login option*

The application contains a form-based authentication mode as a default mode. If you click the login you see a Login child window appear. Enter a user ID and password. You will notice that the progress activity is displayed, and it will verify and return the error message mentioning the user name or password is incorrect, as shown in Figure 13-6.

When you run the project for the first time, it may take a bit longer since it creates the required database in App_Data, which is hidden. You can see it under the web project if you click the "Show All Files" option available under the Solution Explorer window.

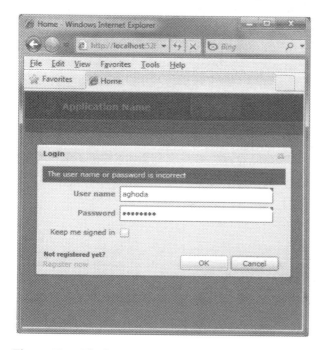

Figure 13-6. The login screen displaying an error message after validating the entered user name and password

So far no user exists; it is obvious that we would get an error message. Now let's register aghoda as a user by clicking the "Register now" link on the login screen (see Figure 13-6). I have registered myself, as shown in Figure 13-7. Now when you click OK, I will become a registered user and automatically logged in to the application. My friendly name will display as a logged-in user, as shown in Figure 13-8.

Figure 13-7. User registration screen of the application

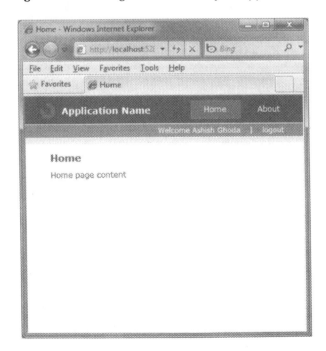

Figure 13-8. Form-based authentication—logged in to the application as Ashish Ghoda

Remember that so far you have only created a project, and, by default, you have received this level of functionality. Isn't that a great way to start building your Silverlight Business Applications using WCF RIA Services?

In the following sections, you will learn how to customize the authentication mode and implement data integration using RIA services.

Implementing Windows Authentication

You can very easily switch the application authentication mode from form-based to windows -based. Visit the Web.config file of the server chapter13.Web project and look for the authentication node. You will notice enabling form-based authentication, as follows.

```
<authentication mode="Forms">
    <forms name=".chapter13_ASPXAUTH" />
</authentication>
```

Change the authentication mode from Forms to Windows and delete the forms element. It should look like this:

```
<authentication mode="Windows">
</authentication>
```

Now visit the App.xaml.cs file of the chapter13 client project. Visit the constructor of the App class and comment the following:

```
webContext.Authentication = new FormsAuthentication();
```

Uncomment the following:

```
webContext.Authentication = new WindowsAuthentication();
```

If you run the project, you will see you are automatically logged in with your Windows account, as shown in Figure 13-9.

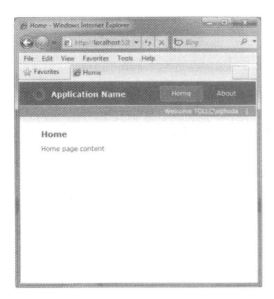

Figure 13-9. Windows authentication—logged in as Windows account TOLLC\aghoda

ADO .NET Entity Data Model for Data Integration

Earlier we created the ApressBooks.mdf SQL database for Chapter 6. We will reuse this database as the data source and map it using the ADO .NET Entity Framework, through which RIA services will perform CRUD operations against the data source and make the application database platform-agnostic.

Go ahead and add an ADO .NET Entity Data Model named ApressBooks.edmx under the Models folder. You will use the "Generate from database" option to link to the ApressBooks.mdf existing database and define the entity connection setting in Web.Config as ApressBooksEntities in the Choose Your Data Connection wizard. Note that you may have to create a connection string for the ApressBooks.mdf file (if it does not exist) to complete this task. Next in the Choose Your Database Objects wizard, select all tables, define the model namespace as ApressBooksModel and keep both options—"Pluralize or singularize generated object names" and "Include foreign key columns in mode"—selected. Now build the solution.

Please look at Figure 13-10 to recollect the schema of the ApressBooks database.

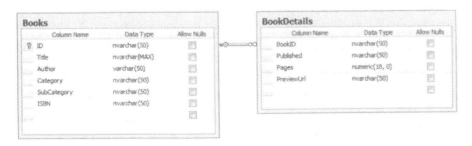

Figure 13-10. ApressBooks database schema

At this point, if you look at the properties of the entity type, for `ApressBooksModel.Book` the entity set name is set to Books and for `ApressBooksModel.BookDetail`, it is set to BookDetails.

Domain Service Class for Data Integration

Domain services are WCF services that will encapsulate the business logic of an application by exposing data operations in the form of a service layer. The domain context communicates with the domain service by using the WCF ChannelFactory to create a channel and pass it a service contract that was generated from the domain service. You can easily create a domain service within the Visual Studio.

Let's create a domain service class under the `Services` folder of the `chapter13.Web` server-side project. For that, right-click the `Services` folder, add a new item, select the domain service class option, and name it `ApressBooksService.cs`. Select only the Books table and make sure you select "Generate associated classes for metadata," as shown in Figure 13-11. By selecting this option it will generate the `ApressBookService.metadata.cs` file, where you can implement the validation and business rules. The code will be automatically copied to the Silverlight client project as soon as you compile the project. Note that here I have selected the "Enable editing" option (see Figure 13-11).

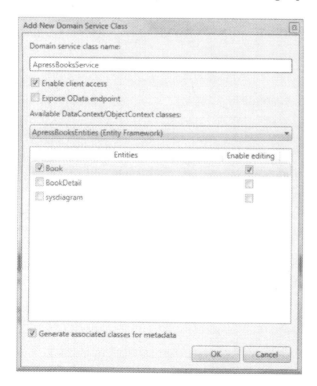

Figure 13-11. Adding and configuring the `ApressBooksService` domain service class

The resultant `ApressBooksService.cs` class will contain the queryable `GetBooks` method that is exposed to the Silverlight client. The following is the default created method. Keep in mind that you can actually update these methods to implement your custom logic such as filtering based on the Book category.

```
[EnableClientAccess()]
public class ApressBooksService :
    LinqToEntitiesDomainService<ApressBooksEntities>
{
    // TODO:
    // Consider constraining the results of your query method.
      // If you need additional input you can
    // add parameters to this method or create additional query
      //methods with different names.
    // To support paging you will need to add ordering to the 'Books'
      //query.
    public IQueryable<Book> GetBooks()
    {
        return this.ObjectContext.Books;
    }
}
```

Reading and Displaying Data from the Data Source

Now let's map this data to a DataGrid control. For that, first make sure you compile the project to expose the added domain service as a Data Source, as shown in Figure 13-12. Note that if you do not get the Data Sources window automatically, click the Data menu item and click the Show Data Sources option.

As shown in Figure 13-12, you will notice that two data sources are available. One is chapter13.Web.UserRegistrationContext.datasource, which is automatically created as part of the Silverlight Business Application template to facilitate user registration with all the fields you have entered to add and register as a new user (see Figure 13-7) supporting user registration domain service. User registration is part of the App_Data database, which is automatically created and is hidden. You can see it under the web project if you click the "Show All Files" option available under the Solution Explorer window.

The second data source is chapter13.Web.Services.ApressBooksContext.datasource, which you have recently created to support required CRUD operations for the ApressBooks.mdf database.

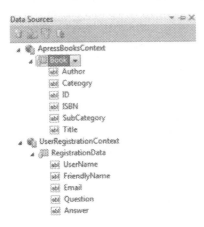

Figure 13-12. Domain data sources of the project

Then add a Grid control to the Home.xaml page available under the Views folder of the chapter13 project. Set appropriate properties to make it of appropriate height and width, and set the AutoGenerateColumns property to true. Now visit the Data Sources window and drag and drop the Book data source to the Grid. If you have design and XAML windows opened side by side, you will notice that dropping the Book data source to the Grid will automatically generate all of the required domain data source code and bind to the Grid. Just run the project and you should see all Books table data populated to the home screen, as shown in Figure 13-13.

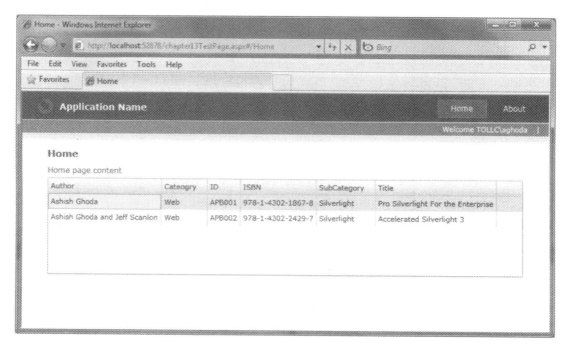

Figure 13-13. Data population using WCF RIA Services and domain data source

If you visit the Home.xaml file, a reference to System.Windows.Controls.DomainServices along with references to the project WCF services and data models are added at the control level, as shown here in the highlighted bold fonts:

```
<navigation:Page
    x:Class="chapter13.Home"
    xmlns="http://schemas.microsoft.com/winfx/2006/xaml/presentation"
    xmlns:x="http://schemas.microsoft.com/winfx/2006/xaml"
    xmlns:d="http://schemas.microsoft.com/expression/blend/2008"
    xmlns:mc="http://schemas.openxmlformats.org/
        markup-compatibility/2006"
    xmlns:navigation="clr-namespace:System.Windows.Controls;assembly=
        System.Windows.Controls.Navigation"
    mc:Ignorable="d" d:DesignWidth="640" d:DesignHeight="480"
    Style="{StaticResource PageStyle}"
    xmlns:sdk="http://schemas.microsoft.com/winfx/2006/xaml/
```

```
      presentation/sdk"
   xmlns:riaControls="clr-namespace:System.Windows.Controls;
      assembly=System.Windows.Controls.DomainServices"
   xmlns:my="clr-namespace:chapter13.Web.Services"
   xmlns:my1="clr-namespace:chapter13.Web.Models">
```

And you will see that the following code has been added to create a Domain Data Source, add the Domain Context, and then define the initial GetBooksQuery to retrieve all records from the Books table and map it to the Grid control.

```
<sdk:DataGrid AutoGenerateColumns="True" Name="Books"
   MinHeight="150" ItemsSource=
      "{Binding ElementName=bookDomainDataSource, Path=Data}"/>
<riaControls:DomainDataSource AutoLoad="True"
   d:DesignData="{d:DesignInstance my1:Book, CreateList=true}"
   Height="0" LoadedData="bookDomainDataSource_LoadedData"
   Name="bookDomainDataSource" QueryName="GetBooksQuery" Width="0">
   <riaControls:DomainDataSource.DomainContext>
      <my:ApressBooksContext />
   </riaControls:DomainDataSource.DomainContext>
</riaControls:DomainDataSource>
```

You can enhance this example by providing filters to the query and adding existing queries to the data domain service class. If you have large data, you can enhance the user experience by providing paging, search, or other business-specific functionalities.

Updating Data to the Data Source

You can extend the application to perform create, update, and delete operations. Remember that you start updating data at the client side, and you must save the changes to the server by explicitly submitting the changes. The easiest way to implement is to call the DomainDataSource.SubmitChanges() method to save the updates and call the DomainDataSource.RejectChanges() method to cancel the changes.

Additional References

Visit the following links to get additional references on this topic:

- A video by Tim Heuer explaining WCF RIA Services support in Visual Studio 2010: www.silverlight.net/learn/videos/all/ria-services-support-visual-studio-2010/

- A video by Tim Heuer explaining the WCF RIA Services implementation approach to perform CRUD operations: www.silverlight.net/learn/videos/all/net-ria-services-intro/

- Online documentation on WCR RIA Services: http://msdn.microsoft.com/en-us/library/ee707344.aspx. This documentation also provides a great overview of how to troubleshoot and deploy RIA Services solutions, as well as security aspects of RIA Services solutions.

- Understanding WCF RIA Services class library template:
  http://msdn.microsoft.com/en-us/library/ee707351.aspx

Silverlight for Windows Mobile

After initial demonstration of Silverlight applications for mobile devices during Silverlight 2 version development, for a while Microsoft shifted the focus from the Silverlight Mobile edition to making the overall Silverlight technology platform (and even the mobile OS platform) more stable and scalable enough to support today's enterprise mobility requirements. Aligning with Silverlight 4, Microsoft released Windows Phone 7, supporting development of out-of-browser Windows Mobile applications using Silverlight and XNA. You can develop high-quality media applications (including integration with video camera and microphone), and data-driven applications to multi-touch and motion-sensing gaming applications (using XNA Framework) for Windows mobile phones. For further details visit www.silverlight.net/getstarted/devices/windows-phone/.

Setting Up a Development Environment

The Mobile Silverlight application development model is very similar to the traditional Silverlight RIA development model; you can use the XAML defining user interface and .NET managed code-behind to integrate with server-side components performing application logic. However, at present you need to use different sets of tools to set up the development environment for Silverlight-based Windows mobile application development.

As of writing this chapter, the Windows Phone Developer Tools CTP April release is available to enable Silverlight-based Windows application development. You can visit the Windows Phone developer home site at http://developer.windowsphone.com/windows-phone-7-series/ and click the "Download the developer tools" link. The Windows Phone Developer Tools CTP provides a Visual Studio-integrated development environment (IDE) to design, develop, and test Windows Phone 7 series phone Silverlight applications.

The Windows Phone Developer Tools CTP (April) release includes the following:

- Visual Studio 2010 Express for Windows Phone CTP

- Windows Phone Emulator

- Silverlight for Windows Phone CTP

- XNA Game Studio 4.0 CTP

Developing a Sample Twitter Application

We will develop a Twitter application very similar to the one we will develop in Chapter 15 explaining cross-domain access. The only the difference is that we will not get the feeds from the authenticated users—we will just pass the user name to get the latest feeds from the defined user name. Note that a similar application is also developed by Scott Guthrie, and you can find it by visiting http://weblogs.asp.net/scottgu/archive/2010/03/18/building-a-windows-phone-7-twitter-application-using-silverlight.aspx.

Create a Windows Phone Application Project

Launch Visual Studio 2010 Express for Windows Phone CTP from the Windows start menu. Create a new project based on the new Silverlight Windows Phone Application template and name it TwitterApp, as shown in Figure 13-14.

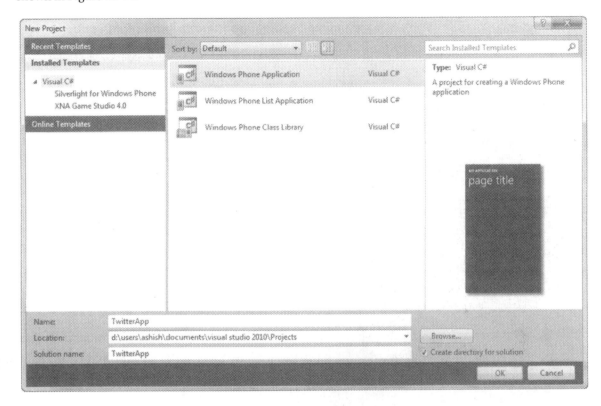

Figure 13-14. Creating a Silverlight Windows Phone Application project using Visual Studio 2010 Express

Defining the User Interface

The next step is to lay out the controls of the application using the Visual Studio designer. We will change the existing application and page titles and add three controls—TextBox, Button, and ListBox—to develop the Twitter application user interface, as shown in Figure 13-15.

Figure 13-15. Silverlight Windows Phone 7 Twitter application user interface

The following is the code snippet of the MainPage.xaml file; the highlighted fonts are the changes I made to develop the Twitter application user interface shown in Figure 13-15.

```
<phoneNavigation:PhoneApplicationPage
    x:Class="TwitterApp.MainPage"
    xmlns="http://schemas.microsoft.com/winfx/2006/xaml/presentation"
    xmlns:x="http://schemas.microsoft.com/winfx/2006/xaml"
    xmlns:phoneNavigation="clr-namespace:Microsoft.Phone.Controls;
        assembly=Microsoft.Phone.Controls.Navigation"
    xmlns:d="http://schemas.microsoft.com/expression/blend/2008"
    xmlns:mc="http://schemas.openxmlformats.org/
```

```
    markup-compatibility/2006"
mc:Ignorable="d" d:DesignWidth="480" d:DesignHeight="800"
FontFamily="{StaticResource PhoneFontFamilyNormal}"
FontSize="{StaticResource PhoneFontSizeNormal}"
Foreground="{StaticResource PhoneForegroundBrush}" >

<Grid x:Name="LayoutRoot"
    Background="{StaticResource PhoneBackgroundBrush}">
    <Grid.RowDefinitions>
        <RowDefinition Height="Auto"/>
        <RowDefinition Height="*"/>
    </Grid.RowDefinitions>

    <!--TitleGrid is the name of the application and page title-->
    <Grid x:Name="TitleGrid" Grid.Row="0">
        <TextBlock Text="Silverlight client for Twitter"
            x:Name="textBlockPageTitle"
            Style="{StaticResource PhoneTextPageTitle1Style}"/>
        <TextBlock Text="Twitter" x:Name="textBlockListTitle"
            Style="{StaticResource PhoneTextPageTitle2Style}"/>
    </Grid>

    <!--ContentGrid is empty. Place new content here-->
    <Grid x:Name="ContentGrid" Grid.Row="1">
        <Grid.RowDefinitions>
            <RowDefinition Height="Auto" />
            <RowDefinition Height="*" />
        </Grid.RowDefinitions>

        <StackPanel Grid.Row="0" Orientation="Horizontal">
            <TextBox x:Name="txtUsername" Height="10" Width="275"
                HorizontalAlignment="Stretch"
                VerticalAlignment="Stretch" Opacity="10"
                Style="{StaticResource PhoneTextBoxStyle}" />
            <Button  x:Name="btnGetTweets" Content="Get Tweets"
                Click="btnGetTweets_Click" Height="60" Width="200"
                Style="{StaticResource PhoneButtonBase}"/>
        </StackPanel>

        <Grid Grid.Row="1">
            <Grid.RowDefinitions>
                <RowDefinition Height="*"/>
                <RowDefinition Height="Auto" />
            </Grid.RowDefinitions>
            <ListBox Grid.Row="0" Height="Auto" Margin="10,0,0,0"
                Name="listBox1" Width="476"
                Style="{StaticResource PhoneListBox}">
                <ListBox.ItemTemplate>
                    <DataTemplate>
                        <StackPanel Orientation="Horizontal"
                            Height="132">
```

```xml
                              <Image
                                  Source="{Binding ImageSource}"
                                  Height="73" Width="73"
                                  VerticalAlignment="Top"
                                  Margin="0,10,8,0"/>
                              <StackPanel Width="370">
                                  <TextBlock
                                    Text="{Binding UserName}"
                                    Foreground="#FFC8AB14"
                                    FontSize="28" />
                                  <TextBlock
                                    Text="{Binding Message}"
                                    TextWrapping="Wrap"
                                    FontSize="24" />
                                  <TextBlock
                                    Text="{Binding CreatedAt}"
                                    FontSize="20"
                                    Foreground="#FFC8AB14" />
                              </StackPanel>
                          </StackPanel>
                      </DataTemplate>
                  </ListBox.ItemTemplate>
              </ListBox>
          </Grid>
      </Grid>
  </Grid>
</phoneNavigation:PhoneApplicationPage>
```

As you can see, I've changed the default application title and page title. Then for the default-created ContentGrid, I have put XAML markup to create a simple UI. I have used data binding for the ListBox ItemTemplate under DataTemplate. Also note the reference added to the `Microsoft.Phone.Controls.Navigation` assembly to support Windows Mobile Phone integration.

Code-Behind for Twitter Integration

First, add a new class named `TwitterMessage` that represents the Twitter status message, as shown here:

```csharp
public class TwitterMessage
{
    public string UserName { get; set; }
    public string Message { get; set; }
    public string ImageSource { get; set; }
    public string CreatedAt { get; set; }
}
```

Next implement the btnGetTweets button's `Click` event, as shown here:

```csharp
private void btnGetTweets_Click(object sender, RoutedEventArgs e)
{
    WebClient client = new WebClient();
```

```
client.DownloadStringCompleted += new
    DownloadStringCompletedEventHandler
        (client_DownloadStringCompleted);
client.DownloadStringAsync(new Uri
    ("http://api.twitter.com/1/statuses/user_timeline.xml?
        screen_name=" + txtUsername.Text));
}
```

Here we created a WebClient to retrieve the Twitter feeds and attach
DownloadStringCompletedEventHandler to process the retrieved Twitter feeds upon receipt. In the end we
call the asynchronous DownloadStringAsync method, passing the Twitter API with the entered user name
as a parameter.

client_DownloadStringCompleted will simply parse the result and bind it to the ListBox listBox1, as
shown here.

```
void client_DownloadStringCompleted
    (object sender, DownloadStringCompletedEventArgs e)
{
    if (e.Error != null)
        return;
    XElement xmlTweets = XElement.Parse(e.Result);
    listBox1.ItemsSource = from tweet in
        xmlTweets.Descendants("status")
            select new TwitterMessage
            {
                ImageSource = tweet.Element("user").
                    Element("profile_image_url").Value,
                Message = tweet.Element("text").Value,
                UserName = tweet.Element("user").
                    Element("screen_name").Value,
                CreatedAt = tweet.Element("created_at").Value
            };
}
```

Testing Silverlight Windows Mobile Application Using
Windows Phone 7 Emulator

Now you are all set to test the application. You get two options to test your developed application. Either
you can use the Windows Phone 7 Emulator to simulate the Windows Phone environment without
having an actual device with you, or you can use the Windows Phone 7 device.

For demonstration purposes we will use the Windows Phone 7 Emulator. Run the application. This
will open a Windows Phone 7 emulator window and launch the application. Enter Ashish Ghoda in the
TextBox and make sure that your desktop computer has Internet access. Then you can test your
application by clicking the Get Tweets button and verifying that the window gets the results from Twitter
and displays them, as shown in Figure 13-16, in the default portrait mode. Note that sometimes when
you run application for the first time, it does not run as expected. In that case, rebuild the application
again and run the application a second time to get the expected results of your application.

Figure 13-16. *Silverlight Windows Phone Twitter application running in portrait mode (default mode) using Windows Phone 7 Emulator*

The Windows Phone 7 Emulator supports the application in landscape and portrait modes, providing a real-time experience. Figure 13-16 shows the application running in the default portrait mode. You can press one of the rotation controls on the emulator to change the application running mode (landscape or portrait). The control will resize to fit the screen automatically. Figure 13-17 shows the application running in the landscape mode.

Figure 13-17. *Silverlight Windows Phone Twitter application running in landscape mode using Windows Phone 7 Emulator*

Note that if the Emulator times out into the lock screen, you can unlock it by clicking at the bottom of the screen and swiping upward. Also, as in other regular applications in Visual Studio, you can set debug breakpoints in the code by placing the cursor on the desired line of code and selecting the Debug | Toggle Breakpoint menu command.

Summary

This chapter provided you a brief overview on the WCF RIA Services implementation approach to make a data-driven application data-platform agnostic and how to handle the application logic in a managed and efficient way for rich Internet applications. We ended the chapter by introducing Silverlight technology platform capabilities to develop the next wave of applications for Windows Mobile. Even though both of these capabilities are still in the initial phase, they seem impressive and promising, and I am looking forward to seeing great enhancements in these areas.

In the next chapter I will introduce you to another notable feature of Silverlight, which is Silverlight support for dynamic languages.

CHAPTER 14

Dynamic Languages and Dynamic .NET for Silverlight

One of the notable features of Silverlight is its support for dynamic languages. A dynamic language is interpreted at runtime, meaning it is possible to add new code while a program is executing. The dynamic language you are likely most familiar with is JScript. Silverlight has direct support for both JScript and Managed Jscript, which is JScript executing on the Dynamic Language Runtime (DLR). Two other dynamic languages are supported: Ruby and Python (called IronRuby and IronPython in the Silverlight/.NET world). This integration capability enables the development of rich Internet applications (RIAs) using the Silverlight platform—XAML for the presentation layer and dynamic languages for the code-behind. This chapter will introduce these dynamic languages, discuss why the DLR is important in the Silverlight picture, and show how to go about using these languages.

Dynamic Languages

The Read-Eval-Print Loop (REPL) environment provides lightweight "play as you go" programming ability for developers through the use of what are known as dynamic programming languages. Dynamic languages are usually dynamically typed and are compiled at runtime. You do not need to declare variables of particular data types. Everything is handled by the runtime through the context of expressions.

The more familiar languages such as C# and Visual Basic are statically typed languages and more rigid in nature. Development and deployment using dynamic languages is more simplified compared to static languages such as C# and Visual Basic, which require compilation and distribution of output. However, you still need to do proper validation and testing type safety and security when using dynamically typed languages.

With dynamic languages, you can create a function and assign it to a variable or pass it as a parameter to another function. This makes things like closures and passing functions as parameters a lot easier. In general, two defining characteristics of closures are your ability to assign a block of code (a function) to a variable, and this block of code's ability to retain access to variables that were accessible where it was created.

If you were to write a traditional method in C# to obtain a subset of a list of words that match a certain criterion, such as a maximum length of three letters or less, the method might look like this:

```
public static List<string> ShortWords(List<string> wordList)
{
    List<string> shortWordList = new List<string>();
    int maximumWordLength = 3;
```

```
    foreach(string word in wordList)
    {
        if(word.Length <= maximumWordLength)
        {
            shortWordList.Add(word);
        }
    }
    return(shortWordList);
}
```

With the use of LINQ you can achieve a similar functionality in a much more effective way. The following code snippet in C# returns a subset of a list of words that match the criterion of a maximum word length of three or less using LINQ:

```
public static List<string> ShortWords(List<string> wordList)
{
    int maximumWordLength = 3;
    return wordList.Where(w => w.Length <=
        maximumWordLength).ToList();
}
```

Implementing the same method in a dynamic language, such as IronRuby, is very similar to the approach of C# using LINQ and is significantly shorter than the traditional approach:

```
def ShortWords(wordList)
  maximumWordLength = 3
  return wordList.select {|w| w.Length <= maximumWordLength}
end
```

Just comparing these two implementations of the same algorithm reveals much about IronRuby (and dynamic languages in general, by extension). The IronRuby code is concise, and nowhere do you see a data type keyword such as string or int. However, the most interesting aspect of this block of IronRuby code is the closure, located between the curly braces. What's going on here is that the closure, essentially a function, is being passed to the select method. The select method uses a closure to extract a subset of a collection. The code that forms the closure actually executes within the select method (here, the closure extracts strings within the collection wordList that meet the criterion), but it retains access to the variables in its original scope (in this case, the maximumWordLength variable). Closures are much more powerful than this simple example illustrates. This is similar to using LINQ or passing a delegate to a method such as Exists or Find in C#, with retaining access to their original scope.

Dynamic Languages for Silverlight

Silverlight supports IronRuby (Ruby for .NET) and IronPython (Python for .NET) dynamic languages. Let us get a quick overview of these dynamic languages.

IronRuby

IronRuby (http://ironruby.net) is an open-source implementation of the Ruby programming language providing integration capabilities of the Ruby language with Microsoft .NET Framework executing through Microsoft's Dynamic Language Runtime (DLR) engine.

Visit the IronRuby home page at http://ironruby.net/ to download the latest 1.0 version of IronRuby supporting .NET Framework 4.0 and Silverlight. You can either use the installable MSI file or extract the ZIP file to your machine at any location. The MSI and ZIP files include all required components required to program, test, and package the IronRuby-based Silverlight applications. They include DLR libraries, IronRuby runtime, Ruby standard libraries, compilation and application execution utilities, and sample files. They also include the IronPython libraries enabling Ruby code calling Python code.

IronRuby has two assemblies—IronRuby.dll and IronRuby.Libraries.dll—that support the IronRuby language, providing capabilities such as parsing the language and communicating with the host environment.

IronPython

IronPython (http://ironpython.net) is an open-source implementation of the Python programming language providing integration capabilities of the Python language with Microsoft .NET Framework executing through Microsoft's Dynamic Language Runtime (DLR) engine.

Visit the IronPython home page at http://ironpython.net/ to download the latest 2.6.1 version of IronPython supporting .NET Framework 4.0 and Silverlight. You can install the MSI file to your machine at any location. The MSI file includes all components required to program, test, and package IronPython-based Silverlight applications. It includes DLR libraries, IronPython runtime, Python standard libraries, compilation and application execution utilities, and sample files.

IronPython has two assemblies—IronPython.dll and IronPython.Modules.dll—that support the IronPython language, providing capabilities such as parsing the language and communicating with the host environment.

Note At present IronRuby and IronPython dynamic languages are in the continuous development and improvement stage. Visit their home pages to access the latest release of the respective languages. You can also get the related source code along with the source code of DLR by visiting http://dlr.codeplex.com/.

Dynamic Language Runtime (DLR) for Silverlight

One of the most technically appealing aspects of the .NET platform on Windows is that it supports a wide variety of languages due to how the Common Language Runtime (CLR) is designed. Despite the many languages .NET supports, one set of languages that aren't as well supported until .NET 4.0 or with Silverlight as they could be are dynamic languages, such as Python and Ruby. This lack of support is based largely on the fact that dynamic languages are not compiled, and for a high-level language to execute on the CLR, it must be translated into Intermediate Language (IL).

Dynamic languages in .NET 4.0 and Silverlight are facilitated by the DLR. The DLR is actually a set of .NET Framework libraries and services for .NET 4.0 and Silverlight that create a bridge between dynamic languages and the CoreCLR in .NET 4.0 and Silverlight. Officially you can define it as a generic platform and hosting model for dynamic languages to run on top of the Microsoft .NET Framework Common Language Runtime (CLR). One of the benefits of code running on a managed platform such as Silverlight is that types can typically be discovered at runtime using reflection. The DLR helps facilitate this discovery so that code written in a dynamic language can perform well. Figure 14-1 shows how applications written in dynamic languages such as Ruby and Python can be executed on the .NET Framework–managed environment using IronRuby, IronPython, and the DLR.

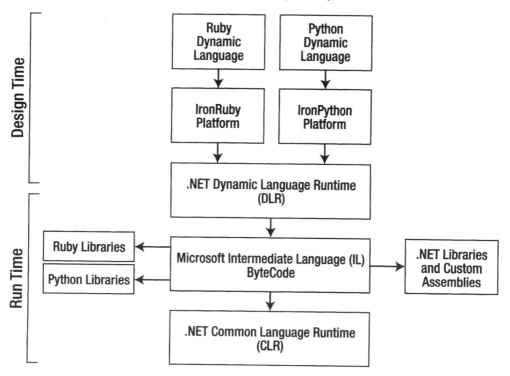

Figure 14-1. Execution model of Silverlight applications based on dynamic languages

DLR Scripting Assemblies

There are five DLR scripting assemblies that provide the runtime scripting environment bridging the dynamic languages with Silverlight.

- `Microsoft.Scripting.dll`: Contains DLR hosting API.

- `Microsoft.Scripting.Core.dll`: Core .NET Framework library to support scripting languages.

- `Microsoft.Scripting.Silverlight.dll`: Enables development of Silverlight applications using dynamic languages.

- `Microsoft.Scripting.ExtensionAttribute.dll`: Contains ExtensionAttribute type to support extension methods.

- `Microsoft.Scripting.Debugging.dll`: Contains a lightweight debugger for DLR-based dynamic languages.

Note that with .NET Framework 4.0, `Microsoft.Scripting.Core.dll` and `Microsoft.Scripting.ExtesionAttribute.dll` are merged with the `System.Core.dll` assembly. However, you need to continue using the preceding assemblies if you would like to support .NET Framework 2.0 SP1 and above versions.

The Microsoft.Scripting.Silverlight.DynamicApplication Class

The `Microsoft.Scripting.Silverlight.dll` scripting assembly contains a set of classes that enable developers to develop Silverlight applications using dynamic languages. One of the key classes is the `DynamicApplication` class, which inherits directly from `System.Windows.Application`. It represents the Silverlight-based dynamic application object by providing access to visual elements from the dynamic language code and also an entry point for dynamic language applications to host on Silverlight hosts. Table 14-1 shows the additional properties this class provides, extending `Host`, `Resources`, and `RootVisual` properties already provided by the `Application` class.

Table 14-1. Key Properties of `Microsoft.Scripting.Silverlight.DynamicApplication`

Property	Type	Description
Current	static DynamicApplication	The `DynamicApplication` instance for the current application.
Debug	bool	true if debugging features are enabled. When debugging is enabled, emitted code is suitable for debugging (it's not optimized) and error reporting is enabled. You can enable debugging by specifying debug=true in the `initParams` parameter in the `object` tag for the application in the HTML.
EntryPoint	string	Gets the name of the code file that contains the application's entry point.
Environment	ScriptRuntime	Gets an instance of `ScriptRuntime` that represents the environment under which the application is executing.
ErrorTargetID	string	The ID of the HTML element where errors/debugging information will be displayed when Debug=true or ReportUnhandledErrors=true.
ReportUnhandledErrors	bool	When true, unhandled exceptions are displayed in the HTML element specified by `ErrorTargetID`. Otherwise, errors are sent to the JScript function specified in the `onerror` property of the `object` tag for the Silverlight application.

This class operates just like the Application class in other Silverlight applications, but provides the extra functionality that dynamic applications need.

Setting Up the Development Environment

The developer community has two options to develop dynamic language-based Silverlight applications.

- *Traditional Approach*: Use of the Chiron.exe development utility. This approach is more or less an obsolete approach and, as a result, this chapter will provide a high-level overview for the readers, who are already familiar with this approach. The high-level introduction will help those readers to migrate from this approach to the "Just-Text" approach.

- *Just-Text Approach*: In-line browser scripting approach.

This chapter will provide an overview of both approaches and then will develop a sample Microsoft Bing Maps application using the newer "Just-Text" approach.

The Traditional Approach with the Chiron.exe File

Note that this section contains only information to support readers who already have used this traditional approach and would like to migrate to the new approach. If you install the latest version of IronRuby and IronPython for .NET Framework 4.0, you will not find the Silverlight folder, and the information mentioned in this section is not applicable as is.

Since Silverlight 2, along with DLR scripting libraries, Microsoft provides a dynamic language-based Silverlight application development environment by providing the Chiron.exe development utility and IronRuby and IronPython Silverlight application project templates.

For this approach, you need DLR and either IronRuby or IronPython from the sites mentioned earlier. Along with samples, documentation, and utilities, some additional important components are installed along with IronRuby and IronPython.

As noted earlier, IronRuby and IronPython (also provided if you install IronRuby) each have two assemblies that support the specific language, providing capabilities such as parsing the language and communicating with the host environment. They are IronPython.dll and IronPython.Modules.dll for IronPython, and IronRuby.dll and IronRuby.Libraries.dll for IronRuby.

The Silverlight templates for dynamic languages provide core application files, which are available under the Silverlight\script\templates\ruby and Silverlight\script\templates\python folders. Table 14-2 provides some details about these application template files.

Table 14-2. Core Application Files for Dynamic Language-Based Silverlight Applications

IronRuby	IronPython Installed with IronRuby upon IronRuby Installation	IronPython Installed Independently	Description
index.html	index.html	index.html	Hosts the dynamic language-based Silverlight application
app\app.rb	app\app.py	python\app.py	Main start-up file for the Silverlight application.
app\app.xaml	app\app.xaml	python\app.xaml	Main XAML user interface file.
css\screen.css	css\screen.css	stylesheets\screen.cs	Defines application styles.
Not provided	Not provided	stylesheets\error.css	Defines application error styles and format.
js\error.js	js\error.js	javascripts\error.js	Manages unhandled application errors.

The Script folder includes the sl.bat file that will help you to create a preliminary dynamic language-based Silverlight application. The following is a command line format:

```
sl [ruby|python] <ApplicationPath>
```

Chiron.exe, the Silverlight development utility, provides two main functions. First, it executes dynamic language applications by providing a development environment and running within the local web server. Second, it dynamically packages a set of files into an XAP file for deployment.

You can execute the developed application in the development environment using Chiron.exe with the /b (browser) option.

```
Chiron /b
```

One of the interesting features of Chiron.exe is that any time you modify a file within the application directory, Chiron.exe will repackage the application into a XAP and reload it. You must still refresh any active browser sessions, though.

The "Just-Text" Approach

The traditional DLR-based development approach makes the use of the Chiron.exe utility mandatory and follows the **Edit Compile (using** Chiron.exe**) Refresh** development model. This approach is still not "the perfect" approach for the dynamic language development community to develop on any operating system.

With the recent Gestalt (visitmix.com/labs/gestalt) prototype developed by the Mix Online Lab (visitmix.com/Lab) team, now it is possible to write IronRuby, IronPython, and XAML code within (X)HTML markup directly —the "Just-Text" approach. There is no need to install any components to create and run the DLR-based application. The "Just-Text" approach follows the **Write Save Refresh** development model and removes the need for the Chiron.exe file.

However, you still need the key DLR scripting and IronRuby and/or IronPython language-specific assemblies that were mentioned earlier.

In addition you need an approach to host Silverlight control(s) and enable DLR integration within the HTML page. The Gestalt project capitalizes on the existing Silverlight.js approach, which uses JavaScript API to create the Object tag to host a Silverlight control and also enables error management and detection of browser and Silverlight (with minimum version) plug-in requirements on the client machine. The Mix Online Lab team enhanced the Silverlight.js file to include in-line scripting and DLR integration capabilities, renamed as dlr.js.

To get started, the Gestalt project provides the cross-browser, cross-platform library built on the DLR. You can get the compressed library file—gestalt.zip—from visitmix.com/labs/gestalt/downloads. Table 14-3 provides details on the core files included in the ZIP file.

Table 14-3. Core Library Files for Dynamic Language-Based Silverlight Applications Using the "Just-Text" Approach

Files	Description
dlr\dlr.js	Enhanced Silverlight.js file to host the dynamic language-based Silverlight application and enable in-line scripting on HTML pages.
dlr\ gestaltmedia.js	Enables HTML5 Video and Audio playback capabilities. We will not need this file for this chapter example.
dlr\dlr.xap	Includes the AppManifest.xaml file referencing the Microsoft.Scripting.slvx file and points to Microsoft.Scripting.Silverlight.dll as an entry point assembly. It also includes the languages.config file. This file provides configuration information for DLR languages (IronRuby and IronPython) that can be used in Silverlight applications. The configuration information includes language file extensions (.py and .rb), language assemblies, and URLs for each language's .slvx file.
dlr\IronRuby.slvx	The IronRuby.slvx file includes the IronRuby.dll and IronRuby.Libraries.dll files to enable development of IronRuby-based Silverlight applications.

dlr\IronPython.slvx	The IronPython.slvx file includes the IronPython.dll and IronPython.Modules.dll files to enable development of IronPython-based Silverlight applications. Since in this chapter we will develop an application using IronRuby, we will not require this file.
dlr\ Microsoft.Scripting .slvx	The Microsoft.Scripting.slvx file includes five DLR scripting assemblies (Microsoft.Scripting.dll, Microsoft.Scripting.Core.dll, Microsoft.Scripting.Silverlight.dll, Microsoft.Scripting.ExtensionAttribute.dll, and Microsoft.Scripting.Debugging.dll) that provide the runtime scripting environment bridging the dynamic languages with Silverlight.
samples/getting.started/* .html	Sample web pages demonstrating in-line scripting IronRuby, IronPython, and XAML capabilities. There are five sample HTML pages included: 01_ruby.html 02_python.html 03_xaml.html 04_animation.html 05_final.html

Note that from Silverlight 3, the "Transparent Silverlight Extensions" capability enables developers to package the commonly used assembly files as a separate reusable library with .slvx (Silverlight Versioned Extension). The SLVX files can be deployed on a common Internet location or client-specific location. The required SLVX files must be referenced in the AppManifest.xaml file within the ExternalParts section as an ExtensionPart with the correct path.

An excellent paper on the "Just-Text" approach was written by Jimmy Schementi. This paper also details how to change default DLR settings of the dlr.js file. For review you can get the paper from http://ironpython.net/browser/sl-back-to-just-text.pdf.

You need to have a web server instance such as IIS or Apache web server to host and run the DLR-based in-line scripted web applications. Once you download the gestalt.zip file, place the dlr and samples (with getting.started subfolder) folders at the root of the web server.

If you do not install these folders at the root of the web server, you need to modify the dlr.js file appropriately.

Next add MIME-types for .rb, .py, and .slvx files as the following:

- For .rb and .py files set the MIME-type to: text/plain

- For .slvx files set the MIME-type to: application/octet-stream

To validate the environment, visit the samples/get.started folder and browse the 05_final.html file. The web page demonstrates the IronPython, HTML, and XAML-based Graphics with animation integration capabilities, as shown in Figure 14-2.

Figure 14-2. Running the sample application of the Gestalt project

Creating Silverlight Applications Using the "Just-Text" Approach

Let's start with defining the skeleton to develop a DLR-based Silverlight application using the "Just-Text" Approach.

Hosting a HTML File

Once you copy the Gestalt files at the web server root level, simply open a text editor and start writing your HTML file. It's that simple!

The good thing is that `dlr.js` adds a Silverlight control on the page and provides all the necessary core requirements to enable dynamic language integration capabilities. For that, simply include the `dlr.js` file to the HTML page.

```
<head>
      <script src="/dlr/dlr.js" type="text/javascript"></script>
</head>
```

Note that this inclusion of the `dlr.js` file will set up default settings for a DLR-based Silverlight application. If you would like to customize the default settings, you need to override the default settings by writing custom script code within the HTML file. For more details, please read Jimmy Schementi's paper on the "Just-Text" approach (`http://ironpython.net/browser/sl-back-to-just-text.pdf`).

In-Line IronRuby/IronPython Code in Hosting HTML File

Now you are all set to write XAML and IronRuby/IronPython code within the HTML file, which you can achieve by writing the XAML and IronRuby/IronPython code within the script tag.

To write in-line IronRuby code you need to add the following script tag with the appropriate type and class information, and place the IronRuby code within the tag.

```
<script type="application/ruby" class="Class Name Goes Here">
    …IronRuby Code Goes Here …
</script>
```

To write in-line IronPython code, you need to add the following script tag with the appropriate type and class information and place the IronPython code within the tag.

```
<script type="application/python" class="Class Name Goes Here">
    …IronPython Code Goes Here …
</script>
```

You can also use text/ruby or text/python script type instead of application/ruby or application/python respectively.

In-Line XAML Code in Hosting HTML File

To write in-line XAML code, you need to add the following script tag with the appropriate type, ID, and width and height information, and place the XAML code within the tag.

```
<script type="application/xml+xaml" id="Place ID here" Width="400" Height="400">
    <UserControl …>
      … XAML Code Goes Here …
    </UserControl>
</script>
```

Here you must define the Width and Height properties values. You can access the XAML controls and implement the event integration using the code, which I will demonstrate while developing the application from the next section.

Once you finish with the code just browse the page and you should see the application outcome right away.

Externalizing XAML and IronRuby/IronPython Code

To modularize your programming model, it is best practice to externalize the XAML and IronRuby/IronPython code as separate files and reference them to the hosting HTML file. For that, you simply need to add the src attribute to the script tag used for defining in-line XAML and IronRuby/IronPython code. The src attribute will define the path for the XAML (*.xaml), IronRuby (*.rb), and IronPython (*.py) files as shown here in the highlighted fonts.

```
<body>
    <script type="application/xml+xaml" src="XAML File Name with Path Information"
        Width="1350" Height="575">
    </script>
    <script type="application/ruby" src="<Ruby File Name with Path Information>"
        class="Class Name Goes Here" >
    </script>
```

```
    <script type="application/python" src="<Python File Name with Path Information>"
        class="Class Name Goes Here" >
    </script>
</body>
```

Note that in this chapter we will have XAML and IronRuby files externalize.

Developing an Interactive Bing Maps Application with Silverlight and IronRuby

Now that you've seen the basic skeleton of the dynamic language Silverlight application using the in-line scripting "Just-Text" approach, let's take it a step further with the integration of Microsoft Bing maps (formerly known as Virtual Earth).

Note The example—Creating Interactive Bing Maps with Silverlight and IronRuby—was originally written by me and published as an article in the February 2010 issue of *MSDN Magazine*. You can review the article and download the code by visiting `http://msdn.microsoft.com/en-us/magazine/ee291739.aspx`. In this section of this book, I have further fine-tuned this example and provided more explanation in details.

Installing Microsoft Bing Maps Silverlight Control SDK

The Microsoft Bing Maps Silverlight Control SDK Version 1 was released in November 2009. To download the latest version 1.0.1 visit `www.microsoft.com/downloads/en/default.aspx` and search for "Bing Maps Silverlight Control SDK." The installer is called `BingMapsSilverlightControlv1.0.1Installer.msi`. Note that you need Silverlight 3 at a minimum to work on this control.

The installation includes `Microsoft.Maps.MapControl.dll` and `Microsoft.Maps.MapControl.xml`, `Microsoft.Maps.MapControl.Common.dll` and `Microsoft.Maps.MapControl.Common.xml`, and offline documentation.

Before you start building applications using this Silverlight Bing Maps control, first you must create a Bing Maps Developer account to receive the application authentication key. You can create an account by visiting `www.bingmapsportal.com/link`.

Include Bing Maps Control to the Solution

There are two ways you can include the Bing Maps control assemblies to the solution. One is making them part of the `dlr.xap` file (for that you need to update the `AppManifest.xaml` file), and the second approach is to create a separate ZIP file and reference it from the hosting HTML file. This section will describe both approaches, however, the second approach is recommended to make the application more flexible and modular.

Include Bing Maps Control within the dlr.xap File

To include Bing Maps control as part of the dlr.xap file, you need to modify the AppManifest.xaml file (available in the dlr.xap file) and include Microsoft.Maps.MapControl.dll and Microsoft.Maps.MapControl.Common.dll files as part of the dlr.xap file to include and load as part of the application start-up.

For that rename dlr.xap to dlr.xap.zip and extract the AppManifest.xaml and languages.config files available in the .xap file. Then add Microsoft.Maps.MapControl.dll and Microsoft.Maps.MapControl.Common.dll files as AssemblyPart as shown here (in the bold letters).

```
<Deployment xmlns="http://schemas.microsoft.com/client/2007/deployment"
    xmlns:x="http://schemas.microsoft.com/winfx/2006/xaml"
    RuntimeVersion="2.0.31005.0"
    EntryPointAssembly="Microsoft.Scripting.Silverlight"
    EntryPointType="Microsoft.Scripting.Silverlight.DynamicApplication"
    ExternalCallersFromCrossDomain="ScriptableOnly">
    <Deployment.Parts>
        <AssemblyPart Source="Microsoft.Maps.MapControl.dll" />
        <AssemblyPart Source="Microsoft.Maps.MapControl.Common.dll" />
    </Deployment.Parts>
    <Deployment.ExternalParts>
        <ExtensionPart Source="Microsoft.Scripting.slvx"/>
    </Deployment.ExternalParts>
</Deployment>
```

Now zip up the modified AppManifest.xaml, existing languages.config, Microsoft.Maps.MapControl.dll, and Microsoft.Maps.MapControl.Common.dll files, and rename the ZIP file to dlr.xap. Overwrite the existing dlr.xap file available (under the /dlr folder) on the web server with the new one.

Include Bing Maps Control As an External ZIP File

The other and recommended alternative is to create an external compressed package as a ZIP file and reference within the hosting file. For that you use the script tag with the type attribute set to application/x-zip-compressed. The src attribute of the script tag contains the ZIP file name with path information, which essentially behaves as a folder, and the files within the ZIP files are referenced and loaded.

In our example, to include the Microsoft.Maps.MapControl.dll and Microsoft.Maps.MapControl.Common.dll files, we first create a ZIP file with the name bingmaps.zip including these files. We then need to add the following script tag including reference to the bingmaps.zip file as shown here to the hosting HTML file. We will create a hosting SilverlightMap.html file in the next section.

```
<script type="application/x-zip-compressed" src="bingmaps.zip">
</script>
```

Here note that the bingmaps.zip file is placed to the application root folder of the web server, where the Bing maps application will be hosted.

Create a SilverlightMap.xaml File

Create a new text file and name it `SilverlightMap.xaml` to add XAML code for this application. Add the UserControl with the name Silverlight_map and reference the to the map control (shown in bold fonts) and to create a necessary namespace:

```
<UserControl x:Name="silverlight_map"
    xmlns="http://schemas.microsoft.com/winfx/2006/xaml/presentation"
    xmlns:x="http://schemas.microsoft.com/winfx/2006/xaml"
        Width="200" Height="280"
    xmlns:d="http://schemas.microsoft.com/expression/blend/2008"
    xmlns:mc="http://schemas.openxmlformats.org/
        markup-compatibility/2006"
    mc:Ignorable="d"
    xmlns:m="clr-namespace:Microsoft.Maps.MapControl;assembly=
        Microsoft.Maps.MapControl">
```

Next add the Canvas control as the main container and the Map element under the Grid control. Notice that I kept the same width and height of Canvas and Grid controls and set the `Width` and `Height` properties of the Map control to 800 and 400 respectively.

```
...
    <Canvas x:Name="container" Width="1350" Height="575">
        <Grid x:Name="layout_root" Width="1350" Height="575">
            <m:Map CredentialsProvider=
                "Your Authentication Key Goes Here"
                Width="800" Height="400" Grid.Column="1"
                HorizontalAlignment="Center"/>
        </Grid>
    </Canvas>
</UserControl>
```

In this code snippet, you need to replace "Your authentication key goes here" with your authentication key for the Map control.

Creating a SilverlightMap.html File

Create a `SilverlightMap.html` file as the hosting file. You need to include the `dlr.js` file and reference to the `bingmaps.zip` and `SilverlightMap.xaml` files (highlighted bold fonts) as shown here.

```
<html>
    <head>
        <script src="dlr.js" type="text/javascript">
        </script>
    </head>
    <body>
        <script type="application/x-zip-compressed" src="bingmaps.zip">
        </script>
        <script type="application/xml+xaml" src="SilverlightMap.xaml"
            id="sl_map" Width="1350" Height="575" defer="true">
```

```
        </script>
    </body>
</html>
```

Copy the `SilverlightMap.html` and `SilverlightMap.xaml` files to the existing root folder on the web server and browse the page. You should see the map in the default road mode (see Figure 14-3).

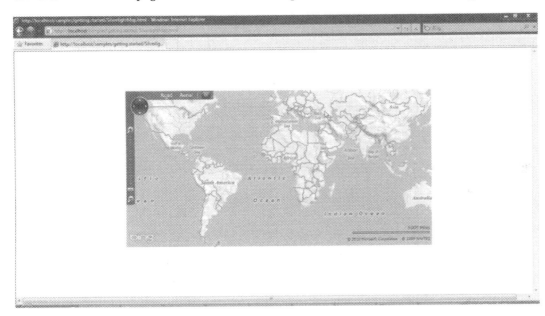

Figure 14-3. DLR-based Bing Map Silverlight application in default road map mode

Adding 3D Animation within the SilverlightMap.xaml File

Let's change the map mode to aerial with labels as the default view, and also introduce 3D animation to the map.

To change the default map mode, first give the Map element a name (in this example I used map_in_ironruby) so that it can be referenced in the IronRuby code. I'll also apply 3D projection to the Map object. To do that I set the `Projection` property of the Map object to `PlanProjection` and set the `RotationX` property to -20. This transforms the Map object, giving a slightly skewed viewing angle.

```
<Grid x:Name="layout_root" Width="1350" Height="575" Background="Black">
    <m:Map x:Name="map_in_ironruby" CredentialsProvider=" Your Authentication Key Goes Here"
        Width="800" Height="400">
        <m:Map.Projection>
            <PlaneProjection RotationX="-20"/>
        </m:Map.Projection>
    </m:Map>
</Grid>
```

Notice that I also changed the background of the Grid to black.

Creating a SilverlightMap.rb IronRuby File and Adding Map Mode

Next create a simple text file named SilverlightMap.rb as an IronRuby file and write the following lines of code to include the required assemblies (including MapControl.dlls) and turn on aerial view with labels of the Map control.

Notice that with the new "Just-Text" approach, I could reference the Map object by name. Any XAML elements with the x:Name set can be accessed through root_visual shorthand as shown here.

```
require "bingmaps/Microsoft.Maps.MapControl"
require "bingmaps/Microsoft.Maps.MapControl.Common"

include System::Windows
include System::Windows::Controls
include Microsoft::Maps::MapControl
include Microsoft::Scripting::Silverlight

DynamicApplication.current.load_root_visual_from_string File.read("SilverlightMap.xaml")

sm = DynamicApplication.current.root_visual.silverlight_map
sm.map_in_ironruby.mode = AerialMode.new(true)
```

As we included a reference of the XAML file to the SilverlightMap.xaml file, we need to include the same for the SilverlightMap.rb file, as shown here in highlighted bold fonts.

```
<html>
    <head>
        <script src="dlr.js" type="text/javascript">
        </script>
    </head>
    <body>
        <script type="application/x-zip-compressed" src="bingmaps.zip">
        </script>
        <script type="application/xml+xaml" src="SilverlightMap.xaml"
            id="sl_map" Width="1350" Height="575" defer="true">
        </script>
        <script type="application/ruby" src="SilverlightMap.rb"
            class="sl_map">
        </script>
    </body>
</html>
```

Now if you copy updated the SilverlightMap.html file and newly created SilverlightMap.rb file to the web server root folder and browse it, you'll see the black background, skewed 3D angle, and labeled aerial view, as shown in Figure 14-4.

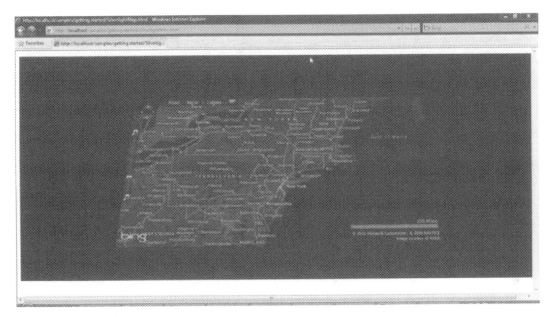

Figure 14-4. *Map mode set to aerial with labels mode and 3D projection*

Add Rotate Map Capabilities

One of the popular demonstrations at the Mix09 conference was Silverlight and Microsoft Bing Map integration with spinning capabilities for the Map object. Let's implement something similar in IronRuby.

To implement this feature, you first need to define the Grid with two columns using ColumnDefinitions.

```
<Grid.ColumnDefinitions>
    <ColumnDefinition Width="200"/>
    <ColumnDefinition Width="1100"/>
</Grid.ColumnDefinitions>
```

Next add three buttons named Rotate Map, Pause, and Stop and Reset, along with title text in the XAML file within the Border. All of this is in the first column on the Grid, as shown here.

```
<StackPanel Grid.Column="0" Orientation="Vertical">
    <Border CornerRadius="20" Margin="0,50,0,5" Width="150"
            Background="DarkBlue" HorizontalAlignment="Center">
        <StackPanel Orientation="Vertical">
            <TextBlock Text="3D Rotation"
                HorizontalAlignment="Center"
                FontSize="12" Foreground="White" Margin="0,5,0,10"/>
            <Button x:Name="rotate_map" Height="25"
                Content="Rotate Map" Width="100" Margin="0,0,0,10"
                Foreground="Black" VerticalAlignment="Center"
                HorizontalAlignment="Center" />
```

```xml
            <Button x:Name="pause_resume" Height="25"
                Content="Pause" Background="DarkGoldenrod"
                Foreground="Black" Width="100" Margin="0,0,0,10"
                VerticalAlignment="Center"
                HorizontalAlignment="Center" />
            <Button x:Name="stop_reset" Height="25"
                Content="Stop and Reset" Background="DarkGoldenrod"
                Foreground="Black" Width="100" Margin="0,0,0,10"
                VerticalAlignment="Center"
                HorizontalAlignment="Center" />
        </StackPanel>
    </Border>
</StackPanel>
```

Now add the Map object to the second column of the Grid.

```xml
<StackPanel Grid.Column="1">
    <m:Map x:Name="map_in_ironruby" CredentialsProvider="Your
        Authentication Key Goes Here"
        Width="800" Height="400" HorizontalAlignment="Center">
        <m:Map.Projection>
            <PlaneProjection RotationX="-20" RotationY="0"
            RotationZ="0"/>
        </m:Map.Projection>
    </m:Map>
</StackPanel>
```

In the next step you'll need to create some rather complex XAML update code. I would recommend creating the XAML file using a development environment such as Visual Studio or Expression Blend to take advantage of their editing and IntelliSense features. Then you can copy the completed XAML to the app.xaml file of your project.

Create a storyboard with the name map_animation targeted for the Map object named map_in_ironruby. The storyboard defines the keyframes for the PlaneProjection animation properties RotationZ, RotationY, GlobalOffsetX, and GlobalOffsetZ. Add the storyBoard as a UserControl resource.

```xml
<UserControl.Resources>
    <Storyboard x:Name="map_animation">
        <DoubleAnimationUsingKeyFrames BeginTime="00:00:00"
            Storyboard.TargetName="map_in_ironruby"
            Storyboard.TargetProperty=
                "(UIElement.Projection).
                (PlaneProjection.RotationZ)">
            <EasingDoubleKeyFrame KeyTime="00:00:00" Value="15"/>
            <EasingDoubleKeyFrame KeyTime="00:00:01" Value="0"/>
            <EasingDoubleKeyFrame KeyTime="00:00:02" Value="-15"/>
            <EasingDoubleKeyFrame KeyTime="00:00:03" Value="0"/>
            <EasingDoubleKeyFrame KeyTime="00:00:04" Value="15"/>
        </DoubleAnimationUsingKeyFrames>
        <DoubleAnimationUsingKeyFrames BeginTime="00:00:00"
            Storyboard.TargetName="map_in_ironruby"
            Storyboard.TargetProperty=
```

```
            "(UIElement.Projection).
              (PlaneProjection.RotationY)">
        <EasingDoubleKeyFrame KeyTime="00:00:00" Value="-90"/>
        <EasingDoubleKeyFrame KeyTime="00:00:01" Value="-180"/>
        <EasingDoubleKeyFrame KeyTime="00:00:02" Value="-270"/>
        <EasingDoubleKeyFrame KeyTime="00:00:03" Value="-360"/>
        <EasingDoubleKeyFrame KeyTime="00:00:04" Value="-270"/>
    </DoubleAnimationUsingKeyFrames>
    <DoubleAnimationUsingKeyFrames BeginTime="00:00:00"
        Storyboard.TargetName="map_in_ironruby"
        Storyboard.TargetProperty=
            "(UIElement.Projection).
              (PlaneProjection.GlobalOffsetX)">
        <EasingDoubleKeyFrame KeyTime="00:00:00" Value="0"/>
        <EasingDoubleKeyFrame KeyTime="00:00:01" Value="200"/>
        <EasingDoubleKeyFrame KeyTime="00:00:02" Value="300"/>
        <EasingDoubleKeyFrame KeyTime="00:00:03" Value="200"/>
        <EasingDoubleKeyFrame KeyTime="00:00:04" Value="0"/>
    </DoubleAnimationUsingKeyFrames>
    <DoubleAnimationUsingKeyFrames BeginTime="00:00:00"
        Storyboard.TargetName="map_in_ironruby"
        Storyboard.TargetProperty=
            "(UIElement.Projection).
              (PlaneProjection.GlobalOffsetZ)">
        <EasingDoubleKeyFrame KeyTime="00:00:00" Value="0"/>
        <EasingDoubleKeyFrame KeyTime="00:00:01" Value="300"/>
        <EasingDoubleKeyFrame KeyTime="00:00:02" Value="0"/>
        <EasingDoubleKeyFrame KeyTime="00:00:03" Value="-300"/>
        <EasingDoubleKeyFrame KeyTime="00:00:04" Value="0"/>
    </DoubleAnimationUsingKeyFrames>
  </Storyboard>
</UserControl.Resources>
```

Next implement the Click events within the IronRuby code to start, pause, resume, and stop the animation. First you need to include a reference to System.Windows.Media and System.Windows.Media.Animation.

```
include System::Windows::Media
include System::Windows::Media::Animation
```

Now load the Disable pause_resume button during the initialization process of the application.

```
sm.pause_resume.is_enabled = false
```

Now implement the Click event of each button. Start with the rotate_map button. First set the Map object to left horizontal alignment in order to best use the available space for the animation. Then set the RepeatBehavior property of the storyboard animation to Forever and begin the animation. Finally enable the pause_resume button and set the button content to Pause.

```
sm.rotate_map.click do |s,e|
    sm.map_in_ironruby.horizontal_alignment =
```

```
            HorizontalAlignment.Left
        sm.map_animation.repeat_behavior = RepeatBehavior.Forever
        sm.map_animation.begin
        sm.pause_resume.is_enabled = true
        sm.pause_resume.content = "Pause"
end
```

Next, implement the pause_resume button Click event. Here, depending on whether you're in a paused state or a running state, you want to either resume or pause the storyboard animation and change the button content.

```
sm.pause_resume.click do |s,e|
        strbtnContent = sm.pause_resume.content.ToString
        if strbtnContent == "Pause"
            sm.pause_resume.content = "Resume"
            sm.map_animation.pause
        else
            sm.pause_resume.content = "Pause"
            sm.map_animation.resume
        end
end
```

Finally, implement the stop_reset button Click event. Here you stop the storyboard animation, disable the pause_resume button, and reset the button content to Pause. You also reset the alignment of the Map object.

```
sm.stop_reset.click do |s,e|
        sm.map_animation.stop
        sm.pause_resume.is_enabled = false
        sm.pause_resume.content = "Pause"
        sm.map_in_ironruby.horizontal_alignment =
            HorizontalAlignment.Center
end
```

Copy and paste the updated files to the web server and browse the SilverlightMap.html file. Figure 14-5 shows the rotating map.

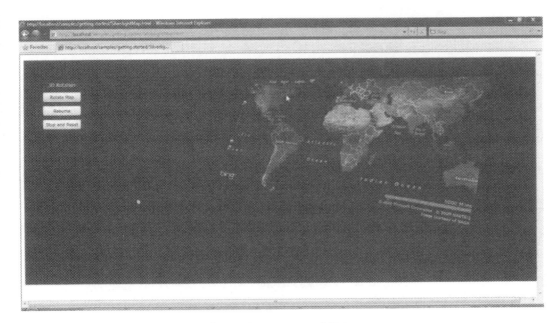

Figure 14-5. 3D Map animation with rotating map capabilities

Targeting Pre-defined Locations

Now let's implement the functionality of highlighting three pre-defined locations on the map: New York, San Francisco, and Vancouver.

First you need revisit the `SilverlightMap.xaml` file to update the XAML code. Add three additional buttons in a new section on the left side of the screen. There is a button for each location (New York, San Francisco, and Vancouver). These are implemented much like the previous buttons. One notable change is the addition of the `Tag` attribute to each `Button` element. The `Tag` attribute defines specific location coordinates and the zoom level of the map.

Add these three buttons within the same StackPanel immediately after the 3D rotation buttons section, as shown here.

```
<Border CornerRadius="20" Margin="0,30,0,0" Width="150"
    Background="DarkBlue" HorizontalAlignment="Center">
    <StackPanel Orientation="Vertical">
        <TextBlock Text="Locate Location"
            HorizontalAlignment="Center" FontSize="12"
            Foreground="White" Margin="0,5,0,10"/>
        <Button x:Name="newyork" Height="25"
            Content="New York" Width="100"
            Margin="0,0,0,10" Foreground="Black"
            VerticalAlignment="Center"
            HorizontalAlignment="Center"
            Tag="40.7199,-74.0030,0.0000 14.0000"/>
        <Button x:Name="sanfrancisco" Height="25"
            Content="San Francisco"
```

```
                    Background="DarkGoldenrod"
                    Foreground="Black" Width="100" Margin="0,0,0,10"
                    VerticalAlignment="Center"
                    HorizontalAlignment="Center"
                    Tag="37.6801,-122.3395,0.0000 11.0000"/>
                <Button x:Name="vancouver" Height="25"
                    Content="Vancouver"
                    Background="DarkGoldenrod" Foreground="Black"
                    Width="100" Margin="0,0,0,10"
                    VerticalAlignment="Center"
                    HorizontalAlignment="Center"
                    Tag="49.2765,-123.1030,0.0000 14.0000"/>
            </StackPanel>
        </Border>
```

Here the Tag attribute provides the coordinate information for each location. When a user clicks the button, this information is used to retarget the map.

Most applications have a title, and this one should be no different. I added the title "Microsoft Bing Maps Silverlight Control and IronRuby Integration" in the second column of the Grid by replacing the existing Map element to place it under the StackPanel, along with the title TextBlock control (see highlighted fonts here).

```
<StackPanel Grid.Column="1" Orientation="Vertical">
    <TextBlock VerticalAlignment="Top"
        HorizontalAlignment="Center" FontSize="20"
        Foreground="Red" Margin="0,5,0,0"
        Text="Microsoft Bing Maps
            Silverlight Control and IronRuby Integration" />
    <m:Map x:Name="map_in_ironruby" Width="800" Height="400"
        HorizontalAlignment="Center" Margin="0,50,0,20">
...
```

Now the presentation layer is complete. If you execute the application at this point, you should see the additional three buttons under the new Locate Location section. However, the map will not be located to the corresponding location if you click on any of the newly added buttons. For that you need to implement code-behind for each button Click event.

The Click events are the same for all three buttons. Based on the value of the Tag property of the corresponding clicked button, pass those coordinates and zoom level as the view specification to create the new map view. Here we used the Split method to split the coordinates and the zoom level, and set the map view using the SetView method of the Maps control. The new map view will show the defined location. Figure 14-6 shows the map located to New York.

```
[:newyork, :sanfrancisco, :vancouver].each do |city|
    sm.send(city).click do |s,e|
        tag_information = s.Tag.split
        location_Converter = LocationConverter.new
        location_info =
            location_Converter.ConvertFrom(tag_information[0].ToString)
        sm.map_in_ironruby.SetView(location_info, tag_information[1]);
    end
end
```

You also need to add the additional reference `Microsoft.Maps.MapControl.Design` to the program to create a new map view.

```
include Microsoft::Maps::MapControl::Design
```

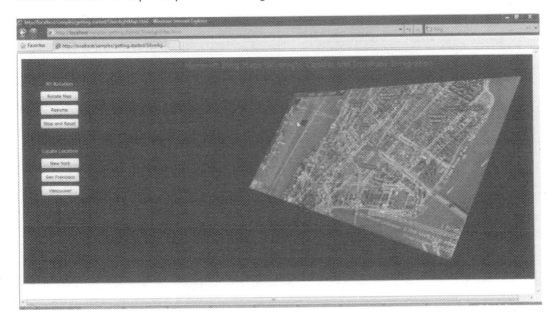

Figure 14-6. Completed DLR-based Bing Maps Silverlight application using the "Just-Text" approach

And that's the finished application. Copy and paste the updated XAML and IronRuby files and browse the `SilverlightMap.html` file to view the completed application. As you can see, it would be easy to customize the views, add additional location targets, and implement other features.

Summary

This chapter introduced the support for dynamic languages that Silverlight provides and showed how to create and deploy dynamic applications. The features of the three supported languages—IronRuby, IronPython, and Managed JScript—were briefly discussed, and a working example of integrating Microsoft Bing Maps control was developed using Silverlight and IronRuby. The next chapter details the security model of Silverlight.

CHAPTER 15

■ ■ ■

Security

The growth of the Internet and the World Wide Web has forever changed the way we use computers. As software engineers, we can no longer ignore security as we did when the average computer wasn't directly connected to a slew of other computers. Silverlight lives online, in users' browsers and other connected devices. No exploration of Silverlight is complete without understanding both the security features it provides and generally how to ensure your Silverlight application has been developed with security in mind. This chapter will go over Silverlight's security model and general techniques for understanding how to design for and evaluate security.

.NET Security in the CLR

While application code executes under the auspices of an environment (the CLR) executing on top of a host operating system, careful thought must still be given to how code is executed.

In .NET, the security model for executable code is called Code Access Security (CAS). There are several important aspects of CAS, including code-making requests for specific security permissions (such as asking for the ability to write to files), stack walks to determine the permission levels granted, and the ability for an administrator to control permission levels granted to applications. For example, if your .NET application wants to modify a file stored in a specific location, it must first ensure that it has the rights to access the directory and modify the file. This permission request can be done declaratively by applying a particular permission-related attribute to a method, or imperatively by invoking the Demand method for a specific permission. In C# on the .NET platform, the imperative approach might look like the following.

```
//additional references
using System.IO;
using System.Security;
using System.Security.Permissions;

public void saveDataToFile(string outputFilename)
{
    FileIOPermission perm = new
      FileIOPermission(FileIOPermission.Write,outputFilename);

    try {
      perm.Demand(); // request permission to write to file
                     // throws exception if we don't have permission
      StreamWriter sw = new StreamWriter(outputFilename);
      // write data to sw
      sw.Close();
```

```
    } catch(SecurityException ex) {
      // handle security exception
    } catch(Exception generalEx) {
      // handle other exceptions
    }
}
```

It's also possible to make security demands declaratively using a CAS-related attribute:

```
[FileIOPermission(SecurityAction.Demand, Write=@"app.config")]
public void saveDataToFile(string outputFilename)
{
    // method code
}
```

The security model within the CLR ensures that the permission being requested can be granted, or the method won't execute. Whether making permission requests imperatively or declaratively, the application code must make specific demands based on what it needs to accomplish. This is a fine-grained approach to ensuring that executable code has only the permissions it needs and works well on the .NET platform.

Silverlight Security Model

The managed execution engine that Silverlight provides is based on .NET—specifically, the CLR for Silverlight. The Silverlight plug-in can interact with the host operating system to communicate over the network, integrate with devices connected to users' machines, modify files on the file system, and display graphics on the screen. The security of the host operating system would be compromised if a Silverlight application were able to use these features directly. Therefore, some mechanism must be in place to ensure a division between application code and code that can affect the host operating system. Silverlight's security model is slightly different compared to regular .NET applications. Instead of Silverlight application code asking for permission to accomplish certain tasks, all custom application code in Silverlight is *security transparent*—that is, it is not trusted in Silverlight applications. Silverlight applications can still interact with the host operating system (e.g., to save and read files in the file system) when initiated by the user, but not directly through code-behind.

Note While there is no CAS available for use by your application, if you explore the online documentation or the assemblies in Reflector, you will come across a namespace related to CAS. This is a holdover from .NET in order to allow the already existing C# compiler to compile Silverlight code, since a CAS-related attribute is emitted by the compiler if the assembly is unverifiable.

Since all application code that you write is security transparent, how is it able to still utilize services offered by the host operating system, such as file system access? There are three categories of code that can execute from the perspective of the Silverlight plug-in. First, there's all the code in a Silverlight application (the code you write and any third-party libraries your application uses). The second and third categories cover code located in the platform assemblies that provide functionality for Silverlight applications, such as isolated storage and network communication. The code in these assemblies either does something high-privilege (e.g., directly modifying a file on disk or invoking a native library on the host operating system) or calls these high-privilege methods. The code in your application invokes the second category of code. This second category is needed because it serves as the middleman between application code (security-transparent code) and the third category, which is the code that is allowed to interact with the host operating system (security-critical code). Figure 15-1 shows the relationship between these three categories of executable code.

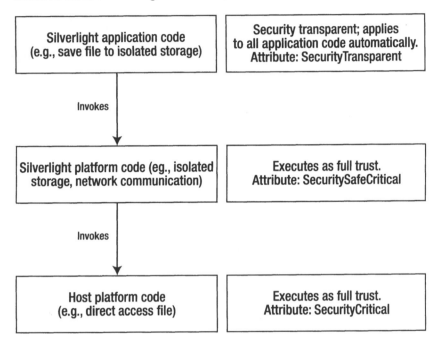

Figure 15-1. Relationship of executable code and security categories

Figure 15-1 also shows the attributes that correspond to each category of code. Your application's code cannot use either the SecuritySafeCritical attribute or the SecurityCritical attribute—if you attempt to use one, it will be ignored, and your code will be treated as security transparent. Any code decorated with the SecuritySafeCritical attribute can be invoked by security-transparent code, and only SecuritySafeCritical code can invoke the SecurityCritical code. Here are several methods from the System.IO.IsolatedStorage.IsolatedStorageFile class that encompass all three categories of executable code:

```
[SecuritySafeCritical]
public void CreateDirectory(string dir);

public IsolatedStorageFileStream CreateFile(string path);

[SecurityCritical]
private string[] DirectoriesToCreate(string fullPath);
```

Both CreateFile and CreateDirectory can be called from your code. Of course, the private visibility of DirectoriesToCreate hides this method from your code regardless, but the SecurityCritical attribute helps to enforce the fact that only SecuritySafeCritical code is a valid invoker. Your code might call the CreateDirectory method, which then subsequently calls the DirectoriesToCreate method.

This brings about another question, though—why does the platform code get to use the SecuritySafeCritical and SecurityCritical attributes, but your code doesn't? This is enforced by the Silverlight plug-in granting the ability to run as SecuritySafeCritical or SecurityCritical only to code that is signed by Microsoft and downloaded from the Microsoft servers. As shown in Figure 15-1, code marked with SecuritySafeCritical acts as a proxy between code that is security transparent and code that is security critical. Without this intermediate layer, application code could make calls to the security-critical code, giving application code far more privilege than it should have. This security model firmly separates platform code (which might be security critical) from application code (which is always security transparent).

Enhancements in Silverlight 4

Using the .NET platform, you can develop partially trusted, elevated-trusted and full-trusted applications. Applications with *partial trust* run in the sandboxed limited-privileged application execution environment with very limited access to the local computer system and resources (e.g., user-initiated access to the file system). Applications with *elevated trust* have an application execution environment with elevated security privileges and thus can have more access to the local computer system and resources (e.g., direct access to folders such as MyDocuments, MyPictures, MyMusic, and MyVideos on the Windows operating system). Applications with *full trust*, such as WPF applications, can have full security privileges and can have full access to local computer system and resources.

The default application mode for Silverlight applications is in-browser mode, where the user is connected to the web server to work on the application. Silverlight 3 and Silverlight 4 also support the out-of-browser mode, enabling applications to run as traditional rich-client windows applications in the connected or disconnected (to the network and thus web server) mode. Silverlight 3 and, by default, Silverlight 4 applications run in in-browser and out-of-browser modes with partial trust in the sandbox environment. That means you have limited access to the local computer resources and file systems.

Silverlight 4 now extends the integration capabilities with local computer resources and file systems by supporting Silverlight 4 applications to run with elevated trust (called trusted applications). As you might have predicted, you can run Silverlight 4 applications with elevated trust only in the out-of-browser mode (not supported in the in-browser mode).

Configuring Silverlight 4 Applications to Run with Elevated Trust

Silverlight 4 applications with elevated trust must run in the out-of-browser mode. As we learned in Chapter 11, to configure elevated trust, first you must enable a Silverlight 4 application to run in out-of-browser mode using project properties (within Visual Studio) and select the "Enable running application out of browser" option. Next, to configure the Silverlight application running out-of-browser with elevated trust, click on the "Out-of-Browser Settings…" button, and select the "Require elevated trust when running outside the browser" option (see Figure 15-2).

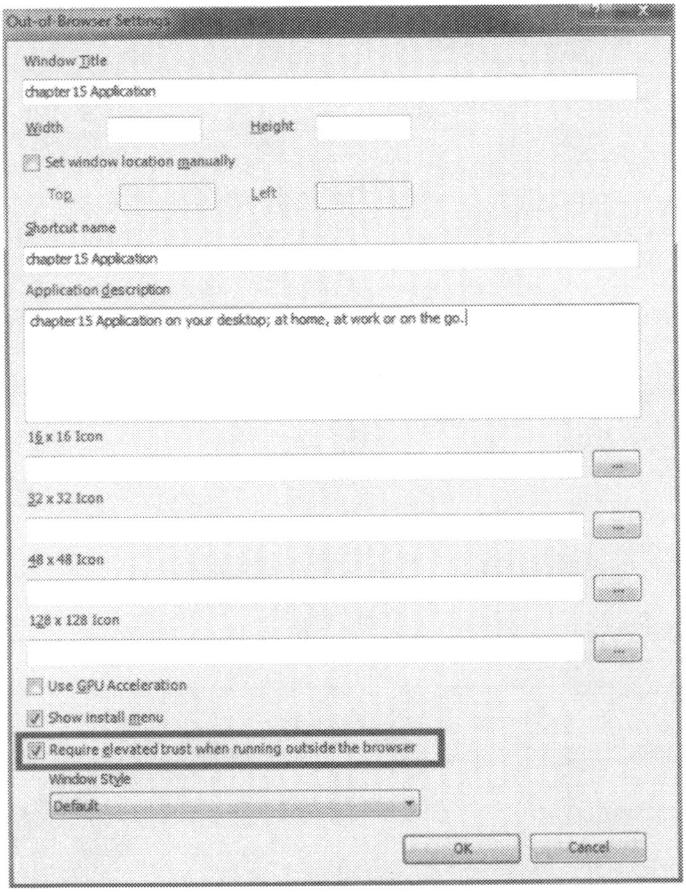

Figure 15-2. *Setting a Silverlight 4 application to run with elevated trust (as a trusted application) in out-of-browser mode*

When you install the Silverlight out-of-browser application with elevated trust, a security-warning window (instead the regular out-of-browser application installation window) will be displayed, warning that the installed application publisher is not verified and potentially can access the local computer data and resources. If you choose to install the application, the Silverlight application will be installed to the computer and you can run the application in the out-of-browser mode with elevated trust.

Figure 15-3 shows the standard out-of-browser application installation window, when the elevated trust is not enabled. Figure 15-4 shows the out-of-browser application installation window with a security warning, when the elevated trust option is enabled and the application is not signed.

Figure 15-3. *Standard out-of-browser application installation window when the elevated trust option is not enabled*

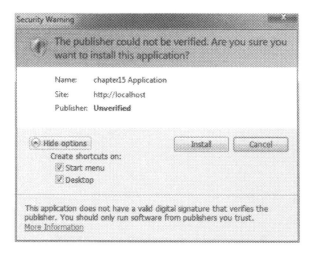

Figure 15-4. *Out-of-browser application installation window with a security warning when the elevated trust option is enabled and the application is not signed with a digital certificate*

Figure 15-4 shows the default security-warning window when the elevated trust option is enabled but the application does not contain a valid digital signature (i.e., the application is not signed). The Silverlight application with elevated trust but without a signed digital certificate will allow you to install the application but will not allow installing new updates. To allow installation of the updates, you must sign your application (e.g., XAP file for Silverlight application) with a valid and unexpired certificate.

The SecuritySettings class available within the System.Windows namespace represents the security configuration of an out-of-browser application. This class contains a read-only (at run time) ElevatedPermissions property indicating whether the out-of-browser application mode is set with elevated trust (returns Required value) or not (returns NotRequired value, a default value). The property contains the value based on the elevated trust settings you set, as shown in Figure 15-2. While you are running the application in the out-of-browser mode, you can determine whether the application is running with elevated trust by using the Application.HasElevatedPermissions property. This property is read-only, and cannot be set through code-behind. Essentially it represents the value of the SecuritySettings.ElevatedPermissions property, which we discussed earlier in this section. It returns true if the application is running with elevated trust, and otherwise it returns false.

Digitally Signing Out-of-Browser Silverlight Applications

It is a three-step process to sign a Silverlight application's (with elevated trust enabled in out-of-browser mode) XAP file with a digital certificate.

1. Create a test certificate or receive the digital certificate (from a certificate authority).

   For demonstration purposes, I will create a test certificate using the MakeCert tool (available in the version-specific Bin folder under Program Files\Microsoft SDKs\Windows on 32-bit OS and Program Files(x86)\Microsoft SDKs\Windows on 64-bit OS). Execute the following command to create a self-signed test certificate with the name TestCert and stored in TestCert.cer. Note that you will need Administrator rights to run this utility.

```
makecert -r -pe -ss PrivateCertStore -n
    "CN=TestCert" TestCert.cer
```

2. Sign the XAP file with the digital certificate and embed the certificate within the XAP file.

   To sign the XAP file with the created self-signed certificate, you will use the SignTool tool (available in the version-specific Bin folder under Program Files\Microsoft SDKs\Windows on 32-bit OS and Program Files(x86)\Microsoft SDKs\Windows on 64-bit OS). Execute the following command to sign the chapter15.xap file by the TestCert certificate. Notice that the XAP file size has grown since the XAP file was signed. It now contains the digital certificate also. You will need to resign the XAP file if you rebuild the project.

```
signtool sign /v /s PrivateCertStore /n TestCert chapter15.xap
```

3. Install the digital certificate to the Trusted Root Certification Authorities store (in the client machine) for verification.

   Your certificate must be trusted to verify the application against the installed digital certificate. For that, you must install the certificate to the Trusted Root Certification Authorities store. You just run the created certificate (TestCert.cer) on the command prompt and select the "Install Certificate…" option on the pop-up window, as shown in Figure 15-5. This should open up the certificate installation wizard. Note that you must select the Trusted Root Certification Authorities store as the installation location within the certificate installation wizard.

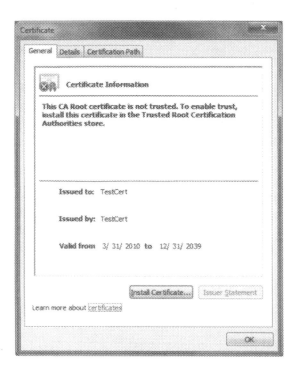

Figure 15-5. Installing a digital certificate to the Trusted Root Certification Authorities store

Figure 15-6 shows the out-of-browser application installation window with a security warning with publisher information (as a trusted application—does not say unverified as in Figure 15-4) when the elevated trust option is enabled and the application is signed with the valid digital certificate.

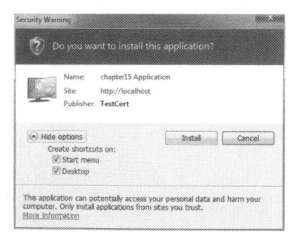

Figure 15-6. Out-of-browser application installation window with a security warning when the elevated trust option is enabled and the application is signed with a digital certificate

Note System administrators can set the local computer policies that disable installation and execution of the out-of-browser Silverlight applications with elevated trust. However, if the OOB application with elevated trust is already installed before the policy is applied or if the application is installed by the system administrator, it will work without any restrictions.

Get more information on group policies settings for Silverlight applications by visiting www.microsoft.com/GetSilverlight/resources/documentation/grouppolicysettings.aspx.

Elevated-Trusted Silverlight Applications vs. Partially Trusted Silverlight Applications

Table 15-1 provides a quick overview of key differences in different features when a Silverlight application is running as a partially trusted application (in in-browser or out-of-browser modes) or when it is running as an elevated-trusted application (in out-of-browser mode).

Table 15-1. Features Capabilities for Partially Trusted Silverlight Applications (In-Browser and Out-of-Browser Mode) and Elevated-Trusted Silverlight Applications (Out-of-Browser Mode Only)

Feature	Partially Trusted Silverlight Application (running in in-browser or out-of-browser mode)	Elevated-Trusted Silverlight Application (running in out-of-browser mode only) (New Feature in Silverlight 4)
Isolated local storage	Full access. For in-browser applications default storage is 1MB. For OOB applications default storage is 25MB.	Full access. For OOB applications default storage is 25MB.
File system access	Restricted file system access. User-initiated actions through open-file dialog and save-file dialog boxes to access file system outside of isolated local storage.	New feature in Silverlight 4. Direct access to file system MyDocuments, MyPictures, MyVideos, and MyMusic folders on Windows platform and related folders on other platforms. No need to use open- and save-file dialog boxes. To access file system you can use System.IO namespace and related classes to manipulate directory, file, properties, path information, and read/write files.
Printing	New feature in Silverlight 4. You can use user-initiated print dialog box for printing.	New feature in Silverlight 4. You can use user-initiated print dialog box for printing.

Clipboard access	New feature in Silverlight 4. User-initiated action. User needs to grant permission (and optionally retain the permission state for the specific application for future uses) to use this functionality. Otherwise the permission ends when user navigates to other page or the page is closed. Access to text clipboard only.	New feature in Silverlight 4. No need for user initiation. Direct access to text clipboard access.
Webcam and microphone integration	New feature in Silverlight 4. User-initiated action. User needs to grant permission (and optionally retain the permission state for the specific application for future uses) to use this functionality. Otherwise the permission ends when user navigates to other page or the page is closed.	New feature in Silverlight 4. No need for user initiation. Direct access to webcam and microphone.
Full-screen mode and keyboard support	Enhanced functionality in Silverlight 4. User-initiated action. Text showing how to exit from the full-screen mode will be displayed. Upon clicking ESC key or switching to other application user automatically exits from the full-screen mode.	New feature in Silverlight 4. No need for user initiation. Text showing how to exit from the full-screen mode will not be displayed. ESC key will not end the full-screen mode. Full keyboard access. However, since ESC key press will not end the full-screen mode, you need to programmatically implement the exit functionality.
Right-click support	New feature in Silverlight 4. Right-click support is enabled in Silverlight 4 applications.	New feature in Silverlight 4. Right-click support is enabled in Silverlight 4 applications.
Out-of-browser application window customization	Not applicable.	New feature in Silverlight 4. You can customize the out-of-browser application window (border, title bar, buttons, window size, and position).
Native integration	Not applicable	New feature in Silverlight 4. Limited access to the programming model and services exposed by the COM automation server (e.g., access to Office system object model).
Cross-domain access restrictions	Requires cross-domain policy file to perform successful cross-domain communication	Can perform cross-domain communication without cross-domain policy file.

Application-Level Security

The security of executable code provided by the CoreCLR is not where the security story ends. While there are guarantees that Silverlight application code cannot gain access to the host operating system or is digitally signed and running with elevated trust in out-of-browser mode, Silverlight applications may still handle confidential information. This information might take the form of a user's credit card data, a user's login credentials, or other information that needs careful handling. This information must be secured in transit, achieved typically via HTTPS, and possibly with a further layer of encryption ensuring that only the intended recipient can decrypt the encrypted information. Secure coding practices combined with the support Silverlight provides can give you confidence that your Silverlight application is secure.

Securing Information in Transit

When a Silverlight application communicates with a server, there is the potential for a third party to listen in on or even tamper with the communication. The established way to secure communication over HTTP is by using the SSL protocol via HTTPS. Silverlight can easily make use of SSL. Both the WebClient and HttpWebRequest classes support HTTPS, and you can also configure the ServiceReferences.ClientConfig class to use SSL.

Configuring a service to communicate over HTTPS is accomplished by setting the mode attribute of the security element to Transport, as shown here. Also, make sure the endpoint's address uses the HTTPS protocol.

```
<configuration>
    <system.serviceModel>
        <bindings>
            <basicHttpBinding>
                <binding name="BasicHttpBinding_AuthenticationService"
                         maxBufferSize="65536"
                         maxReceivedMessageSize="65536">
                    <security mode="Transport" />
                </binding>
            </basicHttpBinding>
        </bindings>
        ...
    </system.serviceModel>
</configuration>
```

Securing Information with Cryptography

While communicating over an encrypted channel ensures that information stays secure in transit, the information arrives unencrypted for the application to handle. Regardless of how the application receives information, you may need to decrypt the information; or if it will be stored locally (such as in isolated storage), it is possible that the information must be encrypted before being written to disk. This is where the System.Security.Cryptography namespace enters the picture. This namespace provides capabilities for encrypting and decrypting data, generating hashes for purposes such as message authentication codes and random number generation suitable for cryptography.

Note Visit the Microsoft MSDN web site to get a detailed overview on cryptography
(http://msdn.microsoft.com/en-us/library/92f9ye3s.aspx).

Hash Algorithms and Message Authentication Codes

A hash algorithm transforms a chunk of data into a small, fixed-length set of bytes known as a *hash* (or *hash code*). As long as the same chunk of data is processed by the same hash algorithm, the resulting hash code will always be the same. If you've heard of CRC codes or digital signatures, you've heard of the result of hash algorithms. Used as a digital signature, a hash code can prove that the data has not changed, since even a small change in the data will result in a completely different hash code.

The base class of hash classes is System.Security.Cryptography.HashAlgorithm. This class provides the main features of a hash algorithm, including hash size and hash value properties, and methods for computing a hash value. It provides additional functionality via the derived class System.Security.Cryptography.KeyedHashAlgorithm—most importantly the addition of a secret password (key) as input to the hash algorithm. This added functionality is important because, otherwise, a chunk of data can be tampered with and a recomputed hash code attached to it.

Taking one more step down the hierarchy brings us to the System.Security.Cryptography.HMAC class, which is derived from KeyedHashAlgorithm. *HMAC* stands for *hash-based message authentication code*. A *message authentication code* (MAC) is another name for a hash value or a digital signature. Changing the data will cause the MAC value to change, thus providing evidence of data tampering. The HMAC class is the one we're most interested in from a class interface perspective since inheritors to HMAC provide specific algorithm implementations. The direct inheritors to HMAC are HMACSHA1 and HMACSHA256, implementations of the SHA-1 and SHA-256 cryptographic algorithms for computing MACs. Tables 15-2 and 15-3 show the properties and methods of these three base classes, which are mainly inherited from the System.Security.Cryptography.HashAlgorithm class.

Table 15-2. Properties of System.Security.Cryptography.HMAC

Property	Type	Description
BlockSizeValue	int	Specifies the size, in number of bits, of the block used by the algorithm.
CanReuseTransform	bool	Returns true if you can reuse the current hash transform. Inherited from the System.Security.Cryptography.HashAlgorithm class.
CanTransformMultipleBlocks	bool	Returns true if the algorithm can transform multiple blocks. Inherited from the System.Security.Cryptography.HashAlgorithm class.
Hash	byte[]	Gets the computed hash value. Inherited from the System.Security.Cryptography.HashAlgorithm class.
HashName	string	Gets/sets the name of the algorithm used for hashing.

HashSize	int	Specifies the size, in number of bits, of the computed hash value. Inherited from the System.Security.Cryptography.HashAlgorithm class.
InputBlockSize	int	Specifies the size, in number of bits, of input blocks. Inherited from the System.Security.Cryptography.HashAlgorithm class.
Key	byte[]	Gets/sets the secret key used in the algorithm, which overrides KeyedHashAlgorithm.Key property.
OutputBlockSize	int	Specifies the size of the output block. Inherited from the System.Security.Cryptography.HashAlgorithm class.

Table 15-3 describes the key methods.

Table 15-3. Key Methods of System.Security.Cryptography.HMAC (et al.)

Method	Description
Clear	Releases all resources used by the algorithm. Inherited from the System.Security.Cryptography.HashAlgorithm class.
ComputeHash	Computes a hash for a byte array (or section thereof) or a Stream. This is the method you use to generate hashes. Inherited from the System.Security.Cryptography.HashAlgorithm class.
Initialize	Initializes an instance of the algorithm. It overrides HashAlgorithm.Initialize().
TransformBlock	Generates a hash value for a section of a byte array and stores it at a specific offset in another byte array. Inherited from the System.Security.Cryptography.HashAlgorithm class
TransformFinalBlock	Generates a hash value for a section of a byte array. Inherited from the System.Security.Cryptography.HashAlgorithm class.

There are two algorithms that provide the specific implementation for the hash algorithms: SHA-1 and SHA-256. Both algorithms can use a key of any length. The SHA-1 algorithm returns a hash value that is 20 bytes (160 bits), and SHA-256 returns a hash value that is 32 bytes (256 bits). As long as the same input bytes and the same key are used, the specific hash algorithm will always generate the same hash value. Here's a helper method that accepts a message (the input bytes) and the key as strings and will use any specific implementation of the HMAC class that you pass in:

```
byte[] calculateHash(string key, string message,
  HMAC hashAlgorithm)
{
    UTF8Encoding encoder = new UTF8Encoding();
    hashAlgorithm.Key = encoder.GetBytes(key);
```

```
    byte[] hash =
      hashAlgorithm.ComputeHash(encoder.GetBytes(message));
    //Convert the hash byte array to Base64 string
    string hashinbase64string =
      System.Convert.ToBase64String(hash);
    return (hash);
}
```

If we pass the string this is a secret message through the HMACSHA256 class, with the secret key p@ssw0rd, and then encode the resulting byte array as a Base64 string, we get the hash value an332+/NeHKDvNIKYiQOokci/ob1xK1eMJYS1yjtwfI=. If we capitalize the first t in the message, the hash value changes to IhbwZnSZXdw95cUbXprjSUAV9VBoFmKdOd9kYT/Et3Y=, which is a significant change. Even changing a single bit in the message or the key will cause a wildly different hash value to be generated.

Note The SHA-1 algorithm is now considered an unsecured algorithm, and SHA-2 (includes SHA-256 and SHA-512 algorithms) is recommended instead. Thus, for Silverlight-based applications, it is recommended to utilize the SHA-256 algorithm instead of SHA-1. Note that Silverlight does not support the SHA-512 algorithm. You can get more details on the SHA algorithm by visiting http://en.wikipedia.org/wiki/SHA.

Encrypting/Decrypting Data

There are two types of encryption algorithms: *symmetric key algorithms* and *asymmetric key algorithms*. A symmetric key algorithm is an algorithm where the key used to encrypt information is the same key used for decryption. An asymmetric key algorithm uses separate keys for encryption and decryption, generally referred to as a *public key* (used for encryption; anyone can obtain the public key to encrypt data for a specific recipient) and a *private key* (this key is kept secret and used to decrypt data encrypted with the public key). Silverlight supports only one encryption algorithm, the symmetric key Advanced Encryption Standard (AES).

The simplest approach to encrypting and decrypting information is to use a single password, as shown in Figure 15-7.

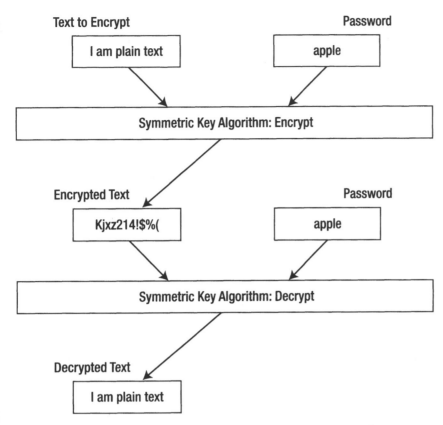

Figure 15-7. Flow of encryption/decryption using a secret password

Since the password is used unmodified, an attacker could conceivably launch a dictionary-based attack to find the password by brute force. For example, if an attacker has the encrypted text and has reason to believe a fruit is used for the password, he could try "banana," "orange," "pear," and finally "apple," and suddenly he'll be staring at the original message, successfully decrypted. One way to go about preventing a dictionary-based attack is to use a *salt*. Salts are random data combined with passwords that make dictionary-based attacks much more expensive, since every word in the dictionary must be combined with every possible salt. The salt is stored with the password (usually a password transformed by a hashing algorithm), so decryption is straightforward since the original salt is known and a human-readable password can pass through the same hashing function again. It's possible to make the attacker's job even harder by using a stronger algorithm to transform a password. One such algorithm is the Public-Key Cryptography Standard (PKCS) #5, defined in RFC 2898, which you can find more about at www.ietf.org/.

PKCS #5 actually defines two modes of operation used for deriving a password. The first is Password-Based Key Derivation Function #1 (PBKDF1), and the second is PBKDF2, which you can find in the cryptography namespace in Silverlight. The main advantage of using PBKDF2 is that although the more rudimentary salt-plus-hash approach makes dictionary attacks computationally infeasible, PBKDF2 requires even more computational resources to successfully crack the password. This is accomplished by applying the hash function multiple times. So, instead of an attacker having to try every possible salt with every possible password in a dictionary, he'd also have to try a variety of iteration counts for rehashing, along with every possible salt and every password in the dictionary. This means that instead of storing just the salt with a hashed password, you store the salt, the hashed password (the output from the PBKDF2 algorithm), and the iteration count.

The Rfc2898DeriveBytes class provides the implementation of the PBKDF2 algorithm. You pass the password (as a string or a byte array), the salt (as a byte array), and, optionally, an iteration count to the constructor. Then you invoke the GetBytes member method with the number of bytes you want returned. Here's an example method that does the work of using the Rfc2898DeriveBytes class for you:

```
private byte[] deriveBytes(string input, byte[] salt, int iterations)
{
    Rfc2898DeriveBytes deriver = new
      Rfc2898DeriveBytes(input, salt, iterations);
    return deriver.GetBytes(16);
}
```

The AesManaged class provides the implementation of the AES algorithm for encrypting/decrypting data. The other important aspect of using the AES algorithm is using an initialization vector, as shown in the preceding code in the second parameter. By default, AES uses a 128-bit block size (a block is a fixed length of data used by certain encryption algorithms such as AES), and the initialization vector is used to initialize the block. Since the default block size is 128 bits, the default size of the initialization vector must be 16 bytes (128 bits / 8 bits per byte = 16 bytes). The initialization vector for the encryption must be the same when decrypting data, so if you send encrypted data over the wire, the other side must somehow know which initialization vector to use. This can be something agreed upon by the encryptor and decryptor in the code design phase. The AesManaged class inherits from Aes, which inherits from SymmetricAlgorithm. Table 15-4 describes the properties of SymmetricAlgorithm.

Table 15-4. Properties of System.Security.Cryptography.SymmetricAlgorithm

Property	Type	Description
BlockSize	int	Size, in number of bits, of the block used by the algorithm.
IV	byte[]	Initialization vector (IV) used by the algorithm; must be BlockSize/8 bytes long. It automatically sets a random value when you create a new instance of the SymmetricAlgorithm class or when you call the GenerateIV method manually.
Key	byte[]	Secret key (e.g., password) used by the algorithm.
KeySize	int	Size, in number of bits, of the secret key.
LegalBlockSizes	KeySizes[]	Array of block sizes that are valid for this algorithm. Certain algorithms, such as AES, support only a few different block sizes.
LegalKeySizes	KeySizes[]	Array of key sizes valid for this algorithm.

Used in conjunction with the CryptoStream class, it's straightforward to encrypt data in a stream such as a MemoryStream or a file stream for working with files from isolated storage. Figure 15-8 shows a simple interface for encrypting and decrypting data. The salt must be at least eight characters long. The password entered, combined with the salt, is used for both encrypting and decrypting.

Password	Iampassword
Salt	Iamsalt
Text to Encrypt	Iamplaintext
	Encrypt
Encrypted Text	W3mTAret+vjbVA3PbuFEgg==
	Decrypt
Decrypted Text	Iamplaintext

Figure 15-8. Demonstration interface for encrypting/decrypting data

Here's a utility encryption method that takes a key, an initialization vector, and the text to encrypt:

```
private string Encrypt(byte[] key, byte[] iv, string plaintext)
{
    AesManaged aes = new AesManaged();
    aes.Key = key;
    aes.IV = iv;
    using (MemoryStream stream = new MemoryStream())
    {
        using (CryptoStream encrypt = new CryptoStream(stream,
                                        aes.CreateEncryptor(),
                                        CryptoStreamMode.Write))
        {
            byte[] plaintextBytes =
                UTF8Encoding.UTF8.GetBytes(plaintext);
            encrypt.Write(plaintextBytes, 0, plaintextBytes.Length);
            encrypt.FlushFinalBlock();
            encrypt.Close();
            return Convert.ToBase64String(stream.ToArray());
        }
    }
}
```

The following demonstrates how to invoke the Encrypt method:

```
private void btnEncrypt_Click(object sender, RoutedEventArgs e)
{
    //generating salt from txtSalt
    byte[] salt=Encoding.Unicode.GetBytes(txtSalt.Text);

    //calling encryption method
    EncryptedText.Text  = Encrypt(deriveBytes(txtPassword.Text, salt, 10),
        initializationVector, txtTextToEncrypt.Text );
}
```

The Decrypt method is implemented similarly, but uses the decryption functionality of the AesManaged class:

```
private string Decrypt(byte[] key, byte[] iv, string encryptedText)
{
    AesManaged aes = new AesManaged();
    byte[] encryptedBytes = Convert.FromBase64String(encryptedText);
    aes.Key = key;
    aes.IV = iv;
    using (MemoryStream stream = new MemoryStream())
    {
        using (CryptoStream decrypt =
                        new CryptoStream(stream, aes.CreateDecryptor(),
                                                  CryptoStreamMode.Write))
        {
            decrypt.Write(encryptedBytes, 0, encryptedBytes.Length);
            decrypt.Flush();
            decrypt.Close();
            byte[] decryptedBytes = stream.ToArray();
            return UTF8Encoding.UTF8.GetString(
                                    decryptedBytes, 0,
                                    decryptedBytes.Length);
        }
    }
}
```

User Access Control

ASP.NET 2.0 introduced a membership database that combines database tables with stored procedures to provide authentication and authorization capabilities. The process of authentication is similar to a guard at a gate, checking identification cards before allowing access. The authentication process has a binary answer: either the user has access or she doesn't. Authorization, however, controls the nature of the access once a user is inside the gate. Ushers at a concert, for example, check concertgoers' tickets to make sure they are permitted access to the concert. This is an example of authentication. Some concert attendees might have access to a VIP section or have a backstage pass. These are varying degrees of access, from a regular concert attendee who can sit and watch to someone who is allowed to go backstage and meet the performers. This is an example of authorization—what access do people have after they get past the gate that separates insiders from outsiders?

In ASP.NET, authorization is accomplished via roles. A user can be a member of zero or more roles, and how roles define access is a detail specified in the application design. ASP.NET 3.5 introduces (and now part of the .NET 4.0 Framework Class library also provides) WCF services to provide clients access to the authentication and authorization databases. Before these services can be used, a web application must be configured to use a membership database. If you want to install the membership capabilities into a database server, you can use the aspnet_regsql utility that comes with the . NET Framework.

The System.Web.ApplicationServices namespace of .NET Framework 4.0 exposes AuthenticationService, RoleService, and ProfileService classes enabling access to ASP .NET forms authentication, roles and profile services as WCF services (visit http://msdn.microsoft.com/en-us/library/system.web.applicationservices.aspx to get more details). Let's take a look at the services for authentication and authorization provided by the AuthenticationService and RoleService classes. Exposing these services in an ASP.NET application is a simple matter of adding the services and bindings in `web.config` and enabling the services in the `system.web.extensions` configuration section. The services must also be referenced in the `ServiceHost` tag in an SVC file. Let's take a closer look at enabling these services and consuming them from Silverlight.

In `web.config`, the `authentication` and `roleManager` elements within the `system.web` section are used to configure and enable authentication and authorization for the web application:

```
<system.web>
    <authentication mode="Forms" />
    <roleManager enabled="true" />
    <!-- ... -->
</system.web>
```

These services must then be enabled in the `system.web.extensions` section. The `RoleService` provides web methods for determining whether a user is a member of a particular role:

```
<system.web.extensions>
   <scripting>
      <webServices>
         <authenticationService enabled="true" requireSSL="false"/>
         <roleService enabled="true"/>
      </webServices>
   </scripting>
</system.web.extensions>
```

It is a good idea to enable SSL for authentication by setting `requireSSL` to `TRUE`. The `system.serviceModel` section contains the services, bindings, and behaviors related to these services:

```
<system.serviceModel>
  <services>
    <service name="System.Web.ApplicationServices.AuthenticationService"
             behaviorConfiguration="authServiceBehaviors">
      <endpoint contract="System.Web.ApplicationServices.AuthenticationService"
                binding="basicHttpBinding"
                bindingConfiguration="serviceBindingConfig"
                bindingNamespace="http://asp.net/ApplicationServices/v200"/>
    </service>
    <service name="System.Web.ApplicationServices.RoleService"
             behaviorConfiguration="roleServiceBehaviors">
      <endpoint contract="System.Web.ApplicationServices.RoleService"
                binding="basicHttpBinding"
                bindingConfiguration="serviceBindingConfig"
                bindingNamespace="http://asp.net/ApplicationServices/v200"/>
    </service>
  </services>
  <bindings>
    <basicHttpBinding>
      <binding name="serviceBindingConfig">
        <security mode="None"/>
      </binding>
    </basicHttpBinding>
  </bindings>
```

```
<behaviors>
  <serviceBehaviors>
    <behavior name="authServiceBehaviors">
      <serviceMetadata httpGetEnabled="true"/>
    </behavior>
    <behavior name="roleServiceBehaviors">
      <serviceMetadata httpGetEnabled="true"/>
    </behavior>
  </serviceBehaviors>
</behaviors>
<serviceHostingEnvironment aspNetCompatibilityEnabled="true"/>
</system.serviceModel>
```

Each service has a corresponding SVC file within the web application in order to connect a service host with the service. For the authentication service, you need to add a Silverlight-enabled WCF service to the web project with the name AuthenticationService.svc for the authentication service, and replace existing content with the following code (you can refer to the "Creating a WCF Service Consumable by Silverlight" section of Chapter 5 for further details on adding WCF service for Silverlight):

```
<%@ ServiceHost Language="C#"
                Service="System.Web.ApplicationServices.AuthenticationService" %>
```

Similarly the following is for the role service, placed in RoleService.svc:

```
<%@ ServiceHost Language="C#"
                    Service="System.Web.ApplicationServices.RoleService" %>
```

Once you have this configuration done, you can attempt to access a service directly from a browser—for example, by browsing to http://localhost:9941/AuthenticationService.svc, as I am running on a local asp.net web server.

Furthermore, you can use the Web Site Administration Tool, shown in Figure 15-9, to manage rules, related to user accounts and user roles, for securing specific resources in the web application. You can access this tool through Visual Studio 2010 by visiting *ASP.NET Configuration Manage*, available under the *Project* menu item.

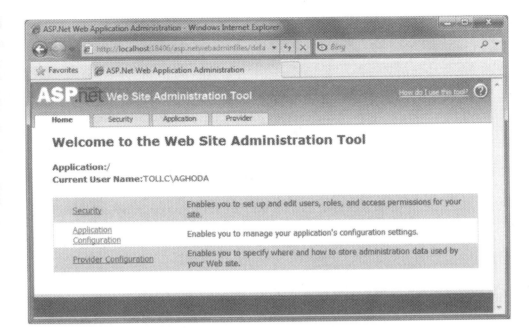

Figure 15-9. Web site administration tool

Visit http://msdn.microsoft.com/en-us/library/ssa0wsyf.aspx to get more details on how to operate this tool to set up appropriate security rules.

Using the Authentication Service

The authentication service provides methods to log in and log out, along with checking whether the user is logged in. When a successful login happens, a cookie is set on the client side to store this state. Let's look closer at the methods the authentication service provides:

IsLoggedIn: Returns true if the user is logged in (authentication cookie is present) and returns false otherwise.

Login: Verifies the user's credentials, and if they are validated successfully, the authentication cookie is set. This method takes the username and password, custom credentials of type string, and a Boolean value specifying whether the authentication cookie persists across sessions.

Logout: Clears the authentication cookie from the browser.

ValidateUser: Verifies the user's credentials. This is similar to Login, but it does not set the authentication cookie if the user's credentials are validated successfully.

Figure 15-10 shows a sample login screen. The login and password shown (testuser/testuser!) are valid with the database distributed with this chapter's code.

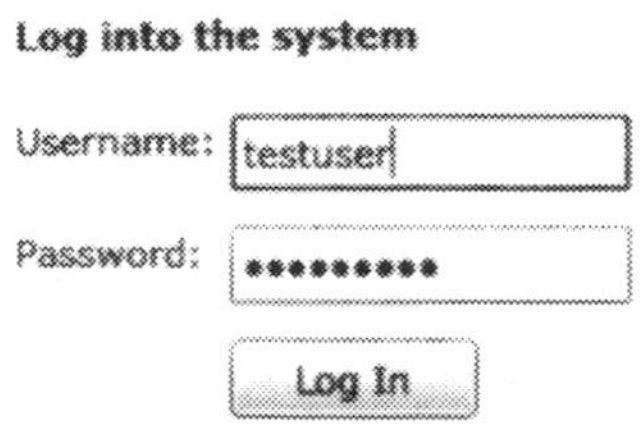

Log into the system

Username: testuser

Password: ••••••••

Log In

Figure 15-10. Sample login screen

In order to transition from a login screen to a screen that represents the main user interface to the application, the XAML that houses the login screen also houses a layout panel that has the main interface. There's a login button on the login screen and a logout button that generally will appear on each screen of the application. See the complete code for the sample login XAML screen.

```xml
<UserControl x:Class="chapter15.UACDemo.LoginScreen"
    xmlns="http://schemas.microsoft.com/winfx/2006/xaml/presentation"
    xmlns:x="http://schemas.microsoft.com/winfx/2006/xaml"
    xmlns:d="http://schemas.microsoft.com/expression/blend/2008"
    xmlns:mc="http://schemas.openxmlformats.org/markup-compatibility/2006"
    mc:Ignorable="d"
    d:DesignHeight="300" d:DesignWidth="400">
    <StackPanel>
        <StackPanel  x:Name="LoginPanel" Background="White">
            <TextBlock Text="Log into the system" Margin="0,0,0,15" FontWeight="Bold"↩
></TextBlock>
            <StackPanel Orientation="Horizontal" Margin="0,0,0,10" >
                <TextBlock Height="23" Text="Username: " />
                <TextBox Height="23" Name="txtUsername" Width="120" />
            </StackPanel>
            <StackPanel Orientation="Horizontal" >
                <TextBlock Height="23" Text="Password:   "   />
                <PasswordBox Height="23" Name="txtPassword" Width="120" />
            </StackPanel>
            <Button Content="Log In" Height="23" HorizontalAlignment="Left"↩
Margin="65,10,0,0"
                Name="btnLogin" Width="75" Click="btnLogin_Click" />
                <TextBlock Height="23" Name="txtResult" HorizontalAlignment="Left"  />
        </StackPanel >
        <StackPanel x:Name="MainPanel" Margin="0,20,0,0" Visibility="Collapsed" >
            <TextBlock Text="You have successfully logged in."/>
            <Button Width="70" Height="26" Content="Logout" x:Name="btnLogout"
                HorizontalAlignment="Left" Click="btnLogout_Click" />
        </StackPanel>
    </StackPanel>
</UserControl>
```

After adding a service reference to the authentication service and including a using statement to the namespace that contains the added service reference, you just need to implement the click event handlers on the buttons for logging in and out:

```
AuthenticationServiceClient client;
public LoginScreen()
{
    InitializeComponent();
    client = new AuthenticationServiceClient();
    client.LoginCompleted +=
            new EventHandler<LoginCompletedEventArgs>(client_LoginCompleted);
    client.LogoutCompleted +=
            new EventHandler<AsyncCompletedEventArgs>(client_LogoutCompleted);
}
```

The login button click handler calls LoginAsync. The third parameter can be custom authentication credentials, but in this case we just pass null. The final parameter is set to true in order to maintain the authentication cookie on the client even after the browser navigates away. This is similar to the "Remember me" check box on the ASP.NET login control.

```
private void btnLogin_Click(object sender, RoutedEventArgs e)
{
    client.LoginAsync( txtUsername.Text,txtPassword.Password, null, true);
}
```

The LoginCompleted event checks the result of the Login call, and if it indicates that the user successfully logged in, the main user interface is shown. Otherwise, an error message is displayed to the user.

```
void client_LoginCompleted(object sender, LoginCompletedEventArgs e)
{
    if (e.Result)
    {
        LoginPanel.Visibility = Visibility.Collapsed;
        MainPanel.Visibility = Visibility.Visible;
    }
    else
    {
        txtResult.Text = "Incorrect username or password";
    }
}
```

The logout button calls the Logout method on the authentication service in order to clear the authentication cookie from the user's browser, and the asynchronous callback handler hides the main user interface and shows the login screen again:

```
private void btnLogout_Click(object sender, RoutedEventArgs e)
{
    client.LogoutAsync();
}
void client_LogoutCompleted(object sender, AsyncCompletedEventArgs e)
{
    LoginPanel.Visibility = Visibility.Visible;
    MainPanel.Visibility = Visibility.Collapsed;
}
```

Since the authentication cookie might be valid when a user first visits the application, your application should call ValidateUser and react accordingly (such as displaying a message that the user is logged in—similar to how web sites display it).

If you don't want to (or can't) use the ASP.NET authentication service, the ASP.NET authentication service serves as a good model for an authentication service you could implement.

Using the RoleService

Once a user is authenticated and logged in, the RoleService is used to obtain the roles the user belongs to and to check whether he belongs to a specified role as part of the authorization process. Let's take a look at the methods the RoleService provides:

GetRolesForCurrentUser: Returns an array of strings containing the roles the currently authenticated user belongs to.

IsCurrentUserInRole: Takes a role name and returns true if the user is a member of the role.

Once the user is authenticated and logged in, you can retrieve the list of roles the user is in using the GetRolesForCurrentUser method. If your application will make a number of role-based decisions, it's better to cache this list of roles locally instead of repeatedly calling the IsCurrentUserInRole service method.

Again, we create an instance of the RoleService client and register the GetRolesForCurrentUser event handler:

```
roleClient = new RoleServiceClient();
roleClient.GetRolesForCurrentUserCompleted +=
    new EventHandler<GetRolesForCurrentUserCompletedEventArgs>
      (roleClient_GetRolesForCurrentUserCompleted);
```

One opportunity to cache the user's roles occurs when the user successfully logs in, although you might want to delay this, since it adds to the amount of time it takes to log the user in. You'd also have to handle loading roles for when the user is already logged in:

```
roleClient.GetRolesForCurrentUserAsync();
```

Once the callback for this web service method occurs, the roles are cached in a List<string>:

```
private List<string> cachedRoles;
private void roleClient_GetRolesForCurrentUserCompleted(object sender,
                            GetRolesForCurrentUserCompletedEventArgs e)
{
    cachedRoles = new List<string>();
    foreach (string role in e.Result)
    {
        cachedRoles.Add(role);
    }
}
public bool isUserInRole(string role)
{
    return(cachedRoles.Contains(role));
}
```

The application can now use the isUserInRole method, instead of the RoleService directly, to make role-based decisions.

Authentication Support with ClientHttpWebRequest

Silverlight supports two different modes for HTTP networking: BrowserHttpWebRequest and ClientHttpWebRequest. By default, HTTP handling is performed by the browser, and you must opt in to client HTTP handling. Get more details by visiting the Microsoft MSDN site, http://msdn.microsoft.com/en-us/library/dd920295.aspx.

Obviously, due to limitations in the browser, the browser stack (BrowserHttpWebRequest) can't use the full set of HTTP verbs and is limited to GET and POST with not much control over cookies or headers. The client stack (ClientHttpWebRequest) enables additional functionality by using the underlying operating system's networking stack. As a result, the client stack will use the operating system's network settings rather than the browser's settings. This opens up the possibility to support NTLM, Basic, and Digest authentication. You can visit http://msdn.microsoft.com/en-us/library/aa292114.aspx to get an overview of all IIS authentication mechanisms.

NTLM Authentication

NTLM is an authentication protocol used in various Microsoft network protocol implementations and is also used throughout Microsoft's systems as an integrated single sign-on mechanism. You can get more information on the NTLM authentication by visiting http://msdn.microsoft.com/en-us/library/aa378749.aspx.

Digest Authentication

The Digest authentication mechanism is very similar to the NTLM mechanism following the challenge/response protocols. It follows standards documented in RFCs 2617 and 2831. You can get more information on the Digest authentication by visiting http://technet.microsoft.com/en-us/library/cc778868(WS.10).aspx.

Basic Authentication

The Basic authentication mechanism provides basic credentials information, through a web-based form-based mechanism providing user id and password. You can get more information on the Basic authentication by visiting http://en.wikipedia.org/wiki/Basic_access_authentication.

As described in Chapter 5, with the release of Silverlight 4, you can pass user credentials as part of the request header of the network request from the application to the server for authentication and authorization. This allows Silverlight applications to set the Credentials API with user-entered credentials (user name and password) for authentication by services such as ADO.NET Data Services or Live Mesh, or a third-party application such as Twitter. This will also allow an integrated authentication scenario (single sign-on) by utilizing the user's logged-in information saved within the client machine operating system.

Developing a Twitter Integration Application

John Papa has demonstrated this enhancement by providing a code snippet of the Twitter integration application, which accesses public Twitter API authenticated by passing the user name and password to retrieve received messages. You can get the entire white paper written by John Papa on new features of Silverlight 4 by visiting http://channel9.msdn.com/learn/courses/Silverlight4/Overview/Overview/Introduction/. In this section we will complete this application.

We will develop a very simple user interface using XAML, which will allow entering your Twitter user name or email id and password to authenticate the Twitter account. We will use a list box, which we will bind to the received Twitter messages of the authorized user as a XML file. In this sample we are binding with the Message and User elements of the retrieved XML file. The following is the related XAML file:

```xml
<UserControl x:Class="chapter15.ClientHttpWebRequestDemo"
    xmlns="http://schemas.microsoft.com/winfx/2006/xaml/presentation"
    xmlns:x="http://schemas.microsoft.com/winfx/2006/xaml"
    xmlns:d="http://schemas.microsoft.com/expression/blend/2008"
    xmlns:mc="http://schemas.openxmlformats.org/markup-compatibility/2006"
    mc:Ignorable="d"
    d:DesignHeight="300" d:DesignWidth="400">
    <StackPanel  x:Name="LayoutRoot" Background="White">
        <TextBlock Text="Enter your twitter username:" Height="26" ></TextBlock>
        <TextBox Height="23" HorizontalAlignment="Left" Name="txtUsername"
            VerticalAlignment="Top" Width="205" />
        <TextBlock Height="26" Text="Enter your twitter password:" />
        <PasswordBox Height="23" HorizontalAlignment="Left" Name="txtPassword"
            VerticalAlignment="Top" Width="203" />
        <Button Content="Get status updates" Height="23" HorizontalAlignment="Left"
            Name="btnGetUpdates" VerticalAlignment="Top" Width="134"
            Click="btnGetUpdates_Click" />
        <ListBox HorizontalAlignment="Left" Name="lstData" >
            <ListBox.ItemTemplate>
                <DataTemplate>
                    <StackPanel Orientation="Horizontal" >
                        <TextBlock Text="{Binding Path=Message}" Foreground="Crimson"  />
                        <TextBlock Text=" : " />
                        <TextBlock Text="{Binding Path=User}" FontWeight="Bold"
    Foreground="Blue" />
                    </StackPanel>
                </DataTemplate>
            </ListBox.ItemTemplate>
        </ListBox>
    </StackPanel>
</UserControl>
```

The code-behind is very straightforward and is shown here.

```csharp
using System;
using System.Collections.Generic;
using System.Linq;
using System.Net;
using System.Windows;
using System.Windows.Controls;
//added
using System.Net.Browser;
using System.Xml.Linq;
```

```
namespace chapter15
{
    public partial class ClientHttpWebRequestDemo : UserControl
    {
        public class StatusUpdates
        {
            public string Message { get; set; }
            public string User { get; set; }
        }
        public ClientHttpWebRequestDemo()
        {
            InitializeComponent();
        }

        private void btnGetUpdates_Click(object sender, RoutedEventArgs e)
        {
            string  username = txtUsername.Text ;
            string password = txtPassword.Password;

            string twitterUri = @"http://twitter.com/statuses/friends_timeline.xml";

            WebClient request = new WebClient();

            //We need to register the prefix to use the ClientHttp networking stack
            WebRequest.RegisterPrefix("http://", WebRequestCreator.ClientHttp);

            //Setting UserDefaultCredentials to false to prevent using credentials↵
from local machine's session
            request.UseDefaultCredentials = false;

            //setting credentials
            request.Credentials = new NetworkCredential(username, password);

            request.DownloadStringCompleted += new
                DownloadStringCompletedEventHandler(request_DownloadStringCompleted);

            request.DownloadStringAsync(new Uri(twitterUri));
        }

        void request_DownloadStringCompleted(object sender,↵
DownloadStringCompletedEventArgs e)
        {
            List<StatusUpdates> stcol = new List<StatusUpdates>();
            XDocument xdoc = XDocument.Parse(e.Result.ToString());
            stcol = (from status in xdoc.Descendants("status")
                             select new StatusUpdates
                             {
                                 Message  = status.Element("text").Value,
                                 User = status.Element("user")↵
.Element("screen_name").Value}).ToList();
                lstData.ItemsSource = stcol;
        }
```

```
        }
    }
```

Here, the `btnGetUpdates` button click event is the key. In this click event, we have registered the prefix `http://` to use `ClientHttp` network stack instead of using the `BrowserHttp` network stack. Also, we have set `UseDefaultCredentials` to `false` to prevent using credentials from local logged-in user credentials. Then you pass the entered user id and password as a header to the request. If authenticated, Twitter will return your account received messages as an XML file. You can retrieve and parse the returned XML file within the `DownloadedStringCompleted` event to retrieve the Message and User elements from each node.

Go ahead and run the project. You will notice that even if you provide the correct user name and password of your Twitter account in your in-browser application session, you will get a security error. What's the problem?

As you have learned in Chapter 5 and will learn in the next section of this chapter, actually you are making a cross-domain call to the publically available Twitter API to access your account and retrieve the messages upon authentication. So, everything depends on how Twitter has set up the cross-domain policy. If you visit `http://twitter.com/crossdomain.xml`, you will receive the XML file shown here.

```
<?xml version="1.0" encoding="UTF-8" ?>
<cross-domain-policy xmlns:xsi="http://www.w3.org/2001/XMLSchema-instance"
    xsi:noNamespaceSchemaLocation="http://www.adobe.com/xml/schemas/PolicyFile.xsd">
    <allow-access-from domain="twitter.com" />
    <allow-access-from domain="api.twitter.com" />
    <allow-access-from domain="search.twitter.com" />
    <allow-access-from domain="static.twitter.com" />
    <site-control permitted-cross-domain-policies="master-only" />
    <allow-http-request-headers-from domain="*.twitter.com" headers="*" secure="true" />
</cross-domain-policy>
```

It is apparent that Twitter's cross-domain policies are pretty strict. So, what can be done? If you revisit the "Elevated-Trusted Silverlight Applications vs. Partially Trusted Silverlight Applications" section of this chapter, you will notice that cross-domain access is relaxed for the elevated-trusted out-of-browser application in Silverlight 4. Go ahead and enable this application in out-of-browser mode with elevated trust (as described in the "Configuring Silverlight 4 Applications to Run with Elevated Trust" section of this chapter). Now run and install a Silverlight application in the out-of-browser mode. If you enter your Twitter user id and password and click the button to retrieve the received messages, you will see them populated in the list box, as shown in Figure 15-11.

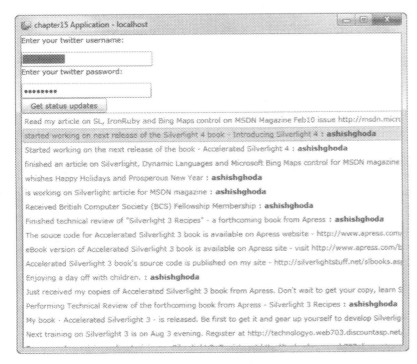

Figure 15-11. *Twitter public API integration using user-entered credentials through* `ClientHttpWebRequest`

Note that here you must run the application in the out-of-browser mode to successfully connect with the cross-domain Twitter API, due to Twitter's restricted cross-domain policy. Every publically available service does not have restricted cross-domain policies. With the relaxed cross-domain policy or trusted cross-domain services, you can apply the similar authentication approach within the in-browser mode.

Same-Domain and Cross-Domain Communication

It is critical to consider different security aspects as a part of your Silverlight application development and deployment strategy. RIAs and social networking are dynamic in nature and need to access different services and data across domains, which exposes you to possible computer security vulnerability such as *cross-site scripting* (XSS) and *cross-site request forgery* (CSRF or XSRF).

XSS is a type of vulnerability where, with the help of client-side scripting of web applications, hackers can gather sensitive user data by accessing stored cookies and session information.

CSRF exploits trusted web sites or services, where hackers can perform unauthorized actions to get data and information from trusted web sites and services by gaining unauthorized control on the logged-in user's web application session. The CSRF threat enables malicious access to web-based controls of the application and executing unauthorized commands to cross-domain applications and services.

Wikipedia explains it like this (`http://en.wikipedia.org/wiki/Cross-site_scripting`):

"Cross-site scripting exploits the trust a user has for a particular site" [whereas] "cross-site request forgery exploits the trust that a site has for a particular user..."

Note Get more information on XSS by visiting `http://en.wikipedia.org/wiki/Cross-site_scripting` and CSRF by visiting `http://en.wikipedia.org/wiki/Cross-site_request_forgery`.

To provide a secured environment that prevents CSRF threats, Silverlight supports same-domain and policy-based cross-domain networking to deploy Silverlight-based enterprise RIAs. Except for images and media, Silverlight allows only site-of-origin (i.e., within the same domain) communication to prevent cross-site request forgery vulnerabilities such as a malicious Silverlight control performing unauthorized actions to cross-domain applications and services. Here the term "same domain" covers the domain name, protocol, and port. As a result, the following scenarios are considered to be cross-domain deployment:

- Same protocol and domain name but different ports—for example, `http://www.technologyopinion.com` and `http://www.technologyopinion.com:81`

- Same domain name and port but different protocol—for example, `http://www.technologyopinion.com` and `https://www.technologyopinion.com`

- Same port and protocol but different domain names—for example, `http://www.technologyopinon.com` and `http://www.apress.com`

Application services must explicitly opt in, detailing the scope of the cross-domain service access by a Silverlight application from all or specific domains by publishing policy files.

Note Get more information on the cross-domain concept from the Microsoft MSDN site by visiting `http://msdn.microsoft.com/en-us/library/cc197955(VS.96).aspx`.

Silverlight enables cross-domain integration by providing two types of declaration policy methods:

- `crossdomain.xml` policy file

- `clientaccesspolicy.xml` policy file

We already discussed `crossdomain.xml` and `clientaccesspolicy.xml` policy files in detail in Chapter 5. I will not repeat the similar content detailing the formatting of these files in this chapter.

When a Silverlight application web client identifies the requirement to access the cross-domain service, it will first look at the existence of the `clientaccesspolicy.xml` file at the root of the deployed service. If it exists, it will authorize against the policy file and, upon successful authorization, can access and utilize the cross-domain deployed service. If the `clientaccesspolicy.xml` file does not exist at the root of the service's domain, next it will look for the `crossdomain.xml` file and authorize against it to gain access.

Division of Responsibility

You should use a secure communication channel with a server by using HTTPS, and enforce application-level access control (such as using the authentication and authorization services provided by ASP.NET 3.5 and 4). This doesn't fully ensure that your application is secure, however. There are several security-related concerns regarding your application's code getting downloaded to the client. These concerns all relate to the possibility that someone can get at the code and resources within a Silverlight application. They can be addressed by application architecture.

The XAP file is just a ZIP archive containing one or more DLL files and resource files. Assume someone wants to take a Silverlight application apart—all they need to do is obtain the XAP file (in the browser's cache or by other means), rename the file extension to zip, and open it in an application that can extract and create ZIP files. The XAP file from this chapter includes chapter15.dll and a manifest file. If you unzip this XAP, someone can now easily get at the DLL.

Once someone has a DLL expanded on disk, it can be disassembled in a utility such as Reflector. Figure 15-12 shows chapter15.dll taken apart in Reflector. It is possible to go a step further and decompile the code, as you can see in Figure 15-13, which shows a method from the LoginScreen class.

Figure 15-12. The methods and classes contained in chapter15.dll as revealed by Reflector

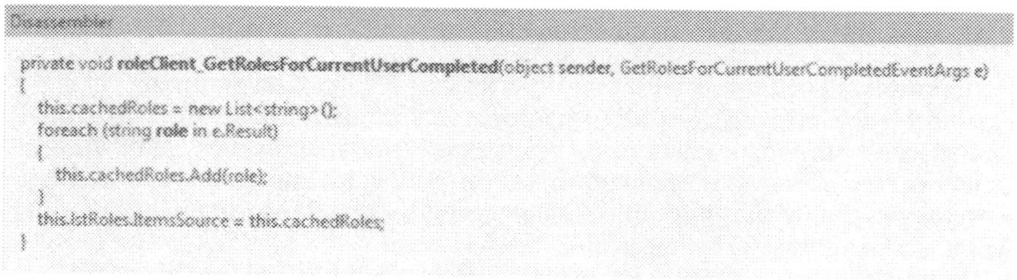

```
Disassembler

private void roleClient_GetRolesForCurrentUserCompleted(object sender, GetRolesForCurrentUserCompletedEventArgs e)
{
    this.cachedRoles = new List<string>();
    foreach (string role in e.Result)
    {
        this.cachedRoles.Add(role);
    }
    this.lstRoles.ItemsSource = this.cachedRoles;
}
```

Figure 15-13. The decompiled `GetRolesForCurrentUser` event callback

Of course, most users won't have the skill or knowledge to disassemble and decompile a Silverlight application, but an application built with security in mind must pay attention to the people who can. The best solution to the disassembling/decompiling of code is to use an obfuscator, such as Dotfuscator, which is distributed with Visual Studio. After running the DLL for this chapter through Dotfuscator, the identifiers are garbled, and the decompiled methods are a challenge to understand unless you're the CoreCLR. Figure 15-14 shows the obfuscated DLL in Reflector.

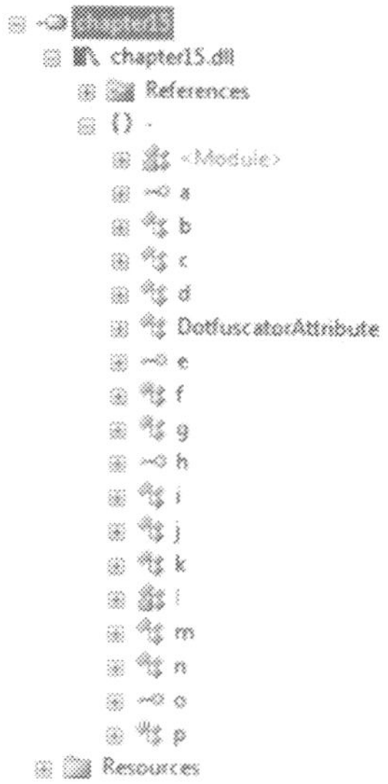

Figure 15-14. The obfuscated `chapter15.dll` file

The method to retrieve and cache roles, after obfuscation, looks like this:

```
private void a(object A_0, m A_1)
{
    this.c = new List<string>();
    foreach (string str in A_1.a())
    {
        this.c.Add(str);
    }
}
```

```
        this.k.ItemsSource = this.c;
}
```

As you can see, obfuscation is great at making it a challenge to understand the code. But make sure as much code related to the application is obfuscated as possible, since some revealed method names or variable names provide clues to what the code nearby is doing.

The simplest application design principle to follow is to place all privileged code on the server side and let the server perform an authentication check before the rest of the method executes. Role-based decisions made on the client side should not create a decision between executing normal-privileged code and high-privileged code. However, you can make role-based decisions on such benign things as the appearance of the user interface.

Another approach to separating different privilege levels of code is to place them behind a traditional web site–login screen for user authentication and then deliver a completely different Silverlight application to the user based on her access level. This is illustrated in Figure 15-15.

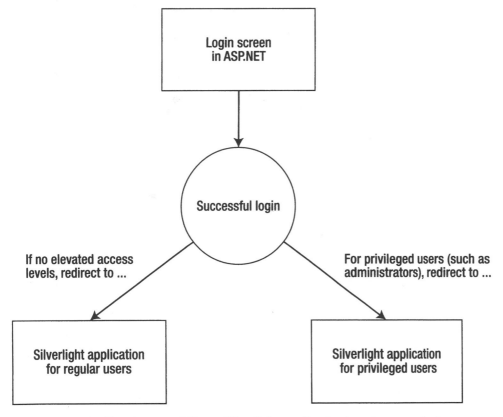

Figure 15-15. Redirecting to a different Silverlight application based on users' roles

If you take this approach, make sure any more highly privileged Silverlight applications are not cached on the client side. This makes it tougher to augment an application to grant a regular user higher privileges. Even if you take this approach, it's wise to place as much high-privilege code on the server side as possible so you can make sure only users with the right access level are allowed to run the code.

Another valid concern is the security of resources used by a Silverlight application. As shown in Figure 15-16, even though the main application assembly has been obfuscated, not only are resources such as the embedded XAML easily viewable, but they can also be easily extracted.

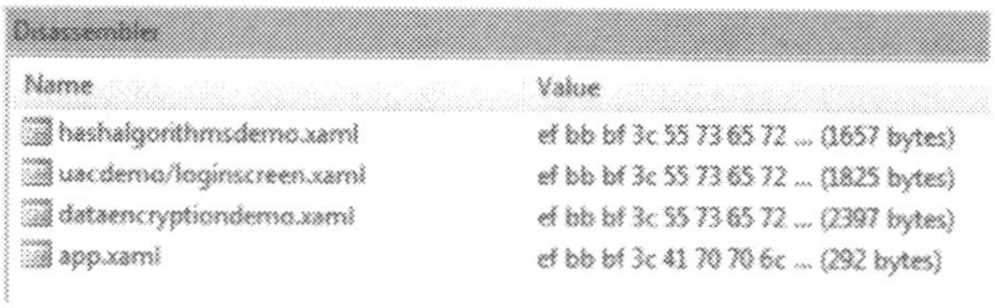

Figure 15-16. *The resources embedded in the application assembly*

One strategy to protect resources is to encrypt them. This is useful for any data files that you want downloaded at the same time as the Silverlight application. You can use the AesManaged class previously detailed with a secret key that is downloaded as part of the Silverlight application (perhaps an authenticated user's data protection password stored with his profile) to encrypt and decrypt data locally.

Another approach to protecting resources is to avoid packaging them with the Silverlight application. Once a user is authenticated, the application can download the appropriate resources on demand. This applies to both resources stored within the application's DLL and resources stored in the XAP file. Your application design must account for this anywhere a resource (such as an image) differs based on a user's access level.

Summary

Applications must be designed and developed with security in mind. This chapter started off by detailing the security model Silverlight provides for executable code, illustrating how partially trusted Silverlight application code cannot directly invoke any code that can interact with the host platform. We also looked at the new elevated-trusted out-of-browser application mode introduced in Silverlight 4, which relaxes the restrictions to access host platform resources, file systems, and services available cross-domain. The rest of this chapter detailed application-level security, such as using HTTPS as a secure channel, encrypting/decrypting information, authenticating and authorizing users, and ensuring your applications are designed well to protect code and resources. Make sure your Silverlight application and surrounding infrastructure (such as an ASP.NET application) are designed and developed with security in mind. Late in development or immediately before deployment are not the times to start thinking about security.

The next chapter is focused on the use of the Silverlight unit testing framework to implement the unit testing strategy during the Silverlight development project life cycle; it also explains key points for debugging Silverlight applications using Visual Studio.

PART 5

Testing and Deploying Silverlight RIAs

CHAPTER 16

Testing and Debugging

Testing and debugging are vital activities in building quality software. From a developer's perspective, unit testing ensures small units of code work. By having a suite of tests, it is easy to catch a bug introduced into code that was previously shown to be bug free. Testing helps ensure software quality by catching as many bugs as possible and proactively ensuring bugs aren't introduced. Debugging, however, is generally done after a bug has been found. Debugging involves tools and an effective problem-solving process to find the root cause of a bug in order to apply a fix. You can build defenses into your application to make debugging easier, such as error logs (to capture errors) and audit logs (to reconstruct what the user of the application did to trigger the bug). This chapter aims to show you how to go about testing Silverlight applications and preparing for and conducting debugging when things do go wrong.

Before I get into details, it is important for readers to know that at the time of writing, there are some known issues in the Silverlight Unit Test Framework. As mentioned on the Silverlight Toolkit site (http://silverlight.codeplex.com/) the April 2010 version of the Silverlight Unit Test Framework is in the Experimental Quality Band. Experimental components are intended for evaluation purposes. The main goal of experimental quality band components is to provide an opportunity for feedback during the earliest stages of development. However, I think it is critical to cover those pre-matured topics in the chapter from conceptual prospective (using an earlier version of the Silverlight toolkit). I am confident that future release of Silverlight Toolkit will resolve such issues and at that time this chapter will offer valuable guidelines to implement and perform unit test of your Silverlight-based applications.

Testing

Testing involves both ensuring applications are error free and verifying applications work according to requirements and design. It is the software developer's job to implement tests, known as *unit tests*, to thoroughly test the code he writes. *Integration testing*, usually the next step after unit testing, is where two or more unit-tested components are integrated together as a part of the larger system or composite component. *Regression testing* features thorough system testing of the software application, and needs to be repeated if a software defect is identified and fixed. Regression testing confirms/validates that the fixed defect does not introduce one or more new defects. Unit testing, integration testing, and regression testing are part of the development phase of the software development project life cycle.

Functional testing verifies the application corresponds to its specifications and requirements, and *usability testing* ensures the application is well designed from a user interface perspective. Unit testing, integration testing, and regression testing can be part of functional testing, usability testing, or both. Functional testing and usability testing generally belong to a quality assurance department.

Unit Testing

The goal of unit testing is to test the smallest possible unit of a system. If you're building an airplane, it's critical to test the smallest units of the airplane, such as verifying that each screw can withstand a certain degree of pressure, or that hoses that pump fluid or oxygen don't disconnect or wear out absurdly fast. These pieces require thorough testing, or the airplane likely won't work. However, the airplane manufacturer can't practically test the tiniest parts; the responsibility of testing lies with the manufacturer of these parts. The screw manufacturer must know how much pressure the screws can withstand and then verify they match the specification. These smallest parts are the units of a system, the building blocks that, when assembled, create something much larger. Just like the screw manufacturer must test his screws, the software developer must test his code at the smallest unit possible—typically methods.

Silverlight Unit Testing Framework

Microsoft provides a Silverlight unit testing framework very similar to the testing framework used by Visual Studio; however, the testing output is not by default integrated with Visual Studio. Microsoft Silverlight Unit Test Framework is part of the Infrastructure and Development tools of Silverlight Toolkit and it gets installed along with the Silverlight Toolkit (http://silverlight.codeplex.com/)

The unit testing framework contains the following two testing framework binaries:

- `Microsoft.Silverlight.Testing.dll`

- `Microsoft.VisualStudio.QualityTools.UnitTesting.Silverlight.dll`

There are two ways to perform unit tests:

- Performing in-browser unit test using Visual Studio 2010 unit test application.

- Running test from Visual Studio command prompt using MSBuild. In this way, you can even supply specific test name to include and exclude tests that are marked with the `Tag` attribute found in `Microsoft.Silverlight.Testing`.

Now let's look at the Silverlight unit testing framework in action and understand both options one by another.

In-browser Unit Testing from Visual Studio 2010

Once you install Silverlight unit test framework by installing Silverlight Toolkit, Visual Studio 2010 will contain a new project template: Silverlight Unit Test Application template, which helps to create a Silverlight unit test application project to perform in-browser unit testing. Create a new Silverlight Unit Test application project named chapter16, as shown in Figure 16-1.

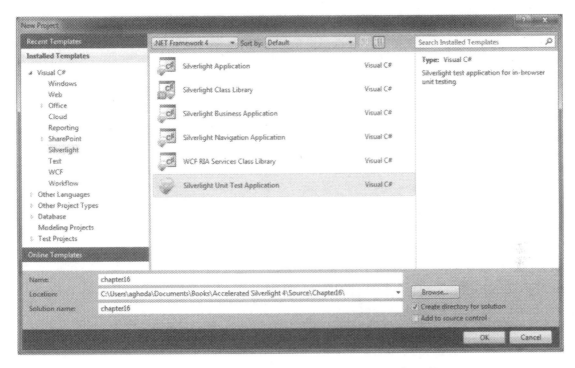

Figure 16-1. Creating Silverlight Unit Test Appliacation product in Visual Studio 2010

The testing framework provides its own user interface that you can connect to your Silverlight testing application by invoking UnitTestSystem.CreateTestPage, which you can see is getting invoked as application startup within App.xaml.cs of chapter16 unit test application project as shown in the following code:

```
private void Application_Startup(object sender, StartupEventArgs e)
{
    this.RootVisual = UnitTestSystem.CreateTestPage();
}
```

Now that you have the unit testing framework ready to go, the next step is to add a reference to the application assembly that is the subject of testing. The rest happens automatically after you apply certain test-related attributes to classes that contain tests. If you're writing a business application, user input typically must be validated to ensure it meets certain criteria. A validation class might be located in a class library assembly and used by any Silverlight applications developed by a company. In the example, you add a Silverlight Class Library project named ValidationLibrary to chapter16 solution. Add a new class named Validators with a single validation method that verifies a value is within a range to the ValidationLibrary project:

```
namespace ValidationLibrary
{
    public class Validators
    {
```

```
        public static bool validateRange
            (int value, int lowBound, int highBound)
        {
            return (value >= lowBound && value < highBound);
        }
    }
}
```

Even a method this simple may have a bug in it. Bugs aren't only due to poorly written code—bugs can also be due to incorrect assumptions or failure to match requirements. Or a bug can be due to a simple typo. In order to know for sure whether a piece of code contains bugs, a set of unit tests must be written. The Validators class is located in the ValidationLibrary assembly. You must add reference to the ValidationLibrary class library project to chapter16 unit test application project using the Add Reference dialog box.

Let's turn to the application that provides the unit testing framework and implement some tests. For that update a class Tests in chapter16 test application project and add the following using statements at the top to add reference to the ValidationLibrary class library:

```
using ValidationLibrary;
```

If you're unfamiliar with unit testing frameworks, they typically work by examining the metadata on classes and methods to get the necessary cues as to what to do. A class that contains test methods is decorated with the TestClass attribute, and individual test methods are decorated with TestMethod, as shown in the following.

```
namespace chapter16
{
    [TestClass]
    public class Tests : SilverlightTest
    {
        [TestMethod]
        public void TestRangeTooLow()
        {
            Assert.IsFalse(Validators.validateRange(0, 10, 20));
        }

        [TestMethod]
        public void TestRangeAtUpperBound()
        {
            Assert.IsTrue(Validators.validateRange(20, 10, 20));
        }
    }
}
```

Initially with the previous two tests, the TestRangeTooLow test will succeed and the TestRangeAtUpperBound will fail, which I will explain in details later in this section. The Assert class provides a number of methods to verify conditions to indicate test success. If the conditions are not met, an exception is thrown automatically and is caught by the unit testing framework, informing you of the test failure.

Now right-click the chapter16TestPage.html page under the chapter16.Web project and select the View Browser option or press ctrl + F5 to run the project without debugging mode. All tests will execute immediately. An `AssertFailedException` exception will be raised if the `TestRangeAtUpperBound` test fails. You will see the output shown in Figure 16-2. Note that, if you hit simply F5 to run the project in the debug mode, it will break on line with exception and again pressing F5 will show the final resultant failed test screen shown in Figure 16-2.

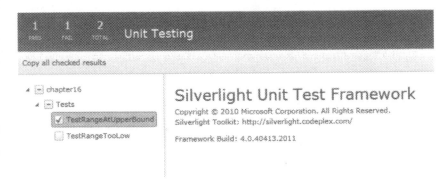

Figure 16-2. Unit testing framework output with a failing test

Now if you click the "Copy all checked results" link in the test output, you can see the failing results in details (as shown in Figure 16-3), which you can copy for further evaluation. You can also view this by clicking on the failing test treeview item in the left-hand side menu.

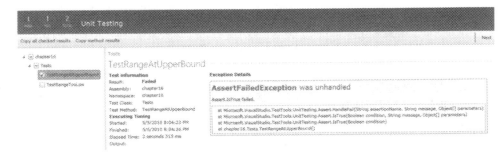

Figure 16-3. Detailed results on the failing test

The reason this test fails is that the requirements for the validator method specify that the lower and upper bounds must both be inclusive. This is easily fixed by changing the < to <= when testing the value against the upper bound. After making this fix, rerunning the testing application shows all tests succeeding, as shown in Figure 16-4.

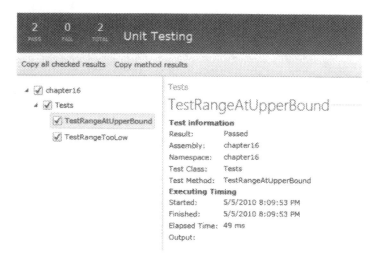

Figure 16-4. *Unit testing framework output with all tests passing*

Unit Testing from Visual Studio 2010 Command Prompt using MSBuild

---

Caution As mentioned on the Silverlight Toolkit site (`http://silverlight.codeplex.com/`), the April 2010 version of the Silverlight Unit Test Framework is in the Experimental Quality Band. Experimental components are intended for evaluation purposes. The main goal of these components is to provide an opportunity for feedback during the earliest stages of development. Unit testing from Visual Studio 2010 Command Prompt using MSBuild, feature is having issues with the April 2010 version.

As acknowledged by Jeff Wilcox on the reported issue (`http://silverlight.codeplex.com/WorkItem/View .aspx?WorkItemId=6054`), running unit test using MSBuild is a known issue with no workarounds for April 2010 release and expected to be fixed in the future builds.

However, it is important to describe this topic. I have used the November 2009 release of the Silverlight Toolkit for this section to explain this feature. Please read this section as a concept, and continue following the Silverlight Toolkit CodePlex site and Jeff Wicox blog to see updates made in the Silverlight Unit Test Framework to fix this known issue.

Performing unit tests from the Visual Studio command prompt enables automation of the tests. Through MSBuild, there is a task that can control the browser and save the log file from the unit tests when they run. Visit your chapter16 project folder and execute the following command to run the test from Visual Studio command prompt as shown here:

```
C:\book\code\chapter16\chapter16>MsBuild /t:test
```

Note that the folder structure might be different based on project set up in your machine. Upon running this command, a new browser window opens and quickly run tests, and then closes the browser. Afterwards, you will see that MSBuild reports success in Visual Studio command prompt (see Figure 16-5). As discussed in the beginning of this section, you will not get the mentioned results with April 2010 Silverlight Toolkit release.

Figure 16-5. MSBuild Reports Unit Test Success in Visual Studio 2010 Command Prompt

Here you run the test using the default browser (on my machine, Internet Explorer). If you want to run tests in specific browser such as Google Chrome or Mozilla Firefox, you pass the desired browser as a parameter to the command as shown in the following code.

For Google Chrome:

```
msbuild /t:test /p:browser=chrome
```

For Mozilla Firefox:

```
msbuild /t:test /p:browser=firefox
```

Using Tag Expressions

Tag Expressions help select a subset of tests by using `tagexpression` switch in the syntax. By specifying a tag expression at the command prompt, you can include and exclude tests that are marked with the `Tag` attribute found in `Microsoft.Silverlight.Testing`. You can use a method name directly if you have not set any Tag attribute for the method. In this case; if you want to run only one test `TestRangeTooLow`, the syntax will look like the following:

```
msbuild /t:test /p:tagexpression=TestRangeTooLow
```

And if you want to run all tests except `TestRangeTooLow`, use the following expression.

```
msbuild /t:test /p:tagexpression=!TestRangeTooLow
```

Test Result Files

Running the tests through MSBuild creates test result files (*.trx) inside the same folder as the test page for the application. In your case the folder is Bin\Debug. If you navigate to this folder, you will see TestResults.trx, TestResults2.trx etc. This file format is similar to the Visual Studio *.trx format but at the time of writing this book, Visual Studio 2010 does not open this file. However, you can open this file in Visual Studio 2008 instead. This test file provides information about test execution times, results with other information related to the test. Please download the code from Apress site to look at the trx file as a sample.

Code Coverage and Instrumentation

Code coverage is a measurement used in software testing that describes the degree to which the source code of a program has been tested. The prime intention of the tests are to verify that your code does what it's expected to, but that it also documents what the code is expected to do. Code coverage can be thought of as an indirect measure of quality because we're talking about the degree to which tests cover the code. Keep in mind that only code coverage test should not be thought as verifying the end product's quality.

All flavors of Visual Studio 2010 product does not support Silverlight code coverage testing. If you have Visual Studio 2010 Ultimate or Premium installed, you are all set for Silverlight code coverage test. For more details on and feature comparison matrix of different products of Visual Studio 2010, visit the Microsoft Visual Studio page at www.microsoft.com/visualstudio/en-us/products.

Code coverage in Silverlight requires static analysis tools located in C:\Program Files (x86)\Microsoft Visual Studio 10.0\Team Tools\Static Analysis Tools on 64bit OS or at C:\Program Files\Microsoft Visual Studio 10.0\Team Tools\Static Analysis Tools in the case of 32bit OS.

To prepare the chapter16 unit test project for code coverage, you need to edit chapter16.csproj file. The safe way to do this is to right-click the chapter16 project in Solution explorer and choose unload project. After project gets unload, right-click the chapter16 project and choose Edit chapter16.csproj. This will open the project file as XML document. Now look for the following lines and uncomment the ItemGroup that enables instrumenting Silverlight assembly by changing the Include property of the InstrumentSilverlightAssemblies from SilverlightClassLibrary1 (default value) to ValidationLibrary (see highlighted text).

```
<!--
  //
  // Silverlight Code Coverage Instrumentation
  // List any libraries or assemblies that you would like
  //to instrument during
  // a code coverage pass. An example, for ClassLibrary1, is provided,
  // and commented out below as a starting point:
  //
-->
<ItemGroup>
    <InstrumentSilverlightAssemblies Include="ValidationLibrary">
        <Visible>false</Visible>
    </InstrumentSilverlightAssemblies>
</ItemGroup>
...
```

Note that in the preceding code, in InstrumentSilverlightAssemblies tag, Include is set to the ValidationLibrary assembly for instrumentation. Now save the file and reload the project. Run the following command to collect the code coverage.

```
C:\book\code\chapter16\chapter16>MsBuild /t:coveragetest
```

If all went well, you will see the Instrumentation messages; CoverageInstrument, RunTests and MergeCoverageData appear and finally the Build succeeded message. You will also see the in between, default browser window opens up quickly and closes showing some flick of test currently running.

Once the test coverage successfully completed, you can run the view target as well. The coverageview command will rerun all the tests and instrument again as well. Now, if you run the following command, you'll see the viewer popup, that lets you drill down into types and methods to see what's covered in test and what's not covered.

```
C:\book\code\chapter16\chapter16>MsBuild /t:coverageview
```

Figure 16-6 shows the Silverlight code coverage window.

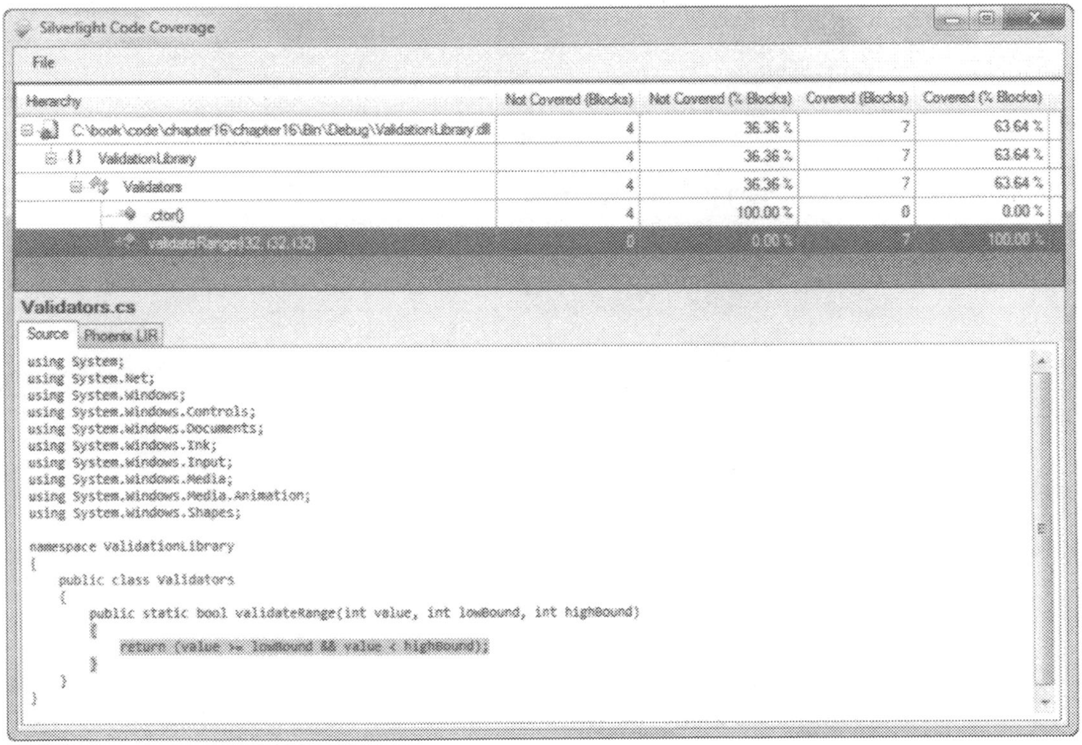

Figure 16-6. Silverlight Code Coverage Viewer

The Silverlight code coverage viewer shows the code coverage in percentage. In this case, it is 63.64% for ValidationLibrary class library. The test coverage data that this viewer application shows can be found in the same directory where the test results go (in your case it is

C:\book\code\chapter16\chapter16\Bin\Debug) and it is named Coverage.xml. If you open this file in Visual Studio, you will see a set of visited blocks and other information in the file.

Note With Visual Studio 2010 and April 2010 version of Silverlight Toolkit, the test results coverage file name is based on the class library. The naming convention is <ClassLibraryName>.Coverage.xml. In this case, it will be ValidationLibrary.Coverage.xml.

Assert Class

The Assert class provides a number of useful methods for conveniently verifying test results, and also provides a way to trigger a failure in case the provided methods are not sufficient. Table 16-1 lists the static methods provided by the Assert class. Note that many methods provide a large set of overloads in order to cover a wide variety of data types. These assertion methods also give the ability to pass in a string parameter as a custom message that will be included in the test execution report.

Table 16-1. Static Methods of the Microsoft.VisualStudio.TestTools.UnitTesting.Assert Class

Method	Description
AreEqual	Tests whether two values are equal.
AreNotEqual	Tests whether two values are not equal.
AreNotSame	Tests whether two object references point to different objects.
AreSame	Tests whether two object references point to the same object.
Fail	Causes a test to immediately fail. Use this to fail a test based on custom logic.
Inconclusive	Causes a test to report "inconclusive" in the report. Use this for tests not implemented or for tests where it's impossible to pass or fail the test.
IsFalse	Tests whether the specified Boolean value is false.
IsInstanceOfType	Tests whether an object is an instance of a given type.
IsNotInstanceOfType	Tests whether an object is not an instance of a given type.
IsNotNull	Tests whether a given reference is not null.
IsNull	Tests whether a given reference is null.
IsTrue	Tests whether the specified Boolean value is true.
ReplaceNullChars	Utility method to replace null characters within a string with \0 so that the null characters can be displayed.

The `Assert` class can throw an `AssertFailedException` or an `AssertInconclusiveException` in the case of Assert.Inconclusive method. It is recommended not to catch these exceptions by your code since they provide the mechanism for communicating test results to the unit testing framework. There are two other `Assert`-related classes: `StringAssert` and `CollectionAssert`. `StringAssert` provides a set of methods useful for string-based conditional tests, and `CollectionAssert` does likewise for collections. Table 16-2 lists the methods of `StringAssert`, and Table 16-3 shows the methods of `CollectionAssert`.

Table 16-2. Static Methods of the Microsoft.VisualStudio.TestTools.UnitTesting.StringAssert Class

Method	Description
Contains	Tests whether one string occurs somewhere within another string
DoesNotMatch	Tests whether two strings do not match
EndsWith	Tests whether one string ends with another string
Matches	Tests whether two strings match
StartsWith	Tests whether one string starts with another string

Table 16-3. Static Methods of the Microsoft.VisualStudio.TestTools.UnitTesting.CollectionAssert Class

Method	Description
AllItemsAreInstancesOfType	Tests whether all items in a collection are instances of a specific type
AllItemsAreNotNull	Tests whether all items in a collection are not null
AllItemsAreUnique	Tests whether all items in a collection are different
AreEqual	Tests whether two collections contain the same items (object values are tested, not references) in the same order
AreEquivalent	Similar to AreEqual, but the items can be in any order as long as two collections contain the same items
AreNotEqual	Tests whether two collections contain a different number of items, a different set of items, or the same items in different orders
AreNotEquivalent	Tests whether two collections contain a different number of items or a different set of items
Contains	Tests whether a collection contains a specified item
DoesNotContain	Tests whether a collection does not contain a specified item

IsNotSubsetOf	Tests whether one collection does not contain a subset of items from another collection
IsSubsetOf	Tests whether one collection contains a subset of items from another collection

Besides TestClass and TestMethod, there are many useful attributes for controlling how tests behave. Table 16-4 lists attributes that are useful for the initialization and cleanup of resources. All attributes shown in Table 16-4 apply to methods.

Table 16-4. *Testing Framework Attributes Related to Resource Initialization and Cleanup*

Attribute	Description
AssemblyCleanup	Marks the method that executes after all tests within the assembly have completed executing; can only be used on one method within an assembly.
AssemblyInitialize	Marks the method that executes before any tests within the assembly have executed; can only be used on one method within an assembly.
ClassCleanup	Marks the method that contains the code to execute after all tests within a class containing tests have completed executing; can only apply to a single method within a class.
ClassInitialize	Marks the method that contains the code to execute before any tests within a class execute; can only apply to a single method within a class.
TestCleanup	Marks the method that contains the code to execute after each test completes executing; can only apply to a single method within a class.
TestInitialize	Marks the method that contains the code to execute before each test executes; can only apply to a single method within a class.

Note that both TestInitialize and TestCleanup execute once per test, ClassInitialize and ClassCleanup execute once per testing class, and AssemblyInitialize and AssemblyCleanup execute once per testing assembly. These attributes provide for a variety of resource management in a test class.

There are several other useful attributes you might encounter a need for when writing your unit tests. These are shown in Table 16-5.

Table 16-5. *Testing Framework Attributes*

Attribute	Description
Description	Describes the test to give more contexts when viewing the test results.
ExpectedException	Normally, exceptions indicate the code under test has failed. When a thrown exception indicates success (such as verifying certain methods aren't implemented yet on purpose), this attribute tells the testing framework that the specific exception is expected and avoids failing the test. You can specify this attribute multiple times.
Ignore	Indicates the test should be skipped.
Owner	Provides information on who is responsible for the test. Note that in the April 2010 version it is not visible in the test output.
Priority	Specifies the integer priority of the test. Note that in the April 2010 version, it seems this property is not working as expected.
Timeout	Specifies a timeout in milliseconds for a test. If an operation takes longer than the timeout value specified, the test fails.

It is also important to perform the user interface-driven test. It would be nice if it were possible to test an application's user interface from an outsider's perspective, and automate this if possible. Fortunately, Silverlight provides for this automation.

Automated User Interface Testing

Testing must be automated. Software is too complex to reliably test well manually on a consistent basis. Test automation carries over to user interfaces. Manually testing user interfaces is boring, tedious, and highly unreliable since test cases may be skipped or the order of operations for tests violated. Optimally, you want user interface testing to happen automatically, instead of a tester having to manually click every button and explore every screen. Another reason for automated user interface testing is the ability to easily capture test results. Fortunately, Silverlight does indeed provide automation capabilities in the form of a framework for programmatically controlling user interfaces. The main supporting infrastructure for user interface automation is a set of automation peer classes that closely mirror user interface classes in Silverlight.

The UI Automation Library (System.Windows.Automation) that works for other types of Windows applications can also be used to work with Silverlight applications. Before you can use the automation classes to interact with user interface elements, you must obtain an AutomationElement that serves as a parent element. You can then search for controls that are descendents of the parent. You could use the desktop as the parent, but this would make it slow when searching for controls and can cause stack overflow. Instead, you want to get as close to your Silverlight application as possible.

The Microsoft .NET Framework class library also includes the System.Diagnostics namespace, which mainly provides a set of classes to perform interaction with system processes, event logs, and performance counters.

UI Spy Tool

For user interface testing, there is the UI Spy (UISpy.exe) tool to install with Microsoft Windows SDK. The UI Spy tool enables developers and testers to view and interact with the user interface (UI) elements of an application. By viewing the application's UI hierarchical structure, property values, and raised events, developers and testers can verify that the UI they are creating is programmatically accessible to assistive technology devices.

If you have Microsoft Windows SDK installed, which you can get by visiting http://msdn.microsoft.com/en-us/windows/bb980924.aspx, you can locate this tool at Start\All Programs\Microsoft Windows SDK v6.0A\Tools\UISpy. If you do not have this installed, you can find UISpy.exe in this chapter's code in UISpy.zip file. If you are curious to know more about UISpy tool, visit Microsoft MSDN site at http://msdn.microsoft.com/en-us/library/ms727247.aspx. You can also get details on Microsoft Windows SDK by visiting the Microsoft Windows SDK official blog at http://blogs.msdn.com/windowssdk/.

Since we don't have a UI for Chapter 16, we are going to be using the Chapter 15 code to test this. Figure 16-7 shows the main UI Spy window. Note that in Control View, it shows "window" titled "chapter15 – Windows Internet Explorer". This is chapter15's sample html test page running in IE 8. From now on, you will develop test methods for automated UI testing by keeping this chapter15 test page in context.

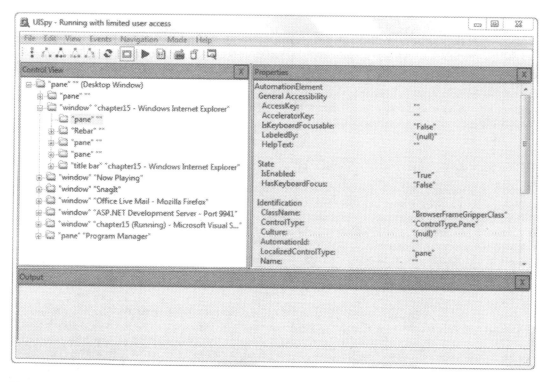

Figure 16-7. Main UI Spy Tool window

Implementing UI Automation Testing

Let's create a C# project of type Test Project in Visual Studio. Note that this is a normal Test Project you will find within the Test tab on Create New project window for Visual Studio 2010 and not Silverlight Unit Test Application project.

To enable UI automation for the clients, you need to add reference to following three UI Automation dlls.

- `UIAutomationClient.dl`: Provides access to the UI Automation client-side APIs.

- `UIAutomationClientSideProviders.dll`: Provides the ability to automate Win32 controls.

- `UIAutomationTypes.dll`: Provides access to the specific types defined in UI Automation.

On Windows 7 x64, the previously mentioned dlls are located at `Program Files (x86)\Reference Assemblies\Microsoft\Framework\.NETFramework\v4.0` and on 32 bit OS, located at Program Files\Reference Assemblies\Microsoft\Framework\.NETFramework\v4.0.

As mentioned earlier, after adding reference to these dlls, you need to add following namespaces.

```
using System.Windows.Automation;
using System.Windows.Automation.Text;
using System.Diagnostics;
```

Once you include references to the UI Automation Library and diagnostics library, you can use the following code to search the currently running processes for a specific window title:

```
Process process = null;
foreach (Process p in Process.GetProcessesByName("iexplore"))
{
    if (p.MainWindowTitle.Contains("(chapter15 - Windows Internet Explorer)"))
    {
        process = p;
        break;
    }
}

if (process != null)
{
    AutomationElement browserInstance =
        System.Windows.Automation.AutomationElement.
          FromHandle(process.MainWindowHandle);
}
```

Once you have an `AutomationElement` that represents a parent to your Silverlight application, you can then search for certain controls of interest. When searching the tree of user interface elements beneath a given `AutomationElement`, you need to define the scope of the search and a condition used to specify what specific elements you want to find. The `AutomationElement` class provides two methods, `FindFirst` and `FindAll`, for finding one or more elements that match the given criteria. The first parameter to these methods is the TreeScope. Table 16-6 shows the different TreeScope values you can use.

Table 16-6. Enumeration Values from System.Windows.Automation.TreeScope

Enumeration Value	Description
Element	Search only within the element
Children	Search within the element and its children
Descendents	Search within the element and all its descendents (its children, its children's children, etc.)
Parent	Search includes the element's descendants (its children, its children's children, etc.)
Descendents	Search includes the element's descendants (its children, its children's children, etc.)
Subtree	Search within the root of the search and all descendents

The second parameter to these methods is the condition. A *condition* is essentially a search criterion. The Condition class itself provides two shortcuts for making searching easy: Condition.TrueCondition and Condition.FalseCondition. By combining the first with a search scope, you can obtain all elements within the scope. The latter will return no elements. By combining one of these with one of the Condition class' four inheritors, you can create sophisticated search criteria.

The AndCondition, OrCondition, and NotCondition classes can be continually nested to support as complicated a search condition as you need.

The other inheritor, PropertyCondition, is used to find elements with certain properties set to certain values. You can use PropertyCondition to search for a value of any of the properties from AutomationElement, such as ClassNameProperty, NameProperty, AcceleratorKeyProperty, and many others.

Revisiting the preceding browserInstance, which now holds a reference to the Internet Explorer (IE) instance that hosts chapter15's Silverlight application, you can search for a specific XAML page control with the name "Silverlight Control" within the application using the FindFirst method, as shown in the following code:

```
//get reference to Silverlight control
AutomationElement uiScreen = browserInstance.FindFirst
    (TreeScope.Descendants, new PropertyCondition
        (AutomationElement.NameProperty, "Silverlight Control"));
//now get reference to the pane named ""
//For this expand UISpy tree of this item
AutomationElement slpan = uiScreen.FindFirst(TreeScope.Descendants,
    new PropertyCondition(AutomationElement.NameProperty, ""));
```

You might wonder how I knew the name of Silverlight control contained in the IE tab? As you can see in Figure 16-8, within the UI Spy tool I have expanded the "pane" "chapter15 – Windows Internet Explorer" control tree and selected the "window" "Silverlight Control" which showing currently loaded page (it is Hash Algorithms example page) in ExampleBrowser root visual page.

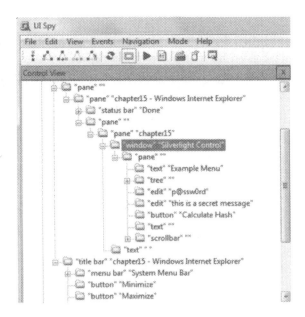

Figure 16-8. UI Spy showing control tree of chapter15 test page

As there can be a lot of items under chapter15 – Windows Internet Explorer, it is better to you get detailed understanding on how to use UI Spy with different modes to locate the desired control in control tree. Visit http://msdn.microsoft.com/en-us/library/ms727247.aspx#UI_Spy_Modes to get more details.

Now you can find the collection of TextBox-type controls available within the "Silverlight Control" XAML page control by utilizing the uiScreen AutomationElement returned in the previous example and the FindAll method shown in the following code snippet. Here you use ControlType.Edit to represent the TextBox control.

```
//get reference to all TextBoxes withing the slpan
AutomationElementCollection uiScreenTextBoxes = slpan.FindAll
    (TreeScope.Children, new PropertyCondition
        (AutomationElement.ControlTypeProperty, ControlType.Edit));
```

Now you will get reference to the only button Calculate Hash using the following code. Here use ControlType.Button to represent the Button control.

```
//get reference to button withing the slpan
AutomationElement uiButton = slpan.FindFirst
    (TreeScope.Children, new PropertyCondition
        (AutomationElement.ControlTypeProperty, ControlType.Button ));
```

Note There are various ways of obtaining AutomationElement objects for user interface (UI) elements. To know more, visit this Microsoft MSDN link: http://msdn.microsoft.com/en-us/library/ms752331.aspx.

The `AutomationProperties` class provides several useful attached properties you can use to provide cues for the automation system while leaving the rest of your object's properties intact. These attached properties are shown in Table 16-7. When developing an application, you can use the `AutomationId` property to uniquely identify elements throughout your application specifically for use by automation clients.

Table 16-7. Attached Properties in AutomationProperties

Name	Type	Description
AcceleratorKey	string	The accelerator key for the element.
AccessKey	string	The access key for the element.
AutomationId	string	A unique identifier for the element; useful as a cue for automation clients in searches.
HelpText	string	Help text for the element; generally the associated tool tip text.
IsColumnHeader	bool	true if the element is a column header (such as in a DataGrid).
IsRequiredForForm	bool	true if the element must be filled out for a given form.
IsRowHeader	bool	true if the element is a row header (such as in a DataGrid).
ItemStatus	string	Indicates the status of the item; generally application specific.
ItemType	string	Describes the type of the element.
LabeledBy	UIElement	Specifies which UIElement acts as a label for this element.
Name	string	The element's name.

As an example, the attached AutomationId for Button control can be set the following way:

```
<Button AutomationProperties.AutomationId="myButton" />
```

Once you have a reference to the element of the Silverlight application, you can use other aspects of the UI Automation Library to simulate keyboard and mouse input for the application under test. So now let's simulate entering values into the textboxes and then simulate clicking the Calculate Hash button, as shown in following code.

```
//perform steps to automate UI testing such as setting text box value
foreach (AutomationElement item in uiScreenTextBoxes)
{
    object valuePattern = null;
        if (item.TryGetCurrentPattern(ValuePattern.Pattern, out valuePattern))
        {
            ((ValuePattern)valuePattern).SetValue("TestValue");
        }
}
//perform steps to automate UI testing such as
//simulating mouse click, keyboard strokes..
object invokePattern = null;
if (uiButton.TryGetCurrentPattern(InvokePattern.Pattern, out invokePattern))
{
    // This event will be invoked ("btnCalcHash_Click");
    ((InvokePattern)invokePattern).Invoke();
}
```

Debugging

The debugging process should not begin when a bug is discovered. Instead, it should start during application design. You should include logging functionality in your application, such as error logs and audit logs. An error log is useful for tracking exceptions thrown by an application. Exceptions also come with stack traces that help in identifying the code path that lead to the exception. Audit logs can be used to reconstruct what users were doing within the application leading up to an error. These are important elements that must go into application design and development, but there are also other approaches you can use to make code easier to debug, such as including extra logging or other features in special debug mode builds of an application. Any time you go about debugging, however, you must take a structured approach to hunting bugs down.

The Debugging Process

Debugging may or may not be your favorite activity when developing software, but the same general frame of mind you use for developing code can be applied to debugging. Debugging is just another form of problem solving. Having a plan of attack to discover the source of a bug is invaluable. Here are the steps you should follow when you know of a bug and need to go about fixing it:

1. *Get to know the system*: If you're unfamiliar with the system you're fixing, you should get enough familiarity to do as good a job as possible at fixing the bug without introducing new bugs. Knowing how the system works, what components it uses, and what technologies are involved (e.g., IIS, ASP.NET, Windows Workflow Foundation) can also possibly give you more clues to narrowing down the bug.

2. *Reproduce the bug*: You must know what you're fixing in order to fix it. Sometimes you're lucky enough to have a consistent reproduction; sometimes you aren't. The goal here is to have the smallest piece of code or the shortest sequence of actions that reveals the bug.

3. *Make a guess:* Sometimes by making a guess you can identify the bug right away. This isn't always possible, but when it works, you appear to have special powers. Raymond Chen calls this "psychic debugging." It's really just a matter of having enough experience to know the source of a bug based on symptoms. If you can't solve the bug immediately, sometimes a guess will at least get you closer to the source of it in the code.

4. *Gather evidence:* Solving a bug isn't the most difficult activity as long as you have a solid plan. Part of this plan is to analyze the evidence at your disposal—usually bug reports, error/audit logs, analysis tools such as file/registry activity monitors, and so on.

5. *Conduct heavy debugging:* If you haven't discovered the source of the bug yet, then now is likely the time to step through code in a debugger. This can be a slow process, depending on how close you can get to the bug, but it will typically give you a clear view of the system at a line-by-line level.

6. *Identify the solution:* By now you've found the source of the bug. Sometimes a bug fix is straightforward; other times you must be careful not to affect other parts of the system. A strong set of unit tests is invaluable at this point. If you fix the bug but introduce a new bug, or reintroduce an old bug (a regression), the unit tests can identify this and you can revisit your solution.

7. *Apply the fix:* You've identified the solution, implemented it, and verified it hasn't broken any existing tests. After applying the fix, you may have to update unit tests or add new unit tests. Accordingly, you will probably perform integration testing and regression testing as part of your functional and usability testing to confirm that there is no adverse effect on the applied fix.

Let's take a closer look at some tools and techniques that can save you time when you are debugging Silverlight applications.

Conditional Compilation

Much like .NET assemblies, Silverlight assemblies can be compiled in a debug mode configuration or a release mode configuration. The main differences between debug and release mode are which conditional symbols are defined and whether symbols are generated along with the assembly. For debug mode, the preprocessor symbol DEBUG and TRACE are automatically defined, and for release mode, TRACE is defined.

Sometimes implementing code only for purposes of debugging can be extremely useful. For example, an application might write a significant amount of information to a log file for debugging only. This code can't run in production applications due to performance reasons, and optimally we want to get rid of this code completely. This can be achieved with conditional compilation. The best approach to conditional compilation is to use #if...#endif to isolate blocks of code that must only appear in certain configurations. Generally, these are used to only put debug code in debug builds—for example, writing to a debug trace log.

```
private void login()
{
#if DEBUG
    traceLog.WriteLine("entered login method");
```

```
#endif
    authService.Login(usernameTB.Text, passwordTB.Text, null, null);
#if DEBUG
    traceLog.WriteLine("leaving login method");
#endif
}
```

The DEBUG symbol is automatically defined for debug mode configurations, and TRACE is automatically defined for release mode configurations. There is one other approach to conditional compilation that is used to limit the type of code that can call a particular method. This is accomplished using the Conditional attribute on a method, as shown here:

```
[Conditional("DEBUG")]
public void debugWriteLine(string message)
{
    debugLog.WriteLine(message);
}
```

A method like this can be extremely useful when providing a public API to a class library that can perform debugging. Any time client code defines the symbol applied to the method via the Conditional attribute, the code is output with the compiled IL but the code with DEBUG attribute is applicable in the debug mode only. This means a client can use the following code with the knowledge the debug writes will only happen when their code is in a debug mode configuration.

```
public void doSomething()
{
    library.debugWriteLine("calling doLongOperation");
    library.doLongOperation();
    library.debugWriteLine("doLongOperation finished");
}
```

When you use the Conditional attribute, the method it applies to is always compiled and included in the finished assembly. This is an important difference between the Conditional attribute and preprocessor symbol testing via the #if command. If you're using Conditional to control code within the same assembly (such as making decisions based on symbols other than DEBUG/TRACE), you can prevent the body of the method from being included in the compilation by combining Conditional with #if:

```
[Conditional("DEBUG")]
public void debugWriteLine(string message)
{
#if DEBUG
    debugLog.WriteLine(message);
#endif
}
```

Debugging Silverlight Applications with Visual Studio

The Visual Studio debugger is an invaluable tool for tracing through code. You need to install Silverlight 4 Tools for Visual Studio 2010 (which you did in Chapter 1 while enabling Silverlight applications development) to enable Silverlight application debugging with Visual Studio.

There's little difference between debugging .NET code on traditional Windows applications and debugging a Silverlight application. The important differences are that the Silverlight plug-in is hosted within a browser (which acts as the host process you debug) and the code on the Silverlight platform runs on the CoreCLR, a runtime completely separate from any other instance of the CLR you have on your system. Silverlight Tools does not support edit-and-continue, just-in-time, or mixed-mode debugging.

Controlling the Debugger

The System.Attribute is a base class for custom attributes including attributes for the System.Diagnostics namespace. Application diagnostic attributes provide cues (such as preventing stepping into certain methods) and more information to the debugger. These attributes are shown in Table 16-8.

Table 16-8. Debug Attributes in System.Diagnostics

Attribute	Description
DebuggableAttribute	Used to provide configuration-related cues to the JIT compiler and debugger, such as disabling optimizations. This is the only class that may affect the compilation process. The others are simply helper classes for debuggers and don't affect the code that is generated.
DebuggerBrowsableAttribute	Controls the display of a member within the debugger. Valid values are Collapsed, Never (member is never shown), and RootHidden (useful for collections; shows individual items without showing the root).
DebuggerDisplayAttribute	Specifies what should be shown in the value column in the debugger for the member this decorates.
DebuggerHiddenAttribute	Used to hide the member from the debugger.
DebuggerNonUserCodeAttribute	Indicates that a type/member is not part of the user code and should be hidden from the debugger, not stepped into. This is effectively a combination of DebuggerHiddenAttribute and DebuggerStepThroughAttribute.
DebuggerStepThroughAttribute	When applied to a method, the debugger steps through the method without stopping in a method; however, it does allow a break point (if set) in the method.

If you have long (or long-running) methods that you don't want to consciously step over in the debugger, using the DebuggerStepThroughAttribute attribute can save significant time. It is used to avoid stepping through code since it prevents the method from being stepped into. Here's an example usage to mark a validation function that is called often. Make sure you use it in a situation like this when you're sure the method isn't the source of any bugs.

```
[DebuggerStepThrough]
private bool validateIpAddress(string ipAddress)
{
    // parse ipAddress and validate that it's a correct IPv4 address
}
```

The `System.Diagnostics.Debug` class provides two useful static methods: `WriteLine`, for sending information to the debugger output, and `Assert`, for testing assumptions. The `WriteLine` method uses the Windows `OutputDebugString` under the covers, so unfortunately this only works when the debugger is on Windows. There are no debug listeners/trace listeners in Silverlight as there are in .NET on Windows, so the `Debug.WriteLine` method is all there really is to writing debug output. Since `OutputDebugString` is used at its core, you can attach a debugger and see the output in the Output window (in Visual Studio) or through another debug viewer.

The other method, `Assert`, is used to test certain assumptions in your code. The `Assert` method (and its overloads) takes a Boolean parameter as a condition to test. When the condition is `false`, you see either a dialog box when running in release mode or the debugger.

Configuring Startup for Debugging

When you're developing a Silverlight application, you can debug the application either by using the development web server or another web server such as IIS or Apache. By including a web site or a web application in your solution when you create a Silverlight project, you can point IIS (or Apache) to this and debug a Silverlight application similar to how it will be deployed on a real server. This can help ensure your configuration is correct on the server side, which will mainly consist of ensuring the web server can serve XAP files and possibly PDB files for debugging purposes. Figure 16-9 shows configuring the web project to start up using an external server. Note that if you are using a development server or IIS, you can separate the base URL from specific pages to make it easier to change from one startup page to the next (such as with the switching of the startup to the second Silverlight application in this chapter).

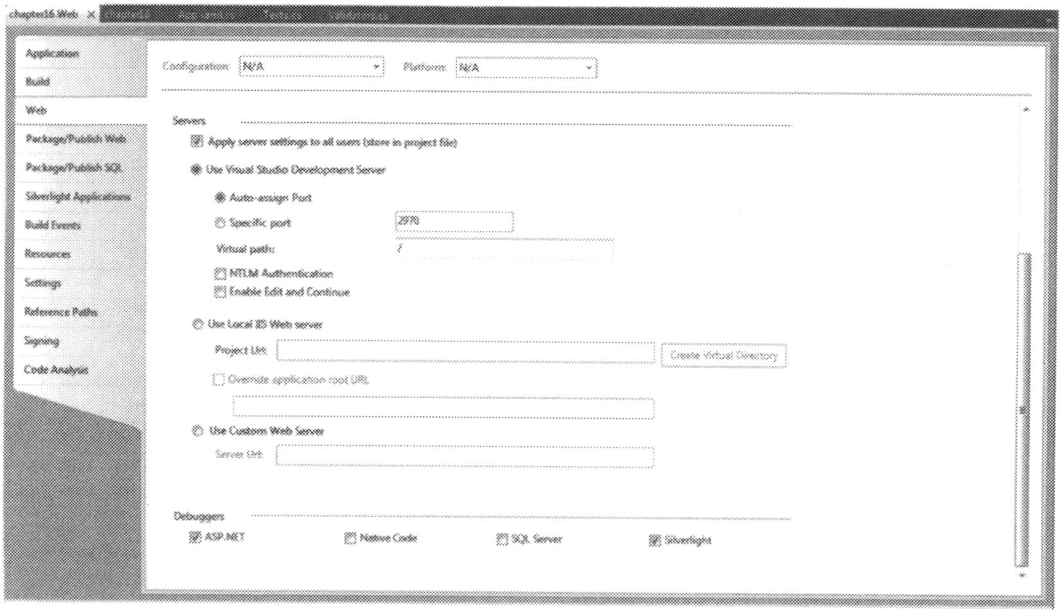

Figure 16-9. Web site startup properties

If you create a Silverlight application with no accompanying web site/web application, you can still debug a Silverlight application from Visual Studio. You can accomplish this by going to the property pages for the Silverlight application itself and ensuring "Dynamically generate a test page" is set (or set to a specific page). This page, and the Silverlight application, will then be hosted in the development web server, and you can debug your application. You can see this property page in Figure 16-10.

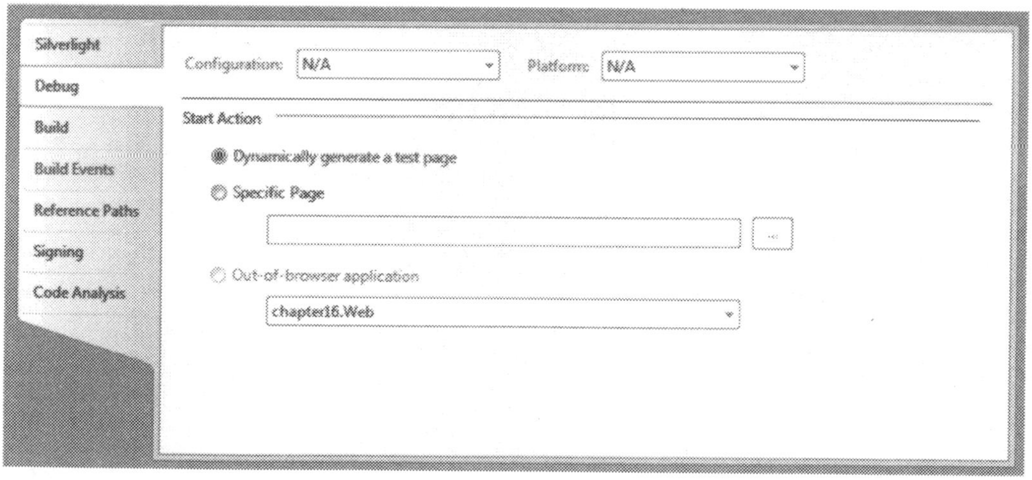

Figure 16-10. Silverlight application startup properties

Once you have your startup properly configured, you can set break points and debug your Silverlight application like any other. If you already have a browser running your Silverlight application outside of Visual Studio, you can attach the debugger to the host process. You can accomplish this by going to the Debug menu in Visual Studio and choosing "Attach to process." If you're debugging ASP.NET, you attach the debugger to the ASP.NET worker process (the browser). Similarly, you attach the Visual Studio debugger to the process that hosts the Silverlight plug-in: the browser. On the Attach to Process dialog (shown in Figure 16-11), you can click Select to limit the type of code the debugger focuses on.

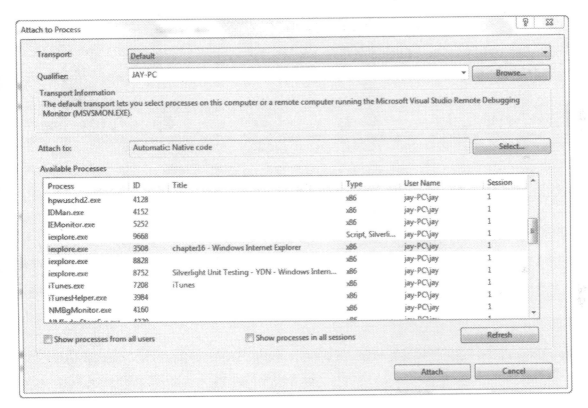

Figure 16-11. The Attach to Process dialog

Figure 16-12 shows the Select Code Type dialog. You can leave this on the default to let the debugger automatically determine the code type, or manually override and focus on Silverlight.

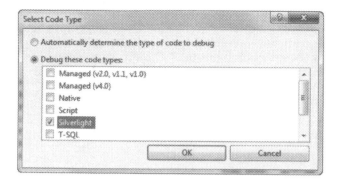

Figure 16-12. Narrowing the type of code to debug via the Select Code Type dialog

The easiest way to find the process you want to debug is by the window title. An instance of iexplore.exe running this chapter's Silverlight application is highlighted in Figure 16-11. Once you've successfully attached to the correct process, using the debugger is no different from starting the browser within the IDE under the debugger. You can set break points, break into the application, and so on.

Debugging Out-of-Browser Applications

With the release of Visual Studio 2010 and Silverlight 4, there is additional support for debugging out-of-browser applications.

In Visual Studio, on the Debug tab of the Silverlight project Properties page, you can set the Start Action to Installed out-of-browser application, then when you start debugging, Visual Studio will launch the out-of-browser application and attach the debugger automatically. To use this feature, you must first run and install the application from the browser. If you have a Web project in your solution, you must also set the Silverlight project as the startup project.

Note Complete discussion of the automated user interface testing using Visual Studio 2010 debugging and testing features are beyond the scope of this book. Visit the video describing this in details at visitmix site: http://videos.visitmix.com/MIX09/T83M.

Handling Unhandled Exceptions

Exceptions happen. It's your mission as a software developer to handle exceptions, such as using isolated storage and reading from a file that doesn't exist. You must handle these in order to build an application that works well and is resistant to expected problems. Sometimes conditions outside your control or conditions you haven't considered will cause an exception, and the Application class provides an unhandled exception handler just for this eventuality. By default (i.e., the default Silverlight application template in Visual Studio), a Silverlight application passes unhandled exceptions on to the browser via the following unhandled exception handler:

```csharp
private void Application_UnhandledException
    (object sender, ApplicationUnhandledExceptionEventArgs e)
{
    // If the app is running outside of the debugger then
     //report the exception using
    // the browser's exception mechanism. On IE this will
     //display it a yellow alert
    // icon in the status bar and Firefox will display
     //a script error.
    if (!System.Diagnostics.Debugger.IsAttached)
    {
        // NOTE: This will allow the application to continue
         //running after an exception has been thrown
        // but not handled.
        // For production applications this error handling
         //should be replaced with something that will
        // report the error to the website and stop the application.
        e.Handled = true;
        Deployment.Current.Dispatcher.BeginInvoke
            (delegate { ReportErrorToDOM(e); });
    }
}

private void ReportErrorToDOM
    (ApplicationUnhandledExceptionEventArgs e)
{
    try
    {
        string errorMsg = e.ExceptionObject.Message +
            e.ExceptionObject.StackTrace;
        errorMsg = errorMsg.Replace('"', '\'').
            Replace("\r\n", @"\n");
        System.Windows.Browser.HtmlPage.Window.Eval
            ("throw new Error(\"Unhandled Error in Silverlight
                Application " + errorMsg + "\");");
    }
    catch (Exception)
    {
    }
}
```

This is a basic unhandled exception handler. The information provided in the browser's error dialog isn't always especially useful, as you can see in Figure 16-13. The dialog isn't too friendly to users, and you won't know your Silverlight application has problems unless users manually report them.

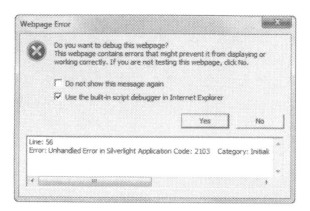

Figure 16-13. The alert dialog in IE displaying the Silverlight exception

This chapter's code includes a static `ErrorHandler` class and `ErrorWindow ChildWindow` control that provides improved handling and display of exceptions. If you download the code, you will find them under ExceptionHandlingDemo folder of the chapter16 project.

When an exception is thrown and goes unhandled, it gets sent to the unhandled exception handler and then passed to the `ErrorHandler`'s `ReportError` Static method. The `ReportError` then displays a simple feedback to users in the form of `ChildWindow`, i.e., `ErrorWindow` control. User can chose to either send the error log to the server or cancel the request. You might want to automatically send exception feedback to the server instead of waiting for the user to do so manually, but there are cases where you'll want the user to have a say. Figure 16-14 shows what this exception pop-up looks like.

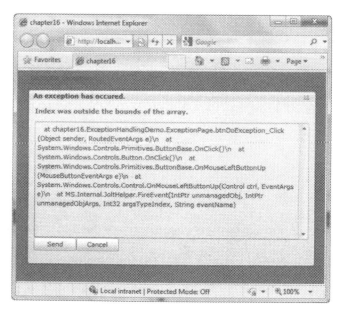

Figure 16-14. The exception dialog as implemented within Silverlight

The ErrorWindow control is made up of three main elements: the txtErrorMsg TextBlock in red font, txtErrorStackTrace TextBlock to display the StackTrace, and buttons for Send and Cancel functionality.

```xml
<controls:ChildWindow
    x:Class="UnitTesting.ExceptionHandlingDemo.ErrorWindow"
    xmlns="http://schemas.microsoft.com/winfx/2006/xaml/presentation"
    xmlns:x="http://schemas.microsoft.com/winfx/2006/xaml"
    xmlns:controls="clr-namespace:System.Windows.Controls;
        assembly=System.Windows.Controls"
    Width="500" Height="300" Title="ErrorWindow">
    <StackPanel  x:Name="LayoutRoot" Margin="2"
        Orientation="Vertical" >
        <TextBlock x:Name="txtErrorMsg" TextWrapping="Wrap"
            Height="26" Foreground="Red" FontWeight="Bold" />
        <ScrollViewer VerticalScrollBarVisibility="Visible"
            Height="200" >
            <TextBlock x:Name="txtErrorStackTrace"
                TextWrapping="Wrap"/>
        </ScrollViewer>
        <StackPanel Orientation="Horizontal" >
            <Button x:Name="btnSend" Content="Send"
                Click="btnSend_Click" Width="75" Height="23"
                HorizontalAlignment="Right" />
            <Button x:Name="btnCancel" Content="Cancel"
                Click="btnCancel_Click" Width="75" Height="23"/>
        </StackPanel>
    </StackPanel>
</controls:ChildWindow>
```

Here you can further extend the Send button Click event to send the error log to the server. The Cancel button Click event will simply close the ErrorWindow child window.

The ErrorHandler static class exposes two public properties that can be set to provide exception details for the static method ReportError. The ReportError method simply sets ErrorWindow's control to these properties and shows the instance of ErrorWindow ChildWindow.

```csharp
public static class ErrorHandler
{
    public static void ReportError(string ErrorMsg, string ErrorStackTrace)
    {
        ErrorWindow errwindow = new ErrorWindow();
        errwindow.Title = "An exception has occured.";
        errwindow.txtErrorMsg.Text  = ErrorMsg;
        errwindow.txtErrorStackTrace.Text  = ErrorStackTrace;
        errwindow.Show();
    }
}
```

Inside the App.xaml.cs in Application_UnhandledException method, you can handle any unhandled exception and call the ErrorHandler.ReportError method to show information about exception to the user.

```
private void Application_UnhandledException
    (object sender, ApplicationUnhandledExceptionEventArgs e)
{
    e.Handled = true;
    ErrorHandler.ReportError(e.ExceptionObject.Message, e.ExceptionObject.
        StackTrace.Replace('"', '\'').Replace("\r\n", @"\n"));
}
```

Now to test this, you just need to raise any exception so it can bubble up to Application level and gets handled in previously defined method and shown to user in the ChildWindow control within Silverlight UI. In the source code of this chapter, I have created and thrown the IndexOutOfRangeException as following.

```
IndexOutOfRangeException ex = new IndexOutOfRangeException();
throw (ex);
```

Now any time your application encounters an exception it can't recover from (otherwise you'd be handling the exception), the user will get immediate feedback and can optionally choose to report the error (if you don't do this automatically or remove this button).

Summary

Testing and debugging are vital activities to develop software effectively. When combined, testing and debugging help form proactive and reactive strategies to reduce the number of defects in software. You saw to how leverage the unit testing libraries and the test harness that you can obtain from Microsoft in order to construct and execute unit tests for Silverlight applications. You also briefly saw how user interface automation is used to interact with Silverlight, and the attached properties you can use to instrument your Silverlight application for user interface automation clients. When it comes to debugging, the class library that comes with Silverlight provides some useful features, such as attributes to control the debugger, and a Debug class useful for sending output to the debugger and testing assumptions within debug mode builds of your application. Finally, you saw an approach to catching unhandled exceptions and displaying them to a user within the Silverlight application itself, providing a prime place to also report unhandled exceptions back to your server.

In the next final chapter of the book, you will see how you can package and deploy Silverlight applications.

■ ■ ■

CHAPTER 17

Packaging and Deploying Silverlight Applications

Silverlight is a client-side technology. This means any server can host a Silverlight application deployment package since there is no dependence on IIS or ASP.NET. For many applications, the only configuration that may be required on the server for the Silverlight application itself is that the MIME type support the Silverlight XAP package. Note that you still have to deploy any resources, custom services, or custom components that are not part of the Silverlight deployment package on the server. While server configuration is straightforward, there remain many aspects to creating and deploying Silverlight applications. We will end the book by exploring in detail parts of Silverlight applications and will discuss Silverlight class assemblies, as well as issues such as versioning and caching.

Client Considerations

Like Adobe Flash plug-in, which you need to install on your local machine to enable Adobe Flash-based applications, you also have to install the Silverlight runtime plug-in on your computer, which is a self-contained managed environment based on .NET. The plug-in itself must be developed (by Microsoft or a third party, such as Novell collaborating with Microsoft for the project Moonlight, http://mono-project.com/Moonlight, a Silverlight implementation for Linux) for each environment that will host it. Visit http://www.silverlight.net/getstarted/ to get Windows and Mac plug-ins.

The two major aspects of supported platforms are the host operating system and the host browser. The minimum memory requirement for all operating systems is 128 MB, though naturally, the more memory you have, the better Silverlight can perform. The supported operating systems are as follows:

- Windows 7

- Windows Vista

- Windows XP with SP2 or later

- Windows Server 2008 and Windows Server 2008 R2

- Windows Server 2003 and Windows Server 2003 R2

- Mac OS X 10.4.8 or higher

- Linux and other Unix/X11-based OS using the Moonlight project

The supported browsers on Windows operating systems are as follows:

- Internet Explorer 6 or later

- Mozilla Firefox 1.5.0.8 or later

- Safari 2.0.4 or later

- Google Chrome (officially supported on Silverlight 4)

The supported browsers on OS X are as follows:

- Firefox 1.5.0.8 or later

- Safari 2.0.4 or later

- Google Chrome (officially supported on Silverlight 4)

Disabling Silverlight Plug-In Using Web Browser

Once Silverlight is installed, it is possible to temporarily disable the add-on (this is a helpful approach for testing and diagnostic purposes). In Microsoft Internet Explorer 8, disabling add-ons is accomplished by going to Tools ➤ Manage Add-Ons ➤ Toolbars and Extensions. You can then disable the add-on by highlighting Microsoft Silverlight and clicking the Disable button, as shown in Figure 17-1.

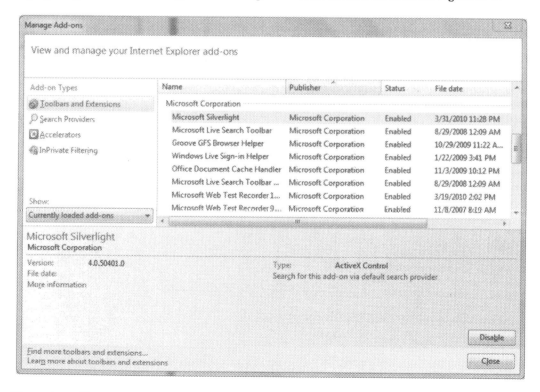

Figure 17-1. The Manage Add-ons dialog in Microsoft Internet Explorer 8

Silverlight Configuration

Every computer that has the Silverlight plug-in installed also has a configuration utility (named Silverlight.Configuration.exe, located in the Silverlight installation directory) to change options related to the Silverlight plug-in, such as automatic updating. Figure 17-2 shows the configuration utility when it first starts. This is a great place to tell your users to look for the full version number of their Silverlight plug-in if you ever need this information.

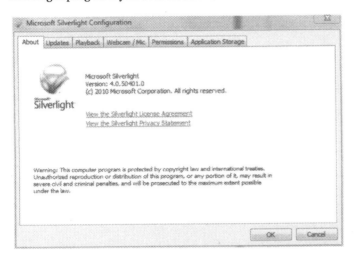

Figure 17-2. The About tab in the Silverlight configuration utility

The second tab, Updates (shown in Figure 17-3), provides options to let the user specify how updates to the Silverlight plug-in are handled.

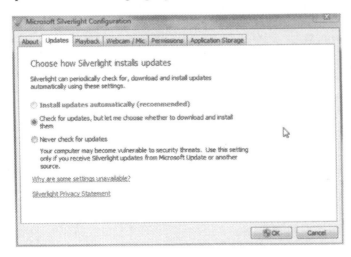

Figure 17-3. The Updates tab in the Silverlight configuration utility

Here, the first option, "Install updates automatically," is disabled on Windows 7 or Vista systems that have User Account Control (UAC) enabled. This is because explicit permission from the user is required before an installation can occur, thus making automatic installation of a Silverlight update impossible. If Silverlight is not running on Windows 7 or Vista (or UAC is disabled), and this option is still unavailable (or "Check for updates" is unavailable), it's likely that the Windows components needed to enable this functionality are not present or are outdated. Visiting Windows Update should fix this problem. You can get more details on Microsoft Silverlight Updater by visiting www.microsoft.com/getsilverlight/resources/documentation/Updater.aspx.

The next tab, shown in Figure 17-4, relates to playback.

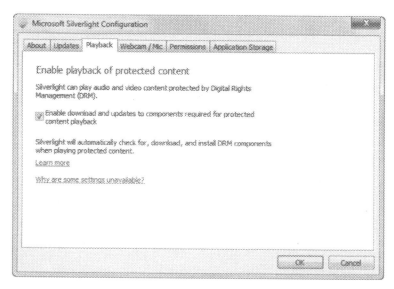

Figure 17-4. The Playback tab in the Silverlight configuration utility

Silverlight has the capability of playing media that is protected with digital rights management (DRM), and this provides the user with a mechanism to explicitly forbid the playing of DRM content.

The next tab shown in Figure 17-5, relates to the Webcam/Mic tab, which is a new tab introduced in Silverlight 4.

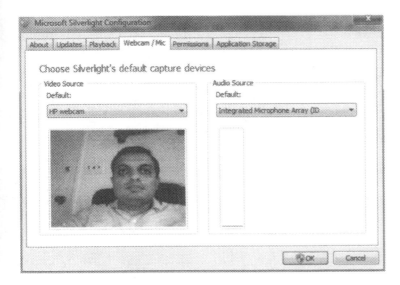

Figure 17-5. The Webcam/Mic tab in the Silverlight configuration utility

The Webcam/Mic tab allows users to choose Silverlight's default audio and video capture devices. When Silverlight attempts to access the selected devices, a user-consent dialog box appears, unless the application is running outside the browser with elevated trust, which we learned in Chapter 11.

The next Permissions tab, shown in Figure 17-6, relates to the permissions and is a new tab introduced in Silverlight 4.

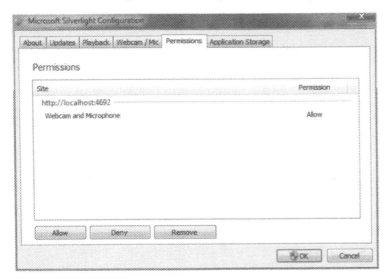

Figure 17-6. The Permissions tab in the Silverlight configuration utility

The permission tab is the place where permissions like Webcam/Mic, Clipboard accesses, etc. are displayed, which can be changed or deleted.

The final tab, shown in Figure 17-7, is Application Storage.

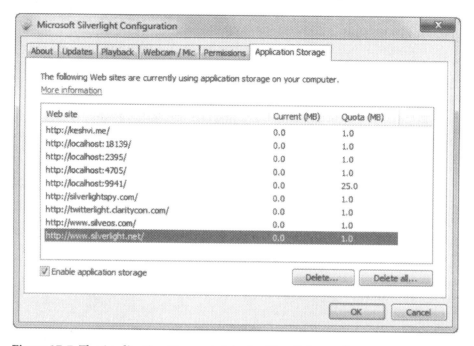

Figure 17-7. The Application Storage tab in the Silverlight configuration utility

This tab shows the list of Silverlight applications that utilize isolated storage, as discussed in Chapter 6. This tab provides a way for a user to see how much space is used and by which applications. The user can also selectively delete (by application) or completely delete the contents of isolated storage. Something important to note, however, is the check box at the bottom. A user can completely turn off isolated storage. If you develop a Silverlight application that has issues using isolated storage that you can't track down, this configuration option is a possible cause.

After looking at the client-side Silverlight plug-in in detail, let's look at the Silverlight application package and the different packaging options.

Silverlight Deployment Package Definition

Table 17-1 summarizes the mandatory and optional components necessary to run any Silverlight application on the browser successfully.

Table 17-1. Silverlight Components for Running Any Silverlight Application Successfully

Mandatory/Optional	Silverlight Component	When Is It Installed/Downloaded?
Mandatory	Silverlight core runtime library (such as System.dll, System.core.dll)	Installed as Silverlight runtime browser plug-in (not application specific)
Mandatory	Silverlight main application package (XAP file), including in-package files such as AppManifest.xaml, application assembly, and other optional assemblies and resource files	Downloaded as a startup package when the user accesses the Silverlight application
Optional	Silverlight SDK library files (in-package or on-demand .NET library files such as System.Xml.Linq.dll)	Downloaded at runtime when referenced
Optional	Application class library assembly files (in-package or on-demand custom class library files developed as part of the Silverlight project)	Downloaded at runtime when referenced
Optional	Other referenced XAP packages, which are part of a partitioned application	Downloaded at runtime when referenced

Core Runtime Library

The *Silverlight core runtime library* is a set of core .NET Framework library components that are required on the client's machine to run any rich Internet application (RIA) based on Silverlight. These components are installed on the client machine as part of the Silverlight runtime installer. As a result, an individual application does not need to include them as part of the Silverlight deployment package file. This helps to reduce the application startup package size and thus improves the application startup performance by reducing the startup download time.

In the "Custom Error Handling for Better User Experience" section of this chapter, we will develop a user-friendly approach to acknowledge that the Silverlight runtime is not installed on the user's machine, and we provide a link to install the required Silverlight runtime plug-in.

Silverlight Application Package (XAP File)

The Silverlight application deployment package is a compressed file called the XAML Application Package (XAP). The Silverlight package is automatically generated as part of the project's build process in Visual Studio 2010. This file is simply a compressed ZIP archive that stores mandatory files, such as the application manifest and the main application DLL, and optional files, such as the auxiliary library DLLs and resource files.

Figure 17-8 shows the chapter3 Silverlight application project (which we developed in Chapter 3) deployment profile—the deployment package file name, application manifest file name, and startup application assembly name with the namespace definition.

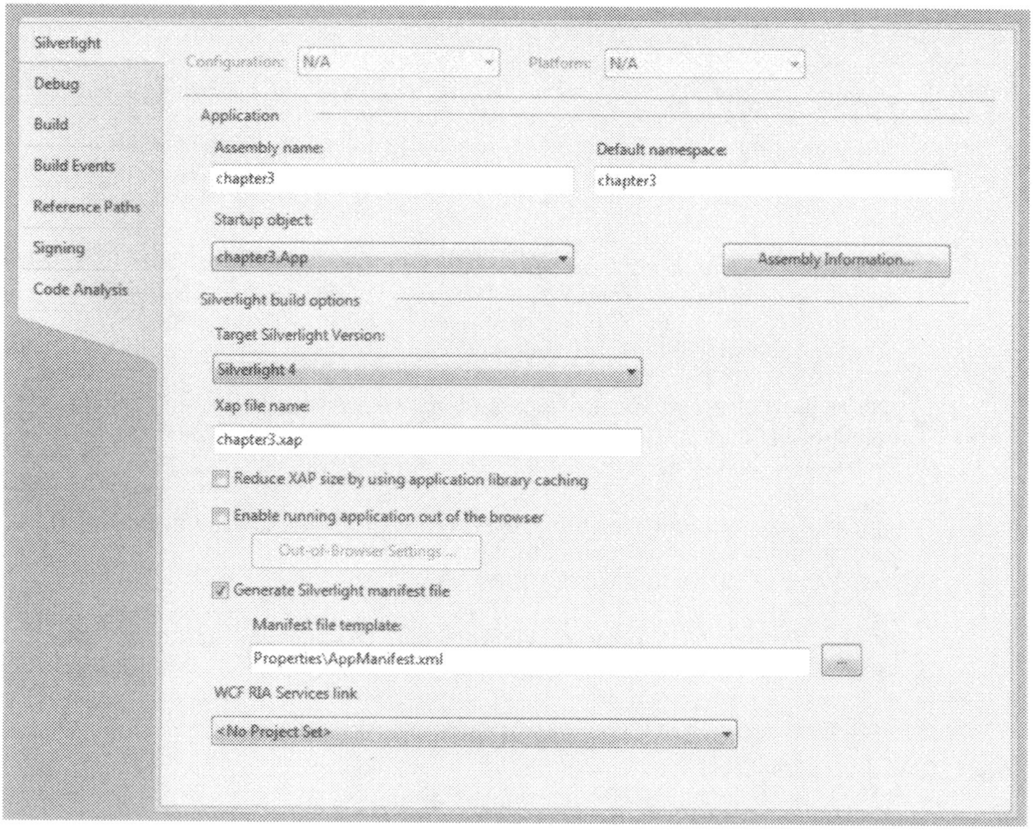

Figure 17-8. chapter3 Silverlight project properties window

As you see in Figure 17-8, there are some new options introduced with Visual Studio 2010. First, you can choose which Silverlight version to target in the Silverlight build options section. The other is to set a new custom name for the XAP file (the default name is <project name>.xap). Also, as you saw in Chapter 11, you can select the application to run in the out-of-browser mode with or without elevated trust. The last option, *WCF RIA Services link*, enables you to set a link to the WCF RIA Service web project.

The selection of the *Reduce XAP size by caching framework extension assemblies* option will reduce the XAP file size by using application library caching, thus improving overall application startup performance. In our case, the chapter3 Silverlight project XAP file size was reduced from 4344KB to only 3830KB after selecting this option. This option will result in multiple zip files, including the framework extension assemblies and other custom assemblies, reducing the XAP file size that will be downloaded upon the first application startup.

If you open the chapter3.xap Silverlight application package file as a ZIP file, it contains the mandatory application manifest (AppManifest.xaml) and startup application assembly (chapter3.dll) files, and the optional .NET library files (such as System.Windows.Controls.dll and System.Windows.Controls.Toolkit.dll).

Application Manifest File

The application manifest file is a XAML file that Visual Studio creates when it creates the Silverlight project. The application manifest file mainly includes a list of assembly files that need to be downloaded upon application startup by defining the Deployment object. The application manifest file of the chapter3 Silverlight application is as follows:

```
<Deployment xmlns="http://schemas.microsoft.com/client/2007/deployment"
  xmlns:x="http://schemas.microsoft.com/winfx/2006/xaml" EntryPointAssembly="chapter3"
  EntryPointType="chapter3.App" RuntimeVersion="4.0.50401.0">
  <Deployment.Parts>
    <AssemblyPart x:Name="chapter3" Source="chapter3.dll" />
    <AssemblyPart x:Name="System.ComponentModel.DataAnnotations"
        Source="System.ComponentModel.DataAnnotations.dll" />
    <AssemblyPart x:Name="System.Windows.Controls.Data.DataForm.Toolkit"
        Source="System.Windows.Controls.Data.DataForm.Toolkit.dll" />
    <AssemblyPart x:Name="System.Windows.Controls.Data"
        Source="System.Windows.Controls.Data.dll" />
    <AssemblyPart x:Name="System.Windows.Controls.Data.Input"
        Source="System.Windows.Controls.Data.Input.dll" />
    <AssemblyPart x:Name="System.Windows.Controls" Source="System.Windows.Controls.dll" />
    <AssemblyPart x:Name="System.Windows.Controls.Input"
        Source="System.Windows.Controls.Input.dll" />
    <AssemblyPart x:Name="System.Windows.Controls.Toolkit"
        Source="System.Windows.Controls.Toolkit.dll" />
    <AssemblyPart x:Name="System.Windows.Data" Source="System.Windows.Data.dll" />
    <AssemblyPart x:Name="System.Reactive" Source="System.Reactive.dll" />
  </Deployment.Parts>
</Deployment>
```

Here the main Deployment element contains attributes such as RuntimeVersion, which defines the Silverlight runtime version required on the client machine, and EntryPointAssembly and EntryPointType, which point toward the Silverlight application startup assembly.

The AssemblyPart element can appear one or more times as a child element of Deployment.Parts. Each AssemblyPart element includes information about an assembly (with the x:Name and Source attributes) that is part of the Silverlight XAP application package. In our case, the first AssemblyPart element defines the startup chapter3 application assembly chapter3.dll. The other optional assemblies, such as System.Windows.Controls.dll and System.Windows.Controls.Toolkit.dll, are Silverlight SDK component libraries, and for this project they are part of the XAP application package. See the complete list of added assemblies in the previously mentioned application manifest file.

Now if you select the *Reduce XAP size by caching framework extension assemblies* option shown in Figure 17-8, all the assemblies except the startup application assembly (chapter3.dll) become external assemblies and packaged as zip files (with <assembly name>.zip naming format) and each are added as ExtensionPart in the application manifest file, as shown here.

```
<Deployment xmlns="http://schemas.microsoft.com/client/2007/deployment"
    xmlns:x="http://schemas.microsoft.com/winfx/2006/xaml" EntryPointAssembly="chapter3"
    EntryPointType="chapter3.App" RuntimeVersion="4.0.50303.0">
<Deployment.Parts>
    <AssemblyPart x:Name="chapter3" Source="chapter3.dll" />
  </Deployment.Parts>
```

```
  <Deployment.ExternalParts>
    <ExtensionPart Source="System.ComponentModel.DataAnnotations.zip" />
    <ExtensionPart Source="System.Windows.Controls.Data.DataForm.Toolkit.zip" />
    <ExtensionPart Source="System.Windows.Controls.Data.zip" />
    <ExtensionPart Source="System.Windows.Controls.Data.Input.zip" />
    <ExtensionPart Source="System.Windows.Controls.zip" />
    <ExtensionPart Source="System.Windows.Controls.Input.zip" />
    <ExtensionPart Source="System.Windows.Controls.Toolkit.zip" />
    <ExtensionPart Source="System.Windows.Data.zip" />
    <ExtensionPart Source="System.Reactive.zip" />
  </Deployment.ExternalParts>
</Deployment>
```

Application Startup Assembly File

Once the Silverlight application plug-in is downloaded, the startup application class assembly (chapter3.dll in our example) containing the Startup event initiates all initialization actions. These initialization actions include displaying the application user interface (driven by the ExampleBrowser class) and other optional application initialization processes, such as retrieving data from a data source and beginning any asynchronous downloads of other on-demand referenced assembly files and resource files.

The defining difference between an application DLL and a library DLL is that the application DLL includes a class that serves as the entry point for the application. If you suspect that this class inherited from Application, you would be correct. You've seen this as part of every application we've developed so far, but I haven't mentioned much about it since the beginning of the book. Your Silverlight application should include both a XAML file and a code-behind file that provide your application with a System.Windows.Application-derived class that will conduct the creation of the user interface. The default application implementation generated by Visual Studio and Expression Blend features the following app.xaml file:

```
<Application xmlns=http://schemas.microsoft.com/winfx/2006/xaml/presentation
        xmlns:x=http://schemas.microsoft.com/winfx/2006/xaml
        x:Class="chapter3.App">
    <Application.Resources>

    </Application.Resources>
</Application>
```

The Application class is a great place to put application-level resources, such as styles and control templates that you want to use throughout the application. The app.xaml.cs code-behind file that follows is also generated:

```
public partial class App : Application
{
    public App()
    {
        this.Startup += this.Application_Startup;
        this.Exit += this.Application_Exit;
        this.UnhandledException += this.Application_UnhandledException;
```

```
        InitializeComponent();
    }
    private void Application_Startup(object sender, StartupEventArgs e)
    {
        this.RootVisual = new MainPage();
    }
    // ...
}
```

The constructor registers default event handlers for the events defined in the Application class. The life cycle of a Silverlight application is shown in Figure 17-9.

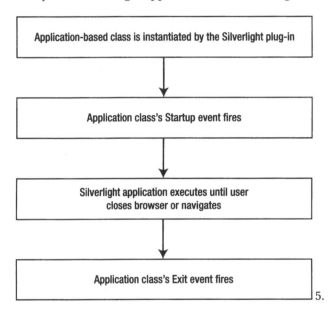

Figure 17-9. Silverlight application life cycle

The Startup event handler is the place to specify the UIElement-based class that provides the main user interface. This is generally a UserControl-based class, such as that generated by default and reflected in setting RootVisual to a new instance of this class (Page). The Exit event handler has no implementation, but the method body is there for you to put any code you want executed when the user exits the Silverlight application (generally by closing the browser or navigating to a different page).

The Application class also provides two useful properties. The Current property is static and returns the one (and only) instance of the Application implementation, making it easy to reference application-level resources from the code-behind. The other property is Host, of type SilverlightHost; it returns a reference to the environment hosting the Silverlight plug-in.

If you do not include an Application-based class, the compiled assembly can be used as a library, either packaged as part of a XAP file containing a Silverlight application or downloaded on demand and loaded via reflection. You can also store other resources, such as data files and media files, outside this XAP file.

Optional Files

The XAP file contains the following optional files:

- *Silverlight SDK library files*: These are additional .NET Framework library files, such as System.Xml.Linq.dll, that we can package so that they will be downloaded at application startup. Alternatively, they can be downloaded when referenced. Only referenced files from the SDK library are required as part of the package or are downloaded on demand.

- *Application class library assembly files*: These are custom class libraries created to introduce reusability. If you have an application class library assembly file, it can be downloaded upon startup or will be downloaded when referenced.

- *Resource files*: The application may refer to different types of resource files such as images and videos. Usually resource files are large (especially image and video files). You can reference these as on-demand, and they will be downloaded when referenced.

- *Additional XAP packages*: In order to support enterprise-level development and maintenance and provide high-performing applications, application partitioning is one way to develop Service-Oriented Architecture (SOA)–based RIAs. Using the application partitioning approach, we can break up larger application modules into more manageable distributed and reusable application modules and deploy them individually. Silverlight enables application partitioning and supports the definition and development of different application modules as separate deployment packages (XAP files) that can be referenced on-demand dynamically. This book does not cover the application partitioning feature in detail. Visit the Silverlight site (www.silverlight.net/learn/handsonlabs/) and look for the hands-on lab *Partitioning Your Silverlight Application for Deployment* to learn more.

In-Package and On-Demand Files

To reduce the initial download time and improve the overall application startup performance, it is crucial to keep the size of the XAP package as small as possible. We need to consider the XAP package definition when we work with an application that has a large number of video or image files in order to provide a better user experience and better performance. If all the files are compiled into the XAP package, it would be a large XAP package that could take significant time to download on the client machine. Silverlight-based RIAs are usually media-rich applications, and it is important to consider different options during application and deployment design to improve overall application performance, stability, and security. Silverlight supports the in-package and on-demand file deployment options to balance initial startup performance and rich media functionality.

At minimum, the application manifest file (AppManifest.xaml), the application class, and other library assemblies and resource files that are required when initializing the application must be part of the Silverlight XAP file. These are called *in-package files*. The package needs to be uploaded on the hosting server.

All other remaining files are optional, and the design team has to decide whether to keep them as part of the application package as in-package files or deploy them on the application hosting server. These files are *on-demand files* and will be downloaded to the client machine when referenced by the application at runtime. The on-demand files can be downloaded with a direct URI reference or using the asynchronous download feature.

Copy Local Property

At design time, you can control the assembly file (.NET library file or custom application class library file) deployment behavior—in-package or on-demand—by setting the Copy Local property of each assembly. If the property value is set to True, the assembly will be part of the XAP deployment package as an in-package file and will be defined in the AppManifest.xaml file. If set to False, you need to deploy it to the hosting server, and it will be downloaded at runtime asynchronously or when referenced. Figure 17-10 demonstrates the Copy Local property for the System.Xml.Linq assembly.

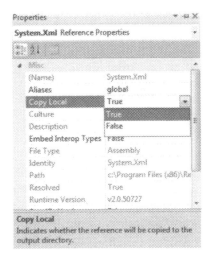

Figure 17-10. Defining in-package/on-demand behavior using the Copy Local property of the assembly file

Using an assembly packaged in the XAP file doesn't require anything special. You add a using reference and then use the types from the assembly. Just to demonstrate referencing an assembly packaged as part of the XAP file, the following code snippet shows chapter17library assembly added as a reference, which is part of the XAP file. You create an instance of ImageUtilities object from the class library:

```
using chapter17library;
// ...
private void loadButton_Click(object sender, RoutedEventArgs e)
{
    ImageUtilities iu = new ImageUtilities();
    statusText.Text = "Successfully created instance from class library";
}
```

If you choose not to package the assembly with your application, it must first be downloaded and then loaded into the application domain using the Load method of AssemblyPart. You can download the assembly using the WebClient class. The following code snippet demonstrates this feature:

```
WebClient webClient = new WebClient();
webClient.OpenReadCompleted +=
                new OpenReadCompletedEventHandler(webClient_OpenReadCompleted);
```

```
webClient.OpenReadAsync(new Uri("/chapter17Web/chapter17library2.dll",
                                UriKind.Relative));
```

Once the assembly is finished downloading, you pass the resulting stream to the Load method. Once the assembly is loaded, you can then create an instance of a member object—in our case, an instance of the custom tree control, as shown here:

```
AssemblyPart part = new AssemblyPart();
Assembly asm = part.Load(e.Result);
Control c = (Control)asm.CreateInstance("chapter17library2.TreeControl");
```

Build Action Property

At design time, you can control the deployment behavior—in-package or on-demand—of resource files (such as image files, video files, and text files) by setting the Build Action property of each resource file. The Build Action property defines how the added file relates to the build and deployment processes. It is an extensible property, and additional options can be added very easily. For Silverlight projects, three Build Action options—None, Resource, and Content—are mainly used. Figure 17-11 shows the possible Build Action property values for the tologo.jpg image file.

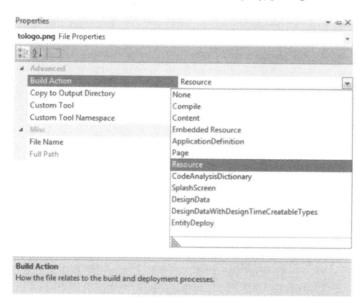

Figure 17-11. *Setting the Build Action property of a resource file*

■ **Note** Get more information on how to add additional custom options for the Build Action property by visiting http://blogs.msdn.com/msbuild/archive/2005/10/06/477064.aspx and the Microsoft MSDN site http://msdn.microsoft.com/en-us/library/ms171468.aspx.

In the following sections, we will discuss the Build Action values that are applicable within the scope of our application.

Build Action As Content

You should use the Content option when a file is large or shared among different applications. The following apply to the file with this Build Action option set:

- Added to the XAP at the application root level.

- Accessible using a URI relative to the application root. You must precede the URI with a leading slash (/)—for example, <Image Source="/tologo.png" />.

Build Action As None with the Copy to Output Directory Property Set Relatively

The None option is a good one when you are working with video files and want to keep them out of the XAP. By default, a video file's Build Action property is set to Content with the Copy to Output Directory property set to Do not copy (which means the file is never to be copied to the output directory). As mentioned earlier for this project, we have set the Build Action property to None. So upon deployment, you must upload the referenced video files alongside the XAP package. You can also use streaming or progressive download to access them efficiently, as well as employ an absolute URI here.

In this case the file

- Is not added to the XAP, but the Copy to Output Directory property will ensure it gets copied to the directory where the XAP is. Setting the value of Copy to Output Directory to Copy always will make the file always copy to the output directory, and a Copy if newer value will copy only if it is a newer version than the current version in the output directory.

- Is accessible using a URI relative to the application root. You must precede the URI with a leading slash (/)—for example, <Image Source="/tologo.png" />.

Build Action As Resource

By default, the XAP package is created in the ClientBin directory as the *<your Project name>*.xap file. If you set the Resource option, it gets embedded into the project DLL. In this case it will not be straightforward to access the resource file. You can retrieve the resource file by decompiling the DLL file using third party tools. There is no need for a leading slash (/) before the URI—for example, <Image Source="tologo.png" />.

This same image can be set from the code-behind by using a relative URI:

```
Image img = new Image();
img.Source = new BitmapImage(new Uri("tologo.png", UriKind.Relative));
```

Hosting Silverlight Applications

If planned and designed properly, deploying Silverlight applications in a secured enterprise environment is very straightforward. As shown in Figure 17-12, to deploy and consume a Silverlight application successfully, you need to follow these steps on the server and client sides:

- Server side:

    1. Set the IIS MIME type related to the Silverlight application deployment package XAP file type (if required, for more details see the section Setting the IIS MIME Type).

    2. Deploy the Silverlight application package (XAP file).

    3. Deploy additional resource files (video files, image files, other files, assembly files). This is an optional application-specific step.

    4. Deploy additional services (with required cross-domain policy files). This is an optional application-specific step.

    5. Deploy the required database (with required cross-domain policy files). This is an optional application-specific step.

    6. Add the Silverlight plug-in or reference the deployed Silverlight application in your ASP.NET or HTML web page.

- Client side:

    7. Install the Silverlight 4 runtime. Note that Silverlight 4 version is backward-compatible and thus Silverlight 3, Silverlight 2, and Silverlight 1 applications should work on Silverlight 4 runtime.

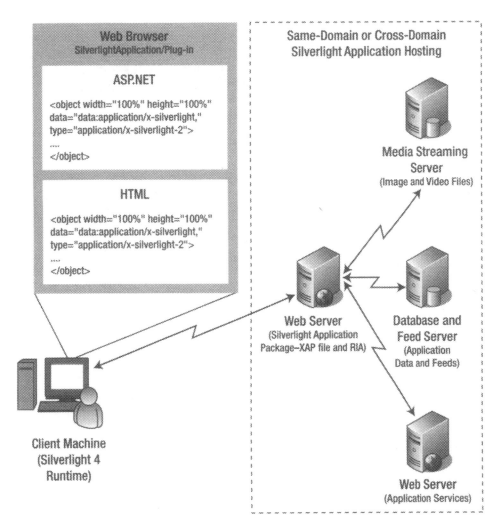

Figure 17-12. Deploying and consuming a Silverlight application

Server-Side Silverlight RIA Deployment

At minimum, you need to host the Silverlight XAP file on the web server. In more complex scenarios, you may have additional resource files, assembly files, databases, and web services to be deployed in the same-domain or cross-domain environment.

The simplest deployment option is to manually copy the deployment package and related resource files to the web server under the `ClientBin` directory.

Setting the IIS MIME Type

If you are using IIS 6 or earlier on the web server (or any other web server), you need to add the MIME type related to the Silverlight application deployment package XAP file type. You can right-click the IIS manager to open the Properties window. Click the MIME Type button to add a new MIME type for the file type XAP with the MIME type `application/x-silverlight-app`. You can visit `http://technet.microsoft.com/en-us/library/bb742440.aspx` to get more information on IIS and MIME type.

■ **Note** If you are using IIS 7, the XAP Silverlight package file type is already related to the `application/x-silverlight-app` MIME type. No additional steps are required.

Same-Domain and Cross-Domain Deployment

As we learned in Chapter 11, it is critical to consider different security aspects as a part of your deployment strategy. RIAs and social networking are dynamic in nature and need to access different services and data across domains, which exposes you to possible computer security vulnerability such as *cross-site scripting* (XSS) and *cross-site request forgery* (CSRF or XSRF).

Except for images and media, Silverlight allows only site-of-origin (i.e., within the same domain) communication to prevent cross-site request forgery vulnerabilities such as a malicious Silverlight control performing unauthorized actions to cross-domain applications and services. Here the term "same domain" covers the domain name, protocol, and port.

Silverlight enables cross-domain integration by providing two types of declaration policy methods:

- `crossdomain.xml` policy file

- `clientaccesspolicy.xml` policy file

Note that Silverlight 4 allows development and deployment of elevated trusted out-of-browser applications, which do not require cross-domain policy files for cross-domain communication.

Visit Chapters 4 and 11 to get more details on how to create and add `crossdomain.xml` and `clientaccesspolicy.xml` policy files.

Using the Policy Files

When a Silverlight application web client identifies the requirement to access the cross-domain service, it will first look at the existence of the `clientaccesspolicy.xml` file at the root of the deployed service. If it exists, it will authorize against the policy file, and upon successful authorization it can access and utilize the cross-domain deployed service. If the `clientaccesspolicy.xml` file does not exist at the root of the service's domain, next it will look for the `crossdomain.xml` file and authorize against it to gain access.

Custom Initialization Parameters

The `initParams` parameter is used to pass a set of delimited properties with their values to Silverlight, and thus to the Silverlight application. Each property takes the form of *Name=Value*, and the properties are separated by commas. These initialization parameters can be accessed from the Silverlight application in the Application class's startup handler. They are accessible via the StartupEventArgs parameter to the Startup event handler in your implementation of the Application class. You can cache these in your App class by handling the Startup event.

```
internal IDictionary<string, string> InitParams;
private void Application_Startup(object sender, StartupEventArgs e)
{
    this.InitParams = e.InitParams;
}
```

Once the parameters are cached in your Application-based class, they can be accessed via the App instance (though you need to cast it to your specific class type in order to access the InitParams member).

```
IDictionary<string,string> initParams = ((App)App.Current).InitParams;
foreach (string key in initParams.Keys)
{
    TextBlock tb = new TextBlock();
    tb.Text = key + " = " + initParams[key];
    LayoutRoot.Children.Add(tb);
}
```

Embedding Silverlight Plug-Ins to the Web Page

In the previous section, we looked at the Silverlight application security settings. Now it's time to embed the Silverlight application plug-in into your web page. Enterprises can embed the Silverlight plug-ins into web applications using the following two options:

- HTML object element
- Silverlight.js JavaScript helper file

Upon creating a Silverlight application project using Visual Studio 2010, if the user selects "Host the Silverlight application in a new web site" as the hosting platform option, a separate ASP.NET web site project with two additional test web pages (.aspx and .html) are added to host the Silverlight application/user control. The naming convention of these test pages is based on the Silverlight application name—<Name of the Silverlight Application>TestPage.aspx for the ASPX file and <Name of the Silverlight Application>TestPage.html for the HTML file.

HTML object Element

The HTML object element enables us to embed the Silverlight plug-in in the HTML web page. The following code snippet demonstrates the Silverlight control added in the chapter3TestPage.html file or chapter3TestPage.aspx file to host the application that will be developed in Chapter 14:

```
<div id="silverlightControlHost">
    <object data="data:application/x-silverlight-2,"
        type="application/x-silverlight-2" width="100%" height="100%">
        <param name="source" value="ClientBin/chapter3.xap"/>
```

```
        <param name="onError" value="onSilverlightError" />
        <param name="background" value="white" />
        <param name="minRuntimeVersion" value="4.0.50401.0" />
        <param name="autoUpgrade" value="true" />
        <a href="http://go.microsoft.com/fwlink/?LinkID=149156&
            v=4.0.50401.0"
              style="text-decoration:none">
              <img src="http://go.microsoft.com/fwlink/?LinkId=161376"
                  alt="Get Microsoft Silverlight"
                  style="border-style:none"/>
        </a>
    </object>
    <iframe id="_sl_historyFrame"
        style="visibility:hidden;height:0px;width:0px;border:0px">
    </iframe>
</div>
```

As shown in this code snippet, you need to define the attributes of the object element in order to run the Silverlight plug-in in all browsers with optimal performance.

- The data attribute is required for some browsers to avoid performance issues. The value ends with a comma, which indicates that the second parameter is an empty value.

- The type attribute defines the MIME type of Silverlight to allow the browser to identify the plug-in and the required Silverlight version.

- The width and height attributes are required (with fixed pixel values or with relative percentages) to run across different types of browsers properly.

A param child element with its name attribute set to source is required. The value attribute of this element contains the location of the Silverlight XAP file (in this example, it is ClientBin/chapter3.xap).

The param child element with the name attribute set to minRuntimeVersion defines the minimum Silverlight runtime version that is required on the client machine to run the Silverlight plug-in successfully. Set the Silverlight version number (e.g., version 4 or 3) as a value of the value attribute of this element.

This particular example of the OBJECT tag includes three optional parameters (onError, background, and autoUpgrade). There are actually many parameters, some of which follow, that can be specified to control and communicate with the Silverlight plug-in (get more details by visiting the Microsoft MSDN web site at http://msdn.microsoft.com/en-us/library/cc838259(VS.96).aspx).

background: Defaults to white. Specifies the color used by the Silverlight plug-in to paint its background. Useful when the content of the Silverlight application does not fill up the entire space specified in the OBJECT tag. This parameter uses the same syntax for colors as in XAML.

enableFramerateCounter: This should not be used with production applications! If this is set to true, the current frame rate is displayed in the host browser's status bar. This is supported only on Internet Explorer on Windows.

enableHtmlAccess: Defaults to true. Boolean value that controls whether the Silverlight application can use the HTML Document Object Model (DOM) bridge classes.

enableRedrawRegions: This should not be used with production applications! If this is set to true, the regions that are being redrawn are specially highlighted.

initParams: This is used to communicate initialization parameters to Silverlight that can be accessed from an application. Properties are comma-separated, and the property value is separated by an equal sign from the property name.

maxFrameRate: This defaults to 60. Integer value specifying an upper limit for the frame rate (the actual frame rate might be lower than what is requested).

onError: This is mandatory. It specifies a JavaScript event handler to handle exceptions from the hosted Silverlight application.

onLoad: This specifies a JavaScript event handler invoked when the root XAML file has completed loading.

onResize: This specifies a JavaScript event handler that is invoked when the Silverlight plug-in's ActionWidth or ActualHeight property is changed.

onSourceDownloadComplete: This is invoked when the application specified in the Source parameter has finished downloading.

onSourceDownloadProgressChanged: This is invoked periodically while the Silverlight application is downloading in order to report download progress.

Source: This is mandatory. Specifies the URI to the XAP file containing the Silverlight application.

splashScreenSource: This specifies the URI to a XAML file to show a splash screen while the Silverlight application is downloading.

windowless: This defaults to false. Only applies to Silverlight running on Windows. Set it to true to run Silverlight as a windowless plug-in.

The other important aspects of this specific OBJECT tag are the links that provide direction to a user who does not have the Silverlight plug-in installed. The URLs corresponding to installer packages for each version of Silverlight are shown in Table 17-2.

Table 17-2. Installer URLs for Silverlight Versions

Silverlight Version	Installer URL
3	http://go2.microsoft.com/fwlink/?LinkId=149156
4	http://go.microsoft.com/fwlink/?LinkID=149156&v=4.0.50401.0

■ **Note** The iframe tag is specified in order to prevent the Safari browser from caching the page. If the page is cached, the Silverlight plug-in will fail to reload correctly.

Several of these properties are exposed via the `App.Current.Host.Settings` object (of type `System.Windows.Interop.Settings`). These settings are shown in Table 17-3.

Table 17-3. Properties of the System.Windows.Interop.Settings Class

Property	Type	Description
EnableAutoZoom	bool	Gets or sets whether the Silverlight plug-in resizes its content based on the current browser setting. The default is true if there is no handler for the Zoomed event; otherwise the default is false.
EnableCacheVisualization	bool	Usually not used in the production. Gets or sets whether to visualize areas of page that are being GPU-accelerated with a color overlay. The default value is false.
EnableFrameRateCounter	bool	Gets or sets whether the frame rate counter is displayed (Microsoft Internet Explorer only). The default value is false.
EnableGPUAcceleration	bool	Gets whether the graphics processor unit (GPU) hardware acceleration is enabled. The default value is false.
EnableHTMLAccess	bool	Gets a value specifying whether HTML DOM access is permitted
EnableRedrawRegions	bool	Gets or sets a value specifying where redraw regions are shown.
MaxFrameRate	int	Gets or sets the maximum frame rate per second. The default value is 60.
Windowless	bool	Gets a value specifying whether the Silverlight plug-in is windowless (only applies to Silverlight running on Windows).

Silverlight.js JavaScript Helper File

You can use the `Silverlight.js` JavaScript helper file and use the `createObject` and `createObjectEx` functions defined in this file to embed the Silverlight plug-in in a web page. This approach can be used if there is a need to have multiple plug-in instances in a single web page by specifying a unique identifier for each embedded Silverlight plug-in.

However, it is recommended you use the HTML `object` element–approach to integrate enterprise SOA-based Silverlight plug-ins in your web pages. This book does not cover this approach in detail.

■ **Note** To get more information on the use of JavaScript to embed a Silverlight plug-in, please visit the Microsoft MSDN web site at `http://msdn.microsoft.com/en-us/library/cc265155(VS.96).aspx`.

Custom HTML Object Element Error Handling for Better User Experience

Clients' machines must have the Silverlight runtime installed in order to run Silverlight plug-ins successfully. However, it is very likely that a user's machine may not have Silverlight installed or may contain the older version (i.e., the required minimum version is not installed). In this scenario, instead of providing the default Microsoft message to install Silverlight, it would be friendlier if we provided a branded explanatory message and a link to the Silverlight runtime installer.

The recommended Silverlight plug-in integration approach is the use of the HTML object element, which supports custom error handling if the Silverlight runtime is not installed on a user's machine. This section describes how to implement HTML object element custom error management for Silverlight RIAs.

You can add the HTML markup representing the branded message with its Silverlight installation link after all param child elements of the HTML object element. If the required version of Silverlight is not installed on the user's machine, the custom message will be displayed; otherwise, the message will be skipped.

The following code snippet (shown in highlighted bold fonts) demonstrates the custom error handling for Silverlight when the HTML object element is used to embed the Silverlight plug-in:

```
<div id="silverlightControlHost">
    <object data="data:application/x-silverlight-2," type="application/x-silverlight-2"
        width="100%" height="100%">
        <param name="source" value="ClientBin/chapter3.xap"/>
        <param name="onError" value="onSilverlightError" />
        <param name="background" value="white" />
        <param name="minRuntimeVersion" value="4.0.50401.0" />
        <param name="autoUpgrade" value="true" />
        <div id="SLNotInstalled">
            Write HTML markup to render in the browser providing
            custom enterprise branded message with Silverlight
            installation link
        </div>
    </object>
    <iframe id="_sl_historyFrame" style="visibility:hidden;height:0px;width:0px;border:0px">
    </iframe>
</div>
```

Silverlight and the Build Process

An important part of an effective software development process includes a strong build and deployment process. The build process, at a minimum, should leverage scripts to make building software easy and primed for automation (either in the form of scheduled builds or continuous integration). Two of the most popular tools used for building software are NAnt and MSBuild. Both of these tools use XML configuration files that specify a series of tasks, including compiling projects, copying build output to different locations, and packaging applications (such as constructing an install package). Silverlight applications must be compiled and packaged into a XAP file for deployment to a web site. MSBuild is the official build tool from Microsoft, and the Silverlight SDK comes with MSBuild-specific tasks related to compiling and packaging Silverlight applications. You must use the version of MSBuild that comes with .NET 4.0 (this version of MSBuild also has the version number 4.0). This section will be most useful to you if you are trying to build Silverlight applications outside the IDE—for example, if you're trying to establish a build process.

Building a Silverlight Application Visual Studio Project (.csproj) with MSBuild

One huge advantage of MSBuild is that it can use project files from Visual Studio as build scripts. A Visual Studio CSPROJ file contains a set of properties, many of which are Silverlight-specific.

Let's briefly dissect one of these Visual Studio project files (chapter3 is shown here) to see the Silverlight-specific additions:

```
<OutputType>Library</OutputType>
<AppDesignerFolder>Properties</AppDesignerFolder>
<RootNamespace>chapter3</RootNamespace>
<AssemblyName>chapter3</AssemblyName>
<TargetFrameworkIdentifier>Silverlight</TargetFrameworkIdentifier>
<TargetFrameworkVersion>v4.0</TargetFrameworkVersion>
<SilverlightVersion>$(TargetFrameworkVersion)</SilverlightVersion>
<SilverlightApplication>true</SilverlightApplication>
<SupportedCultures>
</SupportedCultures>
<XapOutputs>true</XapOutputs>
<GenerateSilverlightManifest>true</GenerateSilverlightManifest>
<XapFilename>chapter3.xap</XapFilename>
<SilverlightManifestTemplate>Properties\AppManifest.xml</SilverlightManifestTemplate>
<SilverlightAppEntry>chapter3.App</SilverlightAppEntry>
<TestPageFileName>TestPage.html</TestPageFileName>
<CreateTestPage>true</CreateTestPage>
<ValidateXaml>true</ValidateXaml>
```

You can see that this project file is configured for Silverlight applications, setting properties related to the XAP file and defining the class that inherits from the IntelliSense class and serves as the entry point to the application. This project file also contains the directive to include the extension for building Silverlight applications. This extension controls how XAML pages are processed and how the XAP file is created. The structure of a Silverlight application as generated by Visual Studio includes the entry point for the application (the App.xaml and App.xaml.cs files), an empty UserControl (ExampleBrowser), an empty application manifest, the AssemblyInfo source file, and of course the project file. Let's look at using MSBuild to build this application. On disk, these files are organized as shown here:

```
chapter3\App.xaml
chapter3\App.xaml.cs
chapter3\chapter3.csproj
chapter3\ExampleBrowserClass\ExampleBrowser.xaml
chapter3\ExampleBrowserClass\ExampleBrowser.xaml.cs
chapter3\Properties
chapter3\Properties\AppManifest.xml
chapter3\Properties\AssemblyInfo.cs
```

Simply executing msbuild.exe with the project file specified as the command-line parameter causes MSBuild to execute, compile, and package this application. The output from msbuild.exe looks like this:

```
C:\book\code\chapter3\chapter3>MsBuild chapter3.csproj
Microsoft (R) Build Engine Version 4.0.30128.1
[Microsoft .NET Framework, Version 4.0.30128.1]
Copyright (C) Microsoft Corporation 2007. All rights reserved.

Build started 4/2/2010 12:24:46 AM.
Project "C:\book\code\chapter3\chapter3\chapter3.csproj" on node 1 (default targets).
MainResourcesGeneration:
Skipping target "MainResourcesGeneration" because all output files are up-to-date with respect
to the input files.
GenerateTargetFrameworkMonikerAttribute:
Skipping target "GenerateTargetFrameworkMonikerAttribute" because all output files are up-to-
date with respect to the input files.
CoreCompile:
  C:\Windows\Microsoft.NET\Framework\v4.0.30128\Csc.exe /noconfig /nowarn:1701,1702 /nostdlib+
/reference:"c:\Program Files (x86)\Reference
Assemblies\Microsoft\Framework\Silverlight\v4.0\mscorlib.dll" /reference:"c:\Program Files
(x86)\Microsoft
SDKs\Silverlight\v4.0\Libraries\Client\System.ComponentModel.DataAnnotations.dll"
/reference:"c:\Program Files (x86)\Reference
Assemblies\Microsoft\Framework\Silverlight\v4.0\System.Core.dll" /reference:"c:\Program Files
(x86)\Reference Assemblies\Microsoft\Framework\Silverlight\v4.0\system.dll"
/reference:"c:\Program Files (x86)\Reference
Assemblies\Microsoft\Framework\Silverlight\v4.0\System.Net.dll" /reference:"c:\Program Files
(x86)\Reference Assemblies\Microsoft\Framework\Silverlight\v4.0\System.Windows.Browser.dll"
/reference:"C:\Program Files (x86)\Microsoft
SDKs\Silverlight\v4.0\Toolkit\Nov09\Bin\System.Windows.Controls.Data.DataForm.Toolkit.dll"
…
…
CopyFilesToOutputDirectory:
  Copying file from "obj\MCD\Debug\chapter3.dll" to "bin\Debug\chapter3.dll".
  chapter3 -> C:\book\code\chapter3\chapter3\bin\Debug\chapter3.dll
  Copying file from "obj\MCD\Debug\chapter3.pdb" to "bin\Debug\chapter3.pdb".
CreateSilverlightAppManifest:
  Begin application manifest generation
  No changes detected. Application manifest file is up to date
XapPackager:
  Begin Xap packaging
  Creating file chapter3.xap
  Adding chapter3.dll
  Adding System.ComponentModel.DataAnnotations.dll
  Adding System.Windows.Controls.Data.DataForm.Toolkit.dll
  Adding System.Windows.Controls.Data.dll
  Adding System.Windows.Controls.Data.Input.dll
  Adding System.Windows.Controls.dll
  Adding System.Windows.Controls.Input.dll
  Adding System.Windows.Controls.Toolkit.dll
  Adding System.Windows.Data.dll
  Adding System.Reactive.dll
  Adding AppManifest.xaml
  Xap packaging completed successfully
CreateHtmlTestPage:
```

```
  Creating test page
  Test page created successfully
Done Building Project "C:\book\code\chapter3\chapter3\chapter3.csproj" (default targets).

Build succeeded.
   0 Warning(s)
   0 Error(s)

Time Elapsed 00:00:02.09t
```

The actual compilation and creation of the DLL and PDB files is done after the `PrepareForBuild` task. After the compilation, a Silverlight-specific application manifest is created, and the contents are packaged into a XAP file. If you examine the contents of the `obj\Debug` directory, you will see the following files:

```
App.g.cs
ExampleBrowserClass\ExampleBrowser.g.cs
chapter3.csproj.FileListAbsolute.txt
chapter3.dll
chapter3.g.resources
chapter3.pdb
ResolveAssemblyReference.cache
XapCacheFile.xml
```

The `App.g.cs` and `ExampleBrowser.g.cs` files are generated based on their corresponding XAML files and should not be edited. These files contain the generated partial class definition for their corresponding class. Much like with Windows Forms, these generated files include the implementation of `InitializeComponent` and objects for any XAML elements with an `x:Name` attribute defined. The DLL and PDB files are the important parts of the output, and exactly what you should be used to from .NET—the code compiled to an assembly and a symbol file for debugging purposes. The `XapCacheFile.xml` file is the Silverlight application manifest and contains instructions for the XAP packaging utility, such as the files to include in the XAP and where to place the generated XAP file.

```
<xapCache source="C:\book\code\chapter3\chapter3\Bin\Debug\chapter3.xap"
    lastWriteTime="4/6/2010 12:24:35 AM">
  <file source="C:\book\code\chapter3\chapter3\obj\Debug\chapter3.dll"
      archivePath="chapter3.dll" lastWriteTime="4/6/2010 12:24:33 AM" />
  <file source="c:\Program Files (x86)\Microsoft
      SDKs\Silverlight\v4.0\Libraries\Client\System.ComponentModel.DataAnnotations.dll"
      archivePath="System.ComponentModel.DataAnnotations.dll"
      lastWriteTime="3/3/2010 1:38:44 AM" />
  …
  …
</xapCache>
```

Building a Silverlight Application MsBuild Project (.proj) with MSBuild

While using Visual Studio project files as the configuration files with MSBuild is a useful approach, sometimes you might need to use the native MSBuild file format. While it does share a lot with the Visual

Studio project file format, there are a few differences. Let's take a look at an MSBuild file that goes a lot further than the preceding simple example. This build file is based on a simple Silverlight 4 Application project, SilverlightApplication1, that I have put in the MsBuildSampleProject folder of this chapter's source code folder. The file, build.proj, is annotated with line numbers and broken up for ease of discussion. Repetitive elements have been removed in the interest of space and clarity, but all the code segments match the build.proj included in this chapter's code.

```
<Project ToolsVersion="4.0" DefaultTargets="Build"
    xmlns="http://schemas.microsoft.com/developer/msbuild/2003">
    <PropertyGroup>
        <SchemaVersion>2.0</SchemaVersion>
        <NoStdLib>true</NoStdLib>
        <NoConfig>true</NoConfig>
        <TargetFrameworkVersion>v4.0</TargetFrameworkVersion>
```

Project is the root element for MSBuild configuration files. TargetFrameworkVersion is set to 4.0, but keep in mind that this has no connection to .NET 4.0 on Windows. This version number is reflective of the time when Silverlight was released .

```
<RootNamespace>SilverlightApplication1</RootNamespace>
<AssemblyName>SilverlightApplication1</AssemblyName>
<OutputType>Library</OutputType>
<OutputPath>ClientBin</OutputPath>
```

The RootNamespace, as its name implies, specifies the root namespace used in the source code being built. The AssemblyName specifies the file name used for the built assembly. Since both Silverlight applications and Silverlight libraries are DLLs, the OutputType will always be set to Library. The OutputPath specifies the directory where the output files of tasks from this configuration file are placed.

```
<SilverlightAppEntry>SilverlightApplication1.App</SilverlightAppEntry>
```

This specifies the class that inherits from the Application class and thus serves as the entry point for the Silverlight application. Without this, the packaged XAP file won't be valid and won't successfully start in Silverlight.

```
<GenerateSilverlightManifest>true</GenerateSilverlightManifest>
<SilverlightManifestTemplate>Properties\AppManifest.xml</SilverlightManifestTemplate>
```

These two properties are required in order to generate a Silverlight manifest file that includes the details of the XAP file. If you don't specify these, no Silverlight manifest is generated, and if you specify the next two properties, the constructed XAP file will contain only the DLL from the build process instead of all the files it should.

```
<XapOutputs>true</XapOutputs>
<XapFilename>SilverlightApplication1.xap</XapFilename>
</ProjectGroup>
```

These two properties instruct MSBuild to create a XAP file with the specified name. The XAP file is placed in the directory specified in the OutputPath property. If these properties are not specified, no XAP file will be produced.

```
<ItemGroup>
  <Reference Include="mscorlib" />
  <Reference Include="System.Windows" />
  <Reference Include="system" />
  <Reference Include="System.Core" />
  <Reference Include="System.Net" />
  <Reference Include="System.Xml" />
  <Reference Include="System.Windows.Browser" />
</ItemGroup>
```

This `ItemGroup` section shows the set of Silverlight assemblies that are required to build a default Silverlight application that results from creating a new Silverlight project in Visual Studio. If the application being built uses assemblies other than these, this section is where they get added.

```
<ItemGroup>
  <Reference Include="SilverlightClassLibrary1, Version=1.0.0.0,
    Culture=neutral, processorArchitecture=MSIL"  >
    <HintPath>libs\SilverlightClassLibrary1.dll</HintPath>
    <SpecificVersion>False</SpecificVersion>
  </Reference>
```

This is the first Silverlight class library. `HintPath` specifies where this library is located.

```
  <Reference Include="SilverlightClassLibrary2, Version=1.0.0.0,
    Culture=neutral, processorArchitecture=MSIL">
    <HintPath>libs\SilverlightClassLibrary1.dll</HintPath>
    <SpecificVersion>False</SpecificVersion>
    <Private>False</Private>
  </Reference>
</ItemGroup>
```

This is the other class library. Setting the value of the `Private` property to `False` is what prevents this assembly from being included in the XAP file.

```
<ItemGroup>
  <Compile Include="App.xaml.cs">
    <DependentUpon>App.xaml</DependentUpon>
  </Compile>
  <Compile Include="MainPage.xaml.cs">
    <DependentUpon>MainPage.xaml</DependentUpon>
  </Compile>
  <Compile Include="Properties\AssemblyInfo.cs" />
</ItemGroup>
```

This is the format used to compile the code-behind files for each XAML page. Since each XAML page is marked as a dependency, the next `ItemGroup`'s contents are built first.

```
<ItemGroup>
  <ApplicationDefinition Include="App.xaml">
    <SubType>Designer</SubType>
    <Generator>MSBuild:Compile</Generator>
```

```
    </ApplicationDefinition>
    <Page Include="MainPage.xaml">
      <SubType>Designer</SubType>
      <Generator>MSBuild:Compile</Generator>
    </Page>
  </ItemGroup>
```

This section includes the part of the build process that turns a XAML page, such as `MainPage.xaml`, into its corresponding generated partial class for the code-behind, such as `MainPage.g.cs`. There's one entry here for each XAML file in the project.

```
  <ItemGroup>
    <Resource Include="imgs\Chrysanthemum.jpg" />
```

This `Resource` element specifies that the resource file is placed into the Silverlight application assembly.

```
    <Content Include="libs\SilverlightClassLibrary1.dll" />
    <Content Include="libs\SilverlightClassLibrary2.dll" />
  </ItemGroup>
```

The `Content` element specifies that the resource file should be packaged in a XAP file that is created at the end of the build process.

```
<Import Project="$(MSBuildExtensionsPath32)\Microsoft\Silverlight\v4.0\
    Microsoft.Silverlight.CSharp.targets" />
```

This part is required to import the Silverlight-related tasks into the build for use by MSBuild. The Silverlight-related tasks used in this build file include compiling XAML and creating a XAP file.

Silent Installer for Silverlight Out-of-Browser Applications

What if you would like to distribute the out-of-browser Silverlight 4 applications (partially trusted and elevated trusted OOB applications) using a local media such a CD drive or from file share or USB? Silverlight 4 introduces the capability to install partially or elevated trusted Silverlight OOB applications using the `sllauncher.exe` program installed as part of the Silverlight runtime installation.

The regular way to install the OOB version of the Silverlight application is to browse to the in-browser version of the Silverlight application and install the OOB version of the application by right-clicking and selecting the install option. If you refer back to Chapter 11, you will notice that during the OOB application installation time, you will first get the security consent dialog box. Silverlight 4 enables you to install the OOB (partially or elevated trusted) applications silently with the `sllauncher.exe` program, using the XAP file available locally (without connecting to the server to access the in-browser version of the application). The silent installation means that during the installation process you do not get the security consent dialog box.

The `sllauncher.exe` program should be available under the folder where Silverlight is installed. On a 32-bit operating system, it will be available under the `C:\Program Files\Microsoft Silverlight` folder, and on a 64-bit operating system, it will be available under the `C:\Program Files (x86)\Microsoft Silverlight` folder.

As part of the `sllauncher.exe` program command line, you need to pass the following parameters to install the OOB version of the Silverlight application:

- The `install` parameter defines the XAP file with the full local path.

- The `origin` parameter defines the server URL where the Silverlight application is hosted. This will help the OOB application get updates from the server.

- The `shortcut` parameter defines the application shortcut on the desktop and/or start menu.

- The `overwrite` parameter indicates to overwrite the installed version of the application (if already installed).

For demonstration purposes, the following command line installs the `SampleOOB.xap` named Silverlight application to your local computer, where the application XAP file is available on `E:\SampleOOB.xap` and originally hosted at `http://www.technologyopinion.com/sampleoob/sampleoob.xap`. Here, we create application shortcuts on the desktop and start menu and indicate to overwrite the application, if already installed.

```
sllauncher.exe
    /install:E:\SampleOOB.xap
    /origin:http://www.technologyopinion.com/sampleoob/sampleoob.xap
    /shortcut:startmenu+desktop
    /overwrite
```

Summary

The final chapter of this book covered the packaging and deployment of Silverlight applications and libraries. The XAP file is the main unit of deployment when delivering Silverlight applications to the user. A XAP file can include the application manifest file, main Silverlight application assembly, resources such as images and video, and library assemblies. We discussed in-package and on-demand files options, the importance of defining and analyzing additional components (Silverlight SDK assemblies, custom application libraries, and resource files), and making a strategic decision to define in-package and on-demand files. A balanced decision considering application needs and startup download package size helps to optimize application performance and the user experience.

Silverlight needs a client-side runtime engine. One of the key components is hosting the application with a better user experience. This chapter explained how easy it is to implement a custom message that's user friendly when the required Silverlight runtime is not installed on the user's machine.

Finally, any complete software engineering process has a build process, so you saw how to leverage MSBuild to include Silverlight in the build. We also learned about the new enhanced feature of Silverlight 4 that installs the partial or elevated trusted out-of-browser Silverlight applications silently using the `sllauncher.exe` program. You've now reached the end of the journey through how Silverlight works and learned all you need to build applications.

The Silverlight technology platform has truly evolved from a basic media player (Silverlight 1 version) to a tool to develop true enterprise-level line of business applications (Silverlight 4 version). I hope that this book will be of great assistance to you to as you gear-up for using Silverlight 4 as a development platform. I wish you good luck in your amazing Silverlight journey. Don't forget to write—send me email at `AskAshish@technologyopinion.com` with your feedback and comments.

Index

Numerics

2D graphics
  geometries
    clipping with, 390
    grouping, 390
    path geometries, 387–389
    simple geometries, 384–386
  overview, 383
  shapes
    Ellipse class, 392–393
    Line class, 393
    overview, 391
    Path class, 393–395
    Polygon class, 393
    Polyline class, 393
    Rectangle class, 393
2D graphics feature, 6
2D vector graphics, 8
3D animation, 452–453
3D effects, 403–405

A

A size rotationAngle isLargeArcFlag
    sweepDirectionFlag endPoint command,
    394
AAC (Advanced Audio Coding), 10, 162–164
Abort method, 211, 518
Aborted state, 518–519
AbortRequested state, 518–519
About page link, 470
About tab, Silverlight configuration utility, 647
About.xaml page, 455–456
AcceptsReturn property, TextBox class, 85–86
access controls
    authentication support with
        ClientHttpWebRequest
      Basic authentication, 603

developing Twitter integration
    application, 603–607
  Digest authentication, 603
  NTLM authentication, 603
overview, 596–598
using authentication service, 599–602
using RoleService, 602–603
Account.cs class, 44
accountList data source, 45
accountListBox class, 45
AcquiringLicense state, 165, 167
ActionWidth property, Silverlight plug-in, 665
Active Server Pages (ASP), 32, 153–154, 356
Active state, ClockState enumeration, 423
ActualHeight property
    FrameworkElement class, 64
    Silverlight plug-in, 665
ActualWidth property, 64, 66
Add method, 289, 528
Add Reference dialog box, 500
addError method, 255–256
AddHandler method, UIElement class, 60
AddLink method, 286
AddMessage method, 230
AddObject method, 286
AddRelatedObject method, 286
AddressFamily property, 215
ADO .NET Entity Data Model, 541–542
Adobe Flash/Flex/AIR framework, 5
Advanced Audio Coding (AAC), 10, 162–164
Advanced Encryption Standard (AES), 10, 163,
    592
Advanced Stream Redirector (ASX), 163–164
AdvanceFeaturesDemoApp project, 455, 465–
    466, 475–476
AES (Advanced Encryption Standard), 10, 163,
    592
Aes class, 594
AesManaged class, 594, 596, 612
AIR framework, 5

AlignmentX property, TileBrush class, 408
AlignmentY property, TileBrush class, 408
All enumeration, 293
AllowDownloading property, 156
AllowDrop property, 23, 61–62, 314–316
AllowedDeviceAccess property,
    CaptureDeviceConfiguration class, 174
AllowedSenderDomains property, 508
allow-from element, 188
AllRead enumeration, 293
AllWrite enumeration, 293
Alpha channel, 413
Amplitude property, 439
Angle property, RotateTransform class, 396
animation, 415–416
    3D, 452–453
    with Expression Blend tool, 448–452
    procedural
        bubble user control, 442–444
        DemoPage user control, 444–447
    Silverlight 1, 7
    Silverlight 3, 9
    storyboards
        animation easing, 438–442
        From/To/By animations, 423–431
        keyframe animations, 432–438
    timelines
        AutoReverse, 418–419
        BeginTime, 419–420
        Duration, 420
        FillBehavior, 421
        overview, 416–417
        RepeatBehavior, 421
        SpeedRatio, 421–422
animation property, 36
Animation.RepeatBehavior property, 421
AnswerValue property, 246
Any Source Multicast (ASM), 232
API (application programming interface), 141,
    164
App class, 540, 663
App_Data folder, 538
app\app.py file, 561
app\app.rb file, 561
app\app.xaml file, 561
App.Current.Host.Settings object, 666
Append option, 306
App.g.cs file, 670
Application class, 50–52, 559, 654–657, 663, 671
application DLL, 654
application partitioning, 656

application programming interface (API), 141,
    164
application screen, printing, 331–333
Application Storage tab, 650
Application-based class, 655, 663
Application.CheckAndDownloadUpdateComp
    leted event, 488
Application.Current.Host.Source property, 143
Application.GetResourceStream event, 210
Application.HasElevatedPermissions property,
    584
ApplicationIdentity section, 478
Application.Install( ) method, 479
Application.InstallState property, 478
Application.IsRunningOutOfBrowser property,
    479
application-level security. *See also*
    Cryptography
    division of responsibility, 609–612
    same-domain and cross-domain
        communication, 607–608
    securing information in transit, 589
ApplicationNameTextBlock, 485
<Application.Resources> tag, 347
applications. *See also* socket-based sample text
    chat application
    configuring to run with elevated trust, 582–
        584
    hosting
        custom HTML object element error
            handling, 667
        custom initialization parameters, 662–
            663
        embedding Silverlight plug-ins to web
            page, 663–666
        overview, 659–660
        server-side Silverlight RIA deployment,
            661–662
    LoB, 313
    out-of-browser, digitally signing, 585–586
    text chat, executing, 230–231
    trusted, 189–191
    Twitter integration, 603–607
ApplicationServiceContext.IsRunningOutOfBr
    owser property, 486
application/x-zip-compressed attribute, 567
ApplyingChanges property, 287
ApplyTemplate method, 64, 67–68
AppManifest.xaml file, 562–563, 566–567, 651–
    652, 656–657

App.xaml file, 41–42, 50, 358, 362–363, 460, 572, 654, 668
App.xaml.cs file, 50, 52, 540, 654, 668
App.xaml.cs to control, 191
ApressBooks database, 541
ApressBooks.edmx .NET Entity Data Model, 541
ApressBooksEntities entity connection, 541
ApressBookService.metadata.cs file, 542
ApressBooks.mdf database, 541, 543
ApressBooksModel namespace, 541
ApressBooksModel.Book entity, 542
ApressBooksModel.BookDetail entity, 542
ApressBooksService class, 542
architecture of Silverlight, 27–28
ArcSegment class, 387–388
Argument property, 524
ArgumentException property, 246–247
Arrange method, UIElement class, 60
ASM (Any Source Multicast), 232
ASMX (ASP.NET web service), 252
ASP (Active Server Pages), 32, 153–154, 356
ASP .NET validation web service, INotifyDataErrorInfo interface, 252–253
AspectRatio property, 156
ASP.NET AJAX, 5
ASP.NET Configuration Manage option, 598
ASP.NET web service (ASMX), 252
aspnet_regsql utility, .NET Framework, 596
AspNetCompatibilityRequirements attribute, 193–194
AspNetCompatibilityRequirementsMode.Allo wed attribute, 194
assemblies, core .NET for Silverlight, 48–49
<assembly name>.zip naming format, 653
AssemblyInfo source file, 668
AssemblyName property, 671
AssemblyPart class, 653, 657
Assert class, and unit testing framework, 624–627
Assets directory, 459–460
Assets folder, 535
ASX (Advanced Stream Redirector), 163–164
asymmetric key algorithms, 592
asynchronous communication, 199–202
asynchronous download feature, 656
asyncResult parameter, 464
AsyncState parameter, 213
AsyncValidationDemo.xaml control, 258

atomic operation, 527
attached property, dependency property system in XAML, 38
AttachLink method, 286
AttachTo method, 287
Attributes property, MediaElement class, 164
audio content. See media integration
AudioCaptureDevice class, 176–177
AudioCaptureDevice property, CaptureSource class, 178
AudioFrameSize property, AudioCaptureDevice class, 177
AudioSink class, 174, 182
AudioStreamCount property, MediaElement class, 164
AudioStreamIndex property, MediaElement class, 164
audio/video pipeline, RAW, 10
authentication element, 597
authentication service, 599–602
authentication support, with ClientHttpWebRequest, 603–607
AuthenticationService class, 596, 598
AuthLoaderAsyncResult class, 467–468
Auto enumeration, 275
AutoCompleteBox control, 10, 91–94
AutoEllipsis property, 271
AutoGenerateColumns property, 544
Automatic value, 136, 420, 462
AutomationFactory class, 497
AutomationPeer object, 60
AutoPlay property, 122, 165
AutoReverse property, 417–419, 423
autoUpgrade parameter, 664
AvailableFreeSpace property, 305

▓ B

BackEase function, 9, 439
background attribute, 39
background parameter, 664
Background property, 39, 54, 66, 106, 123, 148, 370
Background state, 518
BackgroundWorker class, 522–526
Balance property, MediaElement class, 165
Base class Libraries (BCL), 7, 49
BaseAddress property, 208
BasedOn attribute, 360

BasedOn property,
System.Windows.DependencyObject Style
class, 358
BasedOn styles, 358
BaselineOffset property, 85
BaseUri property, 287
Basic authentication, 603
basicHttpBinding method, 192
BCL (Base class Libraries), 7, 49
Before loaded state, 378
Begin method, 423, 428
BeginEdit method, 282
Begin/End method, 199
BeginExecute(T) method, 287
BeginGetAllTitle class, 201
BeginGetRequestStream method, 211, 213
BeginGetResponse method, 211–212, 515
BeginInvoke method, 515, 521–522
BeginJoinGroup method, 233–234
BeginLoadProperty method, 299
BeginPrint event, 330
BeginRead method, 309
BeginReceiveFromGroup method, 233
BeginReceiveFromSource method, 235
BeginSaveChanges class, 296
BeginSaveChanges method, 287
BeginSendTo method, 233
BeginSendToGroup method, 233
BeginSendToSource method, 235
BeginTime property, 417, 419–421, 425
BeginWrite method, 309
behaviorConfiguration attribute, 205
BehaviorExtensionElement element, 203
Bezier curves, 437–438
BezierSegment class, 387, 389
Binding attribute, 283
Binding for Text property, 246
Binding markup extension, 44–46, 238, 241,
281
Binding object, 246
{Binding path, properties}, 46, 239
{Binding path}, 46, 239
{Binding properties}, 46, 239
binding XAML controls, with culture-specific
resource files, 348–350
{Binding}, 46, 239
BindingBase.FallbackValue property, 264–265
BindingBase.StringFormat property, 264
BindingBase.TargetNullValue property, 264–
265
BindingDirection property, 281

BindingExpression.UpdateSource( ) method,
251
Binding.NotifyOnValidationError property,
248–249
bindings element, 196, 198
Binding.ValidatesOnExceptions property, 246–
247
BindingValidationError event handler, 66, 248,
259
BindsDirectlyToSource property, 239
Bing Maps application
adding 3D animation within
SilverlightMap.xaml file, 569
adding rotate Map capabilities, 571–574
creating SilverlightMap.html file, 568–569
creating SilverlightMap.rb IronRuby file
and adding Map mode, 570
creating SilverlightMap.xaml file, 568
including Bing Maps control, 566–567
installing Microsoft Bing Maps Silverlight
control SDK, 566
targeting pre-defined locations, 575–577
Bing Maps control, 566–567
BingMapsSilverlightControlv1.0.1Installer.msi
file, 566
bingmaps.zip file, 567–568
Bitmap
application programming interface (API),
147–152
caching, 153
Bitmap application programming interface
(API), 164
bitmap caching, 154
BitmapImage class, 142–143, 208
BitmapImage instance, 146
BitmapSource class, 147
BlackoutDates property, Calendar class, 119
BlackoutDay state, 377
BlockLineHeight value, 110
Blocks property, RichTextBox class, 89
BlockSize property,
System.Security.Cryptography.SymmetricAl
gorithm class, 594
BlockSizeValue property,
System.Security.Cryptography.HMAC class,
590
BlockSource method, 233
Blue RadioButton control, 513
BlurEffect effect, 405
BlurFactor property, MultiScaleImage control,
156

BookDataGrid _SelectionChanged method, 298

BookDataGrid class, 297–298

BookDataGrid property, 295

BookDataGrid_SelectionChanged method, 299

BookDetail entity, 297

BookDetails property, 291

BookDetailsDataGrid method, 297–299

BookInfo class, 192, 195, 198, 497

BookInfo object array, 193

BookNotFound class, 206

Books property, 506

Books table, 542, 544–545

BookService proxy, 197

Border control, 106–107, 459

BorderBrush property
    Border class, 106
    Control class, 66

Borderless Round Corners option, 484

BorderThickness property
    Border class, 106
    Control class, 66

BounceEase function, 9, 439

Bounces property, 439

Bounds property, 390

BrowserHttp network stack, 606

BrowserHttpWebRequest mode, 603

Brush class, 39, 395, 413

brushes
    gradient brushes
        LinearGradientBrush class, 411
        RadialGradientBrush class, 412
    overview, 407
    SolidColorBrush, 408
    tile brushes, 408–409

brushes and transforms features, 7

btnAddItem button, 296

btnClose_Click event, 321–322

btnConnect button control, 229

btnCopy_Click event, 338

btnExportExcel_Click event, 499

btnExportWord_Click event, 499, 504

btnGetData button, 296

btnGetData Click event, 294

btnGetData_Click method, 297–298

btnGetTweets button, 550

btnGetUpdates button click event, 606

btnPaste_Click event, 338

btnSend button, 229

btnSubmit_Click event, 510

btnUpdateDataSource_Click event, 245

Bubble user control, 442–445

Buffer property, 216

Buffering state, 165, 167

BufferingProgress property, 165, 167

BufferingProgressChanged event, MediaElement class, 167

BufferingTime property, MediaElement class, 165

BufferList property, 216

Build Action property, 143, 658–659

build process
    building Silverlight application MsBuild project (.proj) with MSBuild, 670–673
    building Silverlight application Visual Studio project (.csproj) with MSBuild, 668–670
    overview, 667

BuildAction property, 146–147, 482

build.proj file, 671

Button class, 33, 40, 46–48, 359, 369, 371, 374, 377

Button control, 83, 374–377

Button element, 575

Button icon, 20

Button_Click event, 83

ButtonBase class
    Button control, 83
    HyperlinkButton control, 83
    overview, 81–82
    RepeatButton control, 83–84

ButtonBase controls, 502

By property, 424

By value, 424

BytesReceived method, 210

BytesTransferred property, 216

▓ C

C point1 point2 endPoint command, 394

cache visualization, for image integration in Silverlight, 154

CacheMode attribute, 153

CacheMode property, UIElement class, 61

CacheSize property, 135, 458

Calendar class, 377

Calendar control, 118–120

Calendar property, 339

CalendarButton class, 377

CalendarButton control, 377

CalendarButtonFocused state, 377

CalendarButtonFocusStates class, 377
CalendarButtonStyle property, Calendar class, 119
CalendarButtonUnfocused state, 377
CalendarDayButton class, 377
CalendarItemStyle class, 377
CalendarItemStyle property, Calendar class, 119
CalendarStyle class, 377
Callback function, 469
Cancel property, 524
CancelAsync method, 207
CancelConnectAsync method, 214
CancelEdit method, 282
CancellationPending property, 522, 524
Cancelled property, 200
CanChangePage property, 271
CanExecute method, 503
CanExecuteChanged event, 503
CanGoBack property, 135, 457–458
CanGoForward property, 135, 457–458
CanMoveToFirstPage property, 272
CanMoveToLastPage property, 272
CanMoveToNextPage property, 272
CanMoveToPreviousPage property, 272
CanPause property, MediaElement class, 165
CanRead property, 309
CanReuseTransform property, System.Security.Cryptography.HMAC class, 590
CanSeek property, 165, 309
CanTransformMultipleBlocks property, System.Security.Cryptography.HMAC class, 590
Canvas class, 39, 43
Canvas component, Silverlight 1, 6
Canvas control, 30, 32–33, 39, 54–56, 69, 568
Canvas.Background property, 39
Canvas.Left property, 415, 425–426, 442
Canvas.Top property, 426, 440, 442
CanWrite property, 309
CaptuerSource class, 181
Capture Web Camera button, 181
CaptureDevice class, 176–177
CaptureDeviceConfiguration class, 174–175, 180
CaptureFailed event, CaptureSource class, 178
CaptureImageAsync method, 178, 181
CaptureImageCompleted event, 178, 180
CaptureImageCompletedEventArgs.Result method, 178

CaptureMouse method, UIElement class, 60
CaptureSource class, 177, 181
CaptureSource variable, 179
CaptureVideo button, 179
CaptureVideo_Click event, 180
CAS (Code Access Security), 579
Cascading Style Sheets (CSS), 40, 355, 360
CellEditEnded event, 273
CellEditEnding event, 273
Center property, 386, 390, 412
CenterOfRotationX property, PlaneProjection class, 403
CenterOfRotationY property, PlaneProjection class, 403
CenterOfRotationZ property, PlaneProjection class, 404
CenterX property
    CompositeTransform class, 402
    RotateTransform class, 396
CenterY property
    CompositeTransform class, 402
    RotateTransform class, 396
Central Processor Unit (CPU), 153
Change method, 531
CheckAccess method, 59, 521–522
CheckAndDownloadUpdateAsync event, 488
CheckAndDownloadUpdateCompleted event, 489
CheckBox class, 84–85, 377
CheckBox control, 10, 169
Checked events, 84, 510
checked state, 377–378
Child property
    Border class, 106
    Popup class, 111
    ViewBox class, 80
Child Window template, 125, 131–132
ChildWindow class, 131–133, 321–323
ChildWindow control, 11, 103
Chiron.exe development utility, 560–561
Chiron.exe file, 560–562
Choice class, 247, 249
ChooseAccount user control, 44
ChooseAccount.xaml file, 44–45
CircleEase function, 9, 439
City property, 270
Clear method, System.Security.Cryptography.HMAC class, 591
ClearValue method, DependencyObject class, 59

Click events, 82, 229, 337, 550, 573–574, 576
ClickMode property, ButtonBase class, 82
client access, controlling via socket policy
server, 213–214
client element, 196, 198
client_DownloadStringCompleted event, 551
clientaccesspolicy.xml file, 186–189, 213, 608,
662
ClientAccess.xml file, 13
ClientBin folder, 18, 160–161, 479, 659, 661
ClientConfig class, 236
ClientHttp network stack, 606
ClientHttp stack, 188
ClientHttpWebRequest, authentication
support with, 603–607
Clip property, 61, 390
Clipboard access, 336–338
Clipboard class, 336
Clipboard support, in DataGrid control, 276–
277
Clipboard.ContainsText method, 338
Clipboard.GetText method, 338
Clipboard.SetText method, 338
ClipDemo user control, 336
clipping with geometries, 390
ClockState enumeration, 423
Close method, 131, 212, 215, 484
Closed state, 165, 167–168
Closing event, 483
CLR (Common Language Runtime), 5, 27, 48–
49, 260, 557, 579–580
Code Access Security (CAS), 579
code coverage, and unit testing using MSBuild,
622–624
code-behind
defining user interface in XAML using, 30–
32
and INotifyDataErrorInfo interface, 258–
260
codes, message authentication, 590–592
Collapsed event, TreeViewItem class, 101
CollectionChanged event, 284
/collectionType:<type> option, 197
CollectionViewSource class, 237, 284
Color property, 150, 408, 426
Color type, 39
Color_Checked event, 510
ColorAnimation class, 415, 424, 426
ColorAnimationUsingKeyFrames class, 415
ColorInterpolationMode property,
GradientBrush class, 410

ColorStop object, 443
Column Header Style, 377
Column property, Grid class, 38
column sizing, in DataGrid control, 274–276
ColumnDefinition class, 73, 571
ColumnSpan property, Grid class, 38
COM automation, 497–500
COMAccessDemo.xaml file, 498, 504–505
ComAutomationFactory class, 12
ComboBox control, 10, 98–99
ComboBoxItem class, 99
COMCommand class, 504–506
Command property, 68, 82, 503, 505–506
commanding support
Model class, 504
overview, 502–503
ViewModel class, 504–505
View.xaml file, 505–506
CommandParameter property, 68, 82, 503
CommitEdit( ) method, 284
Common Language Runtime (CLR), 5, 27, 48–
49, 260, 557, 579–580
CommonStates class, 377
communication
asynchronous, 199–202
cross-domain, enabling
cross-domain policy files, 186–189
overview, 185
trusted applications, 189–191
same-domain and cross-domain, 607–608
CompareExchange method, Interlocked class,
528
Completed event, 199, 202, 217, 230, 417, 425,
428
ComponentModel assembly, 277
Compose step, Deep Zoom Composer, 158
composite transformation, 401–403
CompositeTransform class, 401, 403, 450
CompositeTransform node, 383, 401
CompositeTransform type, 383
ComputedHorizontalScroll property,
ScrollViewer class, 114
ComputedVerticalScroll property,
ScrollViewer class, 114
ComputeHash method,
System.Security.Cryptography.HMAC class,
591
Condensed value, 109
conditional compilation, and debugging, 634–
635
Conditional styling, 366

/config:<fileName> option, 197
configuration, Silverlight, 647–650
ConnectAsync method, 214
connected mode, 582
Connected property, 215
ConnectSocket property, 216
Consultant.cs class, adding to implement
    INotifyDataErrorInfo interface, 253–258
consume information, XAML to, 195
consuming web services with WCF
        communicating directly over HTTP
            HttpWebRequest class, 211–213
            WebClient class, 207–210
        creating web services consumable by
            Silverlight, 192–195
        invoking services from Silverlight
            asynchronous communication, 199–
                202
            handling errors, 202–207
            overview, 196
            Silverlight Service Utility tool, 197–198
        overview, 191
        XAML to consume information, 195
Contains value, FilterMode, 95
ContainsCaseSensitive value, FilterMode, 95
ContainsOrdinal value, FilterMode, 95
ContainsOrdinalCaseSensitive value,
    FilterMode, 95
ContainsText method, 336
Content attribute, ListBoxItem class, 33
content attribute syntax, 40
Content element, 40, 673
Content option, Build Action property, 658–
    659
content presenter class, 378
Content property, 79, 103, 105, 276, 368, 494
ContentControl class, 98, 103
ContentFrame_Navigated event, 457, 462
ContentFrame_NavigationFailed event, 457,
    462
ContentGrid control, 550
ContentLength property, 212
ContentLoader property, 135, 457–458, 463,
    470
ContentPresenter class, 48, 368
ContentTemplate property, ContentControl
    class, 103
ContentType property, 211–212
context menu, right-click, 326–329
Continuous check box, 170–171
control bar, timeline editor, 449

Control class, 57, 66–68, 355, 367
control templates
    creating, 366–377
    custom button control using, 374–377
    developing templated control, 378–381
    for other controls, 377–378
    Visual State Manager (VSM), 368–374
control toolbox, Expression Blend, 20
controls. See also access controls; layout
    management and grouping controls; user
    interface controls
    printing, 333–334
    structure of XAML, 32–33
    user
        defining, 315–317
        implementing code behind, 317–320
    XAML, binding with culture-specific
        resource files, 348–350
control-skinning, enhanced, 9
ControlTemplate class, 46, 379
Convert method, 262
ConvertBack method, 262
Converter property, 239
ConverterCulture property, 239
ConverterParameter property, 240
Copy and Paste feature, Silverlight 4, 11
Copy Local property, 657–658
Copy to Output Directory property, 659
CopyFile method, 305
Core architecture feature, Silverlight 1, 6
core runtime library, 651
CornerRadius property, Border class, 106
Count property, 216, 421, 496
count variable, 529
CPU (Central Processor Unit), 153
Create Empty option, Expression Blend tool,
    370
Create option, 306
CreateBubble method, 445, 447
CreateDirectory method, 305, 582
CreateFile method, 305, 309, 582
CreateNew option, 306
createObject function, 666
createObjectEx function, 666
CreateThumbnail method, 493
Credentials property, 288
cross-domain communication
    enabling
        cross-domain policy files, 186–189
        overview, 185
        trusted applications, 189–191

and same-domain communication, 607–608
cross-domain deployment, 662
cross-domain-access element, 188
CrossDomainAcess.xml file, 13
crossdomain.xml file, 186–187, 608, 662
cross-platform frameworks
    Adobe Flash/Flex/AIR, 5
    Java platform, 4
    Microsoft ASP.NET AJAX, 5
    Microsoft Silverlight, 5–6
    Qt, 4
cross-Silverlight application communication
    example in action
        creating receiver Silverlight application, 510–512
        creating sender Silverlight application, 509–510
        hosting sender and receiver applications on same page, 512–514
        overview, 508
    overview, 506
    using System.Windows.Messaging namespace, 507–508
cross-site request forgery (CSRF or XSRF), 607, 662
cross-site scripting (XSS), 607, 662
Cryptography
    authentication support with ClientHttpWebRequest
        Basic authentication, 603
        developing Twitter integration application, 603–607
        Digest authentication, 603
        NTLM authentication, 603
    encrypting/decrypting data, 592–596
    hash algorithms and message authentication codes, 590–592
    overview, 589
    user access control
        overview, 596–598
        using authentication service, 599–602
        using RoleService, 602–603
cryptography namespace, 593
CryptoStream class, 594
CSRF or XSRF (cross-site request forgery), 607, 662
CSS (Cascading Style Sheets), 40, 355, 360
css\screen.css file, 561
cubic Bezier curve, 437

CubicEase easing function, 439
CultureInfo class, 339
CultureInfoDemo user control, 340
CultureList_SelectionChanged event handler, 349
culture-specific resource files, adding, 344–346
Current property
    Application class, 655
    Microsoft.Scripting.Silverlight.DynamicApplication class, 559
CurrentCulture property, 339, 517
CurrentSource property, 135, 458
CurrentState property, 165, 168
CurrentStateChanged event, 167–168, 171
CurrentThread property, Thread class, 517
CurrentUICulture property, 339, 517
Cursor property, FrameworkElement class, 64
custom button control, 374–377
custom HTML object element error handling, 667
custom icons, 482
custom IDictionary support, 354
custom initialization parameters, 662–663
custom navigation
    extending example
        AuthLoaderAsyncResult class, 467–468
        CustomAuthContentLoader class, 468–470
        overview, 465–466
    INavigationContentLoader interface
        BeginLoad method, 463–464
        CancelLoad method, 464
        CanLoad method, 464
        EndLoad method, 464
custom printing, 334–335
Custom value, FilterMode, 95
CustomAuthContentLoader class, 465–470
CustomButton class, 374
CustomContentLoader folder, 466
customizing
    out-of-browser applications
        custom icons, 482
        window manipulation and customization, 483–484
    windows, 483–484
CustomValidation attribute, 278
CustomWorkerArgs class, 524
CustomWorkerArgs instance, 523, 525

■ D

d class, 377
data
  displaying
    BindingBase.FallbackValue property,
      264–265
    BindingBase.TargetNullValue property,
      264–265
    CollectionViewSource, 284
    data binding, 238–262
    DataForm control, 279–283
    DataGrid control, 266–279
    string indexers, binding to, 265–266
    StringFormat property, 263–264
    type converters, 262–263
  encrypting/decrypting, 592–596
  enhancements in Silverlight 4, 237
  integration and data manipulation
    controls, 95–106
    ComboBox, 98–99
    ContentControl, 103
    DataForm, 104–105
    DataGrid, 104
    DataPager, 105
    DescriptionViewer, 105
    HeaderedContentControl, 103–104
    HeaderedItemsControl, 102–103
    ItemsControl, 96
    Label, 105
    ListBox, 96–98
    TreeView, 99–101
    ValidationSummary, 106
  and isolated storage, 303–310
  shared, 526–529
  validation
    Binding.NotifyOnValidationError
      property, 248–249
    Binding.ValidatesOnExceptions
      property, 246–247
    client-side, 249–251
    for DataForm control, 283
    for DataGrid control, 277–279
    FrameworkElement.BindingValidation
      Error event, 248–249
    server-side, asynchronous, 251–260
  WCF Data Services
    Entity Data Model (EDM), 285
    overview, 284
    Silverlight application using, 289–299

    Silverlight client library for, 286–289
  XML data
    overview, 299
    parsing, 300–301
    serializing, 301–302
    using LINQ, 302–303
data binding
  data validation
    asynchronous server-side validation,
      251–260
    Binding.NotifyOnValidationError
      property, 248–249
    Binding.ValidatesOnExceptions
      property, 246–247
    client-side, 249–251
    FrameworkElement.BindingValidation
      Error event, 248–249
  DependencyObject, 261–262
  element-to-element, 260–261
  IDataErrorInfo Interface, for client-side
    validation, 249–251
  INotifyDataErrorInfo interface
    adding Consultant.cs class to
      implement, 253–258
    ASP .NET validation web service, 252–
      253
    and code-behind, 258–260
    overview, 251
  PropertyChanged event, 243–245
  to string indexers, 265–266
  in Visual Studio 2010, 245
  in XAML
    overview, 44–45
    RelativeSource property, 46–47
DataAnnotations assembly, 277
DataContext proeprty, 250
DataContext property, 64, 238, 247, 266
DataForm control
  customized display of fields, 282–283
  data validation for, 283
  IEditableObject interface, 282
  overview, 104–105
DataFormat.FileDrop format, 315
DataGrid class, 377
DataGrid control
  clipboard support in, 276–277
  column sizing in, 274–276
  data validation for
    cell-level, 277
    row-level, 277–279

DataPager control, 271–273
    events in, 273–274
    filtering in, 271
    grouping in, 267–270
    overview, 104
    paging in, using DataPager control, 271–273
    sorting in, 270
DataGridBoundColumn.ClipboardContentBinding event, 277
DataGridCell control, ContentControl class, 103
DataGrid.ClipboardCopyMode event, 276
DataGridClipboardCopyMode.ExcludeHeader event, 276
DataGridClipboardCopyMode.IncludeHeader event, 277
DataGridClipboardCopyMode.None event, 276
DataGrid.CopyingRowClipboardContent event, 277
DataGridLengthUnitType enumeration, 274, 276
DataManipulation controls, 11
DataModel.edmx entity, 291
DataNamespace property, 288
DataObject.GetData(DataFormat.FileDrop) method, 315
DataPager control, 11, 105, 271–273
DataServiceCollection(T) class, 238, 289
DataServiceContext class, 286, 297, 299
DataServiceContext.BeginSaveChanges method, 297
DataServiceContext.EndSaveChanges method, 297
DataServiceQuery class, WCF Data Services, 288
DataServiceQuery method, 297
DataTemplate class, 45, 550
DatePicker class, 377
DatePicker control, 118–120
DateTimeFormat property, 339
DateValidationError event, 120
DBService.svc service, 294
DBService.svc WCF Data Services proxy, 294
DBService.svc.cs file, 292
Debug | Toggle Breakpoint menu command, 553
Debug property,
    Microsoft.Scripting.Silverlight.DynamicApplication class, 559

debugging
    conditional compilation, 634–635
    process explained, 633–634
    unhandled exceptions handling, 640–644
    with Visual Studio
        configuring startup for, 637–640
        controlling debugger, 636–637
        out-of-browser applications, 640
        overview, 635
Decrement method, Interlocked class, 528
Decrypt method, 596
deep linking, 471
Deep Zoom Composer, 8, 16, 155, 158–161
Deep Zoom project, 160
DeepZoomIntegration Silverlight 4 application project, 161
DeepZoomSample project, 158
Default.aspx page, 512–513
DefaultExt property, SaveFileDialog class, 129
DefaultOptions property, 288
DefaultStyleKey property, Control class, 67
DefineImageTransform method, 150–151
DefineOpacityMask method, 150–151
defining user controls, 315–317
Delay property, RepeatButton class, 84
delegate keyword, 521
Delete option, 307
DeleteDirectory method, 305
DeleteFile method, 305
DeleteLink method, 287
DeleteObject method, 287
DeliverMessage method, 225, 227
Demand method, 579
DemoPage user control, 444–447
dependency property system
    dependency property system in XAML, 35–38
    in XAML
        attached property, 38
        dependency property, 35–38
        DependencyObject class, 39
        overview, 34
DependencyObject class
    data binding, 261–262
    dependency property system in XAML, 39
DependencyObjectCollection event handler, 262
DependencyObjects class, 262
DependencyProperty class, 46
DependencyPropertyChangedEventArgs class, 38

DependencyProperty.Register method, 37
deploying Silverlight applications. *See*
    packaging and deploying Silverlight
    applications
Deployment element, 653
Deployment.Parts element, 653
Description property, 105
DescriptionViewer control, 11, 105
design and development tools
    Deep Zoom Composer, 16
    Eclipse Tools for Silverlight (eclipse4SL), 16
    Expression Blend, 15
    Expression Encoder, 16
    SketchFlow, 15
    Visual Studio, 14–15
design surface, Expression Blend, 448–449
DesignHeight property, 22, 148
DesignWidth property, 22, 148
DesiredFormat property, 177
DesiredSize property, UIElement class, 61
Detach method, 287, 289
DetachLink method, 287
determinate state, 378
development tools. *See* design and
    development tools
dialog boxes
    ChildWindow class, 131–133
    OpenFileDialog class, 125–128
    SaveFileDialog class, 128–130
DialogResult property, 131, 133, 322
Dictionary object, 445
Dictionary<string,object>, 40
Digest authentication, 603
Digital Rights Management (DRM), 8, 13, 141,
    163, 165, 648
digitally signing out-of-browser applications,
    585–586
direct content, 353
DirectoriesToCreate method, 582
/directory:<directory> option, 197
DirectoryExists method, 305
DirectX Software Development Kit (SDK), 9,
    405
Disable button, Manage Add Ons dialog box,
    646
Disable pause_resume button, 573
Disabled state, 372, 375, 377–378
disabling Silverlight plug-in using web
    browser, 646
disconnected mode, 582
discrete interpolation, 434–436

Dispatcher object, 515, 521
Dispatcher property, 59, 147, 521–522
Dispatcher.BeginInvoke, 521
DispatcherTimer class, 529–530
DispatcherTimer timer, 171
DisplayAttribute property, 105
DisplayDate property, Calendar class, 119
DisplayDateChanged event, Calendar class,
    119
DisplayDateEnd property, Calendar class, 119
DisplayDateStart property, Calendar class, 119
DisplayMemberPath property, ItemsControl
    class, 96
DisplayMode property, 119, 272
DisplayModeChanged event, Calendar class,
    119
DisplayName property, 339
Dispose method, 215, 233, 235, 305
DLR (Dynamic Language Runtime), 8, 27, 555–
    559
dlr folder, 563, 567
dlr\ gestaltmedia.js file, 562
dlr\dlr.js file, 562
dlr\dlr.xap file, 562
dlr.js file, 562–564, 568
dlr.xap file, 566–567
DnsEndPoint class, 214, 220, 230
Dock enumeration, 79
Dock property, 69, 75–76
DockPanel control, 10, 69, 74–77
Document Object Model (DOM), 664
Document Outline, Visual Studio, 32
DOM (Document Object Model), 664
domain service class, 542
DomainDataSource.RejectChanges( ) method,
    545
DomainDataSource.SubmitChanges( )
    method, 545
doSomething method, 519
DoubleAnimation class, 415, 417, 424, 445, 452
DoubleAnimationUsingKeyFrames class, 415,
    434
DownloadedStringCompleted event, 606
DownloadProgress event, BitmapImage class,
    143
DownloadProgress property, 165, 167
DownloadProgressChanged event, 167, 207–
    209
DownloadProgressChangedEventArgs event
    handler, 209
DownloadProgressEventArgs class, 143

DownloadProgressOffset property, MediaElement class, 165
DownloadStringAsync method, 207, 210, 551
DownloadStringCompleted event, 207
DownloadStringCompletedEventHandler, 551
DoWork event, BackgroundWorker class, 523
DoWorkEventArgs object, 523–524
Drag and Drop feature, Silverlight 4, 11
Drag Indicator Style, 377
drag-and-drop functionality
    adding ChildWindow as image viewer, 321–323
    defining user controls, 315–317
    events of UIElement to enable, 314
    implementing code behind user controls, 317–320
    local image files integration using, 21–26
    processing dropped files, 315
    properties of UIElement to enable, 314
DragEnter event, 62, 314–315
DragEventArgs.Data method, 315
DragEventArgs.GetPosition method, 320
DragEventHandler class, 62
DragLeave event, 62, 314–316, 319
DragnDropDemo user control, 315, 322
DragnDropDemo.xaml page, 348
DragnDrop.xaml.cs file, 317, 349
DragOver event, 62, 315–316, 319
DrawingAttributes class, 122
DrawingAttributes property, 122
DRM (Digital Rights Management), 8, 13, 141, 163, 165, 648
Drop event, 23–24, 62, 315–316
Drop Location Indicator Style, 377
DropDownClosed event, AutoCompleteBox class, 94
DropDownClosing event, AutoCompleteBox class, 94
DropDownOpened event, AutoCompleteBox class, 94
DropDownOpening event, AutoCompleteBox class, 94
dropped files, processing, 315
DroppedFramesPerSecond property, MediaElement class, 165
DropShadowEffect effect, 405
DropShadowEffect property, 405
DropZoneCanvas Canvas control, 315–316
DropZoneCanvas control, 316
DropZoneCanvas_DragLeave event, 320
dueTime parameter, 531

Duration property, 417–418, 420–422, 425
Dynamic Language Runtime (DLR), 8, 27, 555–559
dynamic languages and Dynamic .NET
    creating Silverlight applications using "Just-Text" approach
        externalizing XAML and IronRuby/IronPython code, 565–566
        hosting HTML file, 564
        in-line IronRuby/IronPython code in hosting HTML file, 564–565
        in-line XAML code in hosting HTML file, 565
    developing interactive Bing Maps application
        adding 3D animation within SilverlightMap.xaml file, 569
        adding rotate Map capabilities, 571–574
        creating SilverlightMap.html file, 568–569
        creating SilverlightMap.rb IronRuby file and adding Map mode, 570
        creating SilverlightMap.xaml file, 568
        including Bing Maps control, 566–567
        installing Microsoft Bing Maps Silverlight control SDK, 566
        targeting pre-defined locations, 575–577
    Dynamic Language Runtime (DLR)
        Microsoft.Scripting.Silverlight.Dynamic Application class, 559
        overview, 557
        scripting assemblies, 558–559
    dynamic languages for Silverlight, 556–557
    setting up development environment
        "Just-Text" approach, 561–563
        traditional approach with Chiron.exe file, 560–561
DynamicTitle style, 361–362
dzc_output.xml file, 160–161

▓ E

Ease method, 442
EaseIn mode, EasingMode property, 439–440
EaseInOut mode, EasingMode property, 439
EaseOut mode, EasingMode property, 439–440
EasingColorKeyFrame class, 439
EasingDoubleKeyFrame class, 439
EasingFunctionBase class, 439, 442

EasingMode property, 439–440, 442
Eclipse Tools for Silverlight (eclipse4SL), 16
Edit a Copy option, Expression Blend tool, 371
Edit Repeat Count option, Expression Blend, 451
Edit Repeat dialog, Expression Blend, 451
Effect property, 61, 405
effects, 3D, 403–405
ElasticEase function, 9, 439, 445
ElementName property, 240, 260–261
Element-to-Element Binding feature, 11
element-to-element, data binding, 260–261
ElementToLogicalPoint method, MultiScaleImage control, 157
elevated trust, 582, 606
ElevatedPermissions property, 12, 189–190, 481, 584
elevated-trusted Silverlight applications
    configuring applications to run with, 582–584
    vs. partially trusted, 587
Ellipse class, 392–393
EllipseGeometry class, 334, 384, 386, 390
else block, 526
Email property, 283
embedding Silverlight plug-ins to web page, 663–666
Employee class, 268, 278
emps array, 268
emps Employee class array object, 275
/emulate:"path to xap file" parameter, 479
Enable WCF RIA Services option, 18
EnableAutoZoom, System.Windows.Interop.Settings class, 666
EnableCacheVisualization parameter, 154
EnableCacheVisualization, System.Windows.Interop.Settings class, 666
Enabled value, 137
/enableDataBinding, 197
enableFramerateCounter parameter, 664
EnableFrameRateCounter property, 154
EnableFrameRateCounter, System.Windows.Interop.Settings class, 666
EnableGPUAcceleration property, 153–154, 666
enableHtmlAccess parameter, OBJECT tag, 664
EnableHTMLAccess, System.Windows.Interop.Settings class, 666
enableRedrawRegions parameter, OBJECT tag, 665

EnableRedrawRegions, System.Windows.Interop.Settings class, 666
Encrypt method, 595
encrypting/decrypting data, 592–596
EndEdit method, 282
EndExecute(T) method, 287
EndGetAllTitle class, 201
EndGetRequestStream method, 211, 213
EndGetResponse method, 211–212
EndJoinGroup method, 233, 235
EndLoad( ) method, 463–465, 469
EndLoadProperty property, 299
EndMethod( ), 464
EndPoint property
    LinearGradientBrush class, 411
    LineGeometry class, 385
EndPrint event, 330
EndRead method, 309
EndReceiveFromGroup method, 233
EndReceiveFromSource method, 235
EndSaveChanges method, 287
EndSendTo method, 233
EndSendToGroup method, 234
EndSendToSource method, 235
EndWrite method, 309
EnglishName property, 339
enhanced control-skinning feature, Silverlight 3, 9
enhancements in Silverlight 4, graphics, 383
Entities property, 288
Entity Data Model Wizard, 285, 291
EntitySetRights.All assembly, 292
EntryPoint property, Microsoft.Scripting.Silverlight.DynamicApplication class, 559
EntryPointAssembly attribute, 653
EntryPointType attribute, 653
Environment property, Microsoft.Scripting.Silverlight.DynamicApplication class, 559
Environment.Specialfolder enumeration, 492
Equals value, FilterMode, 95
EqualsCaseSensitive value, FilterMode, 95
EqualsOrdinal value, FilterMode, 95
EqualsOrdinalCaseSensitive value, FilterMode, 95
errMessage TextBlock control, 248
Error property, 200, 249, 488
ErrorCode method, 253
ErrorException property, 142–143, 157
ErrorInfo class, 260

ErrorInfo event, 256–257
ErrorMessage method, 253
ErrorMessage property, 142–143, 157
errors, handling, 202–207
ErrorsChanged event, 251, 255–256
ErrorSummary control, 11
ErrorTargetID property,
    Microsoft.Scripting.Silverlight.DynamicApp
    lication class, 559
ErrorWindow.xaml page, 455, 470
EvenOdd value, 390, 394
EventArgs class, 142–143, 200, 202
EventArgs event, 66
events
    in DataGrid control, 273–274
    in Microsoft .NET for Silverlight, 53–56
    of UIElement to enable drag-and-drop
            functionality, 314
ExampleBrowser class, 654
ExampleBrowser.g.cs file, 670
ExcelExport method, 504–505
Exception instance, 488
ExceptionRoutedEventArgs class, 142–143, 157
Exchange method, Interlocked class, 528
Execute method, 503, 505
Exists method, 556
Exit event handler, 52, 655
Expanded event, TreeViewItem class, 101
Expanded value, 109
exponential function, 439
ExponentialEase function, 9, 439
Export button, Deep Zoom Composer, 160
Export step, Deep Zoom Composer, 158
Express Blend program, 361
Expression Blend tool, 15, 19–21, 448–452
Expression Design tool, 374, 442
Expression Encoder, 16
Expression property, 288
extending user experience of LoB applications.
    See also Silverlight applications
    clipboard access, 336–338
    drag-and-drop functionality
        adding ChildWindow as image viewer,
            321–323
        defining user controls, 315–317
        events of UIElement to, 314
        implementing code behind user
            controls, 317–320
        processing dropped files, 315
        properties of UIElement to, 314
    enhancements in Silverlight 4, 313

enhancements in XAML features
    custom IDictionary support, 354
    direct content, 353
    flexible root XAML namespace, 352
    whitespace handling, 353
    XmlnsDefinitionAttribute, 353
mouse-wheel support, 324–326
printing capabilities
    implementing functions, 331–335
    overview, 329
    PrintDocument class, 330
    PrintPageEventArgs class, 330
right-click context menu support, 326–329
Extensible Application Markup Language. See
    XAML
Extensible Markup Language (XML), 29, 32–33,
    49, 426
Extension property, 24, 318
ExtensionPart element, 653
ExternalParts section, AppManifest.xaml file,
    563
ExternalResources1.xaml file, 43
ExternalResources2.xaml file, 43
external.xaml file, 363
ExtraCondensed value, 109
ExtraExpanded value, 109
extraFields dictionary, 265–266

▒ F

F0 string, 394
FallbackValue markup extension, 265
FallbackValue method, 265
FallbackValue property, 237, 264
fault contract, 205
FaultReason message, 206
features, enhancements in XAML
    custom IDictionary support, 354
    direct content, 353
    flexible root XAML namespace, 352
    whitespace handling, 353
    XmlnsDefinitionAttribute, 353
feesTextBox control, 262
FieldLabel control, 11
File property, OpenFileDialog class, 126
FileExists method, 305
FileInfo object, 24–25, 318
FileInfo type array, 315
FileInfo.OpenRead method, 315
FileInfo.OpenText method, 315

files
    culture-specific resource
        adding, 344–346
        binding XAML controls with, 348–350
    dropped, processing, 315
    MainPage.xaml, 228–230
    management, 490–493
    Message.cs, 228
    policy, cross-domain
        clientaccesspolicy.xml, 187–189
        crossdomain.xml, 187
        overview, 186
    SocketClientAccessPolicy.xml Policy, 222
Files property, OpenFileDialog class, 126
Fill enum value, 144
Fill property, 376, 392, 511
FillBehavior property, 417, 421
Filling state, ClockState enumeration, 423
FillRule enumeration, 394
FillRule property, 390
Filter property
    OpenFileDialog class, 126
    SaveFileDialog class, 129
FilterIndex property
    OpenFileDialog class, 126
    SaveFileDialog class, 129
filtering in DataGrid control, 271
FilterMode property, AutoCompleteBox class,
    92
Find method, 556
FindName method, FrameworkElement class,
    64
first frame button, control bar, 449
FirstApplication project, 21
FirstDayOfWeek property, Calendar class, 119
FirstName property, 238, 245, 264
Flash framework, 5
Flex framework, 5
flexible root XAML namespace, 352
FlowDirection enumeration, 64
FlowDirection event, 349
FlowDirection property, FrameworkElement
    class, 64
Flush method, 309
Focus method, Control class, 67–68
Focused state, 372, 375, 377–378
FocusStates class, 377
FocusStates visual state group, 372
FontFamily property, 47, 67, 109, 356, 360–361
FontSize property, 23, 67, 109, 355–356, 360–
    361, 365, 368

FontSource property, 85, 109
FontStretch property, 67, 109
FontStyle property, 67, 109
FontWeight property, 23, 67, 110, 356, 360–361
foreach loop, 462, 492–493, 499
foreground animation, example of, 424–429
Foreground property, 67, 110, 356, 361, 365,
    370
Forever value, 420–421, 423, 452
formats, of media for integration in Silverlight,
    163–164
Forms controls
    AutoCompleteBox control, 91–94
    Button control, 83
    HyperlinkButton control, 83
    overview, 81–82
    PasswordBox control, 87–88
    RepeatButton control, 83–84
    RichTextBox control, 88–90
    TextBox control, 85–87
FragmentNavigation event, 136, 458
Frame class, 135, 457
Frame control, 103, 462
frame rate counter, for image integration in
    Silverlight, 154
Frame tag, 457
Frame.StopLoading method, 464
FrameworkElement class, 6, 36, 58, 63–66, 68,
    121, 261, 359
FrameworkElement type, 494
FrameworkElement.BindingValidationError
    event, 248–249
FriendlyName property, CaptureDevice class,
    176
From property, 373, 424
From value, 424
From/By properties, 424
From/To properties, 424
From/To/By animations
    foreground animation example, 424–429
    overview, 423
    shimmering effect example, 430–431
functional controls
    Border, 106–107
    Calendar, 118–120
    DatePicker, 118–120
    dialog boxes
        ChildWindow class, 131–133
        OpenFileDialog class, 125–128
        SaveFileDialog class, 128–130
    GridSplitter, 107

Image, 121
InkPresenter, 122–125
MediaElement, 122
MultiScaleImage, 121
Popup, 111–112
RangeBase class
    ProgressBar control, 117–118
    ScrollBar class, 115–116
    Slider control, 116–117
ScrollViewer, 113–114
TextBlock, 109–111
ToolTipService, 112–113
WebBrowser, 134
functionality, drag-and-drop, 314
functions
animation-easing, 440–442
printing, implementing
    custom printing, 334–335
    printing application screen, 331–333
    printing selected control, 333–334

█ G

GeneratedDuration property,
    System.Windows.VisualTransition class, 373
GeneratedEasingFunction property,
    System.Windows.VisualTransition class, 373
GeneratedImages folder, 160–161
GenerateIV method, 594
geometries
clipping with, 390
grouping, 390
path geometries, 387–389
simple, 384–386
Geometry class, 6, 383–385, 387, 390, 395
GeometryGroup class, 390
Gestalt project, 562, 564
Gestalt prototype, 561
gestalt.zip file, 562–563
GET method, 188, 236
get property value formula, 441
Get Tweets button, 551
GetAllTitle class, 201
GetAllTitle method, 193
GetAnimationBaseValue method,
    DependencyObject class, 59
GetAvailableAudioCaptureDevices method,
    CaptureDeviceConfiguration class, 174
GetAvailableVideoCaptureDevices method,
    CaptureDeviceConfiguration class, 174

GetBindingExpression method,
    FrameworkElement class, 64
GetBook proxy, 199
GetBook_GetByTitleCompleted event handler,
    206
GetBookInfo interface, 198
GetBookInfo service, 196–197, 206
GetBookInfo.cs file, 198, 200, 206
GetBookInfo.svc file, 193, 197, 206
GetBooks method, 504, 542
GetBooksQuery method, 545
GetBytes member method, 594
GetByTitle method, 193
GetByTitle operation, 205
GetByTitleAsync method, 199
GetByTitleCompletedEventArgs event, 206
GetCreationTime method, 305
GetCurrentState method, Storyboard class, 423
GetCurrentTime method, Storyboard class,
    423
GetDefaultAudioCaptureDevice method, 174,
    180
GetDefaultVideoCaptureDevice method, 174,
    180
getDetail button, 199
getDetail_Click method, 201
GetDir method, 492
GetDirectoryNames method, 306
GetDomain method, Thread class, 518
GetErrors method, 251, 255
GetFileNames method, 306
GetHostEntry method, 252
GetIsNetworkAvailable static method, 191
GetLastAccessTime method, 306
GetLastWriteTime method, 306
GetPlacement method, ToolTipService class,
    113
GetPlacementTarget method, ToolTipService
    class, 113
GetPosition property, 325
GetResourceStream method, 210
GetResponseStream method, 212–213
GetRolesForCurrentUser event callback, 610
GetRolesForCurrentUser event handler, 602
GetRolesForCurrentUser method, 602
GetTemplateChild event, Control class, 68
GetText method, 336
getting.started subfolder, 563
GetToolTip method, ToolTipService class, 113
GetUserStoreFor method, 306
GetValue method, 37–39, 59

global Silverlight application, 352
globalization, of Silverlight applications, 338–341
GlobalOffsetX property, 404, 572
GlobalOffsetY property, 404
GlobalOffsetZ property, 404, 572
glyph symbol, 105
GoBack( ) method, 136, 457
GoForward( ) method, 136, 457
GotFocus event, UIElement class, 62
GoToState method, 381
goUpBubble animation, 445
GPU (Graphics Processor Unit), 10, 152–155, 666
gradient brushes
    LinearGradientBrush class, 411
    overview, 410
    RadialGradientBrush class, 412
gradient stops, 410
GradientOrigin property, 412
GradientStop class, 443
GradientStops property, GradientBrush class, 410
grant-to element, 188
graphics
    2D, 8
        geometries, 384–390
        overview, 383
        shapes, 391–395
    3D effects, using perspective transforms, 403–405
    brushes
        gradient, 410–412
        overview, 407
        SolidColorBrush class, 408
        tile, 408–409
    enhancements in Silverlight 4, 383
    pixel shaders, 405–406
    transforms
        arbitrary linear transforms, 399–400
        composite transformation, 401–403
        multiple, combining, 401
        overview, 395
        rotation, 396–397
        scaling, 398–399
        skewing, 397
        translation, 396
    transparency and opacity masks, 412–414
Graphics Processor Unit (GPU), 10, 152–155, 666
Grid class, 38, 41, 372

Grid control, 30, 45, 56, 71–74, 146, 153, 569
Grid panel, 89
Grid.Column property, 38, 71, 146
Grid.ColumnSpan property, ControlsGrid class, 71
GridLength class, 73
Grid.Resources namespace, 362–363
Grid.Row property, 38, 71
Grid.RowSpan property, ControlsGrid class, 71
GridSplitter class, 377
GridSplitter control, 107
GroupDescriptions property, 12, 237, 268, 270
grouping
    in DataGrid control, 267–270
    geometries, 390
GroupName attribute, 379
GroupName property, RadioButton class, 85

▓ H

H x command, 394
H.264 format, 162
hardware acceleration, for image integration in Silverlight
    Bitmap caching, 153
    cache visualization, 154
    frame rate counter, 154
    GPU hardware acceleration, 153–154
    overview, 152
HasCloseButton property, ChildWindow class, 131
HasCount property, RepeatBehavior property, 421
HasDuration property, 421
HasErrors property, 251
hash algorithms, 590–592
Hash property, System.Security.Cryptography.HMAC class, 590
HashAlgorithm.Initialize( ) method, 591
hash-based message authentication code (HMAC), 590
HashName property, System.Security.Cryptography.HMAC class, 590
HashSize property, System.Security.Cryptography.HMAC class, 591
HasItems property, TreeViewItem class, 101
HasMorePages property, 331

HaveResponse property, 211
HD (high-definition), 10, 152, 162
Header property, 79, 102, 104
HeaderedContentControl, 103–104
HeaderedItemsControl, 102–103
Headers property, 211
HeaderTemplate property
    HeaderedContentControl class, 104
    HeaderedItemsControl class, 102
height attribute, object element, 664
Height property, 20–21, 65, 73, 148, 392–393,
    565, 568
helper class, 346–347
Helpers folder, 535
Heuer, Tim, 471, 545
high-definition (HD), 10, 152, 162
High-Level Shading Language (HLSL), 9, 405
HintPath property, 672
history of Silverlight
    version 1, 6–7
    version 2, 7
    version 3, 9
    version 4, 11–13
HLSL (High-Level Shading Language), 9, 405
HMAC (hash-based message authentication
    code), 590
HMAC class, 590–591
HMACSHA1 class, 590
HMACSHA256 class, 590, 592
HoldEnd value, FillBehavior property, 417, 421
Home.xaml file, 455–457, 466, 470, 544
horizontal scrollbar class, 378
HorizontalAlignment property, 65, 108
HorizontalContent property, Control class, 67
horizontally-oriented scrollbar class, 378
HorizontalOffset property, 111, 114, 320, 328
HorizontalScroll property, ScrollViewer class,
    114
HorizontalScrollBar property
    RichTextBox class, 89
    TextBox class, 86
Host property, 559, 655
hosting Silverlight applications
    custom HTML object element error
        handling, 667
    custom initialization parameters, 662–663
    embedding Silverlight plug-ins to web
        page, 663–666
    overview, 659–660
    server-side Silverlight RIA deployment,
        661–662

Hover value, 82
HTML (HyperText Markup Language), 153–
    154, 360
HTML object element, 663–666
HtmlPage. Document class, 303
HTTP (Hypertext Transfer Protocol),
    communicating directly over
        HttpWebRequest class, 211–213
        WebClient class, 207–210
http-request-headers attribute, 188
HTTPS (HyperText Transfer Protocol Secure),
    163
HttpStack property, 288
HttpWebRequest class, 185, 207, 211–213, 236,
    515, 589
HttpWebResponse protocol, 49, 522
hub-and-spoke model, 342–343
HyperlinkButton class, 83, 377, 462
HyperlinkButtons class, 459, 461
HyperText Markup Language (HTML), 153–
    154, 360
Hypertext Transfer Protocol. *See* HTTP
HyperText Transfer Protocol Secure (HTTPS),
    163

▓ I

IAsyncResult method, 199
ICommand interface, 502–503
Icon nodes, 482
IDataErrorInfo Interface, 12, 237, 246, 249–251,
    253
IDataErrorInfo object, 237
IDataObject class, 315
IDE (integrated development environment),
    546
identity matrix, 400
IDictionary class, 354
IDispatchMessageInspector method, 202
IDynamicMetaObjectProvider interface, 12
IEasingFunction interface, 438, 442
IEditableObject interface, 282
IEndpointBehavior method, 202–203
IEnumerable collection, 497
IEnumerable data source, 93
IEnumerable interface, 303
IEnumerable<WebDeveloper> collection, 303
IIS (Internet Information Services), 162
IIS manager, 662
IIS Media Services feature, Silverlight 3, 10

IIS MIME type, setting, 662
IL (Intermediate Language), 557
IList interface, 173
Image class, image integration in Silverlight, 142–147
Image control, 121, 141, 150, 261, 405
Image element, 149, 151, 405
image integration
    Bitmap API, 147–152
    Deep Zoom composer, 158–161
    hardware acceleration
        Bitmap caching, 153
        cache visualization, 154
        GPU hardware acceleration, 153–154
        overview, 152
    Image class, 142–147
    multi-scale images, 155–161
Image object, 210, 318
image viewer, adding ChildWindow as, 321–323
ImageBrush class, 408–409
ImageFailed event
    BitmapImage class, 143
    Image class, 142
    MultiScaleImage control, 157
imageFileList List object, 492
ImageOpened event
    BitmapImage class, 143
    Image class, 142
ImageOpenFailed event, MultiScaleImage control, 157
ImageOpenSucceeded event, MultiScaleImage control, 157
Images folder, 160–161
ImageSource class, 143
ImageStage control, 333
ImageStage.RenderTransform property, 324
ImageStage.Source property, 322
ImageUtilities object, 657
ImageViewer project, 146
ImageWindow_MouseWheel event handler, 324
ImageWindow.xaml file, 321, 326, 331, 349
ImageWindow.xmal.cs file, 324
IMEs (Input Method Editors), 63
img_MouseLeftButtonDown event, 322
imgSource ImageSource property, 322
implicit styling, 43–44, 364–365
Import step, Deep Zoom Composer, 158
improved text rendering feature, Silverlight 3, 10

INavigationContentLoader interface
    BeginLoad method, 463–464
    CancelLoad method, 464
    CanLoad method, 464
    EndLoad method, 464
    overview, 463
in-browser mode, 582, 587
in-browser, unit testing, 616–619
includeExceptionDetailInFaults attribute, 205
include-subpaths attribute, 188
IncreaseQuotaTo method, 306
Increment method, Interlocked class, 528
Indeterminate event, ToggleButton class, 84
indeterminate state, 377–378
index.html file, 561
Individualizing state, 165, 167
Inheritable option, 307
inheritance, style (cascading), 360–361
initBooks method, 193
initial position, 429
initialization parameters, custom, 662–663
Initialization vector (IV), 594
Initialize method, System.Security.Cryptography.HMAC class, 591
InitializeComponent method, 49, 53, 151, 670
InitializeService method, 292, 294
initParams parameter, 559, 662, 665
InkPresenter control, 122–125
Inline elements, 89
Inlines property, TextBlock class, 110
InlineUIContainer function, 24, 89
INotifyCollectionChanged interface, 284
INotifyDataErrorInfo event handler, 258
INotifyDataErrorInfo interface
    adding Consultant.cs class to implement, 253–258
    ASP .NET validation web service, 252–253
    and code-behind, 258–260
    overview, 251
INotifyDataErrorInfo object, 237
INotifyDataErrorInfoDemo interface, 251, 253
INotifyPropertyChanged interface, 200, 243, 246, 259, 278, 346–347, 504
in-package and on-demand files
    Build Action property, 658–659
    Copy Local property, 657–658
    overview, 656
input events, 53
Input Method Editors (IMEs), 63

InputBlockSize property,
System.Security.Cryptography.HMAC class,
591
install parameter, sllauncher.exe program, 674
Installed state, 478
InstallFailed state, 479
installing
Microsoft Bing Maps Silverlight control
SDK, 566
out-of-browser applications, 477–480
/install:"path to xap file" parameter, 479
int data type, 556
integrated development environment (IDE),
546
IntelliSense class, 668
IntelliSense window, 103
interfaces, user, 346–347
Interlaced video format, 164
Interlocked class, 528
Intermediate Language (IL), 557
Internet Information Services (IIS), 162
Internet Standard Multicast (ISM), 232
interpolation, 432, 434–438
Interval property, 84, 530
invalid focused state, 377–378
invalid not focused state, 377–378
invalid state, 377
invalid unfocused state, 377–378
Invalidate method, WritableBitmap class, 147
InvalidateArrange method, UIElement class,
60
InvalidateMeasurement method, UIElement
class, 60
InvalidOperation exception, 423
InvalidOperationException exception, 479
InvariantCulture property, 339
IPagedCollectionView, 105
IPagedViewCollection interface, 105
IPEndPoint class, 214, 220
IQueryable interface, 285
IronPython language
externalizing code, 564–565
in-line code in hosting HTML file, 564–565
IronPython.dll assembly, 557, 560, 563
IronPython.Modules.dll assembly, 557, 560,
563
IronPython.slvx file, 563
IronRuby language
developing interactive Bing Maps
application with

adding 3D animation within
SilverlightMap.xaml file, 569
adding rotate Map capabilities, 571–574
creating SilverlightMap.html file, 568–
569
creating SilverlightMap.rb IronRuby file
and adding Map mode, 570
creating SilverlightMap.xaml file, 568
including Bing Maps control, 566–567
installing Microsoft Bing Maps
Silverlight control SDK, 566
targeting pre-defined locations, 575–
577
externalizing code, 564–565
in-line code in hosting HTML file, 564–565
overview, 556–557
IronRuby.dll assembly, 557, 560, 562
IronRuby.Libraries.dll assembly, 557, 560, 562
IronRuby.slvx file, 562
IsAlive property, Thread class, 517
IsBackground property, Thread class, 517
IsBusy property, 208, 522
IsChecked property, 84, 509
IsCorrectImageFileType method, 24–25
IsCurrentUserInRole method, 602
IsDefaultDevice property, CaptureDevice
class, 176
IsDirectionReversed property, Slider class, 117
IsDownloading property, MultiScaleImage
control, 156
IsDropDownOpen property, 92, 94
IsEditable property, ComboBox class, 98
IsEnabled property, 67–68
isEnabled property, 259
IsEnabled property, 305
IsEnabledChanged event, Control class, 68
IsExpanded property, TreeViewItem class, 101
IsFocused property
ButtonBase class, 82
Slider class, 117
IsFullScreen property, 130
IsHitTestVisible property, UIElement class, 61
IsIdle property, MultiScaleImage control, 156
IsIndeterminate property, 117–118
IsLargeArc property, ArcSegment class, 388
IsLoggedIn method, 599
ISM (Internet Standard Multicast), 232
IsMouseOver property, ButtonBase class, 82
IsMuted property, 165, 409
ISO MPEG Layer III (MP3), 163
ISO MPEG-4 AVC, 163

isolated storage, 237, 303–310
IsolatedStorageException class, 304
IsolatedStorageFile class, 304
IsolatedStorageFileStream class, 304, 307, 309
IsolatedStoreFile.GetUserStoreForApplication static method, 307
IsOpen property, Popup class, 111–112
IsPressed property, ButtonBase class, 82
IsReadOnly property
    RichTextBox class, 89
    TextBox class, 86
IsRequired property, Label control, 105
IsSealed property, System.Windows.DependencyObject Style class, 358
IsSelected property, 98–99, 101
IsSelectionActive property, TreeViewItem class, 101
IsTabStop property, Control class, 67
IsTextCompletion property, AutoCompleteBox class, 93
IsThreeState property, ToggleButton class, 84
IsTodayHighlighted property, Calendar class, 119
isToggle variable, 362
IsTotalItemCountFixed property, 272
isUserInRole method, 603
Item property, 249
ItemContainerStyle property
    AutoCompleteBox class, 93
    ComboBox class, 98
    HeaderedItemsControl class, 102
    ListBox class, 96
    TreeView class, 101
ItemCount property, 272
ItemFilter property, AutoCompleteBox class, 93
ItemGroup element, 672
ItemHeight property, WrapPanel class, 78
Items property, ItemsControl class, 96
ItemsControl class, 247
ItemsControl control, 96
ItemSource property, 92, 104, 295
ItemsPanel property, ItemsControl class, 96
ItemsSource property, 45, 93, 96, 103, 267–268, 280
ItemTemplate property
    AutoCompleteBox class, 93
    ItemsControl class, 96
    ListBox class, 98
    Selector class, 99
ItemWidth property, WrapPanel class, 78
IV (Initialization vector), 594
IV property, System.Security.Cryptography.SymmetricAl gorithm class, 594
IValueConverter interface, 262

⬚ **J**

Java platform, 4
JavaScript Object Notation (JSON), 284
javascripts\error.js file, 561
Join method, Thread class, 518
JournalOwnership property, 136, 459, 462
JPEG format, 142
js\error.js file, 561
JSON (JavaScript Object Notation), 284
"Just-Text" approach
    creating Silverlight applications using
        externalizing XAML and
            IronRuby/IronPython code, 565–566
        hosting HTML file, 564
        in-line IronRuby/IronPython code in
            hosting HTML file, 564–565
        in-line XAML code in hosting HTML
            file, 565
    setting up development environment
        using, 561–563

⬚ **K**

Key property
    System.Security.Cryptography.HMAC
        class, 591
    System.Security.Cryptography.SymmetricA
        lgorithm class, 594
KeyDown event, UIElement class, 62
KeyedHashAlgorithm class, 590
KeyedHashAlgorithm.Key property, 591
KeyEventHandler class, 62
keyframe animations
    discrete interpolation, 434–436
    interpolation, 434–438
    linear interpolation, 434
    overview, 432–433
    spline interpolation, 436–438
KeySize property, System.Security.Cryptography.SymmetricAl gorithm class, 594
KeySpline editor, Expression Blend, 450–451

KeyTime property, 434
KeyUp event, UIElement class, 62

▓ L

L endPoint command, 394
Label control, 103, 105
Language Integrated Query (LINQ), 27, 49
Language property, FrameworkElement class, 65
languages.config file, 562, 567
LargeChange property, RangeBase class, 115
LargeTitle style, 363
last frame button, 449
LastChildFill property, DockPanel, 75–76
LastOperation property, 216
Late Binding, Silverlight 4, 12
layout management and grouping controls
    Canvas control, 69
    DockPanel control, 74–77
    Grid control, 71–74
    StackPanel control, 70
    TabControl control, 78–79
    ViewBox control, 80
    WrapPanel control, 77–78
Layout section, 20
LayoutRoot control, 143
LayoutRoot Grid code, 498
LayoutRoot Grid control, 332
LayoutRoot StackPanel control, 247, 266
LayoutRoot_BindingValidationError method, 259
LayoutRoot_MouseLeftButtonDown event, 329
LayoutRoot_MouseRightButtonUp event, 327
LayoutUpdated event, FrameworkElement class, 66
LegalBlockSizes property, System.Security.Cryptography.SymmetricAlgorithm class, 594
LegalKeySizes property, System.Security.Cryptography.SymmetricAlgorithm class, 594
Length property, 309
LicenseAcquirer property, 165
Line class, 393
Line of Business (LoB), 11
linear interpolation, 434
linear transforms, 399–400
LinearDoubleKeyFrame class, 434

LinearGradiantBrush class, 150
LinearGradientBrush class, 150–151, 411
LineBreak element, 89
LineGeometry class, 384–385
LineHeight property, 110
Line-of-Business (LoB), 88
LineSegment class, 387, 389
LineStackingStrategy property, TextBlock class, 110
LinksStackPanel, 462
LINQ (Language Integrated Query), 27, 49
List class, 45
List<string>, 92, 602
List<WebDeveloper> collection, 302
ListBox class, 45
ListBox control, 10–11, 96–98, 238, 377, 547
ListBox ItemTemplate, 550
ListBox listBox1, 551
ListBoxItem class, 33, 98, 377
ListBoxItem control, ContentControl class, 103
ListBoxItem instance, 145
ListenFailedException class, 507
listItems array, 529
ListSortDirection enumeration, 270
Load method, AssemblyPart class, 657–658
LoadAsync method, 289, 295
LoadCompleted event, 289
Loaded event, 179, 260, 418, 428, 434, 444, 447, 485–486, 498
Loader.BeginLoad method, 469
Load(IEnumerable<T>) method, 289
LoadNextPartialSetAsync method, 289
LoB (Line of Business), 11
LoB (Line-of-Business), 88
LoB applications. See extending user experience of LoB applications
local image files integration, using drag-and-drop functionality, 21–26
LocalFileAccessDemo.xaml file, 490, 496
localization, of Silverlight applications
    adding culture-specific resource files, 344–346
    adding helper class to support dynamic culture-specific change in user interfaces, 346–347
    binding XAML controls with culture-specific resource files, 348–350
    hub-and-spoke model, 342–343
    making project aware of localization capabilities, 350

localization, of Silverlight applications (*cont.*)
preparing for global Silverlight application,
352
LocalizedStrings.cs class, 346–347
LocalMessageReceiver class, 507–508, 511
LocalMessageReceiver.MessageReceived
event, 507
LocalMessageSender class, 507–508, 510
LocalMessageSender.SendCompleted event,
507
LocalOffsetX property, PlaneProjection class,
404
LocalOffsetY property, PlaneProjection class,
404
LocalOffsetZ property, PlaneProjection class,
404
Locate Location section, 576
lock keyword, 528–529
logical tree, 32
LogicalToElementPoint method,
MultiScaleImage control, 157
Login method, 599, 601
LoginAsync method, 601
LoginCompleted event, 601
LoginLabelFontStyle property, 42
LoginPage.xaml, 465, 469
LoginScreen class, 609
Logout method, 599, 601
LogReady event, 167
LostFocus event, UIElement class, 62
LostMouseCapture event
InkPresenter class, 122–124
UIElement class, 62

■ M

M11 property, MatrixTransform class, 399
M12 property, MatrixTransform class, 399
M21 property, MatrixTransform class, 399
M22 property, MatrixTransform class, 399
MAC (message authentication code), 590–592
Main Title style, 362
MainPage class, 52–53, 229, 510–511
MainPage constructor, 53, 485
MainPage_Loaded event, 161
MainPage.g.cs file, 673
MainPage.g.i.cs file, 49
MainPage.xaml file, 19, 52, 228–229, 363, 462,
470, 485, 548
MainPage.xaml page, 195, 294, 455, 457

MainPage.xaml.cs button-click event, 199
MainPage.xaml.cs code, 229–230, 461
MainTitle style, 360–362
Make Into Control option, 374
MakeCert tool, 585
Manage Add-ons dialog box, Microsoft
Internet Explorer 8, 646
ManagedMediaHelpers project, 183
ManagedThreadId property, Thread class, 517
Map control, 568
Map element, 568–569, 576
map_in_ironruby Map element, 569
MapControl.dlls assembly, 570
MappedUri attribute, 471
MappingMode property, GradientBrush class,
410
Maps control, 576
Margin property, 23, 65, 148, 179, 356, 358
Marker member, 173
Marker property, 167
MarkerReached event, 167, 173
Markers property, 166, 173
Markers tab, 172–173
markup extensions, in XAML
data binding, 44–47
implicit styling, 43–44
resource dictionaries, 40–44
template binding, 47–48
masks, transparency and opacity, 412–414
MatrixTransform class, 399, 401
maxFrameRate parameter, OBJECT tag, 665
MaxFrameRate,
System.Windows.Interop.Settings class, 666
MaxHeight property, FrameworkElement
class, 65
MaxHeight value, 110
Maximum property, 115, 118
maximumWordLength variable, 556
MaxLength property
PasswordBox class, 87
TextBox class, 86
MaxWidth property, FrameworkElement class,
65
Measure method, UIElement class, 60
media feature, Silverlight 1, 6
media integration
enhancements in Silverlight 4, 141
images
Bitmap API, 147–152
Deep Zoom composer, 155–161
hardware acceleration, 152–154

Image class, 142–147
multi-scale images, 155–161
MediaElement class, 164–171
streaming, 184
supported formats, 163–164
timeline markers, 172–173
unsupported formats, 163–164
video and audio
MediaElement class, 164–171
overview, 162
supported formats, 163–164
timeline markers, 172–173
unsupported formats, 163–164
web camera and microphone
integration, 174–182
web camera and microphone integration
AudioCaptureDevice,class, 176–177
CaptureDevice class, 176–177
CaptureDeviceConfiguration class,
174–175
CaptureSource class, 177
example of, 179–182
VideoCaptureDevice class, 176–177
Windows Azure Platform
publishing video content, 183–184
subscribing to services, 183
MediaElement class, 149, 164–171
MediaElement control, 122, 141, 148–149, 164,
169–170, 173
MediaElement property, 409
MediaElement UIElement class, 149, 151
MediaEnded event, 167, 170–171
MediaFailed event, MediaElement class, 167
MediaIntegration project, 147, 169
MediaOpened event, MediaElement class, 167
MediaStreamSources class, 182
merged resource dictionaries, 42–43, 363
MergedDictionaries property, 43
MergeOption property, 288
message authentication code (MAC), 590–592
Message class, 228
Message element, 606
Message parameter, 511
Message.cs file, 228
MessageReceived event, 508, 511
MessageReceivedEventArgs class, 507
MessengerConnection class, 223, 225–227
MessengerServer class, 223–225
MessengerServer Windows service project
MessengerConnection class, 225–227
MessengerServer class, 223–225

MessengerServer.exe file, 230
Method property, 211
microphone and web camera integration
AudioCaptureDevice,class, 176–177
CaptureDevice class, 176–177
CaptureDeviceConfiguration class, 174–
175
CaptureSource class, 177
example of, 179–182
VideoCaptureDevice class, 176–177
Microsoft ASP.NET AJAX, 5
Microsoft Bing Maps Silverlight control SDK,
566
Microsoft Developer Network (MSDN), 38
Microsoft Expression Blend, 8
Microsoft Media Server (MMS), 163
Microsoft .NET for Silverlight
core .NET assemblies for, 48–49
managed code-behind .NET integration
Application class, 50–52
events in, 53–56
MainPage class, 52–53
overview, 49
Microsoft SDKs/Silverlight folder, 74
Microsoft.Maps.MapControl.Common.dll file,
566–567
Microsoft.Maps.MapControl.Common.xml
file, 566
Microsoft.Maps.MapControl.Design
namespace, 577
Microsoft.Maps.MapControl.dll file, 566–567
Microsoft.Maps.MapControl.xml file, 566
Microsoft.Phone.Controls.Navigation
assembly, 550
Microsoft.Scripting.Core.dll assembly, 558–
559, 563
Microsoft.Scripting.Debugging.dll assembly,
558, 563
Microsoft.Scripting.dll assembly, 558, 563
Microsoft.Scripting.ExtensionAttribute.dll
assembly, 558–559, 563
Microsoft.Scripting.Silverlight.dll assembly,
558–559, 562–563
Microsoft.Scripting.Silverlight.DynamicApplic
ation class, 559
Microsoft.Scripting.slvx file, 562–563
MIME Type button, IIS manager Properties
window, 662
MinHeight property, FrameworkElement
class, 65
Minimum property, 115, 118

MinimumPopulate property, AutoCompleteBox class, 93

MinimumPrefix property, AutoCompleteBox class, 93

MinWidth property, FrameworkElement class, 65

Mix Online Lab team, 561–562

MMS (Microsoft Media Server), 163

mode attribute, 589

Mode property, 46, 240

Model class, 504

Model View Controller (MVC), 502

Model View Presenter (MVP), 502

Model.cs file, 503

Models folder, 535–536, 541

models, of Silverlight security, 580–582

Model-View-View-Model (MVVM), 68, 82, 248, 502, 533

MotionFinished event, 157

MouseButtonEventArgs.GetPosition method, 328

MouseButtonEventArgs.Handled method, 327

MouseButtonEventHandler class, 63

moused over state, 377–378

MouseEnter event, UIElement class, 62

MouseEventHandler class, 62–63

MouseLeave event, UIElement class, 62

MouseLeftButton down event, 53

MouseLeftButtonDown event, 54, 63, 122–125, 149, 151, 322, 493

MouseLeftButtonUp event, 63, 326

MouseMove event
    InkPresenter class, 122–124
    UIElement class, 63

MouseOver event, 381

MouseOver state, 372–373, 375–376

MouseRightButtonDown event, 63, 313, 326–327

MouseRightButtonUp event, 63, 313, 326

MouseWheel event, 63, 324, 326

mouse-wheel support, 324–326

MouseWheelEventArgs.Delta property, 325

MouseWheelEventHandler class, 63

MouseWheelHelper.cs class, 160

MouseWheelHelper.cs file, 161

move command, 394

MoveDirectory method, 306

MoveFile method, 306

movement animation, 429–430

MP3 (ISO MPEG Layer III), 163

MP3 format, 163–164

MP4 format, 162–163

MSBuild
    building MsBuild project (.proj) with, 670–673
    building Visual Studio project (.csproj) with, 668–670
    unit testing using
        code coverage, 622–624
        overview, 620
        test result files, 622
        using tag expressions, 621

MsBuild project (.proj), building with MSBuild, 670–673

msbuild.exe file, 668

MsBuildSampleProject folder, 671

mscorlib assembly, 48

MSDN (Microsoft Developer Network), 38

MSDN Magazine, 566

msgReceiver.Listen( ) method, 511

MulticastLoopback property, 234

multicasts, UDP, 232–235

multiple transforms, combining, 401

multi-scale images, for image integration in Silverlight, 155–161

MultiScaleImage control, 121, 141, 155–156, 160

MultiScaleSubImage class, 156

Multiselect property, OpenFileDialog class, 126

multi-threaded environment, 515

MVC (Model View Controller), 502

MVP (Model View Presenter), 502

MVVM (Model-View-View-Model), 68, 82, 248, 502, 533

My Pictures folder, 490–491

MyDocuments folder, 587

MyMusic folder, 587

mySlider control, 260–261

MyVideos folder, 587

N

Name attribute, 379, 664

<Name of the Silverlight Application>TestPage.aspx naming convention, 663

<Name of the Silverlight Application>TestPage.html naming convention, 663

Name property, 23, 25, 34, 65, 146, 256, 270, 339, 517
name=value syntax, 46
namespaces
    flexible root XAML, 352
    System.Net
        Socket class, 214–215
        SocketAsyncEventArgs class, 216
    in XAML, 33
NaN value, 85
NAnt build tool, 667
NativeName property, 340
NaturalDuration property, MediaElement class, 166
NaturalVideoHeight property, MediaElement class, 166
NaturalVideoWidth property, MediaElement class, 166
Navigate( ) method, 136, 457
Navigated event, 136, 457–458, 461
NavigateToString(String) method, 134
Navigate(Uri) method, 134
NavigateUri property, 83, 461–462
Navigating event, 136, 458
navigation, 135–138. *See also* Silverlight Navigation Framework
NavigationCacheMode enum, 137
NavigationCacheMode property, Page class, 135, 137
NavigationContext property, Page class, 137
NavigationFailed event, 136, 457–458, 461
navigation:Frame tag, 471
NavigationGrid control, 459
NavigationProperty property, 291
NavigationService property, Page class, 137
NavigationService.StopLoading method, 464
NavigationStopped event, 136, 458
.NET, security of in CLR, 579–580
network communication
    considerations for using networking, 236
    consuming web services with WCF. *See also* Silverlight, invoking services from
        communicating directly over HTTP, 207–213
        creating web services consumable by Silverlight, 192–195
        HttpWebRequest class, 211–213
        overview, 191
        WebClient class, 207–210
        XAML to consume information, 195

    enabling cross-domain communication
        overview, 185
        policy files, 186–189
        trusted applications, 189–191
    network-aware applications, 191
    networking enhancements in Silverlight 4, 185
    UDP multicast
        UdpAnySourceMulticastClient class, 232–233
        UdpSingleSourceMulticastClient class, 234–235
    via sockets. *See also* socket-based sample text chat application; System.Net namespace
    via sockets, controlling client access via socket policy server, 213–214
NetworkAddressChange event, 485
NetworkAddressChanged event, 191
network-aware applications, 191
NetworkCredential class, 185
NetworkInterface class, 191
NetworkInterface.GetIsNetworkAvailable method, 485
New Project dialog, Visual Studio 2010, 17
New Silverlight Application dialog box, Visual Studio 2010, 18
next frame button, control bar, 449
No Border option, 484
NoDelay property, 215
None enumeration, 144, 293
None option, 307, 658–659
None value, FilterMode, 94
Nonzero value, 390
Normal state, 372, 375, 377–378
Normal value, 109
NormalDay state, 377
not focused state, 377
NotFoundMessage fault object, 206
notification API, 494–496
NotificationWindow class, 12, 494, 496
NotifyContent.xaml file, 494–495
NotifyOnValidationError event handler, 248, 259
NotifyOnValidationError property, 240, 246
NotifyPropertyChanged property, 278
NotImplementedException exception, 467
NTLM authentication, 603
NumberFormat property, 340
NumericButtonCount property, 272
NumericButtonStyle property, 272

■ O

obj\Debug directory, 670
OBJECT tag, 664–665
ObjectAnimationUsingKeyFrames class, 415, 432, 435
ObjectDisposedException class, 304
Objects and Timeline area, 20
Objects and Timeline pane, Expression Blend tool, 20, 374
Objects pane, Expression Blend, 449
ObservableCollection class, 279, 289
OData (Open Data Protocol), 284
Offset property, 150, 216, 411
OffsetX property, 399–400
OffsetY property, 399–400
Olson, Larry, 183
OnApplyTemplate method, FrameworkElement class, 64
OnConnection method, 220, 224
OnCreateAutomationPeer method, UIElement class, 60
on-demand file deployment option, 656
on-demand files. See in-package and on-demand files
OnDragEnter method, Control class, 68
OnDragLeave method, Control class, 68
OnDragOver method, Control class, 68
OnDrop method, Control class, 68
One Box solutions, 12
onError parameter, OBJECT tag, 664–665
onerror property, object tag, 559
OneTime mode, 238
OneWay mode, 239
OnFragmentNavigation method, Page class, 137
OnGotFocus method, Control class, 68
OnKeyDown method, Control class, 68
OnKeyUp method, Control class, 68
onLoad parameter, OBJECT tag, 665
OnLostFocus method, Control class, 68
OnLostMouseCapture method, Control class, 68
OnMouseEnter method, Control class, 68
OnMouseLeave method, Control class, 68
OnMouseLeftButtonDown method, Control class, 68
OnMouseLeftButtonUp method, Control class, 68
OnMouseMove method, Control class, 68

OnMouseRightButtonDown method, Control class, 68
OnMouseRightButtonUp method, Control class, 68
OnMouseWheel method, Control class, 68
OnMsgReceived method, 225, 227
OnNavigatedFrom method, Page class, 137
OnNavigatedTo method, Page class, 137
OnNavigatingFrom method, Page class, 137
OnReceive method, 222
onResize parameter, OBJECT tag, 665
OnSend method, 222
onSourceDownloadComplete parameter, OBJECT tag, 665
onSourceDownloadProgressChanged parameter, OBJECT tag, 665
OnTextInput method, Control class, 68
OnTextInputStart method, Control class, 68
OnTextInputUpdate method, Control class, 68
OOB (out-of-browser). See out-of-browser
opacity masks, 412–414
Opacity property, 61, 156, 408, 412–413
OpacityMask property, 61, 150–151, 154, 413
Open Data Protocol (OData), 284
Open File Dialog box, 21, 126
Open option, 307
Open Specification Promise (OSP), 9
open-file dialog box, 587
OpenFile method, 128, 306, 309
OpenFileDialog class, 125–128, 131, 490
Opening state, 165, 167–168
OpenOrCreate option, 307
OpenReadAsync method, 207, 210
OpenReadCompleted event, 207, 209
Open/Save file dialog, 482
OperationContract attribute, 194
Orientation property, 70, 78, 116–117, 148–149
/origin:"Uri to origin of the xap file" parameter, 479
OSP (Open Specification Promise), 9
OSSupportsIPv4 property, 215
OSSupportsIPv6 property, 215
/out:<fileName> option, 197
out-of-browser (OOB)
    applications
        debugging, 640
        digitally signing, 585–586
        silent installer for, 673–674
    functionality
        COM automation, 497–500

customizing out-of-browser applications, 482–484
enabling, 475–476
files management, 490–493
incorporating updated version, 488–490
installing out-of-browser applications, 477–480
networking and offline APIs, 484–487
notification API, 494–496
overview, 474
trusted out-of-browser applications, 481–482
uninstalling out-of-browser applications, 480–481
Out-of-Browser Settings button, 475, 582
Out-of-Browser Settings window, 483
<OutOfBrowserSettings.Icons> node, 482
OutOfBrowserSettings.xml file, 12, 189–190, 476, 481–482
Output tab, 173
OutputBlockSize property, System.Security.Cryptography.HMAC class, 591
OutputPath property, 671
OutputType property, 671
OverlayBrush property, ChildWindow class, 131
OverlayOpacity property, ChildWindow class, 132
overriding styles, 361–362
overwrite parameter, 479, 674
OwnsJournal mode, 462
OwnsJournal value, 136

▓ P

packaging and deploying Silverlight applications
  build process
    building Silverlight application MsBuild project (.proj) with MSBuild, 670–673
    building Silverlight application Visual Studio project (.csproj) with MSBuild, 668–670
    overview, 667
  client considerations
    disabling Silverlight plug-in using web browser, 646
    overview, 645
    Silverlight configuration, 647–650

deployment package definition
  core runtime library, 651
  in-package and on-demand files, 656–659
  overview, 650
  Silverlight Application Package (XAP File), 651–656
hosting Silverlight applications
  custom HTML object element error handling, 667
  custom initialization parameters, 662–663
  embedding Silverlight plug-ins to web page, 663–666
  overview, 659–660
  server-side Silverlight RIA deployment, 661–662
silent installer for Silverlight out-of-browser applications, 673–674
Padding property
  Border class, 106
  Control class, 67
  TextBlock class, 110
Page build action, 43
Page class, 19, 135, 137–138, 462, 655
Page property, 456
PageCount property, 273
PagedCollectionView class, 267–268
PagedCollectionView property, 271, 273
PagedCollectionView.Filter property, 271
PageIndex property, 271, 273
PageMargins property, 331
PageResourceContentLoader class, 463, 465, 468
PageSize property, 271, 273
PageVisual control, 333
PageVisual property, 331
Page.xaml file, 19, 160–161
paging in DataGrid control, 271–273
Panel class, 69
Panel Control class, 63
Paragraph class, 89
Paragraph elements, 89
param child element, 664, 667
ParameterizedThreadStart class, 519
Parent property, 65, 340
parsing XML data in, 300–301
partially trusted Silverlight applications, vs. elevated-trusted, 587
Password property, PasswordBox class, 87

Password-Based Key Derivation Function #1 (PBKDF1), 593
PasswordBox class, 378
PasswordBox control, 10, 87–88
PasswordChanged event, 88
PasswordChar property, 87
Path class, 384–387, 391–395, 409
path geometries, 387–389
Path property, 240
PathFigure objects, 387
PathSegment objects, 387
Pause button, 571
Pause method, 165–166, 423
pause_resume button, 573–574
Paused state, 165, 167
pause/resume button, 426, 428
PBKDF1 (Password-Based Key Derivation Function #1), 593
PC (personal computer), 153
performLengthyOperation property, 525
Permission tab, 175, 649–650
personal computer (PC), 153
perspective transforms, 3D effects using, 403–405
PerspectiveTransform effect, 154
Pixel enumeration, 275
pixel shaders, 405–406
Pixel Shaders feature, Silverlight 3, 9
PixelHeight property, 142–143, 147
Pixels property, WritableBitmap class, 147
PixelWidth property, 142–143, 147
PKCS (Public-Key Cryptography Standard), 593
PlaneProjection animation, 572
PlaneProjection class, 403, 452
PlatformNotSupportedException instance, 488
Play method, 166, 170
Playback tab, Silverlight configuration utility, 648
Player controls, Silverlight, 7
Playing state, 165, 167
plus sign, Expression Blend, 448
PNG format, 141–142
Point property
    ArcSegment class, 388
    LineSegment class, 389
PointAnimation class, 415, 424
PointAnimationUsingKeyFrames class, 415
Points property
    PolyBezierSegment class, 389
    Polygon class, 393

PolyLineSegment class, 389
PolyQuadraticBezierSegment class, 389
policy files, cross-domain
    clientaccesspolicy.xml, 187–189
    crossdomain.xml, 187
    overview, 186
PolicyRequestString string, 222
PolicyServer class, 220
PolicyServer Windows service project
    SocketClientAccessPolicy.xml Policy file, 222
    SocketPolicyConnection class, 220–222
    SocketPolicyServer class, 218–220
PolyBezierSegment class, 387, 389
Polygon class, 393
PolyLine class, 374, 393
PolyLineSegment class, 387, 389
PolyQuadraticBezierSegment class, 387, 389
Populating event, 93–94
Popup control, 111–112
Position property, 166, 171, 309
POST method, 188, 236
Power property, 439
PowerEase easing function, 439
PrepareForBuild task, 670
Pressed state, 372, 375–378
PreviewStyle property, GridSplitter class, 107
previous frame button, control bar, 449
Primitives control, 69
Primitives.ButtonBase control, ContentControl class, 103
Primitives.DataGridColumnHeader control, ContentControl class, 103
Primitives.DataGridRowHeader control, ContentControl class, 103
print dialog box, 587
Print method, 330, 333–334
PrintableArea property, 331
PrintDocument class, 313, 330
PrintDocument.Print method, 332
PrintedPageCount property, 330
printing capabilities
    implementing functions
        custom printing, 334–335
        printing application screen, 331–333
        printing selected control, 333–334
    overview, 329
    PrintDocument class, 330
    PrintPageEventArgs class, 330
printing capability feature, Silverlight 4, 11
PrintPage event, 330, 332

PrintPageEventArgs class, 330
PrintPageEventArgs.PageVisual event, 332
printscreen_Click event, 331
private key, 592
Private property, 672
procedural animation
    bubble user control, 442–444
    DemoPage user control, 444–447
ProceduralAnimationDemo folder, 442
processing dropped files, 315
ProfileService class, 596
Progress property, 143
ProgressBar class, 378
ProgressBar control, 117–118
ProgressChanged event, BackgroundWorker
    class, 523
ProgressChangedEventArgs class, 525
ProgressPercentage method, 210
Project menu item, Visual Studio 2010, 598
Project root element, 671
Projection property, 61, 403, 452, 569
ProjectionMatrix property, PlaneProjection
    class, 404
projects, making aware of localization
    capabilities, 350
Projects tab, Expression Blend 4 RC, 19
Properties folder, 476
Properties pane, 20, 23
Properties tab, Expression Blend, 450
Properties window, IIS manager, 662
property attribute syntax, 39–40
Property member, 38
property triggers, 366
PropertyChanged event, 243–245, 346
PropertyLoadCompleted method, 299
ProtocolType property, 215
Provider property, 288
public key, 592
Public-Key Cryptography Standard (PKCS),
    593
python\app.py file, 561
python\app.xaml file, 561

▓ Q

Q point1 endPoint command, 394
Qt framework, 4
quadratic easing function, 440–441
quadratic formula, 440
QuadraticBezierSegment class, 387, 389

QuadraticEase easing function, 439
QuarticEase easing function, 439
Queue class, 48
QueueUserWorkItem method, 520
QuinticEase easing function, 439
Quota property, 305

▓ R

race condition, 516, 526
RadialGradientBrush class, 412, 444
RadioButton class, 84–85, 378
RadioButton control, 10, 510
RadiusX property, 385–386, 390, 412
RadiusY property, 385–386, 390, 412
Random class, 445
RangeBase class
    ProgressBar control, 117–118
    ScrollBar class, 115–116
    Slider control, 116–117
rate of change, linear interpolation, 434
RAW format, 162, 164
Read method, 309
Read option, 307
ReadByte method, 309
Read-Eval-Print Loop (REPL), 555
ReadLocalValue method, DependencyObject
    class, 59
ReadMultiple enumeration, 293
read-only state, 378
ReadSingle enumeration, 293
ReadWrite option, 307
Real Time Streaming Protocol (RTSP), 163
ReceiveAsync method, 214
ReceiveBufferSize property, 215, 234–235
ReceiverApp application, 511
ReceiverApp MainPage.xaml file, 510
ReceiverDomain property, 508
ReceiverName property, 508
Rect property, RectangleGeometry class, 386
Rectangle class, 393
Rectangle element, 413
RectangleGeometry class, 384–386
Red RadioButton control, 509
Reduce XAP size by caching framework
    extension assemblies option, 652–653
/reference:<path> option, 197
reflectedShot rendered bitmap source, 151
Refresh( ) method, 136, 457
Register method, 37–38

Register now link, 538
RegisterAttached method, 38
RegularDay state, 377
RegularExpression attribute, 283
RelativeSource property, 46–47, 240
RelativeTransform property, 395, 408
ReleaseMouseCapture method, UIElement class, 60
Remember my answer checkbox, 175
remote server, connecting to, 230–231
RemoteEndPoint property, 215–216
Remove method, 306
removeError method, 255–256
RemoveHandler method, UIElement class, 60
Render method, WritableBitmap class, 147
RenderedFramesPerSecond property, MediaElement class, 166
RenderSize property, UIElement class, 61
RenderTransform class, 396
RenderTransform property, 61, 324, 395, 452
RenderTransformOrigin property, UIElement class, 61
repeat button, 378
repeat count, Expression Blend, 451–452
RepeatBehavior property, 417, 421, 423, 452, 573
RepeatButton class, 378
RepeatButton control, 83–84, 379
REPL (Read-Eval-Print Loop), 555
ReportErrorToDOM event, 52
ReportProgress method, 524–525
ReportUnhandledErrors property, Microsoft.Scripting.Silverlight.DynamicApplication class, 559
RequestDeviceAccess method, CaptureDeviceConfiguration class, 174
RequestLog method, 167
RequestUri property, 211
RequiredAttribute property, 105
RequirementMode property, 194
requireSSL property, 597
Reset button, 571
resetting styles, 361–362
Resource build action, 43
resource dictionaries
    merged, 363
    in XAML
        merged, 42–43
        overview, 40
        static, 41–42
Resource element, 188, 673

resource files, culture-specific
    adding, 344–346
    binding XAML controls with, 348–350
Resource option, Build Action property, 658–659
ResourceDictionary class, 42, 363
Resources element, Application class, 50
Resources folder, 147, 536
Resources property, 65, 559
ResponseUri property, 212
Result property, 200, 524–526
resultTextBox interface, 520
Resume method, Storyboard class, 423
Return of Investment (ROI), 3
Rfc2898DeriveBytes class, 594
RIAs (Rich Internet Applications), 3, 27, 455, 555, 651
RichTextArea class, 378
RichTextBox control, 11, 23, 68, 81, 88–90
richTextBox_Drop event, 24
right-click context menu feature, Silverlight 4, 11
right-click context menu support, 326–329
ROI (Return of Investment), 3
roleManager element, 597
RoleService class, 596–597, 602–603
RoleService.svc file, 598
root XAML namespace, 352
root_visual shorthand, 570
RootNamespace property, 671
RootVisual property, 52, 559, 655
Rotate Map button, 571
RotateTransform class, 261, 396, 401
rotation, 396–397
Rotation property, CompositeTransform class, 402
RotationAngle property, ArcSegment class, 388
RotationX property, 404, 569
RotationY property, 404, 572
RotationZ property, 404, 572
routed events, 53
RoutedEventExample class, 53
RoutedEventHandler class, 62, 66, 82, 157
RoutedPropertyChangedEventHandler class, 115
Row Details Template, 377
Row Header Style, 377
Row property, Grid class, 38
RowDefinition class, 73
RowEditEnded event, 273
RowEditEnding event, 273

RowSpan property, Grid class, 38
RTSP (Real Time Streaming Protocol), 163
RTSP with TCP (RTSPT), 163
RTSPT (RTSP with TCP), 163
Run control, 6
runtime plug-in, Silverlight 4, 6
RuntimeVersion attribute, 653
RunWorkerAsync method, 524–525
RunWorkerCompleted event, 523–525
RunWorkerCompletedEventArgs class, 525

▓ S

S point2 endPoint command, 394
SafeFileName property, SaveFileDialog class,
    129
same-domain
    communication, 607–608
    deployment, 662
Sample Pictures folder, 25, 146
SampleOOB.xap file, 674
Save as Type drop-down list, 129
Save File Dialog box, 129
Save-As File dialog box, 10
SaveChanges property, 288
SavechangesOptions.Batch option, 297
SaveFileDialog class, 125, 128–131, 490
SaveFileDialog control, 10
SaveFileName property, 128
Sayed, David, 184
ScaleTransform class, 401, 426, 443
ScaleTransform ScaleY property, 150
ScaleTransform.ScaleX property, 398
ScaleTransform.ScaleY property, 398
ScaleX property, 402, 443
ScaleY property, 402, 443
scaling, 398–399
Schementi, Jimmy, 563
screens, application, 331–333
Script folder, 561
scripting assemblies, DLR, 558–559
Scroll event, ScrollBar class, 116
ScrollableHeight property, ScrollViewer class,
    114
ScrollableWidth property, ScrollViewer class,
    114
ScrollBar class, 69, 115–116, 378
ScrollBar control, 379
ScrollContentPresenter class, 378
ScrollEventArgs class, 116

ScrollToHorizontalOffset property, 150
ScrollViewer class, 377–378
ScrollViewer control, 103, 113–114, 148, 169
SDK (Software Development Kit), 9
SDL (Secure Development Lifecycle), 475
Search Engine Optimization (SEO), 11, 455,
    471–474
SearchMode property, 93
SearchText property, AutoCompleteBox class,
    93
SecondClip value, 172
Secure Development Lifecycle (SDL), 475
security
    application-level. *See also* Cryptography
        division of responsibility, 609–612
        same-domain and cross-domain
            communication, 607–608
        securing information in transit, 589
    enhancements
        configuring applications to run with
            elevated trust, 582–584
        digitally signing out-of-browser
            applications, 585–586
        elevated-trusted vs. partially trusted,
            587
    .NET security in CLR, 579–580
    Silverlight security model, 580–582
security consent dialog box, 673
SecurityCritical attribute, 581–582
SecurityException instance, 488
SecuritySafeCritical attribute, 581–582
SecuritySettings class, 481, 584
SecuritySettings.ElevatedPermissions
    property, 584
Seek method, 165, 167, 310, 423
SeekAlignedToLastTick method, Storyboard
    class, 423
select method, 556
SELECT statement, 297
SelectedAdapter property, AutoCompleteBox
    class, 93
SelectedContent property, TabControl class,
    79
SelectedDate property, Calendar class, 119
SelectedDates property, Calendar class, 119
SelectedDatesChanged event, Calendar class,
    119
SelectedIndex property
    ComboBox class, 98
    ListBox class, 96
    TabControl class, 79

SelectedItem property
  AutoCompleteBox class, 93
  ComboBox class, 98
  ListBox class, 96
  TabControl class, 79
  TreeView class, 101
SelectedItemChanged event, 100, 492
SelectedItems property, ListBox class, 96
SelectedText property, TextBox class, 86
SelectedValue property
  ComboBox class, 98
  ListBox class, 97
  Selector class, 97–98
  TreeView class, 101
SelectedValuePath property
  ComboBox class, 98
  ListBox class, 97
  Selector class, 97–98
  TreeView class, 101
Selection property, RichTextBox class, 89
SelectionBackground property, TextBox class, 86
SelectionChanged event, 79, 94, 97–98, 146, 297, 349
SelectionChangedEventArgs class, 79, 97–98
SelectionForeground property, TextBox class, 86
SelectionLength property, TextBox class, 86
SelectionMode property
  Calendar class, 119
  ListBox class, 97
SelectionStart property, TextBox class, 86
Selector class, 96–98
SemiCondensed value, 109
SemiExpanded value, 109
SendAsync method, 214, 508
SendBufferSize property, 215, 234–235
SendCompleted event, 508
SendCompletedEventArgs class, 507
SenderApp MainPage.xaml file, 509
SendFailedException class, 507
SEO (Search Engine Optimization), 11, 455, 471–474
/serializer:<serializer> option, 197
serializing XML data, 301–302
server-side Silverlight RIA deployment, 661–662
ServiceContract attribute, 193–194
ServiceHost tag, 597
Service-Oriented Architecture (SOA), 656

ServiceReferences.ClientConfig file, 196–199, 589
SetBinding method, FrameworkElement class, 64
SetBuffer method, 216
SetColumnSize method, 276
SetLength method, 310
SetPlacement method, ToolTipService class, 113
SetPlacementTarget method, ToolTipService class, 113
SetSaveStream method, 287
SetSource method, 143, 167, 208
Setter element, 42
setter, style, 365–366
Setters property, 358
SetText method, 336
Setting Opacity property, 413
SetTooltip method, 113
SetValue method, 37–39, 59
SetView method, 576
Shape class, 6, 64, 383–384, 387, 391
shapes
  Ellipse class, 392–393
  Line class, 393
  overview, 391
  Path class, 393–395
  Polygon class, 393
  Polyline class, 393
  Rectangle class, 393
Shapes.Path class, 384
shared data, 526–529
shared variable, 527
Shetty, Ashish, 474
shimmering effect, example of, 430–431
Show method, 130–131, 133, 323, 494
showCurrentPosition method, 171
ShowDialog method
  OpenFileDialog class, 126–127
  SaveFileDialog class, 128
ShowGridLines attribute, 72
ShowsPreview property, GridSplitter class, 107
Shutdown method, 215
signing out-of-browser applications, digitally, 585–586
SignTool tool, 585
silent installer, for Silverlight out-of-browser applications, 673–674
silent uninstall option, 480–481
Silverlight
  animation, 415–416

creating Silverlight 4-based application
Expression Blend tool, 19–21
local image files integration using drag-
and-drop functionality, 21–26
overview, 16–18
creating web services consumable by, 192–
195
cross-platform frameworks
Adobe Flash/Flex/AIR, 5
Java platform, 4
Microsoft ASP.NET AJAX, 5
Microsoft Silverlight, 5–6
Qt, 4
design and development tools
Deep Zoom Composer, 16
Eclipse Tools for Silverlight
(eclipse4SL), 16
Expression Blend, 15
Expression Encoder, 16
SketchFlow, 15
Visual Studio, 14–15
enhancements of
configuring applications to run with
elevated trust, 582–584
digitally signing out-of-browser
applications, 585–586
elevated-trusted vs. partially trusted,
587
overview, 313
history of, 11–13
version 1, 6–7
version 2, 7
version 3, 9
version 4, 11–13
invoking services from
asynchronous communication, 199–
202
handling errors, 202–207
overview, 196
Silverlight Service Utility tool, 197–198
networking enhancements in, 185
overview, 3
security models, 580–582
Silverlight Application Package (XAP File)
application manifest file, 653
application startup assembly file, 654–655
optional files, 656
overview, 651–652
Silverlight applications
elevated-trusted vs. partially trusted, 587
globalization of, 338–341

localization of
adding culture-specific resource files,
344–346
adding helper class to support dynamic
culture-specific change in user
interfaces, 346–347
binding XAML controls with culture-
specific resource files, 348–350
hub-and-spoke model, 342–343
making project aware of localization
capabilities, 350
preparing for global Silverlight
application, 352
overview, 338
Silverlight Business Application template
ADO .NET Entity Data Model for data
integration, 541–542
domain service class for data integration, 542
implementing Windows authentication,
540
overview, 535–536
reading and displaying data from data
source, 543–545
running default project, 537–540
updating data to data source, 545
Silverlight for Windows Mobile
developing sample Twitter application
code-behind for Twitter integration,
550–551
creating Windows Phone Application
project, 547
defining user interface, 547–550
overview, 546
testing application using Windows
Phone 7 Emulator, 551
setting up development environment, 546
Silverlight Navigation Framework
Frame class, 457
implementing custom navigation
extending example, 465–470
INavigationContentLoader interface,
463–465
navigation history and integration with
browser, 462–463
navigation pages, 462
overview, 455–456
start-up page and application navigation
features
navigation to pages, 461
overview, 459–460
user-friendly URIs, 461–462

Silverlight Object tag level, 153–154

Silverlight plug-ins

    embedding to web page, 663–666

    using web browser, disabling, 646

Silverlight project properties window, 652

Silverlight SDK library files, 656

Silverlight Service Utility tool, 197–198

Silverlight Unit Test Application template, 17

Silverlight Windows Phone Application
    template, 547

Silverlight_map UserControl, 568

SilverlightApplication1 Silverlight 4
    Application project, 671

<SilverlightApplicationName>.xap naming
    convention, 18

SilverlightFaultBehavior type, 204

SilverlightHost type, 655

Silverlight.js JavaScript helper file, 663, 666

SilverlightMap.html file, 567–569, 574, 577

SilverlightMap.rb file, 570

SilverlightMap.xaml file
    adding 3D animation within, 569
    creating, 568

Silverlight\script\templates\python folder,
    560

Silverlight\script\templates\ruby folder, 560

simple geometries, 384–386

sine formula, 439

SineEase easing function, 439

SineEase function, 9

Size attributes, 482

Size property, 36, 388

SizeChanged event, 66, 418

SizeChangedEventHandler event, 66

SizeToCells enumeration, 275

SizeToHeader enumeration, 275

SketchFlow, 15

skewing, 397

SkewTransform.AngleX property, 397

SkewTransform.AngleY property, 397

SkewX property, CompositeTransform class,
    402

SkewY property, CompositeTransform class,
    402

SkipToFill method, Storyboard class, 423

sl.bat file, 561

Sleep method, Thread class, 518

Slider class, 378

Slider control, 116–117, 171, 261

sllauncher.exe program, 673–674

sllauncher.exe tool, 479–480

SlSvcUtil.exe directory, 198

SLsvcUtil.exe tool, 196

SlSvcUtil.exe tool, 197

SmallChange property, RangeBase class, 115

SMTP network connection, 253

snapShot rendered bitmap source, 149

SOA (Service-Oriented Architecture), 656

Socket class, 214–215, 220

Socket object type variable, 229

SocketArgs_Completed event, 230

SocketAsyncEventArgs class, 216, 220, 230

socket-based sample text chat application

    executing text chat application, 230–231

    MainPage.xaml file, 228–229

    MainPage.xaml.cs code-behind file, 229–
        230

    Message.cs file, 228

    MessengerServer Windows service project
        MessengerConnection class, 225–227
        MessengerServer class, 223–225

    overview, 217

    PolicyServer Windows service project
        SocketClientAccessPolicy.xml Policy
          file, 222
        SocketPolicyConnection class, 220–222
        SocketPolicyServer class, 218–220

SocketClientAccessPolicy.xml file, 218, 222

SocketError property, 217

SocketPolicyConnection class, 218, 220–222

SocketPolicyServer class, 217–220

sockets

    controlling client access via socket policy
        server, 213–214

    overview, 213

    System.Net namespace
        Socket class, 214–215
        SocketAsyncEventArgs class, 216

Software Development Kit (SDK), 9

SolidColorBrush class, 407–408

Solution Explorer window, Visual Studio, 538

SortDescription type, 270

SortDescriptionCollection class, 267

sorting in DataGrid control, 270

Source attribute
    AssemblyPart element, 653
    ResourceDictionary element, 363

Source Code option, 473

source Image control, 150

Source parameter, 665

Source property
    Frame class, 136

Image class, 142
Image control, 142, 151
MediaElement class, 166
MediaElement control, 149
MultiScaleImage control, 156
ResourceDictionary class, 42
SourceChanged event, 167
SourceName property, 409
sourceVideo class, 149
sourceVideo_MouseLeftButton event, 181
sourceVideo_MouseLeftButtonDown event, 149, 152
SpeedRatio property, 417, 421–422
splashScreenSource parameter, OBJECT tag, 665
spline interpolation, 436–438, 449
Split method, 576
SpreadMethod property, GradientBrush class, 410
src attribute, 567
Stack class, 48
StackPanel class, 41, 362, 367, 575
StackPanel control, 22, 45, 54–55, 69–70, 148, 152, 169, 459
Star enumeration, 275
Start method, 178, 180, 227, 518–519, 530
StartPoint property
    LinearGradientBrush class, 411
    LineGeometry class, 385
start/stop button, 426, 428
StartsWith value, FilterMode, 94
StartsWithCaseSensitive value, FilterMode, 94
StartsWithOrdinal value, FilterMode, 95
StartsWithOrdinalCaseSensitive value, FilterMode, 95
startThreadButton button, 519
Startup event handler, 52, 654–655, 663
Startup method, 52
StartupEventArgs parameter, 663
State property, 178, 268, 270
States pane, Expression Blend tool, 371
static IsAvailable property, 497
static resource dictionaries, 41–42
StaticResource markup extension, 42, 48, 359
Stop method, 167, 171, 178, 181, 423, 530
Stop value, FillBehavior property, 417, 421
stop_reset button, 574
StopLoading( ) method, 136, 457–458, 465
Stopped state, 165, 167, 423, 518
StopRequested state, ThreadState class, 518
StoryBoard animation, 154

Storyboard class, 7, 374, 418, 420, 423–424
Storyboard property, 373, 381
storyboards
    animation easing, 438–442
    From/To/By animations
        foreground animation example, 424–429
        overview, 423
        shimmering effect example, 430–431
    keyframe animations
        discrete interpolation, 434–436
        interpolation, 434–438
        linear interpolation, 434
        overview, 432–433
        spline interpolation, 436–438
Storyboard.TargetName property, 424
Storyboard.TargetProperty property, 425
Stream method, 143, 167, 212
streaming video and audio, 184
StreamReader object, 128
StreamResourceInfo class, 184
StreamWriter object, 130
Stretch enumeration, 392
Stretch property
    Image class, 142
    MediaElement class, 166
    Shape class, 392
    TileBrush class, 409
    ViewBox class, 80
Stretch values, 144
StretchDirection property, ViewBox class, 80
String indexer method, 250
string indexers, binding to, 265–266
string type, 280, 599
string variables, 510
String.Format( ) method, 264
StringFormat property, 263–264
Strings class, 346
Strings.Designer.cs file, 345–346
Strings.fr-fr.resx file, 346
Strings.he.resx file, 346
Strings.resx file, 344–346
Stroke class, 122
Stroke property, Shape class, 392
StrokeCollection class, 122
StrokeDashArray property, Shape class, 392
Strokes class, 122–125
Strokes property, InkPresenter class, 122
StrokeThickness property, Shape class, 392
Style attribute, 359, 364
Style class, 358–360

Style element, 42
Style property, 65, 361, 377
StylePoint objects, 122
styles
    components of, 358
    enhancements in Silverlight 4, 355
    implicit, 364–365
    inheritance (cascading), 360–361
    merged resource dictionaries, 363
    overriding/resetting, 361–362
    setter, 365–366
    target type, 358
stylesheets\error.css file, 561
stylesheets\screen.cs file, 561
Styles.xaml file, 459–460
StylusPoints property, 122–125
SubImages property, MultiScaleImage control, 156
SubTitle style, 361
support
    custom IDictionary, 354
    mouse-wheel, 324–326
    right-click context menu, 326–329
SupportedCultures tag, 350
SupportedFormats property, 177
swayBubble animation, 445
SweepDirection property, ArcSegment class, 388
symmetric key algorithms, 592
SymmetricAlgorithm class, 594
synchronization mechanisms, 528
System.Collections namespace, 48, 497
System.Collections.Generic namespace, 48
System.ComponentModel namespace, 267, 347, 522
System.ComponentModel.DataAnnotations event, 277
System.Core namespace, 49
System.Core.dll assembly, 285, 651
System.Data.Services.Client namespace, 286
System.dll library, 651
System.Globalization namespace, 339, 341
System.IO namespace, 23, 48, 128, 130, 587
System.IO type, 490
System.IO.FileAccess enumeration, 307
System.IO.FileMode enumeration, 306
System.IO.FileShare enumeration, 307
System.IO.FileStream class, 307
System.IO.IsolatedStorage namespace, 304
System.IO.IsolatedStorage.IsolatedStorageFile class, 581

System.Linq namespace, 49, 256, 285
System.Net. HttpWebRequest class, 210
System.Net namespace, 49, 214–216
System.Net.DnsEndPoint class, 214
System.Net.HttpWebRequest class, 188, 207, 236
System.Net.IPEndPoint class, 214
System.Net.NetworkInformation namespace, 191, 485
System.Net.Sockets namespace, 232
System.Net.Sockets.Socket class, 214
System.Net.Sockets.SocketAsyncEventArgs class, 214
System.Net.WebClient class, 188, 207
System.Runtime.InteropServices.Automation namespace, 497
System.Security namespace, 48
System.Security.Cryptography namespace, 49, 589
System.Security.Cryptography.HashAlgorithm class, 590–591
System.Security.Cryptography.HMAC class, 590–591
System.Security.Cryptography.KeyedHashAlgorithm class, 590
System.Security.Cryptography.SymmetricAlgorithm class, 594
System.ServiceModel namespace, 198
system.serviceModel section, 195–196, 198, 597
Systems.Windows.Controls.Primitives.Selector class, 96, 98
Systems.Windows.Controls.Toolkit.dll assembly, 74, 77
System.Threading namespace, 529
System.Threading Timer, 531–532
System.Threading.Interlocked class, 527
System.Threading.Thread class, 516
System.Threading.ThreadPool class, 520
System.Web.ApplicationServices namespace, 596
System.Windows assembly, 497
System.Windows namespace, 49, 358, 584
System.Windows.Application class, 50, 559
System.Windows.Application-derived class, 654
System.Windows.Browser namespace, 49
System.Windows.Clipboard class, 313, 336
System.Windows.Controls namespace, 49, 79, 99, 108, 126, 128, 131, 135, 271

System.Windows.Controls.Data assembly, 104–105, 266

System.Windows.Controls.Data namespace, 104–105

System.Windows.Controls.Data.DataForm.Toolkit assembly, 105

System.Windows.Controls.Data.DataForm.Toolkit namespace, 105

System.Windows.Controls.Data.dll assembly, 271

System.Windows.Controls.Data.Input assembly, 105–106, 466

System.Windows.Controls.Data.Input namespace, 105–106

System.Windows.Controls.dll assembly, 652–653

System.Windows.Controls.DomainServices namespace, 544

System.Windows.Controls.Frame class, 457

System.Windows.Controls.MediaElement class, 164

System.Windows.Controls.Navigation assembly, 459, 463

System.Windows.Controls.Primitives namespace, 81

System.Windows.Controls.Toolkit.dll assembly, 653

System.Windows.Controls.Toolkit.dll file, 652

System.Windows.Data namespace, 267

System.Windows.Data.CollectionViewSource namespace, 284

System.Windows.DependencyObject namespace, 358

System.Windows.DependencyObject Style class, 358

System.Windows.Documents namespace, 89

System.Windows.Duration property, 420

System.Windows.Hosting namespace, 49

System.Windows.Ink namespace, 122

System.Windows.Input namespace, 49, 122, 502

System.Windows.InstallState.NotInstalled, 478

System.Windows.Interop.Settings class, 666

System.Windows.Markup namespace, 49

System.Windows.Media namespace, 49, 174, 573

System.Windows.Media.Animation namespace, 573

System.Windows.Media.Animation.Storyboard class, 423

System.Windows.Media.Animation.Timeline class, 416

System.Windows.Media.Brush class, 407

System.Windows.Media.Effects library, 405

System.Windows.Media.Geometry class, 383

System.Windows.Media.Imaging namespace, 23, 146–147, 149

System.Windows.Media.TimelineMarker class, 172

System.Windows.Messaging namespace, 507–508

System.Windows.Navigation namespace, 135, 463

System.Windows.Printing namespace, 330–331

System.Windows.Resources.StreamResourceInfo object, 209

System.Windows.Shapes.Shape class, 383, 391

System.Windows.Threading namespace, 447, 519

System.Windows.UIElement class, 314

System.Windows.VisualTransition class, 373

System.Xml namespace, 49

System.Xml.Linq assembly, 657

System.Xml.Linq namespace, 302

System.Xml.Linq.dll library, 651, 656

System.Xml.Serialization assembly, 229

System.Xml.Serialization namespace, 301

System.Xml.XmlReader class, 300

■ T

T point1 endPoint command, 394

TabControl class, 378

TabControl control, 78–79

TabIndex property, Control class, 67

TabItem control, ContentControl class, 103

TabItem instances, 378

TabNavigation property, Control class, 67

TabPanel class, 69

TabPanel control, 10

TabStripPlacement property, TabControl class, 79

Tag attribute, 524–525, 575–576

tag expressions, using when unit testing with MSBuild, 621

Tag property, 46–47, 65, 576

target Image control, 150

Target property, 105–106

TargetFrameworkVersion property, 671

TargetName property, 83, 425, 461
TargetNullValue binding extension property, 264
TargetNullValue markup extension, 265
TargetNullValue method, 265
TargetNullValue property, 237
TargetProperty property, 425–426
TargetType property, 42–43, 358–359, 364, 374
targetUri value, 464
tbMainTitle control, 362
TED (Technology, Entertainment, Design), 155
template binding, in XAML, 47–48
Template property, Control class, 67, 367
TemplateBinding markup extension, 46, 368
TemplateBindingExample user control, 47
TemplatedParent class, 46–47
TemplatePart attributes, 381
templates, control
    creating, 366–377
    custom button control using, 374–377
    developing templated control, 378–381
    for other controls, 377–378
    Visual State Manager (VSM), 368–374
TemplateVisualState attributes, 378–379, 381
testing, 615–632
    automated user interface
        implementing, 629–632
        overview, 627
        UI Spy tool, 628
    unit testing framework
        and Assert class, 624–627
        in-browser, 616–619
        using MSBuild, 620–624
Text attribute, 39
text chat application, executing, 230–231
Text property
    AutoCompleteBox class, 93
    TextBlock class, 110, 128
    TextBox class, 86
TextAlignment property
    TextBlock class, 110
    TextBox class, 86
TextBlock class, 47–48, 55, 356, 359–362, 368
TextBlock control, 6, 23, 43, 109–111, 171, 261, 362, 405, 576
TextBlock element, 40, 405
TextBox class, 40, 378
TextBox control, 10, 85–87, 547, 551
TextBoxStyle property, AutoCompleteBox class, 93
TextChanged event, 93–94

TextCompositionEventHandler class, 63
TextDecorations property, TextBlock class, 110
TextFilter property, AutoCompleteBox class, 93
TextInput event, UIElement class, 63
TextInputStart event, UIElement class, 63
TextInputUpdate event, UIElement class, 63
TextProperty dependency property, 243
TextSize property, 37–38
TextSizeProperty property, 38
TextTrimming property, 12
TextWrapping property
    RichTextBox class, 89
    TextBlock class, 110, 356
    TextBox class, 86
theme application support feature, Silverlight 3, 9
Themes/Generic.xaml file, 363
Thread class, 516, 520
Thread.Abort method, 519
threading and user interface, 59
Thread.IsBackground property, 518
ThreadPool class, 520
threads
    BackgroundWorker class, 522–526
    creating and managing, 519–521
    Dispatcher property, DependencyObject class, 521–522
    overview, 515
    shared data, 526–529
    Thread class, 516–518
    timers
        DispatcherTimer class, 530
        overview, 529
        System.Threading Timer, 531–532
ThreadStart class, 519–520
Thread.Start method, 518
ThreadState property, 517–518
thumb control, 378
Thumb control, 378
thumbsPanel class, 149–150
thumbsPanel stack panel, 152
ThumbStyle class, 378
Tick event, 171, 530
tile brushes, 408–409
TileBrush class, 408
Timeline class, 416–417, 423
timeline editor, Expression Blend, 449–450
timeline markers, for media integration in Silverlight, 172–173
Timeline pane, Expression Blend, 449

TimelineMarker class, 167
TimelineMarker method, 173
TimelineMarkerRoutedEventArgs class, 173
TimelineMarkerRoutedEventArgs instance, 167
timelines
    AutoReverse property, 418–419
    BeginTime property, 419–420
    Duration property, 420
    FillBehavior property, 421
    overview, 416–417
    RepeatBehavior property, 421
    SpeedRatio property, 421–422
Timer class, 529, 531
Timer constructor, 531
TimerCallback method, 531
TimerCallback parameter, 531
timers
    DispatcherTimer class, 530
    overview, 529
    System.Threading Timer, 531–532
TimeSpan structure, 420
TimeSpan value, 423
Title attribute, 462
Title property, 137, 456, 478
Title style, 360–361
To property, 373, 424
To value, 424
Today state, 377
ToggleButton class, 84–85, 378
tologo.jpg image file, 658
tools, Silverlight Service Utility, 197–198
ToolTip control, ContentControl class, 103
ToolTipService control, 112–113
ToString( ) method, 253, 260
total time span of timeline formula, 422
TotalBytesToReceive method, 210
Transform inheritors, 395
Transform object, 390
Transform property, 395, 408
Transformation class, 46
TransformBlock method, System.Security.Cryptography.HMAC class, 591
TransformFinalBlock method, System.Security.Cryptography.HMAC class, 591
TransformGroup class, 150, 395, 399, 401
transforms
    arbitrary linear transforms, 399–400

composite transformation, 401–403
    multiple, combining, 401
    rotation, 396–397
    scaling, 398–399
    skewing, 397
    translation, 396
TransformToVisual method, UIElement class, 60
TranslateTransform class, 396
TranslateTransform property, 150, 426, 442
TranslateX property, CompositeTransform class, 402, 450
TranslateY property, CompositeTransform class, 402
translation transforms, 396
transparency masks, 412–414
treeDir TreeView control, 491–492, 494, 496
treeDir_SelectedItemChanged event, 496
TreeView control, 99–101
TreeViewItem class, 101
Triggers property, FrameworkElement class, 65
Truncate option, 307
trusted out-of-browser applications, 481–482
Trusted Root Certification Authorities store, 585–586
Ttl property, 215
tunneling, 53
Twitter application
    developing
        code-behind for Twitter integration, 550–551
        creating Windows Phone Application project, 547
        defining user interface, 547–550
        overview, 546
        testing application using Windows Phone 7 Emulator, 551
    integration, 603–607
TwitterApp project, 547
TwitterMessage class, 550
TwoWay data binding, 243
TwoWay mode, 239
TwoWayDataBindingDemo.xaml page, 263
txtAnswer text box, 250–251
txtEmail text box, 260
txtWebsite text box, 260
type attribute, 664
type converters, 39–40, 262–263

U

UAC (User Account Control). *See* User Account Control

UDP (User Datagram Protocol) multicast. *See* User Datagram Protocol multicast

UdpAnySourceMulticastClient class, 172, 232–234

UdpMultiSourceMulticastClient class, 232

UdpSingleSourceMulticastClient class, 172, 234–235

UI Spy tool, and unit testing framework, 628

UIElement class
    drag-and-drop functionality, 314
    overview, 59–61

UIElement.AllowDrop property, 313

UIElement-based class, 655

UIElement.MouseWheel event, 313, 324

UltraCondensed value, 109

UltraExpanded value, 109

UnblockSource method, 234

UNC (Universal Naming Convention), 163

Unchecked event, ToggleButton class, 84

Unchecked state, 377–378

Unfocused state, 372, 375, 377–378

unhandled exceptions, handling, 640–644

UnhandledException event, 52

Uniform enum value, 144

Uniform Resource Identifier (URI), 43, 49, 142–143, 156, 167, 459, 461

UniformToFill enum value, 144

uninstalling out-of-browser applications, 480–481

unit testing framework
    and Assert class, 624–627
    in-browser, 616–619
    using MSBuild
        code coverage, 622–624
        overview, 620
        test result files, 622
        using tag expressions, 621

Universal Naming Convention (UNC), 163

UnsetValue value, 59

UnStarted state, ThreadState class, 518

UpdateApplicationModeStatus method, 486

UpdateAvailable property, 488

UpdateLayout method, UIElement class, 60

UpdateNetworkConnectivityStatus method, 485–486

UpdateObject method, 287

Updates tab, Silverlight configuration utility, 647

UpdateSizing method, 275–276

UpdateSourceTrigger property, 240

UploadProgressChanged event, 207

UploadStringAsync method, 207, 210

UploadStringCompleted event, 207

URI (Uniform Resource Identifier), 43, 49, 142–143, 156, 167, 459, 461

UriMapper control, 471

uriMapper namespace, 471

UriMapper property, 136, 459

UriMapping class, 461

URIs (uniform resource identifier), 461–462

UriSource property, 143

UseDefaultCredentials property, 288, 606

UsedSize property, 305

UseLayoutRounding property, 61

User Account Control (UAC)
    authentication support with
            ClientHttpWebRequest
        Basic authentication, 603
        developing Twitter integration
            application, 603–607
        Digest authentication, 603
        NTLM authentication, 603
    overview, 596–598
    using authentication service, 599–602
    using RoleService, 602–603

user controls
    defining, 315–317
    implementing code behind, 317–320

User Datagram Protocol (UDP) multicast
    UdpAnySourceMulticastClient class, 232–233
    UdpSingleSourceMulticastClient class, 234–235

user interface controls
    building blocks
        Control class, 66–68
        DependencyObject class, 58
        FrameworkElement class, 63–66
        overview, 57
        threading and user interface, 59
        UIElement class, 59–61
    data integration and data manipulation
        controls
        ComboBox, 98–99
        ContentControl, 103
        DataForm, 104–105
        DataGrid, 104

DataPager, 105
DescriptionViewer, 105
HeaderedContentControl, 103–104
HeaderedItemsControl, 102–103
ItemsControl, 96
Label, 105
ListBox, 96–98
overview, 95
TreeView, 99–101
ValidationSummary, 106
enhancements in Silverlight 4, 68
Forms controls
AutoCompleteBox control, 91–94
ButtonBase class, 81–85
PasswordBox control, 87–88
RichTextBox control, 88–90
TextBox control, 85–87
functional controls
Border, 106–107
Calendar, 118–120
DatePicker, 118–120
dialog boxes, 125–133
GridSplitter, 107
Image, 121
InkPresenter, 122–125
MediaElement, 122
MultiScaleImage, 121
Popup, 111–112
ProgressBar, 117–118
ScrollBar, 115–116
ScrollViewer, 113–114
Slider, 116–117
TextBlock, 109–111
ToolTipService, 112–113
WebBrowser, 134
layout management and grouping controls
Canvas control, 69
DockPanel control, 74–77
Grid control, 71–74
StackPanel control, 70
TabControl control, 78–79
ViewBox control, 80
WrapPanel control, 77–78
navigation
Frame class, 135
Page class, 137–138
user interfaces
adding helper class to support dynamic
culture-specific change in, 346–347
defining in XAML, 30–32
userCallback method, 464

UserControl class, 32–33, 47, 50, 52–53, 148,
364–365, 370, 374, 377, 444, 447, 572, 668
UserControl.Resources namespace, 280
UserState method, 210
UserState property, 200, 525
UserToken property, 217
UsesParentJournal value, 136, 462
UseSprings property, MultiScaleImage
control, 157
UseVerboseErrors property, 294

▨ V

V y command, 394
valid state, 377–378
ValidateEmail method, 252, 258
ValidateEmployee property, 278
ValidateEmployee validation class, 277
ValidateOnExceptions property, 247
ValidatesOnDataErrors property, 240
ValidatesOnExceptions property, 241, 246–247
ValidatesOnNotifyData property, 241
ValidatesOnNotifyDataErrors event handler, 259
ValidatesOnNotifyDataErrors interface, 251
ValidateUrl method, 252
ValidateUser method, 599, 602
ValidationErrorEventArgs class, 66
ValidationOnExceptions property, 250
ValidationService interface, 252
ValidationService property, 253, 257
ValidationServiceReference property, 253
ValidationSummary control, 106
Value property, 115, 260
ValueChanged event, RangeBase class, 115
ValueMemberBinding property,
AutoCompleteBox class, 94
ValueMemberPath property,
AutoCompleteBox class, 94
var Error object, 256
VC-1 in MP4 format, 164
vds_ValidateUrlCompleted method, 258
vertical scrollbar class, 378
VerticalAlignment property, 66, 108
VerticalContent property, Control class, 67
vertically-oriented scrollbar class, 378
VerticalOffset property, 111, 114, 320, 328
VerticalScroll property, ScrollViewer class, 114
VerticalScrollBar property
RichTextBox class, 89
TextBox class, 86

video brush, 409
video content, publishing with Windows Azure Platform, 183–184
VideoBrush class, 408
VideoCaptureDevice class, web camera and microphone integration, 176–177
VideoCaptureDevice object, 174, 178
VideoPause event, 180
VideoPlay event, 180
VideoSink class, 174, 182
VideoStop_Click event, 181
View property, 284
ViewBox control, 11–12, 68, 80
ViewModel class, 504–506
ViewModel properties, 504
ViewModel.cs file, 503
ViewportChanged event, MultiScaleImage control, 157
ViewportHeight property, ScrollViewer class, 114
ViewportOrigin property, 156–157
ViewportSize property, ScrollBar class, 116
ViewportWidth property, 114, 156–157
Views folder, 455, 462, 465, 490, 498
View.xaml file, 505–506
Visibility property, 61, 314, 435–436
Visual State Manager (VSM), 10, 368–374
Visual Studio 2010, 14–15, 33, 245
Visual Studio project (.csproj), building with MSBuild, 668–670
VisualState class, 373
VisualStateGroups property, 372
VisualStateManager class, 372, 378, 381
VisualStateTransition class, 373
VisualTransition class, 373
Volume property, MediaElement class, 166
VSM (Visual State Manager), 10, 368–374

■ W

WaitSleepJoin state, ThreadState class, 518
WCF (Windows Communication Foundation), consuming web services with
  communicating directly over HTTP, 207–213
  creating web services consumable by Silverlight, 192–195
  HttpWebRequest class, 211–213
  overview, 191
  WebClient class, 207–210
  XAML to consume information, 195

WCF Data Services
  Entity Data Model (EDM), 285
  overview, 284
  Silverlight application using, 289–299
  Silverlight client library for
    DataServiceCollection (T) class, 289
    DataServiceContext class, 286
    DataServiceQuery class, 288
WCF RIA Service web project, 652
WCF RIA Services class Library template, 17, 534
WCF RIA Services for Silverlight
  additional references, 545
  overview, 533
  setting up development environment, 534
  Silverlight Business Application template
    ADO .NET Entity Data Model for data integration, 541–542
    domain service class for data integration, 542
    implementing Windows authentication, 540
    overview, 535–537
    reading and displaying data from data source, 543–545
    running default project, 537–540
    updating data to data source, 545
WCF RIA Services link option, 652
WCFDataServiceDemo.Web project, 290–291
web browsers
  Google Chrome, 13
  Silverlight plug-in using, 646
web camera and microphone integration
  AudioCaptureDevice,class, 176–177
  CaptureDevice class, 176–177
  CaptureDeviccConfiguration class, 174–175
  CaptureSource class, 177
  example of, 179–182
  VideoCaptureDevice class, 176–177
web pages, embedding Silverlight plug-ins to, 663–666
web services, consuming with WCF
  communicating directly over HTTP, 207–213
  creating web services consumable by Silverlight, 192–195
  HttpWebRequest class, 211–213
  overview, 191
  WebClient class, 207–210
  XAML to consume information, 195

Web Site Administration Tool, 598–599
WebBrowser control, 11, 134
WebBrowserBrush control, 12
WebCameraAndMicroPhoneIntegration class, 179
WebCameraAndMicrophoneIntegration control, 179
Webcam/Mic tab, 176, 648–649
WebClient class, 49, 184–185, 207–210, 236, 589, 657
WebDeveloper class, 238, 243, 262, 264, 300, 302–303
WebDevelopers.xml file, 302
WebRequest class, 211
Website property, 245, 264
whitespace handling, 353
Width property, 20–21, 36, 66, 258, 274, 358, 392–393, 425
Wildermuth, Shawn, 503
Wildlife.wmv, 147, 172
Window class, 483
windowless parameter, OBJECT tag, 665
Windows Azure Platform, and media integration, 183–184
Windows Communication Foundation. *See* WCF
windows, manipulation and customization of, 483–484
Windows Media Audio Professional format, 164
Windows Media Screen format, 164
Windows Media Video format, 164
Windows Media Voice format, 164
Windows Phone 7 Emulator, testing application using, 551
Windows Presentation Foundation (WPF), 3, 27, 29, 33, 39, 53, 360, 364, 366
Windows service project
  MessengerServer
    MessengerConnection class, 225–227
    MessengerServer class, 223–225
  PolicyServer
    SocketClientAccessPolicy.xml Policy file, 222
    SocketPolicyConnection class, 220–222
    SocketPolicyServer class, 218–220
WMA format, 163
WordExport method, 504–505
wordList collection, 556

WorkerReportsProgress property, BackgroundWorker class, 522
WorkerSupportsCancellation property, 522, 525
WorkReportsProgress property, 525
WPF (Windows Presentation Foundation), 3, 27, 29, 33, 39, 53, 360, 364, 366
WrapPanel control, 10, 69, 77–78
WritableBitmap class, 147, 154
Write method, 310
Write option, 307
WriteableBitmap class, 147–149, 151
WriteableBitmapDemonstration class, 150–151
WriteableBitmapDemonstration control, 147
WriteableBitmapDemonstration_Loaded event, 151
WriteableBitmapDemonstrationwithVideoPlayer.cs file, 179
WriteableBitmapDemonstrationwithVideoPlayer.xaml file, 179
WriteableBitmapDemonstration.xaml file, 149, 169
WriteAppend enumeration, 293
WriteByte method, 310
WriteDelete enumeration, 293
WriteMerge enumeration, 293
WriteReplace enumeration, 293
WVC1 format, 163

▓ X

x:) namespace, 33
X property, TranslateTransform class, 396
x radius, 386
x1 point area, KeySpline editor, 451
x2 point area, KeySpline editor, 451
X2 property, Line class, 393
XAML (Extensible Application Markup Language), 30
  to consume information, 195
  controls, binding with culture-specific resource files, 348–350
  enhancements in features
    custom IDictionary support, 354
    direct content, 353
    flexible root XAML namespace, 352
    whitespace handling, 353
    XmlnsDefinitionAttribute, 353

XAML (Extensible Application Markup Language) (*cont.*)
   and Silverlight
      controls structure, 32–33
      defining user interface, 30–32
      dependency property system, 34–39
      markup extensions, 40–48
      namespaces, 33
      sample application, 29–33
      type converters, 39–40
XAML Application Package (XAP), 651
XAML class, 52
XAMLTour Project, 44, 47
XAP (XAML Application Package), 651
XAP file, 18, 651
XAP File (Silverlight Application Package). *See* Silverlight Application Package
XapCacheFile.xml file, 670
x:class attribute, 30
x:class namespace, 34
x:Key attribute, 40, 43, 354, 359, 364
x:Key namespace, 34
XML (Extensible Markup Language), 29, 32–33, 49, 426
   and LINQ, 302–303
   overview, 299
   parsing data, 300–301
   serializing data, 301–302
XmlLanguage class, 65
XmlnsDefinition attribute, 267, 316

XmlnsDefinitionAttribute, 353
XmlReader class, 301
XmlReader.Create method, 300
XmlReaderSettings class, 301
XmlSerializer class, 301
x:Name attribute, 49
   AssemblyPart element, 653
   XAML objects, 670
x:Name namespace, 34
x:Null markup extension, 365
x:Null namespace, 34
XSS (cross-site scripting), 607, 662

Y

y axis, 150
y coordinate, 394
Y property, TranslateTransform class, 396
y radius, 386
y1 point area, KeySpline editor, 451
y2 point area, KeySpline editor, 451
Y2 property, Line class, 393
yellow dots, KeySpline editor, 451

Z

zip file extenxion, 609
ZoomAboutLogicalPoint method, 157
Zoomed event, 666

You Need the Companion eBook

Your purchase of this book entitles you to buy the companion PDF-version eBook for only $10. Take the weightless companion with you anywhere.

We believe this Apress title will prove so indispensable that you'll want to carry it with you everywhere, which is why we are offering the companion eBook (in PDF format) for $10 to customers who purchase this book now. Convenient and fully searchable, the PDF version of any content-rich, page-heavy Apress book makes a valuable addition to your programming library. You can easily find and copy code—or perform examples by quickly toggling between instructions and the application. Even simultaneously tackling a donut, diet soda, and complex code becomes simplified with hands-free eBooks!

Once you purchase your book, getting the $10 companion eBook is simple:

❶ Visit **www.apress.com/promo/tendollars/**.

❷ Complete a basic registration form to receive a randomly generated question about this title.

❸ Answer the question correctly in 60 seconds, and you will receive a promotional code to redeem for the $10.00 eBook.

Apress®
THE EXPERT'S VOICE™

233 Spring Street, New York, NY 10013